Eating Disorders and Obesity: Through the Life Course

Eating Disorders and Obesity: Through the Life Course

Editors

Fernando Fernandez-Aranda
Janet Treasure
Empar Lurbe

MDPI • Basel • Beijing • Wuhan • Barcelona • Belgrade • Manchester • Tokyo • Cluj • Tianjin

Editors

Fernando Fernandez-Aranda
University of Barcelona
Hospital of Bellvitge-IDIBELL
and CIBEROBN
Barcelona
Spain

Janet Treasure
Kings College London
London
UK

Empar Lurbe
University of Valencia
Valencia
Spain

Editorial Office
MDPI
St. Alban-Anlage 66
4052 Basel, Switzerland

This is a reprint of articles from the Special Issue published online in the open access journal *Nutrients* (ISSN 2072-6643) (available at: https://www.mdpi.com/journal/nutrients/special_issues/Eating_Disorders_Obesity_Through_Life_Course).

For citation purposes, cite each article independently as indicated on the article page online and as indicated below:

LastName, A.A.; LastName, B.B.; LastName, C.C. Article Title. *Journal Name* **Year**, *Volume Number*, Page Range.

ISBN 978-3-0365-7464-6 (Hbk)
ISBN 978-3-0365-7465-3 (PDF)

Contents

Preface to "Eating Disorders and Obesity: Through the Life Course"

Eating disorders and obesity are two conditions related to eating behaviors which have a significant impact on an individual's physical and mental health over the lifespan. Although they may seem like opposite ends of the spectrum, there are both shared and differential factors that contribute to the development and maintenance of these conditions.

Shared risk factors for both obesity and eating disorders include a genetic predisposition, environmental factors (such as access to healthy food and physical activity opportunities, cultural attitudes toward body size and shape, and social pressure to conform to certain standards of beauty), psychological factors (such as specific personality traits, namely impulsivity, low self-esteem, poor body image, and difficulties dealing with emotions) and some similar metabolic-hormonal factors.

However, there are some differences in the prevalence, clinical features, and risk factors. For example, there has often been a chronic pattern of overconsumption in obesity, whereas there may be more of an acute, later onset of the intermittent pattern of excessive/restrained pattern of food consumption characteristic of binge eating disorder. Moreover, childhood trauma has been found to be a risk factor for the development of eating disorders, while chronic exposure to social and cultural deprivation and alienation may play a greater role in the development of obesity.

Overall, it is important to recognize that both obesity and eating disorders are complex severe diseases that can interact throughout life (in people with eating disorders, lifetime obesity is present in 40% of cases, and 15–20% patients who have obesity also have a comorbid ED). A personalized approach to treatment targeting the various risk factors may be needed. Early intervention and prevention efforts may help to reduce the prevalence of both conditions and improve overall health outcomes. Individuals with obesity and eating disorders have often been subjected to weight stigma and discrimination, which adversely impact their mental health and self-esteem and serve to perpetuate these problems.

Fernando Fernandez-Aranda, Janet Treasure, and Empar Lurbe
Editors

nutrients

MDPI

Article

Transdiagnostic Perspective of Impulsivity and Compulsivity in Obesity: From Cognitive Profile to Self-Reported Dimensions in Clinical Samples with and without Diabetes

Giulia Testa [1,2,3,†], Bernat Mora-Maltas [1,2,†], Lucía Camacho-Barcia [1,2,3], Roser Granero [3,4], Ignacio Lucas [1,2], Zaida Agüera [1,2,3,5], Susana Jiménez-Murcia [1,2,3,6], Rosa Baños [3,7], Valerie Bertaina-Anglade [8], Cristina Botella [3,9], Mònica Bulló [3,10,11], Felipe F. Casanueva [3,12], Søren Dalsgaard [13], José-Manuel Fernández-Real [3,14], Barbara Franke [15], Gema Frühbeck [3,16], Montserrat Fitó [3,17], Carlos Gómez-Martínez [3,11,18], Xavier Pintó [3,6,19], Geert Poelmans [20], Francisco J. Tinahones [3,21], Rafael de la Torre [3,22,23], Jordi Salas-Salvadó [3,11,18,24], Lluis Serra-Majem [3,25], Stephanie Vos [26], Theresa Wimberley [27] and Fernando Fernández-Aranda [1,2,3,6,*]

1 Department of Psychiatry, University Hospital of Bellvitge, L'Hospitalet de Llobregat, 08907 Barcelona, Spain; gtesta@idibell.cat (G.T.); bmora@idibell.cat (B.M.-M.); lcamacho@idibell.cat (L.C.-B.); ilucas@idibell.cat (I.L.); zaguera@ub.edu (Z.A.); sjimenez@bellvitgehospital.cat (S.J.-M.)
2 Psychiatry and Mental Health Group, Neuroscience Program, Institut d'Investigació Biomèdica de Bellvitge (IDIBELL), L'Hospitalet de Llobregat, 08907 Barcelona, Spain
3 Consorcio CIBER, M.P. Fisiopatología de la Obesidad y Nutrición (CIBERObn), Instituto de Salud Carlos III (ISCIII), 28029 Madrid, Spain; roser.granero@uab.cat (R.G.); rosa.banos@uv.es (R.B.); botella@psb.uji.es (C.B.); monica.bullo@urv.cat (M.B.); felipe.casanueva@usc.es (F.F.C.); jmfreal@idibgi.org (J.-M.F.-R.); gfruhbeck@unav.es (G.F.); mfito@imim.es (M.F.); carlos.gomez@urv.cat (C.G.-M.); xpinto@bellvitgehospital.cat (X.P.); fjtinahones@hotmail.com (F.J.T.); RTorre@imim.es (R.d.l.T.); jordi.salas@urv.cat (J.S.-S.); lluis.serra@ulpgc.es (L.S.-M.)
4 Department of Psychobiology and Methodology, Autonomous University of Barcelona, 08193 Barcelona, Spain
5 Department of Public Health, Mental Health and Perinatal Nursing, School of Nursing, University of Barcelona, L'Hospitalet de Llobregat, 08907 Barcelona, Spain
6 Department of Clinical Sciences, School of Medicine and Health Sciences, University of Barcelona, L'Hospitalet de Llobregat, 08907 Barcelona, Spain
7 Instituto Polibienestar, Universitat de Valencia, 46010 Valencia, Spain
8 Core Lab Department, Biotrial Neurosciences, 35000 Rennes, France; valrie.bertaina-anglade@biotrial.com
9 Department of Basic Psychology Clinic and Psychobiology, Universitat Jaume I, Castellón de la Plana, 12071 Castellón, Spain
10 Department of Biochemistry and Biotechnology, Faculty of Medicine and Health Sciences, University Rovira i Virgili (URV), 43201 Reus, Spain
11 Institut d'Investigació Sanitaria Pere Virgili (IISPV), Hospital Universitari de Sant Joan de Reus, 43204 Reus, Spain
12 Molecular and Cellular Endocrinology Group, Instituto de Investigacion Sanitaria de Santiago de Compostela (IDIS), Complejo Hospitalario Universitario de Santiago de Compostela (CHUS), Santiago de Compostela University (USC) and Centro de Investigacion Biomedica en Red Fisiopatologia de la Obesidad Y Nutricion (Ciberobn), 15705 Santiago de Compostela A Coruña, Spain
13 National Centre for Register-Based Research, Department of Economics and Business Economics, Business and Social Sciences, Aarhus University and iPSYCH, The Lundbeck Foundation Initiative for Integrative Psychiatric Research (Copenhagen-Aarhus), DK-8210 Aarhus, Denmark; sdalsgaard@econ.au.dk
14 Department of Medical Sciences, School of Medicine, Hospital of Girona Dr. Josep Trueta, University of Girona, 17004 Girona, Spain
15 Departments of Human Genetics and Psychiatry, Donders Institute for Brain, Cognition and Behaviour, Radboud University Medical Center, 6525 GA Nijmegen, The Netherlands; Barbara.franke@radboudumc.nl
16 Department of Endocrinology, Instituto de Investigación Sanitaria de Navarra, University of Navarra (IdiSNA), 31008 Pamplona, Spain
17 Unit of Cardiovascular Risk and Nutrition, Hospital del Mar Institute for Medical Research (IMIM), 08003 Barcelona, Spain
18 Universitat Rovira i Virgili, Departament de Bioquímica i Biotecnologia, Unitat de Nutrició, 43201 Reus, Spain
19 Lipids and Vascular Risk Unit, Internal Medicine, University Hospital of Bellvitge (IDIBELL), L'Hospitalet de Llobregat, 08907 Barcelona, Spain
20 Department of Human Genetics, Radboud University Medical Center, 6525 GA Nijmegen, The Netherlands; geert.poelmans@radboudumc.nl

Citation: Testa, G.; Mora-Maltas, B.; Camacho-Barcia, L.; Granero, R.; Lucas, I.; Agüera, Z.; Jiménez-Murcia, S.; Baños, R.; Bertaina-Anglade, V.; Botella, C.; et al. Transdiagnostic Perspective of Impulsivity and Compulsivity in Obesity: From Cognitive Profile to Self-Reported Dimensions in Clinical Samples with and without Diabetes. *Nutrients* **2021**, *13*, 4426. https://doi.org/10.3390/nu13124426

Academic Editor: Roberto Cangemi

Received: 26 October 2021
Accepted: 7 December 2021
Published: 10 December 2021

[21] Department of Endocrinology and Nutrition, Virgen de la Victoria Hospital, Institute of Biomedical Research in Malaga (IBIMA), University of Malaga, 29016 Málaga, Spain
[22] Integrative Pharmacology and Systems Neurosciences Research Group, Institut Hospital del Mar de Investigaciones Médicas Municipal d'Investigació Mèdica (IMIM), 08003 Barcelona, Spain
[23] IMIM-Hospital del Mar Medical Research Institute and CIBER of Physiopathology of Obesity and Nutrition (CIBEROBN), University Pompeu Fabra (DCEXS-UPF), 08003 Barcelona, Spain
[24] Nutrition Unit, University Hospital of Sant Joan de Reus, 43204 Reus, Spain
[25] Nutrition Research Group, Research Institute of Biomedical and Health Sciences (IUIBS), University of Las Palmas de Gran Canaria, 35001 Las Palmas de Gran Canaria, Spain
[26] Alzheimer Centrum Limburg, Department of Psychiatry and Neuropsychology, School for Mental Health and Neuroscience, Maastricht University, 6211 LK Maastricht, The Netherlands; s.vos@maastrichtuniversity.nl
[27] National Centre for Register-Based Research, Department of Economics and Business Economics, Aarhus University, DK-8000 Aarhus, Denmark; tw@econ.au.dk
* Correspondence: ffernandez@bellvitgehospital.cat; Tel.: +34-93-2607227
† These authors contributed equally to this work.

Abstract: Impulsive and compulsive behaviors have both been observed in individuals with obesity. The co-occurrence of obesity and type 2 diabetes (T2D) is more strongly associated with impulsivity, although there are no conclusive results yet. A multidimensional assessment of impulsivity and compulsivity was conducted in individuals with obesity in the absence or presence of T2D, compared with healthy, normal-weight individuals, with highly impulsive patients (gambling disorders), and with highly compulsive patients (anorexia nervosa). Decision making and novelty seeking were used to measure impulsivity, and cognitive flexibility and harm avoidance were used for compulsivity. For impulsivity, patients with obesity and T2D showed poorer decision-making ability compared with healthy individuals. For compulsivity, individuals with only obesity presented less cognitive flexibility and high harm avoidance; these dimensions were not associated with obesity with T2D. This study contributes to the knowledge of the mechanisms associated with diabetes and its association with impulsive–compulsive behaviors, confirming the hypothesis that patients with obesity and T2D would be characterized by higher levels of impulsivity.

Keywords: impulsivity; compulsivity; decision making; cognitive flexibility; type 2 diabetes; novelty seeking; harm avoidance

1. Introduction

The prevalence of obesity worldwide has alarmingly increased, having nearly tripled in the last 50 years, reaching pandemic levels [1]. As one of the major risk factors for noncommunicable diseases, it has been associated with a reduced quality of life, high presence of disabilities, and decreased life expectancy [2]. Obesity is a complex disorder, usually classified as a metabolic, nutritional, and endocrine disease. Several factors contribute to the physiopathology of this disease, including genetic, social, environmental and psychological aspects [3]. According to the body mass index (BMI), obesity is classified in the following three categories: class I obesity (BMI: 30–34.9 kg/m^2), class II obesity (BMI: 35–39.9 kg/m^2), and class III obesity, or morbid obesity (BMI > 39.9 kg/m^2) [4]. The presence of obesity is associated with multiple comorbidities that significantly contribute to higher rates of morbidity and mortality, including type 2 diabetes (T2D) and insulin resistance (IR), among others [5–7].

Excessive food consumption is one of the main contributors to weight gain in obesity. However, appetite and feeding behavior are not only controlled by energy requirements or metabolic need. Food also acts as a natural reinforcer, and its consumption is motivated by its hedonic properties, which rely on mesolimbic dopamine and opioids systems [8,9]. Processed foods, high in fats, sugars, and salt, are believed to stimulate appetite and increase calorie consumption through stimulation of opiates and dopamine receptors in the reward center [10,11]. Given the complexity and multicausality of this pathology, understanding the neurobehavioral mechanisms underpinning obesity is crucial to develop effective specific treatments.

Two constructs that have been suggested to play a role in excessive food intake and weight gain are impulsivity and compulsivity [12]. Impulsivity is typically defined as a tendency to act rashly without giving adequate forethought to the consequences of the behaviors, which, in the case of obesity, is reflected by overeating palatable foods [13]. Impulsivity is multidimensional, including personality traits (e.g., sensation seeking, lack of premeditation, and urgency) [14,15], motor impulsivity (e.g., response inhibition), and choice impulsivity (e.g., decision making and deficits in delay gratification) [16–18]. By contrast, compulsivity is characterized by repetitive and persistent behaviors, often harmful, despite their consequences [19]. In the context of overeating and obesity, this is reflected by repetition of maladaptive habits and a failure to shift behavior, despite its negative effects [20]. An important dimension of compulsivity is cognitive flexibility, which is the ability to flexibly adjust behavior to the demands of a changing environment (e.g., attentional set-shifting and task-shifting) [21,22].

Currently, there is a growing interest in analyzing dimensional models, where a spectrum around a specific construct will be considered, in which different disorders share some characteristics. From this point of view, the term dimension is understood as the set of magnitudes that serve to define a psychological phenomenon [23]. Thus, while the categorical model is based on the process of counting symptoms to an arbitrary number, where the presence of more symptoms becomes meaningless, in dimensional approaches, the number of diagnostic features forms an index of severity by taking into account the daily functioning of patients. The clinical utility of adopting dimensional models has been suggested, especially in the case of personality pathologies [24].

This is the case for the impulsive–compulsive spectrum, in which the dimensional approach is especially relevant. Along this spectrum, some mental disorders typically described in the impulsive pole are gambling disorder (GD) and other impulse control disorders, attention-deficit hyperactivity disorder (ADHD), borderline personality disorder, among others [25–27]. Compulsivity is well represented by anorexia nervosa restrictive type (AN-R), obsessive-compulsive disorder, and obsessive-compulsive personality trait [28,29]. Nonetheless, where obesity and obesity plus T2D comorbidity can be placed along the impulsive–compulsive spectrum is still unknown, which could have important implications for developing specific treatments.

Impulsive personality traits have been associated with a greater body mass index (BMI) and weight gain [30,31]. Moreover, strong evidence exists for a positive relation between obesity and cognitive indices of impulsivity, such as poor decision making [32] and deficits in delay gratification [33]. Similarly, a lack of cognitive flexibility has been shown in individuals with obesity and overweight [34,35]. Personality traits related to compulsivity, such as obsessive-compulsive traits and harm avoidance [36], as well as the ability to cope with negative emotions [37], have been suggested to play an important role in the development and perpetuation of obesity [38,39]. Accordingly, some studies showed elevated harm avoidance in individuals with obesity [40–43].

Type 2 diabetes is a metabolic disorder, characterized by pancreatic β-cell dysfunction and insulin resistance, which result in elevated levels of blood glucose [44]. Impaired glycemic control and IR have been suggested to impact brain dopaminergic systems [45–50], which may contribute to impulsivity and deficits in self-regulation, as well as impairment in cognitive functioning [51–54]. Although there are still no conclusive results, some studies highlight impairments in impulsivity, specifically in motor impulsivity in older adults with T2D [54], and recent research showed more disadvantageous decision making in T2D than in healthy controls in the Iowa gambling task (IGT) [55]. To the best of our knowledge, there are no current studies evaluating the association between compulsivity and T2D in individuals with obesity. Taking all this into account, it is unclear whether the presence of T2D affects different dimensions of impulsivity and compulsivity in individuals with obesity.

The present study aimed to describe and compare different clinical populations along the impulsivity–compulsivity spectrum. It especially focuses on individuals with obesity in the absence or presence of T2D, when compared with highly impulsive patients (namely, patients with GD) highly compulsive patients (namely, patients with AN-R), and healthy, normal-weight individuals. A multiple assessment of various impulsivity and compulsivity dimensions, using self-reported measures and neuropsychological tasks, was conducted to evaluate decision making and novelty seeking as markers of impulsivity, and cognitive flexibility and harm avoidance as markers of compulsivity. Based on the above-mentioned literature, individuals with obesity were expected to present compulsivity-related personality traits and poor cognitive flexibility. For the impulsivity dimensions, we hypothesize an impulsive profile to characterize obesity with T2D, with impulsive decision making and novelty seeking possibly being more pronounced in these individuals than in those with obesity only.

2. Materials and Methods

2.1. Study Design and Population

In the present cross-sectional study, a total of 581 participants along the impulsive–compulsive spectrum were included, as follows: n = 115 individuals with morbid obesity without diabetes (OB-DM), n = 67 individuals with morbid obesity and T2D (OB + DM), n = 107 individuals with anorexia nervosa restrictive subtype (AN-R), n = 121 individuals with gambling disorder (GD) and n = 171 healthy controls (HC). Participants in the AN-R and GD groups who presented with T2D were not included. Seven centers, all part of the Spanish Biomedical Research Centre in Physiopathology of Obesity and Nutrition (CIBERobn), participated in the study. The clinical groups were patients who had been consecutively referred to the clinics mentioned above. Healthy controls were recruited by means of word-of-mouth and advertisements at local universities, from the same catchment area as the clinical groups. The study was conducted according to the guidelines of the Declaration of Helsinki and its amendments, the International Conference on Harmonization Good Clinical Practice guidelines, and local regulatory requirements. The study was approved by the ethics committees of all participating institutions. Informed consent was obtained from all subjects participating in the study.

2.2. Psychometric Measures

The Temperament and Character Inventory—Revised (TCI-R) [56], previously validated in a Spanish adult population [57], consists of 240 items with a five-point Likert scale format. Three character dimensions are evaluated (self-directedness, cooperativeness, and self-transcendence) and also four temperaments (harm avoidance, novelty seeking, reward dependence, and persistence). In this study, harm avoidance and novelty seeking subscales were adopted as measures of compulsivity and impulsivity, respectively. For this sample, the Cronbach's alpha was good, ranging from $\alpha = 0.830$ (for novelty seeking) to $\alpha = 0.889$ (for harm avoidance).

The Symptom Checklist—90 Items—Revised (SCL-90-R) [58], which was validated in a Spanish population [59], was administered for evaluating self-reported psychological distress and psychopathology. The instrument is scored on nine primary symptom dimensions (somatization, obsessive-compulsive behavior, interpersonal sensitivity, depression, anxiety, hostility, phobic anxiety, paranoid ideation, and psychoticism) and three global indices (global severity index (GSI), positive symptom total (PST), and positive symptom distress index (PSDI)). The internal consistency for the global index in our sample was high, $\alpha = 0.980$.

2.3. Neuropsychological Measures

The computerized version of the Wisconsin card sorting test (WCST) [60] was used to evaluate cognitive flexibility through a set-shifting task. The WCST consists of matching stimulus cards within one of three of the following available categories: color, shape, or number. For a correct match, participants must identify the sorting rule, receiving the feedback of "right" or "wrong" after each sort. Following 10 consecutive correct matches, the rule is changed and then a new sorting rule must be identified. There are up to six attempts to detect the sorting rule and five rule shifts during the task. Each rule attainment is referred to as "category completed". Participants do not know the correct rules or changes. The test continues until 128 cards are sorted. The following variables were adopted to measure cognitive flexibility: perseverative errors (i.e., failure to change sorting strategy after negative feedback), non-perseverative errors and the number of completed categories.

The Iowa gambling task (IGT) [61] is a computerized task proposed as a measure of choice impulsivity as it evaluates decision making. It is performed by selecting between four decks where each deck provides a specific amount of play money. It consists of a total of 100 turns in which the rewards interspersed between the decks are probabilistic punishments (monetary losses with different amounts). The final objective of the task is to earn as much money as possible and lose as little money as possible by choosing the cards from any deck, and participants are able to change the deck at any time. The score for this test is obtained by the difference of selected cards from decks A and B, and from decks C and D (CD–AB). Higher scores indicate better performance on the task. This means that the subject will have chosen more cards from decks C and D as they are advantageous (less penalties), while decks A and B are not advantageous (more penalties).

2.4. Procedure

The presence of T2D was diagnosed by a physician and the information was retrieved from medical records. Obesity was defined as BMI $\geq$ 30 kg/m^2, calculated using the formula BMI = weight(kg)/(height(m))^2. AN-R and GD samples were diagnosed according to the DSM-5 criteria [62] by clinical psychologists and psychiatrists with more than 15 years of experience in the field, during a face-to-face clinical interview. Regarding the neuropsychological evaluation, it was administered by a trained psychologist in a single session. In addition, the tests were specifically selected to determine various dimensions of executive functions. Other significant information was collected during the clinical interviews, such as sex, age, and education level.

2.5. Statistical Analysis

Statistical analysis was performed with Stata17 for Windows [63]. Comparison between the groups was performed with analysis of covariance (ANCOVA, adjusted for sex, age, educational level, and BMI) for quantitative measures and with logistic regression (also adjusted for the same covariates) for binary measures. Since the groups were ordered according to their position within the compulsivity–impulsivity continuous dimensional spectrum, these models included polynomial contrasts to assess the presence of patterns in data adjusted by linear, quadratic, cubic, and quartic equation/functions (four polynomial trends were assessed, the maximum allowed for variables categorized in five group levels). Pairwise post hoc comparisons also explored differences between group means and proportions.

The Finner method was employed to control type I error due to multiple null hypothesis tests. This is a correction procedure based on a stepwise multiple-test method aimed to adjust p-values whilst controlling the familywise error rate (FWER, defined as the likelihood of achieving at least k false rejections) [64]. Controlling the k-FWER implies fixing a number of $k-1$ of tolerated erroneous rejections, and then combining the unadjusted p-values to obtain a single testing for the group of null hypothesis tests at α-level.

3. Results

3.1. Descriptive for the Sample

Table 1 displays the distribution of the patients' sex, education levels, age, and BMI, as well as the comparison between the groups. The AN-R group included a high proportion of women and patients with secondary or university education levels, the youngest mean age, and the lowest BMI. The OB-DM group was also characterized by a high proportion of women, patients with primary or secondary study levels, and the highest BMI. OB + DM also included mostly women, the highest proportion of participants with primary education levels, the oldest mean age, and the highest mean BMI. The GD group included mostly men and a high proportion of patients with primary education levels.

Table 1. Descriptive for the sample.

	AN-R *N* = 107		**OB − T2D** *N* = 115		**HC** *N* = 171		**OB + T2D** *N* = 67		**GD** *N* = 121		
	n	%	*n*	%	*n*	%	*n*	%	*n*	%	*p*
Sex											
Women	97	90.7%	107	93.0%	144	84.2%	48	71.6%	19	15.7%	**<0.001** *
Men	10	9.3%	8	7.0%	27	15.8%	19	28.4%	102	84.3%	
Education Primary	29	27.1%	48	41.7%	16	9.4%	48	71.6%	72	59.5%	**<0.001** *
Secondary	48	44.9%	53	46.1%	104	60.8%	17	25.4%	32	26.4%	
University	30	28.0%	14	12.2%	51	29.8%	2	3.0%	17	14.0%	
	Mean	SD	Mean	SD	Mean	SD	Mean	SD	Mean	SD	*p*
Age (years)	25.31	8.30	41.39	11.87	29.71	13.28	54.61	11.33	38.30	13.56	**<0.001** *
BMI (kg/m^2)	16.36	2.17	44.60	6.70	22.34	3.14	41.96	8.59	26.38	5.90	**<0.001** *

Note. AN-R: anorexia nervosa restrictive. OB − T2D: obesity without T2D. HC: healthy control. OB + T2D: obesity without T2D. GD: gambling disorder. SD: standard deviation. * Bold: significant comparison.

3.2. Comparison of Impulsivity and Compulsivity Measures

Table 2 contains the ANCOVA results with a comparison between the means registered in the impulsivity and compulsivity measures, adjusted for the covariates of sex, age, educational level, and BMI (see Figure 1 for the performance line graph for the adjusted mean scores). These results provide evidence for differences between the groups. As expected, the HC achieved the highest performance in the neuropsychological measures (highest means in the IGT and lowest means in the WCST errors and perseverative errors), the lowest mean in harm avoidance, and the lowest psychological distress. AN-R showed the worst performance in the IGT task (the scores were similar to those obtained among GD patients), the lowest mean in the novelty seeking trait, and the highest mean in harm avoidance (for this personality trait, the mean score was quite similar to OB-DM). Regarding the IGT total raw score, patients with OB + DM achieved worse performance compared to the HC group, whereas no differences were found between the participants in the OB-DM group and the HC group. The OB-DM condition reported the worst performance in the WCST task and the highest mean in the harm avoidance scale. The GD patients also achieved poor performance in the neuropsychological task, and the highest mean in the novelty seeking dimension. Figure 2 includes the line chart showing the performance learning curve in the IGT task. HC obtained the best performance, followed by OB-DM and OB + DM, while AN-R and GD achieved the worst results.

Regarding polynomial contrasts, most measures did not adjust to a linear trend, while other quadratic–cubic–quartic functions achieved statistical significance (Table 2). These results indicated that other patterns in data with many fluctuations are more likely to appear than simply increasing or decreasing means within the impulsivity–compulsivity continuous spectrum.

Table 2. Comparison between the groups in impulsivity and compulsivity measurements. ANCOVA adjusted by sex, age, education and BMI.

	AN-R N = 107		**OB − T2D** N = 115		**HC** N = 171		**OB + T2D** N = 67		**GD** N = 121		**Polynomial Contrasts Trends (*p*-Value)**			
Impulsivity	***Mean***	***SD***	***Mean***	***SD***	***Mean***	***SD***	***Mean***	***SD***	***Mean***	***SD***	*O1*	*O2*	*O3*	*O4*
IGT Total raw	−1.62	20.33	7.71	22.12	13.24	28.52	2.10	20.31	1.41	24.58	0.964	**0.004** *	0.106	0.308
IGT Learning	5.84	12.94	6.35	14.65	7.87	16.84	7.08	14.38	3.44	14.38	0.511	0.177	0.477	0.909
IGT Risk index	2.63	13.83	5.89	13.42	8.46	17.02	3.63	13.28	1.96	15.22	0.561	**0.029** *	0.481	0.478
TCI-R Novelty seeking	90.94	12.56	96.53	13.21	100.33	11.45	96.15	12.11	117.82	9.29	**0.001** *	**0.001** *	**0.001** *	**0.035** *
Compulsivity	*Mean*	*SD*	*Mean*	*SD*	*Mean*	*SD*	*Mean*	*SD*	*Mean*	*SD*	*O1*	*O2*	*O3*	*O4*
WCST Errors	27.40	16.71	39.19	25.96	23.06	16.04	27.98	24.61	31.04	24.66	0.636	0.733	**0.001** *	**0.027** *
WCST Errors perseve.	12.94	7.71	19.67	14.61	10.84	7.24	13.96	13.21	13.80	10.88	0.348	0.735	**0.001** *	**0.011**
WCST Categ.compl.	5.11	1.20	4.45	2.22	5.25	1.21	5.37	2.12	4.80	1.97	0.650	0.549	**0.001** *	0.416
TCI-R Harm avoid.	106.02	18.63	108.88	16.87	91.38	16.21	100.21	14.07	103.51	18.77	**0.046** *	**0.002** *	**0.015** *	**0.004** *
SCL-90R Obs.-comp.	1.24	0.91	1.26	0.73	0.70	0.56	1.04	0.67	1.45	0.87	0.505	**0.001** *	**0.016** *	0.055
Pairwise **comparisons**	AN-R/ OB − T2D		AN-R/ HC		AN-R/ OB + T2D		AN-R/ GD	OB − T2D/ HC	OB − T2D/ OB + T2D	OB − T2D/ GD	HC/ OB + T2D	HC/ GD	OB + T2D/ GD	η²
Impulsivity														
IGT Total raw	0.142		**<0.001** *		0.572		0.493	0.291	0.159	0.224	**0.046** *	**0.002** *	0.895	0.048
IGT Learning	0.897		0.307		0.760		0.381	0.638	0.764	0.365	0.821	0.056	0.259	0.008
IGT Risk index	0.407		**0.004** *		0.806		0.807	0.429	0.361	0.222	0.164	**0.005** *	0.605	0.024
TCI-R Novelty seeking	0.068		**<0.001** *		0.102		**<0.001** *	0.133	0.843	**<0.001** *	0.121	**<0.001** *	**<0.001** *	**0.282** †
Compulsivity														
WCST Errors	**0.025** *		0.104		0.915		0.321	**<0.001** *	**0.001** *	0.059	0.288	**0.010** *	0.479	0.043
WCST Errors perseve.	**0.013** *		0.125		0.715		0.647	**<0.001** *	**0.001** *	0.008 *	0.189	0.063	0.943	0.042
WCST Categ.compl.	0.126		0.496		0.555		0.306	**0.023** *	**0.001** *	0.318	0.761	0.072	0.107	0.029
TCI-R Harm avoid.	0.512		**<0.001** *		0.199		0.408	**<0.001** *	**0.002** *	0.132	**0.022** *	**<0.001** *	0.358	**0.124** †
SCL-90R Obs.-comp.	0.937		**<0.001** *		0.314		0.119	**<0.001** *	0.073	0.218	**0.046** *	**<0.001** *	**0.010** *	**0.109** †

Note. AN-R: anorexia nervosa restrictive. HC: healthy control. GD: gambling disorder. OB − T2D: obesity without T2D. OB + T2D: obesity with T2D. IGT: Iowa gambling test. SCL-90: Symptom Checklist—90 Items—Revised. TCI-R: Temperament and Character Inventory–Revised. WCST: Wisconsin card sorting test. SD: standard deviation. O1: order 1, linear. O2: order 2, quadratic. O3: order 3, cubic. O4: order 4, quartic. η^2: partial eta squared. * Bold: significant parameter. † Bold: effect size within the ranges moderate/medium to large/high. Note. AN-R: anorexia nervosa restrictive. OB − T2D: obesity without T2D. HC: healthy control. OB + T2D: obesity with T2D. GD: gambling disorder. IGT: Iowa gambling test. WCST: Wisconsin card sorting test. *Y*-axis represents the means adjusted by sex, age, education, and BMI.

3.3. Comparison of Psychological State

Table S1 (Supplementary) shows the comparison of the psychopathology state between the groups, according to the SCL-90R scales (see Figure S1 for the T-standardized mean scores). A healthier psychology status was registered for the participants within the HC group, followed by the OB + DM patients. On the other hand, the GD and AN-R conditions registered the worse psychology state.

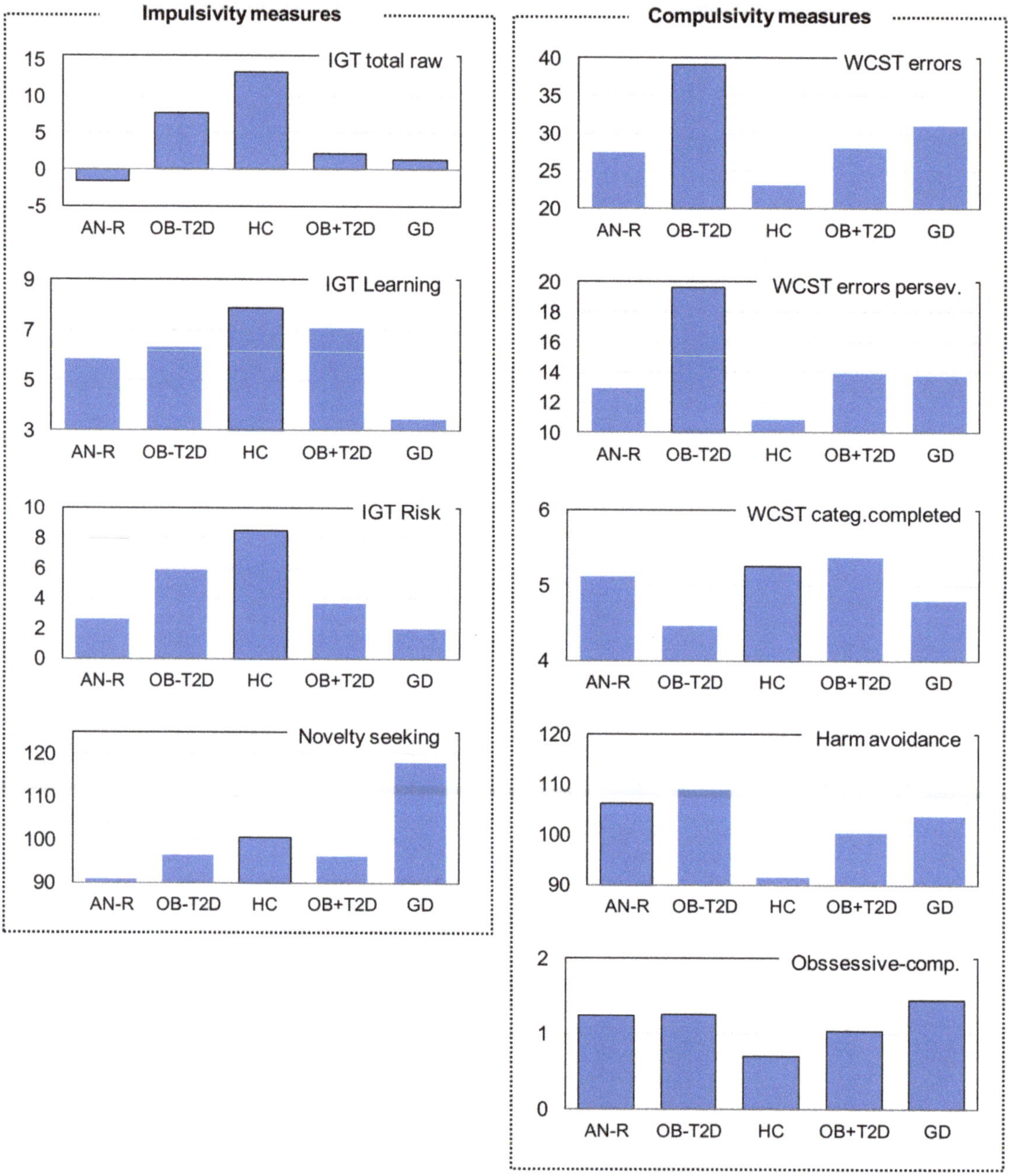

Figure 1. Bar charts with the impulsivity–compulsivity measures in the study (dimensional scores).

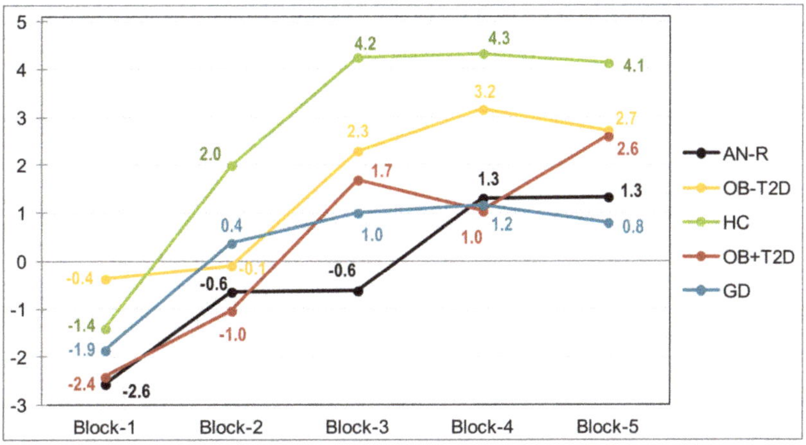

Figure 2. Performance learning curve (IGT task). Note. AN-R: anorexia nervosa restrictive. OB − T2D: obesity without T2D. HC: healthy control. OB + T2D: obesity with T2D. GD: gambling disorder. *Y*-axis represents the means adjusted by sex, age, education, and BMI.

4. Discussion

In the present study, we sought to investigate cognitive and personality traits associated with impulsivity and compulsivity in individuals with obesity in the presence or absence of T2D. Additional groups included in the study were healthy, normal-weight individuals, highly impulsive patients (patients with GD), and underweight, highly compulsive patients (patients with AN-R). Individuals with obesity and T2D showed highly impulsive decision making, whereas the other measure of impulsivity, novelty seeking, was not associated with obesity with T2D, nor with obesity only. For the compulsive pole, individuals with only obesity presented poor cognitive flexibility and high harm avoidance, although these dimensions were not associated with obesity plus T2D.

Impulsive decision making (e.g., choice impulsivity) is characterized by the preference for high immediate reward, despite higher future losses, in terms of both physical and psychological outcomes [17]. Poor decision making, shown by a lower IGT total score, was observed in individuals with obesity in the presence of T2D, when compared with the HC group. This was similar to what was observed in GD and AN-R compared to the HC. By contrast, the IGT total score in individuals with obesity in the absence of T2D did not differ from that of the HC group. Our findings are consistent with a previous study [55], which showed more disadvantageous decisions in the IGT total score in individuals with obesity plus T2D than in the HC. A potential explanation for the relation between obesity plus T2D and cognitive components of impulsivity could be, to some extent, the deficiencies in central insulin signaling, which are thought to impact the brain's dopaminergic (DA) systems [45–49]. Given the central role of DA in cognitive functions related to impulsivity [65–67], it is possible that the presence of T2D and the related alterations in insulin signaling in the brain impact these cognitive dimensions of impulsivity [68,69].

Regarding personality traits related to impulsivity, novelty seeking reflects the tendency to seek out new stimuli and experiences, to be easily bored, and be inclined to avoid monotony [70]. The group of patients with GD were the only group that showed high novelty seeking, whereas individuals with obesity in the presence or absence of T2D were not characterized by high novelty seeking when compared with the HC. Although some studies in the general population reported a positive relation between novelty seeking and BMI [70], this was not found in clinical populations of individuals with obesity, in which novelty seeking was not related to BMI [71] or to successful weight loss [72]. Moreover, it has been suggested that higher novelty seeking is more frequently associated with the presence of eating disorders (e.g., binge eating disorder and night eating disorder) [73], rather than obesity. Impulsive personality traits more strictly linked to decision making, such as urgency [74] and a lack of premeditation [75], may be expected to be more pronounced in individuals with obesity in the presence of T2D, although no studies are available to date.

For the compulsive spectrum, cognitive flexibility refers to the ability to flexibly adapt one's behavior to a changeable environment [76]. We found poor flexibility in individuals with obesity without T2D, compared to the other groups. This is consistent with previous findings, in which deficits in cognitive flexibility have been observed in people with overweight and obesity [34,35]. Difficulties in shifting current behavior in response to different requirements could negatively impact eating behaviors, and this cognitive rigidity could help to maintain unhealthy eating habits and, thus, relate to high body weight [77].

Concerning personality traits, harm avoidance is defined as the tendency to be motivated by a desire to avoid aversive experiences, which is strictly related to compulsive attitudes. We observed higher levels of harm avoidance in the group of individuals with obesity without T2D. This is in line with previous studies in clinical samples, which showed a positive association between harm avoidance and obesity [40–42]. Higher harm avoidance scores have been particularly reported in patients with grade 3 obesity compared with grade 2 and 1 obesity [42]. Nevertheless, higher psychological distress was present in individuals with obesity without T2D compared to the individuals with obesity plus T2D, which could contribute to more rigid behavior and cognition.

Limits and Strengths

The present study was limited by the absence of some important variables, such as the duration of diabetes and the diabetes medication, which could have interfered with the results. Therefore, these findings should be interpreted with caution, and further studies, taking medication and illness duration into account, will need to be undertaken. Furthermore, considering the complex nature of impulsivity and compulsivity, a broader assessment of the other domains of impulsivity/compulsivity would be informative, to better characterize obesity in the presence or absence of T2D.

Despite these limitations, one of the strengths of the study is the inclusion of clinical comparison groups that are representative of impulsivity and compulsivity, such as GD and AN-R. This facilitates the placement of obesity groups along the impulsive–compulsive spectrum. An additional strength is the use of both neurocognitive and personality measures, enabling a more comprehensive assessment.

5. Conclusions

Taken together, the results of this study suggest that the individuals with obesity in the absence of T2D were more rigid in their behavior and showed more compulsive personality traits than those with obesity plus T2D. On the other pole of impulsivity, we found that individuals with obesity in the presence of T2D were more impulsive in their decisions compared to healthy, normal-weight controls; this would allocate them to the impulsive pole of the impulsive–compulsive spectrum. If so, the tendency to make impulsive choices may be expected to negatively impact self-control and diabetes management. However, due to the lack of information about diabetic medication and diabetes duration, which affect insulin signaling in the brain, these findings should be interpreted with caution. Further studies, controlling these variables, are needed to confirm the present findings.

Despite its exploratory nature, this study offers preliminary insights into the personality traits associated with the compulsivity–impulsivity spectrum in individuals with obesity in the presence or absence of T2D. For the health care provider, identifying and understanding the presence of personality traits that could act as a barrier to treatment adherence may improve the success rates of diabetes management and obesity weight loss treatments.

Supplementary Materials: The following are available online at https://www.mdpi.com/article/10.3390/nu13124426/s1: Table S1: comparison between the groups: ANCOVA adjusted for sex, age, education and BMI; Figure S1: line charts with the SCL-90R profile in the study (mean T-scores).

Author Contributions: Conceptualization F.F.-A.; formal statistical analysis, R.G.; writing—original draft preparation, F.F.-A., G.T., B.M.-M., L.C.-B., I.L.; writing—review and editing, F.F.-A., G.T., B.M.-M., L.C.-B., R.G., I.L., Z.A., S.J.-M., R.B., C.B., V.B.-A., M.B., F.F.C., S.D., J.-M.F.-R., B.F., G.F., M.F., C.G.-M., X.P., G.P., F.J.T., R.d.l.T., J.S.-S., L.S.-M., S.V., T.W., F.F.-A. contributed substantially to the data recollection, interpretation of data, and have read and agreed to the published version of the manuscript. All authors have read and agreed to the published version of the manuscript.

Funding: This manuscript and research were supported by grants from the Instituto de Salud Carlos III (ISCIII) (FIS PI14/00290, PI17/01167 and PI20/132) and (PI13/00462, PI16/00501, PI19/00576), by the SLT006/17/00246 grant, funded by the Department of Health of the Generalitat de Catalunya by the call "Acció instrumental de programes de recerca orientats en l'àmbit de la recerca i la innovació en salut" (PERIS) and co-funded by FEDER funds/European Regional Development Fund (ERDF), a way to build Europe. CIBERObn is an initiative of ISCIII. This research was also partially funded by EU-H2020 grants (Eat2beNICE/H2020-SFS-2016-2, Ref 728018; PRIME/H2020-SC1-BHC-2018-2020, Ref: 847879). CG-M receives a predoctoral grant from the University of Rovira i Virgili (2020PMF-PIPF-37). The funders had no role in the study design, data collection and analysis, decision to publish, or preparation of the manuscript.

Institutional Review Board Statement: According to the ethical standards of the Declaration of Helsinki by the research ethics committees, all the participating institutions approved the study protocol and procedures (PR240/13; 2013/5276/I; 13-07-25/7proj2; PR307/06; 2010/3914/I; 111/2010).

Informed Consent Statement: All participants provided written informed consent.

Acknowledgments: We thank CERCA Programme/Generalitat de Catalunya for institutional support. This work is partially supported by ICREA under the ICREA Academia programme.

Conflicts of Interest: FFA received consultancy honoraria from Novo Nordisk and editorial honoraria as EIC from Wiley. BF received educational speaking fees from Medicine. The rest of the authors declare no conflict of interest. The funders had no role in the design of the study; in the collection, analyses, or interpretation of data; in the writing of the manuscript, or in the decision to publish the results.

References

1. World Health Organization. *Obesity and Overweight*; WHO: Geneva, Switzerland, 2021.
2. De Gonzalez, A.B.; Hartge, P.; Cerhan, J.R.; Flint, A.J.; Hannan, L.; MacInnis, R.J.; Moore, S.C.; Tobias, G.S.; Anton-Culver, H.; Freeman, L.B.; et al. Body-Mass Index and Mortality among 1.46 Million White Adults. *N. Engl. J. Med.* **2010**, *363*, 2211–2219. [CrossRef]
3. Blüher, M. Obesity: Global epidemiology and pathogenesis. *Nat. Rev. Endocrinol.* **2019**, *15*, 288–298.
4. Ferrulli, A. Obesity: Classification and Diagnosis. In *Thyroid, Obesity and Metabolism*; Springer: Cham, Switzerland, 2021; pp. 73–93.
5. Neeland, I.J.; Poirier, P.; Després, J.P. Cardiovascular and Metabolic Heterogeneity of Obesity: Clinical Challenges and Implications for Management. *Circulation* **2018**, *137*, 1391–1406. [CrossRef]
6. Piché, M.E.; Tchernof, A.; Després, J.P. Obesity Phenotypes, Diabetes, and Cardiovascular Diseases. *Circ. Res.* **2020**, *126*, 1477–1500. [CrossRef]
7. Heymsfield, S.; Wadden, T. Mechanisms, Pathophysiology, and Management of Obesity. *N. Engl. J. Med.* **2017**, *376*, 1490–1492. [CrossRef]
8. Wenzel, J.M.; Cheer, J.F. Endocannabinoid Regulation of Reward and Reinforcement through Interaction with Dopamine and Endogenous Opioid Signaling. *Neuropsychopharmacology* **2018**, *43*, 103–115.
9. Amin, T.; Mercer, J.G. Hunger and Satiety Mechanisms and Their Potential Exploitation in the Regulation of Food Intake. *Curr. Obes. Rep.* **2016**, *5*, 106–112.
10. Small, D.M.; DiFeliceantonio, A.G. Neuroscience: Processed foods and food reward. *Science* **2019**, *363*, 346–347.
11. Cocores, J.A.; Gold, M.S. The Salted Food Addiction Hypothesis may explain overeating and the obesity epidemic. *Med. Hypotheses* **2009**, *73*, 892–899. [CrossRef]
12. Steward, T.; Miranda-Olivos, R.; Soriano-Mas, C.; Fernández-Aranda, F. Neuroendocrinological mechanisms underlying impulsive and compulsive behaviors in obesity: A narrative review of fMRI studies. *Rev. Endocr. Metab. Disord.* **2019**, *20*, 263–272.
13. Michaud, A.; Vainik, U.; Garcia-Garcia, I.; Dagher, A. Overlapping neural endophenotypes in addiction and obesity. *Front. Endocrinol.* **2017**, *8*, 127.
14. Verdejo-García, A.; Lozano, Ó.; Moya, M.; Alcázar, M.Á.; Pérez-García, M. Psychometric properties of a spanish version of the UPPS-P impulsive behavior scale: Reliability, validity and association with trait and cognitive impulsivity. *J. Pers. Assess.* **2010**, *92*, 70–77. [CrossRef]

15. Whiteside, S.P.; Lynam, D.R. The five factor model and impulsivity: Using a structural model of personality to understand impulsivity. *Pers. Individ. Dif.* **2001**, *30*, 669–689. [CrossRef]
16. Hamilton, K.R.; Littlefield, A.K.; Anastasio, N.C.; Cunningham, K.A.; Fink, L.H.L.; Wing, V.C.; Mathias, C.W.; Lane, S.D.; Schütz, C.G.; Swann, A.C.; et al. Rapid-response impulsivity: Definitions, measurement issues, and clinical implications. *Pers. Disord. Theory Res. Treat.* **2015**, *6*, 168–181. [CrossRef]
17. Hamilton, K.R.; Mitchell, M.R.; Wing, V.C.; Balodis, I.M.; Bickel, W.K.; Fillmore, M.; Lane, S.D.; Lejuez, C.W.; Littlefield, A.K.; Luijten, M.; et al. Choice impulsivity: Definitions, measurement issues, and clinical implications. *Pers. Disord. Theory Res. Treat.* **2015**, *6*, 182–198. [CrossRef]
18. de Water, E.; Mies, G.W.; Figner, B.; Yoncheva, Y.; van den Bos, W.; Castellanos, F.X.; Cillessen, A.H.N.; Scheres, A. Neural mechanisms of individual differences in temporal discounting of monetary and primary rewards in adolescents. *Neuroimage* **2017**, *153*, 198–210. [CrossRef]
19. Robbins, T.; Curran, H.; De Wit, H. Special issue on impulsivity and compulsivity. *Psychopharmacology* **2012**, *219*, 251–252.
20. Moore, C.F.; Sabino, V.; Koob, G.F.; Cottone, P. Pathological Overeating: Emerging Evidence for a Compulsivity Construct. *Neuropsychopharmacology* **2017**, *42*, 1375–1389.
21. Armbruster, D.J.N.; Ueltzhöffer, K.; Basten, U.; Fiebach, C.J. Prefrontal cortical mechanisms underlying individual differences in cognitive flexibility and stability. *J. Cogn. Neurosci.* **2012**, *24*, 2385–2399. [CrossRef]
22. Dajani, D.R.; Uddin, L.Q. Demystifying cognitive flexibility: Implications for clinical and developmental neuroscience. *Trends Neurosci.* **2015**, *38*, 571–578.
23. Widiger, T.A.; Samuel, D.B. Diagnostic categories or dimensions? A question for the Diagnostic and Statistical Manual of Mental Disorders—Fifth edition. *J. Abnorm. Psychol.* **2005**, *114*, 494–504. [CrossRef]
24. Bornstein, R.F.; Natoli, A.P. Clinical utility of categorical and dimensional perspectives on personality pathology: A meta-analytic review. *Pers. Disord. Theory Res. Treat.* **2019**, *10*, 479–490. [CrossRef]
25. Bottesi, G.; Ghisi, M.; Ouimet, A.J.; Tira, M.D.; Sanavio, E. Compulsivity and impulsivity in pathological gambling: Does a dimensional-transdiagnostic approach add clinical utility to DSM-5 classification? *J. Gambl. Stud.* **2015**, *31*, 825–847. [CrossRef]
26. Winstanley, C.A.; Eagle, D.M.; Robbins, T.W. Behavioral models of impulsivity in relation to ADHD: Translation between clinical and preclinical studies. *Clin. Psychol. Rev.* **2006**, *26*, 379–395. [CrossRef]
27. Peters, J.R.; Upton, B.T.; Baer, R.A. Brief Report: Relationships Between Facets of Impulsivity and Borderline Personality Features. *J. Pers. Disord.* **2013**, *27*, 547–552. [CrossRef]
28. Lavender, J.M.; Goodman, E.L.; Culbert, K.M.; Wonderlich, S.A.; Crosby, R.D.; Engel, S.G.; Mitchell, J.E.; Le Grange, D.; Crow, S.J.; Peterson, C.B. Facets of Impulsivity and Compulsivity in Women with Anorexia Nervosa. *Eur. Eat. Disord. Rev.* **2017**, *25*, 309–313. [CrossRef]
29. Fineberg, N.A.; Apergis-Schoute, A.M.; Vaghi, M.M.; Banca, P.; Gillan, C.M.; Voon, V.; Chamberlain, S.R.; Cinosi, E.; Reid, J.; Shahper, S.; et al. Mapping Compulsivity in the DSM-5 Obsessive Compulsive and Related Disorders: Cognitive Domains, Neural Circuitry, and Treatment. *Int. J. Neuropsychopharmacol.* **2018**, *21*, 42–58. [CrossRef]
30. Mobbs, O.; Crépin, C.; Thiéry, C.; Golay, A.; Van der Linden, M. Obesity and the four facets of impulsivity. *Patient Educ. Couns.* **2010**, *79*, 372–377. [CrossRef]
31. Murphy, C.M.; Stojek, M.K.; MacKillop, J. Interrelationships among impulsive personality traits, food addiction, and Body Mass Index. *Appetite* **2014**, *73*, 45–50. [CrossRef]
32. Yang, Y.; Shields, G.S.; Guo, C.; Liu, Y. Executive function performance in obesity and overweight individuals: A meta-analysis and review. *Neurosci. Biobehav. Rev.* **2018**, *84*, 225–244.
33. VanderBroek-Stice, L.; Stojek, M.K.; Beach, S.R.H.; VanDellen, M.R.; MacKillop, J. Multidimensional assessment of impulsivity in relation to obesity and food addiction. *Appetite* **2017**, *112*, 59–68. [CrossRef]
34. Fagundo, A.B.; de la Torre, R.; Jiménez-Murcia, S.; Agüera, Z.; Granero, R.; Tárrega, S.; Botella, C.; Baños, R.; Fernández-Real, J.M.; Rodríguez, R.; et al. Executive functions profile in extreme eating/weight conditions: From Anorexia Nervosa to Obesity. *PLoS ONE* **2012**, *7*, e43382. [CrossRef]
35. Wu, M.; Brockmeyer, T.; Hartmann, M.; Skunde, M.; Herzog, W.; Friederich, H.C. Set-shifting ability across the spectrum of eating disorders and in overweight and obesity: A systematic review and meta-analysis. *Psychol. Med.* **2014**, *44*, 3365–3385.
36. Fineberg, N.A.; Chamberlain, S.R.; Goudriaan, A.E.; Stein, D.J.; Vanderschuren, L.J.M.J.; Gillan, C.M.; Shekar, S.; Gorwood, P.A.P.M.; Voon, V.; Morein-Zamir, S.; et al. New developments in human neurocognition: Clinical, genetic, and brain imaging correlates of impulsivity and compulsivity. *CNS Spectr.* **2014**, *19*, 69–89.
37. Munguía, L.; Lucas, I.; Jiménez-Murcia, S.; Mora-Maltas, B.; Granero, R.; Miranda-Olivos, R.; Sánchez, I.; Testa, G.; Lozano-Madrid, M.; Turton, R.; et al. Executive functions in binge spectrum eating disorders with comorbid compulsive buying. *Eur. Eat. Disord. Rev.* **2021**, *29*, 854–867. [CrossRef]
38. Petry, N.M.; Barry, D.; Pietrzak, R.H.; Wagner, J.A. Overweight and obesity are associated with psychiatric disorders: Results from the national epidemiologic survey on alcohol and related conditions. *Psychosom. Med.* **2008**, *70*, 288–297. [CrossRef]
39. Pavan, C.; Azzi, M.; Lancerotto, L.; Marini, M.; Busetto, L.; Bassetto, F.; Vindigni, V. Overweight/obese patients referring to plastic surgery: Temperament and personality traits. *Obes. Surg.* **2013**, *23*, 437–445. [CrossRef]
40. Fassino, S.; Leombruni, P.; Pierò, A.; Abbate Daga, G.; Amianto, F.; Rovera, G.; Rovera, G.G. Temperament and character in obese women with and without binge eating disorder. *Compr. Psychiatry* **2002**, *43*, 431–437. [CrossRef]

41. López-Pantoja, J.L.; Cabranes, J.A.; Sanchez-Quintero, S.; Velao, M.; Sanz, M.; Torres-Pardo, B.; Ancín, I.; Cabrerizo, L.; Rubio, M.A.; Lopez-Ibor, J.J.; et al. Personality profiles between obese and control subjects assessed with five standardized personality scales. *Actas Esp. Psiquiatr.* **2012**, *40*, 266–274.
42. Sarisoy, G.; Atmaca, A.; Ecemiş, G.; Gümüş, K.; Pazvantoğlu, O. Personality characteristics and body image in obese individuals. *Asia-Pac. Psychiatry* **2014**, *6*, 191–199. [CrossRef]
43. Villarejo, C.; Jiménez-Murcia, S.; Álvarez-Moya, E.; Granero, R.; Penelo, E.; Treasure, J.; Vilarrasa, N.; Gil-Montserrat De Bernabé, M.; Casanueva, F.F.; Tinahones, F.J.; et al. Loss of control over eating: A description of the eating disorder/obesity spectrum in women. *Eur. Eat. Disord. Rev.* **2014**, *22*, 25–31. [CrossRef]
44. Chatterjee, S.; Khunti, K.; Davies, M.J. Type 2 diabetes. *Lancet* **2017**, *389*, 2239–2251.
45. Schoffelmeer, A.N.M.; Drukarch, B.; De Vries, T.J.; Hogenboom, F.; Schetters, D.; Pattij, T. Insulin modulates cocaine-sensitive monoamine transporter function and impulsive behavior. *J. Neurosci.* **2011**, *31*, 1284–1291. [CrossRef]
46. Könner, A.C.; Hess, S.; Tovar, S.; Mesaros, A.; Sánchez-Lasheras, C.; Evers, N.; Verhagen, L.A.W.; Brönneke, H.S.; Kleinridders, A.; Hampel, B.; et al. Role for insulin signaling in catecholaminergic neurons in control of energy homeostasis. *Cell Metab.* **2011**, *13*, 720–728. [CrossRef]
47. Sevak, R.J.; Koek, W.; Galli, A.; France, C.P. Insulin replacement restores the behavioral effects of quinpirole and raclopride in streptozotocin-treated rats. *J. Pharmacol. Exp. Ther.* **2007**, *320*, 1216–1223. [CrossRef]
48. Kleinridders, A.; Cai, W.; Cappellucci, L.; Ghazarian, A.; Collins, W.R.; Vienberg, S.G.; Pothos, E.N.; Kahn, C.R. Insulin resistance in brain alters dopamine turnover and causes behavioral disorders. *Proc. Natl. Acad. Sci. USA.* **2015**, *112*, 3463–3468. [CrossRef]
49. Speed, N.; Saunders, C.; Davis, A.R.; Owens, W.A.; Matthies, H.J.G.; Saadat, S.; Kennedy, J.P.; Vaughan, R.A.; Neve, R.L.; Lindsley, C.W.; et al. Impaired striatal akt signaling disrupts dopamine homeostasis and increases feeding. *PLoS ONE* **2011**, *6*, e25169. [CrossRef]
50. Williams, J.M.; Owens, W.A.; Turner, G.H.; Saunders, C.; Dipace, C.; Blakely, R.D.; France, C.P.; Gore, J.C.; Daws, L.C.; Avison, M.J.; et al. Hypoinsulinemia regulates amphetamine-induced reverse transport of dopamine. *PLoS Biol.* **2007**, *5*, e274. [CrossRef]
51. Mallorquí-Bagué, N.; Lozano-Madrid, M.; Toledo, E.; Corella, D.; Salas-Salvadó, J.; Cuenca-Royo, A.; Vioque, J.; Romaguera, D.; Martínez, J.A.; Wärnberg, J.; et al. Type 2 diabetes and cognitive impairment in an older population with overweight or obesity and metabolic syndrome: Baseline cross-sectional analysis of the PREDIMED-plus study. *Sci. Rep.* **2018**, *8*, 16128. [CrossRef]
52. Mallorquí-Bagué, N.; Lozano-Madrid, M.; Vintró-Alcaraz, C.; Forcano, L.; Díaz-López, A.; Galera, A.; Fernández-Carrión, R.; Granero, R.; Jiménez-Murcia, S.; Corella, D.; et al. Effects of a psychosocial intervention at one-year follow-up in a PREDIMED-plus sample with obesity and metabolic syndrome. *Sci. Rep.* **2021**, *11*, 9144. [CrossRef]
53. Qiao Qiu, W.; Lyn Price, L.; Hibberd, P.; Buell, J.; Collins, L.; Leins, D.; Mkaya Mwamburi, D.; Rosenberg, I.; Smaldone, L.; Scott, T.M.; et al. Executive dysfunction in homebound older people with diabetes mellitus. *J. Am. Geriatr. Soc.* **2006**, *54*, 496–501. [CrossRef]
54. Yeung, S.E.; Fischer, A.L.; Dixon, R.A. Exploring Effects of Type 2 Diabetes on Cognitive Functioning in Older Adults. *Neuropsychology* **2009**, *23*, 1–9.
55. Sun, D.M.; Ma, Y.; Sun, Z.B.; Xie, L.; Huang, J.Z.; Chen, W.S.; Duan, S.X.; Lin, Z.R.; Guo, R.W.; Le, H.B.; et al. Decision-making in primary onset middle-age type 2 diabetes mellitus: A BOLD-fMRI study. *Sci. Rep.* **2017**, *7*, 10246. [CrossRef]
56. Cloninger, C.R. *The Temperament and Character Inventory-Revised*; Center for Psychobiology of Personality, Washington University: St. Louis, MO, USA, 1999.
57. Gutiérrez-Zotes, J.A.; Bayón, C.; Montserrat, C.; Valero, J.; Labad, A.; Cloninger, C.R.; Fernández-Aranda, F. Inventario del Temperamento y el Carácter-Revisado (TCI-R). Baremación y datos normativos en una muestra de población general. *Actas Esp. Psiquiatr.* **2004**, *32*, 8–15.
58. Derogatis, L.R. *SCL-90-R: Symptom Checklist-90-R: Administration, Scoring and Procedures Manuall—II for the Revised Version*; Clinical Psychometric Research: Towson, MD, USA, 1994.
59. Derogatis, L.R. *SCL-90-R Cuestionario de 90 Síntomas Revisado Manual*; González de Rivera y Revuelta, J.L., de las Cuevas, C., Rodríguez-Abuin, M., Rodríguez Pulido, F., Eds.; TEA Ediciones: Madrid, Spain, 2002.
60. Harris, M.E. *Wisconsin Card Sorting Test: Computer Version*; Psychological Assessment Resources: Lutz, FL, USA, 1990; Volume 4.
61. Bechara, A.; Damasio, A.R.; Damasio, H.; Anderson, S.W. Insensitivity to future consequences following damage to human prefrontal cortex. *Cognition* **1994**, *50*, 7–15. [CrossRef]
62. Del Barrio, V. Diagnostic and Statistical Manual of Mental Disorders. In *The Curated Reference Collection in Neuroscience and Biobehavioral Psychology*; American Psychiatric Association: Washington, DC, USA, 2016; ISBN 9780128093245.
63. StataCorp. *Stata Statistical Software: Release 17*; StataCorp LLC: College Station, TX, USA, 2021. Available online: https://www.stata.com/ (accessed on 4 December 2021).
64. Finner, H.; Roters, M. On the False Discovery Rate and Expected Type I Errors. *Biom. J.* **2001**, *43*, 985–1005.
65. Albrecht, D.S.; Kareken, D.A.; Christian, B.T.; Dzemidzic, M.; Yoder, K.K. Cortical dopamine release during a behavioral response inhibition task. *Synapse* **2014**, *68*, 266–274. [CrossRef]
66. Bari, A.; Robbins, T.W. Noradrenergic versus dopaminergic modulation of impulsivity, attention and monitoring behaviour in rats performing the stop-signal task: Possible relevance to ADHD. *Psychopharmacology* **2013**, *230*, 89–111. [CrossRef]

67. Buckholtz, J.W.; Treadway, M.T.; Cowan, R.L.; Woodward, N.D.; Li, R.; Ansari, M.S.; Baldwin, R.M.; Schwartzman, A.N.; Shelby, E.S.; Smith, C.E.; et al. Dopaminergic network differences in human impulsivity. *Science* **2010**, *329*, 532. [CrossRef]
68. Eckstrand, K.L.; Mummareddy, N.; Kang, H.; Cowan, R.; Zhou, M.; Zald, D.; Silver, H.J.; Niswender, K.D.; Avison, M.J. An insulin resistance associated neural correlate of impulsivity in type 2 diabetes mellitus. *PLoS ONE* **2017**, *12*, e0189113. [CrossRef]
69. Eisenstein, S.A.; Gredysa, D.M.; Antenor-Dorsey, J.A.; Green, L.; Arbeláez, A.M.; Koller, J.M.; Black, K.J.; Perlmutter, J.S.; Moerlein, S.M.; Hershey, T. Insulin, central dopamine D_2 receptors, and monetary reward discounting in obesity. *PLoS ONE* **2015**, *10*, e0133621. [CrossRef]
70. Sullivan, S.; Cloninger, C.R.; Przybeck, T.R.; Klein, S. Personality characteristics in obesity and relationship with successful weight loss. *Int. J. Obes.* **2007**, *31*, 669–674. [CrossRef]
71. Gerlach, G.; Herpertz, S.; Loeber, S. Personality traits and obesity: A systematic review. *Obes. Rev.* **2015**, *16*, 32–63. [CrossRef]
72. Dalle Grave, R.; Calugi, S.; El Ghoch, M. Are Personality Characteristics as Measured by the Temperament and Character Inventory (TCI) Associated with Obesity Treatment Outcomes? A Systematic Review. *Curr. Obes. Rep.* **2018**, *7*, 27–36.
73. Dalle Grave, R.; Calugi, S.; Marchesini, G.; Beck-Peccoz, P.; Bosello, O.; Compare, A.; Cuzzolaro, M.; Grossi, E.; Mannucci, E.; Molinari, E.; et al. Personality features of obese women in relation to binge eating and night eating. *Psychiatry Res.* **2013**, *207*, 86–91. [CrossRef]
74. Xiao, L.; Bechara, A.; Grenard, L.J.; Stacy, W.A.; Palmer, P.; Wei, Y.; Jia, Y.; Fu, X.; Johnson, C.A. Affective decision-making predictive of Chinese adolescent drinking behaviors. *J. Int. Neuropsychol. Soc.* **2009**, *15*, 547–557. [CrossRef]
75. Zermatten, A.; Van Der Linden, M.; D'Acremont, M.; Jermann, F.; Bechara, A. Impulsivity and decision making. *J. Nerv. Ment. Dis.* **2005**, *193*, 647–650. [CrossRef]
76. Diamond, A. Executive functions. *Annu. Rev. Psychol.* **2013**, *64*, 135–168.
77. Edwards, C.G.; Walk, A.M.; Thompson, S.V.; Mullen, S.P.; Holscher, H.D.; Khan, N.A. Disordered eating attitudes and behavioral and neuroelectric indices of cognitive flexibility in individuals with overweight and obesity. *Nutrients* **2018**, *10*, 1902. [CrossRef]

nutrients

MDPI

Article

Sex-Specific Mediation Effects of Workplace Bullying on Associations between Employees' Weight Status and Psychological Health Impairments

Hans-Christian Puls [1,*], Ricarda Schmidt [1], Markus Zenger [1,2], Hanna Kampling [3], Johannes Kruse [3], Elmar Brähler [1,4] and Anja Hilbert [1]

1 Integrated Research and Treatment Center AdiposityDiseases, Behavioral Medicine Research Unit, Department of Psychosomatic Medicine and Psychotherapy, University of Leipzig Medical Center, 04103 Leipzig, Germany; ricarda.schmidt@medizin.uni-leipzig.de (R.S.); markus.zenger@h2.de (M.Z.); elmar.braehler@medizin.uni-leipzig.de (E.B.); anja.hilbert@medizin.uni-leipzig.de (A.H.)

2 Faculty of Applied Human Studies, University of Applied Sciences Magdeburg and Stendal, 39576 Stendal, Germany

3 Department of Psychosomatic Medicine and Psychotherapy, Justus Liebig University Giessen, 35390 Giessen, Germany; hanna.kampling@psycho.med.uni-giessen.de (H.K.); johannes.kruse@psycho.med.uni-giessen.de (J.K.)

4 Department of Psychosomatic Medicine and Psychotherapy, University Medical Center of the Johannes Gutenberg University of Mainz, 55131 Mainz, Germany

* Correspondence: hanschristian.puls@hotmail.de; Tel.: +49-341-97-15363; Fax: +49-341-97-15359

Citation: Puls, H.-C.; Schmidt, R.; Zenger, M.; Kampling, H.; Kruse, J.; Brähler, E.; Hilbert, A. Sex-Specific Mediation Effects of Workplace Bullying on Associations between Employees' Weight Status and Psychological Health Impairments. *Nutrients* **2021**, *13*, 3867. https://doi.org/10.3390/nu13113867

Academic Editors: Fernando Fernandez-Aranda, Janet Treasure and Empar Lurbe

Received: 29 September 2021
Accepted: 27 October 2021
Published: 29 October 2021

Publisher's Note: MDPI stays neutral with regard to jurisdictional claims in published maps and institutional affiliations.

Abstract: Background: Individuals with obesity face weight-related discrimination in many life domains, including workplace bullying, especially in female employees with obesity. However, associations between experiences of workplace bullying and psychological health impairments considering weight status and sex remain unclear. Methods: Within a representative population-based sample of $N = 1290$ employees, self-reported experiences of workplace bullying were examined for variations by weight status and sex. Using path analyses, sex-specific mediation effects of workplace bullying on associations between weight status and work-related psychological health impairments (burnout symptoms, quality of life) were tested. Results: Employees with obesity experienced more workplace bullying than those with normal weight. Workplace bullying was positively associated with psychological health impairments and partially mediated the associations between higher weight status and elevated burnout symptoms and lower quality of life in women, but not in men. Conclusions: The result that more experiences of workplace bullying were, compared with weight status, more strongly associated with work-related psychological health impairments in women, but not in men, uniquely extends evidence on sex-specific effects within weight-related discrimination. Continued efforts by researchers, employers, and policy makers are needed to reduce weight-related discrimination in work settings, eventually increasing employees' health and job productivity.

Keywords: weight discrimination; workplace bullying; burnout; sex-specific differences; moderated mediation

1. Introduction

Especially in Western societies, a growing number of individuals with obesity (body mass index (BMI) ≥ 30 kg/m^2 [1]) are at risk of a range of medical and psychological health impairments [2,3]. Although obesity has a complex and multifactorial etiology, it is considered to be the main nutritional disorder, as it ultimately results from an imbalance between caloric intake and caloric expenditure [4]. Aspects that cause additional strain in many life domains (e.g., work settings) of individuals with obesity include weight-related stereotypes (i.e., negative beliefs about a stigmatized group), prejudices (i.e., negative emotions against a stigmatized person), and discrimination (i.e., negative behaviors towards a stigmatized person [5]) such as workplace bullying [6]. The present study aimed to elucidate the intensity of experiences of workplace bullying across the weight range and its associations with psychological health impairments moderated by employees' sex.

In work settings, weight-related stereotypes describe individuals with obesity as, for example, being less effective, less ambitious, and showing more non-medical absenteeism compared with their co-workers with normal weight [7]. Meta-analytic evidence from experimental studies using simulated employment decisions showed that applicants with obesity, compared with those without obesity, were evaluated more negatively on a range of work-related characteristics, including lower hiring recommendations, lower estimated job success, and less job suitability. Most strikingly, the greatest difference in these simulated attributions to applicants with and without obesity was a lower rating of estimated co-worker desirability for those having obesity [8]. In fact, workers with obesity reported frequent experiences of being bullied or socially isolated by their co-workers [7], which was termed workplace bullying [9]. Within a single observational study on two samples of $N = 341$ student employees and $N = 528$ full-time employees, self-reported experiences of workplace bullying were greater in employees with overweight and obesity than in those with normal weight [10]. Nonetheless, more population-based research considering additional moderators (e.g., age and socioeconomic status) would add to the yet limited evidence regarding experiences of workplace bullying across the weight range [11].

The only available study examining sex-specific effects in workplace bullying across the weight range revealed that women with overweight and obesity reported significantly more experiences of workplace bullying than women with normal weight, while this effect was not found in men, thus indicating a weight-by-sex interaction effect on experiences of workplace bullying [10]. In addition, evidence consistently showed women to be more affected by other forms of weight-related discrimination at the workplace than men, especially regarding recruitment and income [12,13]. For example, in a recent population-based study following-up $N = 6000$ middle and high school seniors over four years after graduation, young women with overweight or obesity had less job chances and earned less than those with normal weight, while the opposite effect was found in men [14]. It may be concluded that women experience stronger weight-related discrimination at the workplace, including workplace bullying, than men.

General experiences of weight-related discrimination were associated with a range of medical and psychological health impairments, including eating disturbances (e.g., high-caloric food intake, binge-eating, or emotional eating; [15]). Specific psychological correlates of workplace bullying included elevated symptoms of emotional exhaustion and lower quality of life, both in workers across the weight range [16,17] and in workers with overweight or obesity compared with those with normal weight [18,19]. Further, in the study by Sliter et al. [10], experiences of workplace bullying partially mediated the association between weight status and job withdrawal, with the latter being associated with emotional exhaustion. Alongside depersonalization and reduced perceived accomplishment at work, emotional exhaustion represents a key symptom of the burnout syndrome [20], which itself is known to be an important health issue in work settings [21]. Notably, in sex-specific analyses, experiences of workplace bullying were more strongly associated with weight status in women than in men, and linked to job withdrawal in men, but not in women [10].

Research has only begun to elucidate the prevalence of experiences of workplace bullying and their sex-specific associations with psychological health impairments. Thus, the present study aimed to, firstly, describe the intensity of experiences of workplace bullying in a large population-based sample as a function of employees' weight status and sex. We expected more experiences of workplace bullying in individuals with overweight and obesity than with normal weight and, within participants with overweight or obesity, in women than in men. Secondly, weight status and workplace bullying were evaluated regarding their relative explanatory power for work-related psychological health impairments, hypothesizing a mediating effect of workplace bullying on the association between higher weight status and elevated burnout symptoms as well as lower quality of life. Thirdly, we evaluated whether this mediating effect would be moderated by sex (i.e., evident in women, but not in men).

2. Materials and Methods

2.1. Recruitment and Sample

The present study's data were derived from a 2012 representative survey of the German population with the assistance of the Independent Service for Surveys, Methods, and Analyses (USUMA Berlin). The sampling procedure, as a common and standardized procedure in German representative survey designs [22], included three stages of randomized selection, and thus yielded in a sample representative for the German general population. First, 258 representative sampling areas were selected out of a total of 53,000 areas from all parts of Germany, stratified according to counties and number of inhabitants [23]. Second, 4386 addresses were selected using a random-route-assisted procedure and, third, one randomly selected household member per address was personally contacted and supposed to respond in person for study participation. The survey was approved by the Ethics Committee of the University of Leipzig (Approval No. 072-11-07032011) and followed the ethical guidelines of the International Code of Marketing and Social Research Practice by the International Chamber of Commerce and the European Society for Opinion and Marketing Research. Oral informed assent and consent was obtained from the participants for $\geq$18 years and, for participants <18 years, informed consent was obtained from the parents, which is common in survey research in Germany. Following a face-to-face explanation of the study objectives, the procedure, and data protection, each participant received a questionnaire, which he or she completed himself or herself in the presence of the interviewer.

Of the 2555 participants who responded to the initial contact (response rate 58.3%), n = 1335 (52.3%) participants were employed at the time of the survey and provided data on experiences of workplace bullying derived from the "Intensity of Bullying Coming from Co-Workers" scale (MOB-K, see below [24]). As weight status was a central study variable, we omitted n = 20 participants owing to missing data on weight and height, and we further omitted n = 25 participants with underweight (BMI $\leq$ 18.5 kg/m^2) owing to their small number, finally resulting in a study sample of N = 1290 participants (50.5% out of 2555 eligible individuals; 29.4% out of 4386 initially contacted individuals).

2.2. Measures

Workplace bullying. Experiences of workplace bullying were assessed using the sum score of the MOB-K [24]. The sum score is derived from four items addressing different aspects of workplace bullying (i.e., social isolation, bullying, defamatory statements, and overall quality of interaction), which are rated on a four-point Likert scale (1 = *not at all* to 4 = *very much*). Higher scores indicate higher intensity of experiences of workplace bullying. In the present study, the MOB-K showed good internal consistency (Cronbach's α = 0.83).

Psychological health impairments. To depict work-related psychological health impairments, we focused on work-related symptoms of exhaustion, distress, dysfunctional cognitions, and feelings of decreased efficacy and motivation, all associated with the burnout syndrome [20], and assessed by the "Burnout Screening Scale II" (BOSS II [25]). With 30 items rated on a six-point Likert scale (0 = *not at all* to 5 = *very much*), the BOSS II assesses physical, cognitive, and emotional symptoms occurring within the last seven days. Items are accumulated to a mean score, with higher scores indicating higher impairment. Quality of life was assessed using the sum score of the "EuroQoL 5 Item-index" (EQ-5D [26,27]). Five items addressing impairments in mobility, self-care, usual activities, pain/discomfort, and anxiety/depression are rated on a five-point Likert scale (1 = *not at all* to 5 = *very much*) and accumulated to a sum score, with higher scores indicating a higher quality of life. BOSS

II and EQ-5D showed good to high internal consistency in the present study (Cronbach's $\alpha = 0.83$ and 0.96, respectively).

Weight and socioeconomic status. Participants were categorized into weight status groups according to their BMI (kg/m^2), specifically, normal weight ($18.5 \leq \text{BMI} < 25.0$ kg/m^2), overweight ($25.0 \leq \text{BMI} < 30.0$ kg/m^2), and obesity ($\text{BMI} \geq 30.0$ kg/m^2), based on self-reported weight and height. Participants were further categorized into low, medium, and high socioeconomic status (SES) as derived from a modified Winkler Index, which accumulates information about the highest educational degree, professional degree, current profession, and household net income [28]. Sociodemographic and clinical characteristics of the total sample, sex-specific subsamples, and across the weight range are depicted in Table 1 and Supplementary Table S1, respectively.

Table 1. Sociodemographic and clinical variables for the total sample and sex-specific subsamples, including sex-specific differences using *t*-tests for continuous and χ^2-tests for categorical variables.

Variable	Total Sample ($n = 1290$)	Women ($n = 630$, 48.8%)	Men ($n = 660$, 51.2%)	Sex-Specific Differences		
	M (SD)	*M (SD)*	*M (SD)*	*T*	*df*	*p*
Age (years)	43.06 (12.48)	43.22 (12.21)	42.91 (12.74)	−0.45	1288	0.654
BMI (kg/m^2)	24.86 (3.48)	24.26 (3.65)	25.44 (3.20)	6.19	1288	<0.001
	n (%)	*n* (%)	*n* (%)	χ^2	*df*	*p*
Weight status				70.82	2, 1290	<0.001
Normal weight ($18.5 \leq \text{BMI} < 25.0$ kg/m^2)	714 (55.3)	417 (66.2)	297 (45.0)			
Overweight ($25.0 \leq \text{BMI} < 30.0$ kg/m^2)	494 (38.3)	168 (26.7)	326 (49.4)			
Obesity ($\text{BMI} \geq 30.0$ kg/m^2)	82 (6.4)	45 (7.1)	37 (5.6)			
Socioeconomic status (SES)				86.35	2, 1277	<0.001
Low	312 (24.2)	84 (13.3)	228 (34.5)			
Middle	770 (59.7)	447 (71.0)	323 (49.0)			
High	195 (15.1)	92 (14.6)	103 (15.6)			
German Citizenship				9.89	1, 1290	<0.01
Yes	1226 (95.0)	611 (97.0)	615 (93.2)			
No	64 (5.0)	19 (3.0)	45 (6.8)			
	M (SD)	*M (SD)*	*M (SD)*	*T*	*df*	*p*
Workplace bullying (MOB-K)	4.76 (1.63)	4.76 (1.61)	4.76 (1.64)	−0.07	1288	0.948
Burnout symptoms (BOSS-II)	0.50 (0.60)	0.54 (0.63)	0.44 (0.57)	−2.93	1286	<0.01
Quality of life (EQ-5D)	24.08 (1.65)	23.92 (1.80)	24.24 (1.49)	3.50	1288	<0.001

Notes. BMI = body mass index (kg/m^2); SES = socioeconomic status (Lange et al., 2007); MOB-K = Intensity of Bullying Coming from Co-Workers scale sum score (4–16*, less favorable scores are asterisked; Pfaff, Bentz, & Brähler, 2007); BOSS II = Burnout Screening Scale II mean score (0–5*; Hagemann & Geuenich, 2009); EQ-5D = EuroQoL 5 Item-index sum score (5*–25; Hinz, Kohlmann, Stöbel-Richter, Zenger, & Brähler, 2014; Janssen et al., 2013). Statistical analyses used a two-tailed $\alpha < 0.05$ significance level. *—less favorable scores are asterisked.

2.3. Data Analytics Plan

First, to rule out possible common method variance bias due to the self-report nature of our data [29,30], we applied Harman's single-factor test on all measures prior to data analysis [31]. Based on an eight-factor solution explaining 65.5% of variance, with the first factor accounting for 36.4%, the bias of common method variance in the present data was assumed to be low [30]. Using univariate analyses of covariance (ANCOVA; IBM® SPSS version 25.0; Chicago, IL, USA) on the MOB-K sum score by weight status, sex, and their interaction, weight- and sex-specific differences were identified, controlling for age and SES. Although all dependent variables deviated from normal distribution, which is common in large samples [32], ANCOVA was used because of its robustness against non-normality [33] and the large sample being selected with a high degree of randomization. However, all analyses were repeated using non-parametric methods, specifically the Kruskal–Wallis test, and their results will be reported if deviating from parametric analyses. Post-hoc analyses included unpaired t-tests, applying Bonferroni-corrected significance levels. Cohen's *d* was used as an effect size measure, representing small ($\geq$0.2), medium ($\geq$0.5), and large ($\geq$0.8) effects [34].

Second, using path analysis (IBM® SPSS AMOS® version 25.0; Chicago, IL, USA), we tested the possible mediating effect of experiences of workplace bullying on the association between weight status and psychological health impairments. As a first step, direct effects of weight status on psychological health impairments (BOSS II and EQ-5D) were examined for the total sample (Model 1), controlling for socioeconomic variables (sex, age, and SES). Subsequently, the indirect effects of weight status on mental health variables, possibly mediated by the experiences of workplace bullying (MOB-K sum score), were examined (Model 2).

Third, possible sex-specific mediation effects (i.e., moderated mediation [35,36]) of the experiences of workplace bullying on the associations between weight status and psychological health impairments were examined using the SPSS PROCESS macro version 3.5 [36], which utilizes bootstrapping to assess direct and indirect effects of variables while maximizing power and minimizing concerns about non-normality. Furthermore, 95% confidence intervals were resampled 5000 times for each analysis to test the significance of the indirect effects [37]. To additionally confirm and depict sex-specific differences regarding the explanatory power of weight status and experiences of workplace bullying for psychological health impairments, the final model from the path analysis (Model 2) was applied to subsamples of women (Model 3) and men (Model 4) separately. For path analyses, the following indices were determined for the evaluation of model fit: χ^2 test statistics; the minimum discrepancy, divided by its degrees of freedom (CMIN/DF); the comparative-fit index (CFI); the Tucker–Lewis index (TLI); the normed-fit index (NFI); and the root mean square error of approximation (RMSEA). Good model fit is indicated by non-significant χ^2 statistics; CMIN/DF < 2; CFI, TLI, and NFI > 0.97; and RMSEA < 0.08 [38]. Standardized regression weights were interpreted as indicative of small ($\leq$0.30), medium (between 0.30 and 0.50), or large (>0.50) effects [34]. All analyses used a two-tailed $\alpha < 0.05$ as the significance level.

3. Results

3.1. Weight- and Sex-Specific Differences in Experiences of Workplace Bullying

Regarding experiences of workplace bullying, we found a significant main effect of weight status, F (2, 1276) = 4.24, p = 0.02 (d = 0.16), but no significant main effect of sex, F (1, 1276) = 1.80, p = 0.18 (d = 0.07), and no significant interaction effect of weight status x sex, F (2, 1276) = 0.73, p = 0.48 (d = 0.07). Post-hoc analyses using a Bonferroni-corrected significance level of 0.016 revealed that, compared with participants with normal weight, levels of experiences of workplace bullying were significantly greater in participants with obesity (p = 0.01, d = 0.34). The level of experiences of workplace bullying did not significantly differ between participants with normal weight and those with overweight (p = 0.04, d = 0.12) and between those with overweight and those with obesity (p = 0.15, d = 0.17).

3.2. Associations of Weight Status and Experiences of Workplace Bullying with Psychological Health Impairments

The results of the path analyses are presented in Figure 1 for all models. All models showed good model fit, as depicted in Table 2. In Model 1, a significant direct effect of a higher weight status on elevated burnout symptoms (β = 0.10) and a lower quality of life (β = −0.13) was found. In Model 2, a higher weight status was significantly associated with more experiences of workplace bullying (β = 0.08), with the latter being associated with higher burnout symptoms (β = 0.29) and with a lower quality of life (β = −0.22), showing the indirect effect of weight status on psychological health impairments. In this final model, a higher weight status was still associated with elevated burnout symptoms (β = 0.07) and with a lower quality of life (β = −0.11), thus indicating partial mediation effects of experiences of workplace bullying on the association between higher weight status and elevated burnout symptoms and a lower quality of life.

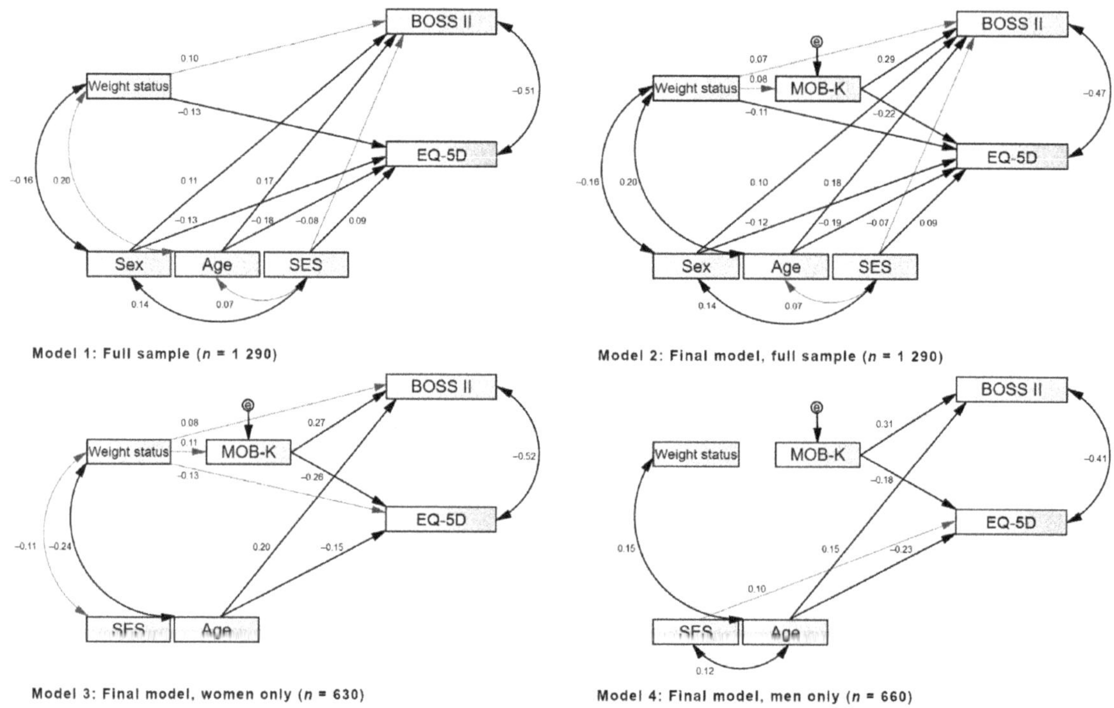

Figure 1. Models 1 to 4: Direct and indirect effects of weight status and workplace bullying on psychological health impairments while controlling for sociodemographic variables. Notes: Standardized regression weights are depicted. Only significant associations are depicted. Different significance levels are depicted with black lines ($p < 0.001$) or gray lines ($p < 0.05$). Burnout symptoms measured by Burnout Screening Scales II. Quality of life measured by Euro-Qol Quality of Life Index. SES = socioeconomic status.

Table 2. Path analysis on the mediating effect of workplace bullying on associations between weight status and psychological health impairments: model fit indices.

Model Fit Indices	*n*	χ^2	*df*	*p*	CMIN/DF	CFI	RMSEA	TLI	NFI
1: Weight status only	1290	0.201	1	0.654	0.201	1.000	0.000	1.025	1.000
2: Final Model, total sample	1290	0.889	3	0.828	0.296	1.000	0.000	1.025	0.999
3: Final Model, women only	630	1.232	1	0.267	1.232	1.000	0.019	0.989	0.997
4: Final Model, men only	660	0.116	1	0.734	0.116	1.000	0.000	1.061	1.000

Notes. *df* = degrees of freedom; BMI = body mass index (kg/m^2); CMIN/DF = minimum discrepancy, divided by degrees of freedom; CFI = comparative-fit index; RMSEA = root mean square error of approximation; TLI = Tucker–Lewis index; NFI = normed fit index.

In sex-specific analyses, we found that weight status was positively associated with experiences of workplace bullying for women (Model 3, β = 0.12), but not for men (Model 4, β = 0.06), thus alone suggesting no mediational effect of experiences of workplace bullying in men. In women, but not in men, a higher weight status was associated with elevated burnout symptoms (β = 0.08) and with a lower quality of life (β = −0.13). Utilizing the PROCESS macro [37], we affirmatively found the mediational effect of experiences of workplace bullying to be moderated by sex. Specifically, while we found direct effects of weight status on burnout symptoms (β = 0.09) and quality of life (β = −0.36) for women and men, indirect effects (i.e., mediated by experiences of workplace bullying) were only evident for women, but not for men, regarding both burnout symptoms (β = 0.03) and quality of life (β = 0.07). Thus, specifically for women, experiences of workplace bullying partially mediated the association between a higher weight status and elevated burnout symptoms and a lower quality of life.

4. Discussion

Derived from a large population-based sample, the present study showed that, in line with our hypotheses and previous research [10], individuals with obesity encounter more frequent experiences of workplace bullying than individuals with normal weight. Experiences of workplace bullying were significantly associated with psychological health impairments and emerged as a partial mediator on the associations between higher body weight and elevated burnout symptoms and a lower quality of life, with this effect being particularly evident in women, but not in men. Based on data from real-life employment settings in Germany, the present results extend previous experimental research on sex-specific weight-related discrimination at the workplace, which mainly focused on recruitment and income [7,8,10–13] by experiences of workplace bullying.

In line with our hypotheses and previous research [16–19,39], more experiences of workplace bullying were associated with elevated burnout symptoms and lower quality of life. These associations were substantially stronger than associations between a higher weight status and a greater risk for psychological health impairments. Experiences of workplace bullying partially mediated the association between a higher weight status and elevated burnout symptoms in the total sample, in line with the mediation effect found by Sliter et al. [10] of workplace bullying on the association between weight status and job withdrawal. Further, experiences of workplace bullying partially mediated the association between a higher weight status and a lower quality of life, altogether indicating that a higher weight status alone is linked to psychological health impairments, while additionally experiencing workplace bullying is associated with a further increased health risk. However, because the associations between weight status and psychological health impairments were only reduced to a small extent (Δβ's ranging from 0.02 to 0.03) after including experiences of workplace bullying, the mediation effects may not be necessarily clinically relevant. Importantly, owing to design, the present results depict cross-sectional associations, leaving unclear the causal mechanisms between weight status, experiences of workplace bullying, burnout symptoms, and quality of life. Thus, all mediation effects must be interpreted considering this important limitation.

Differences in experiences of workplace bullying between women and men across the weight range were shown within sex-specific subsamples in the path analyses, in which a higher weight status was significantly associated with more frequent experiences of workplace bullying in women (Model 3), but not in men (Model 4), replicating findings by Sliter et al. [10] within a larger and representative sample from the general population. However, we found no weight status-by-sex interaction effect on the level of experiences of workplace bullying in the univariate statistics, as previously revealed by Sliter et al. [9]. In the present study, only descriptively, experiences of workplace bullying tended to be increased in women with obesity compared with men with obesity ($p = 0.28$, $d = 0.24$). In contrast to Sliter et al. [10], who showed that men with underweight were more likely to experience workplace bullying than women with underweight, in the present study, we excluded participants with underweight owing to the small sample size ($n = 25$, 1.9%), which may explain the lack of the interaction effect in the present study.

In the present study, derived from both the path analyses and the SPSS PROCESS macro [37], partial mediation effects found in the total sample were evident for women, but not for men, indicating sex-specific differences regarding the adverse psychological health correlates of workplace bullying. In women, but not in men, a higher weight status had direct and indirect effects on elevated burnout symptoms and a lower quality of life, with these associations being partially mediated by experiences of workplace bullying. Thus, while women with obesity were at risk for elevated burnout symptoms and a lower quality of life, those who additionally experienced workplace bullying showed an even increased health risk. Considering the deleterious impact of burnout symptoms on a range of adverse medical conditions (e.g., type 2 diabetes and coronary heart disease), mental health (e.g., insomnia and depressive symptoms), and occupational outcomes (e.g., low job satisfaction and absenteeism) [40], and given that future longitudinal studies could replicate the present findings, employers and policy makers might further address workplace bullying, potentially preventing medical and psychological health impairments for workers and associated productivity losses for organizations [20,41].

Strengths of the present study comprise the use of established measures to depict work-related psychological health impairments within a large sample from the general population, which was representative for the German population both in terms of sex ratio and SES [42,43], and included participants from real-life employment settings, as previously recommended [7]. However, the sample was not generally representative for the prevalence of obesity, as obesity was underrepresented in the present sample (6.4%) as compared with the German general population (23.6% [44]), which might be explained by participants' impression management, specifically by an underreporting of body weight, which was previously found in individuals with BMI $\geq$ 20 kg/m^2, and an overreporting in those with BMI < 20 kg/m^2 [45]. As this bias in self-reported BMI is of high concern for large epidemiological studies within obesity-related research, studies investigating novel methods of large-scale measurement of weight and height are urgently needed (e.g., corrective equations or BMI self-selection [46,47]). A major limitation of the present study is that all analyses used cross-sectional data, leaving unclear the causal mechanisms between body weight, experiences of workplace bullying, and work-related psychological health impairments. Ideally, studies from non-Western countries might replicate our procedures to allow generalization of the results. Finally, as no specific information on participants' occupation was provided, it was not possible to systematically examine the effects considering other possibly relevant work-related variables, such as the number of colleagues or type of work sector.

Most importantly, future research should explore the prospective associations between body weight, experiences of workplace bullying, and psychological health impairments to elucidate their causal relationships. The present result that individuals with obesity, compared with those with normal weight, encounter more frequent experiences of workplace bullying, with the latter being more strongly linked to work-related psychological health impairments than the weight status, suggests continued efforts by researchers and employers to address and eventually reduce experiences of workplace bullying (e.g., by incorporating information on bullying into existing education platforms within the workplace [48,49]). As our study did not focus on discrimination owing to ethnicity or race, future studies should take discriminated features other than weight and sex (e.g., low SES and mental disorders [50,51]) into account when exploring the adverse effects of stigmatization. Our results suggest that, especially in women with obesity, who are at particular risk of experiencing weight-related discrimination in various life domains [52], different discriminated features (i.e., weight status and sex) may add up to multiple layers of stigmatization. Thus, especially in women with obesity, reducing experiences of workplace bullying will likely yield a decreased psychological burden of employees, and might strengthen their health status and lower their odds of adverse occupational outcomes (e.g., job withdrawal or absenteeism).

Supplementary Materials: The following are available online at https://www.mdpi.com/article/10.3390/nu13113867/s1, Supplementary Table S1: Sex-specific experiences of workplace bullying and psychological health impairments across the weight status: Mean values and standard deviations.

Author Contributions: E.B., A.H., J.K. and M.Z. designed and organized the initial survey and participated in selection of measures. H.-C.P., R.S. and A.H. designed the study, H.-C.P. wrote the manuscript. R.S., A.H., M.Z., J.K. and H.K. revised the manuscript. All authors have read and agreed to the published version of the manuscript.

Funding: A.H. and R.S. were supported by the German Federal Ministry of Education and Research (grant 01EO1501).

Institutional Review Board Statement: The study was conducted according to the guidelines of the Declaration of Helsinki, and approved by the Ethics Committee of the University of Leipzig (Approval No. 072-11-07032011), and followed the ethical guidelines of the International Code of Marketing and Social Research Practice by the International Chamber of Commerce and the European Society for Opinion and Marketing Research.

Informed Consent Statement: Oral informed assent and consent was obtained from the participants $\geq$18 years and, for participants <18 years, informed consent was obtained from the parents, which is common in survey research in Germany.

Data Availability Statement: Research data are not shared.

Conflicts of Interest: The authors declare no conflict of interest.

References

1. Chooi, Y.C.; Ding, C.; Magkos, F. The epidemiology of obesity. *Metabolism* **2019**, *92*, 6–10. [CrossRef]
2. Afshin, A.; Sur, P.J.; Fay, K.A.; Cornaby, L.; Ferrara, G.; Salama, J.S.; Mullany, E.C.; Abate, K.H.; Abbafati, C.; Abebe, Z.; et al. Health effects of dietary risks in 195 countries, 1990–2017: A systematic analysis for the Global Burden of Disease Study 2017. *Lancet* **2019**, *393*, 1958–1972. [CrossRef]
3. Gakidou, E.; Afshin, A.; Abajobir, A.A.; Abate, K.H.; Abbafati, C.; Abbas, K.M.; Abd-Allah, F.; Abdulle, A.M.; Abera, S.F.; Aboyans, V.; et al. Global, regional, and national comparative risk assessment of 84 behavioural, environmental and occupational, and metabolic risks or clusters of risks, 1990–2016: A systematic analysis for the Global Burden of Disease Study 2016. *Lancet* **2017**, *390*, 1345–1422. [CrossRef]
4. World Health Organization. *Obesity and Overweight*; World Health Organization: Geneva, Switzerland, 2016; Available online: https://www.who.int/en/news-room/fact-sheets/detail/obesity-and-overweight (accessed on 27 October 2021).
5. Corrigan, P.; Bink, A. The Stigma of Mental Illness. In *Encyclopedia of Mental Health*, 2nd ed.; Elsevier: Amsterdam, The Netherlands, 2016; pp. 230–234. [CrossRef]
6. Puhl, R.; Suh, Y. Stigma and Eating and Weight Disorders. *Curr. Psychiatry Rep.* **2015**, *17*, 1–10. [CrossRef] [PubMed]
7. Giel, K.E.; Thiel, A.; Teufel, M.; Mayer, J.; Zipfel, S. Weight Bias in Work Settings—A Qualitative Review. *Obes. Facts* **2010**, *3*, 33–40. [CrossRef] [PubMed]
8. Roehling, M.V.; Pichler, S.; Bruce, T.A. Moderators of the effect of weight on job-related outcomes: A meta-analysis of experimental studies. *J. Appl. Soc. Psychol.* **2013**, *43*, 237–252. [CrossRef]
9. Gillen, P.A.; Sinclair, M.; Kernohan, W.G.; Begley, C.M.; Luyben, A.G. Interventions for prevention of bullying in the workplace. *Cochrane Database Syst. Rev.* **2017**, *1*, 1465–1858. [CrossRef]
10. Sliter, K.A.; Sliter, M.T.; Withrow, S.A.; Jex, S.M. Employee adiposity and incivility: Establishing a link and identifying demographic moderators and negative consequences. *J. Occup. Health Psychol.* **2012**, *17*, 409–424. [CrossRef]
11. Vanhove, A.; Gordon, R.A. Weight discrimination in the workplace: A meta-analytic examination of the relationship between weight and work-related outcomes. *J. Appl. Soc. Psychol.* **2014**, *44*, 12–22. [CrossRef]
12. Flint, S.W.; Čadek, M.; Codreanu, S.C.; Ivić, V.; Zomer, C.; Gomoiu, A. Obesity Discrimination in the Recruitment Process: "You're Not Hired!". *Front. Psychol.* **2016**, *7*, 647. [CrossRef] [PubMed]
13. Spahlholz, J.; Baer, N.; König, H.-H.; Riedel-Heller, S.G.; Luck-Sikorski, C. Obesity and discrimination—a systematic review and meta-analysis of observational studies. *Obes. Rev.* **2016**, *17*, 43–55. [CrossRef] [PubMed]
14. Lee, H.; Ahn, R.; Kim, T.H.; Han, E. Impact of Obesity on Employment and Wages among Young Adults: Observational Study with Panel Data. *Int. J. Environ. Res. Public Health* **2019**, *16*, 139. [CrossRef]
15. Wu, Y.-K.; Berry, D.C. Impact of weight stigma on physiological and psychological health outcomes for overweight and obese adults: A systematic review. *J. Adv. Nurs.* **2018**, *74*, 1030–1042. [CrossRef]
16. Alshehry, A.S.; Alquwez, N.; Almazan, J.; Namis, I.M.; Moreno-Lacalle, R.C.; Cruz, J.P. Workplace incivility and its influence on professional quality of life among nurses from multicultural background: A cross-sectional study. *J. Clin. Nurs.* **2019**, *28*, 2553–2564. [CrossRef]

17. Viotti, S.; Essenmacher, L.; Hamblin, L.E.; Arnetz, J.E. Testing the reciprocal associations among co-worker incivility, organisational inefficiency, and work-related exhaustion: A one-year, cross-lagged study. *Work Stress* **2018**, *32*, 334–356. [CrossRef]
18. Proper, K.I.; Koppes, L.L.J.; van Zwieten, M.H.J.; Bemelmans, W.J.E. The prevalence of chronic psychological complaints and emotional exhaustion among overweight and obese workers. *Int. Arch. Occup. Environ. Health* **2012**, *85*, 537–545. [CrossRef]
19. Proper, K.I.; Koppes, L.L.; Meijer, S.; Bemelmans, W.J. The Association Between Body Mass Index Status and Sick Leave and the Role of Emotional Exhaustion—A Mediation Analysis Among a Representative Sample of Dutch Employees. *J. Occup. Environ. Med.* **2013**, *55*, 1213–1218. [CrossRef] [PubMed]
20. Aronsson, G.; Theorell, T.; Grape, T.; Hammarström, A.; Hogstedt, C.; Marteinsdottir, I.; Skoog, I.; Träskman-Bendz, L.; Hall, C. A systematic review including meta-analysis of work environment and burnout symptoms. *BMC Public Health* **2017**, *17*, 1–13. [CrossRef] [PubMed]
21. Maslach, C.; Leiter, M.P. Burnout and HealthCare–Editorial. *Burn. Res.* **2014**, *1*, 57–58.
22. Zhang, X.; Kuchinke, L.; Woud, M.; Velten, J.; Margraf, J. Survey method matters: Online/offline questionnaires and face-to-face or telephone interviews differ. *Comput. Hum. Behav.* **2017**, *71*, 172–180. [CrossRef]
23. Von der Heyde, C. The ADM-Sampling-System for Face-to-Face Surveys. 2009. Available online: https://www.adm-ev.de/wp-content/uploads/2018/11/Description-ADM-Stichproben-f2f_EN.pdf (accessed on 27 October 2021).
24. Pfaff, H.; Bentz, J.; Brähler, E. The "Intensity of Bullying Coming from Co-Workers"-scale (MOB-K): Psychometric evaluation on a representative sample from the general population [Die Skala "Mobbingintensität der Kolleginnen und Kollegen"(MOB-K): Teststatistische Überprüfung an einer repräsentativen Bevölkerungsstichprobe]. *Psychosozial* **2007**, *30*, 17–27.
25. Hagemann, W.; Geuenich, K. Burnout screening scales (BOSS). In *Burnout-Screening-Skalen (BOSS)*; Hogrefe: Göttingen, Germany, 2009.
26. Hinz, A.; Kohlmann, T.; Stöbel-Richter, Y.; Zenger, M.; Brähler, E. The quality of life questionnaire EQ-5D-5L: Psychometric properties and normative values for the general German population. *Qual. Life Res.* **2014**, *23*, 443–447. [CrossRef]
27. Janssen, M.F.; Pickard, A.S.; Golicki, D.; Gudex, C.; Niewada, M.; Scalone, L.; Swinburn, P.; Busschbach, J. Measurement properties of the EQ-5D-5L compared to the EQ-5D-3L across eight patient groups: A multi-country study. *Qual. Life Res.* **2013**, *22*, 1717–1727. [CrossRef]
28. Lange, M.; Kamtsiuris, P.; Lange, C.; Rosario, A.S.; Stolzenberg, H.; Lampert, T. Messung soziodemographischer Merkmale im Kinder-und Jugendgesundheitssurvey (KiGGS) und ihre Bedeutung am Beispiel der Einschätzung des allgemeinen Gesundheitszustands. *Bundesgesundheitsblatt Gesundh. Gesundh.* **2007**, *50*, 578–589. [CrossRef] [PubMed]
29. Jakobsen, M.; Jensen, R. Common Method Bias in Public Management Studies. *Int. Public Manag. J.* **2015**, *18*, 3–30. [CrossRef]
30. Tehseen, S.; Ramayah, T.; Sajilan, S. Testing and Controlling for Common Method Variance: A Review of Available Methods. *J. Manag. Sci.* **2017**, *4*, 142–168. [CrossRef]
31. Chang, S.-J.; Van Witteloostuijn, A.; Eden, L. Common Method Variance in International Business Research. *JIBS Spec. Collect.* **2019**, *385–398*, 385–398. [CrossRef]
32. Blanca, M.J.; Alarcón, R.; Arnau, J. Non-normal data: Is ANOVA still a valid option? *Psicothema* **2017**, *29*, 552–557. [CrossRef] [PubMed]
33. Schmider, E.; Ziegler, M.; Danay, E.; Beyer, L.; Bühner, M. Is It Really Robust? *Methodology* **2010**, *6*, 147–151. [CrossRef]
34. Cohen, J. *Statistical Power for the Behavioral Sciences*, 2nd ed.; Laurence Erlbaum and Associates: Hillsdale, NJ, USA, 1988.
35. Hayes, A.F. Beyond Baron and Kenny: Statistical mediation analysis in the new millennium. *Commun. Monogr.* **2009**, *76*, 408–420. [CrossRef]
36. Hayes, A.F. Partial, conditional, and moderated moderated mediation: Quantification, inference, and interpretation. *Commun. Monogr.* **2018**, *85*, 4–40. [CrossRef]
37. Hayes, A.F. *Introduction to Mediation, Moderation, and Conditional Process Analysis: A Regession Approach*; Guilford Press: New York, NY, USA, 2018; pp. 3–4.
38. Schermelleh-Engel, K.; Moosbrugger, H.; Müller, H. Evaluating the fit of structural equation models: Tests of significance and descriptive goodness-of-fit measures. *MPR-Online* **2003**, *8*, 23–74.
39. Khubchandani, J.; Price, J.H. Workplace Harassment and Morbidity Among US Adults: Results from the National Health Interview Survey. *J. Community Health* **2015**, *40*, 555–563. [CrossRef] [PubMed]
40. Salvagioni, D.A.J.; Melanda, F.N.; Mesas, A.E.; González, A.D.; Gabani, F.L.; De Andrade, S.M. Physical, psychological and occupational consequences of job burnout: A systematic review of prospective studies. *PLoS ONE* **2017**, *12*, e0185781. [CrossRef]
41. Sliter, M.; Jex, S.; Wolford, K.; McInnerney, J. How rude! Emotional labor as a mediator between customer incivility and employee outcomes. *J. Occup. Health Psychol.* **2010**, *15*, 468. [CrossRef]
42. German Federal Office of Statistics [Statistisches Bundesamt]. Population and Employment. Households and Families. Results of the Microcensus 2017. Subject 1, Series 3 [Bevölkerung und Erwerbstätigkeit. Haushalte und Familien. Ergebnisse des Mikrozensus 2017. Fachserie 1, Reihe 3]. 2018. Available online: https://www.destatis.de/DE/Themen/Gesellschaft-Umwelt/Bevoelkerung/Haushalte-Familien/Publikationen/Downloads-Haushalte/haushalte-familien-2010300177004.pdf?__blob=publicationFile&v=4 (accessed on 27 October 2021).
43. Lampert, T.; Kroll, L.; Müters, S.; Stolzenberg, H. Measurement of socioeconomic status in the German health interview and examination survey for adults (DEGS1). *Bundesgesundheitsblatt Gesundh. Gesundh.* **2013**, *56*, 631–636. [CrossRef] [PubMed]

44. Mensink, G.; Schienkiewitz, A.; Haftenberger, M.; Lampert, T.; Ziese, T.; Scheidt-Nave, C. Overweight and obesity in Germany: Results of the German Health Interview and Examination Survey for Adults (DEGS1). *Bundesgesundheitsblatt Gesundh. Gesundh.* **2013**, *56*, 131–143. [CrossRef]
45. Gorber, S.C.; Tremblay, M.; Moher, D.; Gorber, B. A comparison of direct vs. self-report measures for assessing height, weight and body mass index: A systematic review. *Obes. Rev.* **2007**, *8*, 307–326. [CrossRef]
46. Flegal, K.M.; Graubard, B.I.; Ioannidis, J.P.A. Evaluation of a suggested novel method to adjust BMI calculated from self-reported weight and height for measurement error. *Obesity* **2021**, *29*, 1700–1707. [CrossRef]
47. Shiely, F.; Millar, S.R. BMI self-selection: Exploring alternatives to self-reported BMI. *Res. Methods Med. Health Sci.* **2021**, *2*, 112–122. [CrossRef]
48. Salas, X.R.; Alberga, A.S.; Cameron, E.; Estey, L.; Forhan, M.; Kirk, S.; Russell-Mayhew, S.; Sharma, A.M. Addressing weight bias and discrimination: Moving beyond raising awareness to creating change. *Obes. Rev.* **2017**, *18*, 1323–1335. [CrossRef] [PubMed]
49. Täuber, S.; Mulder, L.B.; Flint, S.W. The Impact of Workplace Health Promotion Programs Emphasizing Individual Responsibility on Weight Stigma and Discrimination. *Front. Psychol.* **2018**, *9*, 2206. [CrossRef]
50. Makowski, A.C.; Kim, T.J.; Luck-Sikorski, C.; Knesebeck, O.V.D. Social deprivation, gender and obesity: Multiple stigma? Results of a population survey from Germany. *BMJ Open* **2019**, *9*, e023389. [CrossRef] [PubMed]
51. Luck-Sikorski, C.; Schomerus, G.; Jochum, T.; Riedel-Heller, S.G. Layered stigma? Co-occurring depression and obesity in the public eye. *J. Psychosom. Res.* **2018**, *106*, 29–33. [CrossRef] [PubMed]
52. Puhl, R.M.; Himmelstein, M.S.; Pearl, R.L. Weight stigma as a psychosocial contributor to obesity. *Am. Psychol.* **2020**, *75*, 274–289. [CrossRef]

nutrients MDPI

Article

Are Sensitivity to Punishment, Sensitivity to Reward and Effortful Control Transdiagnostic Mechanisms Underlying the Eating Disorder/Obesity Spectrum?

Laurence Claes [1,2,*], Glenn Kiekens [1,3], Els Boekaerts [4], Lies Depestele [5], Eva Dierckx [5,6], Sylvia Gijbels [4], Katrien Schoevaerts [5] and Koen Luyckx [1,7]

1 Faculty of Psychology and Educational Sciences, KU Leuven, 3000 Leuven, Belgium; glenn.kiekens@kuleuven.be (G.K.); koen.luyckx@kuleuven.be (K.L.)
2 Faculty of Medicine and Health Sciences, University Antwerp, 2000 Antwerp, Belgium
3 Center for Contextual Psychiatry, Department of Neurosciences, KU Leuven, 3000 Leuven, Belgium
4 Obesity Centre Hasselt, Jessa Hospital, 3500 Hasselt, Belgium; els.boekaerts@jessazh.be (E.B.); sylvia.gijbels@jessazh.be (S.G.)
5 Psychiatric Hospital Alexianen Zorggroep Tienen, 3300 Tienen, Belgium; lies.depestele@azt.broedersvanliefde.be (L.D.); Eva.Dierckx@vub.be (E.D.); katrien.schoevaerts@azt.broedersvanliefde.be (K.S.)
6 Department of Clinical Psychology, Vrije Universiteit Brussel, 1050 Brussels, Belgium
7 UNIBS, University of the Free State, Bloemfontein 9300, South Africa
* Correspondence: Laurence.claes@kuleuven.be; Tel.: +32-16-32-61-33

Citation: Claes, L.; Kiekens, G.; Boekaerts, E.; Depestele, L.; Dierckx, E.; Gijbels, S.; Schoevaerts, K.; Luyckx, K. Are Sensitivity to Punishment, Sensitivity to Reward and Effortful Control Transdiagnostic Mechanisms Underlying the Eating Disorder/Obesity Spectrum? *Nutrients* **2021**, *13*, 3327. https://doi.org/10.3390/nu13103327

Academic Editors: Fernando Fernandez-Aranda, Janet Treasure and Empar Lurbe

Received: 29 August 2021
Accepted: 20 September 2021
Published: 23 September 2021

Abstract: Although it has been postulated that eating disorders (EDs) and obesity form part of a broad spectrum of eating- and weight-related disorders, this has not yet been tested empirically. In the present study, we investigated interindividual differences in sensitivity to punishment, sensitivity to reward, and effortful control along the ED/obesity spectrum in women. We used data on 286 patients with eating disorders (44.6% AN-R, 24.12% AN-BP, and 31.82% BN), 126 healthy controls, and 640 Class II/III obese bariatric patients (32.81% Class II and 67.19% Class III) with and without binge eating. Participants completed the behavioral inhibition and behavioral activation scales, as well as the effortful control scale, to assess sensitivity to punishment and reward and effortful control. Results showed that patients with EDs scored significantly higher on punishment sensitivity (anxiety) compared to healthy controls and Class II/III obese patients; the different groups did not differ significantly on reward sensitivity. Patients with binge eating or compensatory behaviors scored significantly lower on effortful control than patients without binge eating. Differences in temperamental profiles along the ED/obesity spectrum appear continuous and gradual rather than categorical. This implies that it may be meaningful to include emotion regulation and impulse regulation training in the treatment of both EDs and obesity.

Keywords: sensitivity to reward; sensitivity to punishment; effortful control; eating disorders; obesity; bariatric surgery

1. Introduction

Several authors postulate that eating disorders (EDs) and obesity form part of a broad spectrum of eating- and weight-related disorders [1]. Concerning weight status, anorexia nervosa of the restrictive type (AN-R) and the binge eating/purging type (AN-BP) are characterized by being underweight (BMI < 18.5 kg/m^2), and bulimia nervosa (BN) by normal weight (BMI 18.5–24.9 kg/m^2). Within obesity (BMI $\geq$ 30 kg/m^2), researchers differentiate between Class I (BMI 30–34.9 kg/m^2), Class II (BMI 35–39.9 kg/m^2), and Class III obesity (BMI $\geq$ 40 kg/m^2) [2]. With respect to eating-related behaviors, patients with AN-R mainly engage in severe food restriction, whereas patients with AN-BP also report binge eating and purging behaviors (e.g., vomiting, laxative abuse, etc.) besides food restriction.

Patients with BN and binge eating disorder (BED) are characterized by regular episodes of binge eating with and without compensatory behaviors, respectively [3]. The causes of obesity are diverse, including genetic, environmental, and behavioral aspects of excessive energy intake, partitioning, and expenditure [4]. Obese patients with a comorbid eating disorder (mainly BED, which is reported in 30% of obese patients) report more eating and weight-related pathology, as well as more general and personality psychopathology [1,5,6], compared to obese patients without BED.

The question remains open as to why patients with AN are able to highly restrict their food intake and become emaciated, whereas other patients binge and overconsume with and without purging behaviors [7,8]. Part of the explanation might be found in interindividual differences in reactive (bottom-up) and regulative (top-down) temperament [7,8]. According to dual-process models, ED behaviors result from the interplay of bottom-up processes (e.g., sensitivity to punishment and sensitivity to reward) and top-down processes (e.g., effortful control) [9]. One of the most applied models of reactive temperament that can be used to explain individual variations in food intake is reinforcement sensitivity theory (RST) [7,10,11], which encompasses two primary motivational systems: the behavioral inhibition system (BIS) and the behavioral activation system (BAS). The BIS is sensitive to stimuli that signal conditioned punishment and the omission/termination of reward and is involved in behavioral inhibition [12]. The BIS is related to personality traits, such as the Big Five neuroticism dimension and Cloninger's harm avoidance dimension [13,14]. The BAS is sensitive to stimuli that signal unconditioned reward and relief from punishment and is involved in approach behavior [12]. The BAS is related to personality traits, such as extraversion and novelty seeking [13,14]. Over the years, the RST has included a third system: the fight–flight system [15]. In 2000, Gray and McNaughton [16] presented a revised version of the RST in which the BAS is responsive to (un)conditioned stimuli of reward and the fight–flight–freeze system is responsive to (un)conditioned stimuli of punishment, while the BIS resolves goal conflicts (e.g., approach-avoidance conflicts).

Besides reactive temperament (bottom-up, automatic), regulative (top-down, controlled) temperament or executive control [17] can also play an important role in the regulation of food intake and weight. Self-regulation is often used interchangeably with terms such as effortful control [18] and self-regulation [19]. Effortful control is also related to particular personality traits, such as the Big Five conscientiousness dimension and Cloninger's self-directedness dimension [17]. It is assumed that effortful control can directly influence ED behaviors or moderate the association between reactive temperamental traits and ED psychopathology, in the sense that a high level of effortful control might help individuals control their reactive temperament and decrease their risk of developing ED psychopathology [20].

Up until now, most studies have investigated BISBAS reactivity and effortful control in patients with EDs or obesity with and without BED (often compared to healthy controls) separately; but none of these studies included patients situated over the whole spectrum of ED/Obesity within a single study. In what follows, we present an overview of the literature on the sensitivity of reward/punishment and effortful control in patients with EDs and obesity.

1.1. Punishment Sensitivity

The most applied measures to assess sensitivity to punishment (BIS) and reward (BAS) are the BISBAS scales [21] and the sensitivity to punishment and sensitivity to reward questionnaire (SPSRQ) [22], both based on the original RST theory. The BISBAS scales focus on the general disposition towards reward (e.g., "When I'm doing well, I love to keep at it.") and punishment, whereas the SPSRQ items often include specific situational triggers related to punishment and reward (e.g., "Do you often meet people that you find physically attractive?"). Patients with EDs (AN-R, AN-BP, or BN) typically report significantly higher scores on punishment sensitivity (BIS/SP) compared to healthy controls [8,23–29]. When comparing different ED subtypes, most studies did not find significant differences among AN-R, AN-BP, or BN patients [8,25,29,30]. Two studies [23,27] showed that AN-R patients scored significantly higher on sensitivity to punishment than AN-BP or ED-PB (AN-BP + BN) patients, whereas other studies found the opposite [24] or no significant differences [31].

Studies comparing patients with obesity to healthy controls on punishment sensitivity are rather scarce. Class I obese patients without BED scored significantly lower on punishment sensitivity compared to healthy controls [32], whereas Class I obese patients with BED did not significantly differ from healthy controls [33]. Class II obese patients with and without BED scored significantly higher on punishment sensitivity than healthy controls [32,34]. No study has compared patients with Class III obesity with and without BED to healthy controls with respect to punishment sensitivity. When comparing obese patients (Class II, III) with and without BED on punishment sensitivity, patients with and without BED did not differ from each other [6,34]; no studies were performed in Class I obese patients with and without BED.

Higher punishment sensitivity in patients with EDs, as compared to healthy controls, seems to be linked to their symptomatology. Patients with AN-R relate their self-worth to their weight [35] and are afraid of gaining weight; their strict dieting can be considered as a way to avoid anxiety for weight gain [7,8]. Several studies have demonstrated a positive association between sensitivity to punishment and restrained eating in both adolescents and young adults [20,36]. Patients with binge eating (AN-BP, BN) and obesity, on the contrary, often use food to comfort or soothe themselves and to escape from negative feelings [37]. Davis [38], for example, showed a positive association between sensitivity to punishment and the symptoms of binge eating. The compensatory behaviors of patients with AN-BP/BN can again be considered as a way to avoid weight gain [7,8].

1.2. Reward Sensitivity

When comparing ED patients to healthy controls on reward sensitivity, we need to differentiate between the studies that use the SPSRQ and those that use the BISBAS scales to assess reward sensitivity. As mentioned before, the SPSRQ assesses specific types of rewarding situations (i.e., physical attractiveness, or social approval), whereas the BISBAS scales assess more general reward sensitivity [24]. Studies using the BAS scale to assess reward sensitivity [8,23] have shown that AN-R patients score significantly lower on reward sensitivity compared to healthy controls, whereas AN-BP and BN do not differ significantly from healthy controls. When studies combine AN-R and AN-BP in one group, the difference between them and the healthy controls disappears. Studies using the SR scale show that AN-R, AN-BP, and BN patients score significantly higher on reward sensitivity compared to healthy controls [8,24,26]. However, Glashouwer et al. [24] showed that the differences between EDs and healthy controls disappeared when items that assessed appearance/social reward were removed from the SR scale. When comparing different subtypes of EDs on the BAS scale, most studies did not find significant differences between AN-R and AN-BP [26,27,31] or AN-R, AN-BP, and BN [23,29]. Studies that found significant differences between ED subtypes showed that binge eating/purging patients (AN-BP, BN) scored significantly higher on BAS fun seeking compared to restrictive AN patients [8,23,30]. Comparing ED subtypes utilizing the SR scale showed that patients with AN-R and AN-BP did not differ significantly from each other on the SR scale, whereas BN patients scored significantly higher compared to AN-R patients.

When comparing patients with obesity to healthy controls on reward sensitivity, patients with Class I obesity without BED did not differ from healthy controls on reward sensitivity [32], whereas patients with Class I obesity with BED scored significantly higher on sensitivity to reward when compared to healthy controls [33]. Patients with Class II obesity with and without BED also scored significantly higher on reward sensitivity (both BAS/SR scales) as compared to healthy controls [34]. No study compared patients with Class III obesity with and without BED to healthy controls on sensitivity to reward.

When comparing obese patients, obese patients (Class II/III) with and without BED did not differ significantly from each other on reward sensitivity [6,34]; no studies were performed in Class I obese patients. The higher reward sensitivity in moderate/extreme obese patients makes them possibly more vulnerable to rewarding (fatty/sugary) food in our obesogenic society, which may partially explain the overconsumption of food and their subsequently becoming overweight [7,39]. Several studies have shown positive associations between sensitivity to reward and emotional overeating, preference for high fat food, binge eating, and food cravings [39].

1.3. Effortful Control

Effortful control and its subdimensions (inhibitory, activation, and attentional control) can be measured using the effortful control scale (ECS) from the adult temperament questionnaire short form (ATQ-SF) [40,41]. The perception of low control and the desire for higher control in AN patients (and in particular, patients with AN-R) are psychological variables that were frequently considered in the papers of the original ED theorists, including Bruch [42], Crisp [43], Garfinkel and Garner [44], and Selvini Palazzoli [45]. In the 1980s, Eric Button [46], described AN as a quest for control. Indeed, studies comparing ED subtypes utilizing the ECS show that AN-R patients score significantly higher on effortful control than AN-BP/BN patients, particularly on the subscales for inhibitory and activation control [23,31]. Studies comparing obesity subtypes utilizing Cloninger's self-directedness or Rothbart's effortful control scales do not show differences among Class I, II, and III obesity categories with respect to self-directedness; however, obese patients with BED score significantly lower on self-directedness/effortful control, compared to obese patients without BED [6,47]. Thus, it seems that a lack of effortful control may make ED/obese patients vulnerable to binge eating (and purging).

1.4. The Present Study

The aim of the present study is to investigate temperamental differences on BIS/BAS and effortful control along the ED/obesity spectrum. We collected data from female AN-R, AN-BP, and BN patients, healthy controls, and Class II and Class III obese bariatric patients with and without binge eating within the age range 18–65. Thus, we add to the existing literature by comparing ED, healthy controls, and obesity patients in one study on both executive/top-down and reactivity measures of temperament.

With respect to punishment sensitivity (BIS), we expect that ED and obese patients will score significantly higher compared to healthy controls. Within the ED/obesity subtypes, we do not expect significant differences on punishment sensitivity [48,49].

With respect to reward sensitivity (BAS), we expect no significant differences between ED and healthy controls, with the exception of a potentially lower reward reactivity in AN-R patients compared to healthy controls [48,49]. However, we do expect higher levels of reward sensitivity in obese patients compared to healthy controls. Within obesity subtypes with and without BED, we again do not anticipate differences in BAS reactivity [6,47].

Finally, concerning top-down control, we expect that patients with ED/obesity will score significantly lower than healthy controls [6,23,31,47], whereas patients with binge eating and/or purging (AN-BP, BN, obesity Class II/III with binge eating), are hypothesized to score lower on effortful control compared to patients without binge eating and/or purging (AN-R, obesity Class II/III without binge eating) [6,23,31].

2. Materials and Methods

2.1. Participants & Procedure

Female patients with EDs, healthy controls, and individuals with obesity (from ages 18 to 65) were sampled out of three different data collections.

The sample of ED inpatients consisted of 286 patients, of whom 126 (44.06%) were diagnosed as AN-R, 69 (24.12%) as AN-BP, and 91 (31.82%) as BN through a clinical interview, and cross-validated by the eating disorder evaluation scale (EDES) [50]. The mean age and BMI of all ED subtypes are displayed in Table 1. The three ED subtypes did not differ significantly in age and were significantly younger than healthy controls and patients with obesity. Concerning BMI, AN patients (AN-R/AN-BP) had a significantly lower BMI than BN patients and healthy controls (normal weight) and Class II/III obese patients (severe overweight). All data were collected at the admission of these patients at a specialized inpatient treatment unit for EDs in Flanders, the Dutch-speaking part of Belgium.

The sample of female patients with Class II/III obesity was collected during an intake for a bariatric surgery trajectory at a general hospital in the Dutch-speaking part of Belgium. The presence or absence of binge eating was determined by two items (overeating + loss of control) of the Dutch version of the eating disorder examination questionnaire (EDEQ; see Section 2.2. Instruments). About 210 patients were diagnosed with Class II obesity, of whom 72 (34.29%) engaged in binge eating, and 430 patients with Class III obesity, of whom 141 (32.79%) engaged in binge eating. These comorbidity rates of binge eating are in line with prior research [6]. The mean age and BMI of the individuals with Class II/III obesity with and without binge eating are displayed in Table 1. All patients with obesity were significantly older than patients with ED, and were similar in age to healthy controls (except patients of Class II obesity without BED, who were significantly older). Within the obesity subtypes (Class II and Class III), patients with binge eating were significantly younger than those without binge eating. Concerning BMI, obese patients had significantly higher BMIs compared to patients with AN (underweight), and BN and healthy controls (normal weight). Obesity Class III patients also had a significantly higher BMI than patients with Class II obesity.

Finally, the 126 healthy controls were collected from the Flemish-speaking general population of Belgium, taking into account the distribution of the Flemish population's age, gender, and education. The mean age and BMI of the healthy controls are shown in Table 1. Healthy controls were significantly older than patients with an ED, and similar in age to patients with obesity (except patients of Class II obesity without binge eating, who were older). Concerning BMI, healthy controls had a normal BMI, as did BN patients. However, their BMI was higher than patients with AN, and lower than patients with Class II/III obesity.

All patients and healthy controls gave their informed consent to use their data anonymously for research purposes. The three data collections from which the data were pooled were approved by the ethical committee of the Faculty of Psychology and Educational Sciences (healthy controls) and/or the medical ethical committee of the medical institute in which the patients (with Eds and/or obesity) were treated. Given that the groups did significantly differ regarding age, this variable was included as a confounding variable in all analyses. Although groups also differed with respect to BMI, we did not include BMI as control variable, given that it is an essential characteristic of the diagnostic groups.

Table 1. Means (standard deviations/errors) of Age, BMI, the Behavioral Inhibition and Behavioral Activation Scales and the Effortful Control Scale and subscales for eating disorders, healthy controls and Class II/III obese bariatric groups controlled for age.

	AN-R (*N* = 12)		AN-BP (*N* = 69)		BN (*N* = 89)		HC (*N* = 84)		Class II Obesity − BE (*N* = 138)		Class II Obesity + BE (*N* = 72)		Class III Obesity − BE (*N* = 289)		Class III Obesity + BE (*N* = 140)		*F*
	M	(SD)	M	(SD)	M	(SD)	M	(SD)	M	(SD)	M	(SD)	M	(SD)	M	(SD)	
Age	24.60_{a}	(6.17)	24.52_{b}	(5.04)	24.41_{c}	(5.22)	$38.05_{a,b,c,d}$	(12.15)	$42.07_{a,b,c,d,e}$	(10.19)	$37.19_{a,b,c,e,f}$	(11.07)	$39.42_{a,b,c,e,g}$	(12.74)	$35.53_{a,b,c,e,g}$	(11.75)	58.55 ***
BMI	15.40_{a}	(1.66)	16.27_{b}	(1.67)	$20.96_{a,b,c}$	(1.77)	$21.65_{a,b,d}$	(1.74)	$37.52_{a,b,c,d,e}$	(1.45)	$37.78_{a,b,c,d,f}$	(1.58)	$43.74_{a,b,c,d,e,f,g}$	(4.03)	$43.89_{a,b,c,d,e,f}$	(4.32)	2223.92 ***
	M	(SE)	M	(SE)	M	(SE)	M	(SE)	M	(SE)	M	(SE)	M	(SE)	M	(SE)	
BIS-TOT	3.55_{a}	(0.05)	3.62_{b}	(0.06)	$3.40_{a,b,c}$	(0.06)	$3.19_{a,b,c,d}$	(0.06)	$3.06_{a,b,c,d,e}$	(0.04)	$3.06_{a,b,c,f}$	(0.06)	$3.11_{a,b,c,g}$	(0.03)	$3.26_{a,b,c,e,f,g}$	(0.04)	15.33 ***
BAS-TOT	2.79	(0.04)	2.74	(0.06)	2.78	(0.05)	2.75	(0.05)	2.79	(0.04)	2.85	(0.05)	2.85	(0.03)	2.92	(0.04)	1.91
BAS-DR	2.45_{a}	(0.06)	2.36_{b}	(0.08)	2.37_{c}	(0.07)	2.34_{d}	(0.07)	$2.53_{d,e}$	(0.06)	2.50_{f}	(0.08)	$2.56_{b,c,d,g}$	(0.04)	$2.62_{a,b,c,d}$	(0.05)	2.70 **
BAS-FS	2.60	(0.05)	2.67	(0.07)	2.71	(0.06)	2.65	(0.06)	2.60	(0.05)	2.74	(0.06)	2.64	(0.03)	2.76	(0.05)	1.61
BAS-RR	3.20	(0.04)	3.10	(0.06)	3.16	(0.05)	3.17	(0.05)	3.16	(0.04)	3.23	(0.06)	3.24	(0.03)	3.29	(0.04)	1.80
EC-TOT	4.55_{a}	(0.07)	$4.18_{a,b}$	(0.09)	$3.96_{a,c}$	(0.08)	$4.75_{b,c,d}$	(0.08)	$4.73_{b,c,e}$	(0.06)	$4.36_{c,d,e,f}$	(0.09)	$4.74_{a,b,c,f,g}$	(0.04)	$4.45_{b,c,d,e,g}$	(0.06)	14.45 ***
EC-INH	4.81_{a}	(0.08)	$4.28_{a,b}$	(0.11)	$4.16_{a,c}$	(0.10)	$4.83_{b,c,d}$	(0.10)	$4.61_{b,c,e}$	(0.08)	$4.19_{a,d,e,f}$	(0.11)	$4.62_{b,c,f,g}$	(0.05)	$4.31_{a,d,e,g}$	(0.08)	9.15 ***
EC-ACT	4.85_{a}	(0.09)	$4.52_{a,b}$	(0.11)	$4.12_{a,b,c}$	(0.10)	$4.94_{b,c,d}$	(0.10)	$5.00_{b,c,e}$	(0.08)	$4.70_{c,e,f}$	(0.10)	$4.98_{b,c,f,g}$	(0.06)	$4.73_{c,e,g}$	(0.08)	9.68 ***
EC-ATT	3.79_{a}	(0.10)	3.57_{b}	(0.13)	$3.49_{a,c}$	(0.12)	$4.35_{a,b,c,d}$	(0.11)	$4.52_{a,b,c,e}$	(0.09)	$4.09_{b,c,e,f}$	(0.12)	$4.58_{a,b,c,f,g}$	(0.06)	$4.25_{a,b,c,e,g}$	(0.09)	14.85 ***

Means with the same subscript are significantly different from each other: $_{a}$ different from AN-R; $_{b}$ different from AN-BP; $_{c}$ different from BN; $_{d}$ different from HC; $_{e}$ different from Class II Obesity—BE; $_{f}$ different from Class II Obesity + BE; $_{g}$ different from Class III Obesity—BE. Abbreviations: BMI = body mass index; BIS = behavioral inhibition scale (punishment sensitivity); BAS = behavioral activation scale (reward sensitivity); TOT = total scale; DR = drive; FS = fun seeking; RR = reward sensitivity; EC = effortful control; INH = inhibitory control; ACT = activation control; ATT = attentional control. *** $p < 0.001$, ** $p < 0.01$.

2.2. Instruments

To determine the BMI of the participants, we calculated their weight in kilograms and divided this by their height in m^2. To determine the presence or absence of "binge eating" (not BED), we asked two questions from the EDEQ [51]: "Over the past 28 days, how many times have you eaten what other people would regards as an unusually large amount of food (given the circumstances)?"; and "On how many of these times did you have a sense of having lost control over your eating (at the time you were eating)?". Patients who reported eating unusually large amounts of food while losing control over their eating were considered to cngage in binge eating.

Sensitivity to reward and punishment was measured utilizing the behavioral inhibition/behavioral activation system (BISBAS) scales [21]. The BISBAS scales consist of 20 4-point Likert scale items, ranging from 1 "I strongly agree" to 4 "I strongly disagree". The BIS scale assesses worry concerning potential punishment in the future ($n = 7$, $\alpha = 0.80$ in the present study, e.g., "I worry about making mistakes."), and the BAS scale assesses sensitivity to reward ($n = 13$, $\alpha = 0.81$). The BAS scale (disinhibition) exists of three subscales, measuring BAS drive ($n = 4$, $\alpha = 0.74$, e.g., "When I want something, I usually go all-out to get it"), BAS fun seeking ($n = 5$, $\alpha = 0.52$, e.g., "I often act on the spur of the moment"), and BAS reward responsiveness ($n = 5$, $\alpha = 0.61$, e.g., "When I'm doing well at something, I love to keep at it").

Effortful/executive control was measured using the effortful control scale (ECS) from the adult temperament questionnaire short form (ATQ-SF) [40,41]. The ECS exists of 19 7-point Likert scale items, ranging from 1 "not at all applicable" to 7 "completely applicable" ($\alpha = 0.80$ in the present study). The ECS has three subscales: attention control is the capacity to focus and shift attention when necessary ($n = 5$, $\alpha = 0.73$, e.g., "It is very hard for me to focus my attention when I am distressed."(reversed)); inhibitory control is the capacity to suppress inappropriate approach behavior ($n = 7$, $\alpha = 0.54$, e.g., "I can easily resist talking out of turn, even when I'm excited and want to express an idea."); and finally, activation control refers to the capacity to act when there is a strong tendency to avoid it ($n = 7$, $\alpha = 0.68$, e.g., "If I think of something that needs to be done, I usually get right to work on it.").

2.3. Analyses

Descriptive statistics are reported as means with associated errors. To compare the different ED/HC/obesity groups on the basis of their sensitivity to punishment, sensitivity to reward, and effortful control, we performed ANCOVAs with the group as the independent variable, temperamental dimensions as dependent variables, and age as a covariate. When the ANCOVAs showed significant results, simple contrasts were used to evaluate subgroup differences.

3. Results

The means (standard errors) of the different temperament measures for each ED/HC/obesity group are displayed in Table 1.

3.1. Punishment Sensitivity

With respect to punishment sensitivity (Figure 1), all ED groups scored significantly higher on punishment sensitivity (BIS) compared to healthy controls and patients with obesity. Patients with AN (AN-R+AN-BP) scored significantly higher on punishment sensitivity than patients with BN. Obesity groups did not differ significantly from healthy controls (except Class II obesity—BE) on punishment sensitivity, and scored significantly lower on punishment sensitivity than ED groups. Within the obesity groups, Class III obesity patients with binge eating reported significantly higher punishment sensitivity levels than the other obesity groups.

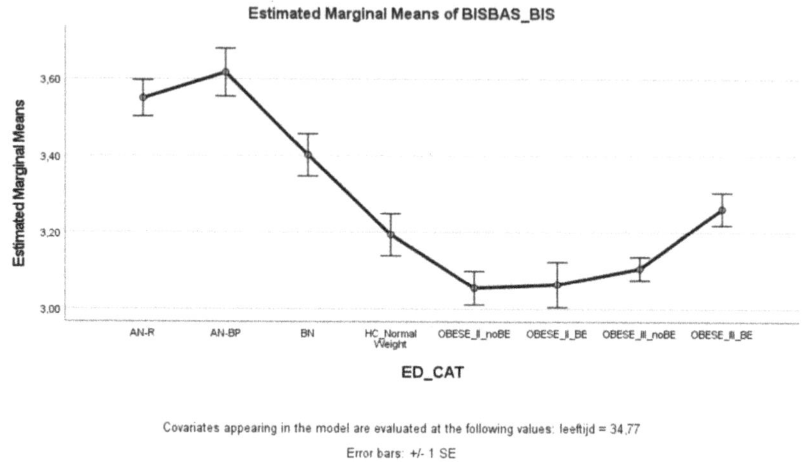

Figure 1. Means (standard errors) of the behavioral inhibition scale scores for eating disorders, healthy controls, and obesity groups, controlled for age.

3.2. *Reward Sensitivity*

With respect to the BAS total score and the fun seeking and reward responsiveness subscales, the ED, healthy controls, and obesity groups did not differ significantly from each other. However, on the BAS drive subscale (Figure 2), patients with Class III obesity with and without binge eating scored significantly higher on drive compared to patients with AN-BP, BN, and healthy controls. Patients with Class III obesity and binge eating also scored higher on the BAS drive subscale than patients with AN-R. There were no significant differences between patients with Class II and Class III obesity.

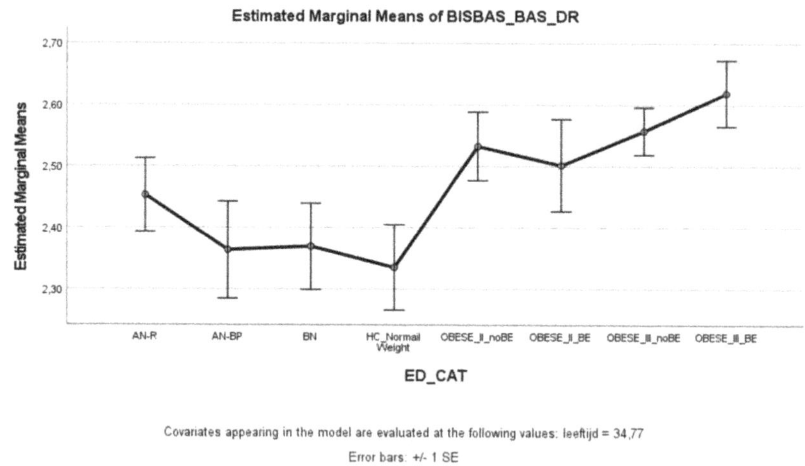

Figure 2. Means (standard errors) of the behavioral activation scale—drive scores for eating disorders, healthy controls, and obesity groups, controlled for age.

3.3. *Effortful Control*

ED and obese groups with binge eating (AN-BP, BN, Class II obesity + BE, Class III obesity + BE) scored significantly lower on effortful control (total score and inhibitory control) compared to healthy controls, whereas ED and obese groups without binge eating

(AN-R, Class II obesity—BE, Class III obesity—BE) did not significantly differ from healthy controls (Figures 3 and 4). Within the ED groups, patients with AN-BP/BN scored significantly lower on effortful control (total, inhibitory, and activation) compared to patients with AN-R (Figures 3–5), whereas in the obesity groups, obese patients with binge eating scored significantly lower on all measures of effortful control compared to obese patients without binge eating. Obese patients without binge eating scored similarly to healthy controls on activation and attentional control (Figures 5 and 6).

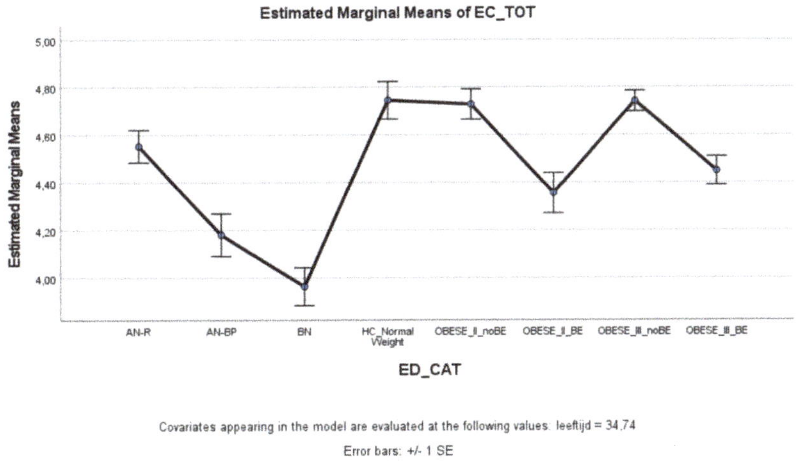

Figure 3. Means (standard errors) of the effortful control scale—total control scores for eating disorders, healthy controls, and obesity groups, controlled for age.

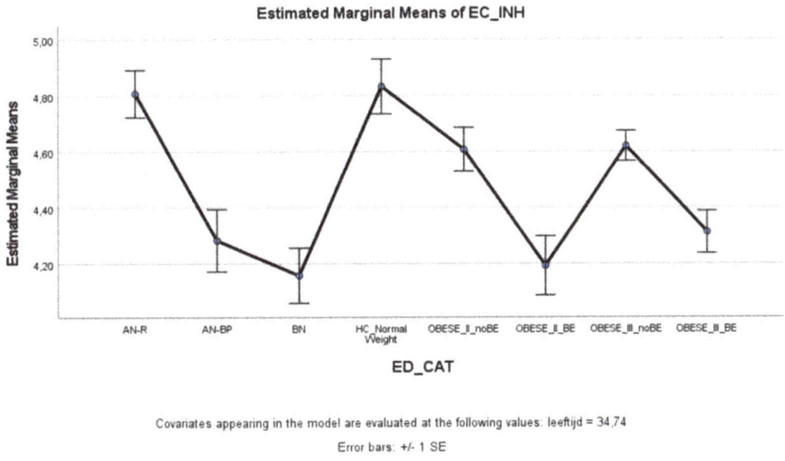

Figure 4. Means (standard errors) of the effortful control scale—inhibitory control scores for eating disorders, healthy controls, and obesity groups, controlled for age.

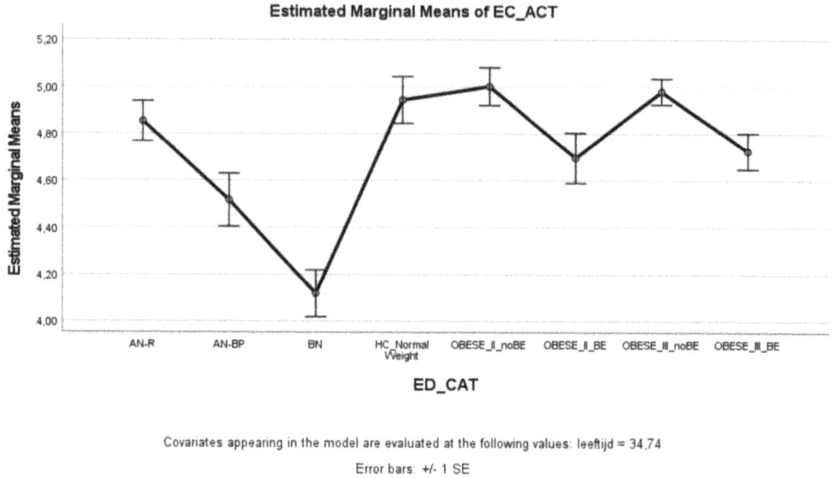

Figure 5. Means (standard errors) of the effortful control scale—activation control scores for eating disorders, healthy controls, and obesity groups, controlled for age.

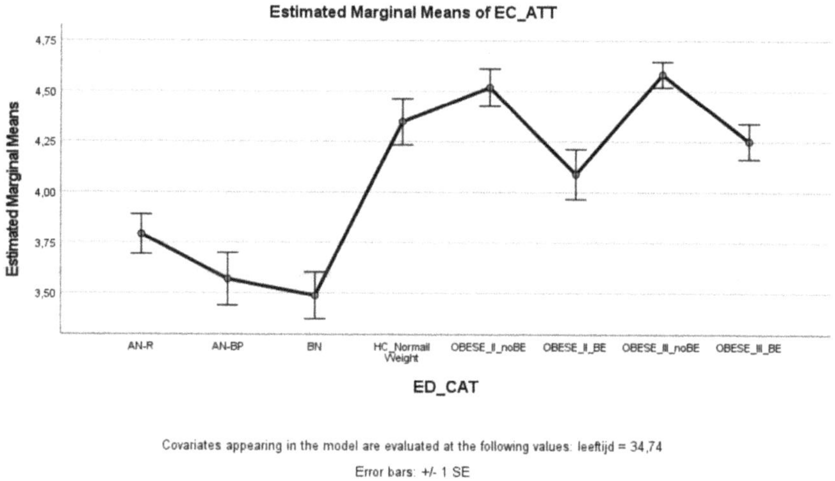

Figure 6. Means (standard errors) of the effortful control scale—attentional control scores for eating disorders, healthy controls, and obesity groups, controlled for age.

4. Discussion

The present study investigated sensitivity to punishment, sensitivity to reward, and effortful control along the ED/obesity spectrum in women. Based on the findings, we can conclude that ED groups are significantly more sensitive to punishment than healthy controls and obese groups. Concerning reward sensitivity, patients with morbid Class III obesity scored significantly higher on BAS drive compared to ED groups (except AN-R) and healthy controls. Finally, all ED/obese groups with binge eating reported significantly lower levels of effortful control (particularly inhibitory control) compared to healthy controls and patients without binge eating.

4.1. Sensitivity to Punishment

The different ED/obese groups' temperamental profiles can help us understand their disturbed eating patterns. The fact that all ED patients are more sensitive to punishment confirms previous studies' findings [25] and can explain the high comorbidity between EDs and anxiety disorders [52]. The high scores on punishment sensitivity can also explain why people with an ED are afraid of weight gain and can resist the temptation to food (as a way to avoid this weight gain) [7,53].

4.2. Effortful Control

Variability in effortful control can also help explain differences between restrictive and binge eating/purging ED subtypes. While restrictive ED patients show similar levels of effortful control as healthy controls (except for attentional control), patients with binge eating/purging behaviors (AN-BP, BN) score significantly lower on effortful control. The lack of effortful control can explain why these patients lose control over their eating behaviors and eat comfort (sugary/fatty) food to deal with their negative effects [37], and then engage in compensatory purging behaviors to avoid weight gain [7,53]. Within this subgroup of obese patients, the lack of effortful control is clearly related to the presence of binge eating behaviors as well. Several studies have shown that obese patients with binge eating tend to have more comorbidity with impulsive psychopathology [54,55] than obese patients without binge eating. Other studies investigating subtypes of obese patients have also found support for the notion of a more resilient subgroup of obese patients and an emotional/behavioral dysregulated group, characterized by low levels of effortful control, psychological complaints, and avoidant and depressive coping patterns [23].

4.3. Reward Sensitivity

Finally, concerning reward sensitivity, we did not find significant differences between the ED, obese, and healthy control groups for BAS reactivity. While we did anticipate a potential difference between AN-R and healthy controls, and between obese patients and healthy controls, some studies also did not find differences when using the BISBAS scales [1,49]. In the present study, only patients with Class II obesity without binge eating and Class III obesity with and without binge eating scored significantly higher on BAS drive than ED and healthy controls. This finding possibly refers to the high drive of obese patients to attain their goal, i.e., the bariatric surgery.

4.4. Clinical Implications

The present study has several clinical implications. Given the high levels of punishment sensitivity, it is essential that the treatment of patients with ED focuses on acquiring emotion regulation skills to help patients cope with emotional distress [37]. This is not surprising, given that EDs are often considered anxiety disorders. Evidence-based treatments of EDs, such as CBT-E and DBT-E [56–59], often include strategies to deal with emotions and to replace maladaptive ED behaviors with more adaptive emotion regulation strategies [37]. Furthermore, for binge eating and/or purging patients, the lack of effortful control certainly needs attention. First of all, it is important that patients focus on the aims of the treatment (which can be complicated by difficulties in attentional control) and learn to steer their behaviors (which can be complicated by difficulties in inhibitory/activation control). Furthermore, we know from prior research that a lack of effortful control/self-directedness can increase drop-out rates and worsen outcomes in patients with ED and obesity [60]. Therefore, impulse regulation strategies are included in evidence treatments for ED and obesity (e.g., CBT) [61]. Dalle Grave et al. [60], for example, conclude that CBT techniques to increase self-control, such as "setting short-term and achievable goals, developing adaptive coping behaviors through problem-solving in order to achieve these goals, and developing the confidence that they possess the resources required to achieve these goals (via progressive increases in self-efficacy through mastery experiences)", could decrease drop-out rates and improve therapy outcomes for patients with obesity [60], (p. 35). Adapting the evidence-based treatments to the temperamental profile of our patients will probably also decrease drop-out rates and further improve our treatments [62,63].

4.5. Limitations and Suggestions for Future Research

Besides the strengths of our study, several limitations need to be discussed and addressed for future studies. First of all, our sample solely consists of female patients with ED/obesity, and healthy controls. Furthermore, we lack a group of outpatients with an ED, 'overweight' people, a group with Class I obesity ± BE, and a group of Class II/III obese patients ± BE who did not apply for bariatric surgery. Therefore, future studies certainly need to include male ED in/outpatients, HC, and overweight people, as well as Class I obese and Class II/III obese ± BE who do and do not seek bariatric surgery. Secondly, binge eating was assessed through two items of the EDE-Q. In future studies, it would be better to use the diagnostic criteria of the DSM-5 binge eating disorder to assess the presence or absence of a BED. Thirdly, all temperament dimensions are assessed by means of self-report questionnaires, which can lead to problems of social desirability, while a few subscales also have rather small internal consistency coefficients (e.g., the BAS fun seeking scale). Therefore, future studies could include interviews or performance-based measures to assess sensitivity to punishment/reward and effortful control [17]. Notwithstanding these limitations, this study is one of few studies which addressed reward and punishment sensitivity and (lack of) effortful control along the weight/eating disordered spectrum in women. Hence, the main finding of our study is that temperamental differences on these dimensions are continuous and gradual, which implies that clinicians should incorporate emotion regulation and impulse regulation training transdiagnostically when working with patients suffering from ED and obesity.

Author Contributions: Conceptualization, L.C., G.K., and K.L.; methodology, L.C.; validation, L.C., G.K., and K.L.; formal analysis, L.C. and G.K.; investigation, E.B., L.D., E.D., S.G., and K.S.; resources, E.B., L.D., E.D., S.G., and K.S.; data curation, L.C.; writing—original draft preparation, L.C.; writing—review and editing, L.C., G.K., E.B., L.D., E.D., S.G., K.S., and K.L.; visualization, L.C.; supervision, L.C. and K.L.; project administration, L.C. All authors have read and agreed to the published version of the manuscript.

Funding: Glenn Kiekens is supported by a Postdoctoral Fellowship from the Research Foundation Flanders (12ZZM21N).

Institutional Review Board Statement: The study was conducted according to the guidelines of the Declaration of Helsinki, and approved by the Ethics Committee of the Faculty of Psychology and Educational Sciences, KU Leuven (09/02/2015: G-2015 02 172 (HC); 22/08/2018: G-2018 08 1312 (ED)) and the Faculty of Medicine and Health Sciences, KU Leuven (15/12/2016: S54997 (ML8926) (Obesity)).

Informed Consent Statement: Informed consent was obtained from all subjects involved in the study.

Data Availability Statement: Data are available upon request at laurence.claes@kuleuven.be.

Conflicts of Interest: The authors declare no conflict of interest.

References

1. Villarejo, C.; Fernández-Aranda, F.; Jiménez-Murcia, S.; Penñas-Lledoó, E.; Granero, R.; Penelo, E.; Tinahones, F.J.; Sancho, C.; Vilarrasa, N.; Montserrat-Gil de Bernabé, M.M.; et al. Lifetime Obesity in Patients with Eating Disorders: Increasing Prevalence, Clinical and Personality Correlates. *Eur. Eat. Disord. Rev.* **2012**, *20*, 250–254. [CrossRef] [PubMed]
2. Keating, C.; Backholer, K.; Gearon, E.; Stevenson, C.; Swinburn, B.; Moodie, M.; Carter, R.; Peeters, A. Prevalence of class-I, class-II and class-III obesity in Australian adults between 1995 and 2011–12. *Obes. Res. Clin. Pract.* **2015**, *9*, 553–562. [CrossRef]
3. Wu, M.; Brockmeyer, T.; Hartmann, M.; Skunde, M.; Herzog, W.; Friederich, H.-C. Set-shifting ability across the spectrum of eating disorders and in overweight and obesity: A systematic review and meta-analysis. *Psychol. Med.* **2014**, *44*, 3365–3385. [CrossRef]
4. Heshka, S.; Allison, D. Is obesity a disease? *Int. J. Obes.* **2001**, *25*, 1401–1404. [CrossRef]

5. Fassino, S.; Leombruni, P.; Pierò, A.; Abbata-Daga, G.A.; Amianto, F.; Rovera, G.; Rovera, G.G. Temperament and character in obese women with and without binge eating disorder. *Compr. Psychiatry* **2002**, *43*, 431–437. [CrossRef] [PubMed]
6. Müller, A.; Claes, L.; Mitchell, J.E.; Fischer, J.; Horbach, T.; De Zwaan, M. Binge Eating and Temperament in Morbidly Obese Prebariatric Surgery Patients. *Eur. Eat. Disord. Rev.* **2011**, *20*, e91–e95. [CrossRef] [PubMed]
7. Dietrich, A.; Federbusch, M.; Grellmann, C.; Villringer, A.; Horstmann, A. Body weight status, eating behavior, sensitivity to reward/punishment, and gender: Relationships and interdependencies. *Front. Psychol.* **2014**, *5*, 1073. [CrossRef] [PubMed]
8. Matton, A.; Goossens, L.; Vervaet, M.; Braet, C. Temperamental differences between adolescents and young adults with or without an eating disorder. *Compr. Psychiatry* **2015**, *56*, 229–238. [CrossRef]
9. Strack, F.; Deutsch, R. Reflective and Impulsive Determinants of Social Behavior. *Personal. Soc. Psychol. Rev.* **2004**, *8*, 220–247. [CrossRef]
10. Gray, J.A. The psychophysiological basis of introversion-extraversion. *Behav. Res. Ther.* **1970**, *8*, 249–266. [CrossRef]
11. Gray, J.A. *The Neuropsychology of Anxiety: An Inquiry into the Functions of the Septal–Hippocampal System*; Oxford University Press: Oxford, UK, 1982.
12. Claes, L.; Bijttebier, P.; Mitchell, J.E.; De Zwaan, M.; Mueller, A. The relationship between compulsive buying, eating disorder symptoms, and temperament in a sample of female students. *Compr. Psychiatry* **2011**, *52*, 50–55. [CrossRef] [PubMed]
13. Mardaga, S.; Hansenne, M. Relationships between Cloninger's biosocial model of personality and the behavioral inhibition/approach systems (BIS/BAS). *Personal. Individ. Differ.* **2007**, *42*, 715–722. [CrossRef]
14. Smits, D.J.M.; De Boeck, P. From BIS/BAS to the big five. *Eur. J. Personal.* **2006**, *20*, 255–270. [CrossRef]
15. Gray, J.A. *The Psychology of Fear and Stress*; Cambridge University Press: Cambridge, UK, 1987.
16. Gray, J.A.; McNaughton, N. *The Neuropsychology of Anxiety: An Inquiry into the Functions of the Septo-Hippocampal System*; Oxford University Press: Oxford, UK, 2000.
17. Nigg, J.T. On inhibition/disinhibition in developmental psychopathology: Views from cognitive and personality psychology and a working inhibition taxonomy. *Psychol. Bull.* **2000**, *126*, 220–246. [CrossRef]
18. Rothbart, M.K. Temperament and Development. In *Temperament in Childhood*; Kohnstamm, G.A., Bates, J.E., Rothbart, M.K., Eds.; John Wiley: Hoboken, NJ, USA, 1989; pp. 187–247.
19. Baumeister, R.F.; Heatherton, T.F.; Tice, D.M. *Losing Control: How and Why People Fail at Self-Regulation*; Academic Press: Cambridge, MA, USA, 1994.
20. Matton, A.; Goossens, L.; Vervaet, M.; Braet, C. Effortful control as a moderator in the association between punishment and reward sensitivity and eating styles in adolescent boys and girls. *Appetite* **2017**, *111*, 177–186. [CrossRef]
21. Carver, C.S.; White, T.L. Behavioral inhibition, behavioral activation, and affective responses to impending reward and punishment: The BIS/BAS Scales. *J. Personal. Soc. Psychol.* **1994**, *67*, 319–333. [CrossRef]
22. Torrubia, R.; Ávila, C.; Molto, J.; Caseras, X. The Sensitivity to Punishment and Sensitivity to Reward Questionnaire (SPSRQ) as a measure of Gray's anxiety and impulsivity dimensions. *Personal. Individ. Differ.* **2001**, *31*, 837–862. [CrossRef]
23. Claes, L.; Nederkoorn, C.; Vandereycken, W.; Guerrieri, R.; Vertommen, H. Impulsiveness and lack of inhibitory control in eating disorders. *Eat. Behav.* **2006**, *7*, 196–203. [CrossRef]
24. Glashouwer, K.A.; Bloot, L.; Veenstra, E.M.; Franken, I.H.; De Jong, P.J. Heightened sensitivity to punishment and reward in anorexia nervosa. *Appetite* **2014**, *75*, 97–102. [CrossRef]
25. Harrison, A.; Treasure, J.; Smillie, L. Approach and avoidance motivation in eating disorders. *Psychiatry Res.* **2011**, *188*, 396–401. [CrossRef]
26. Jappe, L.M.; Frank, G.K.; Bs, M.E.S.; Rollin, M.D.; Pryor, T.; Hagman, J.; Yang, T.T.; Davis, E. Heightened sensitivity to reward and punishment in anorexia nervosa. *Int. J. Eat. Disord.* **2011**, *44*, 317–324. [CrossRef]
27. Jonker, N.C.; Glashouwer, K.A.; Hoekzema, A.; Ostafin, B.D.; De Jong, P.J. Heightened self-reported punishment sensitivity, but no differential attention to cues signaling punishment or reward in anorexia nervosa. *PLoS ONE* **2020**, *15*, e0229742. [CrossRef] [PubMed]
28. Kane, T.A.; Loxton, N.; Staiger, P.K.; Dawe, S. Does the tendency to act impulsively underlie binge eating and alcohol use problems? An empirical investigation. *Personal. Individ. Differ.* **2004**, *36*, 83–94. [CrossRef]
29. Monteleone, P.; Scognamiglio, P.; Monteleone, A.M.; Perillo, D.; Maj, M. Cortisol awakening response in patients with anorexia nervosa or bulimia nervosa: Relationships to sensitivity to reward and sensitivity to punishment. *Psychol. Med.* **2014**, *44*, 2653–2660. [CrossRef]
30. Beck, I.; Smits, D.; Claes, L.; Vandereycken, W.; Bijttebier, P. Psychometric evaluation of the behavioral inhibition/behavioral activation system scales and the sensitivity to punishment and sensitivity to reward questionnaire in a sample of eating disordered patients. *Personal. Individ. Differ.* **2009**, *47*, 407–412. [CrossRef]
31. Claes, L.; Mitchell, J.E.; Vandereycken, W. Out of control? Inhibition processes in eating disorders from a personality and cognitive perspective. *Int. J. Eat. Disord.* **2011**, *45*, 407–414. [CrossRef] [PubMed]
32. Danner, U.N.; Ouwehand, C.; Haastert, N.L.; Hornsveld, H.; Ridder, D.T.D. Decision-making Impairments in Women with Binge Eating Disorder in Comparison with Obese and Normal Weight Women. *Eur. Eat. Disord. Rev.* **2011**, *20*, e56–e62. [CrossRef]
33. Schienle, A.; Schäfer, A.; Hermann, A.; Vaitl, D. Binge-Eating Disorder: Reward Sensitivity and Brain Activation to Images of Food. *Biol. Psychiatry* **2009**, *65*, 654–661. [CrossRef]

34. Davis, C.; Levitan, R.D.; Carter, J.; Kaplan, A.S.; Reid, C.; Curtis, C.; Patte, K.; Kennedy, J.L. Personality and eating behaviors: A case–control study of binge eating disorder. *Int. J. Eat. Disord.* **2007**, *41*, 243–250. [CrossRef]
35. Fairburn, C.G.; Cooper, Z.; Shafran, R. Cognitive behaviour therapy for eating disorders: A "transdiagnostic" theory and treatment. *Behav. Res. Ther.* **2003**, *41*, 509–528. [CrossRef]
36. Jonker, N.C.; Bennik, E.C.; de Jong, P.J. Why Dieters Succeed or Fail: The Relationship Between Reward and Punishment Sensitivity and Restrained Eating and Dieting Success. *Front. Psychol.* **2021**, *12*, 636432. [CrossRef]
37. Ruscitti, C.; Rufino, K.; Goodwin, N.; Wagner, R. Difficulties in emotion regulation in patients with eating disorders. *Bord. Personal. Disord. Emot. Dysregul.* **2016**, *3*, 1–7. [CrossRef]
38. Davis, C. A Narrative Review of Binge Eating and Addictive Behaviors: Shared Associations with Seasonality and Personality Factors. *Front. Psychiatry* **2013**, *4*, 183. [CrossRef]
39. Davis, C.; Fox, J. Sensitivity to reward and body mass index (BMI): Evidence for a non-linear relationship. *Appetite* **2008**, *50*, 43–49. [CrossRef]
40. Evans, D.E.; Rothbart, M.K. Developing a model for adult temperament. *J. Res. Personal.* **2007**, *41*, 868–888. [CrossRef]
41. Rothbart, M.K.; Ahadi, S.A.; Evans, D.E. Temperament and personality: Origins and outcomes. *J. Personal. Soc. Psychol.* **2000**, *78*, 122–135. [CrossRef]
42. Bruch, H. *Anorexia nervosa: The Golden Cage*; Harvard University Press: Cambridge, MA, USA, 1978.
43. Crisp, A.H. *Anorexia nervosa: Patient's Logbook*; Erlbaum: Hove, UK, 1995.
44. Garfinkel, P.E.; Garner, D.M. *Anorexia Nervosa: A Multidimensional Perspective*; Brunner/Mazel: New York, NY, USA, 1982.
45. Selvine-Palazolli, M. *Self-starvation: From the Intrapsychic to the Transpersonal Approach to Anorexia Nervosa*; Human Context Books: London, UK, 1974.
46. Button, E. *Personal Construct Theory and Mental Health: Theory, Research and Practice*; Croom Helm: London, UK, 1985.
47. Dalle Grave, R.D.; Calugi, S.; El Ghoch, M.; Marzocchi, R.; Marchesini, G. Personality Traits in Obesity Associated with Binge Eating and/or Night Eating. *Curr. Obes. Rep.* **2013**, *3*, 120–126. [CrossRef]
48. Bijttebier, P.; Beck, I.; Claes, L.; Vandereycken, W. Gray's Reinforcement Sensitivity Theory as a framework for research on personality–psychopathology associations. *Clin. Psychol. Rev.* **2009**, *29*, 421–430. [CrossRef]
49. Harrison, A.; O'Brien, N.; Lopez, C.; Treasure, J. Sensitivity to reward and punishment in eating disorders. *Psychiatry Res.* **2010**, *177*, 1–11. [CrossRef]
50. Vandereycken, W. The eating disorder evaluation scale (EDES). *Eat. Disord.* **1993**, *1*, 115–122. [CrossRef]
51. Fairburn, C.G.; Beglin, S.J. Assessment of eating disorder psychopathology: Interview or self-report questionnaire? *Int. J. Eat. Disord.* **1994**, *16*, 363–370.
52. Swinbourne, J.; Hunt, C.; Abbott, M.; Russell, J.; St Clare, T.S.; Touyz, S. The comorbidity between eating disorders and anxiety disorders: Prevalence in an eating disorder sample and anxiety disorder sample. *Aust. N. Z. J. Psychiatry* **2012**, *46*, 118–131. [CrossRef]
53. Wierenga, C.E.; Ely, A.; Bischoff-Grethe, A.; Bailer, U.F.; Simmons, A.N.; Kaye, W.H. Are Extremes of Consumption in Eating Disorders Related to an Altered Balance between Reward and Inhibition? *Front. Behav. Neurosci.* **2014**, *8*, 410. [CrossRef]
54. De Zwaan, M.; Gruss, B.; Müller, A.; Philipsen, A.; Graap, H.; Martin, A.; Glaesmer, H.; Hilbert, A. Association between Obesity and Adult Attention-Deficit/Hyperactivity Disorder in a German Community-Based Sample (ADHD). *Obes. Facts* **2011**, *4*, 204–211. [CrossRef]
55. Van Der Oord, S.; Braet, C.; Cortese, S.; Claes, L. Testing the dual pathway model of ADHD in obesity: A pilot study. *Eat. Weight Disord. Stud. Anorex. Bulim. Obes.* **2017**, *23*, 507–512. [CrossRef]
56. Atwood, M.E.; Friedman, A. A systematic review of enhanced cognitive behavioral therapy (CBT-E) for eating disorders. *Int. J. Eat. Disord.* **2019**, *53*, 311–330. [CrossRef]
57. Fairburn, C.G. *Cognitive Behavior Therapy and Eating Disorders*; Guilford Press: New York, NY, USA, 2009.
58. Wisniewski, L.; Kelly, E. The application of dialectical behavior therapy to the treatment of eating disorders. *Cogn. Behav. Pract.* **2003**, *10*, 131–138. [CrossRef]
59. Wisniewski, L.; Safer, D.; Chen, E.; Dimeff, L.A.; Koerner, K. Dialectical behavior therapy and eating disorders. In *Dialectical Behavior Therapy in Clinical Practice: Applications Across Disorders and Settings*; Dimeff, L.A., Koerner, K., Eds.; Guilford Press: New York, NY, USA, 2007; pp. 174–221.
60. Grave, R.D.; Calugi, S.; El Ghoch, M. Are Personality Characteristics as Measured by the Temperament and Character Inventory (TCI) Associated with Obesity Treatment Outcomes? A Systematic Review. *Curr. Obes. Rep.* **2018**, *7*, 27–36. [CrossRef]
61. Castelnuovo, G.; Pietrabissa, G.; Manzoni, G.M.; Cattivelli, R.; Rossi, A.; Novelli, M.; Varallo, G.; Molinari, E. Cognitive behavioral therapy to aid weight loss in obese patients: Current perspectives. *Psychol. Res. Behav. Manag.* **2017**, *10*, 165–173. [CrossRef]
62. Dalle Grave, R.; Sartirana, M.; El Ghoch, M.; Calugi, S. *Treating Obesity with Personalized Cognitive Behavioral Therapy*; Springer: New York, NY, USA; Berlin, Germany, 2018.
63. Kaye, W.H.; Wierenga, C.E.; Knatz, S.; Liang, J.; Boutelle, K.; Hill, L.; Eisler, I. Temperament-based Treatment for Anorexia Nervosa. *Eur. Eat. Disord. Rev.* **2014**, *23*, 12–18. [CrossRef]

nutrients

MDPI

Article

Two of a Kind? Mapping the Psychopathological Space between Obesity with and without Binge Eating Disorder

Laura Marie Sommer [1,†], Georg Halbeisen [2], Yesim Erim [1] and Georgios Paslakis [2,*]

1 Department of Psychosomatic Medicine and Psychotherapy, University Hospital of Erlangen, Friedrich-Alexander-University Erlangen-Nürnberg (FAU), 91054 Erlangen, Germany; laura.marie.sommer@outlook.de (L.M.S.); yesim.erim@uk-erlangen.de (Y.E.)

2 University Clinic for Psychosomatic Medicine and Psychotherapy, Medical Faculty, Campus East-Westfalia, Ruhr-University Bochum, Virchowstr. 65, 32312 Luebbecke, Germany; georg.halbeisen@rub.de

* Correspondence: georgios.paslakis@rub.de

† The present work was performed by L.M.S. in fulfillment of the requirements for obtaining the degree "Dr. Med.".

Abstract: (1) Background: Obesity (OB) is a frequent co-morbidity in Binge Eating Disorder (BED), suggesting that both conditions share phenotypical features along a spectrum of eating-related behaviors. However, the evidence is inconsistent. This study aimed to comprehensively compare OB-BED patients against OB individuals without BED and healthy, normal-weight controls in general psychopathological features, eating-related phenotypes, and early life experiences. (2) Methods: OB-BED patients ($n = 37$), OB individuals ($n = 50$), and controls ($n = 44$) completed a battery of standardized questionnaires. Responses were analyzed using univariate comparisons and dimensionality reduction techniques (linear discriminant analysis, LDA). (3) Results: OB-BED patients showed the highest scores across assessments (e.g., depression, emotional and stress eating, food cravings, food addiction). OB-BED patients did not differ from OB individuals in terms of childhood traumatization or attachment styles. The LDA revealed a two-dimensional solution that distinguished controls from OB and OB-BED in terms of increasing problematic eating behaviors and attitudes, depression, and childhood adversities, as well as OB-BED from OB groups in terms of emotional eating tendencies and self-regulation impairments. (4) Conclusions: Findings support the idea of a shared spectrum of eating-related disorders but also highlight important distinctions relevant to identifying and treating BED in obese patients.

Keywords: binge eating disorder; obesity; food addiction; impulsivity; emotional eating; childhood trauma questionnaire; psychotherapy

Citation: Sommer, L.M.; Halbeisen, G.; Erim, Y.; Paslakis, G. Two of a Kind? Mapping the Psychopathological Space between Obesity with and without Binge Eating Disorder. *Nutrients* **2021**, *13*, 3813. https://doi.org/10.3390/nu13113813

Academic Editors: Fernando Fernandez-Aranda, Janet Treasure and Empar Lurbe

Received: 10 October 2021
Accepted: 24 October 2021
Published: 26 October 2021

1. Introduction

Binge Eating Disorder (BED) is the most common eating disorder (ED) in western countries, with lifetime prevalence averaging 1.57% [1]. In recognition of this growing prevalence, BED was included in the 5th edition of the Diagnostic and Statistical Manual of Mental Disorders (DSM-5) [2]. According to DSM-5 criteria, BED patients suffer from reoccurring binge eating episodes of ingesting large amounts of food in a short period of time, with associated loss of control over their food intake. Negative feelings such as shame or guilt accompany these episodes. The severity of the disorder depends on the frequency of binge eating episodes per week, with thresholds demarcating mild, moderate, severe, and extreme BED.

Obesity is a frequent co-morbidity in BED due to the high volume of food intake and lack of compensatory behaviors in BED patients [3]. In the German general population, 25.9% of men and 24.4% of women are considered obese by a body mass index (BMI) > 30 kg/m^2 [4]. Among individuals with BED symptoms, however, 41.7% are obese, compared with only 15.8% of individuals with no history of an ED [5]. Comorbid obesity in BED patients is a major cause for concern, as obesity is associated with a wide range of physical afflictions, including cardiovascular diseases, type II diabetes, and several cancers [6], as well as with increased psychological burden, such as depression, low self-esteem, body image disturbances, perceived stress, and lowered quality of life [7].

The frequent co-morbidity of BED and obesity may suggest that both conditions are part of a broad spectrum of eating-related behaviors, implying that patients could transition from one condition to another [8]. This idea is consistent with recent studies linking obesity with comorbid BED and obesity without BED to shared phenotypical, in part clinical, features. For example, early life adversities such as trauma have been associated with the development of both BED and obesity [9,10], possibly due to lasting impairments in coping mechanisms and metabolic alterations due to stress [11,12]. In a similar vein, insecure attachment styles that develop in early childhood have been associated with emotional eating, eating unhealthy food, and binge eating [13], which studies link to the pathogenesis of BED and obesity [14,15]. Neurobiological studies also show that dopaminergic and glutamatergic pathways play a crucial role in developing and maintaining both conditions [16], further corroborating the idea of a shared continuum between obesity with comorbid BED and obesity without BED.

Patients with BED and comorbid obesity also differ from obese individuals without BED regarding a variety of phenotypical features. Patients with BED and obesity display higher levels of impulsivity than obese individuals without BED, in general, and especially toward food cues [17,18]. Neurobiological studies have shown that BED patients with obesity show lower activity levels in brain areas responsible for control and self-regulatory processes than obese individuals without BED [17]. Patients with BED have lower response inhibition abilities when presented with food cues in a go-no-go task, a finding associated with decreased activation of the prefrontal control network, which is active during successful no-go (withhold) trials in non-BED obese individuals [19]. Evidence also suggests a more compromised hormonal regulation of hunger and satiety in BED compared to obesity, for example, as mirrored in findings of blunted postprandial ghrelin suppression in BED compared with obesity [20]. In addition, Schulz and Laessle [21] found that depression weakens self-regulation in obese BED patients but not in obese individuals without BED, suggesting a possible link between depression and binge eating behavior. Finally, a recent study from our group showned that negative mood was associated with decreased food avoidance in obese BED patients only, but not in obese individuals without BED [22].

The evidence is less consistent on commonalities and disparities between obese patients with comorbid BED and obese individuals without BED concerning eating-related symptomatology other than binge eating. Strong concerns about shape and weight are core features BED shares with other EDs like anorexia nervosa or bulimia nervosa [23,24], and significant concerns of shape and weight also emerge in connection with obesity without BED in large community samples [25]. Similarly, several eating styles have been associated with obesity and comorbid BED in comparison with obesity without BED, such as emotional eating [22,26–30], eating in response to stress [31], and lower success in dieting and restraint [32], although especially research on the role of restraint has generated inhomogeneous results [33,34]. Newer concepts such as food craving and the strong desire to eat certain foods show stronger correlations with binge eating than obesity [35–37]. Food addiction, which among others, describes a loss of control over eating, cravings, and continued excessive food consumption contrary to the knowledge of adverse consequences [38], is also associated with a higher frequency of binge episodes and emotional eating [39,40]. At the same time, food addiction may play a role in obesity, too [41].

Further exploration of the commonalities and disparities between obesity with comorbid BED and obesity without BED is warranted, considering the results may help identify specific targets of prevention and intervention. Existing therapeutic approaches and weight loss strategies for obesity, such as dietary programs or physical exercise, are often unsuccessful or do not lead to enduring weight reductions [7,42]. Obese patients with BED also exhibit smaller weight reductions compared with obese individuals without an ED following weight-loss surgery [43,44]. Cognitive behavioral therapy (CBT), which functions as the foundation of BED treatment, aims to modify eating behaviors and has been found to lead to a remission of binge episodes among 64.4% of patients, including positive effects in terms of co-occurring psychological impairments [32,45]. However, the evidence for long-term results after cessation of CBT is still disappointing [32,46], suggesting BED treatment needs further improvement.

Thus far, the commonalities and differences in phenotypical features between obese BED patients and obese individuals without BED have been mapped across a range of studies but are seldom explored within a single investigation. One cannot exclude that differences in study design or sample composition account for some inconsistencies across findings, suggesting the need for a more comprehensive investigation. A comprehensive investigation also allows for the assessment the relative contribution of different sets of phenotypical and clinical features in grouping and distinguishing obese patients with BED from obese individuals without BED, aiding in theory development and prognostic application. Here, we conducted an exploratory study in which we assessed eating-related symptomatology (shape and weight concerns [23,24], emotional eating [26–30,47], dieting [32], food craving [37], and food addiction [48]), general psychopathology (impulse control impairments [17], depression [34]), and early life experiences (childhood traumatic events [9,10], attachment styles [14,15]) using standardized questionnaires. Specifically, we aimed to comprehensively compare obese patients with BED against obese individuals without BED as well as healthy, normal-weight controls in terms of these features, using univariate analyses and dimensionality reduction techniques.

2. Materials and Methods

2.1. Participants

A total of 131 German-speaking adults (90 women, 41 men, mean age = 42.7 years, age range: 21 to 82 years) participated in the study: n = 37 obese patients with an active BED (OB-BED; BMI > 30 kg/m^2), n = 50 weight-matched obese controls (OB; BMI > 30 kg/m^2), and n = 44 healthy, normal-weight controls with a BMI between 19.0 and 24.9 kg/m^2 (CO). OB-BED patients were recruited from the psychosomatic ward and day clinic of the Department for Psychosomatic Medicine and Psychotherapy at the University Hospital of Erlangen. Patients were both newly diagnosed individuals as well as individuals who had already received eating disorder-specific treatment in the past. University students, hospital employees, and individuals considering bariatric surgery as an option for weight loss were recruited for the OB and CO groups. For the diagnosis of BED, DSM-5 criteria (e.g., recurrent episodes of binge eating, marked distress, absence of compensatory behaviors) had to be fulfilled [2], which were assessed and confirmed by a physician with longstanding experience in diagnosing and treating eating disorders, in addition to the review of pre-existing documentation and the use of a clinical questionnaire [49]. Common inclusion criteria across groups were: 18 years or older, absence of acute severe psychiatric or somatic concomitant diseases, and no acute suicidal tendencies. ED diagnoses other than BED, or other clinically relevant ED symptoms, served as exclusion criteria; these exclusion criteria were verified before study inclusion during a clinical interview by the physician in charge.

The study was carried out in accordance with the Declaration of Helsinki and was reviewed and approved by the local ethics committee of the Friedrich-Alexander-University Erlangen-Nürnberg (approval no.: 267_17B, 4 December 2017). A sample size of $N \geq 130$ was targeted to achieve a power of 0.70 for detecting medium- or larger-sized (i.e., $f \geq 0.25$) group differences at $p \leq 0.05$ [50]. Participants had no previous experience with the procedure, provided informed, written, and signed consent, and were randomly sampled by convenience among local individuals and patients that were or became available during the recruitment period. Refusals to participate were not recorded; thus, information on participation rate cannot be provided.

2.2. Procedure

All participants completed a battery of paper-and-pencil questionnaires at their own pace, detailed below, to measure different aspects of eating-related symptomatology, general psychopathology, and childhood adversities.

2.3. Assessment of Eating-Related Symptomatology

Problematic eating behaviors and attitudes, such as shape and weight concerns, were assessed using the Eating Disorder Examination—Questionnaire (EDE-Q). The EDE-Q [51] is a self-report questionnaire modeled after the Eating Disorder Examination [52]. It is composed of 22 items and assesses four subcategories: Restraint, Eating Concern, Weight Concern, and Shape Concern. Items are rated on a 6-point scale, based on how often the eating disorder characteristics occurred within the past 28 days. Mean scores are computed for each subcategory, as well as for the overall questionnaire [53].

Emotional eating tendencies were assessed using the Salzburger Emotional Eating Scale (SEES) [54]. The SEES contains twenty items, scored on a 5-point Likert scale and grouped into four subcategories for effects of emotions on eating (happiness, sadness, anger, and anxiety), each yielding a mean score. Mean scores higher than 3 suggest an increased influence of emotion on food intake, while scores below 3 suggest a decreased influence of emotion on food intake.

The Salzburger Stress Eating Scale (SSES) [31] is a ten-item questionnaire that measures general stress eating tendencies, which we included because stress can affect eating even after controlling for the effects of negative emotions [55]. Each item is scored on a 5-point Likert scale ranging from 1 = I eat much less than usual to 5 = I eat much more than usual. A mean score is calculated using all items. Mean scores higher, or lower, than 3 indicate an increased, or decreased, intake when the individual feels stressed, respectively.

As further measures of emotional eating and restraint, we included the Dutch Eating Behavior Questionnaire (DEBQ) [56]. The scale also measures external eating, the tendency to eat after being exposed to food cues. The Emotional Eating scale further splits into effects of diffuse emotions and clearly labeled emotions. The German version has 30 items that are scored on a 5-point Likert Scale [57].

As an additional measure of restraint eating, we included the Perceived Self-Regulatory Success in Dieting (PSRS) [58], a short questionnaire that can be used for distinguishing between successful and unsuccessful dieters [59]. Three brief questions are used to assess whether respondents find it easy to watch their weight, lose weight, or find it challenging to stay in shape. The items are scored on a 7-point Likert scale, with the last item being reversed coded.

Food craving was assessed with the Food Craving Questionnaire—Trait (FCQ-T) [60]. It consists of 39 items scored on a 6-point Likert scale, which in the German version [35] are separated into six subscales: Intentions/Lack of control, Reinforcement, Thoughts/Guilt, Emotions, Cues, and Hunger.

Finally, we also included the Yale Food Addiction Scale (YFAS) 2.0 [61] in order to measure addiction-like eating behavior. The YFAS 2.0 has 35 items which assess how many of the eleven symptoms of food addiction according to DSM-5 addiction criteria (amount, attempts to quit, time, reduced activities, consequences, tolerance, withdrawal, craving, failed obligations, problems, hazardous situations) are present, as well as if the eating behavior causes impairment or distress. The items are scored on a 7-point scale, with each symptom having a specific threshold score. According to the number of symptoms present, the severity of food addiction is considered to be mild (2–3), moderate (4–5), or severe (7 or more symptoms). The endorsement of impairment/distress is necessary for diagnosing addiction at all [62].

2.4. Assessment of General Psychopathology

The Barratt Impulsiveness Scale—Short Version (BIS-15) [63] was used to measure participants' impulsiveness utilizing a three-factor model: non-planning impulsivity, motor impulsivity, and attentional impulsivity. The BIS-15 contains 15 items, each scored on a 4-point Likert scale with six items scored inversely. Accordingly, a sum score of all items ranges between 15 and 60.

The Beck Depression Inventory (BDI-II) [64] was additionally included as a widely used self-report inventory for measuring the severity of depression in adults. The BDI-II contains 21 items, each scored on a 4-point Likert scale, with sum scores ranging between 0 and 63.

2.5. Assessment of Early Life Experiences

Two questionnaires on early life experiences were also included. The short version of the Childhood Trauma Questionnaire (CTQ) [65] contains 28 items and screens for five types of childhood trauma, including physical, sexual, and emotional abuse, as well as physical and emotional neglect. Each subcategory contains five items, and the remaining three items comprise the Minimization/Denial validity scale, which indicates underreporting of maltreatment. All items are rated on a 5-point Likert scale, with some items scored inversely, yielding a sum score for each subcategory.

Finally, the redesigned German version of the Relationship Scales Questionnaire (RSQ) [66] was used to assess attachment style and distinguished between "Separation anxiety", "Closeness anxiety", "Lack of trust," and "Wish to be independent". Each of the 30 items are ranked on a 5-point Likert scale, yielding a mean score for each subcategory of attachment.

2.6. Data Aggregation and Analysis

Participant responses were aggregated according to each questionnaire's specifications. For questionnaire total scores, univariate analyses of variance (ANOVAs) were conducted to assess differences between groups (OB-BED vs. OB vs. CO). To account for multicollinearity among questionnaire subscales, between-group differences on subscales were analyzed using one-way multivariate analysis of variance (MANOVAs). Anthropometric variables (age, BMI) were compared between groups using one-way ANOVA, and a Chi-squared test of independence (for sex ratio), with group as the independent variable. Chi-square tests were also used to analyze symptom severity in the YFAS 2.0.

For assessing the relative contribution of different sets of features in grouping and distinguishing OB-BED patients from OB and CO individuals, a linear discriminant analysis (LDA) was conducted with participant group as the criterion variable and questionnaire scores as predictor variables. The LDA's primary goal is to identify along how many and which dimensions (i.e., the discriminant functions) the participant groups can be distinguished from each other based on a set of predictor variables. Correlations (loadings) between predictors and discriminant functions can be used to indicate the relative value of each questionnaire to the discriminant function. Prior probabilities were adjusted to control for unequal group sizes. Box's M statistic was used to test for violations of the assumption of equal covariance matrices.

The significance level for all analyses was set at $p \leq 0.05$. Effect sizes are reported as η^2. Post hoc pairwise comparisons report Bonferroni-adjusted p-values for multiple comparisons. Variable values are reported as mean $\pm$ standard deviation. Z-standardized values of questionnaires are depicted in Figure 1. Unstandardized means $\pm$ standard deviation for questionnaire responses are summarized in Appendix A (Table A1). All data were analyzed with the Statistical Package for the Social Sciences (SPSS 25; IBM Corp., Armonk, NY, USA).

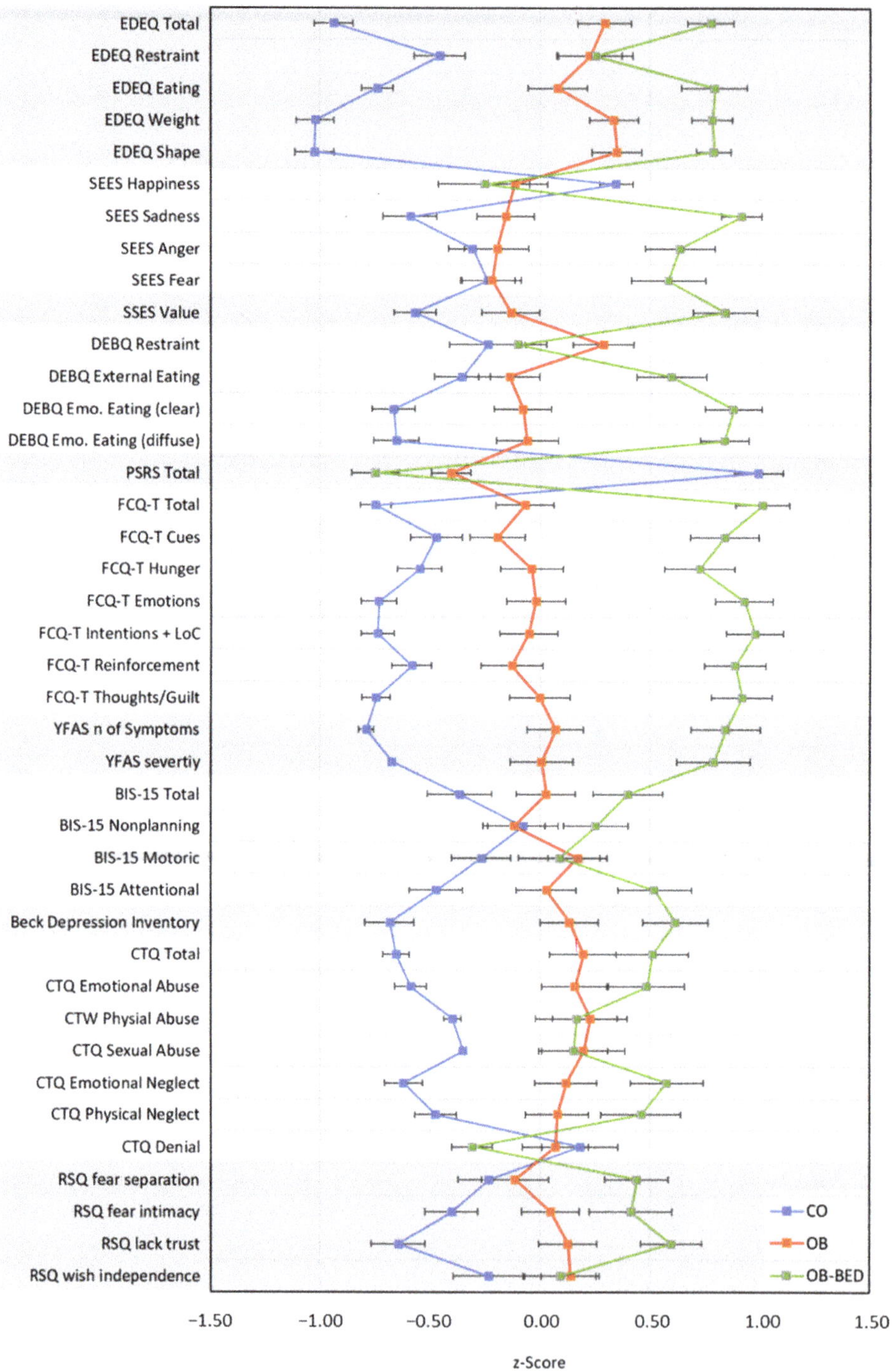

Figure 1. Mean questionnaire scores (z-standardized) and standard errors for the examined groups. CO = control; OB = obese; OB-BED = obese with co-morbid Binge Eating Disorder.

3. Results

3.1. Participant Demographics

Participant demographics are summarized in Table 1. Participant sexes were similarly distributed across participant groups, χ^2 (df = 2) = 0.49, p = 0.78. Groups differed as intended in terms of BMI (post hoc: OB-BED = OB > CO), $F(2, 128) = 125.05$, $p < 0.001$, $\eta^2 = 0.66$, and were similar in age, $F(2, 128) = 3.02$, $p > 0.05$.

Table 1. Demographic information as a function of participant group.

Variable	CO	OB	OB-BED
n (m, f)	14, 30	17, 33	10, 27
age	41.7 ± 16.8	46.1 ± 10.7	39.3 ± 11.2
BMI (kg/m^2)	22.5 ± 1.6	42.9 ± 9.1	46.3 ± 9.3

n = number of participants; m = male; f = female; BMI = body mass index; CO = control; OB = obese; OB-BED = obese with co-morbid Binge Eating Disorder. Values report mean ± standard deviation.

3.2. Eating-Related Symptomatology: EDEQ, SSES, SEES, DEBQ, PSRS, FCTQ, & YFAS 2.0

EDE-Q total scores of disordered eating varied significantly between groups, $F(2, 125) = 62.82$, $p < 0.001$, $\eta^2 = 0.50$, with OB-BED scoring higher than OB and CO, $ps < 0.008$, and OB scoring higher than CO, $p < 0.001$. Expectedly, the analysis of subcategory scores replicated the effect, $F(8, 244) = 20.88$, $p < 0.001$, $\eta^2 = 0.27$, Wilk's $\Lambda = 0.41$, with OB-BED and OB showing higher scores than CO on Restraint, Eating Concern, Weight Concern, and Shape Concern scales, $ps < 0.002$. With the exception of restraint, $p = 1.00$, OB-BED also scored consistently higher than OB, $ps < 0.007$.

Emotional eating according to SEES subscales varied by group, $F(8, 250) = 9.23$, $p < 0.001$, $\eta^2 = 0.23$, Wilk's $\Lambda = 0.60$, with OB-BED scoring lower on the happiness subcategory than CO, $p = 0.02$, but not OB, $p = 1.00$. OB-BED scored higher on the sadness, anger, and fear subcategories than both OB and CO, $ps < 0.001$. With the exception of higher sadness scores for OB than CO, $p = 0.03$, OB and CO were not significantly different, $ps > 0.07$.

SSES mean scores for general stress eating tendencies also differed significantly between groups, $F(2, 127) = 29.77$, $p < 0.001$, $\eta^2 = 0.32$, with CO scoring lower than OB, $p = 0.04$, and OB-BED, $p < 0.001$, and OB scoring lower than OB-BED, $p < 0.001$.

On the DEBQ, scores differed between groups across restraint, external eating and emotional eating subscales, $F(8, 246) = 11.31$, $p < 0.001$, $\eta^2 = 0.27$, Wilk's $\Lambda = 0.53$. CO scored significantly lower on restraint eating behaviors than OB, $p = 0.03$, but not lower than OB-BED, $p = 1.00$, with OB and OB-BED remaining comparable, $p = 0.21$. On the external eating subscale, OB-BED scored higher than OB and CO, $ps < 0.001$, with OB and CO remaining comparable, $p = 0.82$. Finally, on both subscales of emotional eating, OB-BED scored higher than OB and CO, $ps < 0.001$, and OB scored higher than CO, $ps < 0.002$.

In terms of the PSRS perceived success in dieting scores, group differences were obtained, $F(2, 120) = 80.71$, $p < 0.001$, $\eta^2 = 0.57$, due to CO scoring significantly higher than both OB and OB-BED groups, $ps <.001$. OB and OB-BED did not differ in terms of PSRS, $p = 0.07$.

FCTQ food craving total scores differed significantly between groups, $F(2, 121) = 58.02$, $p < 0.001$, $\eta^2 = 0.49$, with OB-BED scoring higher than OB and CO, $ps < 0.001$, and OB scoring higher than CO, $p < 0.001$. This pattern reproduced consistently across FCTQ subscales (OB-BED > OB > CO, $ps < 0.001$), $F(12, 232) = 9.10$, $p < 0.001$, $\eta^2 = 0.32$, Wilk's $\Lambda = 0.46$, with the exception of the food-cue elicited craving, which did not differ between OB and CO, $p = 0.38$.

Finally, food addiction symptoms based on the YFAS 2.0 differed significantly across groups, $F(2, 128) = 45.66$, $p < 0.001$, $\eta^2 = 0.42$, with OB-BED scoring higher than OB and CO, $ps < 0.001$, and OB scoring higher than CO, $p < 0.001$. A Chi-squared test of independence revealed that groups also differed in terms of the clinical significance of food addiction symptoms, χ^2 (df = 2) = 49.97, $p < 0.001$, with 0% of CO, 40% of OB and 76% of OB-BED indicating clinically significant impairments. However, of those classified as severe food addicted ($n = 31$), 61% were in the OB-BED group and 39% were in the OB group, which did not significantly differ from the expected values based on sample size distribution, $p = 0.67$.

3.3. General Psychopathology: BIS-15 & BDI

BIS-15 total impulsivity scores differed significantly between groups, $F(2, 128) = 6.48$, $p < 0.002$, $\eta^2 = 0.09$, with OB-BED scoring higher than CO, $p < 0.001$, whereas OB-BED and OB, and OB and CO remained comparable, *ps* > 0.14. Subscale analysis, $F(6, 252) = 4.56$, $p < 0.001$, $\eta^2 = 0.10$, Wilk's $\Lambda = 0.81$, revealed that overall differences were due to OB-BED scoring higher on attentional impulsivity than OB and CO, *ps* < 0.05, and OB scoring higher than CO, $p = 0.03$. All groups remained comparable on non-planning impulsivity and motor impulsivity subscales, *ps* > 0.10.

On the BDI depression inventory, OB-BED scored higher than OB and CO, *ps* < 0.04, and OB scored higher than CO, $p < 0.001$, $F(2, 126) = 23.78$, $p < 0.001$, $\eta^2 = 0.27$.

3.4. Early Life Experiences: CTQ & RSQ

CTQ total scores for childhood trauma revealed significant groups differences, $F(2, 128) = 19.67$, $p < 0.001$, $\eta^2 = 0.24$, with CO scoring lower than both OB-BED and OB, *ps* < 0.001, and similar scores for OB-BED and OB, $p = 0.30$. In terms of trauma subcategories, group differences were also significant, $F(10, 248) = 4.51$, $p < 0.001$, $\eta^2 = 0.15$, Wilk's $\Lambda = 0.72$, with CO scoring lower than OB-BED and OB in all categories, *ps* < 0.03, except for OB-BED in terms of sexual abuse, $p = 0.06$. OB-BED and OB did not significantly differ in any of the subcategories, *ps* > 0.05. Denial scores indicating underreporting did not differ between groups, $F(2, 128) = 2.70$, $p = 0.07$.

Attachment styles according to RSQ scores differed between groups, $F(8, 244) = 6.32$, $p < 0.001$, $\eta^2 = 0.17$, Wilk's $\Lambda = 0.69$, with differences found on separation anxiety, closeness anxiety, and lack of trust subscales. For separation anxiety, OB-BED revealed elevated scores compared to OB and CO groups, *ps* < 0.03, which themselves remained comparable, $p = 1.00$. Closeness anxiety was only elevated for OB-BED when compared to CO, $p < 0.001$, whereas all other comparisons were not significant, *ps* > 0.15. Finally, all groups differed in lack of trust, *ps* < 0.05, with OB-BED scoring higher than OB and CO, and OB scoring higher than CO. There were no significant differences on the wish to be independent subscale, *ps* > 0.25.

3.5. Discriminant Analysis

Given that in almost all questionnaires and subcategories, significant differences were found between OB-BED, OB and CO groups, a linear discriminant analysis (LDA) was conducted to assess the relative contribution of different sets of psychopathological features in grouping and distinguishing the groups. Given the high internal consistencies of SEES (with happiness reverse-coded), DEBQ, and RSQ subscales (excluding wish for independence, which did not differ between groups), Cronbach's α 0.74, 0.71, and 0.66, respectively, mean total scores for these questionnaires were computed. Thus, eleven total scores for all questionnaires were entered as predictors in the LDA. Because of missing scores on at least one questionnaire, 116 cases were included in the analysis.

Results of the LDA revealed a two-dimensional solution (see Figure 2), with a significant function 1 accounting for 89.6% of the variance, χ^2 (22) = 174.84, $p < 0.001$, and a significant function 2 accounting for the remaining 10.4% of variance, χ^2 (10) = 30.49, $p < 0.001$. Group centroids (i.e., means in multivariate space) suggest a clear distinction between CO (−2.17), OB (0.69) and OB-BED (1.80) groups due to predictors associated with function 1, with predictors related to function 2 primarily distinguishing between OB (−0.68) and OB-BED (0.68) groups, with CO (0.21) in between. In order of importance, predictors primarily associated with function 1 (loadings in parentheses) were EDEQ (0.70), PSRS (−0.69), YFAS (0.49), BDI (0.41), CTQ (0.36), and RSQ (0.34). Function 2 predictors were FCTQ (0.71), SSES (0.64), SEES (0.63), DEBQ (0.45), and BIS-15 (0.24). Because Box's M statistic indicated a significant violation of the assumption of equal covariance at $p < 0.001$, which could render LDA results unstable, a secondary LDA with only OB-BED and OB groups was conducted to confirm the reliability of function 2 predictors. Meeting assumption checks (Box's M $p = 0.30$), the additional analysis yielded a similar solution for the distinction of OB-BED and OB groups, χ^2 (11) = 31.64, $p < 0.001$, with FCTQ (0.87), SSES (0.74), DEBQ (0.70), and SEES (0.69) emerging again as the most important predictors of group differences. Taken together, the LDA findings suggest that CO can be distinguished from OB, and OB-BED groups along a continuum of increasing problematic eating behaviors and attitudes, depression, and childhood adversities, with OB-BED further distinguishable from OB along a continuum of increasing emotional eating tendencies, and eating-related as well as general self-regulation impairments.

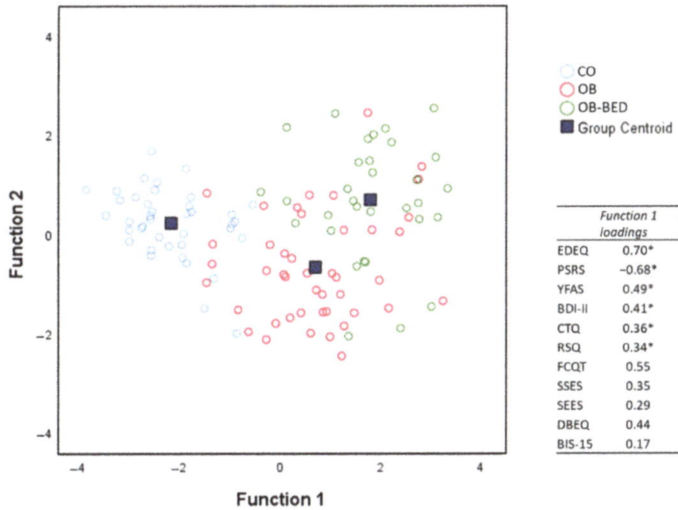

	Function 1 loadings	Function 2 loadings
EDEQ	0.70*	0.06
PSRS	−0.68*	0.13
YFAS	0.49*	0.39
BDI-II	0.41*	0.21
CTQ	0.36*	0.05
RSQ	0.34*	0.21
FCQT	0.55	0.71*
SSES	0.35	0.64*
SEES	0.29	0.63*
DBEQ	0.44	0.45*
BIS-15	0.17	0.24*

Figure 2. Cases and centroids of study groups on the two discriminant functions derived from the linear discriminant analysis (LDA) of questionnaire responses. Asterisks (*) indicate the largest absolute correlation between each predictor and the discriminant functions. CO = control; OB = obese; OB-BED = obese with co-morbid Binge Eating Disorder.

4. Discussion

This study aimed to assess differences and commonalities between obese patients with BED and obese individuals without BED. For that, a battery of questionnaires on early life experiences, general psychopathology, and eating-related symptomatology was assessed on the above-mentioned groups and normal-weight controls, whereby the BED group was a clinically diagnosed sample. In almost all questionnaires and subcategories, significant differences could be found between the groups. However, the findings of the LDA showed that OB-BED, OB, and CO can be grouped along a two-dimensional space, with one continuum primarily distinguishing CO from the OB and OB-BED groups and a second continuum distinguishing between OB and OB-BED groups. Consistent with previous research, aspects of early life experiences emerged as shared features of OB and OB-BED groups, whereas general psychopathology in terms of impulse control impairments distinguished between the groups. However, across both dimensions, features of eating-related symptomatology emerged as the most important predictors of commonalities and disparities between obesity with and without BED. These results are discussed in further detail in the following sections.

4.1. Eating-Related Symptomatology

Although not included in the DSM-5 diagnostic criteria [2], strong concerns about shape and weight are core psychopathologies that BED shares with other EDs like anorexia nervosa or bulimia nervosa [23,24]. Significant concerns of shape and weight and elevated measures of eating disturbances also emerge in connection with obesity in large community samples [25]. For example, Hilbert et al. [67] reported an increased risk of 11 to 20 times for obese individuals to show eating disorder psychopathology compared with individuals with normal weight. Consistent with these findings, OB-BED patients scored consistently higher on the EDEQ than OB participants, who scored higher than controls, with the subscale restraint as the only exception (for similar findings, see [68]). The LDA also suggests that the OB and OB-BED groups can be distinguished from controls along a continuum best described by elevated eating disturbances. Although more research on the relative importance of restraint appears warranted (cf. [69]), these findings suggest that shape and weight concerns in obese BED patients should be of special interest since they may be related to the condition's pathogenesis and can determine the therapy outcome [70].

Related to the question of the role of restraint, we assessed the PSRS. This short questionnaire yields the individuals' self-assessment of their own success in dieting, which has been shown to negatively correlate with BMI, rigid dietary control, food cravings, food addiction symptoms, and binge eating, but to correlate positively with flexible dietary control [59]. In our study, the OB-BED and OB groups reported much lower scores in dieting successfully than controls but remained comparable, which was also indicated by the LDA associating the PSRS with the continuum relevant to the distinction of healthy controls from OB and OB-BED groups. A possible explanation for the lack of distinction between OB-BED and OB groups according to restraint is that the questionnaire measures the attempt to lose weight, rather than actual restraint eating behavior, which more specifically relates to disordered eating [71,72].

However, OB-BED and OB groups were clearly distinguishable according to features of emotional eating, as suggested by the LDA and individual analyses. In the SEES, which was developed with the expectation that persons with lower eating pathologies tend to eat rather more when happy, and persons with higher eating pathologies more when having negative emotions [54]; the average score of eating under negative emotions was increased in OB-BED compared with both OB and controls. Controls, instead, reported eating more when feeling happy. The differences between OB-BED and OB were most pronounced for sadness as a low arousal emotion, which is consistent with similar findings for binge eating in patients with bulimia nervosa [73]. These findings may suggest that mechanisms of decreased food uptake while experiencing high arousal in the form of emotions are decoupled in BED with comorbid obesity but not in obesity without BED. This idea is further supported by similar patterns found for stress eating tendencies in the SSES. Again, the OB-BED group showed the highest score by far, while the OB group reported to eat only slightly more. Controls instead reported eating less under stress. These findings are consistent with laboratory studies showing an increased speed of food uptake after stress exposure in BED patients [74].

In line with the above-summarized findings, the DEBQ, which also measures emotional eating on one subscale, was found to distinguish between OB-BED and OB groups. The OB-BED group in our study showed the highest scores in emotional eating in the DEBQ, including the subscales for diffuse emotions [56]. It stands to reason that these differences hint at the role of emotional dysregulation in predicting binge eating behavior [75].

Further lines of distinction between OB-BED and OB groups emerged along with external eating and food craving tendencies. Consistent with previous findings [75–77], OB-BED patients scored higher than both OB and controls on the DEBQ external eating subscale, which measures the tendency to eat after being exposed to food cues. In a similar vein, OB-BED, OB, and controls were found to differ consistently across FCQT's food craving subscales. Although strong food cravings can be found in healthy individuals, too, it has been shown that those with binge eating symptoms score higher in food craving assessments [37]. Consistent with our findings, this association is stronger for binge eating than for only obesity [35–37]. Innamorati et al. [78] even developed a potential cut-off score (157.5) of the FCQT for identifying clinical-level binge eating. Although our clinically diagnosed BED sample did not meet this criterion on average (142.3), findings from the LDA, which identified FCQT scores among the most important predictors for distinguishing between OB-BED and OB groups, generally support this contention.

As BED has been linked to high impulsivity and related conditions like substance use disorders [32,79], it has been suggested that BED might share features with food addiction [41,48]. Extending this line of research, we compared OB-BED, OB, and controls in terms of food addiction as measured by the YFAS 2.0. In our study, the highest prevalence of 76% for food addiction was found in the OB-BED group, followed by OB (40%) and controls (0%). For the OB-BED group, this is a lower prevalence than shown in previous studies [38,80], though it should be mentioned that food addiction prevalence rates are inhomogeneous across different samples [41]. Given the clear difference in food addiction prevalence between OB-BED and OB groups, it might be considered surprising to find that food addiction in the LDA was associated with the more general distinction between healthy and clinical groups, rather than between OB-BED and OB groups. It should be noted, however, that the LDA included scores for food addiction symptoms rather than scores for food addiction severity, rendering these findings only partly comparable. The decision to include food addiction symptoms rather than severity scores in the LDA was mainly due to statistical reasons, as the absence of variance in severity scores of controls (i.e., none of the controls were classified as food addicted) violated the LDAs assumptions.

4.2. General Psychopathology

Looking at general psychopathology associated with BED, we investigated the role of impulse control impairments in relation to comorbid obesity using the BIS-15. Impulsivity has been frequently investigated in BED in the past. Experimental studies revealed that patients with BED show higher rash-spontaneous behavior, especially toward food, but also in general [17]. Neurobiological findings also link BED to impulsive/compulsive disorders, based on findings of the corticostriatal circuitry regulation of motivation and impulse control [81]. Likewise, the link between impulsivity and obesity has been of interest. A study gathering data about impulsivity in a large sample of the general population showed an association with obesity [82]. However, research suggests that BED surpasses obesity without BED in terms of impulsivity [17], which is consistent with the present findings. Specifically, OB-BED patients scored overall higher than OB and control participants on the BIS-15, with OB participants exceeding controls only on the subscale of attentional impulsivity. This scoring is in line with the findings of Loeber et al. [83], and further supported by the LDA associating impulsivity scores more strongly with the specific distinction between OB-BED and OB groups.

Further replicating previous findings on the relation between depressive symptoms and BED and obesity [84,85], we found that BDI scores of OB-BED patients exceeded those of OB, which exceeded those of controls. Interestingly, and although previous studies associated high BDI scores and depressed moods specifically with BED [21,22], the LDA suggests a linear transition from healthy controls to OB and OB-BED groups with increasing levels of depression. However, the effects of depression on BED are likely mediated through their effect on self-regulation impairments [21,86], which our analysis also suggested are more specific for the distinction of obese patients with and without obesity.

4.3. Early Life Experiences

Finally, adverse childhood events have been repeatedly linked to both obesity and BED [9,10]. It has been argued that adverse experiences may impair coping mechanisms due to mental and emotional perturbations but may also link to metabolic alterations due to stress, and in doing so, promote the development of obesity and BED [11,12]. Consistent with these findings, individual analysis as well as LDA groupings suggest that OB and

OB-BED groups can be distinguished from healthy, normal-weight controls on the basis of overall CTQ trauma scores. However, whereas previous research indicated further distinctions between OB-BED and OB groups in terms of traumatic experiences [11,87] these differences were not significant in the present sample. In part, this may have been caused by a smaller sample size of our study or because the sexual and physical abuse scores were slightly higher in the OB group than in the OB-BED group (for similar findings, see [88]). Though further research on more specific contributions may be required, our findings corroborate childhood trauma as a general risk factor for obesity and BED, which should be considered whilst offering treatment.

In a similar vein, attachment styles, formed in early childhood, have been considered in the pathogenesis of BED and obesity [14,15] and emerged as predicting differences of OB-BED and OB groups towards controls. Specifically, OB-BED patients showed elevated RSQ scores for separation anxiety, closeness anxiety, and lack of trust, whereas OB participants differed from controls only with respect to lack of trust. To our knowledge, this is the first study assessing the RSQ in comparing groups of BED, obesity, and normal-weight controls. The findings could suggest that binge eating in obese individuals might result from poor emotional coping mechanisms [89–91]. However, both individual analysis and the LDA did not identify differences in attachment styles as specifically differentiating between OB-BED and OB groups, suggesting that further research on the role of attachment styles in BED is needed.

4.4. Limitations

Of course, interpreting these findings is subject to limitations. First, the current study investigated the psychopathological space between obese individuals with and without BED in a cross-sectional design. Although the evidence largely supports the idea of BED and obesity forming part of a broad spectrum of eating-related behaviors and disorders in terms of childhood adversities and different aspects of general and eating-related psychopathology, the cross-sectional design prevents any exploration of a transition of individuals from one group to another. This gap may be addressed in studies using similar methods but with a longitudinal design. Second, due to the fact that we included both incident (treatment-naive) as well as prevalent (treatment-experienced) patients, we cannot exclude the possibility that prior recommendations and treated aspects of eating disorder-specific pathology could have modified the answers collected in the questionnaires, limiting interpretations as to whether the observed patterns are sensitive to change. Third, and relatedly, it must be noted that control participants were primarily recruited among individuals considering bariatric surgery as an option for weight loss (OB group), hospital staff, and medical students (normal-weight controls). Although participant groups were comparable in terms of sociodemographic features, we cannot exclude that the observed data pattern is sensitive to sample composition differences.

5. Conclusions

This study sought to show and reproduce specific characteristics of BED with comorbid obesity, especially in comparison with obesity without BED. Importantly, we only tested clinically diagnosed BED patients and obese individuals without a history of ED to make a clear comparison. The findings underline the distinct psychological and psychopathological features that separate OB-BED from obesity. Although OB-BED and OB groups share problematic eating behaviors and attitudes, depression, and adverse early life experiences, increasing emotional eating tendencies and eating-related and general self-regulation impairments appear to specifically relate to the emergence of BED. These results should be considered in therapy and when screening for BED in obese individuals.

Author Contributions: Conceptualization, G.P.; formal analysis, G.P. and G.H.; data curation, L.M.S.; writing—original draft preparation, L.M.S.; writing—review and editing, G.P., Y.E., and G.H.; supervision, G.P. All authors have read and agreed to the published version of the manuscript.

Funding: This research received no external funding.

Institutional Review Board Statement: The study was conducted according to the guidelines of the Declaration of Helsinki, and approved by the Ethics Committee of the Friedrich-Alexander-University Erlangen-Nürnberg (approval no.: 267_17B, 4 December 2017).

Informed Consent Statement: Informed consent was obtained from all subjects involved in the study.

Data Availability Statement: The data presented in this study are available on request from the corresponding author.

Acknowledgments: The present work was performed by L.M.S. in fulfillment of the requirements for obtaining the degree "Dr. med.".

Conflicts of Interest: The authors declare no conflict of interest.

Appendix A

Unstandardized means ± standard deviations of questionnaire responses are summarized in Table A1.

Table A1. Questionnaire responses raw scores as a function of participant group.

Variable		CO	OB	OB-BED
EDEQ				
	Total	0.7 ± 0.86	2.5 ± 1.26	3.2 ± 0.90
	Restraint	0.8 ± 1.13	1.8 ± 1.54	1.8 ± 1.49
	Eating Concern	0.2 ± 0.71	1.5 ± 1.43	2.5 ± 1.35
	Weight Concern	0.7 ± 1.01	3.1 ± 1.43	3.9 ± 1.00
	Shape Concern	1.1 ± 1.08	3.6 ± 1.47	4.4 ± 0.84
SEES				
	Happiness	3.0 ± 0.28	2.7 ± 0.59	2.7 ± 0.71
	Sadness	3.2 ± 0.60	3.5 ± 0.68	4.3 ± 0.42
	Anger	2.9 ± 0.59	2.9 ± 0.88	3.6 ± 0.81
	Fear	2.7 ± 0.70	2.7 ± 0.81	3.4 ± 0.88
SSES				
	Total	2.8 ± 0.53	3.1 ± 0.79	3.9 ± 0.74
DEBQ				
	Restraint	2.3 ± 0.91	2.7 ± 0.79	2.4 ± 0.65
	External Eating	2.9 ± 0.61	3.0 ± 0.73	3.6 ± 0.73
	Emo. Eating total	1.9 ± 0.69	2.6 ± 0.98	3.7 ± 0.74
	Emo. E. Clearly Labelled	1.8 ± 0.73	2.5 ± 1.05	3.6 ± 0.90
	Emo. E. Diffused	2.2 ± 0.78	2.9 ± 1.16	4.0 ± 0.78
PSRS				
	Total	14.8 ± 3.72	7.8 ± 2.99	6.1 ± 3.07
FCQT				
	Total	68.9 ± 18.81	97.2 ± 37.58	142.3 ± 30.03
	Cues	10.2 ± 3.29	11.4 ± 3.64	15.8 ± 3.92
	Hunger	8.8 ± 2.92	11.1 ± 4.29	14.4 ± 4.10
	Emotions	6.5 ± 3.00	10.6 ± 5.24	16.1 ± 4.47
	Intentions/Lack of Control	15.1 ± 5.41	22.8 ± 10.04	34.3 ± 8.57
	Reinforcement	15.0 ± 5.43	19.2 ± 8.88	28.6 ± 7.71
	Thoughts/Guilt	13.3 ± 4.91	22.1 ± 11.17	33.1 ± 9.71
YFAS				
	No. of Symptoms	0.1 ± 0.78	3.1 ± 3.15	5.8 ± 3.35
	Severity, n			
	None	44	32	10
	Mild	0	3	3
	Moderate	0	2	5
	Severe	0	12	19

Table A1. *Cont.*

Variable		CO	OB	OB-BED
BIS				
	Total	29.3 ± 6.40	31.9 ± 6.34	34.4 ± 6.42
	Nonplanning	10.8 ± 3.40	10.6 ± 3.20	11.8 ± 2.84
	Motoric	10.1 ± 2.44	11.3 ± 2.64	11.1 ± 3.14
	Attentional	8.5 ± 2.45	10.0 ± 2.96	11.5 ± 3.13
BDI				
	Total	6.2 ± 7.61	14.7 ± 9.67	19.7 ± 9.30
CTQ				
	Total	31.9 ± 6.16	45.2 ± 16.76	50.2 ± 15.75
	Emotional Abuse	7.2 ± 2.62	11.1 ± 5.58	12.9 ± 5.60
	Physical Abuse	5.3 ± 0.78	7.1 ± 3.54	6.9 ± 3.32
	Sexual Abuse	5.0 ± 0.15	7.0 ± 4.83	6.8 ± 3.47
	Emotional Neglect	8.3 ± 3.02	12.2 ± 5.24	14.6 ± 5.32
	Physical Neglect	6.1 ± 1.83	7.8 ± 3.03	8.9 ± 3.32
	Denial	0.6 ± 0.99	0.5 ± 0.91	0.2 ± 0.48
RSQ				
	Fear Separation	2.5 ± 0.69	2.6 ± 0.79	3.0 ± 0.65
	Fear Intimacy	2.2 ± 0.65	2.5 ± 0.76	2.8 ± 0.94
	Lack Trust	2.0 ± 0.74	2.7 ± 0.85	3.2 ± 0.77
	Wish Independence	3.8 ± 0.75	4.1 ± 0.67	4.0 ± 0.70

CO = control; OB = obese; OB-BED = obese with co-morbid Binge Eating Disorder; EDEQ = Eating Disorder Examination—Questionnaire; SEES = Salzburger Emotional Eating Scale; SSES = Salzburger Stress Eating Scale; DEBQ = Dutch Eating Behavior Questionnaire; PSRS = Perceived Self-Regulatory Success in Dieting; FCQT = Food Craving Questionnaire—Trait; YFAS = Yale Food Addiction Scale; BIS = Barratt Impulsiveness Scale – Short Version; BDI = Beck Depression Inventory; CTQ = Childhood Trauma Questionnaire; RSQ = Relationship Scales Questionnaire. Values report mean ± standard deviation.

References

1. Qian, J.; Wu, Y.; Liu, F.; Zhu, Y.; Jin, H.; Zhang, H.; Wan, Y.; Li, C.; Yu, D. An update on the prevalence of eating disorders in the general population: A systematic review and meta-analysis. *Eat. Weight Disord.* **2021**. [CrossRef]
2. *American Psychiatric Association Diagnostic and Statistical Manual of Mental Disorders*; American Psychiatric Association: Washington, DC, USA, 2013; ISBN 0-89042-555-8.
3. McCuen-Wurst, C.; Ruggieri, M.; Allison, K.C. Disordered eating and obesity: Associations between binge-eating disorder, night-eating syndrome, and weight-related comorbidities. *Ann. N. Y. Acad. Sci.* **2018**, *1411*, 96–105. [CrossRef]
4. World Health Organization. *Country Profiles on Nutrition, Physical Activity and Obesity in the 53 WHO European Region Member States. Methodology and Summary*; WHO Regional Office for Europe: Copenhagen, Denmark, 2013.
5. Kessler, R.C.; Berglund, P.A.; Chiu, W.T.; Deitz, A.C.; Hudson, J.I.; Shahly, V.; Aguilar-Gaxiola, S.; Alonso, J.; Angermeyer, M.C.; Benjet, C.; et al. The prevalence and correlates of binge eating disorder in the World Health Organization World Mental Health Surveys. *Biol. Psychiatr.* **2013**, *73*, 904–914. [CrossRef]
6. Flegal, K.M.; Kit, B.K.; Orpana, H.; Graubard, B.I. Association of all-cause mortality with overweight and obesity using standard body mass index categories: A systematic review and meta-analysis. *JAMA* **2013**, *309*, 71–82. [CrossRef]
7. Chu, D.-T.; Minh Nguyet, N.T.; Nga, V.T.; Thai Lien, N.V.; Vo, D.D.; Lien, N.; Nhu Ngoc, V.T.; Son, L.H.; Le, D.-H.; Nga, V.B.; et al. An update on obesity: Mental consequences and psychological interventions. *Diabetes Metab. Syndr. Clin. Res. Rev.* **2019**, *13*, 155–160. [CrossRef]
8. Villarejo, C.; Fernández-Aranda, F.; Jiménez-Murcia, S.; Peñas-Lledó, E.; Granero, R.; Penelo, E.; Tinahones, F.J.; Sancho, C.; Vilarrasa, N.; Montserrat-Gil De Bernabé, M.; et al. Lifetime obesity in patients with eating disorders: Increasing prevalence, clinical and personality correlates. *Eur. Eat. Disord. Rev.* **2012**, *20*, 250–254. [CrossRef] [PubMed]
9. Palmisano, G.L.; Innamorati, M.; Vanderlinden, J. Life adverse experiences in relation with obesity and binge eating disorder: A systematic review. *J. Behav. Addict.* **2016**, *5*, 11–31. [CrossRef] [PubMed]
10. Caslini, M.; Bartoli, F.; Crocamo, C.; Dakanalis, A.; Clerici, M.; Carrà, G. Disentangling the association between child abuse and eating disorders: A systematic review and meta-analysis. *Psychosom. Med.* **2016**, *78*, 79–90. [CrossRef]
11. Amianto, F.; Spalatro, A.V.; Rainis, M.; Andriulli, C.; Lavagnino, L.; Abbate-Daga, G.; Fassino, S. Childhood emotional abuse and neglect in obese patients with and without binge eating disorder: Personality and psychopathology correlates in adulthood. *Psychiatr. Res.* **2018**, *269*, 692–699. [CrossRef]
12. Ehlert, U. Enduring psychobiological effects of childhood adversity. *Psychoneuroendocrinology* **2013**, *38*, 1850–1857. [CrossRef] [PubMed]

13. Faber, A.; Dubé, L.; Knäuper, B. Attachment and eating: A meta-analytic review of the relevance of attachment for unhealthy and healthy eating behaviors in the general population. *Appetite* **2018**, *123*, 410–438. [CrossRef] [PubMed]
14. Tasca, G.A.; Balfour, L. Attachment and eating disorders: A review of current research. *Int. J. Eat. Disord.* **2014**, *47*, 710–717. [CrossRef]
15. Maras, D.; Obeid, N.; Flament, M.; Buchholz, A.; Henderson, K.A.; Gick, M.; Goldfield, G.S. Attachment Style and Obesity: Disordered Eating Behaviors as a Mediator in a Community Sample of Canadian Youth. *J. Dev. Behav. Pediatr.* **2016**, *37*, 762–770. [CrossRef] [PubMed]
16. Yohn, S.E.; Galbraith, J.; Calipari, E.S.; Conn, P.J. Shared Behavioral and Neurocircuitry Disruptions in Drug Addiction, Obesity, and Binge Eating Disorder: Focus on Group I mGluRs in the Mesolimbic Dopamine Pathway. *ACS Chem. Neurosci.* **2019**, *10*, 2125–2143. [CrossRef]
17. Giel, K.E.; Teufel, M.; Junne, F.; Zipfel, S.; Schag, K. Food-related impulsivity in obesity and binge eating disorder—A systematic update of the evidence. *Nutrients* **2017**, *9*, 1170. [CrossRef]
18. Paslakis, G.; Kühn, S.; Grunert, S.; Erim, Y. Explicit and Implicit Approach vs. Avoidance Tendencies towards High vs. Low Calorie Food Cues in Patients with Obesity and Active Binge Eating Disorder. *Nutrients* **2017**, *9*, 1068. [CrossRef]
19. Hege, M.A.; Stingl, K.T.; Kullmann, S.; Schag, K.; Giel, K.E.; Zipfel, S.; Preissl, H. Attentional impulsivity in binge eating disorder modulates response inhibition performance and frontal brain networks. *Int. J. Obes.* **2015**, *39*, 353–360. [CrossRef]
20. Hernandez, D.; Mehta, N.; Geliebter, A. Meal-Related Acyl and Des-Acyl Ghrelin and Other Appetite-Related Hormones in People with Obesity and Binge Eating. *Obesity* **2019**, *27*, 629–635. [CrossRef]
21. Schulz, S.; Laessle, R.G. Associations of negative affect and eating behaviour in obese women with and without binge eating disorder. *Eat. Weight Disord.* **2010**, *15*, e287–e293. [CrossRef] [PubMed]
22. Krehbiel, J.; Halbeisen, G.; Kühn, S.; Erim, Y.; Paslakis, G. Too hot to handle: Mood states moderate implicit approach vs. avoidance tendencies toward food cues in patients with obesity and active binge eating disorder. *J. Psychiatr. Res.* **2021**, *143*, 302–308. [CrossRef] [PubMed]
23. Wang, S.B.; Jones, P.J.; Dreier, M.; Elliott, H.; Grilo, C.M. Core psychopathology of treatment-seeking patients with binge-eating disorder: A network analysis investigation. *Psychol. Med.* **2019**, *49*, 1923–1928. [CrossRef]
24. Lewer, M.; Bauer, A.; Hartmann, A.; Vocks, S. Different Facets of Body Image Disturbance in Binge Eating Disorder: A Review. *Nutrients* **2017**, *9*, 1294. [CrossRef] [PubMed]
25. Rø, Ø.; Reas, D.L.; Rosenvinge, J. The impact of age and BMI on Eating Disorder Examination Questionnaire (EDE-Q) scores in a community sample. *Eat. Behav.* **2012**, *13*, 158–161. [CrossRef] [PubMed]
26. Wiedemann, A.A.; Ivezaj, V.; Barnes, R.D. Characterizing emotional overeating among patients with and without binge-eating disorder in primary care. *Gen. Hosp. Psychiatr.* **2018**, *55*, 38–43. [CrossRef] [PubMed]
27. Zeeck, A.; Stelzer, N.; Linster, H.W.; Joos, A.; Hartmann, A. Emotion and eating in binge eating disorder and obesity. *Eur. Eat. Disord. Rev.* **2010**, *19*, 426–437. [CrossRef]
28. Ricca, V.; Castellini, G.; Lo Sauro, C.; Ravaldi, C.; Lapi, F.; Mannucci, E.; Rotella, C.M.; Faravelli, C. Correlations between binge eating and emotional eating in a sample of overweight subjects. *Appetite* **2009**, *53*, 418–421. [CrossRef] [PubMed]
29. Davis, C.; Levitan, R.D.; Carter, J.; Kaplan, A.S.; Reid, C.; Curtis, C.; Patte, K.; Kennedy, J.L. Personality and eating behaviors: A case–control study of binge eating disorder. *Int. J. Eat. Disord.* **2008**, *41*, 243–250. [CrossRef]
30. Pinaquy, S.; Chabrol, H.; Simon, C.; Louvet, J.P.; Barbe, P. Emotional eating, alexithymia, and binge-eating disorder in obese women. *Obes. Res.* **2003**, *11*, 195–201. [CrossRef]
31. Meule, A.; Reichenberger, J.; Blechert, J. Development and preliminary validation of the Salzburg Stress Eating Scale. *Appetite* **2018**, *120*, 442–448. [CrossRef] [PubMed]
32. Agüera, Z.; Lozano-Madrid, M.; Mallorquí-Bagué, N.; Jiménez-Murcia, S.; Menchón, J.M.; Fernández-Aranda, F. A review of binge eating disorder and obesity. *Neuropsychiatrie* **2021**, *35*, 57–67. [CrossRef]
33. Johnson, F.; Pratt, M.; Wardle, J. Dietary restraint and self-regulation in eating behavior. *Int. J. Obes.* **2012**, *36*, 665–674. [CrossRef]
34. Spoor, S.T.P.; Stice, E.; Bekker, M.H.J.; Van Strien, T.; Croon, M.A.; Van Heck, G.L. Relations between dietary restraint, depressive symptoms, and binge eating: A longitudinal study. *Int. J. Eat. Disord.* **2006**, *39*, 700–707. [CrossRef] [PubMed]
35. Meule, A.; Lutz, A.; Vögele, C.; Kübler, A. Food cravings discriminate differentially between successful and unsuccessful dieters and non-dieters. Validation of the Food Cravings Questionnaires in German. *Appetite* **2012**, *58*, 88–97. [CrossRef]
36. Meule, A. Twenty Years of the Food Cravings Questionnaires: A Comprehensive Review. *Curr. Addict. Rep.* **2020**, *7*, 30–43. [CrossRef]
37. Van den Eynde, F.; Koskina, A.; Syrad, H.; Guillaume, S.; Broadbent, H.; Campbell, I.C.; Schmidt, U. State and trait food craving in people with bulimic eating disorders. *Eat. Behav.* **2012**, *13*, 414–417. [CrossRef]
38. Carter, J.C.; Van Wijk, M.; Rowsell, M. Symptoms of 'food addiction' in binge eating disorder using the Yale Food Addiction Scale version 2.0. *Appetite* **2019**, *133*, 362–369. [CrossRef]
39. Davis, C.; Curtis, C.; Levitan, R.D.; Carter, J.C.; Kaplan, A.S.; Kennedy, J.L. Evidence that "food addiction" is a valid phenotype of obesity. *Appetite* **2011**, *57*, 711–717. [CrossRef]
40. Davis, C. Compulsive Overeating as an Addictive Behavior: Overlap between Food Addiction and Binge Eating Disorder. *Curr. Obes. Rep.* **2013**, *2*, 171–178. [CrossRef]

41. Penzenstadler, L.; Soares, C.; Karila, L.; Khazaal, Y. Systematic Review of Food Addiction as Measured with the Yale Food Addiction Scale: Implications for the Food Addiction Construct. *Curr. Neuropharmacol.* **2018**, *17*, 526–538. [CrossRef]
42. Hession, M.; Rolland, C.; Kulkarni, U.; Wise, A.; Broom, J. Systematic review of randomized controlled trials of low-carbohydrate vs. low-fat/low-calorie diets in the management of obesity and its comorbidities. *Obes. Rev.* **2009**, *10*, 36–50. [CrossRef]
43. Brownley, K.A.; Berkman, N.D.; Peat, C.M.; Lohr, K.N.; Cullen, K.E.; Bann, C.M.; Bulik, C.M. Binge-Eating Disorder in Adults: A Systematic Review and Meta-analysis. *Ann. Intern. Med.* **2016**, *165*, 409–420. [CrossRef]
44. White, M.A.; Kalarchian, M.A.; Masheb, R.M.; Marcus, M.D.; Grilo, C.M. Loss of control over eating predicts outcomes in bariatric surgery patients: A prospective, 24-month follow-up study. *J. Clin. Psychiatr.* **2010**, *71*, 175–184. [CrossRef]
45. Hilbert, A.; Petroff, D.; Herpertz, S.; Pietrowsky, R.; Tuschen-Caffier, B.; Vocks, S.; Schmidt, R. Meta-Analysis of the Efficacy of Psychological and Medical Treatments for Binge-Eating Disorder. *J. Consult. Clin. Psychol.* **2019**, *87*, 91–105. [CrossRef] [PubMed]
46. Grilo, C.M. Psychological and Behavioral Treatments for Binge-Eating Disorder. *J. Clin. Psychiatr.* **2017**, *78* (Suppl. S1), 20–24. [CrossRef]
47. Escandón-Nagel, N.; Peró, M.; Grau, A.; Soriano, J.; Feixas, G. Alimentación emocional y conflictos cognitivos como predictores del trastorno por atracón en pacientes con obesidad. *Int. J. Clin. Health Psychol.* **2018**, *18*, 52–59. [CrossRef]
48. Gearhardt, A.; White, M.; Potenza, M. Binge eating disorder and food addiction. *Curr. Drug Abuse Rev.* **2011**, *4*, 201–207. [CrossRef] [PubMed]
49. Meule, A. German Version of the Eating Disorder Diagnostic Scale—DSM-5 Version 2015. Available online: https://adrianmeule.files.wordpress.com/2013/05/eddsgerman.pdf (accessed on 10 October 2021).
50. Faul, F.; Erdfelder, E.; Lang, A.G.; Buchner, A. G*Power 3: A flexible statistical power analysis program for the social, behavioral, and biomedical sciences. *Behav. Res. Methods* **2007**, *39*, 175–191. [CrossRef] [PubMed]
51. Fairburn, C.G.; Beglin, S.J. Assessment of eating disorders: Interview or self-report questionnaire? *Int. J. Eat. Disord.* **1994**, *16*, 363–370. [PubMed]
52. Fairburn, C.G.; Cooper, Z. The eating disorder examination. In *Binge Eating: Nature, Assessment and Treatment*; Fairburn, C.G., Wilson, G.T., Eds.; Guilford Press: New York, NY, USA, 1993; pp. 317–360.
53. Hilbert, A.; Tuschen-Caffier, B. *Eating Disorder Examination–Questionnaire: Deutschsprachige Übersetzung*; Münster Verlag Psychotherapie: Münster, Germany, 2006.
54. Meule, A.; Reichenberger, J.; Blechert, J. Development and Preliminary Validation of the Salzburg Emotional Eating Scale. *Front. Psychol.* **2018**, *9*, 88. [CrossRef]
55. Reichenberger, J.; Pannicke, B.; Arend, A.K.; Petrowski, K.; Blechert, J. Does stress eat away at you or make you eat? EMA measures of stress predict day to day food craving and perceived food intake as a function of trait stress-eating. *Psychol. Health* **2021**, *36*, 129–147. [CrossRef]
56. van Strien, T.; Frijters, J.E.R.; Bergers, G.P.A.; Defares, P.B. The Dutch Eating Behavior Questionnaire (DEBQ) for assessment of restrained, emotional, and external eating behavior. *Int. J. Eat. Disord.* **1986**, *5*, 295–315. [CrossRef]
57. Nagl, M.; Hilbert, A.; de Zwaan, M.; Braehler, E.; Kersting, A. The German Version of the Dutch Eating Behavior Questionnaire: Psychometric Properties, Measurement Invariance, and Population-Based Norms. *PLoS ONE* **2016**, *11*, e0162510. [CrossRef] [PubMed]
58. Fishbach, A.; Friedman, R.S.; Kruglanski, A.W. Leading us not unto temptation: Momentary allurements elicit overriding goal activation. *J. Pers. Soc. Psychol.* **2003**, *84*, 296–309. [CrossRef]
59. Meule, A.; Papies, E.K.; Kübler, A. Differentiating between successful and unsuccessful dieters. Validity and reliability of the Perceived Self-Regulatory Success in Dieting Scale. *Appetite* **2012**, *58*, 822–826. [CrossRef] [PubMed]
60. Cepeda-Benito, A.; Gleaves, D.; Williams, T.; Erath, S. The development and validation of the State and Trait Food-Cravings Questionnaire. *Behav. Ther.* **2000**, *31*, 151–173. [CrossRef]
61. Gearhardt, A.N.; Corbin, W.R.; Brownell, K.D. Development of the Yale Food Addiction Scale Version 2.0. *Psychol. Addict. Behav. J. Soc. Psychol. Addict. Behav.* **2016**, *30*, 113–121. [CrossRef] [PubMed]
62. Meule, A.; Müller, A.; Gearhardt, A.N.; Blechert, J. German version of the Yale Food Addiction Scale 2.0: Prevalence and correlates of "food addiction" in students and obese individuals. *Appetite* **2017**, *115*, 54–61. [CrossRef] [PubMed]
63. Meule, A.; Vögele, C.; Kübler, A. Psychometric evaluation of the German Barratt Impulsiveness Scale-Short Version (BIS-15). *Diagnostica* **2011**, *57*, 126–133. [CrossRef]
64. Hautzinger, M.; Keller, F.; Kühner, C. *BDI-II. Beck-Depressions-Inventar*, 2nd ed.; Pearson: London, UK, 2009.
65. Bader, K.; Hänny, C.; Schäfer, V.; Neuckel, A.; Kuhl, C. Childhood Trauma Questionnaire-Psychometrische Eigenschaften einer deutschsprachigen Version. [Childhood Trauma Questionnaire-Psychometric properties of a German version]. *Z. Klin. Psychol. Psychother.* **2009**, *38*, 223–230. [CrossRef]
66. Steffanowski, A.; Oppl, M.; Meyerberg, J.; Juergen, S.; Wittmann, W.; Nübling, R. *Psychometrische Überprüfung einer Deutschsprachigen Version des Relationship Scales Questionaire (RSQ)*; Psychosozial: Giessen, Germany, 2001; pp. 320–342. ISBN 3-89806-081-0.
67. Hilbert, A.; de Zwaan, M.; Braehler, E. How Frequent Are Eating Disturbances in the Population? Norms of the Eating Disorder Examination-Questionnaire. *PLoS ONE* **2012**, *7*, e29125. [CrossRef]
68. Özdin, S.; Karabekiroğlu, A.; Özbalcı, G.S.; Aker, A.A. The effect of cognitive symptoms in binge eating disorder on depression and self-esteem: A cross-sectional study. *Eat. Weight Disord.* **2021**, *26*, 1483–1489. [CrossRef] [PubMed]

69. Çalışır, S.; Çalışır, A.; Arslan, M.; İnanlı, İ.; Çalışkan, A.M.; Eren, İ. Assessment of depressive symptoms, self-esteem, and eating psychopathology after laparoscopic sleeve gastrectomy: 1-year follow-up and comparison with healthy controls. *Eat. Weight Disord.* **2020**, *25*, 1515–1523. [CrossRef]
70. Grilo, C.M.; White, M.A.; Gueorguieva, R.; Wilson, G.T.; Masheb, R.M. Predictive significance of the overvaluation of shape/weight in obese patients with binge eating disorder: Findings from a randomized controlled trial with 12-month follow-up. *Psychol. Med.* **2013**, *43*, 1335–1344. [CrossRef] [PubMed]
71. Gagnon-Girouard, M.P.; Bégin, C.; Provencher, V.; Tremblay, A.; Boivin, S.; Lemieux, S. Can we apply the dual-pathway model of overeating to a population of weight-preoccupied overweight women? *Int. J. Eat. Disord.* **2009**, *42*, 244–252. [CrossRef]
72. Zambrowicz, R.; Schebendach, J.; Sysko, R.; Mayer, L.E.S.; Walsh, B.T.; Steinglass, J.E. Relationship between three factor eating questionnaire-restraint subscale and food intake. *Int. J. Eat. Disord.* **2019**, *52*, 255–260. [CrossRef] [PubMed]
73. Meule, A.; Richard, A.; Schnepper, R.; Reichenberger, J.; Georgii, C.; Naab, S.; Voderholzer, U.; Blechert, J. Emotion regulation and emotional eating in anorexia nervosa and bulimia nervosa. *Eat. Disord.* **2021**, *29*, 175–191. [CrossRef]
74. Schulz, S.; Laessle, R.G. Stress-induced laboratory eating behavior in obese women with binge eating disorder. *Appetite* **2012**, *58*, 457–461. [CrossRef]
75. Benzerouk, F.; Djerada, Z.; Bertin, E.; Barrière, S.; Gierski, F.; Kaladjian, A. Contributions of emotional overload, emotion dysregulation, and impulsivity to eating patterns in obese patients with binge eating disorder and seeking bariatric surgery. *Nutrients* **2020**, *12*, 3099. [CrossRef]
76. Mason, T.B.; Lewis, R.J. Profiles of Binge Eating: The Interaction of Depressive Symptoms, Eating Styles, and Body Mass Index. *Eat. Disord.* **2014**, *22*, 450–460. [CrossRef]
77. Ferrer-Garcia, M.; Pla-Sanjuanelo, J.; Dakanalis, A.; Vilalta-Abella, F.; Riva, G.; Fernandez-Aranda, F.; Sánchez, I.; Ribas-Sabaté, J.; Andreu-Gracia, A.; Escandón-Nagel, N.; et al. Eating behavior style predicts craving and anxiety experienced in food-related virtual environments by patients with eating disorders and healthy controls. *Appetite* **2017**, *117*, 284–293. [CrossRef]
78. Innamorati, M.; Imperatori, C.; Balsamo, M.; Tamburello, S.; Belvederi Murri, M.; Contardi, A.; Tamburello, A.; Fabbricatore, M. Food cravings questionnaire-trait (FCQ-T) discriminates between obese and overweight patients with and without binge eating tendencies: The italian version of the FCQ-T. *J. Pers. Assess.* **2014**, *96*, 632–639. [CrossRef] [PubMed]
79. Grilo, C.M.; White, M.A.; Barnes, R.D.; Masheb, R.M. Psychiatric disorder co-morbidity and correlates in an ethnically diverse sample of obese patients with binge eating disorder in primary care settings. *Compr. Psychiatr.* **2013**, *54*, 209–216. [CrossRef] [PubMed]
80. Fauconnier, M.; Rousselet, M.; Brunault, P.; Thiabaud, E.; Lambert, S.; Rocher, B.; Challet-Bouju, G.; Grall-Bronnec, M. Food addiction among female patients seeking treatment for an eating disorder: Prevalence and associated factors. *Nutrients* **2020**, *12*, 1897. [CrossRef]
81. Kessler, R.M.; Hutson, P.H.; Herman, B.K.; Potenza, M.N. The neurobiological basis of binge-eating disorder. *Neurosci. Biobehav. Rev.* **2016**, *63*, 223–238. [CrossRef]
82. Bénard, M.; Camilleri, G.; Etilé, F.; Méjean, C.; Bellisle, F.; Reach, G.; Hercberg, S.; Péneau, S. Association between Impulsivity and Weight Status in a General Population. *Nutrients* **2017**, *9*, 217. [CrossRef]
83. Loeber, S.; Rustemeier, M.; Paslakis, G.; Pietrowsky, R.; Müller, A.; Herpertz, S. Mood and restrained eating moderate food-associated response inhibition in obese individuals with binge eating disorder. *Psychiatr. Res.* **2018**, *264*, 346–353. [CrossRef]
84. Smith, C.E.; Hawkins, M.A.W.; Williams-Kerver, G.A.; Duncan, J. Depression subtypes, binge eating, and weight loss in bariatric surgery candidates. *Surg. Obes. Relat. Dis.* **2020**, *16*, 690–697. [CrossRef] [PubMed]
85. Udo, T.; McKee, S.A.; Grilo, C.M. Factor structure and clinical utility of the Beck Depression Inventory in patients with binge eating disorder and obesity. *Gen. Hosp. Psychiatr.* **2015**, *37*, 120–125. [CrossRef]
86. Meule, A.; Blechert, J. Interactive and indirect effects of trait impulsivity facets on body mass index. *Appetite* **2017**, *118*, 60–65. [CrossRef]
87. Belli, H.; Ural, C.; Akbudak, M.; Sagaltıcı, E. Levels of childhood traumatic experiences and dissociative symptoms in extremely obese patients with and without binge eating disorder. *Nord. J. Psychiatr.* **2019**, *73*, 527–531. [CrossRef]
88. Palmisano, G.L.; Innamorati, M.; Sarracino, D.; Bosco, A.; Pergola, F.; Scaltrito, D.; Giorgio, B.; Vanderlinden, J. Trauma and dissociation in obese patients with and without binge eating disorder: A case–control study. *Cogent Psychol.* **2018**, *5*, 1–20. [CrossRef]
89. Han, S.; Carole Pistole, M. College student binge eating: Insecure attachment and emotion regulation. *J. Coll. Stud. Dev.* **2014**, *55*, 16–29. [CrossRef]
90. Shakory, S.; Van Exan, J.; Mills, J.S.; Sockalingam, S.; Keating, L.; Taube-Schiff, M. Binge eating in bariatric surgery candidates: The role of insecure attachment and emotion regulation. *Appetite* **2015**, *91*, 69–75. [CrossRef]
91. Blomquist, K.K.; Ansell, E.B.; White, M.A.; Masheb, R.M.; Grilo, C.M. Interpersonal problems and developmental trajectories of binge eating disorder. *Compr. Psychiatr.* **2012**, *53*, 1088–1095. [CrossRef] [PubMed]

nutrients

Review

Impact of Obesity in Kidney Diseases

Vasilios Kotsis [1], Fernando Martinez [2], Christina Trakatelli [1] and Josep Redon [2,3,4,*]

1 3rd Department of Internal Medicine, Hypertension-24h ABPM ESH Center of Excellence, Papageorgiou Hospital, Aristotle University of Thessaloniki, 564 29 Pavlos Melas, Greece; vkotsis@auth.gr (V.K.); ctrak@auth.gr (C.T.)
2 Internal Medicine Hospital Clínico de Valencia, 46010 Valencia, Spain; fernandoctor@hotmail.com
3 Cardiovascular and Renal Research Group, INCLIVA Research Institute, University of Valencia, 46010 Valencia, Spain
4 CIBERObn Carlos III Institute, 28029 Madrid, Spain
* Correspondence: josep.redon@uv.es

Abstract: The clinical consequences of obesity on the kidneys, with or without metabolic abnormalities, involve both renal function and structures. The mechanisms linking obesity and renal damage are well understood, including several effector mechanisms with interconnected pathways. Higher prevalence of urinary albumin excretion, sub-nephrotic syndrome, nephrolithiasis, increased risk of developing CKD, and progression to ESKD have been identified as being associated with obesity and having a relevant clinical impact. Moreover, renal replacement therapy and kidney transplantation are also influenced by obesity. Losing weight is key in limiting the impact that obesity produces on the kidneys by reducing albuminuria/proteinuria, declining rate of eGFR deterioration, delaying the development of CKD and ESKD, and improving the outcome of a renal transplant. Weight reduction may also contribute to appropriate control of cardiometabolic risk factors such as hypertension, metabolic syndrome, diabetes, and dyslipidemia which may be protective not only in renal damage but also cardiovascular disease. Lifestyle changes, some drugs, and bariatric surgery have demonstrated the benefits.

Keywords: obesity; fatty kidney; glomerulopathy; CKD; ESRD; bariatric surgery

Citation: Kotsis, V.; Martinez, F.; Trakatelli, C.; Redon, J. Impact of Obesity in Kidney Diseases. *Nutrients* **2021**, *13*, 4482. https://doi.org/10.3390/nu13124482

Academic Editors: Fernando Fernandez-Aranda, Janet Treasure and Empar Lurbe

Received: 4 November 2021
Accepted: 10 December 2021
Published: 15 December 2021

1. Introduction

The continuous growing of the obesity pandemic introduced a great bulk of disease beyond the classical well recognized metabolic, orthopedic, psychological, and cardiovascular consequences of obesity. Beside these, although in some ways linked to, is the impact of obesity in the kidney, usually silent during the years before producing relevant damage with clinical expressivity. A review in epidemiology, mechanisms, clinical, and therapeutic aspects is presented.

1.1. Epidemiology

In adults within a large, community-based population, in an integrated system of health care delivery in whom serum creatinine had been measured between 1996 and 2000 and who had not been supported with dialysis or undergone kidney transplantation, an independent, ranked association between a reduced estimated GFR and the risk of death, cardiovascular events, and hospitalization was reported. As GFR decreased from 59 to 45 (mL/min/1.73 m^2), the risk of death increased to 1.8 reaching gradually the highest values of almost 6 times more in the end stage renal disease patients [1]. Similar results for the association of CKD progression with cardiovascular disease and death was also reported in metanalysis studies [2,3]. The unadjusted prevalence of stage 3 and 4 CKD in USA increased from the late 1990s to the early 2000s with a rise in the prevalence of diabetes, hypertension, and obesity. However, the overall prevalence has stabilized since 2003 to 2004 and 6.9% of the population has CKD in 2011 to 2012. Reasons for the recent stabilization of overall CKD prevalence despite continued aging of the U.S. population and the increased prevalence of obesity include better control of hypertension, successful glycemic control with the newer drugs, and expanded use of medications blocking the renin–angiotensin system in patients with proteinuria [4]. In the UK, the prevalence of eGFR < 60 mL/min/1–73 m^2 was 7.7%, 7.0% and 7.3% in 2003, 2009/2010, and 2016, respectively initially decreased in 2010 but again increased in 2016 [5]. At the same time in the UK the prevalence of diabetes and obesity increased during 2003–2016, while prevalence of hypertension and smoking fell.

Beyond the impact of diabetes and hypertension on the increased risk of CKD in the obese patients, the direct role of obesity in kidney injury has been demonstrated in animal models and epidemiological studies in humans. BMI has been reported as an independently significant factor for the development of CKD in most studies [6–10] with an odds ratio from the lowest to the highest BMI of 1.273 for developing ESKD, after adjustment for age, sex, systolic blood pressure, and proteinuria [6], but obesity risk appeared largely mediated by diabetes and hypertension in other studies [8] or not to be associated with ESKD [11]. A recent metanalysis of studies from a general population with normal baseline renal function reported that obesity increased the relative risk of developing low eGFR by 1.28 and albuminuria by 1.51 [12]. Table 1 collected studies of CKD risk in adults with metabolic syndrome.

Table 1. Risk of CKD in adults with metabolic syndrome (·MS).

Study	Patients	Study Endpoint	OR (CI 95%) for Chronic Kidney Disease
Chen et al. [13]	6217 US adults	chronic kidney disease and microalbuminuria	2.60 (1.68–4.03) versus non metabolic syndrome
Palaniappan et al. [14]	6217 American adults	microalbuminuria	OR 2.2 (1.44–3.34) and 4.1 (2.45–6.74) for women and men versus non metabolic syndrome.
Chen et al. [15]	15,160 Chinese adults	chronic kidney disease	1.64 (1.16–2.32) versus non metabolic syndrome
Tanaka et al. [16]	6980 Japanese adults	chronic kidney disease	<60 years; 1.69 (i.35–2.11) versus non metabolic syndrome
Chang et al. [17]	60,921 Korean adults	chronic kidney disease	1.68 (0.57–1.80) versus non metabolic syndrome
Ryu et al. [18]	10,685 Korean healthy men/40,616.8 person-years	prospective, chronic kidney disease	2.00 (1.46–2.73)
Kurella et al. [19]	10,096 US adults/9 years of follow-up	prospective, CKD	1.43 (1.18–1.73)
Yang et al. [20]	4248 Chinese adults/5.40 years of follow-up	prospective chronic kidney disease	1.42 (1.03–1.73)
Ninomiya et al. [21]	1440 adults/5 years of follow up	prospective, chronic kidney disease	2.08 (1.23–3.52)
Lucove et al. [22]	1484 Native Americans/10 years follow up	prospective, chronic kidney disease	1.3 (1.10–1.60)
Sun et al. [23]	118,924 Taiwanese/3.7 years follow up	prospective, chronic kidney disease	1.30 (1.24–1.36)
Chen J [24]	26,601 subjects	chronic kidney disease	1.99 (1.57–2.53)
Rashidbeygi E et al. [25]	10,603,067 participants	meta-analysis albuminuria and proteinuria	1.92 (1.71–2.15) and 2.08 (1.85–2.34)
Thomas et al. [24]	30,146 adults	meta-analysis chronic kidney disease	1.55 (1.34–1.80)

Nondiabetic participants with normal baseline kidney function and metabolic syndrome according to the National Cholesterol Education Program who were included in the Atherosclerosis Risk in Communities study had an adjusted risk of developing CKD of

1.43 compared with participants with no features of the metabolic syndrome [19]. Central fat distribution indices, i.e., waist to hip circumference or visceral fat, are better related with the risk of ESKD compared to BMI [26–28]. Meta analyses reported that metabolic syndrome components such as obesity, impaired fasting glucose, elevated blood pressure, and hypertriglyceridemia were associated with significant increases in proteinuria and albuminuria risk [25].

Metabolically healthy obesity (MHO) is an obesity phenotype that obesity is not associated with metabolic complications such as insulin resistance, inflammation, hypertension, or T2D. Compared with metabolically healthy non-obesity phenotype, the odds ratios for incident CKD for MHO were similar to the comparison group, but significantly increased for metabolically abnormal non-obese and obesity phenotype respectively after adjustment for confounders [29–31]. However, other studies reported that MHO may have an intermediate future risk to develop ESKD.

1.2. Pathology

Obesity-Related Glomerulopathy

Physical compression of the kidneys from accumulation of adipose tissue around the organs emphasizes the possible role of visceral obesity in the development of renal disease. Deposition of extracellular matrix throughout the renal medulla is expanded and the tissue surrounding the ducts of Bellini at the vascular pole tends to prolapse. Increased numbers of interstitial cells and material rich in lipids and proteoglycans press the renal parenchyma towards the pole of the kidney resulting in the formation of round-shaped, enlarged kidney in obese subjects. Renal compression affects both vascular (the vasa recta) and tubular (the Henle's loops) elements causing activation of the RAS and increased sodium reabsorption [32–34].

The primary histologic features are few lesions of focal-segmental glomerulosclerosis, profound glomerulomegaly due to glomerular hyalinosis and fibrosis, as well as lipid accumulation in the glomeruli and adhesion to Bowman's capsule [35,36]. Altered fat metabolism in the kidneys induces lipid accumulation, suggesting that high fat intake may have a direct lipotoxicity effect in the kidneys. Ectopic lipid accumulation in the kidneys induces structural and functional changes of the mesangial cells, podocytes, and proximal tubular cells. Perivascular fat in the renal sinus appears to participate in vascular function, modifying the blood flow in the underlying arteries. Obesity increases renal mass and glomerular diameter. Podocytes need to enlarge their processes to cover an expanded area that cause podocyte detachment, loss in protein selectivity, formation of denuded areas that trigger matrix deposition, and podocyte damage.

Glomerular changes in obesity-induced renal injury are unmatched to those of diabetic nephropathy, due to the lower severity in the first in the mesangial space changes. Patients with diabetic nephropathy more frequently have albuminuria, proteinuria, and ESKD compared to obesity induced nephropathy where the results are slower and the progression to end renal disease is less frequent. Other causes of renal injury, apart from high fat intake, could include overexpression of Ang II with a consequent increase in proliferative factors such as transforming growth factor (TGF-β) and plasminogen activator inhibitor and insulinemia giving genesis to cell growth. Hyperfiltration because of sodium reabsorption, increase the blood flow to the kidney causing gradual glomerular wall sclerosis due to physical shear stress and a dangerous circle starts in which nephrons are injured leading to their apoptosis, sodium retention attenuates, while blood pressure increases to maintain sodium balance. Proteinuria of nephrotic range is rare among the obese, but albuminuria may exist [35,37]. These findings suggest that obesity-related renal damage should be defined as a special form of focal-segmental glomerulosclerosis slowly progressing to end stage renal disease. Patients with the metabolic syndrome have high prevalence of microvascular disease manifested as tubular atrophy, interstitial fibrosis, and arterial sclerosis [38].

1.3. Mechanisms

The mechanisms of structural abnormalities of CKD are related to the obesity-comorbidities, i.e., hypertension, insulin resistance, type 2 diabetes, and atherogenic dyslipidemia, that contribute to renal damage through mechanisms that include inflammation, oxidative stress, RAAS upregulation, increased SNS activity, and endothelial dysfunction that finally induce renal damage [39], Figure 1.

A. Hemodynamics

Activation of the sympathetic nervous system (SNS) has been thought to play an important role in the pathogenesis of hypertension and CKD among obese individuals [40]. Plasma renin activity displayed significant increase in obesity and local perivascular adipose tissue angiotensin II is also increased [33]. Angiotensin II raises the efferent arteriole tone in the glomerulus, production of TGF-beta, fibrosis, and apoptosis of the podocytes. In the early stages of kidney damage associated to obesity, e-GFR is increased due to the hyperperfusion from volume overload. Intrarenal increased physical forces, generating from fat accumulation around and into the renal medulla, diminish flow rate of the filtrate at the loop of Henle and sodium retention is observed [33]. These early changes can be reverted by weight loss, salt restriction, and renin-angiotensin system blockade.

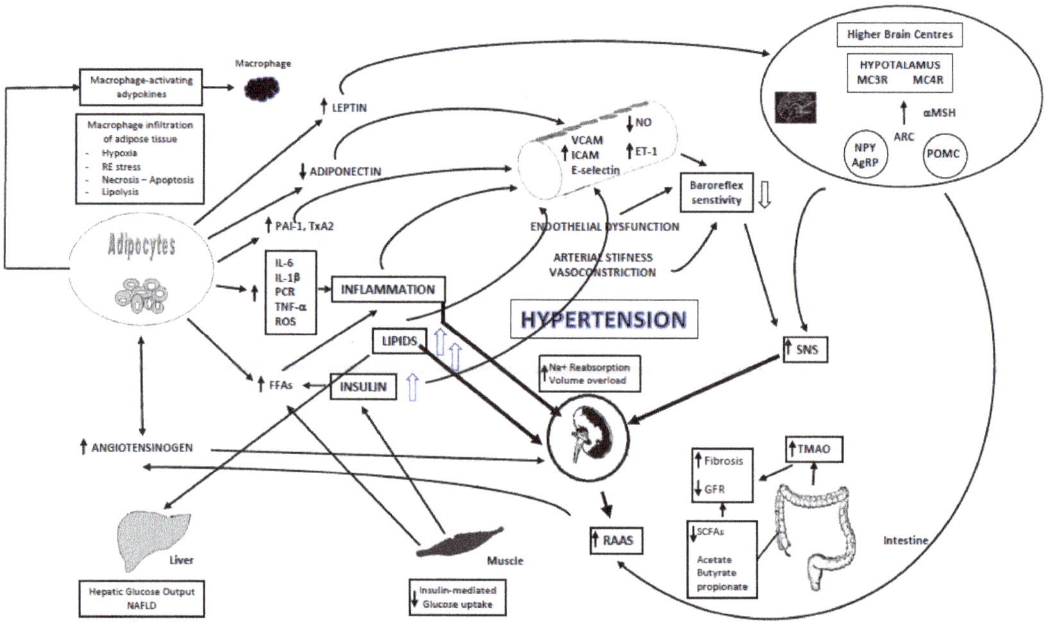

Figure 1. Mechanisms of obesity induced renal damage. Modified from Kotsis V et al., J Hypertens. 2018 Jul; 36(7):1427–1440.

B. Inflammation

Chronic low-grade inflammation develops locally in the expanding adipose cells from macrophage but becomes systemic through the release of pro-inflammatory mediators that include cytokines into the blood stream. Elevated levels of free fatty acids (FFAs) in obese individuals may enhance vascular a-adrenergic sensitivity, inhibit Na^+, K^+-ATPase and the sodium pump increasing vascular smooth muscle tone and vascular resistance, activate epidermal growth factor receptor, and produce reactive oxygen species and protein kinase C. A variety of biologically active cytokines are produced in adipose cells, including reactive oxygen species, proinflammatory and inflammatory molecules (interleukin-1β, interleukin-6, tumor necrosis factor-α, C-reactive protein), angiogenetic factors (vascular endothelial growth factor), hemostasis modulating compounds (plasminogen activator inhibitor-1, thromboxane A2), acute phase reaction proteins (serum amyloid A proteins, C-reactive protein), and activation of nuclear factor kappa-light-chain-enhancer of activated B cells (NF-κB) and IκB kinase (IKK), pathways that promote endothelial dysfunction and microvascular disease [33]. Different pathophysiological mechanisms may contribute to the development of CKD from gut microbiota dysbiosis such as production of uremic toxins mainly trimethylamine-N-oxide (TMAO), reduced prophylactic short-chain fatty acids, enhanced inflammation and immune response, reduced nitric oxide (NO), and peptides that block the angiotensin-I converting enzyme [41].

C. Hormones

Insulin resistance induces glomerular hyperfiltration, endothelial dysfunction, increased vascular permeability, angiogenesis, and other pathways implicated in microvascular damage that is associated with albuminuria [42]. Hyperglycemia activates pathways that increase production of advanced glycation end-products (AGEs), activate protein kinase C isoforms, and increase transforming growth factor β that enhances extracellular matrix production by mesangial cells inducing renal fibrosis [43]. Podocytes block proteinuria through arrangement of actin cytoskeleton in their foot processes. Decreased podocyte number and podocyte foot process effacement have been reported in diabetic patients with early phases of kidney damage. Insulin action in podocytes is critical for the glomerular function and structure affecting morphology, cytoskeleton remodeling, and finally their survival [44].

Leptin is a small peptide hormone that is produced in adipose tissue and increases in the blood of obese subjects. The circulating leptin associates with adipose tissue mass and regulates food intake through its hypothalamic actions that release other neurotransmitters. Leptin can modify insulin actions, induce angiogenesis, reduce endothelial NO synthase, and interact with the immune system. Leptin is cleared by the kidney and is increased in patients with chronic renal failure associated with anorexia and weight loss in ESKD patients. Leptin triggers glomerular endothelial cells secretion of TGF-beta, to which sensitized mesangial cells may respond inducing development of focal glomerulosclerosis and proteinuria [45]. Additional effects of leptin on the kidney include natriuresis, increased sympathetic nervous activity, and stimulation of reactive oxygen species [33].

Adiponectin is an adipose tissue derived peptide hormone, reduced in obese subjects, that acts as lipolytic factor and regulates insulin sensitivity. Adiponectin prevents the atherogenic process by inhibiting foam-cell formation. Adiposity is characterized by adiponectin deficiency. Plasma adiponectin levels are inversely related to insulin levels. Adiponectin knockout mice demonstrate a diet dependent insulin resistance and atherogenesis [33]. Adiponectin increases AMPK activity, reducing podocyte permeability [46,47]. Finally, resistin, an inflammatory adipokine produced by the monocyte macrophage cells, is increased in patients with low GFR [48]. In adults with hypertension and diabetes, circulating resistin levels were associated with reduced estimated glomerular filtration rate and albuminuria [49].

1.4. Endothelial Dysfunction and Changes in Vascular Structure

Endothelial dysfunction plays an important role in the pathogenesis of CKD and albuminuria [50]. Insulin resistance, low levels of adiponectin, high plasma leptin, increased levels of plasma glucose, and FFAs induce an inflammation profile that causes endothelial dysfunction, which causes increased protein loss from the kidneys.

Nitric oxide (NO) is produced from the endothelium, promotes vasodilation, reduces inflammation, and platelet aggregation. Phosphoinositide 3-kinase activation is causing phosphorylation of endothelial NO synthase (e-NOs) that produce NO [51]. Obesity is associated with reduced NO bioavailability. In the presence of insulin resistance this pathway is down-regulated, while hyperinsulinemia increases endothelin-1 levels resulting in imbalance between vasodilator and vasoconstrictor endothelium factors causing hypertension [52,53]. Vascular cell adhesion molecule-1 (VCAM-1), inter-cellular adhesion molecule-1 (ICAM-1), and E-selectin increase monocyte adhesion to the vascular wall, inducing atherosclerosis. These vascular factors promote a cycle that is causing renal damage and hypertension [33].

2. Clinical Consequences

The clinical consequences of obesity on the kidneys, with or without metabolic abnormalities, involve both renal function and structures, Figure 2. Higher prevalence of urinary albumin excretion, sub-nephrotic syndrome, nephrolithiasis, increased risk of developing CKD, and progression to ESKD have been identified as being associated with obesity and having a relevant clinical impact. In renal replacement therapy and kidney transplantation, both the availability of donors and graft survival are also influenced by obesity. At the time of estimating the association and the impact of obesity on renal disease, the presence of sarcopenia, a not infrequent condition, can be misleading, since it can lead to underestimating obesity [54]. Therefore, other parameters beyond BMI should be considered [55].

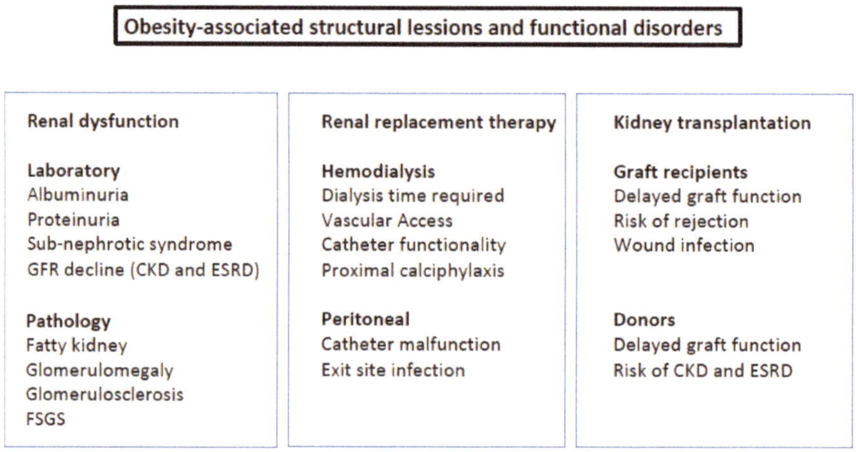

Figure 2. Obesity-associated structural lesions and functional disorders. FSGS: focal segmentary glomerulosclerosis.

2.1. Urinary Albumin Excretion and Proteinuria

In obese subjects, albuminuria is more frequent. A significant association of albuminuria with either obesity or central obesity has been reported [56–58], being higher in the presence of central obesity. The presence of a cluster of cardiovascular risk factors increases the risk [59].

Albuminuria associated with obesity has been observed in children and adolescents. In moderate obese adolescents, the prevalence was reported at 2.4% [60]; however, in severe obesity, 3% displayed proteinuria, 14% microalbuminuria, and 3% had a GFR <60 mL/min/1.73 m^2 [61]. In addition, Goknar et al. [62] reported that severely obese children had a higher number of urinary markers for tubular damage, such as N-acetyl-beta-D-glucosaminidase (NAG), and kidney injury molecule (KIM)-1.

Even though the prevalence of albuminuria in the presence of obesity has been demonstrated, this condition remains underdiagnosed due to the absence of clinical symptoms and lack of specific search of low-grade albuminuria.

2.2. Sub-Nephrotic Syndrome

Obesity-related glomerulopathy is a characteristic syndrome which is categorized by the presence of sub-nephrotic proteinuria, glomerulopathy, and renal function loss. Patients usually do not have proteinuria at the level of nephrotic syndrome in 30% of subjects [63] in which there is sub-nephrotic proteinuria in the absence of edema, hypoalbuminemia, and less hyperlipidemia. The reason for the differences between this syndrome and typical nephrotic syndrome is the indolent development of compensating mechanisms over many years. These mechanisms reduce or limit the systematic and metabolic impact, increasing hepatic synthesis of albumin and other proteins [64]. This is in contrast with nephrotic syndrome due to other etiologies. Biopsies in obese patients reveal glomerulomegaly and some of them also develop an adaptive form of focal segmental glomerulosclerosis, increasing the risk of progression to renal dysfunction [65].

2.3. Progression to CKD and ESRD

Obesity has been associated with a higher incidence of CKD defined by the presence of albuminuria and/or GFR < 60 mL/min/1.73 m^2 as compared to the non-obese population [12,66–68]. The impact of obesity on conditions that favor the progressive decline of renal function has been emphasized. Low birth weight children, low renal endowment, subjects with reduced renal mass due to different origins, or with primary or secondary renal damage, displayed an increased risk of progression toward CKD and ESKD in the presence of obesity [69]. The role of metabolic abnormalities obesity-associated in the increment of risk has received attention. While some studies support that the metabolically healthy obese (MHO) do not have an increased risk of progression toward CKD and ESKD [70,71], or even a reduction in risk [72]. However, other studies are more in favour of MHO being the first stage of obesity [73] and that it is a question of time as to the development of metabolic abnormalities and consequently an increased risk of the development of renal dysfunction.

Individuals who are obese have a more than 3-fold higher risk of developing end-stage kidney disease (ESKD) than those with normal bodyweight [74,75]. In a large cohort from Austria, with a prevalence of obesity of 11.8%, 0.3% developed ESKD in a follow-up of 22 years and an increase of 5 points of BMI increased the risk by 56% [76]. In a cohort of the Kaiser Permanent register with 320,252 subjects followed over 21 years, the hazard risk for ESKD increased through the obesity grade 3.57, 6.10, and 7.07 for obesity 1 to III respectively, as compared with normal weight subjects [74]. However, when the rate of decline of renal function in CKD to develop ESKD was evaluated, controversial data had been reported. While some studies reported a faster decline [77] in the presence of obesity, other did not confirm [78].

2.4. Nephrolithiasis

Prevalence and incidence of nephrolithiasis is increased in obese subjects. Association is facilitated by lower urinary pH, increased urinary oxalate, sodium and phosphate excretion, and uric acid. Other factors such as the effect of insulin resistance on tubular H-Na exchanger and ammoniagenesis promoting urine acidification have also been implicated in the pathogenesis [79]. It is worth commenting that the risk increases after certain weight loss therapies. In fact, after Roux-en-Y, gastric bypass absorption of oxalate in the intestine largely increases and the risk of nephrolithiasis needs to be prevented by reducing dietary oxalate consumption and oral calcium supplementation.

2.5. Renal Replacement Therapy

The increasing prevalence of obesity produces a challenge for optimal care of patients in renal replacement therapy, in both hemo- and peritoneal dialysis [80]. In the case of hemodialysis, at 3 years, adiposity of the subcutaneous tissue produced problems with vascular access and a reduction in the catheter functionality. Moreover, in obese subjects, increased dialysis time or frequency is necessary, and it is more difficult to achieve the dry weight. Proximal calciphylaxis is more frequent in obese than in lean patients. In patients on peritoneal dialysis, catheter malfunction and exit site infections are more prevalent in obese subjects. In some patients with severe adiposity, a prophylactic omentectomy could be useful. In addition, patients with advanced CKD, especially those undergoing dialysis, tend to have severe nutritional disorders, protein-energy wasting, and the presence of obesity may be better in this population, an obesity paradox [81].

2.6. Kidney Transplantation

In the past, obesity was a contraindication for kidney transplantation if weight was not reduced. Despite the fact that cut-off limits have increased, even until a BMI of 40 kg/m^2, obesity is still one of the leading causes of being inactive on the transplant list. The reason for this is that obese subject recipients of transplantation have increased rates of delayed graft function, wound infection, and rejection.

It is also relevant to note the impact of obesity on the living kidney donor pool and the acceptance of organs from obese subjects. In the former, there is a risk for the donor and recipient, since a mass reduction in an obese subject puts them at risk for future ESKD and in the latter, delayed graft function is more frequent if the donor is obese. According to KDIGO recommendations, an individualized decision should be made for a living donor if the BMI > 30 kg/m^2 due to the risk for future development of hypertension, diabetes as well as ESKD [82].

2.7. Renal Cancer

Obesity has been associated with an increased risk of kidney malignancy. Several studies have concluded the increment of risk associated with obesity and it has been estimated that 20% of renal cancer patients were obese. The risk of kidney cancer was increased by 35% in overweight participants and by 76% in obese subjects in comparison to normal weight participants, irrespective of the gender [83]. The association is consistent in both sexes and across populations; however, no clear explanation for the pathogenesis has been found.

2.8. Fatty Kidney

Accumulation of ectopic fat in the kidney is receiving more attention in the last years and will increase with the development of techniques that allow for a better estimation than the classical echography and CT-scan. Apart from intra-renal accumulation in the proximal tubule and in minor grade in the glomeruli, fat in the renal sinus and around the renal capsule seems to play a role in the renal dysfunction of the obese patient. Renal sinus fat has been associated with CKD in the Framingham Heart Study [84]. Moreover, perirenal fat seems to produce lipotoxic effects on the kidney, increasing the glomerular hydrostatic pressure and the activity of the renin-angiotensin-aldosterone system, contributing to the progression of kidney damage [85].

2.9. Other Obesity-Associated Conditions and Renal Damage

Two frequent complications of obesity seem to further increase the risk of renal damage. First is sleep-apnea and nocturnal hypoxemia, which have been associated with loss of kidney function through activation of the renin-angiotensin system [86]. Second is non-alcoholic fatty liver disease (NAFLD). In a meta-analysis of 33 studies, NAFLD, non-alcoholic steatohepatitis, and advanced fibrosis were associated with an increased risk of prevalence and incidence of CKD, with a graded risk from the presence to the severity of NAFLD [87].

3. Treatment of Obesity and Renal Damage

Losing weight is key in limiting the impact that obesity produces on the kidneys by reducing albuminuria/proteinuria, declining rate of eGFR deterioration, delaying the development of CKD and ESKD and improving the outcome of a renal transplant. The resulting effects due to weight reduction are multiple. Aside from a reduction in BP as well as control of other CV risk factors, reduction of leptin, glomerular hyperfiltration, RAAS activity, inflammation, and oxidative stress seem to be the most relevant. Considering the characteristic hyperfiltration hemodynamic profile and the relevance of hyperfiltration-mediated conditions in obesity-induced renal damage, reduction in filtration fraction is the main mechanism that provides a beneficial impact to the subject who has lost weight. In addition, a reduction in the activity of the RAAS has also been observed [88]. Weight reduction may also contribute to appropriate control of cardiometabolic risk factors such as hypertension, metabolic syndrome, diabetes, and dyslipidemia which may be protective not only in renal damage but also cardiovascular disease [89].

3.1. *Life Style Intervention*

Patients with obesity, particularly those with markers of renal injury (albuminuria/ tubular markers or eGFR < 60 mL/min/1.73 m^2), need to be encouraged to lose weight through a combination of diet and physical exercise. If addressed early, a low-calorie diet, with or without physical exercise, is able to reduce albuminuria with a decrease being proportional to the reduced weight. Weight loss achieved through a combination of diet and exercise has also had beneficial effects on the reduction in urinary protein excretion. After diet introduction, it is possible to observe UAE reduction in a few weeks. In a control trial, which lasted for five months, a 4% weight reduction decreased proteinuria in around 50% of subjects [90]. However, data on slowing the progression to CKD were less documented due to difficulties in assessing the outcomes [91,92] and the short-term duration of the studies [55].

A low-calorie diet with salt restriction is recommended since it can contribute to BP reduction [55]. Further salt intake reduction should be implemented if proteinuria is present. Addition of fibre in the diet promotes growth of short-chain fatty acid producing bacteria that have been demonstrated to reduce all-cause mortality in CKD [93] and there seem to be promising results regarding preclinical CKD risk [94]. A high-protein diet is not recommended since it increases GFR and UAE.

A recent manuscript reviewed the randomized clinical trials of lifestyle intervention in patients with CKD [55]. Diet intervention with low-calorie and salt restriction reduce weight and albuminuria; however, no convincing data exist for other specific dietary pattern such as low fat, low carbohydrate, or a Mediterranean diet. Studies performed on the impact of physical exercise demonstrated a reduction in BP, BMI, and improvement in exercise capacity and quality of life; however, no reduction in albuminuria was observed. The limitation of losing weight with lifestyle is that the maximal reduction achieved is 3 to 4% and the maintenance overtime is poor, therefore other additional actions need to be implemented.

3.2. *Medications*

RAAS blockers

In the presence of albuminuria or proteinuria, RAAS blockers should be prescribed to reduce not only the overactivity of the system but also the sympathetic overactivity, HTN, insulin resistance, and low-grade inflammation. The most important effect is to reduce the filtration fraction and consequently albuminuria; however, in CKD patients the reduction in eGFR should be monitored after starting treatment.

Antiobese-drugs

Of the drugs approved for treatment of obesity, Phentermine-Topiramate, GLP-1 receptor agonist, and Bupropion-Naltresone, mainly data about the impact on renal function is available for the GLP1 agonist. This class of drug has been tested for renal protection in diabetic patients. Liraglutide, a GLP1 agonist, introduced initially as a glucose-lowering drug with impact in body-weight, is able to reduce weight and in a recent trial, LEADER, demonstrated reduction in CV risk [95]. A significant decrease in albuminuria, new onset of persistent proteinuria, and no progression of eGFR decline have been reported in diabetic patients. SUSTAIN-6 with semaglutide [96], another member of the GLP1 agonist class, reduces the risk of composite renal outcome largely driven by persistent proteinuria. However, Dulaglutide in the AWARD-7 [97] did not find differences in the reduction of albuminuria. Topiramate in one study did not demonstrate a beneficial impact on renal outcomes in Type 2 diabetes. Lorcaserin, a selective serotonin 2C receptor, in high cardiovascular risk patients, offered a reduced rate of renal impairment in comparison with placebo [98]. The beneficial impact of GLP1 is that it may protect the kidney from progression to CKD and/or ESKD.

Sodium-glucose cotransporter 2 inhibitors

Sodium-glucose cotransporter 2 inhibitor (SGLT2i) is a class of drug released in the last years with a mechanism that produces various beneficial effects in patients with diabetes, obesity, and cardio and renal protection. Inhibition of glucose reabsorption in the proximal tubule produce glucosuria, reducing the caloric burden and the sodium content with reduction of blood volume, and increasing the sodium arrival to the yuxtaglomerular corpus, inhibiting the hyperactivity of the renal angiotensin system and reducing the filtration fraction, giving protection to the kidney [99]. As a consequence, slightly reduced weight, reduced BP, and the GFR that results can protect of renal function at large. Additional mechanisms in NH3, sympathetic activity, and oxidative stress with beneficial effects complete a frame of a very useful drug. Several outcome trials supported the beneficial impact of the drug in the cardiovascular and renal outcomes [100–103]. The last European of Society of Cardiology and the European Society of Diabetes (ESC/EASD) recommended introduction of SGLT2i in the first step of diabetic patients with very high risk or previous cardiovascular events [104]. In patients with obesity associated diabetes, it may be a good choice in order to protect renal function. The same applies in obese subjects with increased urinary albumin excretion or proteinuria. However, in patients with reduced GFR the efficacy of the drug is reduced and the impact on protection is diminished. As GFR < 45 mL/min/1.73 m^2 is almost negligible, it is a challenge to their use. The beneficial impact observed in patients with GFR between 30–45 mL/min/1.73 m^2 in trials and the absence of side effect point to their use off-label [105].

3.3. Bariatric Surgery

Bariatric surgery, also so-called metabolic surgery, refers to methods used to reduce obesity and improve metabolic abnormalities. The most used techniques are the vertical sleeve gastrectomy, Roux-en-Y gastric bypass, adjustable gastric banding, and biliopancreatic diversion/duodenal switch. Selection of the most appropriate procedure needs to consider not only the morbidity/mortality risk during the procedures but also the potential side effects during follow-up [82]. The surgical treatment of obesity improved management of diabetic and non-diabetic CKD and reduced the rate of renal decline toward ESKD. Once ESKD is established, absolute event rates are low and although complications can be present, it remains a safe intervention. Implementing one of the above surgeries pre-transplant increases the potential access to transplantation and, in addition, improves the management of metabolic complications post-transplantation, including new-onset diabetes. Likewise, this may be beneficial as a treatment for potential obese donors [82].

A beneficial impact on obese patients with type 2 diabetes in kidney protection has been emphasized. A large metanalysis concluded that post-surgical reduction in albuminuria is independent of the changes in BMI, HbA1c, and systolic BP [106]. In non-diabetic subjects, randomized studies are not available, but many observational studies have demonstrated the beneficial impact in reducing incidence of albuminuria and the risk for ESKD after an 18 year follow-up [107]. In CKD patients, at the end of the first year post-surgery [108] and after 7 years of follow-up, improvement in the categories of CKD were observed in around half of the patients, and even in patients with very high risk at baseline a quarter of them improved [109].

In patients with ESKD in dialysis, before kidney transplantation, bariatric surgery had a reduction in mortality, incidence of diabetes, and around 60% of cardiac diseases. The preferred method in dialysis patients is the laparoscopic sleeve gastrectomy in which results are more effective with less complications and with the additional advantage of not interfering with pharmacokinetics of immunosuppression drugs [110].

Increment in the incidence of kidney stones has been reported associated with bariatric surgery. Among the factors that contribute to this association are the decrease in urinary volume and citrate, the increased urinary oxalate, and the calcium oxalate saturation. Procedure selection may be critical to mitigate the risks of oxalate nephropathy since more restrictive procedures reduce the risk [111].

4. Conclusions

The impact of obesity on the kidney has received attention after the recognition that BMI is the second most important marker in developing ESKD after proteinuria and one of the most relevant associated with the presence of CKD, since obesity is frequently associated with hypertension, metabolic syndrome, and diabetes. An important impact on subjects with renal replacement therapy and renal transplantation is also present. The pathologic lesions included a characteristic glomerulopathy coupled with cellular fat load and perivascular fat deposit as well as so-called fatty kidney with fat deposits in the perirenal and renal sinus. The mechanisms linking obesity and renal damage are well understood, including several effector mechanisms with interconnected pathways. In the presence of an increment in urinary albumin excretion, it is mandatory to take action in order to reduce overweight and to control hypertension, diabetes, and dyslipidemia to further prevent GFR reduction.

Author Contributions: Conceptualization, V.K. and J.R.; methodology, V.K. and J.R.; resources F.M. and C.T.; writing, V.K. and F.M.; review and editing, C.T., F.M., V.K. and J.R.; supervision, V.K. and J.R. All authors have read and agreed to the published version of the manuscript.

Funding: This research received no external funding.

Institutional Review Board Statement: Not applicable.

Informed Consent Statement: Not applicable.

Data Availability Statement: Not applicable.

Acknowledgments: The study was partially funded by CIBER Fisiopatología Obesidad y Nutrición (CB06/03), Instituto de Salud Carlos III, Spain; supported by grant numbers PI11/00144 and PI14/01781, Instituto de Salud Carlos III.

Conflicts of Interest: The authors declare no conflict of interest.

Abbreviations

MC3R: melanocortin 3 receptor, MC4R: melanocortin 4 receptor, aMSH: Melanocyte Stimulating Hormone, ARC: Arcuate nucleus, NPY: Neuropeptide Y, AgRP: Agouti-related peptide, POMC: Pro-opiomelanocortin, SNS: sympathetic nervous system, NO: Nitric oxide, ET: endothelin, VCAM-1: vascular cell adhesion molecule 1, ICAM-1: intercellular adhesion molecule 1, PAI-1: Plasminogen activator inhibitor-1, TXA2: Thromboxane A2, IL: interleukin, CRP: c reactive protein, TNF: tumor necrosis factor, ROS: Reactive oxygen species, FFA: free fatty acids, Na: sodium, GFR: glomerular filtration rate, TMAO: Trimethylamine N-oxide, RAS: renin angiotensin system, SCFAs: short-chain fatty acids.

References

1. Go, A.S.; Chertow, G.M.; Fan, D.; McCulloch, C.E.; Hsu, C.-Y. Chronic Kidney Disease and the Risks of Death, Cardiovascular Events, and Hospitalization. *N. Engl. J. Med.* **2004**, *351*, 1296–1305. [CrossRef]
2. Matsushita, K.; Van Der Velde, M.; Astor, B.C.; Woodward, M.; Levey, A.S.; De Jong, P.E.; Coresh, J.; Gansevoort, R.T. Association of estimated glomerular filtration rate and albuminuria with all-cause and cardiovascular mortality in general population cohorts: A collaborative meta-analysis. *Lancet* **2010**, *375*, 2073–2081. [CrossRef]
3. Nitsch, D.; Grams, M.; Sang, Y.; Black, C.; Cirillo, M.; Djurdjev, O.; Iseki, K.; Jassal, S.K.; Kimm, H.; Kronenberg, F.; et al. Associations of estimated glomerular filtration rate and albuminuria with mortality and renal failure by sex: A meta-analysis. *BMJ* **2013**, *346*, f324. [CrossRef]

4. Murphy, D.; McCulloch, C.E.; Lin, F.; Banerjee, T.; Bragg-Gresham, J.L.; Eberhardt, M.S.; Morgenstern, H.; Pavkov, M.E.; Saran, R.; Powe, N.R.; et al. Trends in Prevalence of Chronic Kidney Disease in the United States. *Ann. Intern. Med.* **2016**, *165*, 473–481. [CrossRef]
5. Hounkpatin, H.O.; Harris, S.; Fraser, S.D.S.; Day, J.; Mindell, J.S.; Taal, M.W.; O'Donoghue, D.; Roderick, P.J. Prevalence of chronic kidney disease in adults in England: Comparison of nationally representative cross-sectional surveys from 2003 to 2016. *BMJ Open* **2020**, *10*, e038423. [CrossRef] [PubMed]
6. Iseki, K.; Ikemiya, Y.; Kinjo, K.; Inoue, T.; Iseki, C.; Takishita, S. Body mass index and the risk of development of end-stage renal disease in a screened cohort. *Kidney Int.* **2004**, *65*, 1870–1876. [CrossRef]
7. Polemiti, E.; Baudry, J.; Kuxhaus, O.; Jäger, S.; Bergmann, M.M.; Weikert, C.; Schulze, M.B. BMI and BMI change following incident type 2 diabetes and risk of microvascular and macrovascular complications: The EPIC-Potsdam study. *Diabetologia* **2021**, *64*, 814–825. [CrossRef] [PubMed]
8. Stengel, B.; Tarver–Carr, M.E.; Powe, N.R.; Eberhardt, M.S.; Brancati, F.L. Lifestyle Factors, Obesity and the Risk of Chronic Kidney Disease. *Epidemiology* **2003**, *14*, 479–487. [CrossRef] [PubMed]
9. Othman, M.; Kawar, B.; El Nahas, A.M. Influence of Obesity on Progression of Non-Diabetic Chronic Kidney Disease: A Retrospective Cohort Study. *Nephron* **2009**, *113*, c16–c23. [CrossRef]
10. Nowak, K.L.; You, Z.; Gitomer, B.; Brosnahan, G.; Torres, V.E.; Chapman, A.B.; Perrone, R.D.; Steinman, T.I.; Abebe, K.Z.; Rahbari-Oskoui, F.F.; et al. Overweight and Obesity Are Predictors of Progression in Early Autosomal Dominant Polycystic Kidney Disease. *J. Am. Soc. Nephrol.* **2017**, *29*, 571–578. [CrossRef]
11. Brown, R.N.; Mohsen, A.; Green, D.; Hoefield, R.A.; Summers, L.K.; Middleton, R.J.; O'Donoghue, D.J.; Kalra, P.A.; New, D.I. Body mass index has no effect on rate of progression of chronic kidney disease in non-diabetic subjects. *Nephrol. Dial. Transplant.* **2012**, *27*, 2776–2780. [CrossRef]
12. Garofalo, C.; Borrelli, S.; Minutolo, R.; Chiodini, P.; De Nicola, L.; Conte, G. A systematic review and meta-analysis suggests obesity predicts onset of chronic kidney disease in the general population. *Kidney Int.* **2017**, *91*, 1224–1235. [CrossRef]
13. Chen, J.; Muntner, P.; Hamm, L.L.; Jones, D.W.; Batuman, V.; Fonseca, V.; Whelton, P.K.; He, J. The metabolic syndrome and chronic kidney disease in U.S. adults. *Ann. Intern. Med.* **2004**, *140*, 167–174. [CrossRef]
14. Palaniappan, L.; Carnethon, M.; Fortmann, S.P. Association between microalbuminuria and the metabolic syndrome: NHANES III. *Am. J. Hypertens.* **2003**, *16*, 952–958. [CrossRef]
15. Chen, J.; Gu, D.; Chen, C.-S.; Wu, X.; Hamm, L.L.; Muntner, P.; Batuman, V.; Lee, C.-H.; Whelton, P.K.; He, J. Association between the metabolic syndrome and chronic kidney disease in Chinese adults. *Nephrol. Dial. Transplant.* **2007**, *22*, 1100–1106. [CrossRef]
16. Tanaka, H.; Shiohira, Y.; Uezu, Y.; Higa, A.; Iseki, K. Metabolic syndrome and chronic kidney disease in Okinawa, Japan. *Kidney Int.* **2006**, *69*, 369–374. [CrossRef] [PubMed]
17. Chang, I.; Han, J.H.; Myung, S.C.; Kwak, K.W.; Kim, T.-H.; Park, S.W.; Choi, N.Y.; Chung, W.H.; Ahn, S.H. Association between metabolic syndrome and chronic kidney disease in the Korean population. *Nephrology* **2009**, *14*, 321–326. [CrossRef]
18. Ryu, S.; Chang, Y.; Woo, H.-Y.; Lee, K.-B.; Kim, S.-G.; Kim, D.-I.; Kim, W.S.; Suh, B.-S.; Jeong, C.; Yoon, K. Time-Dependent Association Between Metabolic Syndrome and Risk of CKD in Korean Men Without Hypertension or Diabetes. *Am. J. Kidney Dis.* **2009**, *53*, 59–69. [CrossRef] [PubMed]
19. Kurella, M.; Lo, J.C.; Chertow, G.M. Metabolic Syndrome and the Risk for Chronic Kidney Disease among Nondiabetic Adults. *J. Am. Soc. Nephrol.* **2005**, *16*, 2134–2140. [CrossRef]
20. Yang, T.; Chu, C.-H.; Hsu, C.-H.; Hsieh, P.-C.; Chung, T.-C.; Bai, C.-H.; You, S.-L.; Hwang, L.-C.; Lin, C.-M.; Sun, C.-A. Impact of metabolic syndrome on the incidence of chronic kidney disease: A Chinese cohort study. *Nephrology* **2012**, *17*, 532–538. [CrossRef] [PubMed]
21. Ninomiya, T.; Kiyohara, Y.; Kubo, M.; Yonemoto, K.; Tanizaki, Y.; Doi, Y.; Hirakata, H.; Iida, M. Metabolic Syndrome and CKD in a General Japanese Population: The Hisayama Study. *Am. J. Kidney Dis.* **2006**, *48*, 383–391. [CrossRef] [PubMed]
22. Lucove, J.; Vupputuri, S.; Heiss, G.; North, K.; Russell, M. Metabolic Syndrome and the Development of CKD in American Indians: The Strong Heart Study. *Am. J. Kidney Dis.* **2008**, *51*, 21–28. [CrossRef]
23. Sun, F.; Tao, Q.; Zhan, S. Metabolic syndrome and the development of chronic kidney disease among 118 924 non-diabetic Taiwanese in a retrospective cohort. *Nephrology* **2010**, *15*, 84–92. [CrossRef] [PubMed]
24. Thomas, G.; Sehgal, A.R.; Kashyap, S.R.; Srinivas, T.R.; Kirwan, J.P.; Navaneethan, S.D. Metabolic Syndrome and Kidney Disease: A Systematic Review and Meta-analysis. *Clin. J. Am. Soc. Nephrol.* **2011**, *6*, 2364–2373. [CrossRef]
25. Rashidbeygi, E.; Safabakhsh, M.; Aghdam, S.D.; Mohammed, S.H.; Alizadeh, S. Metabolic syndrome and its components are related to a higher risk for albuminuria and proteinuria: Evidence from a meta-analysis on 10,603,067 subjects from 57 studies. *Diabetes Metab. Syndr. Clin. Res. Rev.* **2018**, *13*, 830–843. [CrossRef] [PubMed]
26. França, A.K.T.D.C.; Dos Santos, A.M.; Salgado, J.V.; Hortegal, E.V.; Da Silva, A.A.M.; Filho, N.S. Estimated Visceral Adipose Tissue, but Not Body Mass Index, Is Associated with Reductions in Glomerular Filtration Rate Based on Cystatin C in the Early Stages of Chronic Kidney Disease. *Int. J. Nephrol.* **2014**, *2014*, 574267. [CrossRef]
27. Kittiskulnam, P.; Thokanit, N.S.; Katavetin, P.; Susanthitaphong, P.; Srisawat, N.; Praditpornsilpa, K.; Tungsanga, K.; Eiam-Ong, S. The magnitude of obesity and metabolic syndrome among diabetic chronic kidney disease population: A nationwide study. *PLoS ONE* **2018**, *13*, e0196332. [CrossRef]

28. Zammit, A.R.; Katz, M.J.; Derby, C.; Bitzer, M.; Lipton, R.B. Chronic Kidney Disease in Non-Diabetic Older Adults: Associated Roles of the Metabolic Syndrome, Inflammation, and Insulin Resistance. *PLoS ONE* **2015**, *10*, e0139369. [CrossRef] [PubMed]
29. Yun, H.-R.; Kim, H.; Park, J.T.; Chang, T.I.; Yoo, T.-H.; Kang, S.-W.; Choi, K.H.; Sung, S.; Kim, S.W.; Lee, J.; et al. Obesity, Metabolic Abnormality, and Progression of CKD. *Am. J. Kidney Dis.* **2018**, *72*, 400–410. [CrossRef]
30. Chen, H.-Y.; Lu, F.-H.; Chang, C.-J.; Wang, R.-S.; Yang, Y.-C.; Chang, Y.-F.; Wu, J.-S. Metabolic abnormalities, but not obesity per se, associated with chronic kidney disease in a Taiwanese population. *Nutr. Metab. Cardiovasc. Dis.* **2020**, *30*, 418–425. [CrossRef]
31. Adair, K.E.; Bowden, R.G.; Funderburk, L.K.; Forsse, J.S.; Ylitalo, K.R. Metabolic Health, Obesity, and Renal Function: 2013–2018 National Health and Nutrition Examination Surveys. *Life* **2021**, *11*, 888. [CrossRef] [PubMed]
32. Rocchini, A.P. Obesity hypertension*1. *Am. J. Hypertens.* **2002**, *15*, S50–S52. [CrossRef]
33. Kotsis, V.; Stabouli, S.; Papakatsika, S.; Rizos, Z.; Parati, G. Mechanisms of obesity-induced hypertension. *Hypertens. Res.* **2010**, *33*, 386–393. [CrossRef]
34. Hall, J.E.; Crook, E.D.; Jones, D.W.; Wofford, M.R.; Dubbert, P.M. Mechanisms of Obesity-Associated Cardiovascular and Renal Disease. *Am. J. Med. Sci.* **2002**, *324*, 127–137. [CrossRef] [PubMed]
35. Kambham, N.; Markowitz, G.S.; Valeri, A.M.; Lin, J.; D'Agati, V.D. Obesity-related glomerulopathy: An emerging epidemic. *Kidney Int.* **2001**, *59*, 1498–1509. [CrossRef]
36. Deji, N.; Kume, S.; Araki, S.-I.; Soumura, M.; Sugimoto, T.; Isshiki, K.; Chin-Kanasaki, M.; Sakaguchi, M.; Koya, D.; Haneda, M.; et al. Structural and functional changes in the kidneys of high-fat diet-induced obese mice. *Am. J. Physiol. Renal. Physiol.* **2009**, *296*, F118–F126. [CrossRef] [PubMed]
37. Serra, A.; Romero, R.; Lopez, D.; Navarro, M.; Esteve, A.; Perez, N.; Alastrue, A.; Ariza, A. Renal injury in the extremely obese patients with normal renal function. *Kidney Int.* **2008**, *73*, 947–955. [CrossRef] [PubMed]
38. Alexander, M.P.; Patel, T.V.; Farag, Y.M.; Florez, A.; Rennke, H.G.; Singh, A.K. Kidney pathological changes in metabolic syndrome: A Cross-sectional Study. *Am. J. Kidney Dis.* **2009**, *53*, 751–759. [CrossRef]
39. Redon, J.; Lurbe, E. The Kidney in Obesity. *Curr. Hypertens. Rep.* **2015**, *17*, 43. [CrossRef]
40. Kotsis, V.; Jordan, J.; Micic, D.; Finer, N.; Leitner, D.R.; Toplak, H.; Tokgozoglu, L.; Athyros, V.; Elisaf, M.; Filippatos, T.D.; et al. Obesity and cardiovascular risk. *J. Hypertens.* **2018**, *36*, 1427–1440. [CrossRef] [PubMed]
41. Antza, C.; Stabouli, S.; Kotsis, V. Gut microbiota in kidney disease and hypertension. *Pharmacol. Res.* **2018**, *130*, 198–203. [CrossRef] [PubMed]
42. Groop, P.-H.; Forsblom, C.; Thomas, M.C. Mechanisms of Disease: Pathway-selective insulin resistance and microvascular complications of diabetes. *Nat. Clin. Pract. Endocrinol. Metab.* **2005**, *1*, 100–110. [CrossRef]
43. Dronavalli, S.; Duka, I.; Bakris, G.L. The pathogenesis of diabetic nephropathy. *Nat. Clin. Pract. Endocrinol. Metab.* **2008**, *4*, 444–452. [CrossRef] [PubMed]
44. De Cosmo, S.; Menzaghi, C.; Prudente, S.; Trischitta, V. Role of insulin resistance in kidney dysfunction: Insights into the mechanism and epidemiological evidence. *Nephrol. Dial. Transplant.* **2012**, *28*, 29–36. [CrossRef]
45. Wolf, G.; Chen, S.; Han, D.C.; Ziyadeh, F.N. Leptin and renal disease. *Am. J. Kidney Dis.* **2002**, *39*, 1–11. [CrossRef]
46. Rutkowski, J.M.; Wang, Z.V.; Park, A.S.D.; Zhang, J.; Zhang, D.; Hu, M.C.; Moe, O.W.; Susztak, K.; Scherer, P.E. Adiponectin Promotes Functional Recovery after Podocyte Ablation. *J. Am. Soc. Nephrol.* **2013**, *24*, 268–282. [CrossRef] [PubMed]
47. Przybyciński, J.; Dziedziejko, V.; Puchałowicz, K.; Domański, L.; Pawlik, A. Adiponectin in Chronic Kidney Disease. *Int. J. Mol. Sci.* **2020**, *21*, 9375. [CrossRef]
48. Axelsson, J.; Bergsten, A.; Qureshi, A.; Heimbürger, O.; Bárány, P.; Lönnqvist, F.; Lindholm, B.; Nordfors, L.; Alvestrand, A.; Stenvinkel, P. Elevated resistin levels in chronic kidney disease are associated with decreased glomerular filtration rate and inflammation, but not with insulin resistance. *Kidney Int.* **2006**, *69*, 596–604. [CrossRef]
49. Ellington, A.A.; Malik, A.R.; Klee, G.G.; Turner, S.T.; Rule, A.D.; Mosley, J.T.H.; Kullo, I.J. Association of plasma resistin with glomerular filtration rate and albuminuria in hypertensive adults. *Hypertension* **2007**, *50*, 708–714. [CrossRef]
50. Seliger, S.L.; Salimi, S.; Pierre, V.; Giffuni, J.; Katzel, L.; Parsa, A. Microvascular endothelial dysfunction is associated with albuminuria and CKD in older adults. *BMC Nephrol.* **2016**, *17*, 82. [CrossRef]
51. Rajapakse, N.W.; Karim, F.; Straznicky, N.E.; Fernandez, S.; Evans, R.; Head, G.; Kaye, D.M. Augmented endothelial-specific L-arginine transport prevents obesity-induced hypertension. *Acta Physiol.* **2014**, *212*, 39–48. [CrossRef]
52. Gruber, H.-J.; Mayer, C.; Mangge, H.; Fauler, G.; Grandits, N.; Wilders-Truschnig, M. Obesity reduces the bioavailability of nitric oxide in juveniles. *Int. J. Obes.* **2008**, *32*, 826–831. [CrossRef] [PubMed]
53. Rajapakse, N.; Head, G.; Kaye, D.M. Say NO to obesity-related hypertension: Role of the l-arginine–nitric oxide pathway. *Hypertension* **2016**, *67*, 813–819. [CrossRef] [PubMed]
54. Sharma, D.; Hawkins, M.; Abramowitz, M.K. Association of sarcopenia with eGFR and misclassification of obesity in adults with CKD in the United States. *Clin. J. Am. Soc. Nephrol.* **2014**, *9*, 2079–2088. [CrossRef] [PubMed]
55. Chintam, K.; Chang, A.R. Strategies to Treat Obesity in Patients with CKD. *Am. J. Kidney Dis.* **2021**, *77*, 427–439. [CrossRef] [PubMed]
56. Chen, B.; Yang, D.; Chen, Y.; Xu, W.; Ye, B.; Ni, Z. The prevalence of microalbuminuria and its relationships with the components of metabolic syndrome in the general population of China. *Clin. Chim. Acta* **2010**, *411*, 705–709. [CrossRef]

57. Thoenes, M.; Reil, J.C.; Khan, B.V.; Bramlage, P.; Volpe, M.; Kirch, W.; Böhm, M. Abdominal obesity is associated with microalbuminuria and an elevated cardiovascular risk profile in patients with hypertension. *Vasc. Health Risk Manag.* **2009**, *5*, 577–585. [CrossRef] [PubMed]
58. Chandie Shaw, P.K.C.; Berger, S.P.; Mallat, M.; Frölich, M.; Dekker, F.; Rabelink, T.J. Central Obesity Is an Independent Risk Factor for Albuminuria in Nondiabetic South Asian Subjects. *Diabetes Care* **2007**, *30*, 1840–1844. [CrossRef] [PubMed]
59. Du, N.; Peng, H.; Chao, X.; Zhang, Q.; Tian, H.; Li, H. Interaction of obesity and central obesity on elevated urinary albumin-to-creatinine ratio. *PLoS ONE* **2014**, *9*, e98926. [CrossRef]
60. Lurbe, E.; Torro, M.I.; Alvarez, J.; Aguilar, F.; Fernandez-Formoso, J.A.; Redon, J. Prevalence and factors related to urinary albumin excretion in obese youths. *J. Hypertens.* **2013**, *31*, 2230–2236. [CrossRef] [PubMed]
61. Xiao, N.; Jenkins, T.M.; Nehus, E.; Inge, T.H.; Michalsky, M.; Harmon, C.M.; Helmrath, M.A.; Brandt, M.L.; Courcoulas, A.; Moxey-Mims, M.; et al. Kidney function in severely obese adolescents undergoing bariatric surgery. *Obesity* **2014**, *22*, 2319–2325. [CrossRef]
62. Goknar, N.; Öktem, F.; Özgen, I.T.; Torun, E.; Kucukkoc, M.; Demir, A.D.; Cesur, Y. Determination of early urinary renal injury markers in obese children. *Pediatr. Nephrol.* **2014**, *30*, 139–144. [CrossRef] [PubMed]
63. Lakkis, J.I.; Weir, M.R. Obesity and Kidney Disease. *Prog. Cardiovasc. Dis.* **2018**, *61*, 157–167. [CrossRef] [PubMed]
64. Hernández-Conde, M.; Llop, E.; Carrillo, C.F.; Tormo, B.; Abad, J.; Rodriguez, L.; Perelló, C.; Gomez, M.L.; Martínez-Porras, J.L.; Puga, N.F.; et al. Estimation of visceral fat is useful for the diagnosis of significant fibrosis in patients with non-alcoholic fatty liver disease. *World J. Gastroenterol.* **2020**, *26*, 6658–6668. [CrossRef] [PubMed]
65. D'Agati, V.D.; Chagnac, A.; de Vries, A.; Levi, M.; Porrini, E.; Herman-Edelstein, M.; Praga, M. Obesity-related glomerulopathy: Clinical and pathologic characteristics and pathogenesis. *Nat. Rev. Nephrol.* **2016**, *12*, 453–471. [CrossRef]
66. Fox, C.S.; Larson, M.; Leip, E.P.; Culleton, B.; Wilson, P.W.F.; Levy, D. Predictors of new-onset kidney disease in a community-based population. *JAMA* **2004**, *291*, 844–850. [CrossRef] [PubMed]
67. Ejerblad, E.; Fored, C.M.; Lindblad, P.; Fryzek, J.; McLaughlin, J.K.; Nyrén, O. Obesity and risk for chronic renal failure. *J. Am. Soc. Nephrol.* **2006**, *17*, 1695–1702. [CrossRef] [PubMed]
68. Chang, A.R.; Grams, M.E.; Ballew, S.; Bilo, H.; Correa, A.; Evans, M.; Gutierrez, O.M.; Hosseinpanah, F.; Iseki, K.; Kenealy, T.; et al. Adiposity and risk of decline in glomerular filtration rate: Meta-analysis of individual participant data in a global consortium. *BMJ* **2019**, *364*, k5301. [CrossRef]
69. Gurusinghe, S.; Brown, R.D.; Cai, X.; Samuel, C.S.; Ricardo, S.D.; Thomas, M.C.; Kett, M.M. Does a nephron deficit exacerbate the renal and cardiovascular effects of obesity? *PLoS ONE* **2013**, *8*, e73095. [CrossRef] [PubMed]
70. Hashimoto, Y.; Tanaka, M.; Okada, H.; Senmaru, T.; Hamaguchi, M.; Asano, M.; Yamazaki, M.; Oda, Y.; Hasegawa, G.; Toda, H.; et al. Metabolically Healthy Obesity and Risk of Incident CKD. *Clin. J. Am. Soc. Nephrol.* **2015**, *10*, 578–583. [CrossRef]
71. Song, Y.-M.; Sung, J.; Lee, K. Longitudinal relationships of metabolic syndrome and obesity with kidney function: Healthy Twin Study. *Clin. Exp. Nephrol.* **2015**, *19*, 887–894. [CrossRef]
72. Panwar, B.; Hanks, L.J.; Tanner, R.M.; Muntner, P.; Kramer, H.; McClellan, W.M.; Warnock, D.G.; Judd, S.E.; Gutiérrez, O.M. Obesity, metabolic health, and the risk of end-stage renal disease. *Kidney Int.* **2015**, *87*, 1216–1222. [CrossRef]
73. Chen, S.; Zhou, S.; Wu, B.; Zhao, Y.; Liu, X.; Liang, Y.; Shao, X.; Holthöfer, H.; Zou, H. Association between metabolically unhealthy overweight/obesity and chronic kidney disease: The role of inflammation. *Diabetes Metab.* **2014**, *40*, 423–430. [CrossRef] [PubMed]
74. Hsu, C.-Y.; McCulloch, C.E.; Iribarren, C.; Darbinian, J.; Go, A.S. Body mass index and risk for end-stage renal disease. *Ann. Intern. Med.* **2006**, *144*, 21–28. [CrossRef]
75. Zitt, E.; Pscheidt, C.; Concin, H.; Kramar, R.; Lhotta, K.; Nagel, G. Anthropometric and metabolic risk factors for ESRD are disease-specific: Results from a large population-based cohort study in Austria. *PLoS ONE* **2016**, *11*, e0161376. [CrossRef] [PubMed]
76. Fritz, J.; Brozek, W.; Concin, H.; Nagel, G.; Kerschbaum, J.; Lhotta, K.; Ulmer, H.; Zitt, E. The Triglyceride-Glucose Index and Obesity-Related Risk of End-Stage Kidney Disease in Austrian Adults. *JAMA Netw. Open* **2021**, *4*, e212612. [CrossRef] [PubMed]
77. Lu, J.L.; Molnar, M.Z.; Naseer, A.; Mikkelsen, M.K.; Kalantar-Zadeh, K.; Kovesdy, C.P. Association of age and BMI with kidney function and mortality: A cohort study. *Lancet Diabetes Endocrinol.* **2015**, *3*, 704–714. [CrossRef]
78. Swartling, O.; Rydell, H.; Stendahl, M.; Segelmark, M.; Lagerros, Y.T.; Evans, M. CKD Progression and Mortality among Men and Women: A Nationwide Study in Sweden. *Am. J. Kidney Dis.* **2021**, *78*, 190–199.e1. [CrossRef]
79. Siener, R.; Glatz, S.; Nicolay, C.; Hesse, A. The Role of Overweight and Obesity in Calcium Oxalate Stone Formation. *Obes. Res.* **2004**, *12*, 106–113. [CrossRef] [PubMed]
80. Diwan, T.S.; Cuffy, M.C.; Linares-Cervantes, I.; Govil, A. Impact of obesity on dialysis and transplant and its management. *Semin. Dial.* **2020**, *33*, 279–285. [CrossRef]
81. Kittiskulnam, P.; Johansen, K.L. The obesity paradox: A further consideration in dialysis patients. *Semin. Dial.* **2019**, *32*, 485–489. [CrossRef] [PubMed]
82. Martin, W.P.; White, J.; López-Hernández, F.J.; Docherty, N.G.; Le Roux, C.W. Metabolic Surgery to Treat Obesity in Diabetic Kidney Disease, Chronic Kidney Disease, and End-Stage Kidney Disease; What Are the Unanswered Questions? *Front. Endocrinol.* **2020**, *11*, 289. [CrossRef] [PubMed]
83. Rysz, J.; Franczyk, B.; Ławiński, J.; Olszewski, R.; Gluba-Brzózka, A. The Role of Metabolic Factors in Renal Cancers. *Int. J. Mol. Sci.* **2020**, *21*, 7246. [CrossRef]

84. Foster, M.C.; Hwang, S.-J.; Porter, S.A.; Massaro, J.; Hoffmann, U.; Fox, C.S. Fatty Kidney, Hypertension, and Chronic Kidney Disease: The Framingham Heart Study. *Hypertension* **2011**, *58*, 784–790. [CrossRef]
85. Praga, M.; Morales, E. The Fatty Kidney: Obesity and Renal Disease. *Nephron* **2016**, *136*, 273–276. [CrossRef]
86. Hanly, P.J.; Ahmed, S.B. Sleep Apnea and the Kidney: Is sleep apnea a risk factor for chronic kidney disease? *Chest* **2014**, *146*, 1114–1122. [CrossRef]
87. Musso, G.; Gambino, R.; Tabibian, J.H.; Ekstedt, M.; Kechagias, S.; Hamaguchi, M.; Hultcrantz, R.; Hagström, H.; Yoon, S.K.; Charatcharoenwitthaya, P.; et al. Association of Non-alcoholic Fatty Liver Disease with Chronic Kidney Disease: A Systematic Review and Meta-analysis. *PLoS Med.* **2014**, *11*, e1001680. [CrossRef] [PubMed]
88. Camara, N.; Iseki, K.; Kramer, H.; Liu, Z.-H.; Sharma, K. Kidney disease and obesity: Epidemiology, mechanisms and treatment. *Nat. Rev. Nephrol.* **2017**, *13*, 181–190. [CrossRef]
89. DeBoer, M.D.; Filipp, S.L.; Musani, S.K.; Sims, M.; Okusa, M.D.; Gurka, M.J. Metabolic Syndrome Severity and Risk of CKD and Worsened GFR: The Jackson Heart Study. *Kidney Blood Press. Res.* **2018**, *43*, 555–567. [CrossRef] [PubMed]
90. Morales, E.; Valero, M.A.; León, M.; Hernández, E.; Praga, M. Beneficial effects of weight loss in overweight patients with chronic proteinuric nephropathies. *Am. J. Kidney Dis.* **2003**, *41*, 319–327. [CrossRef] [PubMed]
91. Afshinnia, F.; Wilt, T.J.; Duval, S.; Esmaeili, A.; Ibrahim, H.N. Weight loss and proteinuria: Systematic review of clinical trials and comparative cohorts. *Nephrol. Dial. Transplant.* **2009**, *25*, 1173–1183. [CrossRef] [PubMed]
92. Navaneethan, S.D.; Yehnert, H.; Moustarah, F.; Schreiber, M.J.; Schauer, P.R.; Beddhu, S. Weight Loss Interventions in Chronic Kidney Disease: A Systematic Review and Meta-analysis. *Clin. J. Am. Soc. Nephrol.* **2009**, *4*, 1565–1574. [CrossRef] [PubMed]
93. Krishnamurthy, V.M.R.; Wei, G.; Baird, B.C.; Murtaugh, M.; Chonchol, M.B.; Raphael, K.; Greene, T.; Beddhu, S. High dietary fiber intake is associated with decreased inflammation and all-cause mortality in patients with chronic kidney disease. *Kidney Int.* **2012**, *81*, 300–306. [CrossRef] [PubMed]
94. Vaziri, N.D.; Liu, S.-M.; Lau, W.L.; Khazaeli, M.; Nazertehrani, S.; Farzaneh, S.H.; Kieffer, D.A.; Adams, S.H.; Martin, R.J. High Amylose Resistant Starch Diet Ameliorates Oxidative Stress, Inflammation, and Progression of Chronic Kidney Disease. *PLoS ONE* **2014**, *9*, e114881. [CrossRef] [PubMed]
95. Marso, S.P.; Daniels, G.H.; Brown-Frandsen, K.; Kristensen, P.; Mann, J.F.E.; Nauck, M.A.; Nissen, S.E.; Pocock, S.; Poulter, N.R.; Ravn, L.S.; et al. Liraglutide and Cardiovascular Outcomes in Type 2 Diabetes. *N. Engl. J. Med.* **2016**, *375*, 311–322. [CrossRef]
96. Verma, S.; McGuire, D.K.; Bain, S.C.; Bhatt, D.L.; Leiter, L.A.; Mazer, C.D.; Fries, T.M.; Pratley, R.E.; Rasmussen, S.; Vrazic, H.; et al. Effects of glucagon-like peptide-1 receptor agonists liraglutide and semaglutide on cardiovascular and renal outcomes across body mass index categories in type 2 diabetes: Results of the LEADER and SUSTAIN 6 trials. *Diabetes Obes. Metab.* **2020**, *22*, 2487–2492. [CrossRef] [PubMed]
97. Tuttle, K.; Lakshmanan, M.C.; Rayner, B.; Zimmermann, A.G.; Woodward, D.B.; Botros, F.T. Body weight and eGFR during dulaglutide treatment in type 2 diabetes and moderate-to-severe chronic kidney disease (AWARD-7). *Diabetes Obes. Metab.* **2019**, *21*, 1493–1497. [CrossRef]
98. Scirica, B.M.; Bohula, E.A.; Dwyer, J.P.; Qamar, A.; Inzucchi, S.E.; McGuire, D.K.; Keech, A.C.; Smith, S.R.; Murphy, S.A.; Im, K.; et al. Lorcaserin and Renal Outcomes in Obese and Overweight Patients in the CAMELLIA-TIMI 61 Trial. *Circulation* **2019**, *139*, 366–375. [CrossRef]
99. Janež, A.; Fioretto, P. SGLT2 Inhibitors and the Clinical Implications of Associated Weight Loss in Type 2 Diabetes: A Narrative Review. *Diabetes Ther.* **2021**, *12*, 2249–2261. [CrossRef] [PubMed]
100. Wanner, C.; Inzucchi, S.E.; Lachin, J.; Fitchett, D.; Von Eynatten, M.; Mattheus, M.; Johansen, O.E.; Woerle, H.J.; Broedl, U.C.; Zinman, B.; et al. Empagliflozin and Progression of Kidney Disease in Type 2 Diabetes. *N. Engl. J. Med.* **2016**, *375*, 323–334. [CrossRef]
101. Furtado, R.H.; Bonaca, M.P.; Raz, I.; Zelniker, T.A.; Mosenzon, O.; Cahn, A.; Kuder, J.; Murphy, S.A.; Bhatt, D.L.; Leiter, L.A.; et al. Dapagliflozin and Cardiovascular Outcomes in Patients With Type 2 Diabetes Mellitus and Previous Myocardial Infarction. *Circulation* **2019**, *139*, 2516–2527. [CrossRef] [PubMed]
102. Neal, B.; Perkovic, V.; Mahaffey, K.W.; De Zeeuw, D.; Fulcher, G.; Erondu, N.; Shaw, W.; Law, G.; Desai, M.; Matthews, D.R. Canagliflozin and Cardiovascular and Renal Events in Type 2 Diabetes. *N. Engl. J. Med.* **2017**, *377*, 644–657. [CrossRef] [PubMed]
103. Perkovic, V.; Jardine, M.J.; Neal, B.; Bompoint, S.; Heerspink, H.J.L.; Charytan, D.M.; Edwards, R.; Agarwal, R.; Bakris, G.; Bull, S.; et al. Canagliflozin and Renal Outcomes in Type 2 Diabetes and Nephropathy. *N. Engl. J. Med.* **2019**, *380*, 2295–2306. [CrossRef]
104. Cosentino, F.; Grant, P.J.; Aboyans, V.; Bailey, C.J.; Ceriello, A.; Delgado, V.; Federici, M.; Filippatos, G.; Grobbee, E.D.; Hansen, T.B.; et al. 2019 ESC Guidelines on diabetes, pre-diabetes, and cardiovascular diseases developed in collaboration with the EASD. *Eur. Heart J.* **2020**, *41*, 255–323. [CrossRef] [PubMed]
105. Li, J.; Fagbote, C.O.; Zhuo, M.; Hawley, C.E.; Paik, J.M. Sodium-glucose cotransporter 2 inhibitors for diabetic kidney disease: A primer for deprescribing. *Clin. Kidney J.* **2019**, *12*, 620–628. [CrossRef] [PubMed]
106. Scheurlen, K.M.; Probst, P.; Kopf, S.; Nawroth, P.P.; Billeter, A.T.; Müller-Stich, B.P. Metabolic surgery improves renal injury independent of weight loss: A meta-analysis. *Surg. Obes. Relat. Dis.* **2019**, *15*, 1006–1020. [CrossRef]
107. Shulman, A.; Peltonen, M.; Sjöström, C.D.; Andersson-Assarsson, J.C.; Taube, M.; Sjöholm, K.; Le Roux, C.W.; Carlsson, L.M.S.; Svensson, P.-A. Incidence of end-stage renal disease following bariatric surgery in the Swedish Obese Subjects Study. *Int. J. Obes.* **2018**, *42*, 964–973. [CrossRef] [PubMed]

108. Funes, D.R.; Blanco, D.G.; Gómez, C.O.; Frieder, J.S.; Menzo, E.L.; Szomstein, S.; White, K.P.; Rosenthal, R.J. Metabolic Surgery Reduces the Risk of Progression From Chronic Kidney Disease to Kidney Failure. *Ann. Surg.* **2019**, *270*, 511–518. [CrossRef]
109. Friedman, A.N.; Wahed, A.S.; Wang, J.; Courcoulas, A.P.; Dakin, G.; Hinojosa, M.W.; Kimmel, P.L.; Mitchell, J.E.; Pomp, A.; Pories, W.J.; et al. Effect of Bariatric Surgery on CKD Risk. *J. Am. Soc. Nephrol.* **2018**, *29*, 1289–1300. [CrossRef]
110. Kuo, J.H.; Wong, M.S.; Perez, R.V.; Li, C.-S.; Lin, T.-C.; Troppmann, C. Renal Transplant Wound Complications in the Modern Era of Obesity. *J. Surg. Res.* **2012**, *173*, 216–223. [CrossRef]
111. Abou-Mrad, R.M.; Abu-Alfa, A.K.; Ziyadeh, F.N. Effects of weight reduction regimens and bariatric surgery on chronic kidney disease in obese patients. *Am. J. Physiol. Renal Physiol.* **2013**, *305*, F613–F617. [CrossRef] [PubMed]

nutrients

MDPI

Article

Impact of COVID-19 Lockdown in Eating Disorders: A Multicentre Collaborative International Study

Isabel Baenas [1,2,3,†], Mikel Etxandi [1,†], Lucero Munguía [1,2,3], Roser Granero [2,3,4], Gemma Mestre-Bach [5], Isabel Sánchez [1,2,3], Emilio Ortega [6,7], Alba Andreu [6], Violeta L. Moize [6,7], Jose-Manuel Fernández-Real [2,8,9], Francisco J. Tinahones [2,10], Carlos Diéguez [2,11], Gema Frühbeck [2,12], Daniel Le Grange [13], Kate Tchanturia [14], Andreas Karwautz [15], Michael Zeiler [15], Hartmut Imgart [16], Annika Zanko [16], Angela Favaro [17], Laurence Claes [18,19], Ia Shekriladze [20], Eduardo Serrano-Troncoso [21], Raquel Cecilia-Costa [21], Teresa Rangil [22,23], Maria Eulalia Loran-Meler [22], José Soriano-Pacheco [24,25], Mar Carceller-Sindreu [24,25], Rosa Navarrete [26], Meritxell Lozano [27], Raquel Linares [27], Carlota Gudiol [28,29,30,31], Jordi Carratala [28,29,30,31], Maria T. Plana [25,32,33], Montserrat Graell [25,34], David González-Parra [35], José A. Gómez-del Barrio [25,36,37], Ana R. Sepúlveda [38], Jéssica Sánchez-González [1], Paulo P. P. Machado [39], Anders Håkansson [40,41], Ferenc Túry [42], Bea Pászthy [43], Daniel Stein [44], Hana Papezová [45], Jana Gricova [45], Brigita Bax [46], Mikhail F. Borisenkov [47], Sergey V. Popov [47], Denis G. Gubin [48,49], Ivan M. Petrov [50], Dilara Isakova [51], Svetlana V. Mustafina [52], Youl-Ri Kim [53], Michiko Nakazato [54], Nathalie Godart [55,56,57], Robert van Voren [58], Tetiana Ilnytska [59], Jue Chen [60], Katie Rowlands [14], Ulrich Voderholzer [61], Alessio M. Monteleone [62], Janet Treasure [14], Susana Jiménez-Murcia [1,2,3,30,*] and Fernando Fernández-Aranda [1,2,3,30,*]

1 Department of Psychiatry, Bellvitge University Hospital-IDIBELL, 08907 Barcelona, Spain; ibaenas@bellvitgehospital.cat (I.B.); mikeletxandi@gmail.com (M.E.); laarcreed_lm@hotmail.com (L.M.); isasanchez@bellvitgehospital.cat (I.S.); jsanchezg@bellvitgehospital.cat (J.S.-G.)
2 CIBER Fisiopatología Obesidad y Nutrición (CIBERobn), Instituto de Salud Carlos III, 28029 Barcelona, Spain; Roser.Granero@uab.cat (R.G.); jmfreal@idibgi.org (J.-M.F.-R.); fjtinahones@uma.es (F.J.T.); carlos.dieguez@usc.es (C.D.); gfruhbeck@unav.es (G.F.)
3 Psychoneurobiology of Eating and Addictive Behaviors Group, Neurosciences Programme, Bellvitge Biomedical Research Institute (IDIBELL), 08908 Barcelona, Spain
4 Department of Psychobiology and Methodology, School of Psychology, Universitat Autònoma de Barcelona, 08193 Barcelona, Spain
5 Facultad de Ciencias de la Salud, Universidad Internacional de La Rioja, 26006 La Rioja, Spain; gemma.mestre.bach@gmail.com
6 Endocrinology and Nutrition Division, Hospital Clinic and Institut d'Investigacions Biomèdiques August Pi Sunyer (IDIBAPS), 08036 Barcelona, Spain; eortega1@clinic.cat (E.O.); aandreu@clinic.cat (A.A.); vmoize@clinic.cat (V.L.M.)
7 Centro de Investigación Biomédica en Red de Diabetes y Enfermedades Metabólicas Asociadas (CIBERDEM), 28029 Madrid, Spain
8 Unit of Diabetes, Endocrinology and Nutrition, Hospital de Girona Dr. Josep Trueta-Institut d'Investigació Biomèdica de Girona (IDIBGI), 17007 Girona, Spain
9 Department of Medical Sciences, School of Medicine, University of Girona, 17004 Girona, Spain
10 Department of Endocrinology and Nutrition, Virgen de la Victoria University Hospital-Instituto de Investigación Biomédica de Málaga (IBIMA), 29010 Málaga, Spain
11 Department of Physiology, CIMUS, University of Santiago de Compostela-Instituto de Investigación Sanitaria, 15782 Santiago de Compostela, Spain
12 Metabolic Research Laboratory, Clínica Universidad de Navarra, University of Navarra-IdiSNA, 31008 Pamplona, Spain
13 Eating Disorders Program, Department of Psychiatry, University of California, San Francisco, CA 94143, USA; Daniel.LeGrange@ucsf.edu
14 Section of Eating Disorders, Department of Psychological Medicine, Institute of Psychiatry, Psychology and Neuroscience, King's College London, London WC2R 2LS, UK; kate.tchanturia@kcl.ac.uk (K.T.); katie.rowlands@kcl.ac.uk (K.R.); janet.treasure@kcl.ac.uk (J.T.)
15 Eating Disorders Unit, Department of Child and Adolescent Psychiatry, Medical University of Vienna, 1090 Vienna, Austria; Andreas.karwautz@meduniwien.ac.at (A.K.); michael.zeiler@meduniwien.ac.at (M.Z.)
16 Parkland Klinik, 34537 Bad Wildungen, Germany; Hartmut.imgart@parkland-klinik.de (H.I.); Annika.zanko@parkland-klinik.de (A.Z.)
17 Department of Neuroscience, University of Padua and Neuroscience Center (PNC), 35122 Padua, Italy; angela.favaro@unipd.it

Citation: Baenas, I.; Etxandi, M.; Munguía, L.; Granero, R.; Mestre-Bach, G.; Sánchez, I.; Ortega, E.; Andreu, A.; Moize, V.L.; Fernández-Real, J.-M.; et al. Impact of COVID-19 Lockdown in Eating Disorders: A Multicentre Collaborative International Study. *Nutrients* **2022**, *14*, 100. https://doi.org/10.3390/nu14010100

Academic Editor: Patrick R.M. Lauwers

Received: 29 October 2021
Accepted: 20 December 2021
Published: 27 December 2021

[18] Clinical Psychology, Faculty of Psychology and Educational Sciences, KU Leuven, 3000 Leuven, Belgium; laurence.claes@kuleuven.be
[19] Clinical Psychology, Faculty of Medicine and Health Sciences, University Antwerp, 2000 Antwerp, Belgium
[20] D. Uznadze Institute of Psychology, Ilia State University, 0162 Tbilisi, Georgia; ia.shekriladze@iliauni.edu.ge
[21] Child and Adolescent Psychiatry and Psychology Department, Hospital Sant Joan de Déu- Institut de Recerca Sant Joan de Déu, 08950 Esplugues de Llobregat, Spain; eduardo.serrano@sjd.es (E.S.-T.); raquel.cecilia@sjd.es (R.C.-C.)
[22] Department of Psychiatry, Germans Trias i Pujol University Hospital-IGTP, 08916 Barcelona, Spain; teresa.rangil@uab.cat (T.R.); mloran.germanstrias@gencat.cat (M.E.L.-M.)
[23] Department of Psychiatry and Legal Medicine, Universitat Autònoma de Barcelona, 08193 Barcelona, Spain
[24] Department of Psychiatry, Hospital de la Santa Creu i Sant Pau-Institut d'Investigació Biomèdica Sant Pau (IIB-Sant Pau)-Universitat Autònoma de Barcelona (UAB), 08041 Barcelona, Spain; jsoriano@santpau.cat (J.S.-P.); mar.carceller@e-campus.uab.cat (M.C.-S.)
[25] Centro de Investigación Biomédica en Red de Salud Mental (CIBERSAM), ISCIII, 28029 Madrid, Spain; mtplana@clinic.cat (M.T.P.); montserrat.graell@salud.madrid.org (M.G.); andres.gomez@scsalud.es (J.A.G.-d.B.)
[26] Centro de Diagnóstico de Enfermedades Moleculares, Universidad Autónoma de Madrid, 28049 Madrid, Spain; rnavarrete@cbm.csic.es
[27] FITA Foundation, 08006 Barcelona, Spain; mlozano@fitafundacion.org (M.L.); rlinares@fitafundacion.org (R.L.)
[28] Infectious Diseases Department, Hospital Universitari Bellvitge-Institut de Investigació Biomedica de Bellvitge (IDIBELL)-Institut Català d'Oncologia-Hospitalet, 08908 Barcelona, Spain; cgudiol@bellvitgehospital.cat (C.G.); jcarratala@bellvitgehospital.cat (J.C.)
[29] REIPI (Spanish Network for Research in Infectious Disease), Instituto de Salud Carlos III, 28029 Madrid, Spain
[30] Department of Clinical Sciences, School of Medicine and Health Sciences, University of Barcelona, 08907 Barcelona, Spain
[31] CIBER de Enfermedades Infecciosas (CIBERINFEC), Instituto de Salud Carlos III, 28029 Madrid, Spain
[32] Institute of Neuroscience, Hospital Clínic de Barcelona, 08036 Barcelona, Spain
[33] Department of Child and Adolescent Psychiatry and Psychology, 2017SGR881, Institute of Neurosciences, Hospital Clinic de Barcelona, 08036 Barcelona, Spain
[34] Child and Adolescent Psychiatry and Psychology Service, Child Hospital Niño Jesus, 28009 Madrid, Spain
[35] Psychiatry Service, University of Salamanca Healthcare Complex (USHC)-Institute of Biomedicine of Salamanca (IBSAL)-University of Salamanca, 37008 Salamanca, Spain; dgonzalezp@saludcastillayleon.es
[36] Unidad de Trastornos de la Conducta Alimentaria, Hospital Universitario "Marqués de Valdecilla", Avda, Valdecilla s/n, 39011 Santander, Spain
[37] Instituto de Investigación Valdecilla (IDIVAL), 39011 Santander, Spain
[38] Facultad de Psicología, Universidad Autónoma de Madrid, 28049 Madrid, Spain; anarosa.sepulveda@uam.es
[39] Psychotherapy and Psychopathology Research Unit—Psychology Research Center, School of Psychology, University of Minho, 4710-057 Braga, Portugal; pmachado@psi.uminho.pt
[40] Department of Clinical Sciences Lund, Psychiatry, Faculty of Medicine, Lund University, 221 00 Lund, Sweden; anders_c.hakansson@med.lu.se
[41] Gambling Disorder Unit, Malmö Addiction Center, 205 02 Malmö, Sweden
[42] Institute of Behavioral Sciences, Semmelweis University, 1085 Budapest, Hungary; turyferenc@gmail.com
[43] 1st Department of Paediatrics, Semmelweis University, 1085 Budapest, Hungary; paszthy@gyer1.sote.hu
[44] Safra Children's Hospital, Chaim Sheba Medical Center, Tel Hashomer 52 621, Israel; Daniel.Stein@sheba.health.gov.il
[45] Department of Psychiatry, 1st Medical Faculty of Charles University, 11000 Prague, Czech Republic; hana.papezova@lf1.cuni.cz (H.P.); jana.gricova@lf1.cuni.cz (J.G.)
[46] Eating Disorders Center, Vilnius University Vilnius, 01513 Vilnius, Lithuania; bax.brigita@gmail.com
[47] Institute of Physiology of Komi Science Centre of the Ural Branch of the Russian Academy of Sciences, 167982 Syktyvkar, Russia; borisenkov@physiol.komisc.ru (M.F.B.); s.v.popov@inbox.ru (S.V.P.)
[48] Laboratory for Chronobiology and Chronomedicine, Department of Biology, Tyumen State Medical University, 625023 Tyumen, Russia; gubin@tyumsmu.ru
[49] Tyumen Cardiology Research Institute, Tomsk Research Medical Center, 634009 Tyumen, Russia
[50] Department of Biological & Medical Physics UNESCO, Tyumen State Medical University, 625023 Tyumen, Russia; petrov@tyumsmu.ru
[51] Department of Therapy and Endocrinology, Tyumen State Medical University, 625023 Tyumen, Russia; isakovadn@tyumsmu.ru
[52] Institute of Internal and Preventive Medicine–Branch of the Institute of Cytology and Genetics, Siberian Branch of Russian Academy of Sciences, 630090 Novosibirsk, Russia; svetlana3548@gmail.com
[53] Department of Psychiatry, Seoul Paik Hospital-Inje University, Seoul 01757, Korea; youlri.kim@gmail.com
[54] Department of Psychiatry, School of Medicine, International University of Health and Welfare, Narita 286-8686, Japan; michiko.nakazato@nifty.ne.jp

55 CESP, Université Paris-Saclay, UVSQ, INSERM U 1178, 94805 Villejuif, France; nathalie.godart@fsef.net
56 Department of Psychiatry, Institut Mutualiste Montsouris, School of Medicine, Université Paris Descartes, 75006 Paris, France
57 UFR des Sciences de la Santé Simone Veil (UVSQ), Praticienne Hospitalière, Fondation Santé des Etudiants de France, 78180 Paris, France
58 Department of Political Science, Vytautas Magnus University, 44248 Kaunas, Lithuania; rvvoren@gmail.com
59 Institute of Psychiatry of Taras Shevchenko, National University of Kyiv, 01033 Kyiv, Ukraine; tatiana.ilnitskaya.14@gmail.com
60 Department of Clinical Psychology, Shanghai Mental Health Center, Shanghai Jiao Tong University School of Medicine, 280, Shanghai 200030, China; chenjue2088@163.com
61 Schön Klinik Roseneck, 83209 Prien am Chiemsee, Germany; UVoderholzer@schoen-klinik.de
62 Dipartimento di Salute Mentale e Fisica e Medicina Preventiva, Universitá degli Studi della Campania "Luigi Vanvitelli", 80138 Naples, Italy; alessiomaria.monteleone@unicampania.it
* Correspondence: sjimenez@bellvitgehospital.cat (S.J.-M.); ffernandez@bellvitgehospital.cat (F.F.-A.); Tel.: +34-93-260-7227 (S.J.-M. & F.F.-A.)
† These authors contributed equally to this work.

Abstract: Background. The COVID-19 lockdown has had a significant impact on mental health. Patients with eating disorders (ED) have been particularly vulnerable. Aims. (1) To explore changes in eating-related symptoms and general psychopathology during lockdown in patients with an ED from various European and Asian countries; and (2) to assess differences related to diagnostic ED subtypes, age, and geography. Methods. The sample comprised 829 participants, diagnosed with an ED according to DSM-5 criteria from specialized ED units in Europe and Asia. Participants were assessed using the COVID-19 Isolation Scale (CIES). Results. Patients with binge eating disorder (BED) experienced the highest impact on weight and ED symptoms in comparison with other ED subtypes during lockdown, whereas individuals with other specified feeding and eating disorders (OFSED) had greater deterioration in general psychological functioning than subjects with other ED subtypes. Finally, Asian and younger individuals appeared to be more resilient. Conclusions. The psychopathological changes in ED patients during the COVID-19 lockdown varied by cultural context and individual variation in age and ED diagnosis. Clinical services may need to target preventive measures and adapt therapeutic approaches for the most vulnerable patients.

Keywords: eating disorders; COVID-19 lockdown; COVID-19 Isolation Eating Scale (CIES); eating symptoms; psychological impact

1. Introduction

The COVID-19 pandemic has been a challenge for governments and health care professionals. The lockdown has been a worldwide response to control the spread of the disease. Although the measures taken have been effective in reducing the transmission of the infection, health professionals have expressed concerns about the mental health consequences that can result from social isolation and restrictions to daily life [1–3].

The psychological impact of lockdown in history and in the current context has been considered [4]. Higher levels of negative emotions such as anxiety, depression, anger, guilt or even posttraumatic stress symptoms have been reported [4,5]. A more profound impact has been observed in individuals with chronic diseases and mental illness [1,6,7]. Patients with eating disorders (ED) have been found to be at risk of adverse psychological consequences in the context of the COVID-19 pandemic [8,9].

Several studies have highlighted the emotional distress due to lockdown in patients with an ED, reporting high levels of anxiety, depression, and post-stress traumatic symptoms that may persist after lockdown [10–12]. Social distancing might obstruct adaptive strategies to deal with psychological distress [3,9,13] and maladaptive coping strategies, such as engaging in substance abuse and potentially addictive behaviors (e.g., gaming), may be adopted [14,15].

Changes in eating behaviors, exercise and weight/body mass index (BMI) have been detected both in the general population and in patients with an ED [16,17]. Emotional disturbances secondary to environmental changes and "food insecurity" have been considered as some possible explanatory factors [17–19]. Reduced social support, low self-direction, childhood trauma, and insecure attachment or difficulties in emotion regulation are vulnerability factors leading to psychological distress in lockdown, which can be associated with disturbed eating patterns [11,20–23].

Increased dietary restriction and physical activity in patients with anorexia nervosa (AN) or higher frequency of binge episodes among patients with bulimia nervosa (BN) and binge eating disorder (BED) have been reported during lockdown [10,11,21,24,25]. However, there are few studies focusing on the evolution of ED symptoms after lockdown and these have yielded mixed results [10,11]. A differential impact on eating and general psychopathology has been assessed in patients with an ED when compared with the general population [11,16]. This may vary with the ED subtype [26]. Moreover, age may be a possible factor to consider when evaluating clinical changes in the context of lockdown. In this line, younger age [1,7], together with cultural and socio-demographic factors may modulate them [27,28].

In order to assess the global effect of lockdown due to the COVID-19 pandemic in patients with a current diagnosis of ED, an international group of clinical and research experts developed the COVID Isolation Eating Scale (CIES), which has been translated in nineteen languages [26]. The study by Fernandez-Aranda, Munguía et al. [26] provided evidence of the psychometric robustness of the Spanish version of the CIES, with an adequate goodness-of-fit for the confirmatory factor analysis and good to excellent Cronbach alpha values. Preliminary data suggested that the effects of lockdown differed between ED subtypes, whereby patients with other specified feeding and eating disorders (OSFED) reported the highest global impairment [26].

To the best of our knowledge, this is the first observational study to analyze clinical changes in patients with ED longitudinally during lockdown, from a multicenter and international perspective. Both child/adolescent and adult populations were assessed using the CIES. The aims of the present study were: (1) to explore eating symptoms and behavioral changes, as well as other psychopathological features in the context of lockdown, and (2) to examine whether ED subtypes, age and geography moderated this effect.

2. Materials and Methods

2.1. Participants

The sample comprised $N = 829$ participants, from European (Spain, $n = 300$; Austria, $n = 43$; Germany, $n = 103$; Russia, $n = 119$; Portugal, $n = 28$; Lithuania, $n = 23$; Czech Republic, $n = 50$; Ukraine, $n = 10$) and Asian (China, $n = 92$; Korea, $n = 50$; Japan, $n = 11$) private and public ED units. Participants were diagnosed according to DSM-5 criteria [29] by expert clinical psychologists and psychiatrists using a semi-structured clinical interview (SCID-5) [30].

2.2. Assessment

The COVID Isolation Eating Scale (CIES) [26] is a self-report questionnaire that assesses the impact of lockdown on patients with ED and/or obesity and has been translated in 19 languages [26]. Supplementary Material contains the English version of the scale. It is composed of 4 subscales:

I. Circumstances of the lockdown (eight items).
II. Effects of the lockdown on eating symptoms (thirteen items): it evaluates symptomatology of AN, BN, BED and OSFED, according with the DSM-5. Comorbidity with other psychiatric disorders or diabetes is assessed.
III. Reaction to the lockdown (34 items): it evaluates the effects of the confinement on eating behaviors, attitudes and habits, anxious-depressive symptoms, emotion

dysregulation, and other symptomatology associated with substance use disorders and behavioral addictions.

IV. The evaluation of remote interventions (thirteen items) assesses acceptance, general satisfaction, and motivation for virtual interventions.

The last three subscales are answered in a five-point Likert scale. Sections 2 and 3 consider two moments of time, before confinement and the current moment of time.

According to the factorial analysis [26], five factors were identified. Factor 1 was defined by the items measuring eating related symptoms; Factor 2 by the items measuring the effects of lockdown on the eating-related style; Factor 3 by the items assessing anxiety and depressive symptoms; Factor 4 was defined by the items related to emotion regulation; and Factor 5 by those that evaluate telemedicine.

Only the subscales I, II and III (that correspond to the factor 1, 2, 3 and 4) were used in this study. Therefore, no results referring to the acceptance of virtual are reported (subscale 4, factor 5).

2.3. *Additional Assessment*

Socio-demographic and clinical information (i.e., age, ED subtype, and variables related to COVID-19 and lockdown) were also obtained through the CIES questionnaire.

2.4. *Procedure*

All the participants were already involved in outpatient ED treatment in specialized units of the different countries. The subjects were asked by therapists from each center to voluntarily complete the study questionnaire (i.e., CIES), translated into participants' languages [26]. Data collection took place retrospectively between August 2020 and January 2021.

The study was approved by the Clinical Research Ethics Committee of the leading University Hospital (Bellvitge University Hospital) (PR239/20), and informed written consent was obtained from all participants.

2.5. *Statistical Analysis*

Statistical analysis was performed with Stata17 for Windows [31]. The assessment of the pre-post changes in the quantitative measures was carried out through repeated measures analysis of variance (repeated-ANOVA), while the McNemar test was used for paired nominal data.

Additionally, the differences post-pre values were generated for the scores registered in the CIES, and for the weight (kg) and the BMI (kg/m^2) (values equal to zero in these new variables indicate absence of change; negative values indicate a decreasing pre-post change; and positive values indicate an increasing pre-post change). Next, ANOVA procedures compared the mean differences between the diagnostic subtypes, the groups of age, and the continent.

In this study, the statistical analyses were adjusted by the sociodemographic sex and age, due to the differences between the groups (defined by the diagnostic subtypes and the origin of the samples).The effect size was estimated with Cohen's-h coefficient for the differences between the proportions and with Cohen's-d for the differences between the means (null effect size was considered for $|h| < 0.20$ or $|d| < 0.20$, low-poor for $|h| > 0.20$ or $|d| > 0.20$, moderate-medium for $|h| > 0.50$ or $|d| > 0.50$ and large-high for $|h| > 0.80$ or $|d| > 0.80$) [32,33]. Finner's method controlled the increase in the Type-I error due the use of multiple significance tests [34].

3. Results

3.1. *Characteristics of the Participants*

Table S1 (Supplementary Material) displays sociodemographic and clinical characteristic of the sample during the lockdown, as well as the comparison between the diagnostic types, the age groups, and the different continents. For the total sample, the mean age was 27.9 years old (*SD* = 12.3). Most participants were women (70.4%), lived with other people during the lockdown (78.9%), did not have to take care of others (73.8%), were not infected with COVID-19 (92.8%), did not know anyone close to them who was infected with COVID-19 (84.8%), were working (53.8%), and reported a minimal financial loss (73.5%).

3.2. Comparison between Diagnostic Subtypes of Changes Pre to Post Lockdown

Table 1 contains the changes in the CIES subscales scores between the pre- and post-lockdown within each diagnostic subtype. After adjusting by sex and age, patients with AN reported a significant worsening in eating style and alcohol use. Patients with BN had an increase in weight, and a decrease in ED symptoms, but emotion dysregulation and alcohol use were increased. Individuals with BED reported increased weight, an impaired eating style and had an increase in anxiety-depression symptoms. The group with OSFED reported an increase in anxiety-depression symptoms and emotion dysregulation.

Table 1. Assessment of the post-pre changes stratified by ED subtype.

	Pre		Post			
Anorexia (n = 370)	Mean	SD	Mean	SD	p	|d|
Weight (kg)	48.29	9.02	48.27	8.23	0.954	0.00
BMI (kg/m^2)	17.92	3.06	17.94	3.00	0.862	0.01
CIES-F1 ED symptoms	13.94	6.93	13.32	7.46	0.089	0.09
CIES-F2 Eating style	10.96	8.75	9.98	8.71	0.005 *	0.11
CIES-F3 Anxiety-depression	17.20	9.62	17.93	9.85	0.089	0.07
CIES-F4 Emotion dysregulation	8.51	5.09	8.27	5.26	0.247	0.05
	n	%	n	%	p	|h|
Tobacco	52	14.1%	52	14.1%	1.00	0.00
Alcohol	57	15.4%	38	10.3%	0.001 *	0.15
Other illegal drugs	33	8.9%	26	7.0%	0.143	0.07
Behavioral addictions	244	65.9%	242	65.4%	0.875	0.01
Bulimia (n = 148)	Mean	SD	Mean	SD	p	|d|
Weight (kg)	61.09	14.52	62.26	13.89	0.026 *	0.08
BMI (kg/m^2)	22.27	5.07	22.70	4.84	0.025 *	0.09
CIES-F1 ED symptoms	19.78	6.82	18.39	7.16	0.048 *	0.20
CIES-F2 Eating style	21.96	10.15	20.28	10.79	0.073	0.16
CIES-F3 Anxiety-depression	20.36	9.02	20.84	9.61	0.467	0.05
CIES-F4 Emotion dysregulation	9.91	4.83	9.22	5.28	0.045 *	0.14
	n	%	n	%	p	|h|
Tobacco	42	28.4%	46	31.1%	0.388	0.06
Alcohol	62	41.9%	45	30.4%	<0.001 *	0.24
Other illegal drugs	30	20.3%	22	14.9%	0.115	0.14
Behavioral addictions	108	73.0%	106	71.6%	0.839	0.03
BED (n = 113)	Mean	SD	Mean	SD	p	|d|
Weight (kg)	95.27	33.79	99.18	31.49	<0.001 *	0.12
BMI (kg/m^2)	33.63	10.38	35.08	9.63	<0.001 *	0.14
CIES-F1 ED symptoms	14.10	7.26	14.57	6.72	0.449	0.07
CIES-F2 Eating style	20.88	11.30	18.86	11.60	0.010 *	0.18
CIES-F3 Anxiety-depression	17.66	10.37	19.45	11.37	0.004 *	0.16
CIES-F4 Emotion dysregulation	8.99	5.91	8.88	5.87	0.745	0.02
	n	%	n	%	p	|d|
Tobacco	29	25.7%	28	24.8%	1.00	0.02
Alcohol	36	31.9%	31	27.4%	0.405	0.10
Other illegal drugs	18	15.9%	13	11.5%	0.332	0.13
Behavioral addictions	73	64.6%	79	69.9%	0.263	0.11

Table 1. *Cont.*

	Pre		Post			
OSFED (*n* = 198)	Mean	SD	Mean	SD	*p*	|d|
Weight (kg)	81.68	25.86	82.25	26.29	0.280	0.02
BMI (kg/m^2)	28.58	8.06	28.77	8.13	0.340	0.02
CIES-F1 ED symptoms	13.74	5.95	13.35	5.70	0.266	0.07
CIES-F2 Eating style	13.94	9.14	13.99	9.12	0.924	0.00
CIES-F3 Anxiety-depression	13.99	10.03	16.17	10.90	<0.001 *	0.21
CIES-F4 Emotion dysregulation	6.73	5.08	7.80	5.86	<0.001 *	0.20
	n	%	*n*	%	*p*	|h|
Tobacco	58	29.3%	65	32.8%	0.092	0.08
Alcohol	57	28.8%	51	25.8%	0.286	0.07
Other illegal drugs	13	6.6%	16	8.1%	0.629	0.06
Behavioral addictions	123	62.1%	131	66.2%	0.152	0.08

BMI: body mass index. BED: binge eating disorder. OSFED: other specified feeding eating disorders. SD: standard deviation. * Bold: significant comparison. Results adjusted by sex and age.

Table 2 shows the comparison between the diagnostic ED subtypes for post-pre changes (defined as the difference between the measures at the end of the follow-up and the post lockdown versus the pre lockdown). The first line-plot displayed in Figure 1 also contains the mean changes within each measure (mean values close to the horizontal line at value 0 represent absence of pre-post changes). After adjusting by sex and age, compared with other groups, patients with BED were characterized by the highest increase in weight, BMI, and the CIES-F1 ED symptoms. For the CIES-F2 eating style, BED and BN achieved statistically equal changes, which represented a higher decrease compared with AN, and OSFED. For CIES-F3 anxiety-depression and CIES-F4 emotional dysregulation, OSFED registered the highest increase compared with the other diagnostic conditions.

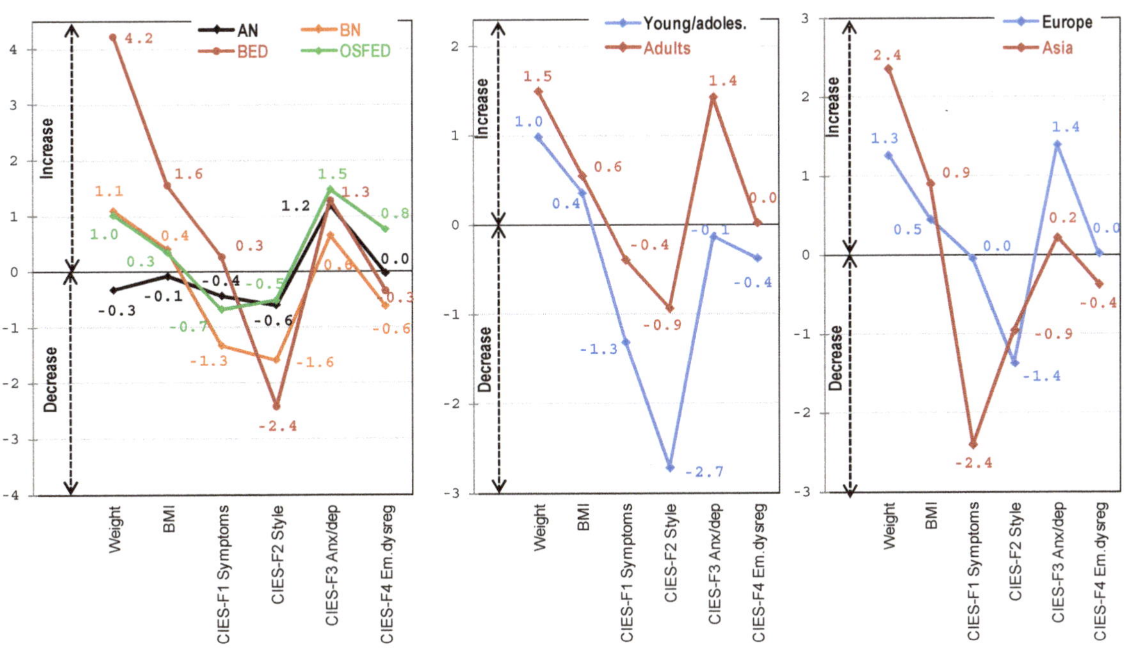

Figure 1. Differences (post-pre changes) for the weight, the BMI and the CIES factors.

Table 2. Comparison of the post-pre differences by the ED subtype.

	Anorexia (AN) $n = 370$		Bulimia (BN) $n = 148$		BED $n = 113$		OSFED $n = 198$		Significant Pairwise Comparisons
	Mean	**SD**	**Mean**	**SD**	**Mean**	**SD**	**Mean**	**SD**	
Weight (kg)	−0.32	6.66	1.10	6.32	4.22	11.58	1.02	7.43	BED ≠ (AN = BN = OSFED)
BMI (kg/m^2)	−0.09	2.54	0.40	2.31	1.55	4.13	0.35	2.71	BED ≠ (AN = BN = OSFED)
CIES-F1 ED symptoms	−0.43	7.03	−1.32	8.52	0.26	6.54	−0.67	4.90	BED ≠ (AN = BN = OSFED)
CIES-F2 Eating style	−0.60	6.72	−1.58	11.34	−2.42	8.12	−0.52	6.69	(BED = BN) ≠ (AN = OSFED)
CIES-F3 Anxiety-dep.	1.19	8.28	0.65	8.28	1.28	6.53	1.47	7.04	OSFED ≠ (AN = BN = BED)
CIES-F4 Emot.dysreg.	−0.03	4.06	−0.62	4.25	−0.34	3.73	0.75	3.94	OSFED ≠ (AN = BN = BED)

BMI: body mass index. BED: binge eating disorder. OSFED: other specified feeding eating disorders. SD: standard deviation.

3.3. Comparison between the Groups of Age for the Changes during the Lockdown

Table 3 contains the results of the repeated-ANOVA assessing the changes between the pre- and post-lockdown within each age group (young/adolescents versus adults). These analyses were adjusted by the ED subtype and sex. Among young/adolescents, a significant decrease was observed for the CIES-F2 eating style. Adult patients reported increased weight, BMI and CIES-F3 anxiety-depression symptoms, decreased CIES-F2 eating style, and the likelihood of alcohol and other illegal drug use.

Table 3. Assessment of the post-pre changes stratified by groups of age.

	Pre		Post			
Age: young/adolescents ($n = 172$)	Mean	SD	Mean	SD	p	|d|
Weight (kg)	63.49	13.52	65.44	13.51	0.073	0.14
BMI (kg/m^2)	22.74	4.00	23.37	3.97	0.119	0.16
CIES-F1 ED symptoms	14.83	6.73	13.32	7.52	0.213	0.21
CIES-F2 Eating style	16.54	9.23	12.75	8.60	0.003 *	0.43
CIES-F3 Anxiety-depression symptoms	15.96	8.89	15.46	8.83	0.701	0.06
CIES-F4 Emotion dysregulation	8.84	5.24	8.39	5.33	0.537	0.09
	n	%	n	%	p	|h|
Tobacco	14	9.6%	16	11.1%	0.566	0.05
Alcohol	18	9.7%	9	3.1%	0.118	0.28
Other illegal drugs	9	6.0%	8	5.8%	0.945	0.01
Behavioral addictions	125	79.7%	127	80.1%	0.948	0.01
Age: adults ($n = 657$)	Mean	SD	Mean	SD	p	|d|
Weight (kg)	72.18	27.82	73.62	27.96	<0.001 *	0.05
BMI (kg/m^2)	25.79	9.00	26.32	9.10	<0.001 *	0.06
CIES-F1 ED symptoms	15.54	7.14	15.22	6.96	0.237	0.04
CIES-F2 Eating style	17.17	10.60	16.32	10.52	0.008 *	0.08
CIES-F3 Anxiety-depression symptoms	17.69	10.13	19.26	10.57	<0.001 *	0.15
CIES-F4 Emotion dysregulation	8.61	5.27	8.70	5.53	0.546	0.02
	n	%	n	%	p	|h|
Tobacco	167	26.2%	175	27.4%	0.235	0.03
Alcohol	194	31.4%	156	25.4%	<0.001 *	0.13
Other illegal drugs	85	13.9%	69	11.0%	0.025 *	0.09
Behavioral addictions	423	65.0%	431	66.6%	0.272	0.03

BMI: body mass index. SD: standard deviation. * Bold: significant comparison. Results adjusted by ED subtype and sex.

The results of the ANOVA procedures comparing between the age group the differences generated between the values measured at post- and pre-lockdown are shown in Table 4 (ANOVA procedures adjusted by the ED subtype and sex) (see also the second line-plot of Figure 1). Statistical differences were achieved by comparing the mean changes in the CIES-F2 eating style and the CIES-F3 anxiety-depression symptoms.

Table 4. Comparison of the post-pre differences by the groups of age.

	Young/Adolescents n = 172		Adults n = 657			
	Mean	**SD**	**Mean**	**SD**	p	|d|
Weight (kg)	0.99	7.16	1.50	7.86	0.480	0.07
BMI (kg/m^2)	0.36	2.66	0.56	2.89	0.471	0.04
CIES-F1 ED symptoms	−1.30	7.94	−0.39	6.50	0.154	0.13
CIES-F2 Eating style	−2.71	8.17	−0.93	7.85	0.017 *	0.22
CIES-F3 Anxiety-depression symptoms	−0.13	8.55	1.43	7.52	0.030 *	0.19
CIES-F4 Emotion dysregulation	−0.37	4.77	0.03	3.84	0.289	0.09

BMI: body mass index. SD: standard deviation. * Bold: significant comparison. Results adjusted by ED subtype and sex.

3.4. Comparison between Continents for the Changes during the Lockdown

Table 5 contains the results of the repeated-ANOVA (adjusted by the ED subtype, sex, and age) assessing the changes between the pre- and post-lockdown in the weight, the BMI and the CIES scores. Separated/stratified analyses have been performed within each continent (Europe and Asia). Among the European patients, a significant increase was observed in weight, BMI and the CIES-F3 anxiety-depression symptoms. Besides, a significant decrease in the CIES-F2 eating style and in the likelihood of alcohol and other illegal drug use was reported. In Asian patients, while an increase in weight and BMI was obtained, a decrease in the CIES-F1 ED symptoms was found.

Table 5. Assessment of the post-pre changes stratified by continent.

	Pre		**Post**			
Europe (n = 676)	Mean	SD	Mean	SD	p	|d|
Weight (kg)	72.99	27.78	74.20	28.24	0.001 *	0.04
BMI (kg/m^2)	26.06	8.95	26.49	9.14	0.001 *	0.05
CIES-F1 ED symptoms	14.94	6.61	15.09	7.06	0.587	0.02
CIES-F2 Eating style	16.29	9.73	15.03	9.82	<0.001 *	0.13
CIES-F3 Anxiety-depression symptoms	17.00	9.65	18.51	10.34	<0.001 *	0.15
CIES-F4 Emotion dysregulation	8.54	5.13	8.58	5.46	0.805	0.01
	n	%	n	%	p	|h|
Tobacco	166	28.2%	173	29.3%	0.306	0.02
Alcohol	172	30.8%	132	22.9%	<0.001 *	0.18
Other illegal drugs	75	14.5%	58	10.2%	0.003 *	0.13
Behavioral addictions	440	66.9%	452	68.4%	0.209	0.03
Asia (n=153)	Mean	SD	Mean	SD	p	|d|
Weight (kg)	56.19	15.41	58.01	14.99	0.038 *	0.12
BMI (kg/m^2)	20.79	4.95	21.51	4.91	0.030 *	0.15
CIES-F1 ED symptoms	17.91	8.14	15.55	7.53	0.006 *	0.30
CIES-F2 Eating style	19.78	12.44	18.61	12.15	0.314	0.10
CIES-F3 Anxiety-depression symptoms	19.02	10.74	19.13	10.59	0.899	0.01
CIES-F4 Emotion dysregulation	9.13	5.75	8.61	5.73	0.241	0.09
	n	%	n	%	p	|h|
Tobacco	15	12.0%	18	14.6%	0.167	0.08
Alcohol	40	28.6%	33	25.6%	0.354	0.07
Other illegal drugs	19	13.6%	19	14.4%	0.736	0.02
Behavioral addictions	108	68.0%	106	73.0%	0.284	0.11

BMI: body mass index. SD: standard deviation. * Bold: significant comparison. Results adjusted by ED subtype, sex, and age.

Finally, the results of the ANOVA comparing the differences post- and pre-lockdown between the geographical area are shown in Table 6 (results adjusted by the ED subtype, sex, and age) (see also the third line-plot of Figure 1). Statistical differences were achieved comparing the mean changes in the CIES-F1 ED symptoms (higher decrease for Asian patients).

Table 6. Comparison of the post-pre differences by continent.

	Europe n = 676		Asia n = 153			
	Mean	**SD**	**Mean**	**SD**	p	$\|d\|$
Weight (kg)	1.27	7.47	2.37	8.73	0.138	0.13
BMI (kg/m^2)	0.46	2.73	0.91	3.28	0.100	0.15
CIES-F1 ED symptoms	−0.04	6.32	−2.40	8.43	<0.001 *	0.32
CIES-F2 Eating style	−1.37	6.90	−0.95	11.48	0.583	0.04
CIES-F3 Anxiety-depression symptoms	1.40	7.54	0.22	8.62	0.113	0.15
CIES-F4 Emotion dysregulation	0.02	3.94	−0.37	4.47	0.309	0.09

BMI: body mass index. SD: standard deviation. * Bold: significant comparison. Results adjusted by ED subtype, sex, and age.

4. Discussion

The aim of this study was to compare the psychopathological effects in the context of lockdown due to the COVID-19 pandemic in patients with ED from different continents (i.e., Europe and Asia). Secondly, we examined if these differences pre/post lockdown varied by ED subtype, age, and continental provenance.

4.1. ED Subtypes and Changes during Lockdown

In line with previous studies [26] the findings highlight a differential psychopathological impact during lockdown according to the ED diagnosis. Patients diagnosed with BN and BED reported weight gain after lockdown, the BED group experiencing the greatest weight changes when comparing by ED subtypes. It is possible that a sedentary lifestyle favored by "stay-at-home" measures and mobility restrictions during lockdown [35] may play a pivotal role in these weight changes [36,37]. Some of the increased eating behaviors related to "food insecurity" or boredom, such as snacking [35], could also lead to weight gain [16,17]. In this line, individuals with BED and BN showed a higher impairment in their eating style in comparison with the other ED subtypes. Moreover, previous studies have recognized an increased vulnerability to weight gain in individuals with overweight and obesity [38], conditions that are usually presented in individuals with BN and BED [39,40].

Eating behaviors have been described as maladaptive strategies to cope with emotional distress [13,18,22]. However, ED symptoms and emotion dysregulation were reduced in BN, which aligns with other findings [10,41]. The continued presence of other people at home and maintaining daily routines [4] are two significant socio-demographic features that characterized our sample, and may have allowed patients with BN to reduce binge episodes and purging. Moreover, the observed decrease in other maladaptive behaviors after lockdown (i.e., alcohol consumption) has been previously described in an international non-clinical study [35].

Individuals with BED reported the highest impact on ED symptoms when comparing ED subtype groups, although no significant changes in ED symptoms pre- and post-lockdown were individually reported in this group. A greater illness perception among these patients together with a higher motivation for change [42], and the weight gain during lockdown, could encourage them to improve their eating style (e.g., non abuse of certain palatable foods).

Changes in eating style have also been described in patients with AN, which may suggest an increased control over food intake during lockdown. Changes in diet habits have been observed both in general and clinical populations during lockdown [16], the restricting pattern being commonly mentioned [24]. Surprisingly, and in contrast to other studies [12,43], they did not report significant modification in weight/BMI, ED symptoms nor other psychological features. Furthermore, a reduction in alcohol use was described in this ED subtype after lockdown.

Regarding OSFED group, both psychopathology and emotion regulation worsened during lockdown. This aligns with previous research which found that individuals with OSFED deteriorated in adverse situations [44,45]. Not only they did experience a greater psychological impairment than subjects from other ED groups but this impairment also persisted after lockdown [10,11,23].

4.2. Age Differences Regarding Changes during Lockdown

Overall young/adolescent patients had a significant improvement in eating habits in comparison to older individuals. The adult group reported significant weight/BMI changes and higher psychological impact than the former one. These results differed from those described in the general population in which younger people had a poorer adjustment to lockdown [1,7]. One possible explanation for our results could be that older age is linked to patients with BED, who in our study reported a greater psychopathological impact than other ED subtypes. Besides, younger people may be supervised and accompanied more frequently by others, constituting a possible protective factor [4]. Furthermore, young people are usually more familiar with the use of social media, which might imply a better adaptation to the online modality, promoting therapeutic adherence and the maintenance of academic/work routines, as well as social contact [4,13].

4.3. Influence of Continental Provenance on the Changes during Lockdown

Both European and Asian patients experienced weight gain during lockdown, as has been described in clinical and general populations [36,37,46], without significant differences between groups. In comparison with European patients, participants from Asia reported an improvement of their ED symptoms. These findings were not in line with other studies exploring the impact of lockdown on the Asian population [46]. Individual differences in personality and coping features have been reported between countries [27,28] which might lead to a differential adjustment to stress such as the COVID-19 pandemic [47].

4.4. Strengths and Limitations

The large sample size with international participation using a validated and homogeneous method of evaluation is a strength of this study. Moreover, the analysis related to age and provenance were adjusted for the ED subtype. However, the observational design of the study and the voluntary nature of participation in it could be some of the limitations of the present work. Furthermore, the presence of memory bias due to the retrospective nature of the assessment and the heterogeneity of the sample must be mentioned. Even though initial evidence regarding clinical changes in ED patients during lockdown has been measured by the CIES, future studies should consider involving other ED severity questionnaires.

5. Conclusions

In this international study of the adjustment of patients with an ED during lockdown, we observed differences that varied according to ED subtype, age, and provenance. Individuals with BED showed higher worsening of eating symptoms and change in weight during lockdown than those from other ED subtypes. The greatest psychological impairment was described in the OSFED group. Finally, young and Asian patients appeared to be more resilient. These findings may enhance preventive and therapeutic approaches in similar future circumstances.

Supplementary Materials: The following supporting information can be downloaded at: https://www.mdpi.com/article/10.3390/nu14010100/s1, Table S1. Descriptive for the age, sex, and the confinement context/ Covid Isolation Eating Scale (CIES)-English version.

Author Contributions: Conceptualization, F.F.-A. and S.J.-M.; Data curation, I.B., M.E., L.M., R.G., G.M.-B., I.S. (Isabel Sánchezand), E.O., A.A., V.L.M., J.-M.F.-R., F.J.T., C.D., G.F., D.L.G., K.T., A.K., M.Z., H.I., A.Z., A.F., L.C., I.S. (Ia Shekriladze), E.S.-T., R.C.-C., T.R., M.E.L.-M., J.S.-P., M.C.-S., R.N., M.L., R.L., C.G., J.C. (Jordi Carratalaand), M.T.P., M.G., D.G.-P., J.A.G.-d.B., A.R.S., J.S.-G., P.P.P.M., A.H., F.T., B.P., D.S., H.P., J.G., B.B., M.F.B., S.V.P., D.G.G., I.M.P., D.I., S.V.M., Y.-R.K., M.N., N.G., R.v.V., T.I., J.C. (Jue Chen), K.R., U.V., A.M.M., J.T., S.J.-M. and F.F.-A.; Formal analysis, R.G.; Methodology, R.G.; Writing–original draft, I.B., M.E., L.M., R.G., G.M.-B., S.J.-M. and F.F.-A.; Writing–review & editing, I.B., M.E., L.M., R.G., G.M.-B., I.S. (Isabel Sánchezand), E.O., A.A., V.L.M., J.-M.F.-R., F.J.T., C.D., G.F., D.L.G., K.T., A.K., M.Z., H.I., A.Z., A.F., L.C., I.S. (Ia Shekriladze), E.S.-T., R.C.-C., T.R., M.E.L.-M., J.S.-P., M.C.-S., R.N., M.L., R.L., C.G., J.C. (Jordi Carratalaand), M.T.P., M.G., D.G.-P., J.A.G.-d.B., A.R.S., J.S.-G., P.P.P.M., A.H., F.T., B.P., D.S., H.P., J.G., B.B., M.F.B., S.V.P., D.G.G., I.M.P., D.I., S.V.M., Y.-R.K., M.N., N.G., R.v.V., T.I., J.C. (Jue Chen), K.R., U.V., A.M.M., J.T., S.J.-M. and F.F.-A. All authors have read and agreed to the published version of the manuscript.

Funding: Fondo Investigación Sanitario-FIS, Grant/Award Numbers: FIS, INT19/00046, PI17/01167; Ministerio de Economía y Competitividad, Grant/Award Number: PSI2015-68701-R; Portuguese Foundation for Science and Technology grant, Grant/Award Number: POCI-01-0145-FEDER-028145; Consejo Nacional de Ciencia y Tecnología; Generalitat de Catalunya; European Regional Development Fund.

Institutional Review Board Statement: The present study was conducted in accordance with the latest version of the Declaration of Helsinki and was approved by the Clinical Research Ethics Committee of Bellvitge University Hospital (PR239/20).

Informed Consent Statement: Written and signed informed consent was obtained from all subjects involved in the study.

Data Availability Statement: Individuals may inquire with Fernández-Aranda regarding availability of the data as there is ongoing studies using the data. To avoid overlapping research efforts, Fernández-Aranda will consider a request on a case-by-case basis.

Acknowledgments: We thank CERCA Programme/Generalitat de Catalunya for institutional support. This manuscript and research was supported by grants from the Department of Health of the Generalitat de Catalunya by the call Pla estratègic de recerca i innovació en salut (PERIS, SLT006/17/00077), the Ministerio de Economía y Competitividad (PSI201568701R), Fondo de Investigación Sanitario (FIS) (INT19/00046, PI17/01167, PI20/132), CIBERINFEC (CB21/13/00009) and co-funded by FEDER funds /European Regional Development Fund (ERDF), a way to build Europe (Eat2beNICE/ H2020-SFS-2016-2; Ref 728018; and PRIME/ H2020-SC1-BHC-2018-2020; Ref: 847879). CIBEROBN, CIBERSAM, CIBERINFEC and CIBERDEM are all initiatives of Instituto de Salud Carlos III (ISCIII). GMB is supported by a postdoctoral grant from FUNCIVA. PPM was supported, in part, by a Portuguese Foundation for Science and Technology grant (POCI-01-0145-FEDER-028145). IB was partially supported by a Post-Residency Grant from the Research Committee of the University Hospital of Bellvitge (HUB; Barcelona, Spain) 2020–2021. The funders had no role in the study design, data collection and analysis, decision to publish, or preparation of the manuscript.

Conflicts of Interest: FFA received consultancy honoraria from Novo Nordisk and editorial honoraria as EIC from Wiley. The rest of the authors declare no conflict of interest. The funders had no role in the design of the study; in the collection, analyses, or interpretation of data; in the writing of the manuscript, or in the decision to publish the results.

References

1. González-Sanguino, C.; Ausín, B.; Castellanos, M.Á.; Saiz, J.; López-Gómez, A.; Ugidos, C.; Muñoz, M. Mental health consequences during the initial stage of the 2020 Coronavirus pandemic (COVID-19) in Spain. *Brain Behav. Immun.* **2020**, *87*, 172–176. [CrossRef] [PubMed]
2. Wang, C.; Pan, R.; Wan, X.; Tan, Y.; Xu, L.; Ho, C.S.; Ho, R.C. Immediate Psychological Responses and Associated Factors during the Initial Stage of the 2019 Coronavirus Disease (COVID-19) Epidemic among the General Population in China. *Int. J. Environ. Res. Public Health* **2020**, *17*, 1729. [CrossRef] [PubMed]
3. Rodgers, R.F.; Lombardo, C.; Cerolini, S.; Franko, D.L.; Omori, M.; Fuller-Tyszkiewicz, M.; Linardon, J.; Courtet, P.; Guillaume, S. The impact of the COVID-19 pandemic on eating disorder risk and symptoms. *Int. J. Eat. Disord.* **2020**, *53*, 1166–1170. [CrossRef] [PubMed]

4. Chew, Q.H.; Wei, K.C.; Vasoo, S.; Chua, H.C.; Sim, K. Narrative synthesis of psychological and coping responses towards emerging infectious disease outbreaks in the general population: Practical considerations for the COVID-19 pandemic. *Singap. Med. J.* **2020**, *61*, 350–356. [CrossRef] [PubMed]
5. Cao, W.; Fang, Z.; Hou, G.; Han, M.; Xu, X.; Dong, J.; Zheng, J. The psychological impact of the COVID-19 epidemic on college students in China. *Psychiatry Res.* **2020**, *287*, 112934. [CrossRef] [PubMed]
6. De Girolamo, G.; Cerveri, G.; Clerici, M.; Monzani, E.; Spinogatti, F.; Starace, F.; Tura, G.; Vita, A. Mental Health in the Coronavirus Disease 2019 Emergency—The Italian Response. *JAMA Psychiatry* **2020**, *77*, 974–976. [CrossRef] [PubMed]
7. Ozamiz-Etxebarria, N.; Dosil-Santamaria, M.; Picaza-Gorrochategui, M.; Idoiaga-Mondragon, N. Stress, Anxiety, and Depression Levels in the Initial Stage of the COVID-19 Outbreak in a Population Sample in the Northern Spain. *Cad. Saúde Pública* **2020**, *36*, e00054020. [CrossRef]
8. Todisco, P.; Donini, L. Eating disorders and obesity (ED&O) in the COVID-19 storm. *Eat. Weight. Disord. Stud. Anorex. Bulim. Obes.* **2021**, *26*, 747–750. [CrossRef]
9. Branley-Bell, D.; Talbot, C.V. Exploring the impact of the COVID-19 pandemic and UK lockdown on individuals with experience of eating disorders. *J. Eat. Disord.* **2020**, *8*, 44. [CrossRef]
10. Nisticò, V.; Bertelli, S.; Tedesco, R.; Anselmetti, S.; Priori, A.; Gambini, O.; Demartini, B. The psychological impact of COVID-19-related lockdown measures among a sample of Italian patients with eating disorders: A preliminary longitudinal study. *Eat. Weight. Disord. Stud. Anorex. Bulim. Obes.* **2021**, *26*, 2771–2777. [CrossRef]
11. Castellini, G.; Cassioli, E.; Rossi, E.; Innocenti, M.; Gironi, V.; Sanfilippo, G.; Felciai, F.; Monteleone, A.M.; Ricca, V. The impact of COVID-19 epidemic on eating disorders: A longitudinal observation of pre versus post psychopathological features in a sample of patients with eating disorders and a group of healthy controls. *Int. J. Eat. Disord.* **2020**, *53*, 1855–1862. [CrossRef]
12. Msc, J.D.T.; Watson, H.J.; Thornton, L.M.; Borg, S.; Ma, R.E.F.; Ba, C.M.M.; Bs, L.E.H.; van Furth, E.; Peat, C.M.; Bulik, C.M. Early impact of COVID-19 on individuals with self-reported eating disorders: A survey of ~1000 individuals in the United States and the Netherlands. *Int. J. Eat. Disord.* **2020**, *53*, 1780–1790. [CrossRef]
13. Fernández-Aranda, F.; Casas, M.; Claes, L.; Bryan, D.C.; Favaro, A.; Granero, R.; Gudiol, C.; Jiménez-Murcia, S.; Karwautz, A.; Le Grange, D.; et al. COVID-19 and implications for eating disorders. *Eur. Eat. Disord. Rev.* **2020**, *28*, 239–245. [CrossRef]
14. Håkansson, A.; Fernández-Aranda, F.; Menchón, J.M.; Potenza, M.N.; Jiménez-Murcia, S. Gambling During the COVID-19 Crisis – A Cause for Concern. *J. Addict. Med.* **2020**, *14*, e10–e12. [CrossRef]
15. King, D.L.; Delfabbro, P.H.; Billieux, J.; Potenza, M.N. Problematic online gaming and the COVID-19 pandemic. *J. Behav. Addict.* **2020**, *9*, 184–186. [CrossRef]
16. Phillipou, A.; Meyer, D.; Neill, E.; Tan, E.J.; Toh, W.L.; Van Rheenen, T.E.; Rossell, S.L. Eating and exercise behaviors in eating disorders and the general population during the COVID -19 pandemic in Australia: Initial results from the COLLATE project. *Int. J. Eat. Disord.* **2020**, *53*, 1158–1165. [CrossRef]
17. Christensen, K.A.; Forbush, K.T.; Richson, B.N.; Thomeczek, M.L.; Perko, V.L.; Bjorlie, K.; Christian, K.; Ayres, J.; Wildes, J.E.; Chana, S.M. Food insecurity associated with elevated eating disorder symptoms, impairment, and eating disorder diagnoses in an American University student sample before and during the beginning of the COVID-19 pandemic. *Int. J. Eat. Disord.* **2021**, *54*, 1213–1223. [CrossRef]
18. Touyz, S.; Lacey, H.; Hay, P. Eating disorders in the time of COVID-19. *J. Eat. Disord.* **2020**, *8*, 19. [CrossRef]
19. Weissman, R.S.; Bauer, S.; Thomas, J.J. Access to evidence-based care for eating disorders during the COVID-19 crisis. *Int. J. Eat. Disord.* **2020**, *53*, 639–646. [CrossRef]
20. Baenas, I.; Caravaca-Sanz, E.; Granero, R.; Sánchez, I.; Riesco, N.; Testa, G.; Vintró-Alcaraz, C.; Treasure, J.; Jiménez-Murcia, S.; Fernández-Aranda, F. COVID -19 and eating disorders during confinement: Analysis of factors associated with resilience and aggravation of symptoms. *Eur. Eat. Disord. Rev.* **2020**, *28*, 855–863. [CrossRef]
21. Machado, P.P.P.; Pinto-Bastos, A.; Ramos, R.; Rodrigues, T.F.; Louro, E.; Gonçalves, S.; Brandão, I.; Vaz, A. Impact of COVID-19 lockdown measures on a cohort of eating disorders patients. *J. Eat. Disord.* **2020**, *8*, 57. [CrossRef] [PubMed]
22. Vuillier, L.; May, L.; Greville-Harris, M.; Surman, R.; Moseley, R.L. The impact of the COVID-19 pandemic on individuals with eating disorders: The role of emotion regulation and exploration of online treatment experiences. *J. Eat. Disord.* **2021**, *9*, 10. [CrossRef] [PubMed]
23. Monteleone, A.M.; Cascino, G.; Marciello, F.; Abbate-Daga, G.; Baiano, M.; Balestrieri, M.; Barone, E.; Bertelli, S.; Carpiniello, B.; Castellini, G.; et al. Risk and resilience factors for specific and general psychopathology worsening in people with Eating Disorders during COVID-19 pandemic: A retrospective Italian multicentre study. *Eat. Weight. Disord. Stud. Anorex. Bulim. Obes.* **2021**, *26*, 2443–2452. [CrossRef]
24. Schlegl, S.; Maier, J.; Meule, A.; Voderholzer, U. Eating disorders in times of the COVID-19 pandemic—Results from an online survey of patients with anorexia nervosa. *Int. J. Eat. Disord.* **2020**, *53*, 1791–1800. [CrossRef] [PubMed]
25. Schlegl, S.; Meule, A.; Favreau, M.; Voderholzer, U. Bulimia nervosa in times of the COVID -19 pandemic—Results from an online survey of former inpatients. *Eur. Eat. Disord. Rev.* **2020**, *28*, 847–854. [CrossRef]
26. Fernández-Aranda, F.; Munguía, L.; Mestre-Bach, G.; Steward, T.; Etxandi, M.; Baenas, I.; Granero, R.; Sánchez, I.; Ortega, E.; Andreu, A.; et al. COVID Isolation Eating Scale (CIES): Analysis of the impact of confinement in eating disorders and obesity—A collaborative international study. *Eur Eat Disord Rev.* **2020**, *28*, 871–883. [CrossRef] [PubMed]

27. Hamamura, T.; Heine, S.J.; Paulhus, D.L. Cultural differences in response styles: The role of dialectical thinking. *Pers. Individ. Differ.* **2008**, *44*, 932–942. [CrossRef]
28. English, T.; Chen, S. Culture and self-concept stability: Consistency across and within contexts among Asian Americans and European Americans. *J. Pers. Soc. Psychol.* **2007**, *93*, 478–490. [CrossRef]
29. American Psychiatric Association. *Diagnostic and Statistical Manual of Mental Disorders*; American Psychiatric Association: Washington, DC, USA, 2013.
30. First, M.B.; Williams, J.B.W.; Karg, R.S.; Spitzer, R.L. *Structured Clinical Interview for DSM-5 Disorders, Clinician Version (SCID-5-CV)*; American Psychiatric Association: Arlington, TX, USA, 2015.
31. *Stata-Corp Stata Statistical Software: Release 17*; Statacorp: College Station, TX, USA, 2021.
32. Cohen, J. *Statistical Power Analysis for the Behavioral Sciences*, 2nd ed.; L. Erlbaum Associates: Hillsdale, NJ, USA, 1988; ISBN 978-0-8058-0283-2.
33. Kelley, K.; Preacher, K.J. On effect size. *Psychol. Methods* **2012**, *17*, 137–152. [CrossRef]
34. Finner, H.; Roters, M. On the false discovery rate and expecte type I errors. *J. Am. Stat. Assoc.* **2001**, *88*, 920–923. [CrossRef]
35. Ammar, A.; Brach, M.; Trabelsi, K.; Chtourou, H.; Boukhris, O.; Masmoudi, L.; Bouaziz, B.; Bentlage, E.; How, D.; Ahmed, M.; et al. Effects of COVID-19 Home Confinement on Eating Behaviour and Physical Activity: Results of the ECLB-COVID19 International Online Survey. *Nutrients* **2020**, *12*, 1583. [CrossRef]
36. Sánchez, E.; Lecube, A.; Bellido, D.; Monereo, S.; Malagón, M.M.; Tinahones, J.F. Leading Factors for Weight Gain during COVID-19 Lockdown in a Spanish Population: A Cross-Sectional Study. *Nutrients* **2021**, *13*, 894. [CrossRef]
37. Bhutani, S.; Cooper, J.A. COVID-19–Related Home Confinement in Adults: Weight Gain Risks and Opportunities. *Obesity* **2020**, *28*, 1576–1577. [CrossRef]
38. Stevenson, J.L.; Krishnan, S.; A Stoner, M.; Goktas, Z.; A Cooper, J. Effects of exercise during the holiday season on changes in body weight, body composition and blood pressure. *Eur. J. Clin. Nutr.* **2013**, *67*, 944–949. [CrossRef]
39. Agüera, Z.; Lozano-Madrid, M.; Mallorquí-Bagué, N.; Jiménez-Murcia, S.; Menchón, J.M.; Fernández-Aranda, F. A review of binge eating disorder and obesity. *Neuropsychiatrie* **2021**, *35*, 57–67. [CrossRef]
40. Villarejo, C.; Fernández-Aranda, F.; Jiménez-Murcia, S.; Peñas-Lledó, E.; Granero, R.; Penelo, E.; Tinahones, F.J.; Sancho, C.; Vilarrasa, N.; Montserrat-Gil de Bernabé, M.; et al. Lifetime Obesity in Patients with Eating Disorders: Increasing Prevalence, Clinical and Personality Correlates. *Eur. Eat. Disord. Rev.* **2012**, *20*, 250–254. [CrossRef]
41. Monteleone, A.M.; Marciello, F.; Cascino, G.; Abbate-Daga, G.; Anselmetti, S.; Baiano, M.; Balestrieri, M.; Barone, E.; Bertelli, S.; Carpiniello, B.; et al. The impact of COVID-19 lockdown and of the following "re-opening" period on specific and general psychopathology in people with Eating Disorders: The emergent role of internalizing symptoms. *J. Affect. Disord.* **2021**, *285*, 77–83. [CrossRef]
42. Agüera, Z.; Riesco, N.; Valenciano-Mendoza, E.; Granero, R.; Sánchez, I.; Andreu, A.; Jiménez-Murcia, S.; Fernández-Aranda, F. Illness perception in patients with eating disorders: Clinical, personality, and food addiction correlates. *Eat. Weight. Disord.—Stud. Anorex. Bulim. Obes.* **2021**, *26*, 2287–2300. [CrossRef]
43. Bryan, D.C.; Macdonald, P.; Ambwani, S.; Cardi, V.; Rowlands, K.; Willmott, D.; Treasure, J. Exploring the ways in which COVID-19 and lockdown has affected the lives of adult patients with anorexia nervosa and their carers. *Eur. Eat. Disord. Rev.* **2020**, *28*, 826–835. [CrossRef]
44. Claes, L.; Boekaerts, E.; Verschueren, M.; Boukaert, W.; Luyckx, K. Identity statuses in prebariatric patients with obesity: Associations with eating disorder symptoms, psychological complaints, and coping behaviour? *Eur. Eat. Disord. Rev.* **2019**, *27*, 410–420. [CrossRef]
45. Riesco, N.; Agüera, Z.; Granero, R.; Jiménez-Murcia, S.; Menchón, J.M.; Fernández-Aranda, F. Other Specified Feeding or Eating Disorders (OSFED): Clinical heterogeneity and cognitive-behavioral therapy outcome. *Eur. Psychiatry* **2018**, *54*, 109–116. [CrossRef] [PubMed]
46. He, M.; Xian, Y.; Lv, X.; He, J.; Ren, Y. Changes in Body Weight, Physical Activity, and Lifestyle During the Semi-lockdown Period After the Outbreak of COVID-19 in China: An Online Survey. *Disaster Med. Public Heal. Prep.* **2021**, *15*, e23–e28. [CrossRef] [PubMed]
47. Rajkumar, R.P. COVID-19 and mental health: A review of the existing literature. *Asian J. Psychiatry* **2020**, *52*, 102066. [CrossRef] [PubMed]

nutrients

MDPI

Article

Are Peripheral Biomarkers Determinants of Eating Styles in Childhood and Adolescence Obesity? A Cross-Sectional Study

Lorena Desdentado [1,2,3], Jaime Navarrete [2], María Folgado-Alufre [2,3], Ana de Blas [4], Jéssica Navarro-Siurana [2], Francisco Ponce [1,4], Guadalupe Molinari [1], Andrea Jimeno-Martínez [1,5], Azahara I. Rupérez [1,5], Gloria Bueno-Lozano [1,5,6], Aida Cuenca-Royo [1,7], Emili Corbella [1,8], Zaida Agüera [1,9], Rosa M. Baños [1,2,3] and Julio Álvarez-Pitti [1,4,*]

1 CIBER Fisiopatología Obesidad y Nutrición (CIBEROBN), Instituto de Salud Carlos III, Av. Monforte de Lemos, 3-5. Pabellón 11, Planta 0, 28029 Madrid, Spain; lorena.desdentado@uv.es (L.D.); siscopz80@gmail.com (F.P.); guadalupemolinari@gmail.com (G.M.); andreajimenotic@gmail.com (A.J.-M.); airuperez@unizar.es (A.I.R.); mgbuenol@unizar.es (G.B.-L.); acuenca@imim.es (A.C.-R.); emilic@bellvitgehospital.cat (E.C.); zaguera@bellvitgehospital.cat (Z.A.); banos@uv.es (R.M.B.)

2 Polibienestar Research Institute, University of Valencia, Calle Serpis, 29, 46022 Valencia, Spain; nahijai@uv.es (J.N.); maria.folgado@uv.es (M.F.-A.); jessica.navarro-siurana@uv.es (J.N.-S.)

3 Department of Personality, Evaluation, and Psychological Treatments, University of Valencia, Avda. Blasco Ibañez, 21, 46010 Valencia, Spain

4 Pediatric Department, Consorcio Hospital General Universitario de Valencia, Avda. Tres Cruces, 2, 46014 Valencia, Spain; adeblaszapata@gmail.com

5 Growth, Exercise, Nutrition and Development (GENUD) Research Group, Facultad de Ciencias de la Salud, Instituto Agroalimentario de Aragón, Universidad de Zaragoza, Calle Miguel Servet, 177, 50013 Zaragoza, Spain

6 Paediatric Endocrinology Department, Clinical Hospital Lozano Blesa, Zaragoza, Avda. San Juan Bosco, 50009 Zaragoza, Spain

7 Integrative Pharmacology and Systems Neurosciences Research Group, Neurosciences Research Program, Hospital del Mar Medical Research Institute (IMIM), 08003 Barcelona, Spain

8 Cardiovascular Risk Unit, Internal Medicine Department, Bellvitge University Hospital—IDIBELL, Feixa Llarga, s/n, 08907 Barcelona, Spain

9 Department of Public Health, Mental Health and Perinatal Nursing, Health Sciences Campus Bellvitge, School of Nursing, University of Barcelona, Feixa Llarga, s/n, 08907 Barcelona, Spain

* Correspondence: alvarez_jul@gva.es; Tel.: +34-96-1820772

Citation: Desdentado, L.; Navarrete, J.; Folgado-Alufre, M.; de Blas, A.; Navarro-Siurana, J.; Ponce, F.; Molinari, G.; Jimeno-Martínez, A.; Rupérez, A.I.; Bueno-Lozano, G.; et al. Are Peripheral Biomarkers Determinants of Eating Styles in Childhood and Adolescence Obesity? A Cross-Sectional Study. *Nutrients* **2022**, *14*, 305. https://doi.org/10.3390/nu14020305

Academic Editor: Dina Bellizzi

Received: 21 October 2021
Accepted: 30 November 2021
Published: 12 January 2022

Abstract: Disturbances in eating behaviors have been widely related to obesity. However, little is known about the role of obesity-related biomarkers in shaping habitual patterns of eating behaviors (i.e., eating styles) in childhood. The objective of the present study was to explore the relationships between several biomarkers crucially involved in obesity (ghrelin, insulin resistance, and leptin/adiponectin ratio) and eating styles in children and adolescents with obesity. Seventy participants aged between 8 and 16 (56.2% men) fulfilled the Spanish version of the Dutch Eating Behavior Questionnaire for Children to measure external, emotional, and restrained eating styles. In addition, concentrations of ghrelin, leptin, adiponectin, insulin, and glucose were obtained through a blood test. Hierarchical multiple regression analyses controlling for age and sex were computed for each eating style. Results indicated that individuals with higher ghrelin concentration levels showed lower scores in restrained eating ($\beta = -0.61$, $p < 0.001$). The total model explained 32% of the variance of the restrained pattern. No other relationships between obesity-related biomarkers and eating behaviors were found. This study highlights that one of the obesity-risk factors, namely lower plasma ghrelin levels, is substantially involved in a well-known maladaptive eating style, restraint eating, in childhood obesity.

Keywords: obesity; children; adolescents; ghrelin; insulin resistance; leptin; adiponectin; leptin/adiponectin ratio; eating behavior; eating styles

1. Introduction

Obesity is a multifactorial disease that is currently considered a public health problem. Specifically, the prevalence of obesity has increased rapidly in childhood and adolescence (5–19 years old), with more than 100 million affected in 2016 [1]. Although recent literature has suggested maintenance, even slight decrease, of childhood obesity prevalence in Spain, it continues to be one of the highest prevalence of obesity and overweight in Europe [2].

These high prevalence figures are partly because there is currently no effective treatment for obesity, which can be generalized to most children and adolescents [3]. Recently, the American Association of Clinical Endocrinologists [4] and the European Association for the Study of Obesity [5] has proposed a new diagnostic term, namely "adiposity-based chronic disease" (ABCD). The phrase "adiposity-based" is justified because the disease is primarily due to abnormalities in the mass, distribution, and/or function of adipose tissue. This fact reinforces the concept of obesity as a chronic, complex, multifactorial, and incurable disease at present. For this reason, it is important to continue exploring the different roots of obesity since this is the only way to develop individualized treatments that ensure a higher success rate.

Eating behaviors stand out as crucial proximal determinants of body weight and the motivation to eat since childhood [6,7]. Eating styles represent dispositional tendencies of food intake and have been closely related to obesity in adults [8] and children and adolescents [9,10]. According to the three main theories about impaired food consumption (i.e., the external, psychosomatic, and restraint theories), three predominant eating styles have been identified [11]. External eating refers to the predominance of external environmental factors, such as smell or sight, as determinants of eating behavior, independently of the internal bodily state (i.e., feeling hungry or satiated) [12,13]. Emotional eating emphasizes the influence of emotional factors so that eating behavior is prompted in response to emotional arousal states, such as fear, anxiety, or anger, again without considering internal physiological signals of hunger and satiety [14]. Restraint eating concerns the attempt to control eating behavior through cognitive control and suppression of internal hunger signals to lose weight or avoid weight gain [13].

Previous research has shown that emotional eating can be considered an "obese" eating pattern, since it has been consistently found that higher emotional eating is related to overweight and long-term weight gain in both adults [8,15,16] and children [17], although the prevalence in childhood (7 to 12 years old) is actually low [11]. Emotional eating seems to emerge in adolescence [18,19] and is more prevalent in females than in males [20].

Restrained eating is also conceptualized as an "obese" eating style [21]. Overall, the distinctive features of restrained eaters are restricting food intake for long periods of time to lose or maintain weight and expressing dissatisfaction towards their body size and/or shape [22]. According to the restraint theory, when the cognitive control of eating is disrupted, restrained eaters tend to show a more disinhibited behavior, increasing their food intake and overeating [23]. Hence, although paradoxical, the involvement of restrained eating in obesity, as well as eating disorders, is not surprising [24].

Unlike emotional and restrained eating, some studies suggest that external eating might not be an "obese eating" pattern (i.e., an eating tendency related to a higher body mass index (BMI)) since levels of external eating seem to be similar between normal-weight and overweight individuals [8,25]. Moreover, it has been argued that external eating could represent an adaptive response that helped survive whenever food is available in periods of food shortage [26]. However, it should be noted that these findings contrast with evidence indicating that overweight and obese individuals show poor interoceptive abilities (i.e., awareness of internal bodily cues accompanying homeostatic states such as satiety) [27], which might predispose them to rely on external cues rather than internal signals of satiety and, therefore, to less adaptive eating behaviors [28]. In this line, Mata and colleagues found that external eating was positively related to the insula activation—which is considered a crucial brain hub for interoceptive processing [29]—in adolescents with excess weight, whereas this relationship was negative among healthy weight adolescents [30].

These results suggest the presence of an altered relationship between insula function and interoceptive/exteroceptive processing in adolescents with excess weight. Moreover, it is known that children with higher reward sensitivity (including sensitivity towards external cues of appetitive stimuli) are more vulnerable to become overweight [31], although this relationship is not straightforward. Specifically, external eating and food responsive behavior mediate the relationship between weight and reward sensitivity in childhood [32].

In the regulation of appetite, not only the central nervous system (CNS), but the adrenal glands, the pancreas, and the gastrointestinal tract are involved, and the adipose tissue also plays a relevant role [33]. Adipose tissue is a metabolically active organ involved in multiple biological processes and communicates through the secretion of peptides and hormones, known as adipokines [34]. As mentioned above, obesity is characterized by a pathological expansion and/or unhealthy distribution of body fat, producing adipose tissue dysfunction. This dysfunction produces a disbalance in the homeostasis of children and adolescents with obesity, favoring a profile characterized by resistance to insulin action (with a secondary elevation of insulin), resistance to leptin action (which favors hyperleptinemia), and low adiponectin and ghrelin values [35]. This profile increases the risk of developing associated cardiometabolic diseases [36] but also could be involved in (maladaptive) eating behaviors in childhood obesity. However, no previous studies have examined this relation.

Ghrelin is a well-known gut hormone involved not only in food intake, but also in energy storage, stimulating adipogenesis [37,38]. Specifically, circulating ghrelin levels increase during intake restriction, leading to increased appetite [39] and then fall quickly after ingestion [39]. Thus, it is postulated that one primary role of ghrelin is to act as a meal initiator. However, to our best knowledge, research on its association with eating styles is scarce in normal-weight [40,41] and obese adults [42] and even absent in obese children and adolescents.

The main metabolic disturbance driven by obesity is insulin resistance (IR) [43]. Insulin levels rise and fall rapidly in response to feeding and starvation. These changing insulin levels orchestrate the metabolic switch between anabolism and catabolism. Glucose is the main regulator of insulin, but also other nutrients, hormones, and the autonomic nervous system, influence its serum levels [44].

As insulin, leptin, which is mostly released by adipose tissue, is well-known to reduce appetite and increase energy expenditure. In obesity, leptin resistance is produced due to the excess adiposity, and, therefore, leptin does not properly reduce food consumption, leading to increased body weight [45]. Circulating leptin levels throughout the day do not undergo large variations, showing a circadian rhythm and oscillatory pattern [46].

Adiponectin is also almost exclusively produced in adipose tissue [47]. The mechanisms of this adipokine in appetite regulation are intricate, and it could be an appetite stimulator or inhibiting factor depending on feeding status, the content of glucose in cerebrospinal fluid, and the degree of fatness [48]. In contrast to other adipokines, the circulating levels of adiponectin are inversely proportional to total fat mass [49], and also with fasting insulin concentration and plasma triglycerides, but positively with the plasma cholesterol contained in HDL [50].

Leptin and adiponectin are regulated in an opposite manner in most cases. Children and adolescents with obesity tend to have higher leptin levels and lower adiponectin levels [51]. This unfavorable leptin/adiponectin ratio has been proposed as a functional biomarker of adipose tissue inflammation and seems to be a good indicator of cardiometabolic risk associated with obesity and metabolic syndrome [52]. However, it remains unknown whether this biomarker acts as an underlying factor of eating styles in obesity.

Thus, eating behavior is modulated by both external and internal signals from the body [53]. External cues include environmental factors such as the hedonic properties of food, as well as social factors such as other people's behavior [54]. Internal signals usually refer to physiological processes underlying feelings of hunger and satiety, such as the blood concentrations of ghrelin, glucose, and leptin [55]. At this point, it becomes evident that eating behavior and, ultimately, obesity are highly complex. Disentangling the multiple factors involved and the relationships between them can help us better understand obesity and, therefore, develop more effective prevention and treatment methods, especially in the early stages of human development. As pointed out by Verbiest and colleagues [10], interdisciplinary work is needed to do so.

Despite a certain amount of research focused on the regulatory role of these hormonal biomarkers in eating behavior in obese samples, most studies have considered imminent appetite and food intake as outcome variables. However, little is known regarding the contribution of peripheral obesity-related biomarkers to eating styles, that is, to (relatively) well-established patterns of eating behaviors such as emotional, external, and restrained eating.

The aim of this study is to explore the relationship between several peripheral obesity-related biomarkers (i.e., ghrelin, IR, and leptin/adiponectin ratio) and eating styles (i.e., external, emotional, and restrained) in a Spanish sample of obese children and adolescents. Specifically, based on preliminary research on this field, it is hypothesized that poorer obesity-related biomarkers in obese children and adolescents, namely lower ghrelin, higher IR, and higher leptin/adiponectin ratio, will be associated with higher scores on external, emotional, and restrained eating.

2. Materials and Methods

2.1. Participants

Participants in the current study were recruited from the Obesity and Cardiovascular Risk Unit at General University Hospital Consortium of Valencia (CHGUV) and Pediatric Endocrinology Department at the University Clinical Hospital "Lozano Blesa" (HCULB) in Zaragoza (Spain). Data were collected between November 2019 and September 2021 as a part of the Eat4HealthyLife research project, a multicentered study that explores potential risk factors of obesity and eating disorders (EDs). Eligible criteria considered were the following: aged between 8 and 16 years old, diagnosis of obesity (BMI Z-score > 2 standard deviations according to the scales of their reference group by age and sex), and not having received or not currently receiving obesity treatment in our outpatient clinic. None of the subjects included suffer from any other disease or eating disorder. The sample consisted of 70 children and adolescents with obesity. The mean age of the sample was 12.36 (SD = 2.19), and 56.2% were boys.

2.2. Measures

2.2.1. Sociodemographic Data and Anthropometrics

Anthropometric measurements were collected under standardized conditions with patients wearing light clothing and no shoes. Bioelectrical impedance analysis, using a TANITA TBF-410 M over a horizontal and hard surface and to the nearest 0.1 kg, was the selected method to measure body weight and composition. Height was measured to the nearest 0.5 cm using a portable height board (SECA 216). BMI z-score (BMIz) was calculated for each patient. BMIz correlates to growth percentile charts and allows children's relative weight follow-up from childhood up to adolescence. Participants' obesity was defined with BMIz scores greater than 2 SD following World Health Organization (WHO) growth charts [56].

2.2.2. Metabolic Assessment

Blood samples were collected from fasting participants scheduled early in the morning. Glucose and insulin measurements and a lipid panel were requested for every patient. The homeostatic model assessment (HOMA) index of IR was measured as the product of insulin (μU/mL) and glucose (mmol/L) divided by 22.5. Hyperinsulinism was defined according to pubertal stage normative data [57].

Adipokine laboratory measurements were obtained from the Cardiovascular Risk Unit Laboratory at Hospital General of Valencia (Valencia, Spain). Ghrelin, leptin, and adiponectin were measured using commercially available BMS 2192, BMS 2039, and BMS 2032/2 eBioscience ELISA kits. The leptin assay detection limit was set at 894 ng/L. Adiponectin assay range was set from 764 μg/L to 16,893 μg/L. The ghrelin assay was set from a mean value of 915 pg/mL.

2.2.3. Eating Styles

The Dutch Eating Behavior Questionnaire for Children (DEBQ-C) [11,58] was used to measure eating styles, which is a 20 item self-report questionnaire rated in a 3-point Likert scale from 1 to 3 (1 = "no", 2 = "sometimes", 3 = "yes") that assess three different eating behavior patterns: external (e.g., "Does walking past a candy store make you feel eating? "), emotional (e.g., "Does worrying make you feel like eating?"), and restrained (e.g., "Do you intentionally eat food that helps you lose weight?") eating. Higher scores on each subscale are indicative of greater emotional, external, or restrained eating. Emotional eating and restrained eating subscales are composed of 7 items each, whereas external eating is composed of 6 items. Total scores for each subscale are computed with the mean score of their corresponding items. In this sample, the internal consistency of each scale was acceptable ($\alpha = 0.87$, $\alpha = 0.78$, and $\alpha = 0.65$, respectively). EDs were ruled out according to the diagnostic criteria of the DSM-5 [59].

2.3. Procedure

New patients arriving at the Obesity Risk Units were considered potential candidates to participate in this study. At their first appointment at the Unit, participants were weighed and measured to calculate BMIz. Once the patients were diagnosed with obesity, parents were offered the possibility for their children to voluntarily participate in the study. All parents of participants signed the informed consent documents before starting the assessment, in accordance with the Declaration of Helsinki. The study was approved by the Ethics Committee at CHGUV (reference number: 4/2019) and the Research Ethics Committee of the Autonomous Community of Aragon (CEICA) (reference number: PI19/269). Then, patients who agreed to participate were scheduled to come to the hospital in a second session. In this session, participants underwent a blood test to measure biomarkers, and one hour later (after having breakfast), they completed several psychological measures in the context of the Eat4HealthyLife project, including the DEBQ-C, assisted by a trained psychologist. Specifically, the assessment protocol of this project included some neurocognitive measurements, including the Kaufman Brief Intelligence Test Second Edition [60] and the Digit span subtest of the Wechsler Intelligence Scale for Children [61]. However, they are not reported herein because they are not relevant for the objective of this study.

It should be noted that recruitment of participants was stopped during the lockdown period (between March and June 2020), as well as during the third wave of COVID-19 in Spain (between January and March 2021) when the incidence of cases was very high. From the beginning of the pandemic, the study sessions took place with appropriate safety measures, such as mask and ventilation in the room. None of the participants presented symptoms compatible with an infectious process either at the time of the evaluation or in the previous week.

2.4. Statistical Analyses

Data analyses were conducted using the SPSS v26 software (IBM, Armonk, NY, USA). First, descriptive statistics (mean, standard deviation) were performed to analyze the sociodemographic data of the sample. Second, Cronbach's alpha was calculated to establish the internal consistency of the psychometrical measures, with coefficients above 0.70 being considered adequate [62].

Finally, three hierarchical multiple regressions were conducted to determine whether external, emotional, and restrained eating styles (DEBQ-C) were explained by ghrelin, IR, and leptin/adiponectin ratio after controlling for sex and age. Thus, the control variables (sex and age) were entered at Block 1, and the rest of the independent variables were entered at Block 2. Preliminary analyses were performed to check normality, linearity, homoscedasticity, and multicollinearity assumptions, with no serious violations noted.

3. Results

3.1. Descriptive Statistics

The means, standard deviations, ranges, and percentiles 25, 50, and 75 of the different measures for eating styles and the peripheral obesity-related biomarkers, as well as height and weight, are displayed in Table 1.

Table 1. Descriptive statistics for study measures (n = 70).

Measure	M	SD	Range	Percentiles		
				P_{25}	P_{50}	P_{75}
Height (cm)	158.22	11.12	133.90–181.20	151.00	158.40	166.30
Weight (kg)	77.86	18.71	39.80–115.40	64.80	76.70	91.90
External eating	1.99	0.55	1–3	1.50	2.00	2.50
Emotional eating	1.53	0.62	1–3	1.00	1.21	1.86
Restrained eating	1.91	0.45	1–3	1.57	1.86	2.18
Ghrelin (pg/mL)	1497.84	1109.36	90.40–4386.18	690.65	1084.36	2076.84
HOMA index	5.24	5.73	0.89–39.24	2.53	4.14	5.86
Leptin/adiponectin ratio	1.64	2.03	0.04–9.68	0.48	0.94	1.76

Notes. n = number of participants; M = mean; SD = standard deviation.

3.2. Hierarchical Multiple Regressions

3.2.1. External Eating

Regarding the first hierarchical multiple regression model, sex and age explained 5% of the variance of external eating, which did not reach statistical significance: F (2, 50) = 1.32, p = 0.277, R^2 = 0.050. After entering ghrelin, IR, and leptin/adiponectin ratio at Block 2, the total model did not statistically significantly explain external eating: F (5, 47) = 1.25, p = 0.303, R^2 = 0.117. Table 2 shows the regression coefficients of the independent variables on external eating.

Table 2. Regression coefficients of sex, age, ghrelin, IR, and leptin/adiponectin ratio on external eating.

Variables	B	SE B	β	p	R^2	ΔR^2
Block 1					0.05	0.05
Constant	1.38	0.47		0.005		
Sex	0.22	0.15	0.20	0.164		
Age	0.02	0.04	0.10	0.494		
Block 2					0.12	0.07
Constant	1.60	0.59		0.010		
Sex	0.26	0.16	0.24	0.099		
Age	−0.00	0.04	−0.01	0.967		
Ghrelin	−0.00	0.00	−0.11	0.508		
IR	0.02	0.01	0.19	0.213		
Leptin/adiponectin ratio	0.02	0.04	0.07	0.638		

Notes. B = unstandardized beta values; SE B = standard error of B; β = standardized beta values; R^2 = coefficient of determination; ΔR^2 = coefficient of determination change.

3.2.2. Emotional Eating

In the second hierarchical multiple regression model, sex and age explained 13% of the variance of emotional eating: F (2, 50) = 3.63 p = 0.034, R^2 = 0.127. However, after entering ghrelin, IR, and leptin/adiponectin ratio at Block 2, the total model did not statistically explain emotional eating: F (5, 47) = 2.36, p = 0.054, R^2 = 0.201. Table 3 shows regression coefficients of the independent variables on emotional eating.

Table 3. Regression coefficients of sex, age, ghrelin, IR, and leptin/adiponectin ratio on emotional eating.

	Model					
Variables	**B**	**SE B**	**β**	***p***	R^2	ΔR^2
Block 1					0.13	0.13 *
Constant	0.50	0.51		0.311		
Sex	0.40	0.17	0.32	0.020		
Age	0.04	0.04	0.13	0.318		
Block 2					0.20	0.07
Constant	0.23	0.63		0.713		
Sex	0.42	0.17	0.34	0.015		
Age	0.03	0.04	0.12	0.448		
Ghrelin	0.00	0.00	0.12	0.454		
IR	0.02	0.02	0.19	0.191		
Leptin/adiponectin ratio	0.06	0.04	0.19	0.188		

Notes. B = unstandardized beta values; SE B = standard error of B; β = standardized beta values; R^2 = coefficient of determination; ΔR^2 = coefficient of determination change. * $p < 0.05$.

3.2.3. Restrained Eating

The third hierarchical multiple regression model showed that sex and age (Block 1) did not significantly explain the variance in restrained eating: F (2, 50) = 0.32 p = 0.727, R^2 = 0.013. After entry of ghrelin, IR, and leptin/adiponectin ratio at Block 2, the total model statistically significantly explained restrained eating: F (5, 47) = 4.37, p = 0.002, R^2 = 0.317. Among them, ghrelin was the unique significant predictor of restrained eating (β = −0.61; $p < 0.001$), indicating that individuals with higher ghrelin levels showed lower scores on restrained eating, explaining 31% of its variance. Table 4 shows regression coefficients of the independent variables on restrained eating.

Table 4. Regression coefficients of sex, age, ghrelin, IR, and leptin/adiponectin ratio on restrained eating.

	Model					
Variables	**B**	**SE B**	**β**	***p***	R^2	ΔR^2
Block 1					0.01	0.01
Constant	1.63	0.39		0.000		
Sex	0.08	0.13	0.08	0.558		
Age	0.01	0.03	0.07	0.622		
Block 2					0.32	0.31 **
Constant	2.64	0.42		0.000		
Sex	0.14	0.11	0.16	0.198		
Age	−0.05	0.03	−0.23	0.102		
Ghrelin	0.00	0.00	−0.61	<0.001		
IR	0.01	0.01	0.09	0.506		
Leptin/adiponectin ratio	−0.01	0.03	−0.04	0.758		

Notes. B = unstandardized beta values; SE B = standard error of B; β = standardized beta values; R^2 = coefficient of determination; ΔR^2 = coefficient of determination change. ** $p < 0.01$.

4. Discussion

The present study was aimed at examining the involvement of different peripheral obesity-related biomarkers (namely, ghrelin, IR, and leptin/adiponectin ratio) to explain different eating styles, i.e., external, emotional, and restrained patterns, in childhood and adolescence obesity.

Our findings show that plasma ghrelin concentrations were negatively related to restrained eating after controlling for sex and age (nonsignificant) effects. In other words, a poor obesity-related biomarker (i.e., lower ghrelin concentrations) was related to restrained eating in childhood and adolescence obesity, as expected. These findings extend previous research that supports the restraint theory [21,23] by suggesting that restrained eating is not only an "obese" eating style, but also a "higher-risk-obesity" eating style. It should be noted that our results contrast with some previous studies conducted in normal-weight adults, indicating that restrained eating is positively correlated [41] or not correlated [40] with ghrelin. According to preliminary research, this discrepancy in the direction of the relationship could be due to the obesity status [63]. Moreover, different measures of restrained eating could reflect distinct conceptualizations of what it means, which might also explain inconsistencies in the literature in this regard. Mainly, scales measuring restrained eating differ in the purpose for which authors developed them [22], i.e., to assess chronic dieters who cyclically restrain their intake or over-eat [64], or individuals who success in reducing their intake [11]. Future studies should be cautious in this concern and simultaneously include individuals with normal and excess weight through different life course stages to disentangle the nature of this relationship. Finally, IR and leptin/adiponectin ratio were not significantly related to restrained eating. In the study conducted by Schur and colleagues [41], leptin and insulin were also measured, but they were not related to cognitive restraint, similar to our results.

External eating was hypothesized to be underlaid by high-risk peripheral biomarkers, specifically lower ghrelin levels, higher IR, and higher inflammation indicators (i.e., leptin/adiponectin ratio). However, our results showed no significant contribution from these biochemical indices to explain external eating once sex and age effects were partialized out. Although there are no previous studies examining the role of ghrelin, IR, leptin, and adiponectin in self-report eating styles in obesity, preliminary evidence exists regarding the influence of ghrelin on the brain activity involved in processing external food cues. In this regard, Malik and colleagues found an increased brain activity response to food-related visual cues after ghrelin administration, which was indeed correlated with self-reported hunger ratings [65]. However, our results suggest that this effect is not extended to the habitual external eating style in childhood obesity.

Similarly, contrary to what was hypothesized, emotional eating was not significantly related to any obesity-related biomarkers in our sample. Sex was the only statistically significant predictor of emotional eating, indicating that women showed higher scores on emotional eating than men, which is consistent with previous findings [20]. Noteworthy in this regard is a previous cohort study that found that higher leptin was cross-sectionally related to emotional overeating at age 7 years, but it was not prospectively associated with emotional overeating three years later after controlling for BMIz. However, this study used a parent-reported instead of a self-report measure of eating styles, that is, parents (or main caregivers) responded to the questionnaire instead of the children on their own (e.g., "My child eats more when annoyed"). Therefore, some biases of their parents could have influenced these results.

To our knowledge, this is the first study to comprehensively consider both physiological risk indicators of obesity and eating styles in a young sample. Theoretically, this study suggests that metabolic dysfunction of adipokines and IR might not yet be involved in eating behavior patterns in obesity in the early stages of development (i.e., childhood and adolescence). This fact promisingly implies that these hormonal disruptions could not have impaired the usual eating responses yet, even if they might be affecting current satiety perceptions, as pointed out by previous research [66]. Given the predictive role of eating styles on prospective weight in adults [15], it can be thought that the clinical condition of obese children and adolescents could still be reversed without consequences in their way of relating to food. In particular, this can be applied to eating styles that involve appropriate processing of interoceptive satiety signals, namely the absence of eating as a maladaptive emotion regulation strategy (emotional eating) and the adaptive levels of sensitivity towards food-related rewards (external eating). However, this is not the case with the cognitive suppression of these internal hunger signals, as evidenced by the negative association between restrained eating and ghrelin levels. In other words, it seems that cognitively ignoring the interoceptive signs of hunger is not a good eating strategy in children and adolescents with obesity, since it is related to a poorer ghrelin profile.

Although interoceptive cues might be ignored at a cognitive level in those with lower ghrelin concentrations, it might be plausible that interoceptive abilities are not yet disturbed in young obese individuals, unlike obese adults [27]. This could explain why emotional and external eating styles were not related to metabolic biomarkers in our sample. Taking all into account, and in light of preliminary research on the role of interoceptive processing as an underlying mechanism of eating styles in adults [67], future studies should examine the interaction between peripheral biomarkers involved in satiety, their perception and processing in the central nervous system (i.e., interoception), and eating styles, in childhood obesity. From a clinical point of view, our findings suggest that dietary treatments mainly focused on restricting the amount of food intake (which inevitably involves ignoring the sensations of appetite) rather than on eating healthy food are contraindicated. In this line, previous research has shown the negative effects of dieting for healthy management of obesity during childhood and adolescence in the long term [68].

The current study presents some limitations that should be noted. First, the sample size was not very large, so the statistical power might be compromised, leading to not finding a statistical effect in this sample that could exist in the population. Second, the age range of participants in this study covered two different developmental stages (childhood and adolescence). Although statistical control has been applied over the potential effect of age (and sex) on the relationships of interest, future studies should replicate this research throughout the different development stages. Third, our results refer only to children and adolescents with moderate and severe obesity (BMIz > 2), so they cannot be generalized to other populations such as children and adolescents with normal weight or overweight (BMIz < 2), nor to adults. Fourth, our findings may be biased by the recruitment period, which was characterized by the COVID-19 pandemic for a portion of our sample. In this regard, a recent longitudinal study showed that external, emotional, and restrained eating styles remained stable during the lockdown in college students [69], supporting the notion of eating styles as trait-like rather than state-like patterns. Although these findings might be different in children and adolescents with obesity, to our best knowledge, there is no evidence to think that the associations between eating styles and biomarkers may vary according to circumstantial factors. Finally, given the cross-sectional nature of the design of the current study, causal relationships cannot be established. Future studies should adopt longitudinal designs to determine the directionality between ghrelin and restrained eating in childhood obesity and the mediating mechanisms by which this relationship occurs.

Despite these limitations, this study contributes substantially to a better understanding of the interactions between two different types of crucial factors (biochemical and psychological) involved in childhood and adolescent obesity, namely circulating hormones and eating styles.

5. Conclusions

This is the first study to report the link between the low ghrelin concentrations (which is a well-known biomarker of risk in obesity) and high dispositional tendency to cognitively suppress internal signals of hunger, i.e., restraint eating, which is an eating style considered maladaptive and widely related to obesity across the lifespan. Expanding on previous research, our study indicates that dietary restraint, in addition to being an obesity-related eating style, is also a behavioral pattern of increased risk within the obesity spectrum.

Author Contributions: Conceptualization, L.D., J.N., M.F.-A., J.N.-S., G.M., A.d.B., A.C.-R., E.C., Z.A., R.M.B. and J.Á.-P.; methodology, L.D., J.N., M.F.-A., J.N.-S., G.M., A.d.B., R.M.B., A.J.-M., A.I.R., G.B.-L. and J.Á.-P.; validation, L.D., J.N., M.F.-A., J.N.-S., G.M., A.d.B., R.M.B. and J.Á.-P.; formal analysis, L.D., J.N., M.F.-A. and J.N.-S.; investigation, L.D., J.N., M.F.-A., J.N.-S., A.d.B., F.P., A.J.-M., A.I.R., G.B.-L. and J.Á.-P.; resources, G.M., R.M.B. and J.Á.-P.; data curation, L.D., J.N., M.F.-A., J.N.-S., A.d.B., F.P., A.J.-M., A.I.R. and J.Á.-P.; writing—original draft preparation, L.D., J.N., M.F.-A., J.N.-S., A.d.B. and J.Á.-P.; writing—review and editing, L.D., J.N., M.F.-A., J.N.-S., G.M., A.d.B., R.M.B. and

J.Á.-P.; supervision, J.Á.-P., G.M. and R.M.B.; project administration, J.Á.-P., G.M., Z.A. and R.M.B.; funding acquisition, J.Á.-P., Z.A. and R.M.B. All authors have read and agreed to the published version of the manuscript.

Funding: This research was funded by Centro de Investigación Biomédica en Red de Fisiopatología de la Obesidad y Nutrición (CIBEROBN), Instituto de Salud Carlos III, Spain, through the EAT4HEALTHYLIFE project (Obesity and abnormal eating behavior across the lifespan. A cross sectional and longitudinal approach of environmental and neurobiological factors). In addition, L.D. and M.F.-A. are supported by their grants FPU18/01690 and FPU19/03720, respectively, funded by Ministerio de Ciencia e Innovación/Agencia Estatal de Investigación/10.13039/501100011033 and by "European Social Fund – Investing in your future".

Institutional Review Board Statement: The study was conducted according to the guidelines of the Declaration of Helsinki and approved by the Ethics Committee of the General University Hospital Consortium of Valencia (CHGUV) (reference number: 4/2019) and the Research Ethics Committee of the Autonomous Community of Aragon (CEICA) (reference number: PI19/269).

Informed Consent Statement: Written informed consent was obtained from all participants involved in this study.

Data Availability Statement: The dataset generated and analyzed is available from the corresponding author on reasonable request.

Acknowledgments: We thank the families who kindly participated in the Eat4HealthyLife research project.

Conflicts of Interest: The authors declare no conflict of interest.

References

1. NCD Risk Factor Collaboration (NCD-RisC). Worldwide Trends in Body-Mass Index, Underweight, Overweight, and Obesity from 1975 to 2016: A Pooled Analysis of 2416 Population-Based Measurement Studies in 128.9 Million Children, Adolescents, and Adults. *Lancet* **2017**, *390*, 2627–2642. [CrossRef]
2. Buoncristiano, M.; Spinelli, A.; Williams, J.; Nardone, P.; Rito, A.I.; García-Solano, M.; Grøholt, E.K.; Gutiérrez-González, E.; Klepp, K.I.; Starc, G.; et al. Childhood Overweight and Obesity in Europe: Changes from 2007 to 2017. *Obes. Rev.* **2021**, e13226. [CrossRef] [PubMed]
3. Al-Khudairy, L.; Loveman, E.; Colquitt, J.L.; Mead, E.; Johnson, R.E.; Fraser, H.; Olajide, J.; Murphy, M.; Velho, R.M.; O'Malley, C.; et al. Diet, Physical Activity and Behavioural Interventions for the Treatment of Overweight or Obese Adolescents Aged 12 to 17 Years. *Cochrane Database Syst. Rev.* **2017**, *2017*, CD012691. [CrossRef]
4. Mechanick, J.I.; Hurley, D.L.; Garvey, W.T. Adiposity-Based Chronic Disease as a New Diagnostic Term: The American Association of Clinical Endocrinologists and American College of Endocrinology Position Statement. *Endocr. Pract.* **2017**, *23*, 372–378. [CrossRef] [PubMed]
5. Frühbeck, G.; Busetto, L.; Dicker, D.; Yumuk, V.; Goossens, G.H.; Hebebrand, J.; Halford, J.G.C.; Farpour-Lambert, N.J.; Blaak, E.E.; Woodward, E.; et al. The ABCD of Obesity: An EASO Position Statement on a Diagnostic Term with Clinical and Scientific Implications. *Obes. Facts* **2019**, *12*, 131–136. [CrossRef] [PubMed]
6. Blundell, J.E. The Contribution of Behavioural Science to Nutrition: Appetite Control. *Nutr. Bull.* **2017**, *42*, 236–245. [CrossRef]
7. Llewellyn, C.; Fildes, A. Behavioural Susceptibility Theory: Professor Jane Wardle and the Role of Appetite in Genetic Risk of Obesity. *Curr. Obes. Rep.* **2017**, *6*, 38–45. [CrossRef] [PubMed]
8. Van Strien, T.; Herman, C.; Verheijden, M. Eating Style, Overeating, and Overweight in a Representative Dutch Sample. Does External Eating Play a Role? *Appetite* **2009**, *52*, 380–387. [CrossRef]
9. Obregón, A.M.; Pettinelli, P.P.; Santos, J.L. Childhood Obesity and Eating Behaviour. *J. Pediatr. Endocrinol. Metab.* **2015**, *28*, 497–502. [CrossRef] [PubMed]
10. Verbiest, I.; Michels, N.; Tanghe, A.; Braet, C. Inflammation in Obese Children and Adolescents: Association with Psychosocial Stress Variables and Effects of a Lifestyle Intervention. *Brain Behav. Immun.* **2021**, *98*, 40–47. [CrossRef]
11. Van Strien, T.; Frijters, J.; Bergers, G.; Defares, P. The Dutch Eating Behavior Questionnaire (DEBQ) for Assessment of Restrained, Emotional, and External Eating Behavior. *Int. J. Eat. Disord.* **1986**, *5*, 295–315. [CrossRef]
12. Schachter, S. The Interaction of Cognitive and Physiological Determinants of Emotional State. *Adv. Exp. Soc. Psychol.* **1964**, *1*, 49–80. [CrossRef]
13. Elfhag, K.; Morey, L. Personality Traits and Eating Behavior in the Obese: Poor Self-Control in Emotional and External Eating but Personality Assets in Restrained Eating. *Eat. Behav.* **2008**, *9*, 285–293. [CrossRef] [PubMed]
14. Bruch, H. *Eating Disorders. Obesity, Anorexia Nervosa, and the Person within*; Routledge & Kegan Paul: Oxfordshire, UK, 1974.
15. Koenders, P.G.; Van Strien, T. Emotional Eating, Rather than Lifestyle Behavior, Drives Weight Gain in a Prospective Study in 1562 Employees. *J. Occup. Environ. Med.* **2011**, *53*, 1287–1293. [CrossRef]

16. Sung, J.; Lee, K.; Song, Y. Relationship of Eating Behavior to Long-Term Weight Change and Body Mass Index: The Healthy Twin Study. *Eat. Weight Disord.* **2009**, *14*, e98–e105. [CrossRef] [PubMed]
17. Sleddens, E.F.; Kremers, S.P.; Thijs, C. The Children's Eating Behaviour Questionnaire: Factorial Validity and Association with Body Mass Index in Dutch Children Aged 6–7. *Int. J. Behav. Nutr. Phys. Act.* **2008**, *5*, 49. [CrossRef] [PubMed]
18. Van Strien, T.; Snoek, H.; van der Zwaluw, C.; Engels, R. Parental Control and the Dopamine D2 Receptor Gene (DRD2) Interaction on Emotional Eating in Adolescence. *Appetite* **2010**, *54*, 255–261. [CrossRef] [PubMed]
19. Van Strien, T.; van der Zwaluw, C.; Engels, R. Emotional Eating in Adolescents: A Gene (SLC6A4/5-HTT)—Depressive Feelings Interaction Analysis. *J. Psychiatr. Res.* **2010**, *44*, 1035–1042. [CrossRef]
20. Van Strien, T.; Konttinen, H.; Homberg, J.R.; Engels, R.C.M.E.; Winkens, L.H.H. Emotional Eating as a Mediator between Depression and Weight Gain. *Appetite* **2016**, *100*, 216–224. [CrossRef]
21. Varela, C.; Andrés, A.; Saldaña, C. The Behavioral Pathway Model to Overweight and Obesity: Coping Strategies, Eating Behaviors and Body Mass Index. *Eat. Weight Disord.* **2019**, *25*, 1277–1283. [CrossRef]
22. Polivy, J.; Herman, C.; Mills, J. What Is Restrained Eating and How Do We Identify It? *Appetite* **2020**, *155*, 104820. [CrossRef] [PubMed]
23. Herman, C.P.; Polivy, J. A Boundary Model for the Regulation of Eating. *Psychiatr. Ann.* **1983**, *13*, 918–927. [CrossRef]
24. Baños, R.; Cebolla, A.; Moragrega, I.; Van Strien, T.; Fernández-Aranda, F.; Agüera, Z.; de la Torre, R.; Casanueva, F.; Fernández-Real, J.; Fernández-García, J.; et al. Relationship between Eating Styles and Temperament in an Anorexia Nervosa, Healthy Control, and Morbid Obesity Female Sample. *Appetite* **2014**, *76*, 76–83. [CrossRef] [PubMed]
25. Wardle, J. Eating Style: A Validation Study of the Dutch Eating Behaviour Questionnaire in Normal Subjects and Women with Eating Disorders. *J. Psychosom. Res.* **1987**, *31*, 161–169. [CrossRef]
26. Van Strien, T. Causes of Emotional Eating and Matched Treatment of Obesity. *Obesity* **2018**, *18*, 35. [CrossRef] [PubMed]
27. Herbert, B.M.; Pollatos, O. Attenuated Interoceptive Sensitivity in Overweight and Obese Individuals. *Eat. Behav.* **2014**, *15*, 445–448. [CrossRef]
28. Herbert, B.M.; Blechert, J.; Hautzinger, M.; Matthias, E.; Herbert, C. Intuitive Eating Is Associated with Interoceptive Sensitivity. Effects on Body Mass Index. *Appetite* **2013**, *70*, 22–30. [CrossRef] [PubMed]
29. Craig, A.D. (Bud) How Do You Feel—Now? The Anterior Insula and Human Awareness. *Nat. Rev. Neurosci.* **2009**, *10*, 59–70. [CrossRef]
30. Mata, F.; Verdejo-Roman, J.; Soriano-Mas, C.; Verdejo-Garcia, A. Insula Tuning towards External Eating versus Interoceptive Input in Adolescents with Overweight and Obesity. *Appetite* **2015**, *93*, 24–30. [CrossRef] [PubMed]
31. Rollins, B.Y.; Loken, E.; Savage, J.S.; Birch, L.L. Measurement of Food Reinforcement in Preschool Children. Associations with Food Intake, BMI, and Reward Sensitivity. *Appetite* **2014**, *72*, 21–27. [CrossRef] [PubMed]
32. Vandeweghe, L.; Verbeken, S.; Vervoort, L.; Moens, E.; Braet, C. Reward Sensitivity and Body Weight: The Intervening Role of Food Responsive Behavior and External Eating. *Appetite* **2017**, *112*, 150–156. [CrossRef]
33. Hellström, P.M.; Geliebter, A.; Näslund, E.; Schmidt, P.T.; Yahav, E.K.; Hashim, S.A.; Yeomans, M.R. Peripheral and Central Signals in the Control of Eating in Normal, Obese and Binge-Eating Human Subjects. *Br. J. Nutr.* **2004**, *92*, S47–S57. [CrossRef]
34. Funcke, J.-B.; Scherer, P.E. Beyond Adiponectin and Leptin: Adipose Tissue-Derived Mediators of Inter-Organ Communication. *J. Lipid Res.* **2019**, *60*, 1648. [CrossRef] [PubMed]
35. Mechanick, J.I.; Zhao, S.; Garvey, W.T. The Adipokine-Cardiovascular-Lifestyle Network: Translation to Clinical Practice. *J. Am. Coll. Cardiol.* **2016**, *68*, 1785–1803. [CrossRef] [PubMed]
36. Gadde, K.M.; Martin, C.K.; Berthoud, H.R.; Heymsfield, S.B. Obesity: Pathophysiology and Management. *J. Am. Coll. Cardiol.* **2018**, *71*, 69–84. [CrossRef] [PubMed]
37. Wiedmer, P.; Nogueiras, R.; Broglio, F.; D'Alessio, D.; Tschöp, M.H. Ghrelin, Obesity and Diabetes. *Nat. Clin. Pract. Endocrinol. Metab.* **2007**, *3*, 705–712. [CrossRef] [PubMed]
38. Austin, J.; Marks, D. Hormonal Regulators of Appetite. *Int. J. Pediatr. Endocrinol.* **2009**, *2009*, 41753. [CrossRef]
39. Cummings, D.; Purnell, J.; Frayo, R.; Schmidova, K.; Wisse, B.; Weigle, D. A Preprandial Rise in Plasma Ghrelin Levels Suggests a Role in Meal Initiation in Humans. *Diabetes* **2001**, *50*, 1714–1719. [CrossRef]
40. Langlois, F.; Langlois, M.F.; Carpentier, A.C.; Brown, C.; Lemieux, S.; Hivert, M.F. Ghrelin Levels Are Associated with Hunger as Measured by the Three-Factor Eating Questionnaire in Healthy Young Adults. *Physiol. Behav.* **2011**, *104*, 373–377. [CrossRef]
41. Schur, E.A.; Cummings, D.E.; Callahan, H.S.; Foster-Schubert, K.E. Association of Cognitive Restraint with Ghrelin, Leptin, and Insulin Levels in Subjects Who Are Not Weight-Reduced. *Physiol. Behav.* **2008**, *93*, 706–712. [CrossRef]
42. Buss, J.; Havel, P.J.; Epel, E.; Lin, J.; Blackburn, E.; Daubenmier, J. Associations of Ghrelin with Eating Behaviors, Stress, Metabolic Factors, and Telomere Length among Overweight and Obese Women: Preliminary Evidence of Attenuated Ghrelin Effects in Obesity? *Appetite* **2014**, *76*, 94. [CrossRef]
43. Ten, S.; Maclaren, N. Insulin Resistance Syndrome in Children. *J. Clin. Endocrinol. Metab.* **2004**, *89*, 2526–2539. [CrossRef]
44. Flier, J.S. Starvation in the Midst of Plenty: Reflections on the History and Biology of Insulin and Leptin. *Endocr. Rev.* **2019**, *40*, 1–16. [CrossRef]
45. Obradovicm, M.; Sudar-Milovanovic, E.; Soskic, S.; Essack, M.; Arya, S.; Stewart, A.; Gojobori, T.; Isenovic, E. Leptin and Obesity: Role and Cinical Implication. *Front. Endocrinol.* **2021**, *12*, 585887. [CrossRef] [PubMed]

46. Sinha, M.K.; Sturis, J.; Ohannesian, J.; Magosin, S.; Stephens, T.; Heiman, M.L.; Polonsky, K.S.; Caro, J.F. Ultradian Oscillations of Leptin Secretion in Humans. *Biochem. Biophys. Res. Commun.* **1996**, *228*, 733–738. [CrossRef] [PubMed]
47. Scherer, P.; Williams, S.; Fogliano, M.; Baldini, G.; Lodish, H. A Novel Serum Protein Similar to C1q, Produced Exclusively in Adipocytes. *J. Biol. Chem.* **1995**, *270*, 26746–26749. [CrossRef] [PubMed]
48. Tang, N.; Zhang, X.; Chen, D.; Li, Z. The Controversial Role of Adiponectin in Appetite Regulation of Animals. *Nutrients* **2021**, *13*, 3387. [CrossRef]
49. Silha, J.; Krsek, M.; Skrha, J.; Sucharda, P.; Nyomba, B.; Murphy, L. Plasma Resistin, Adiponectin and Leptin Levels in Lean and Obese Subjects: Correlations with Insulin Resistance. *Eur. J. Endocrinol.* **2003**, *149*, 331–335. [CrossRef]
50. Zhao, S.; Kusminski, C.M.; Scherer, P.E. Adiponectin, Leptin and Cardiovascular Disorders. *Circ. Res.* **2021**, 136–149. [CrossRef]
51. Martos-Moreno, G.Á.; Barrios, V.; Chowen, J.A.; Argente, J. *Adipokines in Childhood Obesity*; Elsevier: London, UK, 2013; Volume 91, ISBN 9780124077669.
52. Frühbeck, G.; Catalán, V.; Rodríguez, A.; Ramírez, B.; Becerril, S.; Salvador, J.; Colina, I.; Gómez-Ambrosi, J. Adiponectin-Leptin Ratio Is a Functional Biomarker of Adipose Tissue Inflammation. *Nutrients* **2019**, *11*, 454. [CrossRef]
53. Freitas, A.; Albuquerque, G.; Silva, C.; Oliveira, A. Appetite-Related Eating Behaviours: An Overview of Assessment Methods, Determinants and Effects on Children's Weight. *Ann. Nutr. Metab.* **2018**, *73*, 19–29. [CrossRef]
54. Vartanian, L.R.; Spanos, S.; Peter Herman, C.; Polivy, J. Conflicting Internal and External Eating Cues: Impact on Food Intake and Attributions. *Health Psychol.* **2017**, *36*, 365–369. [CrossRef]
55. De Graaf, C.; Blom, W.; Smeets, P.; Stafleu, A.; Hendriks, H. Biomarkers of Satiation and Satiety. *Am. J. Clin. Nutr.* **2004**, *79*, 946–961. [CrossRef]
56. De Onis, M.; Onyango, A.; Borghi, E.; Siyam, A.; Nishida, C.; Siekmann, J. Development of a WHO Growth Reference for School-Aged Children and Adolescents. *Bull. World Health Organ.* **2007**, *85*, 660–667. [CrossRef]
57. Peplies, J.; Jiménez-Pavón, D.; Savva, S.; Buck, C.; Günther, K.; Fraterman, A.; Russo, P.; Iacoviello, L.; Veidebaum, T.; Tornaritis, M.; et al. Percentiles of Fasting Serum Insulin, Glucose, HbA1c and HOMA-IR in Pre-Pubertal Normal Weight European Children from the IDEFICS Cohort. *Int. J. Obes.* **2014**, *38*, 39–47. [CrossRef]
58. Baños, R.M.; Cebolla, A.; Etchemendy, E.; Felipe, S.; Rasal, P.; Botella, C. Validation of the Dutch Eating Behavior Questionnaire for Children (DEBQ-C) for Use with Spanish Children. *Nutr. Hosp.* **2011**, *26*, 890–898. [CrossRef]
59. American Psychiatric Association. *Diagnostic and Statistical Manual of Mental Disorders*, 5th ed.; American Psychological Association: Washington, DC, USA, 2013.
60. Kaufman, A.S.; Kaufman, N.L. *K-BIT, Test Breve de Inteligencia de Kaufman*; TEA Ediciones: Madrid, Spain, 2011.
61. Wechsler, D. *WISC-IV: Escala Wechsler de Inteligencia Para Niños-IV*; Pearson: Madrid, Spain, 2005.
62. DeVellis, R. *Scale Development: Theory and Applications*; SAGE Publications: Los Angeles, CA, USA, 2016.
63. Konttinen, H.; Haukkala, A.; Sarlio-Lähteenkorva, S.; Silventoinen, K.; Jousilahti, P. Eating Styles, Self-Control and Obesity Indicators. The Moderating Role of Obesity Status and Dieting History on Restrained Eating. *Appetite* **2009**, *53*, 131–134. [CrossRef]
64. Herman, C.; Polivy, J. Experimental and clinical aspects of restrained eating. In *Obesity: Basic Mechanisms and Treatment*; Stunkard, A., Ed.; W.B. Saunders: Philadelphia, PA, USA, 1980; pp. 208–225.
65. Malik, S.; McGlone, F.; Bedrossian, D.; Dagher, A. Ghrelin Modulates Brain Activity in Areas That Control Appetitive Behavior. *Cell Metab.* **2008**, *7*, 400–409. [CrossRef] [PubMed]
66. Kullmann, S.; Heni, M.; Veit, R.; Scheffler, K.; Machann, J.; Häring, H.-U.; Fritsche, A.; Preissl, H. Intranasal Insulin Enhances Brain Functional Connectivity Mediating the Relationship between Adiposity and Subjective Feeling of Hunger. *Sci. Rep.* **2017**, *7*, 1627. [CrossRef] [PubMed]
67. Young, H.A.; Williams, C.; Pink, A.E.; Freegard, G.; Owens, A.; Benton, D. Getting to the Heart of the Matter: Does Aberrant Interoceptive Processing Contribute towards Emotional Eating? *PLoS ONE* **2017**, *12*, e0186312. [CrossRef]
68. Dulloo, A.; Montani, J. Pathways from Dieting to Weight Regain, to Obesity and to the Metabolic Syndrome: An Overview. *Obes. Rev.* **2015**, *16*, 1–6. [CrossRef] [PubMed]
69. Escrivá-Martínez, T.; Miragall, M.; Herrero, R.; Rodríguez-Arias, M.; Baños, R.M. *Eating Behaviors and Body Mass Index before and during COVID-19 Confinement: A Predictive Model*; Polibienestar Research Institute, University of Valencia: Valencia, Spain, 2021; Unpublished.

nutrients

MDPI

Article

Psychopathological Symptoms and Well-Being in Overweight and Underweight Adolescents: A Network Analysis

Michael Zeiler [1,*], Julia Philipp [1], Stefanie Truttmann [1], Karin Waldherr [2], Gudrun Wagner [1,†] and Andreas Karwautz [1,†]

[1] Eating Disorder Unit, Department for Child and Adolescent Psychiatry, Medical University of Vienna, 1090 Vienna, Austria; julia.philipp@meduniwien.ac.at (J.P.); stefanie.truttmann@meduniwien.ac.at (S.T.); gudrun.wagner@meduniwien.ac.at (G.W.); andreas.karwautz@meduniwien.ac.at (A.K.)

[2] Department for Research and Development, Ferdinand Porsche FernFH-Distance Learning University of Applied Sciences, 2700 Wiener Neustadt, Austria; karin.waldherr@fernfh.ac.at

* Correspondence: Michael.zeiler@meduniwien.ac.at; Tel.: +43-1-40400-21270

† Senior authors.

Abstract: Overweight and underweight adolescents have an increased risk of psychological problems and reduced quality of life. We used a network analysis approach on a variety of psychopathology and well-being variables to identify central factors in these populations. The network analysis was conducted on data of 344 overweight adolescents (>90th BMI-percentile) and 423 underweight adolescents (<10th BMI-percentile) drawn from a large community sample (10–19 years) including behavioral and emotional problems (Youth Self-Report), eating disorder risk (SCOFF) and well-being variables (KIDSCREEN). Additionally, psychopathology and well-being scores of overweight and underweight individuals were compared with 1.560 normal weight adolescents. Compared to their normal weight peers, overweight adolescents showed elevated psychopathology and eating disorder risk as well as reduced well-being. Underweight adolescents reported increased levels of internalizing problems but no increased eating disorder risk or reduced well-being. The network analysis revealed that anxious/depressed mood and attention problems were the most central and interconnected nodes for both overweight and underweight subsamples. Among underweight individuals, social problems and socially withdrawn behavior additionally functioned as a bridge between other nodes in the network. The results support psychological interventions focusing on improving mood, coping with negative emotions and tackling inner tension.

Keywords: overweight; obesity; underweight; adolescents; mental health; psychopathology; quality of life; eating disorder risk; network analysis

Citation: Zeiler, M.; Philipp, J.; Truttmann, S.; Waldherr, K.; Wagner, G.; Karwautz, A. Psychopathological Symptoms and Well-Being in Overweight and Underweight Adolescents: A Network Analysis. *Nutrients* **2021**, *13*, 4096. https://doi.org/10.3390/nu13114096

Academic Editors: Fernando Fernandez-Aranda, Janet Treasure and Empar Lurbe

Received: 9 October 2021
Accepted: 12 November 2021
Published: 16 November 2021

1. Introduction

It is well known that overweight or obese children and adolescents are at increased risk of psychopathological symptoms, behavioral and emotional problems as well as reduced quality of life. Previous evidence shows elevated symptoms of depression [1–3], anxiety [2] and conduct disorders [4], more emotional difficulties and peer problems [3], lower self-esteem [5] as well as higher school absenteeism [6] for overweight or obese children and adolescents compared to their normal weight peers. A higher prevalence of disordered eating, particularly binge eating behavior, and reduced body satisfaction were found in overweight/obese adolescents [7–9]. Furthermore, reduced quality of life in physical, mental and social domains was consistently reported [10,11].

While less intensively discussed in the literature, children and adolescents at the lower end of the weight spectrum have also become a focus of attention. Apart from disordered eating [12] and body dissatisfaction [13] reported in this subgroup (which may represent problems indicating symptoms of anorexia nervosa), internalizing problems in particular, including depression and socially withdrawn behavior, were reported for underweight adolescents [14,15]. Moreover, previous studies have shown that weight-related teasing occurs for overweight and underweight adolescents, which consequently may increase the risk of social isolation and mental health problems for both groups [16,17].

Due to these multiple mental health concerns, psychological factors have been identified as an important target for selective prevention and treatment of obesity in adolescents [18] but also in underweight adolescents. Some authors even point to integral prevention and intervention approaches for individuals at both ends of the weight spectrum because of shared environmental risk factors for (severe) underweight and obesity, which, for example, include teasing, peer problems and negative family relationships [19–21]. Of note, in the latest Cochrane review on dietary and physical activity interventions for preventing obesity in youths, including more than 150 randomized-controlled trials, only a few interventions included components targeting psychological factors such as depression, anxiety, self-esteem, support by peers, stress and body image [22]. This is all the more interesting because another review focusing on psychological interventions for overweight or obese individuals revealed significant improvements in depression, self-esteem, body-image, anxiety, stress, disordered eating and general well-being while reaching similar weight loss compared to dietary and physical activity interventions directly targeting the weight [23].

Thus, there is evidence that psychological interventions for adolescents with weight-related problems should be provided. However, due to the variety of psychological problems and well-being variables associated with overweight and underweight, which also opens up a variety of possible targets for prevention and treatment interventions, one may ask whether there exist specific 'core' mental health domains that such interventions should focus on and that may be most beneficial regarding the intervention outcomes. One method to tackle this question is psychological network analysis. A network analysis is a relatively new statistical approach to model the complex interactions between a large number of different variables (called 'network'). It allows the identification of specific associations between variables in the network on the one hand, and the identification of central variables on the other hand (c.f. [24]). In brief, a central variable in a network is highly associated with other variables in the network. Thus, it can be assumed that if a central variable is changed, this also has effects on many other variables in the network whereby these effects are usually not directly proportional. Consequently, a network analysis on psychopathological symptoms and well-being variables obtained in overweight and underweight adolescents should help identifying central symptoms and characteristics. For example, if body dissatisfaction turns out to be a central variable in a network including different mental health problems in overweight adolescents, this variable would be a promising target for interventions as reducing body dissatisfaction would presumably also affect other psychopathological symptoms in the network (e.g., depression and anxiety).

In recent years, psychological network analyses have been performed in patients with diagnosed eating disorders including anorexia nervosa and bulimia nervosa with the aim to identify central symptoms of the eating disorder pathology. Studies including a variety of eating disorder symptoms in their network analysis found that shape and weight concerns, desiring weight loss, desire to be thinner, feeling ineffective, worries that feeling will get out of control and guilt after overeating were the most central symptoms [25–27]. Other studies on eating disorder patients which additionally included general psychopathology showed that depressive and anxiety symptoms, interpersonal sensitivity and personal alienation had the highest centrality in the network [28,29]. Authors of these studies concluded that these symptoms represent important targets for effective treatment. Studies using a network approach on mental health in overweight and obese individuals are scarce and have focused on adult individuals only. Calugi and Dalle Grave [30] reported that interpersonal sensitivity and shape-weight concerns were the most central variables in adult patients with obesity, while disordered eating symptoms including binge eating and dietary restraint were the most peripheral and least connected symptoms in the network. Another network analysis on physical performance and quality of life variables emphasized the importance of mental health as a key factor in adults with obesity [31]. Moreover, in a very small sample of obese children, aspects of unhealthy eating behavior, physical activity habits and low mood turned out to be central variables [32]. In another network analysis among a general sample of adolescents including different variables on executive function and disinhibited eating, emotional eating emerged as the most central symptom [33]. So far, no study has used a network analysis approach to explore the interconnection of psychopathology and quality of life variables obtained in overweight/obese or underweight adolescents.

Thus, the present study has the following aims: First, we aimed to investigate psychopathological symptoms and well-being/quality of life in overweight or obese adolescents from a large representative community sample. We hypothesized that overweight or underweight adolescents would show higher levels of psychopathology and reduced well-being compared to their normal weight peers. Second, using a network analysis approach we aimed to identify central factors among a variety of psychopathological symptoms and well-being variables, which will inform about potential beneficial targets for psychological interventions (e.g., indicated prevention approaches) for overweight and underweight adolescent populations.

2. Materials and Methods

2.1. Sampling and Recruitment

In this study, we used data from the 'Mental Health in Austrian Teenagers' (MHAT, [34]) study, an epidemiological survey that aimed to obtain the prevalence of mental health problems in a large representative sample of Austrian adolescents aged 10 to 18 years. The main part of the sample was recruited via schools (n = 261 schools, including all school types in all regions of Austria). School classes of the 5th, 7th, 9th and 11th grade were randomly selected from participating schools and all students within these classes were invited to participate. A total of 3.615 adolescents from the school sample participated in this study (response rate: 47.3%). The participants completed a comprehensive questionnaire to obtain sociodemographic information, behavioral and emotional problems and well-being/quality of life (see Section 2.2). The school sample was complemented by a small sample of adolescents who dropped out of school and who were recruited from training courses for unemployed adolescents (n = 43, 1.1% of the total sample) and by a small sample of adolescents currently in inpatient treatment due to a psychiatric disorder who were recruited from child and adolescent psychiatry wards across Austria (n = 133, 3.5% of the total sample). This was done to also cover adolescents from the population who cannot be reached via the regular school setting (due to early school dropout and severe mental health problems). This sample composition reflects the general population of Austrian adolescents including all levels of psychopathological symptoms and quality of life. Thus, this sample allows to adequately tackle the main research question of this paper (identifying central mental health aspects that may be promising targets for indicated prevention strategies for overweight and underweight adolescent populations). Written informed consent was collected from all participants and legal representatives prior to the inclusion in the study. Ethical approval was obtained from the Ethics Committee of the Medical University of Vienna (#1134/2013). Details about the sampling, recruitment strategy and procedures are published in Zeiler et al. [34] and Wagner et al. [35].

For the purpose of this study, we used subsamples of the entire dataset and included overweight adolescents defined by body-mass index (BMI) $\geq$ 90th sex and age specific percentile (n = 344) as well as underweight adolescents defined by BMI $\leq$ 10th sex and age specific percentile (n = 423). Data from normal weight adolescents (25th < BMI percentile > 75th, n = 1.560) were used as a reference to enable a classification of psychopathology and well-being scores of the overweight/underweight subsamples. Weight and height measures were derived from the adolescents' self-reports. Participants who did not provide any (valid) height/weight information were excluded.

2.2. Instruments

Apart from sociodemographic information (e.g., sex, age, migration background, living situation, diagnosed somatic and psychiatric disorders in the family) that was used to describe the sample, we obtained data from three validated and often used instruments to assess psychopathological symptoms and quality of life. The strength of a network analysis lies in exploring complex associations among a large number of diverse psychological features. Thus, we selected instruments that assess many different aspects of psychopathology and quality of life in a dimensional/continuous way. While network estimation approaches to handle categorical and ordinal data exists, such data types are still regarded as suboptimal [36]. Moreover, the selection of instruments was driven by the limited time provided by the schools to complete the entire questionnaire battery (max. one school hour of 50 min).

Specifically, data obtained through the following instruments were included in the network analysis:

The Youth Self-Report (YSR, [37,38]) is a widely used self-report instrument to measure a wide range of behavioral and emotional problems (112 items rated on a three-point scale). Item ratings are summed up in eight syndrome scales ('socially withdrawn', 'somatic complaints', 'anxious/depressed', 'social problems', 'thought problems', 'attention problems', 'dissocial behavior' and 'aggressive behavior'). Additionally, the items can be aggregated to three broadband scales, a total problem score, an internalizing problem score and an externalizing problem score. The YSR raw scores were used in this study. However, we also calculated the percentage of clinically relevant problem scores by using the available norms (cut-off: T-score > 63 for broadband scales). Internal consistencies were excellent for the broadband scales (Cronbach's alpha > 0.86) and acceptable for the syndrome scales (Cronbach's alpha between 0.56–0.86).

We used the SCOFF questionnaire [8,39] to screen for eating disorders, an aspect that is not covered in the YSR questionnaire but which is particularly relevant for overweight and underweight populations). It assesses five core features of eating disorders, including significant weight loss, intentional vomiting, body dissatisfaction, loss of control over food and food intrusive thought. The presence/absence of each symptom is rated on a dichotomous scale ('yes' vs. 'no'). The total score representing the number of present eating disorder symptoms (possible score range 0–5) was used in the present study. According to the authors of the original SCOFF version [39], a score ≥ 2 represents an increased risk for eating disorders. A recently published meta-analysis reported a pooled sensitivity of 86% and specificity of 83% using full-syndrome eating disorders or other established eating disorder questionnaires as reference [40].

Moreover, we used the KIDSCREEN scales [41] to obtain well-being and quality of life in different domains including 'self-perception' (satisfaction with own body and appearance), 'parent relation and home life' (assessing the quality of relationship with parents, feeling understood by them, being able to talk with them), 'social support and peers' (assessing the quality of peer relationship, spending joyful time with friends, helping each other, being able to rely on friends), 'school environment' (satisfaction with the school environment, getting along well with teachers, being able to concentrate well) and 'social acceptance' (assessing the absence of bullying). Items are rated on a five-point scale; higher subscale scores indicate higher levels of well-being/quality of life. In addition to the subscales, a general measure of well-being ('KIDSCREEN-10') was calculated. In the present study, the raw scores of the general and subscale measures were used. Internal consistencies of the scales ranged from 0.77 to 0.89.

2.3. Data Analysis

Descriptive analyses and comparative analyses of the overweight, underweight and normal weight subsamples were performed using IBM SPSS Statistics 27.0. The network analysis was conducted using JASP (version 0.12.2.0) [42] which makes use of the *R* packages '*bootnet*' [43] and '*qgraph*' [44].

First, we compared YSR, SCOFF and KIDSCREEN (general and subscale) scores obtained from the overweight and underweight subsamples with the normal weight reference group using general linear models controlling for sex. Differences between the overweight/underweight and normal weight samples were analyzed using Tukey tests. We further used Chi^2-tests to compare the percentages of clinically relevant YSR scores and eating disorder risk (SCOFF ≥ 2) between the overweight, underweight and normal weight reference samples.

The network analysis for overweight and underweight adolescents was performed on general psychopathology variables (YSR syndrome scales), eating disorder risk (SCOFF total score) and well-being/quality of life variables (KIDSCREEN scores, not using the KIDSCREEN-10 general quality of life score). Due to the correlational nature of this approach and as age-/sex-standardized scores are not available for all of the included instruments, we used the raw scores of these questionnaires in this analysis. A network is defined as a set of variables (called 'nodes') which are reciprocally connected through 'edges' (most commonly some kind of correlation) that do not imply a priori direction or allow causal inference. In the present study, we estimated partial correlation networks using the graphical Least Absolute Shrinkage and Selection Operator (gLASSO [45]). Using the gLASSO estimation, small or unstable correlations within the network are set to zero, resulting in a more parsimonious and better interpretable network only depicting the most robust associations between the nodes. Each edge represents the thus regularized partial correlation between two nodes. In contrast to non-regularized partial correlations (all edges between all nodes are estimated and included in the network plot), regularized partial correlations are used to effectively assess the sparse and interpretable network structure. The stronger the partial correlation between two nodes (either positive or negative), the thicker the edge presented in the network plot. As gLASSO produces a collection of network solution, the Extended Bayesian Information Criterion (EBIC, [46]) was used to select the optimal network model. The Fruchterman–Reingold algorithm [47] was used to organize the network plot. Nodes with more or stronger connections are placed closer together while nodes with less connection are placed further apart.

The centrality of the nodes was estimated with the node strength, betweenness and closeness centrality indices. Node 'strength' refers to the weighted number and strength of all connections of a specific node and thus represents the overall influence of a node in the network. 'Betweenness' represents the number of shortest paths that pass through the node of interest, respectively, the number of times that the node represents the shortest path between other nodes; thus, a node with high betweenness is important in the connection that other nodes have between them (node acting as a bridge). 'Closeness' quantifies the number of direct and indirect links between the node of interest to all other nodes in the network; thus, a node with high closeness will be affected quickly by changes in any part of the network and vice versa (c.f. [24]). *z*-Standardized centrality indices (mean = 0, SD = 1) are reported.

Moreover, we performed the Network Comparison Test (NCT, [48]) using the '*NetworkComparisonTest*' package in *R* to compare the network structure and the global network strength between the overweight and underweight samples.

2.4. Sample Size Considerations and Network Stability/Edge Accuracy Calculations

Currently, there is no established method for a formal power analysis available for psychological network analyses, nor is there a minimal sample size required for this type of analysis [43]. Rather, there are established methods to evaluate the network stability (e.g., stability of central indices) and edge accuracy which should be reported along a psychological network analysis. Providing evidence for the stability of a network solution is an important prerequisite to reasonably interpret the network. In general, there is a larger chance to find stable network solutions in larger samples than in smaller samples.

The accuracy of the network solution was evaluated by the two following analyses: First, the case-dropping subset bootstrap approach was used to analyze the stability of central indices after observing only subsamples of the data. The correlation stability (CS) coefficient quantifies the stability of central indices and represents the maximum proportion of cases that can be dropped from the full dataset so that the correlation between the original central indices and central indices calculated from bootstrap subsets has a 95% probability of being $r = 0.7$ or higher. Ideally, the CS-coefficients should be above 0.5 [43]. Second, the accuracy of edge weights was evaluated by calculating 95% confidence intervals based on non-parametric bootstrapping (n = 1.000 boots) which is recommended for LASSO regularized edges [43]. In case of excessively large bootstrapped confidence intervals, the edge strengths should be interpreted with caution.

3. Results

3.1. Sample Description

Key characteristics of the overweight and underweight subsamples in reference to adolescents with normal weight are provided in Table 1. Compared to the overweight and normal weight samples, there were more females in the underweight group. The percentage of adolescents with migration background was highest among overweight adolescents. Moreover, the percentage of adolescents with parents where both are employed was lowest in the overweight subsample. Compared to the normal weight reference group, the percentage of adolescents with any diagnosed psychiatric disorder was elevated in the overweight and underweight subsamples. The mean BMI of the overweight group was 27.00 (1.83 standard deviations above the BMI expected according to sex and age). The mean BMI of the underweight group was 15.67 (1.92 standard deviations below the BMI expected according to sex and age).

Table 1. Sample description.

	Overweight Sample (n = 344)	Underweight Sample (n = 423)	Reference (Normal Weight Sample) (n = 1.560)
Female sex (%)	52.6%	66.9%	53.8%
Age (Mean, SD)	14.79 (2.34)	14.30 (2.38)	14.77 (2.27)
Migration background [1] (%)	31.7%	22.6%	25.3%
Living with both parents (%)	69.3%	71.3%	74.3%
Residency (living in urban region) [2] (%)	54.6%	55.5%	58.8%
Employment status of parents			
Both parents employed (%)	70.2%	77.3%	79.1%
No or one parent employed (%)	29.8%	22.7%	20.9%
BMI (Mean, SD)	27.00 (3.30)	15.67 (1.42)	19.82 (1.64)
BMI-SDS [3] (Mean, SD)	1.83 (0.46)	−1.92 (0.63)	−0.01 (0.38)
Any diagnosed psychiatric disorder (%)	8.0%	11.3%	4.0%
Any diagnosed chronic somatic illness (%)	13.3%	14.1%	10.7%
Diagnosed psychiatric disorders in family (%)	6.2%	7.0%	4.0%
Diagnosed chronic somatic illness in family (%)	19.0%	15.4%	16.4%

[1] Either adolescent or one parent born in a country other than Austria; [2] An urban region is defined as living in a city with >10.000 inhabitants; [3] SDS = Standard Deviation Score.

3.2. Psychopathology and Well-Being of Overweight and Underweight Adolescents

Compared to normal weight adolescents, overweight adolescents showed significantly higher YSR total and internalizing scores as well as higher levels of psychopathology in most YSR subscales (except in those related to the externalizing problem domain) (Table 2). Moreover, overweight adolescents reported significantly more symptoms of eating disorders and lower levels of well-being in all domains compared to the normal weight group. Underweight adolescents showed significantly higher scores in the YSR internalizing problem domain and the socially withdrawn subscale compared to the normal weight group. Regarding externalizing problems (including the dissocial and aggressive behavior subscales) and the SCOFF, underweight adolescents even reported problem scores significantly lower than normal weight adolescents. There were no other statistically significant differences between the underweight and normal weight group.

Table 2. Differences in psychopathology, eating disorder risk and well-being scores of overweight and underweight adolescents compared to a normal weight reference group.

	Overweight Sample (Mean, SD)	Underweight Sample (Mean, SD)	Reference (Normal Weight Sample) (Mean, SD)	Overweight vs. Normal Weight (Tukey Test [1])	Underweight vs. Normal Weight (Tukey Test [1])
General Psychopathology					
Total Problems	41.06 (23.85)	33.84 (20.72)	34.64 (20.48)	$p < 0.001$	$p = 0.766$
Internalizing Problems	13.16 (11.13)	12.27 (9.21)	11.11 (8.70)	$p < 0.001$	$p = 0.041$
Externalizing Problems	11.22 (6.69)	8.90 (10.47)	10.53 (6.67)	$p = 0.186$	$p < 0.001$
Socially withdrawn	3.46 (2.77)	3.39 (2.73)	2.90 (2.58)	$p = 0.001$	$p = 0.002$
Somatic Complaints	3.50 (3.18)	3.20 (2.82)	3.04 (2.78)	$p = 0.014$	$p = 0.543$
Anxious/Depressed	6.71 (6.48)	6.14 (5.56)	5.56 (5.22)	$p = 0.001$	$p = 0.115$
Social Problems	2.66 (2.44)	2.17 (2.14)	1.99 (2.02)	$p < 0.001$	$p = 0.264$
Thought Problems	1.71 (2.09)	1.41 (1.88)	1.53 (1.93)	$p = 0.284$	$p = 0.509$
Attention Problems	5.10 (3.03)	4.53 (3.07)	4.58 (2.93)	$p = 0.008$	$p = 0.952$
Dissocial Behavior	3.56 (2.53)	2.78 (2.45)	3.36 (2.66)	$p = 0.412$	$p < 0.001$
Aggressive Behavior	7.66 (4.76)	6.12 (4.38)	7.17 (4.66)	$p = 0.174$	$p < 0.001$
Eating Disorder Risk					
SCOFF score	1.33 (1.18)	0.74 (1.07)	0.88 (1.04)	$p < 0.001$	$p = 0.047$
Well-being/Quality of Life					
KIDSCREEN-10	38.08 (7.54)	37.74 (7.19)	40.01 (6.77)	$p < 0.001$	$p = 0.775$
Self-Perception	17.39 (4.60)	19.42 (4.46)	19.10 (4.27)	$p < 0.001$	$p = 0.321$
Parent-Relation & Home-Life	24.90 (5.29)	25.97 (4.59)	25.86 (4.64)	$p = 0.002$	$p = 0.900$
Social support & Peers	16.28 (3.46)	16.68 (17.05)	17.03 (2.92)	$p < 0.001$	$p = 0.094$
School Environment	14.67 (3.57)	15.60 (3.25)	15.31 (3.28)	$p = 0.004$	$p = 0.283$
Social Acceptance/Bullying	13.15 (2.62)	13.99 (1.81)	13.86 (2.01)	$p < 0.001$	$p = 0.484$

[1] controlled for sex.

Considering the established cut-off scores for the YSR instrument, 26.7% of overweight adolescents showed clinically relevant total problem scores which was a significantly higher percentage than in the underweight (15.6%) and normal weight (16.2%) subsamples ($Chi^2(2) = 22.927$, $p < 0.001$). Clinically relevant internalizing problems were reported in 24.7% of overweight adolescents which was similar to underweight adolescents (22.3%) but higher than in the normal weight reference group (19.0%) ($Chi^2(2) = 6.841$, $p < 0.033$). A significantly lower number of underweight adolescents (5.5%) showed clinically relevant externalizing problems compared to overweight (10.5%) and normal weight adolescents (8.8%) ($Chi^2(2) = 6.953$, $p = 0.031$). Eating disorder risk (defined as SCOFF score ≥ 2) was reported in 41.3% of overweight adolescents which was significantly higher than in the underweight (16.5%) and normal weight (23.1%) sample ($Chi^2(2) = 68.189$, $p < 0.001$).

3.3. *Results of the Network Analysis*

3.3.1. General Network Structure

Figure 1 shows the network plots based on the EBIC gLASSO estimation for the (**a**) overweight and (**b**) underweight group. In the overweight group, anxious/depressed mood is placed very central in the network with strong associations to socially withdrawn behavior and moderate associations to other psychopathological symptoms (e.g., thought problems) and well-being variables (particularly self-perception). Attention problems was another node with several associations to other nodes in the network, especially aggressive behavior and social problems. Aggressive and dissocial behavior were clustered at the periphery of the network. Interestingly, eating disorder risk obtained with the SCOFF was one of the most peripheral nodes in the network. However, it was placed next to self-perception (assessing satisfaction with body and appearance) and somatic complaints. Moreover, nodes related to the contact, problems and satisfaction with peers were plotted next to each other.

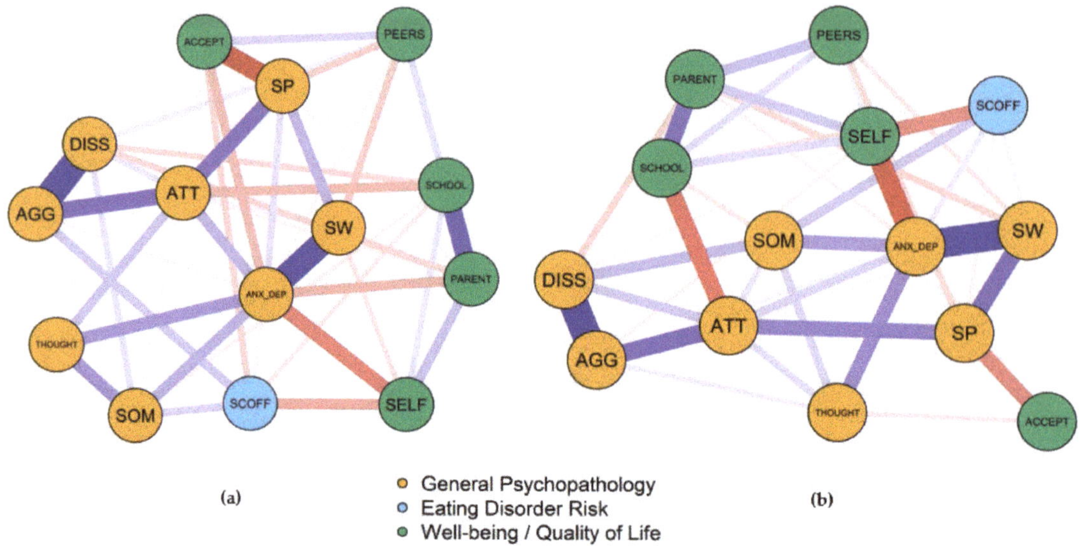

Figure 1. Network plots of the estimated EBIC gLASSO networks of (**a**) overweight adolescents; (**b**) underweight adolescents. Each node represents a variable of the YSR, SCOFF or KIDSCREEN scales. Each link ('edge') represents the partial correlation (blue = positive correlation, red = negative correlation). Thicker edges represent stronger associations. Variable abbreviations: ACCEPT Social Acceptance, AGG Aggressive Behavior, ANX_DEP Anxious Depressed, ATT Attention Problems, DISS Dissocial Behavior, PARENT Parent Relation and Home Life, PEERS Social Support and Peers, SCHOOL School Environment, SCOFF SCOFF Score, SELF Self Perception, SOM Somatic Complaints, SP Social problems, SW Socially Withdrawn, THOUGHT Thought Problems.

In the underweight group, again, anxious/depressed mood was strongly associated to several other nodes in the network including socially withdrawn behavior, self-perception, somatic complaints and thought problems. Attention problems were strongly positively associated with aggressive behavior and social problems and negatively linked to satisfaction with the school environment. With the exception of the social acceptance domain of the KIDSCREEN questionnaire, well-being variables seem to form a cluster within the network, with well-being regarding school being strongly negatively associated with attention problems and self-perception being negatively associated with anxious/depressed mood and eating disorder risk. As in the overweight group, the SCOFF was one of the most peripheral nodes in the network.

3.3.2. Centrality Indices

The central indices for all nodes in the network are shown in Figure 2. Anxious/depressed mood (overweight group: $z = 2.76$, underweight group: $z = 2.47$) and attention problems (overweight group: $z = 1.14$, underweight group: $z = 1.18$) were by far the nodes with the highest strength (named 'degree' in the centrality plot), thus representing the nodes with the highest overall influence in the network. These nodes also had the highest betweenness (anxious/depresses: $z = 2.72/z = 2.16$, attention problems: $z = 1.53/z = 1.30$) and closeness (anxious/depresses: $z = 2.28/z = 1.48$, attention problems: $z = 1.76/z = 1.29$), indicating that they also function as a bridge between other nodes of the network. For the underweight group, betweenness and closeness was also relatively high for the social problems (betweenness: $z = 1.01$, closeness: $z = 0.98$) and socially withdrawn (betweenness: $z = 0.73$, closeness: $z = 1.09$) nodes. The exact standardized centrality coefficients for all nodes (separated by the overweight and underweight groups) are provided in Supplementary Table S1.

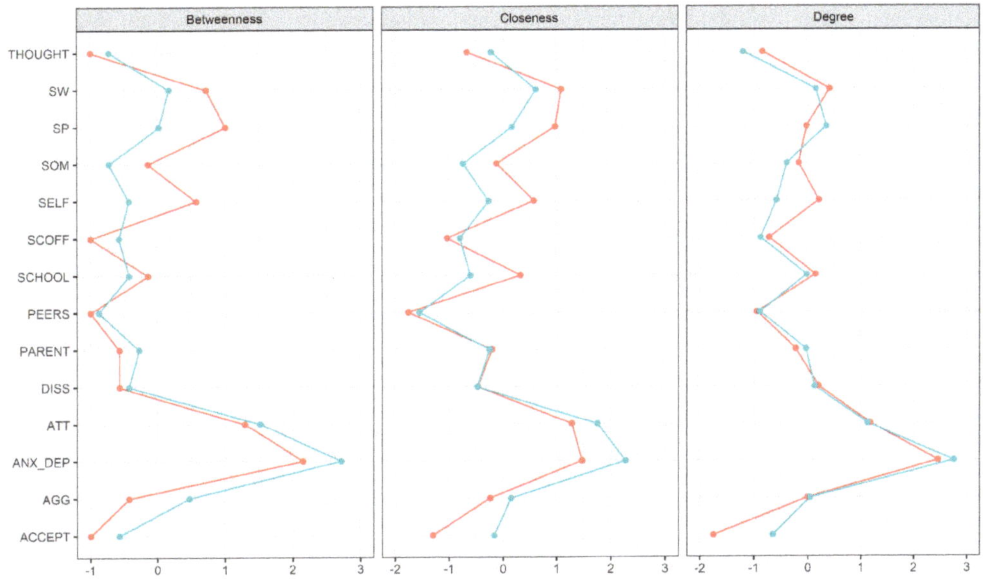

Figure 2. Centrality plot depicting standardized centrality indices (betweenness, closeness, degree = strength) of psychopathological symptoms, eating disorder risk and well-being measures in overweight (blue lines) and underweight (red lines) adolescents. See footnote of Figure 1 for variable abbreviations.

3.3.3. Comparison between Overweight and Underweight Adolescents

The network comparison test revealed no statistically significant difference between the networks for overweight and underweight adolescents regarding the structural invariance (M = 0.118, p = 0.967) and the global network strength (S = 0.470, p = 0.159).

3.3.4. Stability of Central Indices and Edge Accuracy

For the overweight group, the CS coefficients were 0.75 for strength, 0.67 for betweenness and 0.67 for closeness. For the underweight group, the CS coefficients were 0.75, 0.59 and 0.67, respectively. Furthermore, the correlation stability plots (Figures S1 and S2 in the Supplementary Material) show that the correlation with the original centrality indices decreases slowly when an increasing number of participants are dropped from the full dataset. This indicates that the stability of all centrality indices in both samples are sufficiently high and can be reliably interpreted.

Figures S3 and S4 (Supplementary Material) show the bootstrapped 95% confidence intervals of edge weights for the network of the overweight and underweight groups. The edge accuracy plots reveal that the confidence intervals of edge weights are not excessively large; thus, the estimations of the edge weights seem to be sufficiently accurate to be reasonably interpreted.

3.3.5. Network Structure in Normal Weight Adolescents

While this was not the focus of this study, we additionally estimated the EBIC *g*LASSO network for the normal weight reference group (25th < BMI percentile > 75th) to explore whether the centrality indices are similar to those estimated from the overweight and underweight subsamples and whether the network of psychopathology and well-being variables holds regardless of the adolescent weight status. Indeed, anxious/depressed mood showed the highest strength followed by attention problems and social problems. Regarding betweenness and closeness, attention problems turned out to be by far the most central variable followed by anxious/depressed mood, social problems and satisfaction with the school environment. The network and centrality plots for the normal weight sample are provided in Supplementary Figure S5. Thus, in normal weight adolescents, attention problems as well as satisfaction with the school environment seem to play a slightly more pronounced role compared to the overweight and underweight groups. However, the formal test of network comparison yielded no statically significant differences in structural invariance and global network strength between the normal weight group and adolescents at the lower and upper end of the weight spectrum.

4. Discussion

Consistent with the literature e.g., [2,9], the present findings provide clear evidence that overweight adolescents represent a specific risk group for mental health problems. Elevated psychopathological symptoms were observed primarily in the internalizing domain while a similar study in overweight/obese adolescents, which also used the YSR instrument, reported increased psychopathology in both internalizing and externalizing behavioral domains [15]. Most obvious, the eating disorder risk in overweight adolescent was about twice as high as in the normal weight population, which supports previously published literature emphasizing the high prevalence of binge eating and compensatory and unhealthy weight control behavior in overweight and obese adolescent populations [8,49,50]. In this regard, the present results mirror other results in the literature pointing to the shared risk factors for obesity and eating disorders [19,21]. Furthermore, the reduced quality of life scores regarding satisfaction with one's own body and appearance, relationship to peers and parents and satisfaction with the school environment reported by overweight adolescents and which has been also found in other studies [10,11], points to the urgent need for interventions promoting well-being and mental health in this group.

The question whether underweight adolescents also have an increased risk for mental health problems is much less easy to answer based on the present results. Elevated psychopathological symptoms were found for internalizing problems only (with more socially withdrawn behavior), while quality of life scores were comparable to those of normal weight adolescents and even lower levels of externalizing problems were reported compared to the reference sample. Indeed, whether or not underweight is associated with increased mental health concerns has been controversially discussed in the literature [10,14,51]. As in our study, Drosopoulou et al. [15] reported increased socially withdrawn behavior in underweight adolescents, while they found no differences in other psychopathological symptoms compared to normal weight youth. While underweight is a core characteristic of anorexia nervosa, we found that the eating disorder risk was minimally but significantly lower in underweight compared to normal weight adolescents. This may be surprising; however, a similar result was also found in another large population study where a different instrument to assess eating disorder risk was used [49]. This indicates that underweight per se is not a sign of increased eating disorder risk and that underweight adolescents (provided there are no additional risk factors) would not need specific (preventive) interventions targeting eating disorder symptoms.

The core aim of this study, which also represents the novelty of this research, was the use of psychological network analysis to identify central factors among mental health and well-being variables which inform about potential key targets for interventions for overweight and underweight adolescents. As psychopathological symptoms were most prevalent in overweight adolescents, the following discussion primarily focuses on what can be done for this risk group. The most central variables in the network were anxious/depressed mood and attention problems, while variables associated with eating disorder risk and body dissatisfaction were rather peripheral nodes. At first glance, this seems surprising, but this finding is consistent with another network analysis based on adult individuals with obesity showing that variables directly related to eating disorders were rather placed in the periphery of a network including different psychological characteristics [30]. This may—to some extent—reflect that particularly anxiety problems, but also symptoms of attention-deficit-hyperactivity disorder constitute the most prevalent mental health problems among children and adolescents in general [35,52]. However, it must be emphasized that variables that turn out as most central in psychological network analyses do not necessarily correspond to the most prevalent symptoms of mental health disorders. The main finding from this study (depressive/anxious mood, attention problems as central symptoms in a psychological network, thus representing promising key targets for intervention) contradicts the current practice of many psychological (preventive) interventions among overweight/obese adolescents which primarily aim to reduce disordered eating behavior and weight/shape concerns [53]. Rather, our results indicate that broader intervention approaches, not solely focusing on eating disorder symptoms but (also) incorporating contents to positively impact mood and reduce feelings of depression and anxiety might be most promising. This seems all the more appropriate considering the role emotions and emotion regulation play in individuals with overweight and obesity. Negative affect and stress, for example triggered by weight-related teasing and negative body image, may challenge existing emotion regulation strategies which in turn may result in maladaptive coping such as emotional eating that is often reported in overweight individuals [54,55]. Strengthening skills towards awareness, understanding and acceptance of emotions, self-support and self-compassion may improve resilience, self-efficacy, self-esteem and assertiveness among overweight and obese adolescents [54]. This is in line with a systematic review pointing to the causal link between negative emotions (depression, anxiety, stress) and the development of obesity concluding that adolescents' anxiety and depression are therefore important targets for preventive interventions of obesity [56].

Apart from anxious/depressed mood, the 'attention problems' subscale of the YSR was also a central variable in the network analysis. On the one hand, this may be linked to the association between attention-deficit-hyperactivity disorder and obesity (e.g., higher levels of impulsivity which may reinforce disregulated eating behaviors) often reported in the literature [57]. Apart from impulsivity and problems with concentration, this scale also assesses inner restlessness and tension. This indicates that intervention components tackling these problems, like the use of relaxation techniques, may be promising concerning promoting well-being in overweight or obese adolescents. This is in line with previous randomized-controlled trials that have shown a beneficial effect of stress management and relaxation intervention (progressive muscle relaxation, guided imagery, diaphragmatic breathing) to reduce general psychopathology, anxiety and depression symptoms in children and adolescents with obesity compared to interventions solely focusing on the change of dietary and physical activity habits [58,59].

Of note, the factors contributing to the development and maintenance of overweight and obesity in childhood and adolescents are manifold as, for example, shown in the 'Foresight Obesity System Map' where different biological, medical, psychological, developmental, social and economic factors as well as factors related to diet, physical activity, media and infrastructure have been put together and correlated [60]. The present study provides a contribution to the question of the relative importance of psychological factors in overweight and obesity.

Finally, we found that the network structure of the overweight, underweight and normal weight groups was quite similar. While social problems, socially withdrawn behavior and satisfaction with the school environment tend to play a slightly more central role in the networks of underweight and normal weight compared to overweight adolescents, anxious/depressed mood and attention problems were by far the most important factors within the networks across all groups. Interestingly, in a usability study and survey assessing the adolescents' and stakeholders' perspectives on Internet-based prevention for mental health problems in general and for eating disorders and obesity specifically, coping with stress and negative mood were mentioned as the most important topics to address while topics directly related to eating disorders (e.g., healthy nutrition, physical activity) were perceived as less relevant [61,62], which supports the findings of the present study. This has implications for the conceptualization of prevention initiatives in general. Rather than having to focus on different psychological targets for different weight groups, focusing on mood, depression, anxiety and inner restlessness might be promising targets for mental health promotion and preventive interventions across the whole weight spectrum. This is especially important for large-scale interventions to prevent obesity and eating disorders in school settings [63,64], where individualized interventions dependent on the individuals' weight status are difficult to implement.

The findings from this study must be interpreted in line with the following limitations: First, as in every network analysis, the findings strongly depend on the (variety of) variables that are considered. In this study, we focused on general psychopathological symptoms and well-being variables. Eating disorder symptoms were obtained with a brief screening questionnaire only and we did not obtain detailed information on restraint eating, binge eating or weight/shape concerns using more specific instruments. Due to time constraints, we used the YSR questionnaire assessing different behavioral and emotion problems rather than different instruments assessing different psychopathological symptoms (e.g., depression, anxiety, conduct problems, attention problems) separately (and probably more specifically). Moreover, other (non-psychological) variables like physical activity or dietary habits, which were not addressed in this study, might have provided additional information regarding the interplay between mental health and lifestyle behaviors among overweight and underweight adolescents. Second, weight and height information to calculate the BMI and classify the individual into the overweight, underweight and normal weight groups was obtained via adolescent self-report; thus, these data might lack accuracy to some extent. However, a study based on a general sample of adolescents demonstrated that the difference between self-reported and objectively measured height and weight is marginal [65]. Hence, self-report information should be sufficiently accurate for the purpose of the present study where adolescents were classified into broad weight categories and these data are not used for the diagnosis of anorexia nervosa or obesity. Third, it may be argued that the size of the subsamples of overweight and underweight adolescents may be small given the large number of variables and associations to be estimated. However, to tackle this potential limitation, we used the LASSO estimation which is particularly suitable for smaller samples as it returns a sparse network model where the number of parameters that need to be estimated is reduced [43]. Furthermore, the network stability and edge accuracy measures indicate that the achieved centrality indices and edge weights can be reliably interpreted with the obtained sample size. Finally, it should be noted that we have drawn a community sample of adolescents. Thus, the network analysis primarily informs about promising targets for indicated preventive interventions implemented in community (e.g., school) settings. Future studies may also focus on treatment seeking samples of adolescents with severe obesity or severe underweight which may better inform about important targets for clinical interventions for more severely ill adolescents.

5. Conclusions

Psychopathological symptoms and reduced well-being are especially pronounced in overweight or obese adolescents. Thus, stand-alone psychological interventions for this risk group should be considered. At least, mental health components should be an integral part of any intervention for overweight and obese adolescents which primarily focus on promoting healthy dietary and physical activity habits, respectively, concerning losing weight. Our network analysis indicates that psychological interventions focusing on improving mood (respectively, reducing symptoms of depression and anxiety), coping with negative emotions and tackling inner tension, restlessness and stress might be the most promising targets. These variables might also be promising targets for preventive interventions to promote mental health in adolescents across the whole weight spectrum which can be implemented through large-scale school-based initiatives.

Supplementary Materials: The following are available online at https://www.mdpi.com/article/10.3390/nu13114096/s1, Table S1: Standardized centrality indices of the EBIC graphical LASSO network for the overweight and underweight subsamples, Figure S1: Correlation stability plot measuring the stability of betweenness, closeness and strength indices in the overweight subsample,

Figure S2: Correlation stability plot measuring the stability of betweenness, closeness and strength indices in the underweight subsample, Figure S3: Edge accuracy plot depicting 95% confidence obtained from 1.000 bootstrap samples drawn from the population overweight adolescents, Figure S4: Edge accuracy plot depicting 95% confidence obtained from 1.000 bootstrap samples drawn from the population underweight adolescents, Figure S5: Network plot and centrality indices plot for adolescents with normal weight.

Author Contributions: Conceptualization, K.W., A.K., G.W.; methodology, M.Z., J.P.; formal analysis, M.Z.; investigation, J.P., S.T., M.Z.; resources, A.K., G.W.; data curation, M.Z., J.P.; writing—original draft preparation, M.Z.; writing—review and editing, K.W., G.W., A.K., J.P., S.T.; visualization, M.Z.; supervision, A.K., G.W., K.W.; project administration, M.Z., J.P., S.T.; funding acquisition, A.K. All authors have read and agreed to the published version of the manuscript.

Funding: This research was funded by "Gemeinsame Gesundheitsziele-Pharma Master Agreement (a co-operation of the Austrian pharma industry and Austrian social insurances); grant number: 99901001300.

Institutional Review Board Statement: The study was conducted according to the guidelines of the Declaration of Helsinki, and approved by the Ethics Committee of the Medical University of Vienna (reference number: #1134/2013, date of approval: 13 May 2013).

Informed Consent Statement: Informed consent was obtained from all subjects involved in the study including legal representatives for subjects below the age of 18.

Data Availability Statement: The data that support the findings of this study are available from the corresponding author upon reasonable request.

Conflicts of Interest: The authors declare no conflict of interest. The funder had no role in the design of the study; in the collection, analyses, or int erpretation of data; in the writing of the manuscript, or in the decision to publish the results.

References

1. Sutaria, S.; Devakumar, D.; Yasuda, S.S.; Das, S.; Saxena, S. Is obesity associated with depression in children? Systematic Review and meta-analysis. *Arch. Dis. Child.* **2019**, *104*, 64–74. [CrossRef]
2. Wang, S.; Sun, Q.; Zhai, L.; Bai, Y.; Wei, W.; Jia, L. The prevalence of depression and anxiety symptoms among overweight/obese and non-overweight/non-obese children/adolescents in China: A systematic review and meta-analysis. *Int. J. Environ. Res. Public Health* **2019**, *16*, 340. [CrossRef] [PubMed]
3. Sanders, R.H.; Han, A.; Baker, J.S.; Cobley, S. Childhood obesity and its physical and psychological co-morbidities: A Systematic review of australian children and adolescents. *Eur. J. Pediatr.* **2015**, *174*, 715–746. [CrossRef]
4. Nujić, D.; Musić Milanović, S.; Milas, V.; Miškulin, I.; Ivić, V.; Milas, J. Association between Child/adolescent overweight/obesity and conduct disorder: A systematic review and meta-analysis. *Pediatr. Obes.* **2021**, *16*, e12742. [CrossRef] [PubMed]
5. Moradi, M.; Mozaffari, H.; Askari, M.; Azadbakht, L. Association between overweight/obesity with depression, anxiety, low self-esteem, and body dissatisfaction in children and adolescents: A systematic review and meta-analysis of observational studies. *Crit. Rev. Food Sci. Nutr.* **2020**, 1–16. [CrossRef]
6. An, R.; Yan, H.; Shi, X.; Yang, Y. Childhood obesity and school absenteeism: A systematic review and meta-analysis. *Obes. Rev.* **2017**, *18*, 1412–1424. [CrossRef] [PubMed]
7. He, J.; Cai, Z.; Fan, X. Prevalence of binge and loss of control eating among children and adolescents with overweight and obesity: An exploratory meta-analysis. *Int. J. Eat. Disord.* **2017**, *50*, 91–103. [CrossRef]
8. Zeiler, M.; Waldherr, K.; Philipp, J.; Nitsch, M.; Dür, W.; Karwautz, A.; Wagner, G. Prevalence of eating disorder risk and associations with health-related quality of life: Results from a large school-based population screening. *Eur. Eat. Disord. Rev.* **2016**, *24*, 9–18. [CrossRef] [PubMed]
9. Herpertz-Dahlmann, B.; Dempfle, A.; Konrad, K.; Klasen, F.; Ravens-Sieberer, U. The BELLA study group eating disorder symptoms do not just disappear: The implications of adolescent eating-disordered behaviour for body weight and mental health in young adulthood. *Eur. Child Adolesc. Psychiatry* **2015**, *24*, 675–684. [CrossRef]
10. Baile, J.I.; Guevara, R.M.; González-Calderón, M.J.; Urchaga, J.D. The relationship between weight status, health-related quality of life, and life satisfaction in a sample of spanish adolescents. *Int. J. Environ. Res. Public. Health* **2020**, *17*, 3106. [CrossRef]
11. Meixner, L.; Cohrdes, C.; Schienkiewitz, A.; Mensink, G.B.M. Health-related quality of life in children and adolescents with overweight and obesity: Results from the German KIGGS survey. *BMC Public Health* **2020**, *20*, 1722. [CrossRef]
12. Bjornelv, S.; Nordahl, H.M.; Holmen, T.L. Psychological factors and weight problems in adolescents. The role of eating problems, emotional problems, and personality traits: The Young-HUNT study. *Soc. Psychiatry Psychiatr. Epidemiol.* **2011**, *46*, 353–362. [CrossRef] [PubMed]

13. De Oliveira Figueiredo, R.A.; Simola-Ström, S.; Isomaa, R.; Weiderpass, E. Body dissatisfaction and disordered eating symptoms in finnish preadolescents. *Eat. Disord.* **2019**, *27*, 34–51. [CrossRef] [PubMed]
14. Cimino, S.; Cerniglia, L.; Almenara, C.A.; Jezek, S.; Erriu, M.; Tambelli, R. Developmental trajectories of body mass index and emotional-behavioral functioning of underweight children: A longitudinal study. *Sci. Rep.* **2016**, *6*, 20211. [CrossRef] [PubMed]
15. Drosopoulou, G.; Sergentanis, T.N.; Mastorakos, G.; Vlachopapadopoulou, E.; Michalacos, S.; Tzavara, C.; Bacopoulou, F.; Psaltopoulou, T.; Tsitsika, A. Psychosocial health of adolescents in relation to underweight, overweight/obese status: The EU NET ADB survey. *Eur. J. Public Health* **2021**, *31*, 379–384. [CrossRef]
16. Kohlmann, C.-W.; Eschenbeck, H.; Heim-Dreger, U.; Hock, M.; Platt, T.; Ruch, W. Fear of being laughed at in children and adolescents: Exploring the importance of overweight, underweight, and teasing. *Front. Psychol.* **2018**, *9*, 1447. [CrossRef]
17. Jacobs, W.; Merianos, A.L.; Lee Smith, M.; Nabors, L.; Fajayan, A.; Valente, T.W. Examining the role of weight status and Individual attributes on adolescent social relations. *J. Adolesc. Health* **2020**, *67*, 108–114. [CrossRef]
18. Hemmingsson, E. A new model of the role of psychological and emotional distress in promoting obesity: Conceptual review with implications for treatment and prevention. *Obes. Rev.* **2014**, *15*, 769–779. [CrossRef]
19. Krug, I.; Villarejo, C.; Jiménez-Murcia, S.; Perpiñá, C.; Vilarrasa, N.; Granero, R.; Cebolla, A.; Botella, C.; Montserrat-Gil de Bernabe, M.; Penelo, E.; et al. Eating-related environmental factors in underweight eating disorders and obesity: Are there common vulnerabilities during childhood and early adolescence? *Eur. Eat. Disord. Rev.* **2013**, *21*, 202–208. [CrossRef]
20. Sánchez-Carracedo, D.; Neumark-Sztainer, D.; López-Guimerà, G. Integrated prevention of obesity and eating disorders: Barriers, developments and opportunities. *Public Health Nutr.* **2012**, *15*, 2295–2309. [CrossRef] [PubMed]
21. Haines, J.; Neumark-Sztainer, D. Prevention of obesity and eating disorders: A consideration of shared risk factors. *Health Educ. Res.* **2006**, *21*, 770–782. [CrossRef] [PubMed]
22. Brown, T.; Moore, T.H.; Hooper, L.; Gao, Y.; Zayegh, A.; Ijaz, S.; Elwenspoek, M.; Foxen, S.C.; Magee, L.; O'Malley, C.; et al. Interventions for preventing obesity in children. *Cochrane Database Syst. Rev.* **2019**, *7*, CD001871. [CrossRef] [PubMed]
23. MacDonald, D.E.; Cassin, S.E. Nondieting psychological interventions for individuals who are overweight or obese: A systematic review of the evidence. *Psychopathol. Rev.* **2017**, *a4*, 290–318. [CrossRef]
24. Hevey, D. Network analysis: A brief overview and tutorial. *Health Psychol. Behav. Med.* **2018**, *6*, 301–328. [CrossRef]
25. Schlegl, S.; Smith, K.E.; Vierl, L.; Crosby, R.D.; Moessner, M.; Neumayr, C.; Voderholzer, U. Using network analysis to compare diagnosis-specific and age-specific symptom networks in eating disorders. *Int. J. Eat. Disord.* **2021**, *54*, 1463–1476. [CrossRef]
26. Forrest, L.N.; Jones, P.J.; Ortiz, S.N.; Smith, A.R. Core psychopathology in anorexia nervosa and bulimia nervosa: A network analysis. *Int. J. Eat. Disord.* **2018**, *51*, 668–679. [CrossRef]
27. Calugi, S.; Sartirana, M.; Misconel, A.; Boglioli, C.; Dalle Grave, R. Eating Disorder psychopathology in adults and adolescents with anorexia nervosa: A network approach. *Int. J. Eat. Disord.* **2020**, *53*, 420–431. [CrossRef]
28. Solmi, M.; Collantoni, E.; Meneguzzo, P.; Degortes, D.; Tenconi, E.; Favaro, A. network analysis of specific psychopathology and psychiatric symptoms in patients with eating disorders. *Int. J. Eat. Disord.* **2018**, *51*, 680–692. [CrossRef]
29. Monteleone, A.M.; Mereu, A.; Cascino, G.; Criscuolo, M.; Castiglioni, M.C.; Pellegrino, F.; Patriciello, G.; Ruzzi, V.; Monteleone, P.; Vicari, S.; et al. Re-conceptualization of anorexia nervosa psychopathology: A network analysis study in adolescents with short duration of the illness. *Int. J. Eat. Disord.* **2019**, *52*, 1263–1273. [CrossRef]
30. Calugi, S.; Dalle Grave, R. Psychological features in obesity: A network analysis. *Int. J. Eat. Disord.* **2020**, *53*, 248–255. [CrossRef]
31. Dalle Grave, R.; Soave, F.; Ruocco, A.; Dametti, L.; Calugi, S. Quality of life and physical performance in patients with obesity: A network analysis. *Nutrients* **2020**, *12*, 602. [CrossRef]
32. Brogan, A.; Hevey, D.; Wilson, C.; Brinkley, A.; O'Malley, G.; Murphy, S. A network analysis of the causal attributions for obesity in children and adolescents and their parents. *Psychol. Health Med.* **2019**, *24*, 1063–1074. [CrossRef]
33. Byrne, M.E.; Tanofsky-Kraff, M.; Lavender, J.M.; Parker, M.N.; Shank, L.M.; Swanson, T.N.; Ramirez, E.; LeMay-Russell, S.; Yang, S.B.; Brady, S.M.; et al. Bridging executive function and disinhibited eating among youth: A network analysis. *Int. J. Eat. Disord.* **2021**, *54*, 721–732. [CrossRef] [PubMed]
34. Zeiler, M.; Wagner, G.; Philipp, J.; Nitsch, M.; Truttmann, S.; Dür, W.; Karwautz, A.; Waldherr, K. The Mental Health in Austrian Teenagers (MHAT) study: Design, methodology, description of study population. *Neuropsychiatrie* **2018**, *32*, 121–132. [CrossRef] [PubMed]
35. Wagner, G.; Zeiler, M.; Waldherr, K.; Philipp, J.; Truttmann, S.; Dür, W.; Treasure, J.L.; Karwautz, A.F.K. Mental health problems in Austrian adolescents: A nationwide, Two-stage epidemiological study applying DSM-5 criteria. *Eur. Child Adolesc. Psychiatry* **2017**, *26*, 1483–1499. [CrossRef]
36. Borsboom, D.; Deserno, M.K.; Rhemtulla, M.; Epskamp, S.; Fried, E.I.; McNally, R.J.; Robinaugh, D.J.; Perugini, M.; Dalege, J.; Costantini, G.; et al. Network analysis of multivariate data in psychological science. *Nat. Rev. Methods Primer* **2021**, *1*, 58. [CrossRef]
37. Achenbach, T.M.; Rescorla, L.A. *Manual for the ASEBA School-Age Forms & Profiles*; University of Vermont, Research Center for Children, Youth, & Families: Burlington, VA, USA, 2001.
38. Döpfner, M.; Plück, J.; Bölte, S.; Lenz, K.; Melchers, P.; Heim, K. *Fragebogen für Jugendliche. Deutsche Bearbeitung des Youth Self-Report (YSR) der Child Behavior Checklist. Einführung und Anleitung zur Handauswertung.*; Arbeitsgruppe Kinder, Jugend- und Familiendiagnostik: Köln, Germany, 1998.

39. Morgan, J.F.; Reid, F.; Lacey, J.H. The SCOFF questionnaire: Assessment of a new screening tool for eating disorders. *BMJ* **1999**, *319*, 1467–1468. [CrossRef] [PubMed]
40. Kutz, A.M.; Marsh, A.G.; Gunderson, C.G.; Maguen, S.; Masheb, R.M. Eating disorder screening: A systematic review and meta-analysis of diagnostic test characteristics of the SCOFF. *J. Gen. Intern. Med.* **2020**, *35*, 885–893. [CrossRef]
41. Ravens-Sieberer, U.; Gosch, A.; Rajmil, L.; Erhart, M.; Bruil, J.; Power, M.; Duer, W.; Auquier, P.; Cloetta, B.; Czemy, L.; et al. The KIDSCREEN-52 quality of life measure for children and adolescents: Psychometric results from a cross-cultural survey in 13 European countries. *Value Health* **2008**, *11*, 645–658. [CrossRef]
42. JASP Team JASP. 2020. Available online: https://jasp-stats.org (accessed on 15 September 2021).
43. Epskamp, S.; Borsboom, D.; Fried, E.I. Estimating psychological networks and their accuracy: A tutorial paper. *Behav. Res. Methods* **2018**, *50*, 195–212. [CrossRef]
44. Epskamp, S.; Cramer, A.O.J.; Waldorp, L.J.; Schmittmann, V.D.; Borsboom, D. Qgraph: Network visualizations of relationships in psychometric data. *J. Stat. Softw.* **2012**, *48*, 1–18. [CrossRef]
45. Friedman, J.; Hastie, T.; Tibshirani, R. Sparse inverse covariance estimation with the graphical lasso. *Biostat. Oxf. Engl.* **2008**, *9*, 432–441. [CrossRef]
46. Chen, J.; Chen, Z. Extended bayesian information criteria for model selection with large model spaces. *Biometrika* **2008**, *95*, 759–771. [CrossRef]
47. Fruchterman, T.M.J.; Reingold, E.M. Graph drawing by force-directed placement. *Softw. Pract. Exp.* **1991**, *21*, 1129–1164. [CrossRef]
48. Van Borkulo, C.; van Bork, R.; Boschloo, L.; Kossakowski, J.; Tio, P.; Schoevers, R.; Borsboom, D.; Waldorp, L. Comparing network structures on three aspects: A permutation test. **2017**. [CrossRef]
49. Lipson, S.; Sonneville, K. Eating disorder symptoms among undergraduate and graduate students at 12 U.S. colleges and universities. *Eat. Behav.* **2017**, *24*, 81–88. [CrossRef]
50. Vander Wal, J.S. Unhealthy weight control behaviors among adolescents. *J. Health Psychol.* **2012**, *17*, 110–120. [CrossRef]
51. Cui, W.; Zack, M.M.; Wethington, H. Health-related quality of life and body mass index among US adolescents. *Qual. Life Res.* **2014**, *23*, 2139–2150. [CrossRef]
52. Ihle, W.; Esser, G. Epidemiology of mental disorders in childhood and adolescence: Prevalence, course, comorbidity and gender differences. *Psychol. Rundsch.* **2002**, *53*, 159–169. [CrossRef]
53. Leme, A.C.B.; Haines, J.; Tang, L.; Dunker, K.L.L.; Philippi, S.T.; Fisberg, M.; Ferrari, G.L.; Fisberg, R.M. Impact of strategies for preventing obesity and risk factors for eating disorders among adolescents: A systematic review. *Nutrients* **2020**, *12*, 3134. [CrossRef]
54. Aparicio, E.; Canals, J.; Arija, V.; De Henauw, S.; Michels, N. The role of emotion regulation in childhood obesity: Implications for prevention and treatment. *Nutr. Res. Rev.* **2016**, *29*, 17–29. [CrossRef]
55. Farhat, T. Stigma, Obesity and adolescent risk behaviors: Current Research and future directions. *Curr. Opin. Psychol.* **2015**, *5*, 56–66. [CrossRef]
56. Rankin, J.; Matthews, L.; Cobley, S.; Han, A.; Sanders, R.; Wiltshire, H.D.; Baker, J.S. Psychological consequences of childhood obesity: Psychiatric comorbidity and prevention. *Adolesc. Health Med. Ther.* **2016**, *7*, 125–146. [CrossRef]
57. Cortese, S.; Moreira-Maia, C.R.; St Fleur, D.; Morcillo-Peñalver, C.; Rohde, L.A.; Faraone, S.V. Association between ADHD and obesity: A systematic review and meta-analysis. *Am. J. Psychiatry* **2016**, *173*, 34–43. [CrossRef]
58. Stavrou, S.; Nicolaides, N.C.; Papageorgiou, I.; Papadopoulou, P.; Terzioglou, E.; Chrousos, G.P.; Darviri, C.; Charmandari, E. The effectiveness of a stress-management intervention program in the management of overweight and obesity in childhood and adolescence. *J. Mol. Biochem.* **2016**, *5*, 63–70.
59. Emmanouil, C.-C.; Pervanidou, P.; Charmandari, E.; Darviri, C.; Chrousos, G.P. The Effectiveness of a health promotion and stress-management intervention program in a sample of obese children and adolescents. *Horm. Athens Greece* **2018**, *17*, 405–413. [CrossRef]
60. Vandenbroeck, P.; Goossens, J.; Clemens, M. *Tackling Obesities: Future Choices—Building the Obesity System Map*; Department of Innovation Universities and Skills: London, UK, 2007.
61. Nitsch, M.; Adamcik, T.; Kuso, S.; Zeiler, M.; Waldherr, K. Usability and engagement evaluation of an unguided online program for promoting a healthy lifestyle and reducing the risk for eating disorders and obesity in the school setting. *Nutrients* **2019**, *11*, 713. [CrossRef] [PubMed]
62. Zeiler, M.; Kuso, S.; Nitsch, M.; Simek, M.; Adamcik, T.; Herrero, R.; Etchemendy, E.; Mira, A.; Oliver, E.; Jones Bell, M.; et al. Online Interventions to prevent mental health problems implemented in school settings: The perspectives from key stakeholders in Austria and Spain. *Eur. J. Public Health* **2021**, *31*, i71–i79. [CrossRef] [PubMed]
63. Jones Bell, M.; Zeiler, M.; Herrero, R.; Kuso, S.; Nitsch, M.; Etchemendy, E.; Fonseca-Baeza, S.; Oliver, E.; Adamcik, T.; Karwautz, A.; et al. Healthy teens @ school: Evaluating and disseminating transdiagnostic preventive interventions for eating disorders and obesity for adolescents in school settings. *Internet Interv.* **2019**, *16*, 65–75. [CrossRef]

64. Jones, M.; Lynch, K.T.; Kass, A.E.; Burrows, A.; Williams, J.; Wilfley, D.E.; Taylor, C.B. Healthy weight regulation and eating disorder prevention in high school students: A universal and targeted web-based intervention. *J. Med. Internet Res.* **2014**, *16*, e57. [CrossRef] [PubMed]
65. De Vriendt, T.; Huybrechts, I.; Ottevaere, C.; Van Trimpont, I.; De Henauw, S. Validity of self-reported weight and height of adolescents, its impact on classification into BMI-categories and the association with weighing behaviour. *Int. J. Environ. Res. Public. Health* **2009**, *6*, 2696–2711. [CrossRef] [PubMed]

nutrients

MDPI

Review

Unveiling Metabolic Phenotype Alterations in Anorexia Nervosa through Metabolomics

Laura Mayo-Martínez [1], Francisco J. Rupérez [1], Gabriel Á. Martos-Moreno [2,3,4,5], Montserrat Graell [6,7], Coral Barbas [1], Jesús Argente [2,3,4,5,8,*] and Antonia García [1,*]

1 Centre for Metabolomics and Bioanalysis (CEMBIO), Faculty of Pharmacy, Universidad San Pablo-CEU, Montepríncipe Campus, 28660 Madrid, Spain; l.mayo1@usp.ceu.es (L.M.-M.); ruperez@ceu.es (F.J.R.); cbarbas@ceu.es (C.B.)
2 Departments of Pediatrics & Pediatric Endocrinology, Hospital Infantil Universitario Niño Jesús, 28009 Madrid, Spain; gabrielangelmartos@yahoo.es
3 La Princesa Research Institute, 28006 Madrid, Spain
4 Department of Pediatrics, Universidad Autónoma de Madrid, 28006 Madrid, Spain
5 Centro de Investigación Biomédica en Red de Fisiopatología de la Obesidad y Nutrición (CIBEROBN), Instituto de Salud Carlos III, 28029 Madrid, Spain
6 Department of Psychiatry, Hospital Infantil Universitario Niño Jesús, 28009 Madrid, Spain; montserratgraell1@gmail.com
7 Centro de Investigación Biomédica en Red Salud Mental (CIBERSAM), Instituto de Salud Carlos III, 28029 Madrid, Spain
8 IMDEA Food Institute, CEI UAM & CSIC, 28049 Madrid, Spain
* Correspondence: jesus.argente@uam.es (J.A.); antogar@ceu.es (A.G.)

Citation: Mayo-Martínez, L.; Rupérez, F.J.; Martos-Moreno, G.Á.; Graell, M.; Barbas, C.; Argente, J.; García, A. Unveiling Metabolic Phenotype Alterations in Anorexia Nervosa through Metabolomics. *Nutrients* **2021**, *13*, 4249. https://doi.org/10.3390/nu13124249

Academic Editors: Fernando Fernandez-Aranda, Janet Treasure and Empar Lurbe

Received: 6 October 2021
Accepted: 25 November 2021
Published: 26 November 2021

Abstract: Anorexia nervosa (AN) is a mental disorder characterized by an intense fear of weight gain that affects mainly young women. It courses with a negative body image leading to altered eating behaviors that have devastating physical, metabolic, and psychological consequences for the patients. Although its origin is postulated to be multifactorial, the etiology of AN remains unknown, and this increases the likelihood of chronification and relapsing. Thus, expanding the available knowledge on the pathophysiology of AN is of enormous interest. Metabolomics is proposed as a powerful tool for the elucidation of disease mechanisms and to provide new insights into the diagnosis, treatment, and prognosis of AN. A review of the literature related to studies of AN patients by employing metabolomic strategies to characterize the main alterations associated with the metabolic phenotype of AN during the last 10 years is described. The most common metabolic alterations are derived from chronic starvation, including amino acid, lipid, and carbohydrate disturbances. Nonetheless, recent findings have shifted the attention to gut-microbiota metabolites as possible factors contributing to AN development, progression, and maintenance. We have identified the areas of ongoing research in AN and propose further perspectives to improve our knowledge and understanding of this disease.

Keywords: anorexia; metabolomics; metabolic phenotype; metabolism; microbiota; mass spectrometry

1. Introduction

1.1. Metabolomics: Basic Concepts and Methodological Aspects

Over the last decades, there has been a shift towards precision and personalized medicine that has led to the development of new ways to approach research in health and disease. New technologies, the so-called "omics", have emerged to increase the understanding of disease onset and development in a holistic way [1,2].

Metabolomics is the comprehensive analysis of the metabolites included in a specific biological compartment at a specific time (metabolome). The metabolome is highly dynamic and provides valuable information about the ongoing processes in the human body. Since metabolites are the downstream effectors in the molecular pathways (genome—transcriptome—proteome—metabolome), they reflect the changes that have occured at prior stages of these pathways and give an accurate description of the phenotype. In this context, metabolomics has been extensively applied to the discovery of biomarkers for diagnosis, prognosis, and progression of disease in the clinic [3,4].

Importantly, the term metabolomics has been widely applied to studies that cover the metabolic alterations present in different conditions. The most important analytical techniques for the study of the metabolome are nuclear magnetic resonance (NMR) and mass spectrometry (MS). NMR spectroscopy is an analytical technique in which a strong magnetic field is applied to excite the nuclei of the molecular atoms. After that, the atoms return to their lower-energy state, remitting a radiofrequency that is measured by the detector. NMR has been extensively used for the quantitative measurement of metabolites within complex biological matrices [5,6]. MS is an analytical technique based on the formation of ionic species and its later separation according to mass-to-charge ratios under the application of electric or magnetic fields. Additionally, MS-based metabolomics is usually coupled to high-resolution separation techniques: gas chromatography-MS (GC-MS), liquid chromatography-MS (LC-MS), or capillary electrophoresis-MS (CE-MS). It can also be directly performed without metabolite separation by direct infusion (DI) or flow injection analysis (FIA) [7]. Although NMR provides highly accurate and reproducible results in a short time, MS offers higher sensitivity and wider metabolomics coverage, being a powerful platform for metabolomics analyses. Moreover, MS appears to be the optimum technique for targeted approaches, and it has become the most employed technique in metabolomics in recent years [1,8].

According to their scope, metabolomics studies can be generally divided into untargeted and targeted, although sometimes there is an overlap between these approaches [1,9]. Untargeted metabolomics focuses on the global detection and qualitative analysis of all the metabolites present in one sample. These studies are usually performed under discovery stages, where the objective is to gather all the possible information to unveil compounds that could be of interest in a given alteration [1]. Untargeted studies present a complex workflow that comprises analytical procedures but also advanced chemometric analysis to untangle the large amount of information obtained. Due to the wide chemical variability and heterogeneity between the compounds that can be analyzed, multiplatform strategies are employed to broadly cover the metabolome. It is common to combine LC-MS, GC-MS, and CE-MS strategies to analyze all the possible compounds within one single sample, as each technique is best suited for a subset of metabolites with similar physicochemical properties. The main challenge of this first approach is to process all the information that is extracted from each sample, and the main limiting step is the identification and annotation of the compounds found [4,7,10].

On the contrary, targeted metabolomics aims to cover a concrete set of chemically defined metabolites. This is the classical metabolomics approach in which the compounds of interest are previously selected, and then strategies for analysis are defined. The main advantage of targeted metabolomics is that it can be quantitative (absolute concentrations are determined) or semi-quantitative (comparative measurement of metabolite abundances/intensities between groups) [11–13], while untargeted metabolomics is a comparative approach, usually between patients and controls. The determining step in targeted metabolomics is to optimize the analytical conditions to enhance the method sensitivity and selectivity to measure the subset of compounds of interest. This approach is usually employed in biomarker validation after a first discovery step, which implies the combination of both metabolomics strategies [3,4].

Metabolomics is therefore a useful methodology to identify novel therapeutic targets and progression or severity biomarkers to develop effective strategies for the treatment or diagnosis of many different diseases, including anorexia nervosa (AN).

1.2. Anorexia Nervosa

Anorexia nervosa is a psychiatric disorder characterized by excessive dieting, some compensatory behaviors (excessive exercise, vomiting, and use of laxatives) and, specific psychopathological symptoms (disturbances in the perception of body weight and/or image and fear of becoming fat) that leads to severe and maintained weight loss, which results in progressive malnutrition. The American Psychiatry Association, in the fifth edition of the Diagnostic and Statistical Manual of Mental Disorders (DSM-5) [14], proposed the existence of other restrictive eating disorders such as avoidant/restrictive food intake disorder (ARFID) that presents no specific eating psychopathological symptoms of anorexia (weight concerns and body image disturbance) but features eating or feeding alteration. ARFID includes individuals who meet criteria for the Feeding Disorder of Infancy and Early Childhood DSM-IV category, but also other individuals with clinically significant eating problems who are not included in former DSM categories or therefore must be assigned a diagnosis of eating disorder not otherwise specified (EDNOS), such as selective eating and/or dysphagia [14]. DSM-5 also introduces a new category "Other Specified Feeding or Eating Disorder" (OSFED) for individuals who do not meet criteria for anorexia nervosa, bulimia nervosa or binge disorder and includes five disorders: atypical anorexia, purging disorder, subthreshold bulimia, subthreshold binge eating disorder, and night eating disorder.

AN can be further classified into two main subtypes, restricting and binge/purging disorder. Restrictive anorexia nervosa (AN-R) courses mainly with reduced food intake and excessive exercise, while binge/purging anorexia nervosa (AN-BP) also presents severe energy intake restriction but is combined with recurrent episodes of binge eating or purging behaviors [14,15]. Regardless of the subtype, AN has become one of the most predominant eating disorders with a lifetime prevalence in the general population of 0.6%, being three times higher among females (0.9%) than males (0.3%) [16,17].

The more inclusive DSM-5 criteria reduce the proportion of EDNOS diagnoses regarding DSM-IV and increase the proportion of anorexia and bulimia nervosa, with the new cases probably tending to have a higher minimum body mass index (BMI) and a more benign course [14]. Moreover, it is the eating disorder with the highest mortality rate, mainly due to cardiac complications or suicide [18–20].

Although the etiology of AN remains unclear, there is evidence for disturbed appetite and behavioral pathways that could suggest the physiological origin. Furthermore, it is well established that neurological and genetic predispositions, as well as biological and psychological traits and early experiences in life, might sensitize the individual to stress and hypothalamic-pituitary-adrenal (HPA) axis dysregulation. This sensibility can be further aggravated with environmental and socio-cultural factors that may favor the onset of an eating disorder [21,22]. Thus, AN is postulated to have a multifactorial etiology, and certain conditions may promote the onset in a predisposed population (Figure 1).

Once the disease starts, the maintained weight loss and the altered eating behaviors of the patients lead to wide metabolic dysfunctions complicating the overall clinical picture of the disorder. Among the metabolic alterations, individuals with anorexia nervosa are commonly found to present mild plasma hyper aminoacidemia [23], increased cholesterol levels [24,25], electrolyte imbalances leading to hyponatremia and hypokalemia [26], and profound endocrine disturbances [27–29]. AN patients are reported to have lower triiodothyronine (T3) and thyroxine (T4), showing an altered hypothalamic-pituitary-thyroid axis [26]. In addition, increased cortisol levels in serum and urine have been found, suggesting hyperstimulation of the HPA axis [30,31]. Moreover, patients also have distorted appetite-regulating mechanisms, characterized by increased levels of peptide PYY and ghrelin and decreased concentrations of leptin [26,31–34]. Finally, their extreme eating behaviors lead to micronutrient deficiencies, including reduced levels of zinc, copper, vitamin C, riboflavin, and vitamin B6 [26,35]. Nutritional deprivation can eventually lead to severe complications, including cardiac problems, which is one of the principal causes of death in this disease.

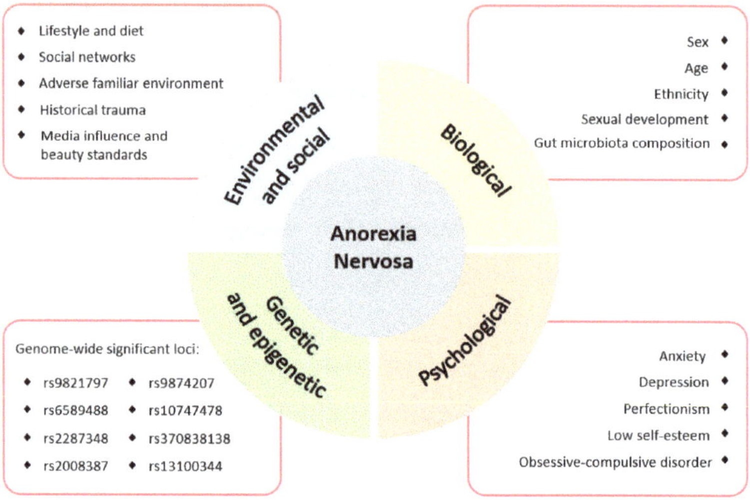

Figure 1. Main factors predisposing to the development of anorexia nervosa [21,22].

Recent findings in the alteration of intestinal microbiota due to eating behavior and diet have led to increasing interest in microbiota in eating disorders. Few studies have analyzed the microbiota composition in AN, and modifications in microbiome composition and their by-products are scarcely described [18,36,37]. Several fecal metabolites are involved in mood modulation, learning, and memory mechanisms. Regarding this, short-chain fatty acids, lipopolysaccharides from gram-negative bacteria, and neurotransmitters are microbiota metabolites that have autocrine or paracrine functions in the human body [18,38,39]. Moreover, there are chiral metabolites that can have different stereoisomers D and L, with very different biological activity. Amongst these, amino acids and hydroxy acids are involved in neuro-immuno endocrine regulation. The sources of D-amino acids and D-hydroxy acids are food, endogenous enzymatic processes, and the microbiome. The D form of some amino acids, mainly D-serine and D-aspartate, is altered in psychiatric diseases such as schizophrenia or bipolar disorder, but also depression, a common feature in AN [40–43]. Lactate, a hydroxy acid, is also modified in schizophrenia, depression, and stress disorders [44,45]. Some of these compounds act on receptors in intestinal endothelial cells, and others reach the systemic circulation and can enter the central nervous system, where they mediate different responses [18,38,39]. Thus, the analysis of these microbiota by-products could be relevant for improving our knowledge of the psychopathology of AN. Whether dysbiosis and altered microbiota metabolites are a consequence of malnutrition or if they are involved in AN onset and progression requires further research [21].

To date, the treatment for AN is based on renourishment therapies, as well as psychotherapy and psychopharmacological interventions, to reduce the core psychopathology and the associated disorders (mainly anxiety, depressive and obsessive–compulsive). Unfortunately, specific treatments that target the origin of the disease are still lacking. Thus, there is an increased probability of relapse and to develop a chronic state of the disease, and around 50% of the patients do not achieve full recovery even during a long follow-up period [46]. Treatment objectives should have a strict priority: prevent the death of the patient, prevent the disease from becoming chronic, and attainment of physical and mental recuperation. An integral treatment program should be carried out by a multidisciplinary and coordinated team, including a pediatrician, endocrinologist, psychiatrist, psychologist, and nutritionist.

As a result, the elucidation of the etiology of the disease is of enormous interest to improve treatment and disease outcomes [21]. The pathophysiology of AN could be better elucidated by combining different "omics" approaches to obtain an accurate characterization of the alterations present. In this context, metabolomics appears to be an excellent tool to characterize the metabolic profile of AN patients, leading to the identification of potential alterations that could be useful for the clinical management of anorexia.

The present review aims to present and discuss the information contained in the metabolomics studies that have been performed to date on AN patients with two main objectives: (1) To clearly define the metabolic phenotype of individuals with anorexia nervosa, which is essential for providing new insight into the etiology and pathophysiology of the disease, and (2) To identify the areas that are still uncovered by metabolomics and need further research in the field, with the final purpose of improving disease management and prognosis.

2. Background

After a thorough bibliographic query including the terms "Metabolomics" or "Metabonomics" and "Mass Spectrometry" or "Nuclear Magnetic Resonance" and "Anorexia Nervosa", we found 72 records. Only studies that performed metabolomics (either targeted or untargeted, by NMR or MS) of human samples of AN patients from the last 10 years were included. Thirteen studies were therefore selected for the narrative review and they are summarized in Table 1.

Four studies out of thirteen employed a targeted metabolomics approach: only [47–50]. Other studies used a combined targeted and untargeted metabolomics approach in their analyses [51–54]. Most of the studies included used MS for the instrumental analysis. Prochazkova et al. used a combination of NMR and MS for metabolite identification and quantification [54]. Salehi et al. performed serum profiling of AN samples by ^{1}H NMR [55].

All the included studies were performed on young adult human females. All the studies performed, with the exception of one, were based on case vs. control analyses, comparing a healthy control group to AN patients. However, ten of them also included patients after treatment, either in the short-term, the long-term, or fully recovered patients [47–49,52–58]. Bulant et al. studied the evolution of the steroid profile of hospitalized women with anorexia nervosa with no control group [50]. One study also performed a timeline analysis including fasting and postprandial samples [56]. Four studies specified that the patients had the restricting type of AN [47,48,51,54]. Moreover, two studies included AN-R and AN-BP patients and established comparisons between them and the healthy controls [37,49]. Three more studies identified both types of AN in their patients, but they did not perform any differential analysis between them [57,58].

Regarding the type of sample analyzed, plasma/serum samples were selected in nine studies [47–53,55,56], and fecal samples from AN patients were analyzed in the rest of the investigations [37,54,57,58].

Table 1. Metabolomics studies on AN in human.

Methodology	Instrumental Analysis	Sample	Study Design	Findings	Ref.
Targeted	FIA-MS/MS	Serum	Evaluation of the metabolic profile of patients during weight recovery. Female adolescents. Healthy controls (n= 25) AN patients at inpatient admission (n = 35) Short-term weight recovery (n = 26) Long-term weight recovery (n = 22)	• Mild hyper aminoacidemia in patients • Increased AC, PC, and SM in patients at different time points • Lower sum of hexoses in patients compared to controls • FDR	[47]
Targeted	FIA-MS/MS	Serum	Comparison of the metabolic profile of acute patients and short-term weight recovered patients. Young females. Healthy controls (n = 16) Acute AN patients (n = 29) Short-term weight recovery (n = 29)	• Mild hyper aminoacidemia in patients • Altered lipidic profile: increased AC, LPC and PC, and SM in patients • Increased hexoses in patients • FDR	[48]
Targeted	LC-MS/MS	Plasma	Analysis of one-carbon metabolism in AN-R and AN-BP patients, in recovered AN patients, and healthy controls. Young women. No eating-disorder history (controls) (n = 36) AN-R patients (n = 30) AN-BP patients (n = 23) AN remitted patients (n = 40; 36 with AN-BP history, and 9 with AN-R history)	• Increased B12 and betaine in AN active patients compared to controls • No differences in choline and Met • FDR	[49]
Targeted	GC-MS (SIM)	Serum	Changes in BMI, and psychopathology and steroid metabolome profiling in AN patients before and after hospitalization. Young women. AN patients (n = 33)	• Increased 20α-dihydro-pregnenolone sulfate and pregnenolone sulfate after treatment • 5-androstene-3β,7β,17β-triol, 7β-OH-DHEA, epietiocholanolone, and epipregnanolone were decreased after renourishment	[50]
Untargeted Targeted	UPLC-MS CE-MS LC-MS/MS	Serum	Comparison of the metabolic profile of AN-R patients with age-matching healthy controls. Young females. Healthy controls (n = 10) AN-R patients (n = 10)	• Lower amino acidic levels in patients • Decreased AC in patients • Lower levels of cis-aconitate, betaine, choline, methyl-2-oxovalerate, and oxovalerate • Increased N-phenylacetylglutamine and guanidinosuccinate • FDR	[51]

Table 1. *Cont.*

Methodology	Instrumental Analysis	Sample	Study Design	Findings	Ref.
Untargeted Targeted	GC-MS HPLC-MS/MS	Plasma	Multiomics study of AN (genomics, proteomics, and metabolomics). Multiplatform metabolomics study of the lipidome and eicosanoid metabolome of acute AN patients, recovered patients, and healthy controls. Healthy controls (n= 36 for PUFAs analysis, n = 38 for eicosanoid analysis) Ill AN patients (n= 30 for PUFAs analysis, n = 10 for eicosanoid analysis) Recovered AN patients (n= 30 for PUFAs analysis, n = 10 for eicosanoid analysis)	• EPHX2 genetic variation is associated with AN development • The activity of sEH is elevated in AN compared to controls • AN present altered postprandial metabolism of PUFAs and sEH-dependent eicosanoids	[52]
Untargeted Targeted	GC-MS HPLC-MS/MS	Plasma	Evaluation of the lipidomic profile of AN patients compared to healthy controls and recovered patients. Young females. Healthy controls (n = 36) Ill AN patients (n = 30) Recovered AN patients (n = 30)	• Increased n-3 and n-6 PUFAs • Decreased n-3: n-6 ratios in AN • Increased oxylipins from CYP450 pathway	[53]
Untargeted Targeted	^{1}H NMR MS (SIM)	Feces	Multiomics approach for analyzing the intestinal microbiota and its metabolites in patients before and after treatment compared to healthy controls. Young females. Healthy controls (n = 67) AN-R patients (n = 59)	• Acetate is decreased before and after treatment • Butyrate is decreased in acute patients but increases with renourishment therapy • Propionate is lower after treatment and presents no difference in acute patients • Decreased dopamine and GABA in acute patients compared to controls • Decreased serotonin in recovered patients • FDR	[54]
Untargeted	^{1}H NMR	Serum	Metabolome profiling of acute AN patients, recovered patients, and healthy controls. Young women. Healthy controls (n = 65) AN patients (n = 65) Recovered AN patients (n = 65)	• Gln is higher in acute patients when compared to controls and recovered patients, with no difference between the last two groups • Thr is increased only in recovered patients when compared with the acute patients • Ala, Gly, Pro, and Ser showed no differences between groups • FDR	[55]

Table 1. *Cont.*

Methodology	Instrumental Analysis	Sample	Study Design	Findings	Ref.
Untargeted	GC-MS	Plasma	Evaluation of the fatty acid profile after renourishment therapy in AN patients. Young women. Healthy controls (n= 47) Ill AN patients (n = 30) Recovered AN patients (n = 20)	• DPA, EPA, and laurate were increased at fasting compared to controls • ALA was increased at both time points compared to controls • FDR	[56]
Untargeted	GC-MS	Feces	Comparison of metabolic profiles of patients in an acute state, after recovery, and healthy controls. Young females. Healthy controls (n = 20) AN patients (n = 24; 18 with AN-R, 6 with AN-BP) AN patients after short-term weight restoration (n = 16)	• Higher Phe in patients after treatment • Higher laurate, hydroxy stearate, and stearate in acute patients • Lower fucose, rhamnose, and xylose in acute patients • FDR	[57]
Untargeted	GC-MS	Feces	Analysis of the microbiome and the metabolome of AN patients before and after treatment compared to healthy controls. Young females. Healthy controls (n = 20) AN patients before treatment (n = 21; 16 with AN-R and 5 AN-BP) AN patients after short-term weight restoration (n = 16)	• Lower Asp, Met, Phe, and Ser in AN patients before and after weight recovery • Lower Leu only in acute patients compared to controls • Lower fucose, rhamnose, and xylose in patients and their values are restored after treatment • Lower arabinose and tagatose in acute patients and increased levels after therapy • FDR	[58]
Untargeted	GC-MS	Feces	Evaluation of the microbiome and the metabolic profile of AN-R and AN-BP patients and healthy controls. Young females. Healthy controls (n = 20) AN-R patients (n = 17) AN-BP patients (n = 6)	• Lower pyro-Glu, Ile, Leu, and Val in AN-R and AN-BP • Lower Thr and Tyr in AN-R • Lower palmitate in AN-R and AN-BP • Lower glycerol in AN-R • Lower allose, arabinose, lactose, rhamnose, scyllo-inositol, sorbose, tagatose, and xylose in AN-R and AN-BP • Lower malate in AN-R and AN-BP • Lower succinate in AN-R • FDR	[37]

3. Metabolic Alterations in Anorexia Nervosa

Individuals with anorexia nervosa present severe metabolic disturbances as a consequence of abnormal eating behaviors. Alterations in biochemical parameters have been described in AN (cortisol, cholesterol, electrolytes, etc.). However, the metabolic phenotype or fingerprinting of AN has been scarcely studied. Predominantly, plasma and serum samples are analyzed due to the ease of sample acquisition and the information they provide about the metabolic status. Generally, studies are focused on small groups of metabolites such as amino acids, lipids, or carbohydrates. Hence, wide untargeted metabolomics analyses are still lacking in AN. The main metabolomics alterations found in plasma from AN patients are summarized in Figure 2 and detailed below. Additionally, in Supplementary Table S1 there is a compilation of all the described alterations in human samples of AN found by metabolomics.

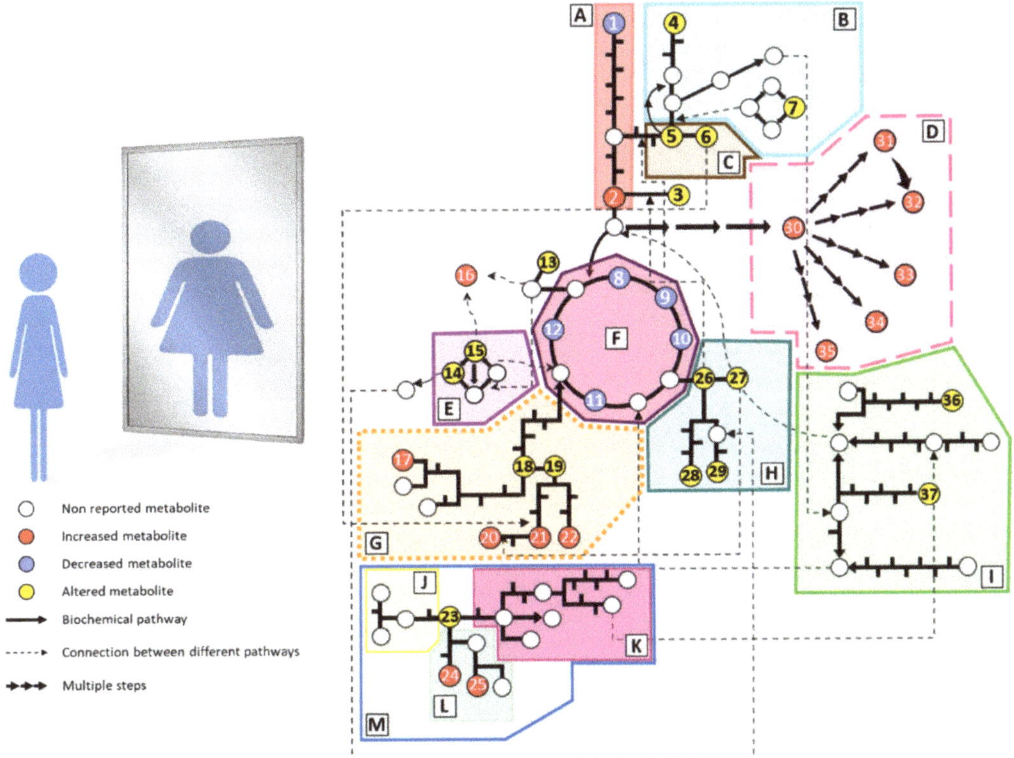

Figure 2. Summary of the main metabolomic alterations found in plasma or serum samples from AN patients in the included studies. Altered pathways: (**A**) glycolysis and gluconeogenesis, (**B**) methionine and cysteine metabolism, (**C**) serine and glycine metabolism, (**D**) lipid metabolism, (**E**) urea cycle, (**F**) tricarboxylate cycle, (**G**) phenylalanine and tyrosine metabolism, (**H**) glutamate, glutamine, proline and histidine metabolism, (**I**) branched-chain amino acids metabolism, (**J**) serotonin pathway, (**K**) kynurenine pathway, (**L**) indole pathway, (**M**) tryptophan metabolism. Metabolites: (1) glucose, (2) pyruvate, (3) alanine, (4) taurine, (5) serine, (6) glycine, (7) methionine, (8) citrate, (9) cis-aconitate, (10) isocitrate, (11) succinate, (12) malate, (13) asparagine, (14) ornithine, (15) arginine, (16) guanidinosuccinate, (17) *p*-cresyl sulfate, (18) tyrosine, (19) phenylalanine, (20) phenylacetylglutamine, (21) phenylacetate, (22) hippurate, (23) tryptophan, (24) indole-3-acetate, (25) indoxyl sulfate, (26) glutamate, (27) glutamine, (28) histidine, (29) proline, (30) fatty acids, (31) phosphatidylcholines, (32) lysophosphatidylcholines, (33) sphingomyelins, (34) acylcarnitines, (35) oxylipins, (36) leucine, (37) isoleucine.

3.1. Amino Acids

Amino acid dysregulation is usually found in patients with AN, probably related to chronic starvation and altered dietary habits. Some studies have analyzed the amino acid profile in AN patients and the results are inconsistent. However, only a few studies have used metabolomics to assess the amino acidic profile.

3.1.1. Plasma and Serum

M. Föcker et al. performed a **targeted** metabolomics assay to determine 163 metabolites in serum of acute patients, weight-restored patients, and controls. The analysis was done by FIA-MS/MS (Flow injection analysis with tandem mass spectrometry) using the AbsoluteIDQkit® p150 from Biocrates (Innsbruck, Austria). They found mild hyper aminoacidemia in patients, with significantly increased concentrations of glutamine, glycine, histidine, leucine, methionine, ornithine, phenylalanine, serine, and tryptophan [48]. However, in a second study a few years later with the AbsoluteIDQkit® p180, they only reported a significant increase in glutamine, glycine, histidine, serine, and tryptophan [47]. Surprisingly, they described more important metabolic alterations in the weight-restored patients than in the acute phase compared to controls, meaning either that the acute patients adapt to chronic starvation or that the rapid weight gain has a huge impact on metabolism.

Conversely, Miyata et al. studied serum amino acids of individuals with anorexia nervosa through an **untargeted** approach combining UPLC-MS and CE-MS. They found significantly lower values of alanine, asparagine, betaine, histidine, allo-isoleucine, isoleucine, leucine, methionine, proline, taurine, and tyrosine. They also described decreasing tendencies in some other amino acids such as arginine, aspartate, phenylalanine, serine, tryptophan, valine, and threonine. The authors mentioned increasing tendencies in the levels of glutamate, glutamine, glycine, and lysine, although they were not statistically significant. Cysteine levels were not assessed [51].

Burdo et al., in their study on plasma levels of carbon metabolism in AN, reported increased levels of betaine and no variation in methionine in acute patients compared with controls and recovered women [49], contrary to what Miyata et al. and M. Föcker et al. have described [48,51].

Salehi et al. performed a metabolomics study based on ^{1}H NMR on serum samples. They compared the profile of acute AN patients (AN) with recovered patients (RecAN) and healthy controls. Five out of twenty-one metabolites were significantly different between the groups. Glutamine was higher in AN when compared to the other groups, but it did not show significant differences between healthy controls and RecAN. Threonine was significantly increased only in RecAN when compared with the AN group. Proline, alanine, serine, and glycine did not show significant variations between the groups [55].

3.1.2. Feces

Monteleone et al. performed an **untargeted** metabolomics assay by GC-MS of fecal samples in acute AN patients, weight restored patients, and healthy controls. They studied 224 identified metabolites, and phenylalanine was significantly decreased in weight-restored patients but acute patients had normal levels compared to healthy controls [57]. However, one year later, Monteleone et al. described decreased levels of phenylalanine, aspartate, serine, and methionine in acute and weight restored AN patients. Leucine was decreased but only in acute patients compared to healthy controls [58]. In 2021, this group performed a new study by using an **untargeted** metabolomics approach with GC-MS in fecal samples comparing both types of AN [37]. They found that isoleucine, leucine, valine, and pyroglutamate are decreased in both types of AN, but the AN-BP subtype presents lower levels than the restricting type compared to controls. Nonetheless, tyrosine and threonine were decreased in AN-R but increased in AN-BP patients.

Although the described amino acid disturbances are not consistent between studies, there is a clear disorder in the amino acidic profile of AN patients. Despite the direction of those variations, we can presume that the mechanisms for homeostasis of amino acids are altered in AN, which in turn leads to modified concentrations of these metabolites in patients. Free amino acid concentrations are the result of the relationship between the incoming sources of amino acid, which include dietary uptake, endogenous synthesis, and gut-bacteria metabolism, and amino acid depletion by protein synthesis and catabolism to increase energy uptake. The altered amino acid pattern is therefore associated with these processes, and whether it is a consequence of chronic starvation or a marked trait of AN that could play a role in the biological origin needs to be clarified.

3.2. Lipids

Alterations in the lipid profiles in the plasma, serum, and feces of AN patients have also been described. Distorted eating behaviors, related to fasting and reduction of carbohydrates and fats, produce massive disturbances in metabolism, increasing lipolysis, gluconeogenesis, fatty acid oxidation, and proteolysis [59]. These variations are reflected in the lipidome of individuals with anorexia nervosa. Different strategies have been used to assess the lipid profile in AN.

3.2.1. Plasma and Serum

Föcker et al. studied the serum lipidome by targeted metabolomics. In a first approach, they reported increased lipid concentrations in AN patients during acute starvation and after weight recovery compared to healthy controls. Glycerophospholipids, including phosphatidylcholines (PC), lysophosphatidylcholines (LPC) and sphingomyelins (SM) were significantly increased in patients (e.g., LPC(14:0), LPC(17:0), PC(32:2), PC(32:3), SM(16:0), SM(18:1). In addition, they also observed increased concentrations of some carnitines in serum of AN patients at both time points (e.g., carnitine, acetyl-carnitine) [48]. These results are consistent with previous studies that described the lipid profile of plasma in AN by non-metabolomics approaches [60]. However, Miyata et al. reported that by untargeted metabolomics lower concentrations of some acylcarnitines (AC), such as palmitoylcarnitine, butyrylcarnitine, O-acetylcarnitine, and octanoylcarnitine are observed [51]. Additionally, the changes found by Föcker et al. after renourishment therapy were higher than in the acute state, similar to that found with amino acids, meaning that metabolism is highly susceptible to maintained starvation but even more to the subsequent weight recovery [48]. Nonetheless, in a subsequent study, Föcker et al. found fewer differences between controls and the acute starvation state. The most significant changes were between the starvation state and short-term weight recovery. After complete renourishment therapy, the metabolome was restored, reaching values close to those of the healthy controls. Hence, metabolism seems to adapt to long starvation and renourishment processes, reaching stable metabolic states. The discordances between these studies were justified by the methodological differences and the small sample size in both cases. The most relevant findings in this second study are some compounds that are proposed as potential biomarkers of different states in disease and treatment of AN. These compounds showed significant associations with their respective states and homogeneous time-course behavior in the tested samples. For the starvation state, PC(34:4) and PC(38:3) are significantly decreased and are restored after therapy. In short-term weight recovery, LPC(16:1) and LPC(20:3) are increased, while PC(38:6) and pimelylcarnitine are decreased, suggesting that they could serve as possible markers of the metabolic state during renourishment therapies in AN [47].

Shih et al. used an **untargeted** metabolomics approach by using GC-MS for the determination of polyunsaturated fatty acids (PUFAs) and a **targeted** metabolomics analysis (HPLC-MS/MS) for oxylipins measurement in plasma. Oxylipins are derived from PUFAs by enzymatic (cyclooxygenases, lipoxygenases, and cytochrome P450) or non-enzymatic oxidations, and they are the most relevant mediators of PUFAs functions in the human body. The concentrations of the free fatty acids n-3 (alpha-linolenate-ALA, stearidonate-SDA, eicosapentaenoate-EPA, and docosahexaenoate-DHA) and n-6 (gamma-linolenate-GLA, dihomo-gamma-linolenate-DGLA, arachidonate-ARA, and osbond acid-OBA) were reported to be increased in the plasma of individuals with AN compared to controls. They analyzed the two major ratios between n-3 and n-6 PUFAs (LA (linolenate): ALA and ARA: EPA), which are significantly decreased in AN compared to controls. Moreover, those ratios were inversely correlated with anxiety in individuals with anorexia nervosa, and ARA: EPA was significantly correlated with BMI in patients as well. They also reported significant differences in individual oxylipins and oxylipins ratios. The eicosanoids significantly altered in AN included DHA and ARA metabolites, which belong to the CYP450 pathway. They also studied sEH (soluble epoxide hydrolase) activity which is an enzyme involved in the inactivation of epoxy-fatty acids from CYP catabolism of PUFAs. They finally suggested a greater in vivo activity, concentration, or efficiency of sEH in AN patients when compared to controls. The higher activity of this enzyme, involved in the CYP oxylipin pathway, has been related to increased inflammation and psychiatric disorders such as depression or anxiety, which are comorbidities of AN [61]. As a general overview, individuals with AN showed altered lipidome profiles that were correlated with increased neuroinflammation, anxiety disorders, and lower BMI [52,53].

Nguyen et al. also studied the plasma lipidic profile in acute and recovered individuals with anorexia nervosa compared to healthy controls at two different time points: fasting and postprandial. They examined 26 compounds, including saturated and unsaturated FA by GC-MS. Out of these 26 FA, AN patients presented significant increases in four species under fasting conditions and in only one of them after food intake. Similar to what Shih et al. described, laurate, EPA, and DPA (docosapentaenoate) were increased under fasting while ALA was increased at both timepoints in AN patients [52,56].

Bulant et al. analyzed the steroid profile of serum samples from 33 hospitalized women with AN. The aim was to determine the steroid variations after renourishment therapy. By GC-MS in selected ion monitoring (SIM) mode, they found significantly decreased concentrations of 7β-hydroxy-metabolites of C19Δ5steroids (7β-hydroxydehydroepiandrosterone and 5-androstene-3β,7β,17β-triol) which have been related to immunostimulation and anti-inflammatory properties. They also observed increased concentrations of the steroids at the beginning of the steroidogenic pathway, pregnenolone sulfate, and 20α-dihydropregnenolone sulfate after treatment [50].

3.2.2. Feces

Monteleone et al. determined the concentration of some FA in feces by GC-MS. They described lower levels of palmitate in AN-R and AN-BP when compared to healthy controls. Glycerol was also found to decrease in AN-R but not in AN-BP patients. Glycerol depletion can occur as a consequence of starvation due to shifts in the energy sources in carbohydrate deficiency [37]. Monteleone et al. also described increased concentrations of laurate as well as stearic and hydroxystearates in acute patients, but levels were restored after treatment [57].

Overall, the plasma/serum lipidome of individuals with AN is characterized by altered concentrations of n-3 and n-6 FA, glycerophospholipids (PC and LPC), sphingophospholipids (SM), carnitines (AC), steroids; and oxylipins [47,48,50–53,56]. Additionally, hypercholesterolemia and hyperlipoproteinemia have been widely described in AN patients [24,25,62]. Therefore, LPC, PC, and SM as components of lipoproteins are expected to increase, which is supported by some of the studies mentioned above [47,48]. Moreover, during starvation the lipolysis rate is increased to provide energy substrates for the organism. Hence, triglycerides are hydrolyzed, and FA are mobilized by AC to produce energy through β-oxidation. Therefore, it is plausible that there is an increase of FA and AC in starvation states [48,59,62]. Lipid metabolism is complex and highly variable and can be associated with the state of the disease, sex, age, and more importantly, diet. However, follow-up studies have shown that lipidic profiles are completely restored after treatment, supporting the existence of underlying alterations that need further research [62,63].

3.3. Sugars

3.3.1. Plasma and Serum

Carbohydrate profiles also differ in patients and controls. By using ^{1}H NMR, Salehi et al. reported lower glucose levels in AN patients compared to controls, but it did not follow the same trend in the recovered patients [55]. In addition, the sum of hexoses determined by Föcker et al. was significantly decreased in acute patients compared to long-term treated patients and controls. In the short-term treated group, hexoses were diminished compared only to healthy controls [47]. In contrast, their previous study showed a higher concentration of hexose in acute and weight-restored patients than in healthy women. However, there were no differences between the patients, either in the acute phase or after treatment [48].

3.3.2. Feces

Monteleone et al. compared the fecal profile of AN-R and AN-BP patients to controls and found that allose, arabinose, lactose, rhamnose, scylloinositol, and xylose were decreased in both groups, but AN-BP presented lower levels when compared to controls. On the contrary, sorbose and tagatose levels were lower in the AN-R group, although both types of patients had significantly decreased concentrations. In summary, a general decrease of carbohydrates was found in the plasma of AN patients independently of their type [37]. Accordingly, in a previous study, they determined that fucose, rhamnose, and xylose were diminished in patients, but normal levels were recovered after renourishment therapy [57,58]. These authors also found that arabinose and tagatose were lower in acute patients, reaching the highest concentration after weight restoration [58].

Altered carbohydrate metabolism is expected in AN. The dietary habits in AN are usually characterized by a low intake of fat and carbohydrate, which makes the organism rely on other sources of energy. Carbohydrate depletion is generally described in undernutrition and starvation. Under fasting conditions, the physiological response involves glycogen breakdown to resort to glucose fuels, which are the main energy source for the cells. Thus, during the early stages of AN, we might find a temporary increase of the carbohydrates in blood that are rapidly consumed. Nevertheless, in chronic starvation, glycogen deposits are exhausted, and there is a shift towards lipolysis and muscle breakdown as energy sources [59].

3.4. Tricarboxylate Cycle

Profound metabolic alterations that affect energy metabolism will also impact the tricarboxylate (TCA) cycle. Therefore, disturbances in metabolites within this pathway have been found in AN.

3.4.1. Plasma and Serum

Miyata et al. reported lower levels of intermediates of the TCA cycle in the serum of individuals with AN compared to healthy controls, including malate, succinate, and cis-aconitate [51].

3.4.2. Feces

Likewise, Monteleone et al., in their study of fecal samples from AN patients, reported lower levels of malate in AN-BP and AN-R, while succinate was decreased in AN-R and increased in the AN-BP group [37].

3.5. Uremic Toxins

Miyata et al. performed a **targeted** metabolomics analysis of six uremic toxins in serum samples by LC-MS/MS. They found that all, *p*-cresyl sulfate, hippurate, indoxyl sulfate, indole-3-acetate, phenylacetate, and phenyl sulfate, were significantly higher in AN patients versus the control group. Moreover, by an **untargeted** approach, they were able to identify increased concentrations of another two toxins in the AN-R group:

guanidinosuccinate and N2-phenylacetylglutamine. Although there was no signal of renal damage in the patients, uremic toxins were increased. As some gut microbiota species can produce uremic toxins, it has been suggested that this increase could be potentially linked to gut dysbiosis in AN patients [51].

3.6. Microbial Metabolites

Recent research has focused the attention on the gut-microbiota-brain axis. The impact of gut microbiota on health and disease has recently been described and appears to be an important biological factor in the development and maintenance of EDs. Gut microbiota is defined as the heterogeneous, unique, and dynamic ecosystem of the intestine that depends on complex interactions between genetic and environmental factors [21,64]. Its role in normal physiology and homeostasis is unquestionable. The microbiota is mainly constituted of bacteria, although there are other organisms such as archaea or protozoa. The composition is highly variable among individuals depending on endogenous and exogenous factors such as sex, age, physical activity, genetic features of the host, and infections, among others. However, it has been demonstrated that the predominant factor determining microbiota composition is the diet [36].

The numerous implications of gut microbiota on host health and wellness range from nutrient/energy metabolism to brain function and mood regulation pathways [65]. Moreover, complex direct and indirect interactions between the microbiota, gut, and brain, have been described constituting the termed "microbiota-gut-brain axis"; and microbiota appears to be involved in the regulation of behaviors and emotions, such as learning, stress, depression, and anxiety, that are common traits in AN [39,66].

Once established that the host diet is critical in the gut microbial composition [21] and that patients with EDs have altered nutritional patterns, it can be assumed that these patients will present a modified microbiota [39] and indeed, this has been described in AN. This dysbiosis results from starvation and malnutrition, but the impact on the onset and progression of the disease needs to be further elucidated [18,67–72]. Gut microbiota produces a set of bioactive molecules that can induce different responses in the host. Experimental data suggest that an important part of the circulating metabolites in the human body are derived from gut microbiota [73]. Some of these metabolites can interact with receptors in enteroendocrine cells (EECs), and some others can enter systemic circulation performing paracrine functions [74]. Among those metabolites, short-chain fatty acids (SCFAs), neurotransmitters, and lipopolysaccharides are widely studied due to their autocrine and paracrine effects.

To assess the putative effect of dysbiosis on the physiopathology of AN, a combined analytical strategy that determines the composition of the microbiota and its subproducts should be performed. Metabolomics tools can be applied to analyze the products of bacterial metabolism that develop important functions in the human body. To do so, the patient's fecal sample constitutes a high-value specimen and should be analyzed. However, alterations in feces have been poorly studied for AN.

SCFAs, such as butyrate, propionate, and acetate, are one of the main products of bacterial metabolism. They come from the fermentation of non-digestible carbohydrates, fiber, and resistant starch. SCFAs can target the ENS stimulating the sympathetic nervous system, which is implicated in energy consumption [73,75].

P. Monteleone et al. and A.M. Monteleone et al. performed **untargeted** metabolomics of fecal samples by GC-MS. In their comparative analysis between both anorexia types, they found that acetate was decreased in AN-R patients but not in the AN-BP group [37]. Moreover, they described increased propionate in AN patients that is restored after treatment, contrary to butyrate that is unchanged in patients and decreases after weight recovery [57,58].

Prochazkova et al. performed a multi-omics study with fecal samples from individuals with AN before and after renourishment compared to healthy controls. They determined the composition of gut microbiota and performed **targeted** metabolomics assays for the analysis of fecal SCFAs and neurotransmitters. Butyrate, acetate, and propionate were analyzed by NMR while the neurotransmitters were determined by MS on selective reaction monitoring (SRM). Butyrate was diminished in the ill patients but showed partial recovery after renourishment therapies, although normal values were not achieved. On the contrary, propionate was significantly decreased in patients after treatment, but there were no significant differences in acute patients compared to controls. Acetate levels were significantly lower in both groups of patients, which implies that renourishment does not restore the normal SCFAs profile.

As suggested previously, the changes in fecal metabolites in patients with AN may result from either their chronic malnutrition and/or changes in their gut microbiota composition [37,57]. Regarding this, butyrate has been related to a reduction of anxiety and depressive-like symptoms and to lower neuroinflammation [76–79]. Thus, decreased butyrate levels might increase susceptibility to depressive-like symptoms. Moreover, the administration of the three SCFAs to mice showed decreased stress-related behaviors [78]. Propionate has also been found to exert direct functions in the central nervous system, it can cross the blood-brain barrier acting on different receptors related to the protection of neuroinflammation mainly [80].

Regarding neurotransmitters, ill patients showed a significant decrease in γ-aminobutyrate (GABA) and dopamine levels. A.M Monteleone et al. also reported significantly decreased GABA levels in both types of AN patients (AN-R and AN-BP) [37]. However, serotonin was only significantly lower in renourished patients. Contrary to expected, the comparison between the patients before and after weight restoration did not yield any significant variation. Tyramine, kynurenine, and hydroxytryptophan concentrations did not vary between groups and they did not change during the course of hospitalization. As a result, novel therapeutic approaches are required to be combined with renourishment to improve the metabolic state of patients [54].

3.7. Covariates

A very important issue in clinical trials is the impact of the covariates. In the studies about anorexia discussed in the present review, covariates such as age, BMI, leptin levels are usually recorded and reported, as part of the diagnosis, prognosis and follow-up criteria for the evaluation and management of the disease. Only a few studies included a detailed specific statistical analysis of the impact and association of covariates. Burdo et al. [49] further tested for several associations between nutrient levels and BMI, as well as eating-disorder symptoms, and they reported that vitamin B12 was negatively associated with BMI in AN. Traits of highly specific markers such as the epoxy-fatty acids and other oxylipins were considered together for ANOVA with other covariates such as age, BMI or anxiety [52,53]. Covariates such as BMI and psychiatric comorbidities were also considered [56], but only to evaluate their correlation with the metabolomics findings (individual fatty acids).

4. Conclusions and Further Perspectives

AN is a devastating and complex disease with a multifactorial origin. Through targeted and untargeted metabolomics mainly based on 1H NMR or MS, the metabolic phenotype of individuals with anorexia nervosa provided has shed light on the metabolic alterations beyond the classical tests. Alterations in pathways such as glycolysis and gluconeogenesis, methionine and cysteine metabolism, serine and glycine metabolism, lipid metabolism, urea cycle, tricarboxylate cycle, phenylalanine and tyrosine metabolism, glutamate, glutamine, proline and histidine metabolism, branched-chain amino acids metabolism, serotonin pathway, kynurenine pathway, indole pathway, and tryptophan metabolism have been revealed. In particular, gut-microbiota metabolites emerge as possible factors contributing to AN development, progression, and maintenance, and deserve further research.

However, validation is a critical point in untargeted metabolomics studies to avoid chance findings. Discrepancies among different studies can be due to the small sample size and the selection of the control group. For this reason, studies with larger sample sizes considering all possible covariates, and validation of results with targeted analytical methods are compulsory to obtain reliable results. Large cohort studies will diminish chance findings, enforcing the statistical significance of the obtained results. Nonetheless, the recruitment of patients with eating disorders is complicated and hinders the capability of obtaining consistent metabolomic findings.

Moreover, given the intestinal dysbiosis in patients with AN and the two-way communication between the gut microbiota and the brain, known as the "gut-brain axis", this relationship could be an interesting aim for new studies on the mechanism and development of AN. In this line, putting together information about different samples such as plasma and feces and integrating different omics as well as psychiatric data will give an understanding of this disease and help to design personalized treatments.

In the articles reviewed, sometimes D- or L- amino acids are referred to in the list of metabolites. After careful reading of the full text, no chiral analysis is described, which makes such chiral assignation doubtful and therefore, D- or L- chiral assignation has not been included in this review. Furthermore, up to now, as a global evaluation, chiral assessment in biological samples from patients is scarcely available, and absent in the case of feces samples; thus, it requires further research and development to unveil the role of chirality in anorexia.

Additionally, longitudinal studies have demonstrated that long term starvation has important metabolic consequences in AN patients. Thus, as discussed throughout this review, whether the described metabolic phenotype is a trait marker of the disease or is a consequence of the food deprivation needs to be further elucidated. Importantly, the application of metabolomics approaches could provide more and better information in longitudinal studies about the development of nutritional disorders, such as the Avon Longitudinal Study [81]. Nevertheless, metabolomics in anorexia nervosa has been almost exclusively employed to study single time points, when the disease is already diagnosed, and comparing versus healthy controls.

Notwithstanding the foregoing, although technological advances in the field of omics sciences are making important progress in the application of precision medicine in most medical diseases, further research in the comprehension of the etiology, pathogenesis, and pathophysiology of eating disorders in general and, in the area of AN in particular, are still required. These studies are necessary to facilitate the future successful application of specific targeted therapies for individuals and thus allowing the groundwork for a new era of precision medicine.

Supplementary Materials: The following are available online at https://www.mdpi.com/article/10.3390/nu13124249/s1, Table S1: Metabolites altered in human samples of individuals with AN.

Author Contributions: Funding acquisition, A.G. and J.A.; Project administration, F.J.R. and A.G.; Resources Provision, C.B., J.A. and A.G.; Supervision, F.J.R., A.G., J.A. and C.B.; Visualization, L.M.-M.; Writing—original draft, L.M.-M.; Writing—review & editing, L.M.-M., G.Á.M.-M., M.G., F.J.R., J.A., C.B. and A.G. All authors have read and agreed to the published version of the manuscript.

Funding: This research was funded by the Ministry of Science, Innovation and Universities of Spain (MICINN) and the European Regional Development Fund FEDER, grant number RTI2018-095166-B-I00. supported through, as well as Comunidad de Madrid (B-2017/BMD-3751 "NOVELREN-CM" and Ref. S2017/BMD3684 MOIR-2) and Instituto de Salud Carlos III, European FEDER (grant number FIS-PI19/00166) and CIBEROBN. LMM is recipient of MCINN FPU grant (FPU19/05505).

Institutional Review Board Statement: Not applicable.

Informed Consent Statement: Not applicable.

Data Availability Statement: Not applicable.

Conflicts of Interest: The authors declare no conflict of interest.

Abbreviations

^{1}H NMR	proton nuclear magnetic resonance
7β-OH-DHEA	7β-hydroxy dehydroepiandrosterone
AC	acylcarnitines
Ala	alanine
ALA	alpha-linolenic acid
AN	anorexia nervosa
AN-BP	anorexia nervosa-binge/purging
AN-R	anorexia nervosa-restricting
Arg	arginine
Asp	aspartate
BMI	body-mass index
CE-MS	capillary electrophoresis-mass spectrometry
DPA	docosapentaenoic acid
EPHX2	epoxide hydrolase 2
EPA	eicosapentaenoic acid
FDR	false discovery rate
FIA-MS/MS	flow injection analysis-tandem mass spectrometry
GABA	γ-amino butyrate
GC-MS	gas chromatography-mass spectrometry
Gln	glutamine
Glu	glutamate
Gly	glycine
HPLC-MS/MS	high performance liquid chromatography-tandem mass spectrometry
Ile	isoleucine
LC-MS	liquid chromatography-mass spectrometry
LC-MS/MS	liquid chromatography-tandem mass spectrometry
Leu	leucine
LPC	lysophosphatidylcholines
Met	methionine
MS	mass spectrometry
NMR	nuclear magnetic resonance
Orn	ornithine
PC	phosphatidylcholines
Phe	phenylalanine
Pro	proline
PUFAs	polyunsaturated fatty acids
sEH	soluble epoxide hydrolase
Ser	serine
SIM	selected ion monitoring
SM	sphingomyelins
Thr	threonine
Trp	tryptophan
Tyr	tyrosine
UPLC-MS	ultra-performance liquid chromatography-mass spectrometry
Val	valine

References

1. González-Riaño, C.; Dudzik, D.; García, A.; Gil-De-La-Fuente, A.; Gradillas, A.; Godzien, J.; López-Gonzálvez, Á.; Rey-Stolle, F.; Rojo, D.; Ruperez, F.J.; et al. Recent Developments along the Analytical Process for Metabolomics Workflows. *Anal. Chem.* **2020**, *92*, 203–226. [CrossRef]
2. Dunn, W.B.; Broadhurst, D.I.; Atherton, H.J.; Goodacre, R.; Griffin, J.L. Systems Level Studies of Mammalian Metabolomes: The Roles of Mass Spectrometry and Nuclear Magnetic Resonance Spectroscopy. *Chem. Soc. Rev.* **2011**, *40*, 387–426. [CrossRef]
3. Dudley, E.; Yousef, M.; Wang, Y.; Griffiths, W.J. 2-Targeted Metabolomics and Mass Spectrometry. *Adv. Protein Chem. Struct. Biol.* **2010**, *80*, 45–83. [CrossRef]
4. Roberts, L.D.; Souza, A.L.; Gerszten, R.E.; Clish, C.B. Targeted Metabolomics. *Curr. Protoc. Mol. Biol.* **2012**, *98*, 30.2.1–30.2.24. [CrossRef] [PubMed]

5. Bharti, S.K.; Roy, R. Quantitative 1H NMR Spectroscopy. *TrAC-Trends Anal. Chem.* **2012**, *35*, 5–26. [CrossRef]
6. Barhoum, A.; García-Betancourt, M.L.; Rahier, H.; van Assche, G. Physicochemical characterization of nanomaterials: Polymorph, composition, wettability, and thermal stability. In *Emerging Applications of Nanoparticles and Architectural Nanostructures: Current Prospects and Future Trends*; Elsevier Inc.: Amsterdam, The Netherlands, 2018; pp. 255–278. ISBN 9780128135167.
7. Goodacre, R.; Vaidyanathan, S.; Dunn, W.B.; Harrigan, G.G.; Kell, D.B. Metabolomics by Numbers: Acquiring and Understanding Global Metabolite Data. *Trends Biotechnol.* **2004**, *22*, 245–252. [CrossRef] [PubMed]
8. Emwas, A.H.M. The Strengths and Weaknesses of NMR Spectroscopy and Mass Spectrometry with Particular Focus on Metabolomics Research. *Methods Mol. Biol.* **2015**, *1277*, 161–193. [CrossRef]
9. Dunn, W.B.; Hankemeier, T. Mass Spectrometry and Metabolomics: Past, Present and Future. *Metabolomics* **2013**, *9*, 1–3. [CrossRef]
10. Fiehn, O. Combining Genomics, Metabolome Analysis, and Biochemical Modelling to Understand Metabolic Networks. *Comp. Funct. Genom.* **2001**, *2*, 155–168. [CrossRef]
11. Hata, K.; Soma, Y.; Yamashita, T.; Takahashi, M.; Sugitate, K.; Serino, T.; Miyagawa, H.; Suzuki, K.; Yamada, K.; Kawamukai, T.; et al. Calibration-Curve-Locking Database for Semi-Quantitative Metabolomics by Gas Chromatography/Mass Spectrometry. *Metabolites* **2021**, *11*, 207. [CrossRef]
12. Liu, X.; Locasale, J.W. Metabolomics—A Primer. *Trends Biochem. Sci.* **2017**, *42*, 274. [CrossRef]
13. Kapoore, R.V.; Vaidyanathan, S. Towards Quantitative Mass Spectrometry-Based Metabolomics in Microbial and Mammalian Systems. *Philos. Trans. Ser. A Math. Phys. Eng. Sci.* **2016**, *374*, 1–14. [CrossRef] [PubMed]
14. American Psychiatric Association. *Diagnostic and Statistical Manual of Mental Disorders*, 5th ed.; American Psychiatric Association: Washington, DC, USA, 2013.
15. Peterson, C.B.; Pisetsky, E.M.; Swanson, S.A.; Crosby, R.D.; Mitchell, J.E.; Wonderlich, S.A.; le Grange, D.; Hill, L.; Powers, P.; Crow, S.J. Examining the Utility of Narrowing Anorexia Nervosa Subtypes for Adults. *Compr. Psychiatry* **2016**, *67*, 54–58. [CrossRef]
16. Smink, F.R.; van Hoeken, D.; Hoek, H.W. Epidemiology of Eating Disorders: Incidence, Prevalence and Mortality Rates. *Curr. Psychiatry Rep.* **2012**, *14*, 406–414. [CrossRef] [PubMed]
17. Bulik, C.M.; Flatt, R.; Abbaspour, A.; Carroll, I. Reconceptualizing Anorexia Nervosa. *Psychiatry Clin. Neurosci.* **2019**, *73*, 518–525. [CrossRef]
18. Borgo, F.; Riva, A.; Benetti, A.; Casiraghi, M.C.; Bertelli, S.; Garbossa, S.; Anselmetti, S.; Scarone, S.; Pontiroli, A.E.; Morace, G.; et al. Microbiota in Anorexia Nervosa: The Triangle between Bacterial Species, Metabolites and Psychological Tests. *PLoS ONE* **2017**, *12*, 1–17. [CrossRef] [PubMed]
19. Arcelus, J.; Mitchell, A.J.; Wales, J.; Nielsen, S. Mortality Rates in Patients with Anorexia Nervosa and Other Eating Disorders a Meta-Analysis of 36 Studies. *Arch. Gen. Psychiatry* **2011**, *68*, 724–731. [CrossRef]
20. Chesney, E.; Goodwin, G.M.; Fazel, S. Risks of All-Cause and Suicide Mortality in Mental Disorders: A Meta-Review. *World Psychiatry* **2014**, *13*, 153. [CrossRef]
21. Lam, Y.Y.; Maguire, S.; Palacios, T.; Caterson, I.D. Are the Gut Bacteria Telling Us to Eat or Not to Eat? Reviewing the Role of Gut Microbiota in the Etiology, Disease Progression and Treatment of Eating Disorders. *Nutrients* **2017**, *9*, 602. [CrossRef]
22. Watson, H.J.; Yilmaz, Z.; Thornton, L.M.; Hübel, C.; Coleman, J.R.I.; Gaspar, H.A.; Bryois, J.; Hinney, A.; Leppä, V.M.; Mattheisen, M.; et al. Genome-Wide Association Study Identifies Eight Risk Loci and Implicates Metabo-Psychiatric Origins for Anorexia Nervosa. *Nat. Genet.* **2019**, *51*, 1207–1214. [CrossRef]
23. Moyano, D.; Vilaseca, M.A.; Artuch, R.; Lambruschini, N. Plasma Amino Acids in Anorexia Nervosa. *Eur. J. Clin. Nutr.* **1998**, *52*, 684–689. [CrossRef] [PubMed]
24. Rigaud, D.; Tallonneau, I.; Vergès, B. Hypercholesterolaemia in Anorexia Nervosa: Frequency and Changes during Refeeding. *Diabetes Metab.* **2009**, *35*, 57–63. [CrossRef] [PubMed]
25. Ohwada, R.; Hotta, M.; Oikawa, S.; Takano, K. Etiology of Hypercholesterolemia in Patients with Anorexia Nervosa. *Int. J. Eat. Disord.* **2006**, *39*, 598–601. [CrossRef] [PubMed]
26. Winston, A.P. The Clinical Biochemistry of Anorexia Nervosa. *Ann. Clin. Biochem.* **2012**, *49*, 132–143. [CrossRef] [PubMed]
27. Muñoz-Calvo, M.T.; Argente, J. Nutritional and Pubertal Disorders. *Endocr. Dev.* **2016**, *29*, 153–173. [CrossRef] [PubMed]
28. Muñoz, M.T.; Argente, J. Anorexia Nervosa in Female Adolescents: Endocrine and Bone Mineral Density Disturbances. *Eur. J. Endocrinol.* **2002**, *147*, 275–286. [CrossRef]
29. Argente, J.; Caballo, N.; Barrios, V.; Muñoz, M.T.; Pozo, J.; Chowen, J.A.; Morandé, G.; Hernández, M. Multiple Endocrine Abnormalities of the Growth Hormone and Insulin-like Growth Factor Axis in Patients with Anorexia Nervosa: Effect of Short-and Long Term-Weight Recuperation. *J. Clin. Endocrinol. Metab.* **1997**, *82*, 2084–2092. [CrossRef]
30. da Luz Neto, L.M.; de Vasconcelos, F.M.N.; da Silva, J.E.; Pinto, T.C.C.; Sougey, É.B.; Ximenes, R.C.C. Differences in Cortisol Concentrations in Adolescents with Eating Disorders: A Systematic Review. *J. De Pediatr.* **2019**, *95*, 18–26. [CrossRef]
31. Schorr, M.; Miller, K.K. The Endocrine Manifestations of Anorexia Nervosa: Mechanisms and Management. *Nat. Rev. Endocrinol.* **2017**, *13*, 174–186. [CrossRef]
32. Soriano-Guillén, L.; Barrios, V.; Campos-Barros, Á.; Argente, J. Ghrelin Levels in Obesity and Anorexia Nervosa: Effect of Weight Reduction or Recuperation. *J. Pediatrics* **2004**, *144*, 36–42. [CrossRef]
33. Martos-Moreno, G.Á.; Chowen, J.A.; Argente, J. Metabolic Signals in Human Puberty: Effects of over and Undernutrition. *Mol. Cell. Endocrinol.* **2010**, *324*, 70–81. [CrossRef]

34. Argente, J.; Barrios, V.; Chowen, J.; Sinha, M.; Considine, R. Leptin Plasma Levels in Healthy Spanish Children and Adolescents, Children with Obesity, and Adolescents with Anorexia Nervosa and Bulimia Nervosa. *J. Pediatrics* **1997**, *131*, 833–838. [CrossRef]
35. Naureen, F.; Masroor, K.; Khatoon, F.; Ayub, S.; Ahmed, M.I.; Hasnat, A.; Samad, N. Zinc and Tryptophan Levels in Anorexia Nervosa; a Co-Relational Study. *Int. J. Biomed. Eng. Sci.* **2014**, *1*, 27–33.
36. Iannone, L.F.; Preda, A.; Blottière, H.M.; Clarke, G.; Albani, D.; Belcastro, V.; Carotenuto, M.; Cattaneo, A.; Citraro, R.; Ferraris, C.; et al. Microbiota-Gut Brain Axis Involvement in Neuropsychiatric Disorders. *Expert Rev. Neurother.* **2019**, *19*, 1037–1050. [CrossRef]
37. Monteleone, A.M.; Troisi, J.; Serena, G.; Fasano, A.; Grave, R.D.; Cascino, G.; Marciello, F.; Calugi, S.; Scala, G.; Corrivetti, G.; et al. The Gut Microbiome and Metabolomics Profiles of Restricting and Binge-Purging Type Anorexia Nervosa. *Nutrients* **2021**, *13*, 507. [CrossRef]
38. Mörkl, S.; Butler, M.I.; Holl, A.; Cryan, J.F.; Dinan, T.G. Probiotics and the Microbiota-Gut-Brain Axis: Focus on Psychiatry. *Curr. Nutr. Rep.* **2020**, *9*, 171–182. [CrossRef]
39. Seitz, J.; Dahmen, B.; Keller, L.; Herpertz-Dahlmann, B. Gut Feelings: How Microbiota Might Impact the Development and Course of Anorexia Nervosa. *Nutrients* **2020**, *12*, 3295. [CrossRef]
40. MacKay, M.B.; Kravtsenyuk, M.; Thomas, R.; Mitchell, N.D.; Dursun, S.M.; Baker, G.B. D-Serine: Potential Therapeutic Agent and/or Biomarker in Schizophrenia and Depression? *Front. Psychiatry* **2019**, *10*, 25. [CrossRef] [PubMed]
41. Billard, J.M. D-Amino Acids in Brain Neurotransmission and Synaptic Plasticity. *Amino Acids* **2012**, *43*, 1851–1860. [CrossRef] [PubMed]
42. Otte, D.M.; Barcena de Arellano, M.L.; Bilkei-Gorzo, A.; Albayram, Ö.; Imbeault, S.; Jeung, H.; Alferink, J.; Zimmer, A. Effects of Chronic D-Serine Elevation on Animal Models of Depression and Anxiety-Related Behavior. *PLoS ONE* **2013**, *8*, e67131. [CrossRef]
43. Fuchs, S.A.; Berger, R.; Klomp, L.W.J.; de Koning, T.J. D-Amino Acids in the Central Nervous System in Health and Disease. *Mol. Genet. Metab.* **2005**, *85*, 168–180. [CrossRef]
44. Zhang, K.; Fujita, Y.; Chang, L.; Qu, Y.; Pu, Y.; Wang, S.; Shirayama, Y.; Hashimoto, K. Abnormal Composition of Gut Microbiota Is Associated with Resilience versus Susceptibility to Inescapable Electric Stress. *Transl. Psychiatry* **2019**, *9*, 231. [CrossRef]
45. Dogan, A.E.; Yuksel, C.; Du, F.; Chouinard, V.-A.; Öngür, D. Brain Lactate and PH in Schizophrenia and Bipolar Disorder: A Systematic Review of Findings from Magnetic Resonance Studies. *Neuropsychopharmacology* **2018**, *43*, 1681. [CrossRef] [PubMed]
46. Zipfel, S.; Löwe, B.; Reas, D.L.; Deter, H.C.; Herzog, W. Long-Term Prognosis in Anorexia Nervosa: Lessons from a 21-Year Follow-up Study. *Lancet* **2000**, *355*, 721–722. [CrossRef]
47. Föcker, M.; Cecil, A.; Prehn, C.; Adamski, J.; Albrecht, M.; Adams, F.; Hinney, A.; Libuda, L.; Bühlmeier, J.; Hebebrand, J.; et al. Evaluation of Metabolic Profiles of Patients with Anorexia Nervosa at Inpatient Admission, Short-and Long-Term Weight Regain—Descriptive and Pattern Analysis. *Metabolites* **2021**, *11*, 7. [CrossRef] [PubMed]
48. Föcker, M.; Timmesfeld, N.; Scherag, S.; Knoll, N.; Singmann, P.; Wang-Sattler, R.; Bühren, K.; Schwarte, R.; Egberts, K.; Fleischhaker, C.; et al. Comparison of Metabolic Profiles of Acutely Ill and Short-Term Weight Recovered Patients with Anorexia Nervosa Reveals Alterations of 33 out of 163 Metabolites. *J. Psychiatr. Res.* **2012**, *46*, 1600–1609. [CrossRef] [PubMed]
49. Burdo, J.; Booij, L.; Kahan, E.; Thaler, L.; Israël, M.; Agellon, L.B.; Nitschmann, E.; Wykes, L.; Steiger, H. Plasma Levels of One-Carbon Metabolism Nutrients in Women with Anorexia Nervosa. *Int. J. Eat. Disord.* **2020**, *53*, 1534–1538. [CrossRef]
50. Bulant, J.; Hill, M.; Velíková, M.; Yamamotová, A.; Martásek, P.; Papežová, H. Changes of BMI, Steroid Metabolome and Psychopathology in Patients with Anorexia Nervosa during Hospitalization. *Steroids* **2020**, *153*, 108523. [CrossRef]
51. Miyata, N.; Hata, T.; Takakura, S.; Yoshihara, K.; Morita, C.; Mikami, K.; Nomoto, K.; Miyazaki, K.; Tsuji, H.; Sudo, N. Metabolomics Profile of Japanese Female Patients with Restricting-Type Anorexia Nervosa. *Physiol. Behav.* **2021**, *228*. [CrossRef]
52. Shih, P.-A.B. Integrating Multi-Omics Biomarkers and Postprandial Metabolism to Develop Personalized Treatment for Anorexia Nervosa. *Prostaglandins Other Lipid Mediat.* **2017**, *132*, 69–76. [CrossRef]
53. Shih, P.; Yang, J.; Morisseau, C.; German, J.; Scott-Van Zeeland, A.; Armando, A.; Quehenberger, O.; Bergen, A.; Magistretti, P.; Berrettini, W.; et al. Dysregulation of Soluble Epoxide Hydrolase and Lipidomic Profiles in Anorexia Nervosa. *Mol. Psychiatry* **2016**, *21*, 537–546. [CrossRef]
54. Prochazkova, P.; Roubalova, R.; Dvorak, J.; Kreisinger, J.; Hill, M.; Tlaskalova-Hogenova, H.; Tomasova, P.; Pelantova, H.; Cermakova, M.; Kuzma, M.; et al. The Intestinal Microbiota and Metabolites in Patients with Anorexia Nervosa. *Gut Microbes* **2021**, *13*, 1–25. [CrossRef]
55. Salehi, A.M.; Nilsson, I.A.; Figueira, J.; Thornton, L.M.; Abdulkarim, I.; Palsson, E.; Bulik, C.M.; Landen, M. Serum Profiling of Anorexia Nervosa. A 1 H NMR-Based Metabolomics Study. *Eur. Neropsychopharmacol.* **2021**, *49*, 1–10. [CrossRef] [PubMed]
56. Nguyen, N.; Dow, M.; Woodside, B.; German, J.B.; Quehenberger, O.; Shih, P.B. Food-Intake Normalization of Dysregulated Fatty Acids in Women with Anorexia Nervosa. *Nutrients* **2019**, *11*, 2208. [CrossRef]
57. Monteleone, P.; Monteleone, A.M.; Troisi, J.; Dalle Grave, R.; Corrivetti, G.; Calugi, S.; Scala, G.; Patriciello, G.; Zanetti, A.; Maj, M. Metabolomics Signatures of Acutely Ill and Short-Term Weight Recovered Women with Anorexia Nervosa. *Mol. Psychiatry* **2021**, *26*, 3980–3991. [CrossRef] [PubMed]
58. Monteleone, A.M.; Troisi, J.; Fasano, A.; Dalle Grave, R.; Marciello, F.; Serena, G.; Calugi, S.; Scala, G.; Corrivetti, G.; Cascino, G.; et al. Multi-Omics Data Integration in Anorexia Nervosa Patients before and after Weight Regain: A Microbiome-Metabolomics Investigation. *Clin. Nutr.* **2020**, *40*, 1137–1146. [CrossRef]

59. Berg, J.M.; Tymoczko, J.L.; Stryer, L. Food Intake and Starvation Induce Metabolic Changes. In *Biochemistry*; W H Freeman: New York, NY, USA, 2002.
60. Žák, A.; Vecka, M.; Tvrzická, E.; Hrubý, M.; Novák, F.; Papežová, H.; Lubanda, H.; Veselá, L.; Staňková, B. Composition of Plasma Fatty Acids and Non-Cholesterol Sterols in Anorexia Nervosa. *Physiol. Res.* **2005**, *54*, 443–451.
61. Ren, Q. Soluble Epoxide Hydrolase Inhibitor: A Novel Potential Therapeutic or Prophylactic Drug for Psychiatric Disorders. *Front. Pharmacol.* **2019**, *10*, 420. [CrossRef] [PubMed]
62. Hussain, A.A.; Hübel, C.; Hindborg, M.; Lindkvist, E.; Kastrup, A.M.; Yilmaz, Z.; Støving, R.K.; Bulik, C.M.; Sjögren, J.M. Increased Lipid and Lipoprotein Concentrations in Anorexia Nervosa: A Systematic Review and Meta-Analysis. *Int. J. Eat. Disord.* **2019**, *52*, 611–629. [CrossRef]
63. Weinbrenner, T.; Züger, M.; Jacoby, G.E.; Herpertz, S.; Liedtke, R.; Sudhop, T.; Gouni-Berthold, I.; Axelson, M.; Berthold, H.K. Lipoprotein Metabolism in Patients with Anorexia Nervosa: A Case–Control Study Investigating the Mechanisms Leading to Hypercholesterolaemia. *Br. J. Nutr.* **2004**, *91*, 959–969. [CrossRef]
64. Breton, J.; Déchelotte, P.; Ribet, D. Intestinal Microbiota and Anorexia Nervosa. *Clin. Nutr. Exp.* **2019**, *28*, 11–21. [CrossRef]
65. Lozupone, C.A.; Stombaugh, J.I.; Gordon, J.I.; Jansson, J.K.; Knight, R. Diversity, Stability and Resilience of the Human Gut Microbiota. *Nature* **2012**, *489*, 220–230. [CrossRef] [PubMed]
66. Cryan, J.F.; O'Riordan, K.J.; Cowan, C.S.M.; Sandhu, K.V.; Bastiaanssen, T.F.S.; Boehme, M.; Codagnone, M.G.; Cussotto, S.; Fulling, C.; Golubeva, A.V.; et al. The Microbiota-Gut-Brain Axis. *Physiol Rev.* **2019**, *99*, 1877–2013. [CrossRef] [PubMed]
67. Mörkl, S.; Lackner, S.; Müller, W.; Gorkiewicz, G.; Kashofer, K.; Oberascher, A.; Painold, A.; Holl, A.; Holzer, P.; Meinitzer, A.; et al. Gut Microbiota and Body Composition in Anorexia Nervosa Inpatients in Comparison to Athletes, Overweight, Obese, and Normal Weight Controls. *Int. J. Eat. Disord.* **2017**, *50*, 1421–1431. [CrossRef] [PubMed]
68. Morita, C.; Tsuji, H.; Hata, T.; Gondo, M.; Takakura, S.; Kawai, K.; Yoshihara, K.; Ogata, K.; Nomoto, K.; Miyazaki, K.; et al. Gut Dysbiosis in Patients with Anorexia Nervosa. *PLoS ONE* **2015**, *10*, e0145274. [CrossRef]
69. Kleiman, S.C.; Watson, H.J.; Bulik-Sullivan, E.C.; Huh, E.Y.; Tarantino, L.M.; Bulik, C.M.; Carroll, I.M. The Intestinal Microbiota in Acute Anorexia Nervosa and during Renourishment: Relationship to Depression, Anxiety, and Eating Disorder Psychopathology. *Psychosom. Med.* **2015**, *77*, 969–981. [CrossRef]
70. Mack, I.; Cuntz, U.; Grmer, C.; Niedermaier, S.; Pohl, C.; Schwiertz, A.; Zimmermann, K.; Zipfel, S.; Enck, P.; Penders, J. Weight Gain in Anorexia Nervosa Does Not Ameliorate the Faecal Microbiota, Branched Chain Fatty Acid Profiles, and Gastrointestinal Complaints. *Sci. Rep.* **2016**, *6*, 26752. [CrossRef]
71. Pfleiderer, A.; Lagier, J.C.; Armougom, F.; Robert, C.; Vialettes, B.; Raoult, D. Culturomics Identified 11 New Bacterial Species from a Single Anorexia Nervosa Stool Sample. *Eur. J. Clin. Microbiol. Infect. Dis.* **2013**, *32*, 1471–1481. [CrossRef]
72. Armougom, F.; Henry, M.; Vialettes, B.; Raccah, D.; Raoult, D. Monitoring Bacterial Community of Human Gut Microbiota Reveals an Increase in Lactobacillus in Obese Patients and Methanogens in Anorexic Patients. *PLoS ONE* **2009**, *4*, e7125. [CrossRef]
73. Holzer, P.; Farzi, A. Neuropeptides and the Microbiota- Gut-Brain Axis. *Adv. Exp. Med. Biol.* **2014**, *817*, 196–219. [CrossRef]
74. Gribble, F.M.; Reimann, F. Function and Mechanisms of Enteroendocrine Cells and Gut Hormones in Metabolism. *Nat. Rev. Endocrinol.* **2019**, *15*, 226–237. [CrossRef]
75. Kimura, I.; Inoue, D.; Maeda, T.; Hara, T.; Ichimura, A.; Miyauchi, S.; Kobayashi, M.; Hirasawa, A.; Tsujimoto, G. Short-Chain Fatty Acids and Ketones Directly Regulate Sympathetic Nervous System via G Protein-Coupled Receptor 41 (GPR41). *Proc. Natl. Acad. Sci. USA* **2011**, *108*, 8030–8035. [CrossRef]
76. Qiu, J.; Liu, R.; Ma, Y.; Li, Y.; Chen, Z.; He, H.; Chen, J.; Tong, L.; Huang, C.; You, Q. Lipopolysaccharide-Induced Depression-Like Behaviors Is Ameliorated by Sodium Butyrate via Inhibiting Neuroinflammation and Oxido-Nitrosative Stress. *Pharmacology* **2020**, *105*, 550–560. [CrossRef] [PubMed]
77. Schroeder, F.A.; Lin, C.L.; Crusio, W.E.; Akbarian, S. Antidepressant-Like Effects of the Histone Deacetylase Inhibitor, Sodium Butyrate, in the Mouse. *Biol. Psychiatry* **2007**, *62*, 55–64. [CrossRef] [PubMed]
78. van de Wouw, M.; Boehme, M.; Lyte, J.M.; Wiley, N.; Strain, C.; O'Sullivan, O.; Clarke, G.; Stanton, C.; Dinan, T.G.; Cryan, J.F. Short-Chain Fatty Acids: Microbial Metabolites That Alleviate Stress-Induced Brain–Gut Axis Alterations. *J. Physiol.* **2018**, *596*, 4923–4944. [CrossRef]
79. Han, A.; Sung, Y.; Chung, S.; Kwon, M. Possible Additional Antidepressant-like Mechanism of Sodium Butyrate: Targeting the Hippocampus. *Neuropharmacology* **2014**, *81*, 292–302. [CrossRef] [PubMed]
80. Hoyles, L.; Snelling, T.; Umlai, U.-K.; Nicholson, J.K.; Carding, S.R.; Glen, R.C.; McArthur, S. Microbiome–Host Systems Interactions: Protective Effects of Propionate upon the Blood–Brain Barrier. *Microbiome* **2018**, *6*, 55. [CrossRef]
81. Ferreira, D.L.S.; Hübel, C.; Herle, M.; Abdulkadir, M.; Loos, R.J.F.; Bryant-Waugh, R.; Bulik, C.M.; de Stavola, B.L.; Lawlor, D.A.; Micali, N. Associations between Blood Metabolic Profile at 7 Years Old and Eating Disorders in Adolescence: Findings from the Avon Longitudinal Study of Parents and Children. *Metabolites* **2019**, *9*, 191. [CrossRef]

nutrients

MDPI

Review

Obesity and Eating Disorders in Children and Adolescents: The Bidirectional Link

Stella Stabouli [1], Serap Erdine [2], Lagle Suurorg [3], Augustina Jankauskienė [4] and Empar Lurbe [5,6,*]

1 First Department of Pediatrics, Hipnmpokration Hospital, Aristotle University, 54124 Thessaloniki, Greece; sstaboul@auth.gr
2 Hypertension and Arteriosclerosis Research and Implementation Center, School of Medicine, Marmara University, Istanbul 34722, Turkey; serap.erdine@gmail.com
3 Tallinn Children's Hospital, 2813419 Estonia, Estonia; lsuurorg@gmail.com
4 Pediatric Center, Institute of Clinical Medicine, Vilnius University, 01513 Vilnius, Lithuania; augustina.jankauskiene@santa.lt
5 Department of Pediatrics, University of Valencia, 1346010 Valencia, Spain
6 CIBER Fisiopatologia Obesidad y Nutricion, Instituto de Salud Carlos III, 28029 Madrid, Spain
* Correspondence: empar.lurbe@uv.es; Tel.: +34-96-3131800

Abstract: Obesity, eating disorders and unhealthy dieting practices among children and adolescents are alarming health concerns due to their high prevalence and adverse effects on physical and psychosocial health. We present the evidence that eating disorders and obesity can be managed or prevented using the same interventions in the pediatric age. In the presence of obesity in the pediatric age, disordered eating behaviors are highly prevalent, increasing the risk of developing eating disorders. The most frequently observed in subjects with obesity are bulimia nervosa and binge-eating disorders, both of which are characterized by abnormal eating or weight-control behaviors. Various are the mechanisms overlying the interaction including environmental and individual ones, and different are the approaches to reduce the consequences. Evidence-based treatments for obesity and eating disorders in childhood include as first line approaches weight loss with nutritional management and lifestyle modification via behavioral psychotherapy, as well as treatment of psychiatric comorbidities if those are not a consequence of the eating disorder. Drugs and bariatric surgery need to be used in extreme cases. Future research is necessary for early detection of risk factors for prevention, more precise elucidation of the mechanisms that underpin these problems and, finally, in the cases requiring therapeutic intervention, to provide tailored and timely treatment. Collective efforts between the fields are crucial for reducing the factors of health disparity and improving public health.

Keywords: obesity; eating disorders; children; adolescents

Citation: Stabouli, S.; Erdine, S.; Suurorg, L.; Jankauskienė, A.; Lurbe, E. Obesity and Eating Disorders in Children and Adolescents: The Bidirectional Link. *Nutrients* **2021**, *13*, 4321. https://doi.org/10.3390/nu13124321

Academic Editor: Stefano Erzegovesi

Received: 22 September 2021
Accepted: 25 November 2021
Published: 29 November 2021

1. Introduction

Obesity, eating disorders (EDs) and unhealthy dieting practices among children and adolescents are alarming health concerns due to their high prevalence, more than 1 hundred million [1], and adverse effects on physical and psychosocial health. Even when, traditionally, obesity and EDs have been looked at as separate conditions, there is emerging evidence highlighting important overlaps, among others, etiology, comorbidity, risk factors and prevention approaches [2]. Environmental and social factors, weight-related teasing by family or peers, thin beauty ideal perceptions by social environment or media may enable transition from obesity to EDs and vice versa [3]. In the presence of obesity and its cardiometabolic adverse health consequences, possible additional EDs could further trigger the burden of current health status and future outcomes [4]. In the present review, we outline the rationale for the awareness and recognition of risk factors that increase vulnerability of obese children and adolescents to EDs and cover several aspects starting with definitions, common pathogenesis, as well as possible implications on treatment outcomes.

Finally, we present the evidence that EDs and obesity can be managed or prevented using the same interventions in the pediatric age.

2. Obesity

Obesity, characterized by the deposition of excessive fat in the body, has been well documented in both sexes, all age groups, and for every geographical and ethnic group. A straightforward method to assess body fat indirectly is body mass index (BMI). According to BMI, weight status is classified in children and adolescents as overweight >85th percentile to <95th percentile and obesity 95th percentile or greater [5]. The WHO recommends the use of BMI z-score defining overweight as having a BMI z-score >1 but less than 2 and obesity z-score as having a BMI z-score equal to or >2 [6].

The prevalence of overweight and obesity among children has increased substantially worldwide since the 1990s. According to the WHO, in 2016, one hundred and twenty-four million children and youth between 5 and 19 years of age were obese and 41 million under the age of 5 were overweight or obese [1]. Childhood obesity is more prevalent in developed countries, although an upwards trend is also seen in developing countries [1]. This issue deserves more attention due to the long-term health effects it may bring on, including obesity persisting into adulthood and increased risk of chronic diseases. Immediate and long-term psychosocial health consequences can also be present, including the potential for reduced self-esteem and depression.

Linked to the development of obesity is the interaction among environmental, behavioral, genetic and metabolic factors [7]. This complex interaction leads to a multifactorial chronic disease with a variety of phenotypes and clinical presentations. All of these combined explain the difficulties in management and treatment responses [8]. Factors contributing to the rise in obesity prevalence world-wide mostly focus on environmental and behavioral elements. Changes in the child's environment in terms of easy affordability of high-calorie fast food, increased portion size, intake of sugar-sweetened beverages (SSBs) and a sedentary lifestyle are associated with increased incidence of obesity [9].

One of the extensively studied causes for obesity is dietary patterns. Even in early life, feeding patterns have been linked to an increased incidence of obesity. In an observational study by Gillman et al. [10], it was reported that in pre-school age children of mothers who did not smoke or gain excessive weight during pregnancy, breast fed for 12 months, and slept 12 h/day, presented an obesity prevalence of 6% at age 3 years compared to a prevalence of 29% among children with the opposite of these four mother/child behaviors. Diet pattern and quality are important issues in the development of obesity. Considering diet, it is important to name discretionary food, a relevant element contributing to childhood obesity. One of the typical examples of this kind of food is SSBs containing a high amount of sugar [11]. In a birth cohort followed from age 2 to 17, investigators reported a significant association between SSBs consumption and increasing BMI z-scores [12].

Together with diet, the other pivotal element is physical activity. Advancements in technology have contributed to more sedentary behavior in children and adolescents. Screen time includes time spent viewing television, computer use, playing electronic games, and using mobile phones. Currently, screen time is the most common sedentary behavior, starting even in infancy [13]. Time spent on screen-based activities can replace time for physical activity and may affect physical and mental health in youth [14]. Adverse effects of excessive screen time on physical strength, obesity, and sleep disturbances have been documented in many studies [15]. Sleep disturbance is a commonly overlooked risk factor associated with high BP in children and adolescents. Lower levels of parental education, regular enforcement of rules about caffeine, and presence of electronics in the child's bedroom overnight are among the factors related to poor sleep [16]. Along with the above well-recognized factors, the presence of socioeconomic adversity, family dysfunction, offspring distress and junk food should be considered [17].

The role of genetics and its contribution to obesity has been filled with a large amount of research. The susceptibility of weight gain varies among individuals, suggesting that there is a heritable component of obesity that interacts with environmental factors [18]. Considering genetic factors, most cases of obesity are polygenic in nature, with multiple genes making small contributions to the overall phenotype. Therefore, genetic susceptibility may affect weight when coupled with other contributing environmental and behavioral factors. In contrast, monogenic obesity is uncommon, accounting for 3 to 5% of obese children, presenting early weight gain often between the first and second year of life [18]. A mutation in the melanocortin 4 receptor gene (MC4 R) is the most common gene defect, which is associated with a severe, early form of obesity in children [19].

Adverse childhood experience (ACE) and its link with obesity has received more attention in the last years. In a recent study, children who had high intrafamilial adversity scores were more prone to be obese than children with low scores [20]. These results are in agreement with the findings of a meta-analysis of 41 studies in which the association of child maltreatment and obesity was assessed [21]. Nowadays, ACE is known to be a potentially modifiable risk factor for obesity.

3. Eating Disorders

Disordered eating behaviors and EDs both cover a broad group of dimensional maladaptive cognitions and behaviors relating to eating and weight, but differ in their diagnosis [22]. Eating disorders refer to psychiatric disorders characterized by abnormal eating or weight control behaviors [23]. According to the Diagnostic and Statistical Manual of Mental Disorders Fifth Edition, specific EDs include anorexia nervosa, bulimia nervosa (BN) and binge eating (BE) [24]. Although the prevalence of EDs varies according to study populations and the criteria used to define them [25], they are of great concern given their serious health consequences that may lead to significant impairments in health, psychosocial functioning, and quality of life [26]. The onset of EDs is usually during adolescence, with the highest prevalence in girls, but EDs may be present in children as young as 5 to 12 years [27]. Recognition of EDs may help to prevent obesity or help weight loss in cases of sustained obesity [28]. Eating disorders may accompany childhood and adolescent obesity or may evolve after intensive interventions to treat obesity.

Putative risk factors for EDs have been investigated, testing a wide range of environmental [29–31] and genetic factors [32,33]. A recent umbrella review of published meta-analyses, including 50 associations from nine meta-analyses, found evidence for childhood sexual abuse as a risk factor for BN and appearance-related teasing victimization for any ED [34]. There were no ED risk factors supported by convincing evidence possibly due to the small number of large-scale collaborative longitudinal studies assessing the relationship between conditions preceding the onset of the disorder and the development of EDs [34].

A new element has come into play, which is food insecurity, characterized by limited or uncertain means of accessing nutritious food in a safe and socially acceptable manner. Emerging evidence consistently indicates that food insecurity is cross-sectionally associated with the bulimic-spectrum among adults. This has been shown in a national representative sample of US adults. During a 12-month period, diagnoses of bulimic-spectrum disorders, mood disorders, and anxiety disorders were more common among individuals who have experienced food insecurity than among those who were food secure. The study highlighted that the greatest difference was observed for bulimic-spectrum eating disorders [35]. Considering these findings, it may be necessary to take the pediatric population into consideration. This emerging evidence needs much more research to better understand this issue.

Whether ACEs are true risk factors for the development of eating disorders remains unclear due to the scarcity of not only prospective studies but also the potential selection bias in clinical samples. In currently available studies, inconsistent results have been reported. In a population-based study, the authors stated that experiences of life events are associated with specific eating behaviors in children aged 10 years [36]. These findings sustain the fact that a link between adverse life events and emotional overeating exists [37,38].

4. Links between Obesity and EDs

In the presence of obesity in the pediatric age, disordered eating behaviors are highly prevalent, increasing the risk of developing EDs. The EDs that have been most frequently observed in subjects with obesity are BN and BE, both of which are characterized by abnormal eating or weight-control behaviors [39,40]. The typical characteristics of BN and binge-eating disorder (BED) are recurrent BE episodes, defined as losing control over eating amounts of food that are objectively large. While attempts to prevent weight gain through inappropriate compensatory behaviors such as self-induced vomiting is characteristic of BN, BED does not share this characteristic [40,41].

Both obesity and EDs are generally studied and treated as independent disorders; however, obesity and EDs can have a bidirectional impact. Among the different EDs, BE is the one with the highest prevalence of comorbid obesity, followed by BN, and almost 30% of female patients with EDs had lifetime obesity [42].

Several mechanisms linking obesity with EDs and vice versa have been proposed, among other environmental and individual risk factors.

4.1. Environmental Risk Factors

Some specific socioenvironmental conditions may act as common risk factors for EDs and obesity. The most common are family and peer teasing, perceived social pressure, frequent criticism or bullying [43]. Also, images on television or social media focus on the ideals of slimness and beauty contribute to body dissatisfaction [44,45], which can act as a risk factor. Beside the most common factors, many others can be related with family BE behaviours, parental mood, anxiety or substance use disorder, family dissonance, high parental demands or perfectionism, and parental separation, identified as possibilities that play a role in the onset of obesity and EDs. Finally, traumatic life events and negative childhood experiences (sexual and physical abuse) also increase the risks [46].

4.2. Individual Risk Factors

4.2.1. Biological-Genetic Risk Factors

The strongest known susceptibility locus for obesity is the fat mass and obesity-associated (FTO) gene [47–49]. Even though it is not fully clear how FTO variants influence obesity, FTO associations with several EDs, including BED, are apparent [50]. Indeed, variants of the FTO gene are associated with poor behavioural regulation and BED, suggesting a genetic role in the pathogenesis of this disorder [50]. Genetic factors notably influence the regulation of neural circuits by controlling the appetite and satiety pathways, as well as the regulation of brain reward systems. Single-Nucleotide Polymorphisms in genes linked to hypothalamic appetite and satiety mechanisms may be involved in the development of EDs related to obesity such as BED and BN [51].

4.2.2. Psychological and Personality Risk Factors

Some specific psychological characteristics such as low self-esteem, negative self-evaluation, and high body dissatisfaction may contribute to the development of EDs and obesity [52]. Research suggests a link between emotional regulation and BE, as well as food addiction [53,54]. When negative affect and emotional dysregulation precede the occurrence of BE episodes, it exacerbates guilt and shame, creating a vicious cycle of losing control over eating [55].

4.2.3. Neuropsychological and Brain Activity Risk Factors

The brain is central to basic research, prevention and treatment in the context of obesity and EDs [56]. Until very recently, little was known about the neuropsychological mechanisms of EDs and obesity. Mesocorticolimbic mechanisms that increase "liking" include brain hedonic hotspots, specific subregions that can causally increase the hedonic effect of palatable tastes. In contrast, a much larger mesocorticolimbic circuit generates the motivation to "want" or induce to obtain and consume food rewards [57].

Theorists focused on the reward circuit because eating palatable food increases activation in reward-related regions, including the ventral and dorsal striatum, midbrain, amygdala, and orbitofrontal cortex, and causes dopamine release in the dorsal striatum in both humans and other animals [58]. Functional, molecular and genetic neuroimaging has highlighted the existence of brain abnormalities and neural fragility factors associated with obesity and EDs, such as overeating or anorexia nervosa [58]. A better understanding of wanting and linking mechanisms tailored to individual types of EDs and obesity could lead to better therapeutic strategies, and perhaps help people who wish to more effectively create stop signals to their own needs [57].

4.2.4. Behavioural Risk Factors

Body dissatisfaction is a well-documented psychological aspect of obesity, especially for women, and research with female college students found that lifetime experiences of weight stigma significantly mediated the relationship between BMI and body dissatisfaction [55].

Diet is the most significant behavioural risk factor for the onset of BED. It is well documented that dieting increases the risk of overeating to counter calorie deprivation and executive function, weight gain over time [42].

Social isolation can be inherently stressful, depressing, and anxiety-provoking. To heal these distressing feelings, an individual can engage in emotional eating, where the food serves as a source of comfort. This has gained special attention during the COVID pandemic [59,60].

4.2.5. Biochemical

Eating behaviour is a complex process controlled by the neuroendocrine system, of which the hypothalamic–pituitary–adrenal axis (HPA axis) is the main component and dysregulation of the HPA axis has been associated with EDs [61,62].

Serotonin also has an inhibitory executive function on eating behaviour [63]. Several studies have assessed the relationship between the noradrenergic system and EDs. A recent systematic review identified a series of key data on the relationship between the noradrenergic system and EDs. Besides its relevant direct, hypothalamus-based actions on feeding regulation, the noradrenergic system is indirectly implied in various endocrine networks controlling human nutrition [64]. Dopamine is a neurotransmitter that regulates the rewarding nature of food [65]. Neuropeptide Y is a hormone that promotes eating and reduces metabolic rate [66]. Leptin has an inhibitory executive function that affects appetite by inducing a feeling of satiety [67]. Ghrelin is an appetizing hormone produced in the stomach and upper part of the small intestine [68]. Circulating leptin and ghrelin levels are an important factor in weight control. Although often associated with obesity, both hormones and related executive functions have been implicated in the pathophysiology of anorexia nervosa and BN [67,68].

4.2.6. Gut Bacteria and Immune System

There is increasing interest in the association of gut bacteria with diseases such as diabetes, obesity, inflammatory bowel disease, and psychiatric disorders. The gut microbiota influences nutrient fermentation, body weight regulation, gut permeability, hormones, inflammation, immunology, and behaviour (gut–brain axis) [69].

The gut microbiome plays a vital role, not only in regulating mood and behaviour, but also in regulating metabolic function, appetite control and weight [70]. Studies have shown that most patients with anorexia and BN have elevated levels of autoantibodies that affect hormones and neuropeptides that regulate appetite control and stress response. A link between the gut microbiome and EDs affecting up to 10 percent of the population has been shown [71].

5. Management

Evidence-based treatments for obesity and EDs in childhood include as first-line approaches weight loss with nutritional management and lifestyle modification via behavioral psychotherapy, as well as treatment of psychiatric comorbidities if those are not a consequence of the ED [27]. The majority of children and adolescents under supervised obesity treatment may have improvements or no change to ED risk profiles [72]. Higher baseline dietary restraint scores in obese children have been associated with increased rates of premature drop out from the intervention program compared to children who completed the program, independent of gender, age, and BMI z-score at baseline and mother's education level [73]. On the other hand, in a secondary analysis of an RCT focusing on changes in energy intake and diet quality during obesity treatment with post-treatment eating pathology in adolescents, there was no association between intensity of diet and EDs [74]. In a systematic review, current measures of dietary restraint and dieting are not associated with ED risk in the short term; however, long-term data are limited [75].

5.1. *Weight Loss, Diet, Behavioral Therapy, Lifestyle Modification*

Most organizations support weight maintenance or weight loss as a treatment goal for the management of pediatric obesity. Lifestyle intervention programs for youth with some degree of overweight recommend considering a wide multidimensional approach covering eating and dietary habits. Suffering from weight-related teasing during childhood and adolescence might lead to emotional eating which, in turn, could impair long-term weight loss maintenance [76]. Even when programs aiming to treat shared risk factors did not result in significant differences in terms of weight status, it had an impact on body dissatisfaction, dieting and weight-control behaviors [22].

Cognitive behavioral therapy (CBT) emphasizes on restructuring of the harmful patterns that infiltrate daily functioning and changing habits and attitudes that maintain psychological disorders. CBT has been suggested as a promising treatment approach for EDs and obesity [77]. However, CBT would be considered as a second-line option when family-based multicomponent behavioral weight loss treatment (FBT) has not been effective or could not be applied [77,78].

Multicomponent interventions are regarded to have higher rates of weight loss. FBT is considered effective at treating childhood obesity and a treatment option for disordered eating and obesity in children [79]. Compared to an adolescent-focus intervention, a healthy family-based lifestyle modification could result in increased sustainably of changes [27]. The results of a clinical trial including adolescents on 4-month FBT and subsequent 8-month weight maintenance interventions showed that weight change following FBT and maintenance were reported to be independent of concurrent physiopathology and EDs in the short or long term [80].

5.2. *Motivational Interviewing*

Frequent counseling may be required in order to help patients maintain motivation to achieve a healthy weight [81]. Motivational interviewing (MI) focus on engagement by establishing a working relationship with the patient in order to explore and plan the need for changes, while at the same time avoiding stigmatizing language regarding weight that may negatively impact a teen and result in BE, decreased physical activity, social isolation, avoidance of health care services, and increased weight gain [27]. Effective health provider–patient communication using MI techniques have been proved useful to encourage positive behavior changes [5].

Even when there is a constant interest for a better approach to prevent and treat obesity among the youth, the actual population-oriented interventions and traditional medical care have not had the expected impact. This shows us that new alternatives are needed in order to fight obesity effectively. As an example, a personalized approach and more intense family-based multi-professional weight management called "*Personalized approach in obesity management*" was initiated in Estonia, being a successful long-term project for dealing with overweight children. Using the motivational interview method, the self-motivation of parents and the child for lifestyle changes was examined using the LINE chair Visual Analogue Scale (VAS—1–10 points), real goals for the child's lifestyle change were selected [82]. According to self-assessment, only 14% of children had similar aspects of health compared to healthy children and, as for the parents, the corresponding figure was 9%. Quality of life estimated that the indicator of children's physical and emotional health is the most frequently disturbed (in 90–92% of respondents). The relevance of the project's results can be seen by its nomination as an example of best practice in Estonia in the EU Joint Action on Nutrition and Physical activity (JANPA) [83].

5.3. APPs and MHealth

Feasibility of medicine-based mHealth intervention targeted for adolescents have been assessed in order to increase high retention and adherence rates in weight loss interventions [84]. The intervention using new technologies, mHealth, may contribute to reduce the degree of overweight in a more cost-effective manner compared to the classical intervention at the clinic [84].

5.4. Public Health Approaches

One of the main risk factors for disordered eating is body dissatisfaction. However, most countries' public health approaches to confront overweight and obesity frequently use messages that may increase body dissatisfaction in children and adolescents [85]. Thus, it remains a challenge for policy makers to balance between sociocultural pressure for thinness and obesogenic environment. The role of the schools at the time to promote health and educational attainment has been highlighted by the World Health Organization's (WHO) Health Promoting Schools (HPS) framework. In a Cochrane review, the WHO HPS framework was found to be effective at improving aspects of student health including BMI z-score at the population level [86].

5.5. Drugs

In combination with lifestyle interventions, the only medication for the treatment of obesity in youth 12 years and older approved by FDA is Orlistat. However, it should be used with caution in the presence of ED psychopathology to avoid misuse as a purging agent [87,88]. Orlistat is the only available anti-obesity drug that does not involve the mechanisms of appetite. It induces weight reduction via the inhibition of lipases in the mucous membranes of the stomach, small intestine, and pancreas, thereby preventing the breakdown of triglycerides into fatty acids and their absorption in the intestines [88].

5.6. Bariatric Surgery

Few studies have assessed the effect of bariatric surgery on disordered eating symptoms. In a study that included 19 adolescents with severe obesity who underwent a reversible bariatric procedure, improvements of emotional and behavioral factors were documented [89]. In a sub-study of the Teen-LABS Consortium, the application of bariatric surgery in adolescents demonstrated better outcomes 1 year after, not only in weight reduction but also in disordered eating symptoms, as compared to those who were under the lifestyle modification program [90]. Participants in the Adolescent Morbid Obesity Surgery (AMOS) study, 5 years of follow-up after Roux-en-Y gastric bypass surgery showed that BE and uncontrolled eating were moderately improved at the end of the period [91]. A small decrease in emotional eating and a small increase in cognitive restraint were also noted between baseline and 5 years after surgery. Higher scores for BE and emotional eating at Lang 2 years and 5 years, and for uncontrolled eating at 2 years after surgery, were also significantly associated with smaller percentage changes in BMI at 5 years relative to baseline. These data suggest that bariatric surgery alone does not improve adolescents' eating behavior and the need for a multidisciplinary team for long-term health support after adolescent bariatric surgery [91].

5.7. Screening for Adverse Childhood Experiences

There are limited data on the effect of structured intervention models to treat obesity and EDs in children who have experienced ACEs. Since there is an association of ACEs with obesity and EDs, the healthcare team should consider the possibility of having an ACE. Screening for ACEs would be regularly performed using validated tools [92,93]. In the case of an affected child, multicomponent intervention strategies should include appropriate psychosocial support and counseling to manage anxiety due to trauma that would impede the effectiveness of obesity and ED treatment. Of note, prevention policies for ACEs that may chance self-confidence, social and emotional skills could accompany healthy eating education on an individual and family level.

6. Conclusions

The rising tide of obesity and EDs and the link between them outlines the rationale for awareness and recognition of amenable risk factors that increase vulnerability. The importance of early detection is unquestionable and pediatricians are in a unique position to identify early and disrupt their progression. Despite well-researched links between the physical and mental health of youth in the presence of obesity, the resulting mental health toll is largely ignored. The importance of identifying risk factors shared by both obesity and EDs may serve as an important focal point for an intervention aimed at simultaneously addressing both of them. Obesity and EDs are important health challenges in children and adolescents; therefore, future research is necessary for early detection of risk factors for prevention, more precise elucidation of the mechanisms that underpin these problems and, finally, in the cases requiring therapeutic intervention, to provide tailored and timely treatment. Collective efforts between the fields are crucial for reducing the factors of health disparity and improving public health.

Author Contributions: Conceptualization, S.S., E.L.; writing—original draft preparation, S.S., S.E., L.S., A.J.; writing—review and editing, E.L. All authors have read and agreed to the published version of the manuscript.

Funding: This work has not received any funding.

Acknowledgments: This publication is based on the work of the COST Action HyperChildNET (CA19115), with the support of COST (European Cooperation in Science and Technology) and the Horizon 2020 Framework Program of the European Union.

Conflicts of Interest: The authors declare no conflict of interest.

References

1. Prevalence of Obesity. World Obesity Federation. Available online: https://www.worldobesity.org/about/about-obesity/prevalence-of-obesity (accessed on 15 November 2021).
2. Rancourt, D.; McCullough, M.B. Overlap in Eating Disorders and Obesity in Adolescence. *Curr. Diab. Rep.* **2015**, *15*, 78. [CrossRef]
3. Taylor, S.A.; Ditch, S.; Hansen, S. Identifying and Preventing Eating Disorders in Adolescent Patients with Obesity. *Pediatr. Ann.* **2018**, *47*, e232–e237. [CrossRef]
4. Hay, P.; Mitchison, D. Eating Disorders and Obesity: The Challenge for Our Times. *Nutrients* **2019**, *11*, 1055. [CrossRef]
5. Kansra, A.R.; Lakkunarajah, S.; Jay, M.S. Childhood and Adolescent Obesity: A Review. *Front. Pediatr.* **2021**, *8*, 581461. [CrossRef] [PubMed]
6. Anderson, L.N.; Carsley, S.; Lebovic, G.; Borkhoff, C.M.; Maguire, J.L.; Parkin, P.C.; Birken, C.S. Misclassification of child body mass index from cut-points defined by rounded percentiles instead of Z-scores. *BMC Res. Notes* **2017**, *10*, 639. [CrossRef] [PubMed]
7. Haqq, A.M.; Kebbe, M.; Tan, Q.; Manco, M.; Salas, X.R. Complexity and Stigma of Pediatric Obesity. *Child. Obes.* **2021**, *17*, 229–240. [CrossRef] [PubMed]
8. Lee, E.Y.; Yoon, K.H. Epidemic obesity in children and adolescents: Risk factors and prevention. *Front. Med.* **2018**, *12*, 658–666. [CrossRef] [PubMed]

9. Di Cesare, M.; Sorić, M.; Bovet, P.; Miranda, J.J.; Bhutta, Z.; Stevens, G.A.; Laxmaiah, A.; Kengne, A.P.; Bentham, J. The epidemiological burden of obesity in childhood: A worldwide epidemic requiring urgent action. *BMC Med.* **2019**, *17*, 212. [CrossRef]
10. Gillman, M.W.; Rifas-Shiman, S.L.; Kleinman, K.; Oken, E.; Rich-Edwards, J.W.; Taveras, E.M. Developmental origins of childhood overweight: Potential public health impact. *Obesity* **2008**, *16*, 1651–1656. [CrossRef]
11. Bucher Della Torre, S.; Keller, A.; Laure Depeyre, J.; Kruseman, M. Sugar-Sweetened Beverages and Obesity Risk in Children and Adolescents: A Systematic Analysis on How Methodological Quality May Influence Conclusions. *J. Acad. Nutr. Diet.* **2016**, *116*, 638–659. [CrossRef]
12. Marshall, T.A.; Curtis, A.M.; Cavanaugh, J.E.; Warren, J.J.; Levy, S.M. Child and adolescent sugar-sweetened beverage intakes are longitudinally associated with higher body mass index z scores in a birth cohort followed 17 years. *J. Acad. Nutr. Diet.* **2019**, *119*, 425–434. [CrossRef] [PubMed]
13. Falkner, B.; Lurbe, E. Primordial Prevention of High Blood Pressure in Childhood: An Opportunity Not to be Missed. *Hypertension* **2020**, *75*, 1142–1150. [CrossRef]
14. Liu, M.; Wu, L.; Yao, S. Dose-response association of screen time-based sedentary behaviour in children and adolescents and depression: A meta-analysis of observational studies. *Br. J. Sports Med.* **2016**, *50*, 1252–1258. [CrossRef] [PubMed]
15. Lissak, G. Adverse physiological and psychological effects of screen time on children and adolescents: Literature review and case study. *Environ. Res.* **2018**, *164*, 149–157. [CrossRef]
16. Buxton, O.M.; Chang, A.M.; Spilsbury, J.C.; Bos, T.; Emsellem, H.; Knutson, K.L. Sleep in the modern family: Protective family routines for child and adolescent sleep. *Sleep Health* **2015**, *1*, 15–27. [CrossRef] [PubMed]
17. Hemmingsson, E. Early Childhood Obesity Risk Factors: Socioeconomic Adversity, Family Dysfunction, Offspring Distress, and Junk Food Self-Medication. *Curr. Obes. Rep.* **2018**, *7*, 204–209. [CrossRef]
18. Van der Klaauw, A.A.; Farooqi, I.S. The hunger genes: Pathways to obesity. *Cell* **2015**, *161*, 119–132. [CrossRef] [PubMed]
19. Loos, R.J.F.; Yeo, G.S.H. The genetics of obesity: From discovery to biology. *Nat. Rev. Genet.* **2021**, *23*, 1–14. [CrossRef]
20. Kaufman, J.; Montalvo-Ortiz, J.L.; Holbrook, H.; O'Loughlin, K.; Orr, C.; Kearney, C.; Yang, B.Z.; Wang, T.; Zhao, H.; Althoff, R. Adverse Childhood Experiences, Epigenetic Measures, and Obesity in Youth. *J. Pediatr.* **2018**, *202*, 150–156. [CrossRef]
21. Danese, A.; Tan, M. Childhood maltreatment and obesity: Systematic review and meta-analysis. *Mol. Psychiatry* **2014**, *19*, 544–554. [CrossRef]
22. Leme, A.C.B.; Haines, J.; Tang, L.; Dunker, K.L.L.; Philippi, S.T.; Fisberg, M.; Ferrari, G.L.; Fisberg, R.M. Impact of Strategies for Preventing Obesity and Risk Factors for Eating Disorders among Adolescents: A Systematic Review. *Nutrients* **2020**, *12*, 3134. [CrossRef] [PubMed]
23. Treasure, J.; Duarte, T.A.; Schmidt, U. Eating disorders. *Lancet* **2020**, *395*, 899–911. [CrossRef]
24. American Psychiatric Association. *Diagnostic and Statistical Manual of Mental Disorders*, 5th ed.; American Psychiatric Press: Washington, DC, USA, 2013.
25. Smink, F.R.; van Hoeken, D.; Hoek, H.W. Epidemiology of eating disorders: Incidence, prevalence and mortality rates. *Curr. Psychiatry Rep.* **2012**, *14*, 406–414. [CrossRef]
26. Hilbert, A. Childhood Eating and Feeding Disturbances. *Nutrients* **2020**, *12*, 972. [CrossRef]
27. Golden, N.H.; Schneider, M.; Wood, C.; Committee on Nutrition; Committee on Adolescence. Section on Obesity. Preventing Obesity and Eating Disorders in Adolescents. *Pediatrics* **2016**, *138*, e20161649. [CrossRef]
28. Horsager, C.; Færk, E.; Gearhardt, A.N.; Lauritsen, M.B.; Østergaard, S.D. Food addiction comorbid to mental disorders in adolescents: A nationwide survey and register-based study. *Eat. Weight Disord.* **2021**. epub ahead of print. [CrossRef]
29. Stice, E. Risk and maintenance factors for eating pathology: A meta-analytic review. *Psychol. Bull.* **2002**, *128*, 825–848. [CrossRef]
30. Stice, E.; Ng, J.; Shaw, H. Risk factors and prodromal eating pathology. *J. Child Psychol. Psychiatry* **2010**, *51*, 518–525. [CrossRef]
31. Wildes, J.E.; Emery, R.E.; Simons, A.D. The roles of ethnicity and culture in the development of eating disturbance and body dissatisfaction: A meta-analytic review. *Clin. Psychol. Rev.* **2001**, *21*, 521–551. [CrossRef]
32. Collantoni, E.; Solmi, M.; Gallicchio, D.; Santonastaso, P.; Meneguzzo, P.; Carvalho, A.F.; Stubbs, B.; Clementi, M.; Pinato, C.; Forzan, M.; et al. Catechol-O-Methyltransferase (COMT) Val158Met Polymorphism and Eating Disorders: Data from a New Biobank and Meta-Analysis of Previously Published Studies. *Eur. Eat. Disord. Rev.* **2017**, *25*, 524–532. [CrossRef] [PubMed]
33. Hinney, A.; Kesselmeier, M.; Jall, S.; Volckmar, A.L.; Föcker, M.; Antel, J.; Heid, I.M.; Winkler, T.W.; Grant, S.F.; Guo, Y.; et al. Evidence for three genetic loci involved in both anorexia nervosa risk and variation of body mass index. *Mol. Psychiatry* **2017**, *22*, 192–201. [CrossRef] [PubMed]
34. Solmi, M.; Radua, J.; Stubbs, B.; Ricca, V.; Moretti, D.; Busatta, D.; Carvalho, A.F.; Dragioti, E.; Favaro, A.; Monteleone, A.M.; et al. Risk factors for eating disorders: An umbrella review of published meta-analyses. *Braz. J. Psychiatry* **2021**, *43*, 314–323. [CrossRef]
35. Hazzard, V.M.; Barry, M.R.; Leung, C.W.; Sonneville, K.R.; Wonderlich, S.A.; Crosby, R.D. Food insecurity and its associations with bulimic-spectrum eating disorders, mood disorders, and anxiety disorders in a nationally representative sample of U.S. adults. *Soc. Psychiatry Psychiatr. Epidemiol.* **2021**, *27*, 1–8. [CrossRef]
36. Thomas, R.; Siliquini, R.; Hillegers, M.H.; Jansen, P.W. The association of adverse life events with children's emotional overeating and restrained eating in a population-based cohort. *Int. J. Eat. Disord.* **2020**, *53*, 1709–1718. [CrossRef] [PubMed]
37. Bjørklund, O.; Wichstrøm, L.; Llewellyn, C.H.; Steinsbekk, S. Emotional over- and Undereating in Children: A Longitudinal Analysis of Child and Contextual Predictors. *Child Dev.* **2019**, *90*, e803–e818. [CrossRef]

38. Michels, N.; Sioen, I.; Braet, C.; Eiben, G.; Hebestreit, A.; Huybrechts, I.; Vanaelst, B.; Vyncke, K.; De Henauw, S. Stress, emotional eating behaviour and dietary patterns in children. *Appetite* **2012**, *59*, 762–769. [CrossRef] [PubMed]
39. Krug, I.; Villarejo, C.; Jiménez-Murcia, S.; Perpiñá, C.; Vilarrasa, N.; Granero, R.; Cebolla, A.; Botella, C.; Montserrat-Gil de Bernabe, M.; Penelo, E.; et al. Eating-related environmental factors in underweight eating disorders and obesity: Are there common vulnerabilities during childhood and early adolescence? *Eur. Eat. Disord. Rev.* **2013**, *21*, 202–208. [CrossRef]
40. Hornberger, L.L.; Lane, M.A.; Committee on Adolescence. Identification and Management of Eating Disorders in Children and Adolescents. *Pediatrics* **2021**, *147*, e2020040279. [CrossRef] [PubMed]
41. Agüera, Z.; Vintró-Alcaraz, C.; Baenas, I.; Granero, R.; Sánchez, I.; Sánchez-González, J.; Menchón, J.M.; Jiménez-Murcia, S.; Treasure, J.; Fernández-Aranda, F. Lifetime Weight Course as a Phenotypic Marker of Severity and Therapeutic Response in Patients with Eating Disorders. *Nutrients* **2021**, *13*, 2034. [CrossRef]
42. Agüera, Z.; Lozano-Madrid, M.; Mallorquí-Bagué, N.; Jiménez-Murcia, S.; Menchón, J.M.; Fernández-Aranda, F. A review of binge eating disorder and obesity. *Neuropsychiatrie* **2021**, *35*, 57–67. [CrossRef]
43. Libbey, H.P.; Story, M.T.; Neumark-Sztainer, D.R.; Boutelle, K.N. Teasing, disordered eating behaviors, and psychological morbidities among overweight adolescents. *Obesity* **2008**, *16* (Suppl. 2), S24–S29. [CrossRef]
44. Macpherson-Sánchez, A.E. Integrating fundamental concepts of obesity and eating disorders: Implications for the obesity epidemic. *Am. J. Public Health* **2015**, *105*, e71–e85. [CrossRef]
45. Field, A.E.; Camargo, C.A., Jr.; Taylor, C.B.; Berkey, C.S.; Roberts, S.B.; Colditz, G.A. Peer, parent, and media influences on the development of weight concerns and frequent dieting among preadolescent and adolescent girls and boys. *Pediatrics* **2001**, *107*, 54–60. [CrossRef] [PubMed]
46. Striegel-Moore, R.H.; Fairburn, C.G.; Wilfley, D.E.; Pike, K.M.; Dohm, F.A.; Kraemer, H.C. Toward an understanding of risk factors for binge-eating disorder in black and white women: A community-based case-control study. *Psychol. Med.* **2005**, *35*, 907–917. [CrossRef] [PubMed]
47. Manfredi, L.; Accoto, A.; Couyoumdjian, A.; Conversi, D. A Systematic Review of Genetic Polymorphisms Associated with Binge Eating Disorder. *Nutrients* **2021**, *13*, 848. [CrossRef]
48. Castellini, G.; Franzago, M.; Bagnoli, S.; Lelli, L.; Balsamo, M.; Mancini, M.; Nacmias, B.; Ricca, V.; Sorbi, S.; Antonucci, I.; et al. Fat mass and obesity-associated gene (FTO) is associated to eating disorders susceptibility and moderates the expression of psychopathological traits. *PLoS ONE* **2017**, *12*, e0173560. [CrossRef]
49. Loos, R.J.; Bouchard, C. FTO: The first gene contributing to common forms of human obesity. *Obes. Rev.* **2008**, *9*, 246–250. [CrossRef]
50. Cameron, J.D.; Tasca, G.A.; Little, J.; Chyurlia, L.; Ritchie, K.; Yeh, E.; Doucette, S.; Obregon, A.M.; Bulman, D.E.; Doucet, É.; et al. Effects of fat mass and obesity-associated (FTO) gene polymorphisms on binge eating in women with binge-eating disorder: The moderating influence of attachment style. *Nutrition* **2019**, *61*, 208–212. [CrossRef]
51. Nicoletti, C.F.; Delfino, H.B.P.; Ferreira, F.C.; Pinhel, M.A.S.; Nonino, C.B. Role of eating disorders-related polymorphisms in obesity pathophysiology. *Rev. Endocr. Metab. Disord.* **2019**, *20*, 115–125. [CrossRef] [PubMed]
52. Goldschmidt, A.B.; Aspen, V.P.; Sinton, M.M.; Tanofsky-Kraff, M.; Wilfley, D.E. Disordered eating attitudes and behaviors in overweight youth. *Obesity* **2008**, *16*, 257–264. [CrossRef]
53. Dingemans, A.; Danner, U.; Parks, M. Emotion Regulation in Binge Eating Disorder: A Review. *Nutrients* **2017**, *9*, 1274. [CrossRef]
54. Gearhardt, A.N.; White, M.A.; Masheb, R.M.; Morgan, P.T.; Crosby, R.D.; Grilo, C.M. An examination of the food addiction construct in obese patients with binge eating disorder. *Int. J. Eat. Disord.* **2012**, *45*, 657–663. [CrossRef]
55. Puhl, R.M.; Himmelstein, M.S.; Pearl, R.L. Weight stigma as a psychosocial contributor to obesity. *Am. Psychol.* **2020**, *75*, 274–289. [CrossRef]
56. Val-Laillet, D.; Aarts, E.; Weber, B.; Ferrari, M.; Quaresima, V.; Stoeckel, L.E.; Alonso-Alonso, M.; Audette, M.; Malbert, C.H.; Stice, E. Neuroimaging and neuromodulation approaches to study eating behavior and prevent and treat eating disorders and obesity. *Neuroimage Clin.* **2015**, *8*, 1–31. [CrossRef]
57. Morales, I.; Berridge, K.C. 'Liking' and 'wanting' in eating and food reward: Brain mechanisms and clinical implications. *Physiol. Behav.* **2020**, *227*, 113152. [CrossRef]
58. Berridge, K.C.; Ho, C.Y.; Richard, J.M.; DiFeliceantonio, A.G. The tempted brain eats: Pleasure and desire circuits in obesity and eating disorders. *Brain Res.* **2010**, *1350*, 43–64. [CrossRef] [PubMed]
59. Cecchetto, C.; Aiello, M.; Gentili, C.; Ionta, S.; Osimo, S.A. Increased emotional eating during COVID-19 associated with lockdown, psychological and social distress. *Appetite* **2021**, *160*, 105122. [CrossRef] [PubMed]
60. Rodgers, R.F.; Lombardo, C.; Cerolini, S.; Franko, D.L.; Omori, M.; Fuller-Tyszkiewicz, M.; Linardon, J.; Courtet, P.; Guillaume, S. The impact of the COVID-19 pandemic on eating disorder risk and symptoms. *Int. J. Eat. Disord.* **2020**, *53*, 1166–1170. [CrossRef] [PubMed]
61. Gross, M.J.; Kahn, J.P.; Laxenaire, M.; Nicolas, J.P.; Burlet, C. Corticotropin-releasing factor and anorexia nervosa: Reactions of the hypothalamus-pituitary-adrenal axis to neurotropic stress. *Ann. Endocrinol.* **1994**, *55*, 221–228.
62. Licinio, J.; Wong, M.L.; Gold, P.W. The hypothalamic-pituitary-adrenal axis in anorexia nervosa. *Psychiatry Res.* **1996**, *62*, 75–83. [CrossRef]
63. Hainer, V.; Kabrnova, K.; Aldhoon, B.; Kunesova, M.; Wagenknecht, M. Serotonin and norepinephrine reuptake inhibition and eating behavior. *Ann. N. Y. Acad. Sci.* **2006**, *1083*, 252–269. [CrossRef]

64. Pruccoli, J.; Parmeggiani, A.; Cordelli, D.M.; Lanari, M. The role of Noradrenergic system in eating disorders: A systematic review. *Int. J. Mol. Sci.* **2021**, *22*, 11086. [CrossRef] [PubMed]
65. Wang, G.J.; Volkow, N.D.; Logan, J.; Pappas, N.R.; Wong, C.T.; Zhu, W.; Netusil, N.; Fowler, J.S. Brain dopamine and obesity. *Lancet* **2001**, *357*, 354–357. [CrossRef]
66. Carlson, N. Ingestive Behavior. In *Physiology of Behavior*; University of Massachusetts, Amherst: Pearson, GA, USA, 2013; pp. 428–432. ISBN 978-0-205-23939-9.
67. Frederich, R.; Hu, S.; Raymond, N.; Pomeroy, C. Leptin in anorexia nervosa and bulimia nervosa: Importance of assay technique and method of interpretation. *J. Lab. Clin.. Med* **2002**, *139*, 72–79. [CrossRef] [PubMed]
68. Atalayer, D.; Gibson, C.; Konopacka, A.; Geliebter, A. Ghrelin and eating disorders. *Prog. Neuropsychopharmacol. Biol. Psychiatry* **2013**, *40*, 70–82. [CrossRef] [PubMed]
69. Seitz, J.; Trinh, S.; Herpertz-Dahlmann, B. The Microbiome and Eating Disorders. *Psychiatr. Clin. N. Am.* **2019**, *42*, 93–103. [CrossRef]
70. Biedermann, L.; Rogler, G. The intestinal microbiota: Its role in health and disease. *Eur. J. Pediatr.* **2015**, *174*, 151–167. [CrossRef]
71. Carbone, E.A.; D'Amato, P.; Vicchio, G.; De Fazio, P.; Segura-Garcia, C. A systematic review on the role of microbiota in the pathogenesis and treatment of eating disorders. *Eur. Psychiatry* **2020**, *64*, e2. [CrossRef]
72. Lister, N.B.; Baur, L.A.; Paxton, S.J.; Jebeile, H. Contextualising Eating Disorder Concerns for Paediatric Obesity Treatment. *Curr. Obes. Rep.* **2021**, *10*, 322–331. [CrossRef]
73. Albayrak, Ö.; Pott, W.; Hebebrand, J.; de Zwaan, M.; Pauli-Pott, U. Baseline Dietary Restraint Predicts Negative Treatment Outcomes after 12 Months in Children and Adolescents with Obesity Participating in a Lifestyle Intervention. *Obes. Facts* **2019**, *12*, 179–189. [CrossRef]
74. Raynor, H.A.; Mazzeo, S.E.; LaRose, J.G.; Adams, E.L.; Thornton, L.M.; Caccavale, L.J.; Bean, M.K. Effect of a High-Intensity Dietary Intervention on Changes in Dietary Intake and Eating Pathology during a Multicomponent Adolescent Obesity Intervention. *Nutrients* **2021**, *13*, 1850. [CrossRef]
75. House, E.T.; Gow, M.L.; Lister, N.B.; Baur, L.A.; Garnett, S.P.; Paxton, S.J.; Jebeile, H. Pediatric weight management, dietary restraint, dieting, and eating disorder risk: A systematic review. *Nutr. Rev.* epub ahead of print. **2021**. [CrossRef] [PubMed]
76. Hübner, C.; Baldofski, S.; Crosby, R.D.; Müller, A.; de Zwaan, M.; Hilbert, A. Weight-related teasing and non-normative eating behaviors as predictors of weight loss maintenance. A longitudinal mediation analysis. *Appetite* **2016**, *102*, 25–31. [CrossRef]
77. Dalle Grave, R.; Eckhardt, S.; Calugi, S.; Le Grange, D. A conceptual comparison of family-based treatment and enhanced cognitive behavior therapy in the treatment of adolescents with eating disorders. *J. Eat. Disord.* **2019**, *7*, 42. [CrossRef]
78. Craig, M.; Waine, J.; Wilson, S.; Waller, G. Optimizing treatment outcomes in adolescents with eating disorders: The potential role of cognitive behavioral therapy. *Int. J. Eat. Disord.* **2019**, *52*, 538–542. [CrossRef]
79. Hayes, J.F.; Fitzsimmons-Craft, E.E.; Karam, A.M.; Jakubiak, J.; Brown, M.L.; Wilfley, D.E. Disordered Eating Attitudes and Behaviors in Youth with Overweight and Obesity: Implications for Treatment. *Curr. Obes. Rep.* **2018**, *7*, 235–246. [CrossRef]
80. Grammer, A.C.; Best, J.R.; Fowler, L.A.; Balantekin, K.N.; Stein, R.I.; Conlon, R.P.K.; Saelens, B.E.; Welch, R.R.; Perri, M.G.; Epstein, L.H.; et al. General and Eating Disorder Psychopathology in Relation to Short- and Long-Term Weight Change in Treatment-Seeking Children: A Latent Profile Analysis. *Ann. Behav. Med.* **2021**, *55*, 698–704. [CrossRef] [PubMed]
81. Bravender, T.; Lyna, P.; Coffman, C.J.; Bodner, M.E.; Østbye, T.; Alexander, S.C.; Lin, P.H.; Pollak, K.I. Physician Weight-Related Counseling Is Unrelated to Extreme Weight Loss Behaviors Among Overweight and Obese Adolescents. *Clin. Pediatr.* **2018**, *57*, 954–957. [CrossRef] [PubMed]
82. Woolford, S.J.; Clark, S.J.; Sana Ahmed Davis, M.M. Feasibility and Acceptability of a 1-Page Tool to Help Physicians Assess and Discuss obesity With Parents of Preschoolers. *Clin. Pediatric* **2009**, *48*, 954–995. [CrossRef]
83. Overview of the Joint Action, J.A.NPA HLG/EU Platform. DG Santé Luxembourg 29 November 2017. Dr Michel Chauliac, Direction Générale de la Santé. Available online: www.janpa-toolbox.eu (accessed on 19 September 2021).
84. Vidmar, A.P.; Pretlow, R.; Borzutzky, C.; Wee, C.P.; Fox, D.S.; Fink, C.; Mittelman, S.D. An addiction model-based mobile health weight loss intervention in adolescents with obesity. *Pediatr. Obes.* **2019**, *14*, e12464. [CrossRef]
85. Bray, I.; Slater, A.; Lewis-Smith, H.; Bird, E.; Sabey, A. Promoting positive body image and tackling overweight/obesity in children and adolescents: A combined health psychology and public health approach. *Prev. Med.* **2018**, *116*, 219–221. [CrossRef]
86. Langford, R.; Bonell, C.; Jones, H.; Pouliou, T.; Murphy, S.; Waters, E.; Komro, K.; Gibbs, L.; Magnus, D.; Campbell, R. The World Health Organization's Health Promoting Schools framework: A Cochrane systematic review and meta-analysis. *BMC Public Health* **2015**, *15*, 130. [CrossRef] [PubMed]
87. Powers, P.S.; Cloak, N.L. Psychopharmacologic treatment of obesity and eating disorders in children and adolescents. *Child Adolesc. Psychiatr. Clin.* **2012**, *21*, 831–859. [CrossRef] [PubMed]
88. Son, J.W.; Kim, S. Comprehensive Review of Current and Upcoming Anti-Obesity Drugs. *Diabetes Metab. J.* **2020**, *44*, 802–818. [CrossRef]
89. Klemenčič, S.; Bujišić, A.; Hribernik, N.; Battelino, T.; Homan, M.; Orel, R.; Kotnik, P. Psychological Outcomes and Predictors of Weight Loss in Adolescents With Severe Obesity Following a Reversible Endoscopic Bariatric Procedure. *Front. Pediatr* **2021**, *9*, 688287. [CrossRef]

90. Sarwer, D.B.; Dilks, R.J.; Spitzer, J.C.; Berkowitz, R.I.; Wadden, T.A.; Moore, R.H.; Chittams, J.L.; Brandt, M.L.; Chen, M.K.; Courcoulas, A.P.; et al. Changes in Dietary Intake and Eating Behavior in Adolescents After Bariatric Surgery: An Ancillary Study to the Teen-LABS Consortium. *Obes. Surg.* **2017**, *27*, 3082–3091. [CrossRef] [PubMed]
91. Järvholm, K.; Bruze, G.; Peltonen, M.; Marcus, C.; Flodmark, C.E.; Henfridsson, P.; Beamish, A.J.; Gronowitz, E.; Dahlgren, J.; Karlsson, J.; et al. 5-year mental health and eating pattern outcomes following bariatric surgery in adolescents: A prospective cohort study. *Lancet Child Adolesc. Health* **2020**, *4*, 210–219. [CrossRef]
92. Chu, W.W.; Chu, N.F. Adverse childhood experiences and development of obesity and diabetes in adulthood-A mini review. *Obes. Res. Clin. Pract.* **2021**, *15*, 101–105. [CrossRef]
93. Isohookana, R.; Marttunen, M.; Hakko, H.; Riipinen, P.; Riala, K. The impact of adverse childhood experiences on obesity and unhealthy weight control behaviors among adolescents. *Compr. Psychiatry* **2016**, *71*, 17–24. [CrossRef] [PubMed]

nutrients

MDPI

Review

Obesity and Cardiometabolic Risk Factors: From Childhood to Adulthood

Dorota Drozdz [1,*,†], Julio Alvarez-Pitti [2,3,4,†], Małgorzata Wójcik [5], Claudio Borghi [6], Rosita Gabbianelli [7], Artur Mazur [8], Vesna Herceg-Čavrak [9], Beatriz Gonzalez Lopez-Valcarcel [10], Michał Brzeziński [11], Empar Lurbe [2,3,4,‡] and Elke Wühl [12,*,‡]

1 Department of Pediatric Nephrology and Hypertension, Pediatric Institute, Jagiellonian University Medical College, 30-663 Cracow, Poland
2 Pediatric Department, Consorcio Hospital General, University of Valencia, 46014 Valencia, Spain; alvarez_jul@gva.es (J.A.-P.); empar.lurbe@uv.es (E.L.)
3 CIBER Fisiopatología Obesidad y Nutrición (CIBEROBN), Instituto de Salud Carlos III, 28029 Madrid, Spain
4 INCLIVA Biomedical Research Institute, Hospital Clínico, University of Valencia, 46010 Valencia, Spain
5 Department of Pediatric and Adolescent Endocrinology, Pediatric Institute, Jagiellonian University Medical College, 30-663 Cracow, Poland; malgorzata.wojcik@uj.edu.pl
6 Department of Medical and Surgical Sciences, University of Bologna-IRCCS S. Orsola, 40126 Bologna, Italy; claudio.borghi@unibo.it
7 Unit of Molecular Biology and Nutrigenomics, School of Pharmacy, University of Camerino, 62032 Camerino, Italy; rosita.gabbianelli@unicam.it
8 Department of Pediatrics, Pediatric Endocrinology and Diabetes, Medical Faculty, University of Rzeszów, 35-310 Rzeszów, Poland; drmazur@poczta.onet.pl
9 Children's Hospital Zagreb, Libertas International University, 10000 Zagreb, Croatia; vherceg@gmail.com
10 Department of Quantitative Methods for Economics and Management, University of Las Palmas de Gran Canaria; 35017 Las Palmas, Spain; beatriz.lopezvalcarcel@ulpgc.es
11 Department of Pediatrics, Gastroenterology, Allergology and Pediatric Nutrition, Medical University of Gdansk, 80-210 Gdansk, Poland; brzezinski@gumed.edu.pl
12 Division of Pediatric Nephrology, Center for Pediatrics and Adolescent Medicine, Heidelberg University Hospital, 69120 Heidelberg, Germany
* Correspondence: dorota.drozdz@uj.edu.pl (D.D.); elke.wuehl@med.uni-heidelberg.de (E.W.); Tel.: +48-604787415 (D.D.); +49-6221-5639318 (E.W.)
† These authors contributed equally to this work.
‡ These authors contributed equally to this work.

Citation: Drozdz, D.; Alvarez-Pitti, J.; Wójcik, M.; Borghi, C.; Gabbianelli, R.; Mazur, A.; Herceg-Čavrak, V.; Lopez-Valcarcel, B.G.; Brzeziński, M.; Lurbe, E.; et al. Obesity and Cardiometabolic Risk Factors: From Childhood to Adulthood. *Nutrients* **2021**, *13*, 4176. https://doi.org/10.3390/nu13114176

Academic Editor: Ana Baylin

Received: 22 October 2021
Accepted: 19 November 2021
Published: 22 November 2021

Abstract: Obesity has become a major epidemic in the 21st century. It increases the risk of dyslipidemia, hypertension, and type 2 diabetes, which are known cardiometabolic risk factors and components of the metabolic syndrome. Although overt cardiovascular (CV) diseases such as stroke or myocardial infarction are the domain of adulthood, it is evident that the CV continuum begins very early in life. Recognition of risk factors and early stages of CV damage, at a time when these processes are still reversible, and the development of prevention strategies are major pillars in reducing CV morbidity and mortality in the general population. In this review, we will discuss the role of well-known but also novel risk factors linking obesity and increased CV risk from prenatal age to adulthood, including the role of perinatal factors, diet, nutrigenomics, and nutri-epigenetics, hyperuricemia, dyslipidemia, hypertension, and cardiorespiratory fitness. The importance of 'tracking' of these risk factors on adult CV health is highlighted and the economic impact of childhood obesity as well as preventive strategies are discussed.

Keywords: obesity; cardiometabolic risk factors; hypertension; dyslipidemia; tracking phenomenon; nutrigenomics

1. Introduction

The increasing prevalence of overweight and obesity, key components of the metabolic syndrome (MetS), in the pediatric and adult population poses a high risk of health complications and is associated with social and economic consequences.

According to the World Health Organization (WHO), the worldwide overall prevalence of obesity has nearly tripled since 1975. In 2016, 39% of adults aged 18 years and over were overweight and 13% were obese. However, among children and adolescents aged 5 to 19, the prevalence of overweight and obesity has risen even more dramatically: overweight increased from just 4% in 1975 to over 18% in 2016, while obesity increased from under 1% in 1975, to 6% in girls and 8% in boys. This is equivalent to more than 340 million overweight and 124 million obese children and adolescents worldwide in 2016 [1].

Obesity is associated with a high incidence of well-known cardiovascular (CV) risk factors such as dyslipidemia, hypertension (HTN) and diabetes. Numerous studies have shown the existence of a CV continuum, in which pathological processes begin as a result of various risk factors and lead to permanent changes and CV complications through endothelial damage, vascular and myocardial remodeling, and atherosclerotic processes. These changes may begin in early childhood and over time significantly increase the CV risk in young adults. This is of even greater concern in patients with already otherwise increased CV risk, e.g., in patients with chronic kidney disease (CKD), in whom the influence of classical and uremic risk factors is cumulative. The question arises, whether in the pediatric population early intervention in obesity will reduce the future CV risk in adulthood.

In this review we will discuss the importance of an early diagnosis and effective treatment of childhood obesity and the linked early and potentially reversible cardiovascular damage in children and adolescents to prevent CV complications, which remain the main cause of morbidity and mortality in the general population.

2. Cardiometabolic Risk Factors

2.1. Perinatal and Early Life Risk Factors

The concept that perinatal conditions, both intrauterine and early life increase the risk of many diseases later in life has gained traction over the last decades. The impact of early life on the development of obesity is a relevant issue due to its high prevalence and association with cardiometabolic risk factors. The greater propensity for obesity in later life seen in children heavier at birth, and an increase in central fat distribution in those with low birth weight (BW), suggest that fetal life is a critical window for programming later body adiposity. Scientific interest has grown regarding the associations of preconception, maternal and paternal health with childhood obesity. Furthermore, early child growth patterns have been emphasized as indicators of future child risks. The precise mechanisms of early programming of such disease states have only partially been elucidated; however, there is evidence to suggest that a window of opportunity may exist in the infant before and during pregnancy, and up to two years of age.

2.1.1. Maternal Risk Factors

Epidemiologic and prospective cohort studies have identified maternal and gestational conditions that confer increased risk for subsequent cardiometabolic disorders [2].

Global rates of childhood obesity have increased dramatically. Evidence suggests that exposure in utero to maternal obesity or gestational diabetes mellitus (GDM) may contribute to these alarming trends [3,4]. Children born to mothers with GDM or obesity during pregnancy have an increased likelihood of developing obesity and metabolic disorders compared with unexposed children [3,4]. It is challenging to distinguish the effects of maternal obesity and diabetes in the preconception period compared to the gestational period, as these characteristics generally track over time. Effects and associated mechanisms could differ for preconception vs. gestational exposure, resulting in a complex interaction between the effects of both periods [5]. The epidemiological evidence supports the need for preconception and early-life interventions to reduce the obesity and diabetes burden in later life [6].

The potential role of the paternal metabolic contribution to a child's later risk of disease has progressively gained more attention. Parental obesity is also a strong predictor of childhood obesity, and even more so when both parents are obese, this risk appears to be even greater [7]. Children of parents with obesity likely share not only genetic risks but also extra-uterine, environmental and lifestyle-related exposures that could explain some of the associations observed with parental preconception obesity and the offspring's obesity risk.

There is some evidence that environmental exposures during pregnancy influence fetal growth and later risk of obesity on offspring. Maternal smoking during pregnancy is associated with restricted fetal growth [2]. Additionally, in later childhood, children of these mothers have a 1.5-fold greater risk for overweight and obesity as compared to those born to mothers who did not smoke [8]. Air pollution and exposure to synthetic chemicals occurring in utero and early childhood have been linked to effects on life-long risk of obesity and metabolic abnormalities [9].

The matter of artificial reproductive techniques (ART) and their impact on childhood obesity has received increased attention [10]. An increase in body fat in children born by "in vitro" fertilization was reported by Ceelen et al., as compared to the controls [11]. Although there is little data, the findings are sufficiently compelling to add ART to the list of prenatal risk factors related to long-term outcomes.

2.1.2. Early Childhood Risk Factors

Birth weight (BW) is a sentinel marker of fetal health reflecting both, the intrauterine growth and the length of gestation. Not only does low BW merits consideration but also high BW which is a consequence of intrauterine overnutrition. Based on recent findings, the associations of abnormal fetal growth with heightened risk for cardiovascular and metabolic disease extend across a range of birth weights and postnatal growth patterns [9].

Early childhood growth trajectories and rapid catch-up growth have been shown to influence the development of risk factors. The impact of BW and postnatal growth on the presence of overweight or obesity, blood pressure (BP) values, metabolic parameters, HTN and type 2 diabetes (T2D), was assessed in a systematic review [12]. Some studies had a significant association with BW and/or postnatal growth while others did not. The most frequent association was seen with BP values and fasting insulin, with the greatest adverse levels present in those who were born with low BW but then became relatively heavy [12]. In one meta-analysis, the odds ratio for overweight and obesity was 3.66 [95% CI 2.59–5.17] in the presence of rapid weight gain before 2 years of age, even higher odds were observed when rapid weight gain occurred before 1 year of age [13].

The above findings underscore the importance of regular growth monitoring. The use of obesity criteria to identify children at risk will miss many at-risk persons. An upward crossing of BMI percentiles during childhood, that does not necessarily connote childhood obesity, also increases the risk.

Early-life feeding practices such as being breastfeed or not, timing of introduction and type of complementary feeding along with the association with obesity has been analyzed in observational studies. Some suggest a lower prevalence of overweight and obesity in children who were fed breast milk compared with infant formula, however, optimal duration of breastfeeding to provide substantial benefits remains unknown [14].

2.1.3. Molecular Techniques and Their Contribution to Understanding Programming

Even when the precise mechanisms of early programming of such diseases later in life has not yet been fully understood, molecular studies can offer the opportunity to dive in depth. The molecular era allowed for the capacity to perform rapid nucleic acid sequencing and microarray studies, as well as other molecular techniques and has provided the potential for far more understanding of developmental origins of health and disease (DOHaD) [9].

There is now a growing literature concerning the role of epigenetics in DOHaD, the majority of which has been carried out in experimental models, particularly in rodents. The degree of adiposity in adult life has been correlated with changes in methylation of DNA at birth or early in life, suggesting that epigenetic markers might be sought as a predictor [15].

The microbiome and its contribution to health and disease have recently been of interest to the scientific community. It has been suggested that the microbiome influences postnatal programming and obesity. Increasingly, the concept that it may play a role in DOHaD seems appealing [16].

2.2. Diet as a Risk Factor for Obesity and Cardiovascular Complications

There is no doubt that a high intake of *sugar* causes weight gain, and therefore is associated with the development of obesity, insulin resistance, and dyslipidemia. All of them are the most important risk factors for the development of HTN and CV disorders. The analysis of the data from the National Health and Nutrition Examination Surveys (NHANES) 1988–1994, 1999–2004, and 2005–2010 (n = 31,147) revealed a significant direct relationship between added sugar consumption and increased risk for CV morbidity and mortality in adults [17]. Most of the added sugar are glucose, fructose, and sucrose (in the intestine sucrose is broken down into glucose and fructose, which are absorbed as such). Glucose excess is directly associated with hyperinsulinemia, while fructose excess increases uric acid levels and very-low-density lipoprotein (VLDL) levels leading to hyperuricemia and liver steatosis [18]. Moreover, it has been shown, that simultaneous consumption of sugar and salt by obese patients is a greater risk factor for developing high blood pressure than consuming each of them separately [19].

'Salt', properly sodium chloride (NaCl) is the main form of sodium intake. It is added to most of the processed food. Additionally, the source of sodium may be different food additives, such as sodium bicarbonate or sodium nitrate added to bread and meat products respectively [20]. The relationship between salt consumption and arterial HTN has been known since the beginning of the 20th century [21]. According to the traditional model, the relationship between sodium excess and the development of HTN in obese individuals is based on the increase of extracellular fluid volume and higher blood flow in the kidney [22]. High glomerular filtration rate and renal blood flow increase renal sodium reabsorption. Glomerular hyperfiltration and neurohumoral activation, within activation of the sympathetic nervous system, lead to the development of severe HTN, subsequent glomerular injury, and impaired renal sodium excretion capacity, resulting in the gradual loss of nephron function [22]. According to that classical theory of 'salt sensitive' arterial HTN development, massive salt restriction should be of universal benefit. On this basis, recommendations were made for general salt reduction [23]. More recent studies, however, show that dietary salt restriction only has a beneficial effect in certain groups, including patients with obesity and/or with HTN [24,25]. Moreover, not only sodium dose, but its ratio to potassium intake might be important. High Na^+/K^+ ratio intake is considered to be a stronger risk factor of HTN and cardiovascular disease than each of these nutrients alone [26]. Contrary, the Na^+/K^+ ratio positively affects the physiological rise of BP in childhood, resulting in smaller BP slopes [26]. Potassium increases urinary sodium excretion which diminishes total sodium content. In addition, potassium is thought to induce vascular smooth muscle relaxation and thus decrease peripheral resistance [27]. Therefore, the so-called DASH (Dietary Approaches to Stop Hypertension) diet, rich in fruits and vegetables, low-fat dairy products, and low saturated and total fat, is an effective tool in the treatment of HTN. It helps not only to reduce sodium load, but also to increase potassium intake.

Uric acid is the final product of purine metabolism in humans, and its production is largely dependent on the activity of xanthine-oxidoreductase (XOR) that is responsible for the final steps of the conversion of xantine to uric acid [28]. The serum levels of uric acid are also influenced by the renal excretion rate of urate that is controlled by renal tubular transport systems (mainly URAT-1 and GLUT-9) that are more directly involved in the global handling of uric acid metabolism [29]. The activation of XOR is leading to an increase in the production of pro-oxidative compounds that have been reported to be involved in the development of HTN, insulin resistance, MetS, diabetes as well as CV and renal disease [30,31]. In children, the increase in serum urate levels has been proven to be responsible for a significant increase in body weight and BP values that can contribute to cardiometabolic abnormalities early in life [32]. In particular, a close correlation has been reported between the fructose intake (a well-known precursor of uric acid) and the increase in body mass index (BMI) in US children and adolescents with a negative impact on the natural history of HTN and MetS [33]. According to the evidence provided by the Bogalusa Heart study [34] the increase in uric acid can antedate and predict the increase in body weight and BP values in childhood suggesting a primary pathogenetic role for elevated uric acid and/or for the mechanisms involved in its production (e.g., XOR activity). This has been recently confirmed by some interesting studies based on the analysis of temporal trajectories of serum urate and showing and increase in cardiac and metabolic disorders in those subjects bearing serum urate levels persistently elevated or progressively increase while the opposite was observed in subjects with serum urate levels persistently normal or undergoing a progressive reduction [35]. Thus, an increase in serum urate levels in children and adolescents may contribute to promote overweight and CV risk factors with a negative prognostic implication on the risk of cardiometabolic disease later in life.

2.3. Nutrigenomics and Nutri-Epigenetics

The nutrigenomics-impact of dietary components starts early in life and can influence health and disease across life. Dietary components are used to produce metabolites that can impact gene expression directly or through epigenetic mechanisms. Functional groups (i.e., methyl-, acetyl-, phosphate-group, etc.) able to modulate gene expression without any changes in DNA sequence, can be synthesized by dietary components [36]. Folate, vitamins (B12, B2, B6) betaine and choline are necessary to synthesize S-adenosine methionine (SAM), the universal methyl group donor, by one carbon cycle. The availability of methyl groups depends on a folate-rich diet (i.e., green leaves, peas, beans, lentils, liver, etc.) and on folic acid supplementation during pregnancy. B12 is present only in animal food (i.e., eggs, meat, fish), so vegans need oral sublingual treatment (to avoid its hydrolysis by the liver). Reduced level of substrates required for one carbon cycle during pregnancy, has been associated to impaired DNA methylation at promoter level of genes that regulate growth and metabolic diseases (i.e., IL10, LEP, ABCA1, GNASAS and MEG3) in siblings [37]. Differences in DNA promoter methylation (i.e., INSIGF, LEP and GNASAS) were measured also according to sibling gender and gestational timing of the malnutrition, and were associated with increased risk in developing obesity in men and glucose intolerance in women later in life. DNA methylation has a key role in the cell differentiation and the methylation of carbon 5 at the cytosine of CpG island of promoter region is associated to gene silencing [38]. Furthermore, an epigenetic memory of multiple environmental conditions (i.e., diet, air pollution, noise pollution, life style, work, family, education, physical activities, etc.) acquired during early life, remains longer and it can influence adult phenotype as well as be epigenetically inherited from generation to generation [39].

High fat diet, low or high protein intake can address epigenetic responses associated to metabolic diseases (i.e., cardiovascular diseases (CVD), T2DM, obesity, HTN, etc.) in adulthood [40]. The nutrigenomic impact of dietary lipids has been extensively studied [41]. Longitudinal analysis shows that chronic uses of high dietary saturated fatty acids (SFAs) or/and sugars increase the risk to develop CVD [42]. Exposure to palmitic acid, a SFA contained in several types of food (i.e., meat, eggs, butter, palm and coconut oils etc.,) is able to activate inflammatory responses by inflammasome activation (i.e., NLRP3, IL-1β, IL-18), while this effect was not observed after monounsaturated fatty acid exposure with oleic acid [43]. Overall, the consumption of ultra-processed food, rich in fats and sugars, low in fiber and antioxidant/anti-inflammatory bioactive compounds, was associated with a rise of caloric intake (about 500 Kcal/day) [44] and with an increase of risk of CVD and all-causes mortality [45]. These findings should serve as an incentive for limiting consumption of ultra-processed food, and encouraging natural or minimally processed foods, as several national policies recommend.

Furthermore, nutrigenomic impact of high protein intake has been investigated; high protein intake (more than the recommended daily intake (RDI) of 0.8 g/Kg per day) increases the risk of prediabetes and T2DM [46]. In addition, the source of proteins is important; Mediterranean, vegan or whole-food plant-based diets significantly increase high-density lipoprotein cholesterol (HDL-C) and may reduce incidence and mortality of CVD. Adherence to the Mediterranean diet has been associated with a metabolic signature useful to predict CVD risk [47], and new epigenetic biomarkers have been identified to predict the risk and the severity of CVD [48].

Additionally, not only strict vegetarian diets, but also a less strict plant-based diets with limited animal products have been associated with low systolic and diastolic BP [49]. A large prospective cohort study has demonstrated that the replacement of animal protein with plant protein (3% of the energy) decreases the CVD mortality (risk reduction 11% in men and 12% in women) [50]. The positive effect of plant-based food is associated to the nutrigenomic activity (i.e., antioxidant, anti-inflammatory, etc.) of polyphenols contained in plants, the positive impact of fiber on gut microbiota richness and diversity, the folic acid and the essential fatty acid content [51].

In summary, nutrigenomics and nutri-epigenetics outcomes have demonstrated how and when animal and plant-based food contribute to influence molecular responses (with beneficial or detrimental effects), supporting the positive role of high adherence to the Mediterranean and/or plant-based diet to reduce the risk to develop CVD. Strategies for prevention should take into account also the inheritance of epigenetic biomarkers across generations.

2.4. *Dyslipidemia, Insulin Resistance, Hypertension and Cluster of CV Risk Factors*

Dyslipidemias are disorders of lipoprotein metabolism that can result in the following abnormalities: high total cholesterol (TC), high low-density lipoprotein cholesterol (LDL-C), high non-high-density lipoprotein cholesterol (non-HDL-C), high triglycerides (TGs), and low HDL-C [52]. Lipid levels vary by age and sex and reference lipid and lipoprotein values have been derived from the population-based Lipid Research Clinical Prevalence Study, which obtained between 1972 and 1976 fasting lipoprotein profiles in more than 15,000 children and adolescents (age range 0 to 19 years), and from the United States National Health and Nutrition Examination Surveys (NHANES), which analyzed lipid levels in 7000 children between 1988 and 1994 [53–56]. In most patients with hyperlipidemia this condition is caused by some underlying "non-lipid" etiology rather than by a primary disorder of lipoprotein metabolism. Among the CV risk factors, lipids and lipoproteins are of special importance and in many studies, childhood obesity has been shown to be associated which increased levels of TC, LDL-C and TGs and decreased level of HDL-C [57,58]. CVD is the number one cause of death in the United States and 38% of adults affected by CVD have risk factors such as elevated serum lipid levels, diabetes, and high blood pressure. Many studies have confirmed an additional role of body fat distribution and in particular of excess visceral fat even in the adolescent age group [59,60].

Atherosclerosis can start at young age, and the number of young individuals developing atherosclerosis is on the rise, especially in children with risk factors such as familial hypercholesterolemia (FH), type 1 diabetes mellitus, chronic kidney disease and HTN. Furthermore, many studies have identified dyslipidemia as a risk for premature atherosclerosis, even in children and adolescents. In the Bogalusa Heart Study, autopsy studies performed in 204 young subjects demonstrated fatty streaks in 50 percent of cases between 2 and 15 years of age and in 85 percent of older subjects between 21 and 39 years of age [61]. The prevalence of raised fibrous plaques in the aorta and coronary arteries also increased with age from approximately 20 percent in subjects between 2 and 15 years of age to 70 percent in those between 26 and 39 years of age. The prevalence and the extent of atherosclerosis found in the aorta and coronary arteries were greater with increasing BMI, BP, and levels of serum TC and LDL-C. The degree of atherosclerotic changes increased with worsening severity and greater numbers of risk factors [62].

Similarly, the Pathobiological Determinants of Atherosclerosis in Youth (PDAY) study [63] reported raised fatty streaks in 10 percent of coronary arteries and 30 percent of aortas in subjects aged 15 to 19. The extent of fatty streaks increased with increasing age, elevated BP, higher serum LDL-C, and lower serum HDL-C. Female patients lagged by five years behind male patients in the progression of the extent of raised lesions in the right coronary arteries. In a subsequent report, individuals with early and more severe atherosclerotic changes were more likely to have had one or more CVD risk factor (including dyslipidemia, obesity, hyperglycemia, HTN, or smoking) [64].

Several longitudinal studies reported tracking of adverse lipid levels from childhood to adulthood. In a cohort of 725 adults (age range 33 to 42 years) in the Muscatine Study, childhood TC levels positively predicted adult carotid intima-media thickness (cIMT). In women, childhood BMI was also a significant predictor of cIMT [65,66]. In the Cardiovascular Risk in Young Finns study, elevated childhood levels of LDL-C and insulin, as well as obesity, were predictive of increased cIMT (observation period 27 years). In subsequent studies, carotid artery elasticity decreased as the number of childhood CVD risk factors increased and flow-mediated dilation was lower in male patients who had elevated BP during adolescence. In this cohort, exposure to CVD risk factors over time correlated with the extent of coronary artery calcification by computed tomography [67]. Similarly, in a cohort of patients involved in the CARDIA study, initially recruited at age 18 to 30 years and followed for 15 years, baseline CVD risk factors (smoking and higher LDL-C, glucose, and systolic blood pressure levels) were associated with increased risk of coronary artery calcium later in life [68]. The International Childhood Cardiovascular Cohort Consortium has performed a meta-analysis that combined data from the four prospective studies mentioned above. In this analysis, the number of childhood CVD risk factors (e.g., increased cholesterol, TGs, BP, and BMI), even in children as young as nine years of age, was predictive of elevated adult cIMT with progressive strengthening of the association through adolescence [69]. Further studies have shown that dyslipidemia in adolescence predicts increased adult cIMT, even after accounting for sex, obesity, and HTN. Screening of lipid levels in children may reveal both genetic lipid abnormalities (e.g., including familial hypercholesterolemia, which affects 1 in 250 people), and dyslipidemia, which responds favorably to lifestyle changes [70]. Even a small weight loss is associated with a significant decrease in the concentration of TG and an increase in the concentration of HDL-C. In addition to the recommended diet, physical activity (PA) is strongly recommended. According to the National Heart, Lung and Blood Institute (NHLBI) recommendations, in patients in whom non-pharmacological management has no effect, the use of lipid-lowering drugs should be considered [71].

The relationship between obesity and its complications, in particular insulin resistance, and arterial hypertension was first noticed in the 1950s [72]. Many studies over the years have confirmed that excess of fat tissue regardless of age and gender is associated with an increase of blood pressure [73–75]. Among children with obesity, the prevalence of arterial HTN is up to 30%, in contrast to less than 3 (5) % in the normal weight pediatric population [76–79] and weight gain is accounted for up to 75% of the risk for primary HTN [80].

The pathogenesis of HTN in obese individuals is complex and still not fully understood. Currently, it is believed that the abnormally increased activity of adipose tissue in the production of hormones and adipokines is of key importance. Pro-inflammatory substances as tumor necrosis factor-α, interleukin-6, C-reactive protein may lead to macrophage recruitment, which could increase pathological lipolysis. Subsequently excess lipid delivery could promote ectopic lipid accumulation leading to the associated impairments in insulin signaling, mainly in the liver and skeletal muscles, that in turn may also contribute to development of insulin resistance [81]. Insulin resistance and hyperinsulinemia are independent activators of the sympathetic nervous system. Other factors with a documented independent role in activating sympathetic nervous system in obese individuals are: leptin excess and intermittent hypoxia caused by sleep-disordered breathing [82–84]. The enhanced activity of sympathetic nervous system causes vasoconstriction and reduced renal blood flow, which is a trigger for renin release, and subsequent activation of the renin–angiotensin–aldosterone system (RAAS) results in sodium and water retention [82]. Additionally, it causes β2-adrenergic receptors dependent activation of the NaCl-cotransporter in the distal tubule, that is considered to be one of the most important mechanisms for the development of salt-sensitive HTN [85]. Although the activation of the RAAS has been well documented in adults and in experimental models, data regarding the role of this mechanism in the development of HTN are contradictory [86]. Interestingly, not only does the classic way of activating the RAAS play an important role in the development of obesity-related arterial HTN, but also plasma aldosterone concentration seems to be positively correlated with the amount of visceral adipose tissue, independent of plasma renin activity [87,88]. Contrary to lean hypertensive subjects, patients with obesity show a positive paradoxical correlation between sodium intake and aldosterone levels. It has been suggested, that some adipokines, as yet unidentified, may directly stimulate aldosterone release from adrenals in angiotensin II-independent manner [87,88]. It has also been proven that adipose tissue can produce angiotensinogen, angiotensin, and angiotensin II itself, stimulating aldosterone secretion by adipocytes in a paracrine/autocrine way independently from the inhibitory effect of high salt consumption [88,89]. Moreover, the results of genetic studies of humans suggest the association of obesity-related HTN with the variants of several genes involved in aldosterone secretion and metabolism, such as glucocorticoid receptor, aldosterone synthase (CYP11B2), and serum and glucocorticoid-regulated kinase 1 [90–92]. Variants of the latter are described to be associated with predisposition to HTN, hyperinsulinism and high salt intake [92]. An additional element may be the excessive stimulation of renin production in vitamin D deficiency, a condition often found in obese people [93,94]. Finally, cortisol production by adipose tissue may stimulate renin production exerting aldosterone-like effects through its mineralocorticoid activity and, moreover, may increase insulin resistance [95]. Undoubtedly, aldosterone is not only a hormone that regulates electrolytes and fluid volume, but can be an important mediator of obesity development independently of calorie intake and target-organ damage. Excess of aldosterone contributes to insulin resistance, and leptin resistance [96]. In the kidney, aldosterone causes podocyte injury, which leads to proteinuria and glomerulosclerosis, and proinflammatory responses, mediating perivascular and interstitial fibrosis [97,98].

Hyperinsulinemia has a similar effect leading to direct kidney damage by impairment in insulin metabolic signaling resulting in reduced NO production, associated impairment of tubuloglomerular feedback, and subsequently hyperfiltration and sodium retention [99]. Hyperinsulinemia is also directly related to the reduction in uric acid excretion. In a number of clinical trials, such as NHANES I, the Framingham Study and the Bogalusa Heart Study (including the pediatric population), it was shown that serum uric acid concentration is an independent prognostic factor for the development of arterial HTN [34,80,100]. Hyperuricemia causes renal vasculitis by the stimulation of nuclear transcription factors, release of pro-inflammatory cytokines, and pre-glomerular arteriolopathy due to e.g., increasing the proliferation of vascular smooth cells and causing inflammation and tubulointerstitial fibrosis. These changes further activate the RAAS and may additionally favor the adverse effect of urates on the glomerular vessels [82]. Additionally, direct compression of the renal parenchyma by perinephric fat may reduce intrarenal blood flow and increase sodium reabsorption, leading to volume expansion, increase of cardiac output and decrease in blood flow reserve [82]. This phenomenon occurs even in the absence of signs of glomerular sclerosis or chronic kidney disease [82]. While in the early stage of obesity induced HTN, the increased glomerular filtration rate and renal blood flow induce an increase in renal sodium absorption, with prolonged HTN, renal vasodilation, glomerular hyperfiltration, and neurohumoral activation led to further increase of BP, glomerular injury, and an impaired renal capacity for sodium excretion, resulting in the gradual loss of nephron and kidney function. In this way, obese subjects require a higher BP than lean subjects to maintain the sodium balance, indicating impaired renal-pressure natriuresis ('salt-sensitive' HTN) [86]. Also, pro-inflammatory substances formed in adipose tissue play a direct role in endothelial damage and increased vascular stiffness. Since HTN itself is also a factor leading to endothelial pathology a "vicious circle" phenomenon should be taken into account. With respect to the above-mentioned mechanisms of the development of HTN in obese children, it seems obvious that the basis of treatment and prevention of complications should be effective reduction of adipose tissue [101,102]. Limiting salt intake is a crucial element in the treatment of obesity-associated HTN. If pharmacotherapy has to be introduced, first-line drugs are antagonists of the RAAS (angiotensin-converting enzyme inhibitors, angiotensin receptor blockers [101,102], but also mineralocorticoid receptor antagonists may be considered in selected cases [103,104]).

2.5. Obesity or Cardiorespiratory Fitness—What Does Really Matter?

Cardiorespiratory fitness (CRF), also known as cardiorespiratory endurance, cardiovascular fitness, aerobic capacity, or aerobic fitness, refers to the "capacity of the circulatory and respiratory systems to supply oxygen to skeletal muscle mitochondria for energy production during PA" [105,106]. This is only 1 of 4 distinct health-related fitness components (CRF, muscular fitness, flexibility and body composition). Although often confused, PA and CRF are related but distinct concepts. "PA is voluntary movement produced by skeletal muscles that results in energy expenditure" [106], while "Exercise refers to a subset of PA in which the goal is to improve performance, health, or both" [106]. While CRF is having the capacity to perform or not perform a certain type of PA, PA is an action or behavior.

Over the last few years, CRF has acquired special scientific interest in the evaluation of youth´s health because it has been shown that it is a predictor of various indicators such as cardiometabolic health [107,108], premature CVD [109], academic achievement [110], and mental wellness [111]. In a cohort of overweight, obese, and control participants, Redon et al. concluded that CRF was inversely related with fasting insulin and the HOMA index, which is considered as a fingerprint for future metabolic disease [112]. In a systematic review and meta-analysis, low CRF in children and adolescents was notably associated with the development of metabolic syndrome [113].

CRF is able to be measured objectively and it can be tracked over time and compared over different populations [114]. Even though the cardiopulmonary exercise test (CPETs) is considered the gold standard method to evaluate CRF, it is not easily implemented [105]. There are also questionnaires designed for examining CRF in youth, but they are only recommended for epidemiological studies and not for estimating CRF in individuals [115]. As a result, outdoor or field procedures have been conveniently developed, among them, the 20m shuttle run test and the Cooper test [116,117] which are the most common. Additionally, there are some suitable tests for use in office settings such as the 6-Minute Walk Test and the Step Test. The Step Test could be an alternative to CPETs in order to estimate office-CRF, because it is easy to administer in limited indoor spaces and requires minimal equipment and training to be implemented [118].

CRF in youth is affected by non-modifiable factors as genetics, age, sex, race/ethnicity and prematurity and by modifiable factors as habitual PA and training, sedentary time, diet, social-economic-environmental factors and obesity. Many obese children and adolescents meet these modifiable factors, and it is shown that youth with obesity have lower CRF than their normal-weight peers [119]. Nevertheless, there is evidence that improvement in CRF in obese children and adolescents increases CV health, even among those who do not improve their body composition [120]. Moreover, overweight children and adolescents with a high fitness level (fat-but-fit subjects) have a healthier CV profile than their overweight, low fit peers and a similar profile to their normal-weight low-fit peers [121]. This suggests that high fitness levels may compensate the negative consequences attributed to body fat.

Unfortunately, in a large epidemiological study conducted in the USA, it was found that just 1 in 5 obese youth has healthy CRF [122]. Therefore, physical exercise programs aimed at improving CRF in this group of patients can be of enormous health interest. Among these programs, those that include high-intensity interval training have demonstrated an increased impact on youth's CRF [123,124].

Considering the high prognostic power of CRF, the American Heart Association proposes to measure it as a vital sign, as is done with the assessment of other risk factors such as BP, tobacco use, alcohol consumption, blood glucose or blood lipid levels [125]. Another factor to be aware of is that overweight/obese youths may have some limitations in performing moderate and vigorous PA. In this context, personalized interventions should be designed according to the subject's objective and up-to-date scientific knowledge. Therefore, the measurement of CRF in obese children and adolescents is not only of prognostic importance, but also allows for the personalization of the treatment according to the physical condition of each individual.

2.6. The Role of Tracking in Increased CV Risk in Adulthood

There is a strong correlation between childhood and adult obesity, and a large number of obese children transfer their adiposity into adulthood. Obese children and adolescents are five times more likely to become obese adults. About 55% of obese children continue being obese in adolescence, around 80% of obese adolescents will continue being obese in adulthood, particularly those suffering from severe obesity. About 70% of them will continue being obese over the age of 30 [126–128]. Age of the child, severity of obesity, and presence of parental obesity affect the tracking of obesity into adulthood. Most adolescents with obesity will continue being obese in adulthood, as persistence of obesity transfer into adulthood is associated with older age. In children under the age of 10, the risk of being obese is doubled if they have obese parents [129].

On the other hand, childhood and adolescent BMI is not a good predictor of adult obesity incidence. Only 20% of adults with obesity were obese as children or adolescents, and over 80% of obese people over the age of 30 were not obese as adolescents. Therefore, BMI has poor sensitivity to predict adult obesity [127]. Childhood obesity is not the only and primary factor that contributes to adult obesity. Adult obesity carries an increased risk of CVD. The link between obesity and CVD is explained by the CVD risk-factor profile that is often observed in obese adults. The profile includes increased rates of dyslipidemia, HTN, as well as T2D. Childhood obesity is a CVD risk-factor, and may lead to early atherosclerosis and premature CVD in adulthood. Even though CVD rarely manifests itself until adulthood, CVD risk factors have been observed in childhood [130]. HTN, dyslipidemia, impaired glucose metabolism, as well as systemic inflammation, have all been associated with vascular changes in childhood. If not adequately treated, they may contribute to an increased risk of adverse CV events in adulthood [131]. Nevertheless, it is important to determine what kind of independent effects childhood obesity has on CVD in adulthood. Many studies and meta-analyses have been conducted, all pointing to obese children being at higher risk for obesity as adults [132,133]. However, a large number of studies did not considered the effect of adulthood-incurred obesity, so it is impossible to form a precise conclusion of the relationship between childhood obesity and CV events in adulthood [134]. Studies that took into consideration the effect of obesity incurred in adulthood on CV events pointed to the fact that the effect of childhood obesity, as an independent factor, might not be great [135]. Those studies showing an association of obesity in childhood with CVD in adulthood, identified weight as a significant independent determinant [65].

However, there are other factors in favor of an association of early obesity with increased CVD risk:

Atherogenesis, a process leading to the development of atherosclerosis begins at an early stage of life [136]. Obesity in childhood accelerates this process and causes changes in blood vessels, especially in adolescence. The earliest sign of atherosclerosis is the appearance of fatty streaks, and atherosclerotic wall lesions are in direct connection to childhood obesity [136–138].

Clustering of CVD risk factors has been highly associated with obesity in childhood, including increased systolic blood pressure, elevated LDL-C, elevated TGs and reduced HDL-C [138,139].

Obesity with multiple CVD risk factors during adolescence is associated with an almost 15-fold increased risk of developing CVD before the age of 50 [140].

In an extensive study conducted on 276,000 children, Baker et al. note that an increased BMI in childhood correlates with the appearance of CVD in adults, and at the same time isn't related to an increased BMI in adults [141].

BMI in late adolescence is directly related to atherosclerosis in middle age measured by coronary angiography—this relationship persisted even when BMI was adjusted for adults, as well as CVD risk factors [142].

Childhood obesity is a moderate risk-factor for adult obesity-related morbidity. However, the risk increase is not significant enough for childhood BMI to serve as a reliable predictor of the incidence of adult morbidities [132].

It is important to note, that the risks of T2DM, HTN, dyslipidemia, and carotid-artery atherosclerosis among overweight or obese children who became nonobese by adulthood were similar to those among persons who were never obese [143].

Table S1 summarizes the given evidence for tracking of CV risk factors from childhood to adulthood.

2.7. The Economic Impact of Childhood Obesity

A search in Pubmed found 264 articles published between 2001 and 2021 on the economic evaluation of prevention and treatment of childhood obesity and overweight. Out of them, 57 are cost-effectiveness studies of interventions aimed at reducing high BP among children and adolescents, or protocols for planned interventions with no results [144].

Two of the studies evaluated interventions to reduce obesity/overweight [145] and promote PA [146]. BP reduction was in both studies a secondary outcome. The Children's Health Interventional Trial was an 11-month outpatient multidisciplinary family-based program implemented with 248 children with obesity or overweight in Germany [145]. The main focus was reducing weight, but the secondary objectives was the improvement of obesity-related health parameters as BP. The intervention obtained a reduction of systolic blood pressure (SBP) by −1.76 mmHg and diastolic blood pressure (DBP) by −2.82 mmHg. The program was cost-effective: on an aggregated level, future savings amounted to between €1859 and €1926 per person, and the return on investment was between 3.3% and 7.0%.

A school-based intervention study evaluated the effect of reduced salt intake among children and their families in China [147]. The focus was on BP of adults in the household rather than children. The intervention was very effective in lowering SBP in adults (−2.3 mmHg), but also in children, and even more in adults older than 60 years (−9.5 mmHg). It was also cost-effective (around $1358 per QALY [Quality adjusted life years] gained). Another study evaluated the cost-effectiveness of an early nutrition program—supplementing infant formula with long-chain polyunsaturated fatty acids—on health consequences in adulthood, more specifically high BP and the risk of HTN-related diseases in later life. The study results showed that the program is dominant (cost saving); it increases life expectancy by 1.2 QALY, with an incremental cost-effectiveness ratio (discounted to present value) of—€630.

Two of the most relevant studies perform an economic evaluation of screening and BP measuring of children and adolescents. The first one [148] compares costs and effectiveness of BP screening programs for adolescents in the US with population-wide preventive interventions, as reductions in salt intake or increasing physical education. Finding and treating the adolescents at highest risk (e.g., left ventricular hypertrophy) is the most cost-effective screening strategy with cost per QALY of $18,000 for boys and $47,000 for girls. Universal screening of all adolescents is dominated by specific population-wide strategies such as salt reduction (cost-saving [boys] and $650/QALY [girls]) and increasing physical education ($11,000/QALY [boys] and $35,000/QALY [girls]).

The second study [149] is a retrospective one that evaluated the initial use of ambulatory BP pressure monitoring for children with clinic BP measurements suggesting stage 1 HTN. It concludes that it is highly cost-effective (cost-savings in the long term of $2.4 million per 1000 patients).

In summary, the evidence so far has shown that some targeted interventions to prevent obesity and high BP in children and adolescents are potentially highly cost-effective.

2.8. Preventive Strategies for Hypertension in Children

There is limited literature regarding preventive strategies or intervention in children and adolescents with elevated blood pressure focusing on BP as the major end point [101,150]. In most cases, the main risk factor for HTN—increased body mass/fat mass is being targeted [2,101]. Similarly, there is limited evidence on population based primary prevention strategies in healthy children to reduce the future risk of HTN [2].

There are well established risk factors for developing HTN in children and adolescents. The major risk is overweight and obesity, additionally the nutritional scheme (quality and quantity of macronutrients), the amount of PA time (as a marker of CRF), parental-factors, sedentary/screen time and sleep time can independently increase prevalence of abnormal BP [151,152].

According to the Nuffield public health intervention ladder and it's modifications, the interventions can be made on different level of individual or population impact [153]. Prevention strategies can be divided into three main groups: individual/family-based, local-community-based and nationally-based activities. Most of those actions are universal for all non-communicable diseases (NCD's) or NCD's risk factors.

Individual, family and school-based level interventions should be mainly focus on education on pro-health behaviors and building ability and capacity/consciousness to put PA and health-supporting diet as one of priorities. There is limited evidence on this in HTN yet similar activities are effective in increased body mass/fat interventions [154,155]. For example, as presented by Farpour-Lambert et al., even 3 months of regular PA can decrease SBP by 7–12 mmHg and DBP by 2–7 mmHg. Others reported similar or smaller effects of SBP/DBP reduction of 2–8 mmHg during different time of intervention or observation time [155–158].

On local/community level policy makers need to focus on the availability of healthy nutritional options, and the availability and places to perform PA (playing fields, recreational areas, biking lanes, etc.) [159]. Additionally, professional trainers support in different sports availability to children during/after school increases their PA hours during the week [160–162], as well as building availability for healthy food choices at schools by limiting vending machines, and improving quality and availability of healthy food at cafeterias/canteens [163–166].

National preventing strategies should focus on the availability of healthy nutritional choices, e.g., through taxation policies, products formulas modification (ex. reducing sodium) [167–170], education campaigns build and delivered for separate age groups, and supporting local authorities in building healthy environments [171,172].

The effectiveness of single strategies/activities is usually limited or low from the clinical perspective, yet addition of several multi-level activities can importantly influence the burden of CVD in children/youth as well as future costs—both health and economic [101,152,173].

3. Conclusions

Cardiovascular disorders with their origin in childhood obesity have multiple medical, social, and economic consequences that might be incurable at a later stage. Thus, the only effective strategy seems to be prevention.

Preventive strategies should include entire families and start ideally before conception. Families with obese members likely share not only genetic risks but also environmental and lifestyle-related exposures. The increased risk of obesity starts as early as before and during pregnancy. The results of numerous clinical trials indicate the influence of parental health on the development of the fetus and the risk of obesity in childhood and adolescence, while obesity and related metabolic risk factors are tracked to adulthood and increase the cardiovascular risk in the general population. Recent studies proved the role of childhood obesity-connected dyslipidemia, hyperinsulinism, or hypertension on increased CV risk. Some new risk factors like maternal smoking, postnatal growth patterns, the impact of diet components on gene expression or fructose intake on uric acid level, are also important elements. As the role of diet is complex, restriction of consumption of highly processed foods should be promoted and consumption of natural or minimally processed foods should be encouraged. Personalized interventions in improving cardiorespiratory fitness are recommended.

Supplementary Materials: The following are available online at https://www.mdpi.com/article/10.3390/nu13114176/s1, Table S1: Evidence for tracking of CV risk factors from infancy and childhood to adulthood. Exemplary studies, reviews or meta-analyses are given for strength of evidence.

Author Contributions: Conceptualization, D.D., J.A.-P., E.W. and E.L.; writing—original draft preparation, all authors; writing—review and editing, all authors. All authors have read and agreed to the published version of the manuscript.

Funding: This publication is based on the work of the COST Action HyperChildNET (CA19115), with the support of COST (European Cooperation in Science and Technology) and the Horizon 2020 Framework Program of the European Union.

HyperChildNET COST Action

COST EUROPEAN COOPERATION IN SCIENCE & TECHNOLOGY

Funded by the Horizon 2020 Framework Programme of the European Union

Institutional Review Board Statement: Not applicable.

Informed Consent Statement: Not applicable.

Conflicts of Interest: The authors declare no conflict of interest.

References

1. Obesity and Overweight. Available online: https://www.who.int/news-room/fact-sheets/detail/obesity-and-overweight (accessed on 12 October 2021).
2. Falkner, B.; Lurbe, E. Primordial Prevention of High Blood Pressure in Childhood an Opportunity Not to Be Missed. *Hypertension* **2020**, *75*, 1142–1150. [CrossRef] [PubMed]
3. Page, K.A.; Luo, S.; Wang, X.; Chow, T.; Alves, J.; Buchanan, T.A.; Xiang, A.H. Children Exposed to Maternal Obesity or Gestational Diabetes Mellitus during Early Fetal Development Have Hypothalamic Alterations That Predict Future Weight Gain. *Diabetes Care* **2019**, *42*, 1473–1480. [CrossRef] [PubMed]
4. Godfrey, K.M.; Reynolds, R.M.; Prescott, S.L.; Nyirenda, M.; Jaddoe, V.W.V.; Eriksson, J.G.; Broekman, B.F.P. Influence of Maternal Obesity on the Long-Term Health of Offspring. *Lancet Diabetes Endocrinol.* **2017**, *5*, 53–64. [CrossRef]

5. Holland, S.L., Reader, T., Dyer, P.S.; Avery, S.V. Phenotypic heterogeneity is a selected trait in natural yeast populations subject to environmental stress. *Environ. Microbiol.* **2014**, *16*, 1729–1740. [CrossRef]
6. Gingras, V.; Hivert, M.F.; Oken, E. Early-Life Exposures and Risk of Diabetes Mellitus and Obesity. *Curr. Diab. Rep.* **2018**, *18*, 89. [CrossRef] [PubMed]
7. Whitaker, K.L.; Jarvis, M.J.; Beeken, R.J.; Boniface, D.; Wardle, J. Comparing Maternal and Paternal Intergenerational Transmission of Obesity Risk in a Large Population-Based Sample. *Am. J. Clin. Nutr.* **2010**, *91*, 1560–1567. [CrossRef]
8. Oken, E.; Levitan, E.B.; Gillman, M.W. Maternal Smoking during Pregnancy and Child Overweight: Systematic Review and Meta-Analysis. *Int. J. Obes.* **2008**, *32*, 201–210. [CrossRef] [PubMed]
9. Lurbe, E.; Ingelfinger, J. Developmental and Early Life Origins of Cardiometabolic Risk Factors: Novel Findings and Implications. *Hypertension* **2021**, *77*, 308–318. [CrossRef]
10. Chen, M.; Heilbronn, L.K. The Health Outcomes of Human Offspring Conceived by Assisted Reproductive Technologies (ART). *J. Dev. Orig. Health Dis.* **2017**, *8*, 388–402. [CrossRef] [PubMed]
11. Ceelen, M.; Van Weissenbruch, M.M.; Roos, J.C.; Vermeiden, J.P.W.; Van Leeuwen, F.E.; Delemarre-van De Waal, H.A. Body Composition in Children and Adolescents Born after in Vitro Fertilization or Spontaneous Conception. *J. Clin. Endocrinol. Metab.* **2007**, *92*, 3417–3423. [CrossRef]
12. Kelishadi, R.; Haghdoost, A.A.; Jamshidi, F.; Aliramezany, M.; Moosazadeh, M. Low Birthweight or Rapid Catch-up Growth: Which Is More Associated with Cardiovascular Disease and Its Risk Factors in Later Life? A Systematic Review and Cryptanalysis. *Paediatr. Int. Child Health* **2015**, *35*, 110–123. [CrossRef] [PubMed]
13. Zheng, M.; Lamb, K.E.; Grimes, C.; Laws, R.; Bolton, K.; Ong, K.K.; Campbell, K. Rapid Weight Gain during Infancy and Subsequent Adiposity: A Systematic Review and Meta-Analysis of Evidence. *Obes. Rev.* **2018**, *19*, 321–332. [CrossRef] [PubMed]
14. Oken, E.; Fields, D.A.; Lovelady, C.A.; Redman, L.M. TOS Scientific Position Statement: Breastfeeding and Obesity. *Obesity* **2017**, *25*, 1864–1866. [CrossRef] [PubMed]
15. Bianco-Miotto, T.; Craig, J.M.; Gasser, Y.P.; Van Dijk, S.J.; Ozanne, S.E. Epigenetics and DOHaD: From Basics to Birth and Beyond. *J. Dev. Orig. Health Dis.* **2017**, *8*, 513–519. [CrossRef]
16. Stiemsma, L.T.; Michels, K.B. The Role of the Microbiome in the Developmental Origins of Health and Disease. *Pediatrics* **2018**, *141*, e20172437. [CrossRef]
17. Yang, Q.; Zhang, Z.; Gregg, E.W.; Flanders, W.D.; Merritt, R.; Hu, F.B. Added Sugar Intake and Cardiovascular Diseases Mortality among Us Adults. *JAMA Intern. Med.* **2014**, *174*, 516–524. [CrossRef] [PubMed]
18. Genovesi, S.; Giussani, M.; Orlando, A.; Orgiu, F.; Parati, G. Salt and Sugar: Two Enemies of Healthy Blood Pressure in Children. *Nutrients* **2021**, *13*, 697. [CrossRef]
19. Alaagib, N.; Sukkar, M.; Kardash, M. The Effects of Salt and Glucose Intake on Angiotensin II and Aldosterone in Obese and Nonobese Patients with Essential Hypertension. *Int. J. Hypertens.* **2020**, *2020*, 6017105. [CrossRef]
20. Turck, D.; Castenmiller, J.; de Henauw, S.; Hirsch-Ernst, K.; Kearney, J.; Knutsen, H.K.; Maciuk, A.; Mangelsdorf, I.; McArdle, H.J.; Pelaez, C.; et al. Dietary Reference Values for Sodium. *EFSA J.* **2019**, *17*, e05778. [CrossRef]
21. Ambard, L.; Beaujard, E. Causes de l'hypertension Artérielle. *Arch. Gén. Méd.* **1904**, *81*, 520–533.
22. Hall, J.E. The Kidney, Hypertension, and Obesity. *Hypertension* **2003**, *41*, 625–633. [CrossRef] [PubMed]
23. WHO. *Guideline: Sodium Intake for Adults and Children*; WHO: Geneva, Switzerland, 2012.
24. Stolarz-Skrzypek, K.; Staessen, J.A. Reducing Salt Intake for Prevention of Cardiovascular Disease-Times Are Changing. *Adv. Chronic Kidney Dis.* **2015**, *22*, 108–115. [CrossRef]
25. Mente, A.; O'Donnell, M.; Rangarajan, S.; Dagenais, G.; Lear, S.; McQueen, M.; Diaz, R.; Avezum, A.; Lopez-Jaramillo, P.; Lanas, F.; et al. Associations of Urinary Sodium Excretion with Cardiovascular Events in Individuals with and without Hypertension: A Pooled Analysis of Data from Four Studies. *Lancet* **2016**, *388*, 465–475. [CrossRef]
26. Umesawa, M.; Iso, H.; Date, C.; Yamamoto, A.; Toyoshima, H.; Watanabe, Y.; Kikuchi, S.; Koizumi, A.; Kondo, T.; Inaba, Y.; et al. Relations between Dietary Sodium and Potassium Intakes and Mortality from Cardiovascular Disease: The Japan Collaborative Cohort Study for Evaluation of Cancer Risks. *Am. J. Clin. Nutr.* **2008**, *88*, 195–202. [CrossRef]
27. Stein, P.P.; Black, H.R. The Role of Diet in the Genesis and Treatment of Hypertension. *Med. Clin. N. Am.* **1993**, *77*, 831–847. [CrossRef]
28. Bardin, T.; Richette, P. Definition of Hyperuricemia and Gouty Conditions. *Curr. Opin. Rheumatol.* **2014**, *26*, 186–191. [CrossRef]
29. Reginato, A.M.; Mount, D.B.; Yang, I.; Choi, H.K. The Genetics of Hyperuricaemia and Gout. *Nat. Rev. Rheumatol.* **2012**, *8*, 610–621. [CrossRef]
30. Ndrepepa, G. Uric Acid and Cardiovascular Disease. *Clin. Chim. Acta* **2018**, *484*, 150–163. [CrossRef]
31. Borghi, C.; Agabiti-Rosei, E.; Johnson, R.J.; Kielstein, J.T.; Lurbe, E.; Mancia, G.; Redon, J.; Stack, A.G.; Tsioufis, K.P. Hyperuricaemia and Gout in Cardiovascular, Metabolic and Kidney Disease. *Eur. J. Intern. Med.* **2020**, *80*, 1–11. [CrossRef]
32. Lurbe, E.; Torro, M.I.; Alvarez-Pitti, J.; Redon, J.; Borghi, C.; Redon, P. Uric Acid Is Linked to Cardiometabolic Risk Factors in Overweight and Obese Youths. *J. Hypertens.* **2018**, *36*, 1840–1846. [CrossRef]
33. Caliceti, C.; Calabria, D.; Roda, A.; Cicero, A.F.G. Fructose Intake, Serum Uric Acid, and Cardiometabolic Disorders: A Critical Review. *Nutrients* **2017**, *9*, 395. [CrossRef]
34. Alper, A.B.; Chen, W.; Yau, L.; Srinivasan, S.R.; Berenson, G.S.; Hamm, L.L. Childhood Uric Acid Predicts Adult Blood Pressure: The Bogalusa Heart Study. *Hypertension* **2005**, *45*, 34–38. [CrossRef] [PubMed]

35. Borghi, C.; Piani, F. Uric Acid and Risk of Cardiovascular Disease. A Question of Start and Finish. *Hypertension* **2021**, *78*, 1219–1221. [CrossRef]
36. Khot, V.; Chavan-Gautam, P.; Joshi, S. Proposing Interactions between Maternal Phospholipids and the One Carbon Cycle: A Novel Mechanism Influencing the Risk for Cardiovascular Diseases in the Offspring in Later Life. *Life Sci.* **2015**, *129*, 16–21. [CrossRef] [PubMed]
37. Tobi, E.W.; Lumey, L.H.; Talens, R.P.; Kremer, D.; Putter, H.; Stein, A.D.; Slagboom, P.E.; Heijmans, B.T. DNA Methylation Differences after Exposure to Prenatal Famine Are Common and Timing- and Sex-Specific. *Hum. Mol. Genet.* **2009**, *18*, 4046–4053. [CrossRef] [PubMed]
38. Bordoni, L.; Gabbianelli, R. Primers on Nutrigenetics and Nutri(Epi)Genomics: Origins and Development of Precision Nutrition. *Biochimie* **2019**, *160*, 156–171. [CrossRef]
39. Bordoni, L.; Nasuti, C.; Mirto, M.; Caradonna, F.; Gabbianelli, R. Intergenerational Effect of Early Life Exposure to Permethrin: Changes in Global DNA Methylation and in Nurr1 Gene Expression. *Toxics* **2015**, *3*, 451–461. [CrossRef] [PubMed]
40. Barabási, A.L.; Menichetti, G.; Loscalzo, J. The Unmapped Chemical Complexity of Our Diet. *Nat. Food* **2020**, *1*, 33–37. [CrossRef]
41. Bordoni, L.; Petracci, I.; Zhao, F.; Min, W.; Pierella, E.; Assmann, T.S.; Martinez, J.A.; Gabbianelli, R. Nutrigenomics of Dietary Lipids. *Antioxidants* **2021**, *10*, 994. [CrossRef]
42. Lottenberg, A.M.; da S. Afonso, M.; Lavrador, M.S.F.; Machado, R.M.; Nakandakare, E.R. The Role of Dietary Fatty Acids in the Pathology of Metabolic Syndrome. *J. Nutr. Biochem.* **2012**, *23*, 1027–1040. [CrossRef]
43. Finucane, O.M.; Lyons, C.L.; Murphy, A.M.; Reynolds, C.M.; Klinger, R.; Healy, N.P.; Cooke, A.A.; Coll, R.C.; Mcallan, L.; Nilaweera, K.N.; et al. Monounsaturated Fatty Acid-Enriched High-Fat Diets Impede Adipose NLRP3 Inflammasome-Mediated IL-1β Secretion and Insulin Resistance despite Obesity. *Diabetes* **2015**, *64*, 2116–2128. [CrossRef]
44. Hall, K.D.; Ayuketah, A.; Brychta, R.; Cai, H.; Cassimatis, T.; Chen, K.Y.; Chung, S.T.; Costa, E.; Courville, A.; Darcey, V.; et al. Ultra-Processed Diets Cause Excess Calorie Intake and Weight Gain: An Inpatient Randomized Controlled Trial of Ad Libitum Food Intake. *Cell Metab.* **2019**, *30*, 67–77.e3. [CrossRef] [PubMed]
45. Bonaccio, M.; Di Castelnuovo, A.; Costanzo, S.; De Curtis, A.; Persichillo, M.; Sofi, F.; Cerletti, C.; Donati, M.B.; de Gaetano, G.; Iacoviello, L. Ultra-Processed Food Consumption Is Associated with Increased Risk of All-Cause and Cardiovascular Mortality in the Moli-Sani Study. *Am. J. Clin. Nutr.* **2021**, *113*, 446–455. [CrossRef]
46. Mittendorfer, B.; Klein, S.; Fontana, L. A Word of Caution against Excessive Protein Intake. *Nat. Rev. Endocrinol.* **2020**, *16*, 59–66. [CrossRef] [PubMed]
47. Li, J.; Guasch-Ferré, M.; Chung, W.; Ruiz-Canela, M.; Toledo, E.; Corella, D.; Bhupathiraju, S.N.; Tobias, D.K.; Tabung, F.K.; Hu, J.; et al. The Mediterranean Diet, Plasma Metabolome, and Cardiovascular Disease Risk. *Eur. Heart J.* **2020**, *41*, 2645–2656. [CrossRef]
48. Bordoni, L.; Petracci, I.; Pelikant-Malecka, I.; Radulska, A.; Piangerelli, M.; Samulak, J.J.; Lewicki, L.; Kalinowski, L.; Gabbianelli, R.; Olek, R.A. Mitochondrial DNA Copy Number and Trimethylamine Levels in the Blood: New Insights on Cardiovascular Disease Biomarkers. *FASEB J.* **2021**, *35*, e21694. [CrossRef]
49. Gibbs, J.; Gaskin, E.; Ji, C.; Miller, M.A.; Cappuccio, F.P. The Effect of Plant-Based Dietary Patterns on Blood Pressure: A Systematic Review and Meta-Analysis of Controlled Intervention Trials. *J. Hypertens.* **2021**, *39*, 23–37. [CrossRef]
50. Huang, J.; Liao, L.M.; Weinstein, S.J.; Sinha, R.; Graubard, B.I.; Albanes, D. Association Between Plant and Animal Protein Intake and Overall and Cause-Specific Mortality. *JAMA Intern. Med.* **2020**, *180*, 1173. [CrossRef] [PubMed]
51. Tang, G.-Y.; Meng, X.; Li, Y.; Zhao, C.-N.; Liu, Q.; Li, H.-B. Effects of Vegetables on Cardiovascular Diseases and Related Mechanisms. *Nutrients* **2017**, *9*, 857. [CrossRef]
52. De Jesus, J.M. Expert Panel on Integrated Guidelines for Cardiovascular Health and Risk Reduction in Children and Adolescents: Summary Report. *Pediatrics* **2011**, *128*, S213.
53. Jolliffe, C.J.; Janssen, I. Distribution of Lipoproteins by Age and Gender in Adolescents. *Circulation* **2006**, *114*, 1056–1062. [CrossRef]
54. Dai, S.; Yang, Q.; Yuan, K.; Loustalot, F.; Fang, J.; Daniels, S.R.; Hong, Y. Non-High-Density Lipoprotein Cholesterol: Distribution and Prevalence of High Serum Levels in Children and Adolescents: United States National Health and Nutrition Examination Surveys, 2005–2010. *J. Pediatr.* **2014**, *164*, 247–253. [CrossRef]
55. Kit, B.K.; Carroll, M.D.; Lacher, D.A.; Sorlie, P.D.; DeJesus, J.M.; Ogden, C.L. Trends in Serum Lipids among US Youths Aged 6 to 19 Years, 1988–2010. *JAMA J. Am. Med. Assoc.* **2012**, *308*, 591–600. [CrossRef]
56. Perak, A.M.; Ning, H.; Kit, B.K.; De Ferranti, S.D.; Van Horn, L.V.; Wilkins, J.T.; Lloyd-Jones, D.M. Trends in Levels of Lipids and Apolipoprotein B in US Youths Aged 6 to 19 Years, 1999–2016. *JAMA J. Am. Med. Assoc.* **2019**, *321*, 1895–1905. [CrossRef] [PubMed]
57. Stewart, J.; McCallin, T.; Martinez, J.; Chacko, S.; Yusuf, S. Hyperlipidemia. *Pediatr. Rev.* **2020**, *41*, 393–402. [CrossRef] [PubMed]
58. Khan, L. Overview of Dyslipidemia in Childhood and Adolescence: Why Does It Matter and What Do We Do about It? *Pediatr. Ann.* **2021**, *50*, e4–e9. [CrossRef] [PubMed]
59. Caprio, S.; Hyman, L.D.; McCarthy, S.; Lange, R.; Bronson, M.; Tamborlane, W.V. Fat Distribution and Cardiovascular Risk Factors in Obese Adolescent Girls: Importance of the Intraabdominal Fat Depot. *Am. J. Clin. Nutr.* **1996**, *64*, 12–17. [CrossRef]
60. Caprio, S.; Perry, R.; Kursawe, R. Adolescent Obesity and Insulin Resistance: Roles of Ectopic Fat Accumulation and Adipose Inflammation. *Gastroenterology* **2017**, *152*, 1638–1646. [CrossRef]

61. Berenson, G.S.; Srinivasan, S.R.; Bao, W.; Newman, W.P.; Tracy, R.E.; Wattigney, W.A. Association between Multiple Cardiovascular Risk Factors and Atherosclerosis in Children and Young Adults. *N. Engl. J. Med.* **1998**, *338*, 1650–1656. [CrossRef]
62. Webber, B.J.; Seguin, P.G.; Burnett, D.G.; Clark, L.L.; Otto, J.L. Prevalence of and Risk Factors for Autopsy-Determined Atherosclerosis among US Service Members, 2001–2011. *JAMA J. Am. Med. Assoc.* **2012**, *308*, 2577–2583. [CrossRef]
63. McGill, H.C.; McMahan, C.A.; Zieske, A.W.; Sloop, G.D.; Walcott, J.V.; Troxclair, D.A.; Malcom, G.T.; Tracy, R.E.; Oalmann, M.C.; Strong, J.P.; et al. Associations of Coronary Heart Disease Risk Factors With the Intermediate Lesion of Atherosclerosis in Youth. *Arterioscler. Thromb. Vasc. Biol.* **2000**, *20*, 1998–2004. [CrossRef] [PubMed]
64. McMahan, C.A.; Gidding, S.S.; Malcom, G.T.; Schreiner, P.J.; Strong, J.P.; Tracy, R.E.; Williams, O.D.; McGill, H.C.; Pathobiological Determinants of Atherosclerosis in Youth (PDAY) Research Group. Comparison of Coronary Heart Disease Risk Factors in Autopsied Young Adults from the PDAY Study with Living Young Adults from the CARDIA Study. *Cardiovasc. Pathol.* **2007**, *16*, 151–158. [CrossRef]
65. Mahoney, L.T.; Burns, T.L.; Stanford, W.; Thompson, B.H.; Witt, J.D.; Rost, C.A.; Lauer, R.M. Coronary Risk Factors Measured in Childhood and Young Adult Life Are Associated with Coronary Artery Calcification in Young Adults: The Muscatine Study. *J. Am. Coll. Cardiol.* **1996**, *27*, 277–284. [CrossRef]
66. Davis, P.H.; Dawson, J.D.; Riley, W.A.; Lauer, R.M. Carotid Intimal-Medial Thickness Is Related to Cardiovascular Risk Factors Measured from Childhood through Middle Age the Muscatine Study. *Circulation* **2001**, *104*, 2815–2819. [CrossRef]
67. Koskinen, J.S.; Kytö, V.; Juonala, M.; Viikari, J.S.A.; Nevalainen, J.; Kähönen, M.; Lehtimäki, T.; Hutri-Kähönen, N.; Laitinen, T.; Tossavainen, P.; et al. Childhood Risk Factors and Carotid Atherosclerotic Plaque in Adulthood: The Cardiovascular Risk in Young Finns Study. *Atherosclerosis* **2020**, *293*, 18–25. [CrossRef] [PubMed]
68. Pletcher, M.J.; Bibbins-Domingo, K.; Liu, K.; Sidney, S.; Lin, F.; Vittinghoff, E.; Hulley, S.B. Nonoptimal Lipids Commonly Present in Young Adults and Coronary Calcium Later in Life: The CARDIA (Coronary Artery Risk Development in Young Adults) Study. *Ann. Intern. Med.* **2010**, *153*, 137–146. [CrossRef]
69. Koskinen, J.; Juonala, M.; Dwyer, T.; Venn, A.; Thomson, R.; Bazzano, L.; Berenson, G.S.; Sabin, M.A.; Burns, T.L.; Viikari, J.S.A.; et al. Impact of Lipid Measurements in Youth in Addition to Conventional Clinic-Based Risk Factors on Predicting Preclinical Atherosclerosis in Adulthood International Childhood Cardiovascular Cohort Consortium. *Circulation* **2018**, *137*, 1246–1255. [CrossRef]
70. Haney, E.M.; Huffman, L.H.; Bougatsos, C.; Freeman, M.; Steiner, R.D.; Nelson, H.D. Screening and Treatment for Lipid Disorders in Children and Adolescents: Systematic Evidence Review for the US Preventive Services Task Force. *Pediatrics* **2007**, *120*, e189–e214. [CrossRef]
71. De Ferranti, S.D.; Steinberger, J.; Ameduri, R.; Baker, A.; Gooding, H.; Kelly, A.S.; Mietus-Snyder, M.; Mitsnefes, M.M.; Peterson, A.L.; St-Pierre, J.; et al. Cardiovascular Risk Reduction in High-Risk Pediatric Patients: A Scientific Statement From the American Heart Association. *Circulation* **2019**, *139*, E603–E634. [CrossRef]
72. Vague, J. The Degree of Masculine Differentiation of Obesities: A Factor Determining Predisposition to Diabetes, Atherosclerosis, Gout, and Uric Calculous Disease. *Am. J. Clin. Nutr.* **1956**, *4*, 20–34. [CrossRef]
73. Muntner, P.; He, J.; Cutler, J.A.; Wildman, R.P.; Whelton, P.K. Trends in Blood Pressure among Children and Adolescents. *J. Am. Med. Assoc.* **2004**, *291*, 2107–2113. [CrossRef]
74. Cheung, E.L.; Bell, C.S.; Samuel, J.P.; Poffenbarger, T.; Redwine, K.M.; Samuels, J.A. Race and Obesity in Adolescent Hypertension. *Pediatrics* **2017**, *139*, e20161433. [CrossRef]
75. Koebnick, C.; Black, M.H.; Wu, J.; Martinez, M.P.; Smith, N.; Kuizon, B.; Cuan, D.; Young, D.R.; Lawrence, J.M.; Jacobsen, S.J. High Blood Pressure in Overweight and Obese Youth: Implications for Screening. *J. Clin. Hypertens.* **2013**, *15*, 793–805. [CrossRef] [PubMed]
76. Valdés Pizarro, J.; Royo-Bordonada, M.A. Prevalence of Childhood Obesity in Spain: National Health Survey 2006–2007. *Nutr. Hosp.* **2012**, *27*, 154–160. [CrossRef] [PubMed]
77. Kollias, A.; Skliros, E.; Stergiou, G.S.; Leotsakos, N.; Saridi, M.; Garifallos, D. Obesity and Associated Cardiovascular Risk Factors among Schoolchildren in Greece: A Cross-Sectional Study and Review of the Literature. *J. Pediatr. Endocrinol. Metab.* **2011**, *24*, 929–938. [CrossRef]
78. Sorof, J.M.; Lai, D.; Turner, J.; Poffenbarger, T.; Portman, R.J. Overweight, Ethnicity, and the Prevalence of Hypertension in School-Aged Children. *Pediatrics* **2004**, *113*, 475–482. [CrossRef]
79. Flynn, J. The Changing Face of Pediatric Hypertension in the Era of the Childhood Obesity Epidemic. *Pediatr. Nephrol.* **2013**, *28*, 1059–1066. [CrossRef]
80. Garrison, R.J.; Kannel, W.B.; Stokes, J.; Castelli, W.P. Incidence and Precursors of Hypertension in Young Adults: The Framingham Offspring Study. *Prev. Med.* **1987**, *16*, 235–251. [CrossRef]
81. Samuel, V.T.; Shulman, G.I. Mechanisms for Insulin Resistance: Common Threads and Missing Links. *Cell* **2012**, *148*, 852–871. [CrossRef]
82. Kotsis, V.; Stabouli, S.; Papakatsika, S.; Rizos, Z.; Parati, G. Mechanisms of Obesity-Induced Hypertension. *Hypertens. Res.* **2010**, *33*, 386–393. [CrossRef]
83. Grøntved, A.; Steene-Johannessen, J.; Kynde, I.; Franks, P.W.; Helge, J.W.; Froberg, K.; Anderssen, S.A.; Andersen, L.B. Association between Plasma Leptin and Blood Pressure in Two Population-Based Samples of Children and Adolescents. *J. Hypertens.* **2011**, *29*, 1093–1100. [CrossRef]

84. Mu, S.; Shimosawa, T.; Ogura, S.; Wang, H.; Uetake, Y.; Kawakami-Mori, F.; Marumo, T.; Yatomi, Y.; Geller, D.S.; Tanaka, H.; et al. Epigenetic Modulation of the Renal β-Adrenergic–WNK4 Pathway in Salt-Sensitive Hypertension. *Nat. Med.* **2011**, *17*, 573–580. [CrossRef]
85. Hall, J.E.; do Carmo, J.M.; da Silva, A.A.; Wang, Z.; Hall, M.E. Obesity, Kidney Dysfunction and Hypertension: Mechanistic Links. *Nat. Rev. Nephrol.* **2019**, *15*, 367–385. [CrossRef] [PubMed]
86. Shatat, I.F.; Flynn, J.T. Relationships between Renin, Aldosterone, and 24-Hour Ambulatory Blood Pressure in Obese Adolescents. *Pediatr. Res.* **2011**, *69*, 336–340. [CrossRef] [PubMed]
87. Goodfriend, T.L.; Kelley, D.E.; Goodpaster, B.H.; Winters, S.J. Visceral Obesity and Insulin Resistance Are Associated with Plasma Aldosterone Levels in Women. *Obes. Res.* **1999**, *7*, 355–362. [CrossRef]
88. Kawarazaki, W.; Fujita, T. The Role of Aldosterone in Obesity-Related Hypertension. *Am. J. Hypertens.* **2016**, *29*, 415–423. [CrossRef]
89. Briones, A.M.; Cat, A.N.D.; Callera, G.E.; Yogi, A.; Burger, D.; He, Y.; Corrêa, J.W.; Gagnon, A.M.; Gomez-Sanchez, C.E.; Gomez-Sanchez, E.P.; et al. Adipocytes Produce Aldosterone through Calcineurin-Dependent Signaling Pathways: Implications in Diabetes Mellitus-Associated Obesity and Vascular Dysfunction. *Hypertension* **2012**, *59*, 1069–1078. [CrossRef]
90. Di Blasio, A.M.; Van Rossum, E.F.C.; Maestrini, S.; Berselli, M.E.; Tagliaferri, M.; Podestà, F.; Koper, J.W.; Liuzzi, A.; Lamberts, S.W.J. The Relation between Two Polymorphisms in the Glucocorticoid Receptor Gene and Body Mass Index, Blood Pressure and Cholesterol in Obese Patients. *Clin. Endocrinol.* **2003**, *59*, 68–74. [CrossRef]
91. Bellili, N.M.; Foucan, L.; Fumeron, F.; Mohammedi, K.; Travert, F.; Roussel, R.; Balkau, B.; Tichet, J.; Marre, M. Associations of the 344 T>C and the 3097 G>A Polymorphisms of CYP11B2 Gene with Hypertension, Type 2 Diabetes, and Metabolic Syndrome in a French Population. *Am. J. Hypertens.* **2010**, *23*, 660–667. [CrossRef] [PubMed]
92. Lang, F.; Stournaras, C. Serum and Glucocorticoid Inducible Kinase, Metabolic Syndrome, Inflammation, and Tumor Growth. *Hormones* **2013**, *12*, 160–171. [CrossRef]
93. Cat, A.N.D.; Friederich-Persson, M.; White, A.; Touyz, R.M. Adipocytes, Aldosterone and Obesity-Related Hypertension. *J. Mol. Endocrinol.* **2016**, *57*, F7–F21.
94. Castrop, H.; Höcherl, K.; Kurtz, A.; Schweda, F.; Todorov, V.; Wagner, C. Physiology of Kidney Renin. *Physiol. Rev.* **2010**, *90*, 607–673. [CrossRef]
95. Reinehr, T.; Andler, W. Cortisol and Its Relation to Insulin Resistance before and after Weight Loss in Obese Children. *Horm. Res.* **2004**, *62*, 107–112. [CrossRef] [PubMed]
96. Lanaspa, M.A.; Kuwabara, M.; Andres-Hernando, A.; Li, N.; Cicerchi, C.; Jensen, T.; Orlicky, D.J.; Roncal-Jimenez, C.A.; Ishimoto, T.; Nakagawa, T.; et al. High Salt Intake Causes Leptin Resistance and Obesity in Mice by Stimulating Endogenous Fructose Production and Metabolism. *Proc. Natl. Acad. Sci. USA* **2018**, *115*, 3138–3143. [CrossRef] [PubMed]
97. Shibata, S.; Nagase, M.; Yoshida, S.; Kawachi, H.; Fujita, T. Podocyte as the Target for Aldosterone: Roles of Oxidative Stress and Sgk1. *Hypertension* **2007**, *49*, 355–364. [CrossRef]
98. Nishiyama, A.; Yao, L.; Nagai, Y.; Miyata, K.; Yoshizumi, M.; Kagami, S.; Kondo, S.; Kiyomoto, H.; Shokoji, T.; Kimura, S.; et al. Possible Contributions of Reactive Oxygen Species and Mitogen-Activated Protein Kinase to Renal Injury in Aldosterone/Salt-Induced Hypertensive Rats. *Hypertension* **2004**, *43*, 841–848. [CrossRef]
99. Whaley-Connell, A.; Sowers, J.R. Insulin Resistance in Kidney Disease: Is There a Distinct Role Separate from That of Diabetes or Obesity. *CardioRenal Med.* **2017**, *8*, 41–49. [CrossRef]
100. Freedman, D.S.; Williamson, D.F.; Gunter, E.W.; Byers, T. Relation of Serum Uric Acid to Mortality and Ischemic Heart Disease. *Am. J. Epidemiol.* **1995**, *141*, 637–644. [CrossRef]
101. Lurbe, E.; Agabiti-Rosei, E.; Cruickshank, J.K.; Dominiczak, A.; Erdine, S.; Hirth, A.; Invitti, C.; Litwin, M.; Mancia, G.; Pall, D.; et al. 2016 European Society OfHypertension Guidelines for Themanagement of High Blood Pressure in Children and Adolescents. *J. Hypertens.* **2016**, *34*, 1887–1920. [CrossRef] [PubMed]
102. Wühl, E. Hypertension in Childhood Obesity. *Acta Paediatr. Int. J. Paediatr.* **2019**, *108*, 37–43. [CrossRef] [PubMed]
103. Bełtowski, J. Salt Intake, Aldosterone Secretion, and Obesity: Role in the Pathogenesis of Resistant Hypertension. *Am. J. Hypertens.* **2021**, *34*, 588–590. [CrossRef]
104. Garg, R.; Kneen, L.; Williams, G.H.; Adler, G.K. Effect of Mineralocorticoid Receptor Antagonist on Insulin Resistance and Endothelial Function in Obese Subjects. *Diabetes Obes. Metab.* **2014**, *16*, 268–272. [CrossRef] [PubMed]
105. Ross, R.; Blair, S.N.; Arena, R.; Church, T.S.; Després, J.P.; Franklin, B.A.; Haskell, W.L.; Kaminsky, L.A.; Levine, B.D.; Lavie, C.J.; et al. Importance of Assessing Cardiorespiratory Fitness in Clinical Practice: A Case for Fitness as a Clinical Vital Sign: A Scientific Statement from the American Heart Association. *Circulation* **2016**, *134*, e653–e699. [CrossRef] [PubMed]
106. Caspersen, C.J.; Christenson, G.M. Physical Activity, Exercise, and Physical Fitness: Definitions and Distinctions for Health-Related Research. *Public Health Rep.* **1985**, *100*, 126–131.
107. Lang, J.J.; Belanger, K.; Poitras, V.; Janssen, I.; Tomkinson, G.R.; Tremblay, M.S. Systematic Review of the Relationship between 20 m Shuttle Run Performance and Health Indicators among Children and Youth. *J. Sci. Med. Sport* **2018**, *21*, 383–397. [CrossRef] [PubMed]
108. Ortega, F.B.; Ruiz, J.R.; Castillo, M.J.; Sjöström, M. Physical Fitness in Childhood and Adolescence: A Powerful Marker of Health. *Int. J. Obes.* **2008**, *32*, 1–11. [CrossRef]

109. Högström, G.; Nordström, A.; Nordström, P. High Aerobic Fitness in Late Adolescence Is Associated with a Reduced Risk of Myocardial Infarction Later in Life: A Nationwide Cohort Study in Men. *Eur. Heart J.* **2014**, *35*, 3133–3140. [CrossRef]
110. Santana, C.C.A.; Azevedo, L.B.; Cattuzzo, M.T.; Hill, J.O.; Andrade, L.P.; Prado, W.L. Physical Fitness and Academic Performance in Youth: A Systematic Review. *Scand. J. Med. Sci. Sports* **2017**, *27*, 579–603. [CrossRef]
111. Lubans, D.; Richards, J.; Hillman, C.; Faulkner, G.; Beauchamp, M.; Nilsson, M.; Kelly, P.; Smith, J.; Raine, L.; Biddle, S. Physical Activity for Cognitive and Mental Health in Youth: A Systematic Review of Mechanisms. *Pediatrics* **2016**, *138*, e20161642. [CrossRef]
112. Redón, P.; Grassi, G.; Redon, J.; Álvarez-Pitti, J.; Lurbe, E. Sympathetic Neural Activity, Metabolic Parameters and Cardiorespiratory Fitness in Obese Youths. *J. Hypertens.* **2017**, *35*, 571–577. [CrossRef]
113. De Oliveira, R.G.; Guedes, D.P. Physical Activity, Sedentary Behavior, Cardiorespiratory Fitness and Metabolic Syndrome in Adolescents: Systematic Review and Meta-Analysis of Observational Evidence. *PLoS ONE* **2016**, *11*, e0168503. [CrossRef]
114. Olds, T.S.; Tomkinson, G.R.; Ferrar, K.E.; Maher, C. A Trends in the Prevalence of Childhood Overweight and Obesity in Australia between 1985 and 2008. *Int. J. Obes.* **2010**, *34*, 57–66. [CrossRef]
115. Ortega, F.B.; Ruiz, J.R.; España-Romero, V.; Vicente-Rodriguez, G.; Martínez-Gómez, D.; Manios, Y.; Béghin, L.; Molnar, D.; Widhalm, K.; Moreno, L.; et al. The International Fitness Scale (IFIS): Usefulness of Self-Reported Fitness in Youth. *Int. J. Epidemiol.* **2011**, *40*, 701–711. [CrossRef]
116. Ruiz, J.R.; Silva, G.; Oliveira, N.; Ribeiro, J.C.; Oliveira, J.F.; Mota, J. Criterion-Related Validity of the 20-m Shuttle Run Test in Youths Aged 13-19 Years. *J. Sports Sci.* **2009**, *27*, 899–906. [CrossRef] [PubMed]
117. Artero, E.G.; España-Romero, V.; Castro-Piñero, J.; Ruiz, J.R.; Jiménez-Pavón, D.; Aparicio, V.A.; Gatto-Cardia, M.C.; Baena, P.A.; Vicente-Rodríguez, G.; Castillo, M.J.; et al. Criterion-Related Validity of Field-Based Muscular Fitness Tests in Youth. *J. Sports Med. Phys. Fitness* **2012**, *52*, 263–272. [CrossRef]
118. Hayes, R.M.; Maldonado, D.; Gossett, T.; Shepherd, T.; Mehta, S.P.; Flesher, S.L. Developing and Validating a Step Test of Aerobic Fitness among Elementary School Children. *Physiother. Can.* **2019**, *71*, 187–194. [CrossRef] [PubMed]
119. Pate, R.R.; Wang, C.Y.; Dowda, M.; Farrell, S.W.; O'Neill, J.R. Cardiorespiratory Fitness Levels among US Youth 12 to 19 Years of Age: Findings from the 1999-2002 National Health and Nutrition Examination Survey. *Arch. Pediatr. Adolesc. Med.* **2006**, *160*, 1005–1012. [CrossRef] [PubMed]
120. García-Artero, E.; Ortega, F.B.; Ruiz, J.R.; Mesa, J.L.; Delgado, M.; González-Gross, M.; García-Fuentes, M.; Vicente-Rodríguez, G.; Gutiérrez, Á.; Castillo, M.J. Lipid and Metabolic Profiles in Adolescents Are Affected More by Physical Fitness than Physical Activity (AVENA Study). *Rev. Esp. Cardiol.* **2007**, *60*, 581–588. [CrossRef]
121. Castillo-Garzón, M.; Ruiz, J.; Ortega, F.; Gutierrez-Sainz, A. A Mediterranean Diet Is Not Enough for Health: Physical Fitness Is an Important Additional Contributor to Health for the Adults of Tomorrow. *World Rev. Nutr. Diet.* **2007**, *97*, 114–138.
122. Gahche, J.; Fakhouri, T.; Carroll, D.D.; Burt, V.L.; Wang, C.-Y.; Fulton, J.E. *Cardiorespiratory Fitness Levels among U.S. Youth Aged 12–15 Years: United States, 1999–2004 and 2012*; NCHS Data Brief; U.S. Department of Health and Human Services, Centers for Disease Control and Prevention, National Center for Health Statistics: Atlanta, GA, USA, 2014; pp. 1–8.
123. Costigan, S.A.; Eather, N.; Plotnikoff, R.C.; Taaffe, D.R.; Lubans, D.R. High-Intensity Interval Training for Improving Health-Related Fitness in Adolescents: A Systematic Review and Meta-Analysis. *Br. J. Sports Med.* **2015**, *49*, 1253–1261. [CrossRef]
124. Liu, J.; Zhu, L.; Su, Y. Comparative Effectiveness of High-Intensity Interval Training and Moderate-Intensity Continuous Training for Cardiometabolic Risk Factors and Cardiorespiratory Fitness in Childhood Obesity: A Meta-Analysis of Randomized Controlled Trials. *Front. Physiol.* **2020**, *11*, 214. [CrossRef]
125. Raghuveer, G.; Hartz, J.; Lubans, D.R.; Takken, T.; Wiltz, J.L.; Mietus-Snyder, M.; Perak, A.M.; Baker-Smith, C.; Pietris, N.; Edwards, N.M. Cardiorespiratory Fitness in Youth: An Important Marker of Health: A Scientific Statement from the American Heart Association. *Circulation* **2020**, *142*, E101–E118. [CrossRef] [PubMed]
126. Freedman, D.S.; Khan, L.K.; Dietz, W.H.; Srinivasan, S.R.; Berenson, G.S. Relationship of Childhood Obesity to Coronary Heart Disease Risk Factors in Adulthood: The Bogalusa Heart Study. *Pediatrics* **2001**, *108*, 712–718. [CrossRef] [PubMed]
127. Simmonds, M.; Llewellyn, A.; Owen, C.G.; Woolacott, N. Predicting Adult Obesity from Childhood Obesity: A Systematic Review and Meta-Analysis. *Obes. Rev.* **2016**, *17*, 95–107. [CrossRef]
128. Di Cesare, M.; Sorić, M.; Bovet, P.; Miranda, J.J.; Bhutta, Z.; Stevens, G.A.; Laxmaiah, A.; Kengne, A.P.; Bentham, J. The Epidemiological Burden of Obesity in Childhood: A Worldwide Epidemic Requiring Urgent Action. *BMC Med.* **2019**, *17*, 212. [CrossRef]
129. Kumar, S.; Kelly, A.S. Review of Childhood Obesity: From Epidemiology, Etiology, and Comorbidities to Clinical Assessment and Treatment. *Mayo Clin. Proc.* **2017**, *92*, 251–265. [CrossRef] [PubMed]
130. Rodrigues, A.N.; Abreu, G.R.; Resende, R.S.; Goncalves, W.L.S.; Gouvea, A.S. Cardiovascular Risk Factor Investigation: A Pediatric Issue. *Int. J. Gen. Med.* **2013**, *6*, 57–66. [CrossRef]
131. McPhee, P.G.; Singh, S.; Morrison, K.M. Childhood Obesity and Cardiovascular Disease Risk: Working Toward Solutions. *Can. J. Cardiol.* **2020**, *36*, 1352–1361. [CrossRef] [PubMed]
132. Llewellyn, A.; Simmonds, M.; Owen, C.G.; Woolacott, N. Childhood Obesity as a Predictor of Morbidity in Adulthood: A Systematic Review and Meta-Analysis. *Obes. Rev.* **2016**, *17*, 56–67. [CrossRef]
133. Singh, A.S.; Mulder, C.; Twisk, J.W.R.; Van Mechelen, W.; Chinapaw, M.J.M. Tracking of Childhood Overweight into Adulthood: A Systematic Review of the Literature. *Obes. Rev.* **2008**, *9*, 474–488. [CrossRef]

134. Reilly, J.J.; Kelly, J. Long-Term Impact of Overweight and Obesity in Childhood and Adolescence on Morbidity and Premature Mortality in Adulthood: Systematic Review. *Int. J. Obes.* **2011**, *35*, 891–898. [CrossRef]
135. Park, M.H.; Falconer, C.; Viner, R.M.; Kinra, S. The Impact of Childhood Obesity on Morbidity and Mortality in Adulthood: A Systematic Review. *Obes. Rev.* **2012**, *13*, 985–1000. [CrossRef]
136. Berenson, G.S.; Wattigney, W.A.; Tracy, R.E.; Newman, W.P.; Srinivasan, S.R.; Webber, L.S.; Dalferes, E.R.; Strong, J.P. Atherosclerosis of the Aorta and Coronary Arteries and Cardiovascular Risk Factors in Persons Aged 6 to 30 Years and Studied at Necropsy (the Bogalusa Heart Study). *Am. J. Cardiol.* **1992**, *70*, 851–858. [CrossRef]
137. Daniels, S.R. Cardiovascular Disease Risk Factors and Atherosclerosis in Children and Adolescents. *Curr. Atheroscler. Rep.* **2001**, *3*, 479–485. [CrossRef] [PubMed]
138. Cook, S.; Kavey, R.E.W. Dyslipidemia and Pediatric Obesity. *Pediatr. Clin. N. Am.* **2011**, *58*, 1363–1373. [CrossRef] [PubMed]
139. Smoak, C.G.; Burke, G.L.; Webber, L.S.; Harsha, D.W.; Srinivasan, S.R.; Berenson, G.S. Relation of Obesity to Clustering of Cardiovascular Disease Risk Factors in Children and Young Adults: The Bogalusa Heart Study. *Am. J. Epidemiol.* **1987**, *125*, 364–372. [CrossRef]
140. Morrison, J.A.; Friedman, L.A.; Gray-McGuire, C. Metabolic Syndrome in Childhood Predicts Adult Cardiovascular Disease 25 Years Later: The Princeton Lipid Research Clinics Follow-up Study. *Pediatrics* **2007**, *120*, 340–345. [CrossRef]
141. Baker, J.L.; Olsen, L.W.; Sørensen, T.I.A. Childhood Body-Mass Index and the Risk of Coronary Heart Disease in Adulthood. *N. Engl. J. Med.* **2007**, *357*, 2329–2337. [CrossRef]
142. Tirosh, A.; Shai, I.; Afek, A.; Dubnov-Raz, G.; Ayalon, N.; Gordon, B.; Derazne, E.; Tzur, D.; Shamis, A.; Vinker, S.; et al. Adolescent BMI Trajectory and Risk of Diabetes versus Coronary Disease. *N. Engl. J. Med.* **2011**, *364*, 1315–1325. [CrossRef] [PubMed]
143. Juonala, M.; Magnussen, C.G.; Berenson, G.S.; Venn, A.; Burns, T.L.; Sabin, M.A.; Srinivasan, S.R.; Daniels, S.R.; Davis, P.H.; Chen, W.; et al. Childhood Adiposity, Adult Adiposity, and Cardiovascular Risk Factors. *N. Engl. J. Med.* **2011**, *365*, 1876–1885. [CrossRef]
144. Serra-Paya, N.; Ensenyat, A.; Real, J.; Castro-Viñuales, I.; Zapata, A.; Galindo, G.; Solé-Mir, E.; Bosch-Muñoz, J.; Mur, J.M.; Teixidó, C. Evaluation of a Family Intervention Programme for the Treatment of Overweight and Obese Children (Nereu Programme): A Randomized Clinical Trial Study Protocol. *BMC Public Health* **2013**, *13*, 1000. [CrossRef]
145. Lier, L.M.; Breuer, C.; Ferrari, N.; Friesen, D.; Maisonave, F.; Schmidt, N.; Graf, C. Cost-Effectiveness of a Family-Based Multicomponent Outpatient Intervention Program for Children with Obesity in Germany. *Public Health* **2020**, *186*, 185–192. [CrossRef]
146. Clemes, S.A.; Bingham, D.D.; Pearson, N.; Chen, Y.L.; Edwardson, C.; McEachan, R.; Tolfrey, K.; Cale, L.; Richardson, G.; Fray, M.; et al. Stand out in Class: Restructuring the Classroom Environment to Reduce Sedentary Behaviour in 9–10-Yearolds—Study Protocol for a Pilot Cluster Randomised Controlled Trial. *Pilot Feasibility Stud.* **2018**, *4*, 103. [CrossRef]
147. Li, X.; Jan, S.; Yan, L.L.; Hayes, A.; Chu, Y.; Wang, H.; Feng, X.; Niu, W.; He, F.J.; Ma, J.; et al. Cost and Cost-Effectiveness of a School-Based Education Program to Reduce Salt Intake in Children and Their Families in China. *PLoS ONE* **2017**, *12*, e0183033. [CrossRef] [PubMed]
148. Wang, Y.C.; Cheung, A.M.; Bibbins-Domingo, K.; Prosser, L.A.; Cook, N.R.; Goldman, L.; Gillman, M.W. Effectiveness and Cost-Effectiveness of Blood Pressure Screening in Adolescents in the United States. *J. Pediatr.* **2011**, *158*, 257–264.e7. [CrossRef]
149. Swartz, S.J.; Srivaths, P.R.; Croix, B.; Feig, D.I. Cost-Effectiveness of Ambulatory Blood Pressure Monitoring in the Initial Evaluation of Hypertension in Children. *Pediatrics* **2008**, *122*, 1177–1181. [CrossRef]
150. Flynn, J.T.; Kaelber, D.C.; Baker-Smith, C.M.; Blowey, D.; Carroll, A.E.; Daniels, S.R.; de Ferranti, S.D.; Dionne, J.M.; Falkner, B.; Flinn, S.K.; et al. Clinical Practice Guideline for Screening and Management of High Blood Pressure in Children and Adolescents. *Pediatrics* **2017**, *140*, e20171904. [CrossRef] [PubMed]
151. Falkner, B.; Gidding, S.S.; Ramirez-Garnica, G.; Wiltrout, S.A.; West, D.; Rappaport, E.B. The Relationship of Body Mass Index and Blood Pressure in Primary Care Pediatric Patients. *J. Pediatr.* **2006**, *148*, 195–200. [CrossRef]
152. Falkner, B.; Lurbe, E.; Schaefer, F. High Blood Pressure in Children: Clinical and Health Policy Implications. *J. Clin. Hypertens.* **2010**, *12*, 261–276. [CrossRef] [PubMed]
153. Griffiths, P.E.; West, C. A Balanced Intervention Ladder: Promoting Autonomy through Public Health Action. *Public Health* **2015**, *129*, 1092–1098. [CrossRef]
154. Gamage, D.G.; Riddell, M.A.; Joshi, R.; Thankappan, K.R.; Chow, C.K.; Oldenburg, B.; Evans, R.G.; Mahal, A.S.; Kalyanram, K.; Kartik, K.; et al. Effectiveness of a Scalable Group-Based Education and Monitoring Program, Delivered by Health Workers, to Improve Control of Hypertension in Rural India: A Cluster Randomised Controlled Trial. *PLoS Med.* **2020**, *17*, e1002997. [CrossRef] [PubMed]
155. Farpour-Lambert, N.J.; Aggoun, Y.; Marchand, L.M.; Martin, X.E.; Herrmann, F.R.; Beghetti, M. Physical Activity Reduces Systemic Blood Pressure and Improves Early Markers of Atherosclerosis in Pre-Pubertal Obese Children. *J. Am. Coll. Cardiol.* **2009**, *54*, 2396–2406. [CrossRef] [PubMed]
156. Xu, H.; Li, Y.; Shang, X.; Du, S.; Zhang, Q.; Liu, A.; Ma, G. Effect of Comprehensive Interventions Including Nutrition Education and Physical Activity on High Blood Pressure among Children: Evidence from School-Based Cluster Randomized Control Trial in China. *Int. J. Environ. Res. Public Health* **2020**, *17*, 8944. [CrossRef]
157. Ketelhut, S.; Ketelhut, S.R.; Ketelhut, K. School-Based Exercise Intervention Improves Blood Pressure and Parameters of Arterial Stiffness in Children: A Randomized Controlled Trial. *Pediatr. Exerc. Sci.* **2021**, *33*, 1–7. [CrossRef] [PubMed]

158. Angelopoulos, P.D.; Milionis, H.J.; Grammatikaki, E.; Moschonis, G.; Manios, Y. Changes in BMI and Blood Pressure after a School Based Intervention: The CHILDREN Study. *Eur. J. Public Health* **2009**, *19*, 319–325. [CrossRef]
159. Straub, N.; Grunert, P.; Von Kries, R.; Koletzko, B. Health Economic Potential of Early Nutrition Programming: A Model Calculation of Long-Term Reduction in Blood Pressure and Related Morbidity Costs by Use of Long-Chain Polyunsaturated Fatty Acid-Supplemented Formula. *Am. J. Clin. Nutr.* **2011**, *94*, 2030S–2035S. [CrossRef]
160. Gelius, P.; Messing, S.; Goodwin, L.; Schow, D.; Abu-Omar, K. What Are Effective Policies for Promoting Physical Activity? A Systematic Review of Reviews. *Prev. Med. Rep.* **2020**, *18*, 101095. [CrossRef]
161. Institute of Medicine (US); National Research Council (US) Committee on Childhood Obesity Prevention Actions for Local Governments; Parker, L.; Burns, A.C.; Sanchez, E. *Actions for Increasing Physical Activity*; National Academies Press (US): Washington, DC, USA, 2009.
162. WHO. *Physical Activity Strategy for the WHO European Region 2016–2025*; WHO: Geneva, Switzerland, 2015; p. 1.
163. Hannan, P.; French, S.A.; Story, M.; Fulkerson, J.A. A Pricing Strategy to Promote Sales of Lower Fat Foods in High School Cafeterias: Acceptability and Sensitivity Analysis. *Am. J. Health Promot.* **2002**, *17*, 1–6. [CrossRef]
164. French, S.A. Pricing Effects on Food Choices. *J. Nutr.* **2003**, *133*, 841S–843S. [CrossRef]
165. Matos, R.S.; Siqueira, J.H.; Cunha, D.B.; del C.B. Molina, M. Impact of a Randomized School-Based Intervention Program on Blood Pressure Levels. *Rev. Bras. Saude Matern. Infant.* **2020**, *20*, 965–974. [CrossRef]
166. Heimuli, J.; Sundborn, G.; Rush, E.; Oliver, M.; Savila, F. Parental Perceptions of Their Child's Weight and Future Concern: The Pacific Islands Families Study. *Pac. Health Dialog* **2011**, *17*, 33–49.
167. Bricarello, L.P.; Poltronieri, F.; Fernandes, R.; Retondario, A.; de Moraes Trindade, E.B.; de Vasconcelos, F.D. Effects of the Dietary Approach to Stop Hypertension (DASH) Diet on Blood Pressure, Overweight and Obesity in Adolescents: A Systematic Review. *Clin. Nutr. ESPEN* **2018**, *28*, 1–11. [CrossRef]
168. Malik, V.S.; Hu, F.B. Sugar-Sweetened Beverages and Cardiometabolic Health: An Update of the Evidence. *Nutrients* **2019**, *11*, 1840. [CrossRef]
169. Popkin, B.M.; Ng, S.W. Sugar-Sweetened Beverage Taxes: Lessons to Date and the Future of Taxation. *PLoS Med.* **2021**, *18*, e1003412. [CrossRef] [PubMed]
170. Appel, L.J.; Lichtenstein, A.H.; Callahan, E.A.; Sinaiko, A.; Van Horn, L.; Whitsel, L. Reducing Sodium Intake in Children: A Public Health Investment. *J. Clin. Hypertens.* **2015**, *17*, 657–662. [CrossRef] [PubMed]
171. Hyseni, L.; Guzman-Castillo, M.; Kypridemos, C.; Collins, B.; Schwaller, E.; Capewell, S.; Boland, A.; Dickson, R.; O'Flaherty, M.; Gallacher, K.; et al. Engaging with Stakeholders to Inform the Development of a Decision-Support Tool for the NHS Health Check Programme: Qualitative Study. *BMC Health Serv. Res.* **2020**, *20*, 394. [CrossRef]
172. Wolfenden, L.; Jones, J.; Williams, C.M.; Finch, M.; Wyse, R.J.; Kingsland, M.; Tzelepis, F.; Wiggers, J.; Williams, A.J.; Seward, K.; et al. Strategies to Improve the Implementation of Healthy Eating, Physical Activity and Obesity Prevention Policies, Practices or Programmes within Childcare Services. *Cochrane Database Syst. Rev.* **2016**, *2016*, CD011779. [CrossRef]
173. Gilmer, T.P.; O'Connor, P.J.; Sinaiko, A.R.; Kharbanda, E.O.; Magid, D.J.; Sherwood, N.E.; Adams, K.F.; Parker, E.D.; Margolis, K.L. Impact of Hypertension on Healthcare Costs among Children. *Am. J. Manag. Care* **2014**, *20*, 622–628. [PubMed]

nutrients

MDPI

Article

Conservative Treatment for Childhood and Adolescent Obesity: Real World Follow-Up Profiling and Clinical Evolution in 1300 Patients

Gabriel Á. Martos-Moreno [1,2,3,4,†], Julián Martínez-Villanueva Fernández [1,†], Alicia Frías-Herrero [1], Álvaro Martín-Rivada [1] and Jesús Argente [1,2,3,4,5,*]

1 Departments of Pediatrics & Pediatric Endocrinology, Hospital Infantil Universitario Niño Jesús, E-28009 Madrid, Spain; gabrielangelmartos@yahoo.es (G.Á.M.-M.); jmvfernandez@gmail.com (J.M.-V.F.); alicia_fh96@hotmail.com (A.F.-H.); amartinrivada@gmail.com (Á.M.-R.)
2 La Princesa Research Institute, E-28009 Madrid, Spain
3 Department of Pediatrics, Universidad Autónoma de Madrid, E-28049 Madrid, Spain
4 Centro de Investigación Biomédica en Red de Fisiopatología de la Obesidad y Nutrición (CIBEROBN), Instituto de Salud Carlos III, E-28029 Madrid, Spain
5 IMDEA Food Institute, CEI UAM & CSIC, E-28049 Madrid, Spain
* Correspondence: jesus.argente@uam.es
† These authors contributed equally to this work.

Citation: Martos-Moreno, G.Á.; Martínez-Villanueva Fernández, J.; Frías-Herrero, A.; Martín-Rivada, Á.; Argente, J. Conservative Treatment for Childhood and Adolescent Obesity: Real World Follow-Up Profiling and Clinical Evolution in 1300 Patients. *Nutrients* **2021**, *13*, 3847. https://doi.org/10.3390/nu13113847

Academic Editors: Fernando Fernandez-Aranda, Janet Treasure, Empar Lurbe and J. Mark Brown

Received: 6 October 2021
Accepted: 26 October 2021
Published: 28 October 2021

Publisher's Note: MDPI stays neutral with regard to jurisdictional claims in published maps and institutional affiliations.

Abstract: Background: Limited therapeutic tools and an overwhelming clinical demand are the major limiting factors in pediatric obesity management. The optimal protocol, environment, body mass index (BMI) change targets and duration of obesity-oriented interventions remain to be elucidated. **Aims:** We aimed to characterize the singularities of follow-up, anthropometric and metabolic evolution of a large cohort of pediatric patients with obesity in a specialized university hospital outpatient obesity unit. **Patients and methods:** Follow-up duration (up to seven years), attrition rate and anthropometric and metabolic evolution of 1300 children and adolescents with obesity were studied. An individualized analysis was conducted in patients attaining a high level of weight loss (over 1.5 BMI-SDS (standard deviation score) and/or 10% of initial weight; $n = 252$; 19.4%) as well as in "metabolically healthy" patients ($n = 505$; 38.8%). **Results:** Attrition rate was high during the early stages (11.2% prior to and 32.5% right after their initial metabolic evaluation). Mean follow-up time was 1.59 ± 1.60 years (7% of patients fulfilled 7 years). The highest BMI reduction occurred in the first year (-1.11 ± 0.89 SDS, $p < 0.001$ in 72.5% of patients). At the end of the follow-up, improvements in glucose and lipid metabolism parameters were observed (both $p < 0.05$), that were highest in patients with the greatest weight reduction (all $p < 0.01$), independent of the time spent to achieve weight loss. The pubertal growth spurt negatively correlated with obesity severity ($r = -0.38$; $p < 0.01$) but patients attaining adult height exceeded their predicted adult height ($n = 308$, $+1.6 \pm 5.4$ cm; $p < 0.001$). "Metabolically healthy" patients, but with insulin resistance, had higher blood pressure, glucose, uric acid and triglyceride levels than those without insulin resistance (all $p < 0.05$). Preservation of the "metabolically healthy" status was associated with BMI improvement. **Conclusions:** Behavioral management of children with obesity can be effective and does not impair growth but is highly conditioned by high attrition. The best results regarding BMI reduction and metabolic improvement are achieved in the first year of intervention and can be preserved if follow-up is retained.

Keywords: childhood obesity; attrition rate; follow-up; success rate; metabolically healthy

1. Introduction

Management and follow-up of children and adolescents affected with obesity are crucial clinical challenges worldwide due to both high prevalence and the limited available therapeutic resources. Additionally, obesity management is highly influenced by a number of barriers both, from the patient's side (stigma, gaps in medical education, misperceptions of the disease or weight status, etc.) and from the healthcare system (insufficient staff, time and facilities to provide timely and patient/family-personalized assistance). These barriers strongly impair the probability of therapeutic success [1].

Despite the recent approval (June 2021) by the European Medicine Agency of liraglutide as the first drug for obesity treatment above 18 years of age, management of obesity in childhood and adolescent largely remains based on combined nutritional and exercise behavioral counseling, ideally involving a multidisciplinary intervention [2,3]. Although primary care assistance is recommended for childhood obesity management, the low rate of successful weight loss in these patients and the increasing prevalence of obesity associated comorbidities has resulted in obesity being one of the most frequent causes for consultation in specialized pediatric endocrinology or obesity clinics in our environment, thus generating increasing delays in patient attention [4]. Nevertheless, there is no consensus regarding the best environment to manage childhood obesity to achieve a high success in weight loss and its maintenance with, for example, primary care assistance allows for higher accessibility and proximity to patients [5] while tertiary care centers normally have more available resources and the possibility to develop multidisciplinary care units [6].

In contrast, there is robust consensus and evidence that the major factor limiting success in childhood obesity management programs is the high withdrawal rate observed throughout follow-up at all levels of assistance [7], reaching up to 92% after 2 years in some reports [8], with sociodemographic and anthropometric features being potential predictors of a higher risk of attrition [9,10]. Among these factors, the perception that obesity is not a disease state [9], initial weight loss wrongly assumed as "curation" [9,10] and, most importantly, lack of sustained weight loss [11], have been postulated as the main risk factors for early termination of intervention programs in children and adolescents with obesity. Consequently, the combination of some of these factors (early weight loss + high drop-out rate + lack of sustained weight loss), can result in selection bias in the analysis of the results of these programs in the long term.

An additional concern of parents upon intervention for childhood obesity is the potential effect on growth and pubertal development of their child. These patients usually exhibit some degree of advancement in skeletal maturation and overgrowth in relation to their target height [12,13] and this is directly correlated with the severity of their obesity and inversely proportional to the magnitude of their pubertal growth spurt [13] but does not impair the attainment of their predicted adult height [13–15]. Consequently, although severe caloric restriction is not usually included in childhood and adolescent obesity interventions [2,3] and evidence indicates that conventional strategies for weight control in this age range do not impair growth or puberty [15], this can be a factor underlying the reluctance of some parents to intervene.

Some points of discussion in childhood obesity management protocols include the degree of weight loss needed to achieve clinically significant improvements, the role (if any) of the time to attain weight loss and the amount of time this BMI reduction should be sustained for in order to preserve the beneficial effect of the intervention. A decrease in BMI Z-score of 0.25 or more has been suggested to be sufficient to improve cardiometabolic risk factors [16], whereas a duration over 3 years of intervention, beginning at the earliest age possible, has been associated with more successful outcomes [17]. However, there is limited knowledge regarding what should be considered an excellent degree of weight reduction under conservative treatment and what is an acceptable evolution after attaining this degree of weight loss [18].

A subgroup of patients with obesity that has raised special interest are those classified in some studies as "metabolically healthy" [19]. This concept of "metabolically healthy" in children with obesity was inherited from the concept first postulated in adults where a patient with excess fat mass, but normal blood pressure, lipid profile and glycemia was proposed to be metabolically healthy [20]. However, the evidence that insulin resistance is the first step of carbohydrate metabolism impairment in childhood obesity, often preceding the rise of blood glucose levels [12,21,22] and the data supporting the role of uric acid as a potential marker of metabolic impairment in children [23] have lead to the question of whether these parameters should also be considered before assuming that a child with obesity is "metabolically healthy" [20–22].

Based on the above observations, we hypothesized that the time required to obtain a significant reduction in BMI affects both the attrition rate and the degree of improvement in metabolic impairment in children with obesity. Thus, the aims of this study were: (1) To analyze the duration of follow-up, the drop-out rate and its causes and the behavioral changes implemented, along with the patient's BMI Z-score, growth and metabolic evolution up to a maximum of 7 years in the regular outpatient care in an obesity clinic in a tertiary hospital, with a particular emphasis on BMI changes and attrition rate. (2) To study the features of patients achieving a large reduction in BMI ("excellent responders"), characterizing their weight loss and metabolic changes, the evolution of their BMI in the 5 years following weight reduction and exploring how the time required to attain weight loss affects the metabolic changes observed. (3). To compare the features of patients with obesity, with or without metabolic comorbidities during their first evaluation, as well as the evolution of their metabolic status according to BMI changes during follow-up, while evaluating the role of insulin resistance in the definition of a "metabolically healthy status".

2. Patients and Methods

2.1. Study Cohort

One thousand and three hundred children and adolescents [mainly Caucasians (75.8%) and Latinos (19.0%)] with standardized BMI above +2 SDS for national and international references [24,25] were enrolled during a period of 6 years after potential underlying pathological or syndromic causes of obesity were ruled out. Patients above 12 years of age and their parents or guardians gave informed consent as required by the local ethics committee, which had previously approved the study in accordance with the "Ethical Principles for Medical Research Involving Human Subjects" adopted in the Declaration of Helsinki by the World Medical Association.

At the first visit of all patients (baseline, B) weight, height, BMI, pubertal status and systolic and diastolic blood pressure were recorded and standardized when indicated [26]. A left wrist/hand X-ray was used to estimate bone age according to the Greulich & Pyle method [27] and a 12-h fasting serum sample (serum stored at −80 °C until assayed) was used to determine glucose, insulin, HbA1c (hemoglobin A1c), the lipid profile and uric acid levels by standardized assays and to calculate the HOMA homeostatic model assessment) index as previously reported (cohort characterization displayed in Table 1) [12].

Table 1. Clinical features of the entire cohort and in the two main ethnicities.

	Total Cohort (n = 1300)		Caucasians (n = 986/75.8%)		Latinos (n = 247/19.0%)	
	Prepubertal	**Pubertal**	**Prepubertal**	**Pubertal**	**Prepubertal**	**Pubertal**
n	693 (53.3%)	607 (46.7%)	525 (53.2%)	461 (46.8%)	130 (52.6%)	117 (47.4%)
Sex	**F** 263 (38.0%) **M** 430 (62.0%)	**F** 351 (57.8%) **M** 256 (42.2%)	**F** 192 (36.6%) **M** 333 (63.4%)	**F** 271 (58.8%) **M** 190 (41.2%)	**F** 56 (43.1%) **M** 74 (56.9%)	**F** 66 (56.4%) **M** 51 (43.6%)
Age (years)	8.26 ± 2.54	12.96 ± 1.97	8.47 ± 2.38	13.10 ± 1.94	7.68 ± 2.82	12.53 ± 2.05
BMI-SDS	4.21 ± 1.52	3.77 ± 1.43	4.14 ± 1.42	3.71 ± 1.36	4.38 ± 1.84	3.81 ± 1.39
Glucose (mg/dL)	91.65 ± 7.00	93.44 ± 6.70	91.34 ± 7.08	93.27 ± 6.70	92.83 ± 6.58	94.17 ± 6.85
HbA1c (%)	5.45 ± 0.34	5.47 ± 0.30	5.45 ± 0.34	5.45 ± 0.30	5.43 ± 0.34	5.53 ± 0.28
Insulin (μU/mL)	11.78 ± 6.94	17.19 ± 10.74	11.47 ± 6.37	16.51 ± 10.44	13.01 ± 8.46	18.98 ± 11.39
HOMA	2.70 ± 1.65	4.01 ± 2.66	2.63 ± 1.56	3.85 ± 2.63	2.99 ± 1.86	4.43 ± 2.67

Table 1. *Cont.*

	Total Cohort (n = 1300)		Caucasians (n = 986/75.8%)		Latinos (n = 247/19.0%)	
	Prepubertal	**Pubertal**	**Prepubertal**	**Pubertal**	**Prepubertal**	**Pubertal**
LDL-c (mg/dL)	99.72 ± 26.31	93.36 ± 24.27	99.87 ± 26.03	93.56 ± 24.42	101.97 ± 27.58	93.16 ± 24.30
HDL-c (mg/dL)	47.33 ± 11.10	43.93 ± 9.84	47.83 ± 10.85	44.50 ± 9.99	45.34 ± 11.56	40.94 ± 8.51
Triglycerides (mg/dL)	74.64 ± 44.34	85.63 ± 53.60	72.75 ± 43.51	82.69 ± 53.78	82.61 ± 45.90	97.2 ± 54.40
Uric acid (mg/dL)	4.47 ± 0.92	5.28 ± 1.11	4.51 ± 0.89	5.30 ± 1.05	4.30 ± 0.92	5.11 ± 1.12

Abbreviations: BMI-SDS: Standardized body mass index (Z-score); F: Female; HDL-c: High density lipoprotein cholesterol; HOMA: Homeostatic model assessment; LDL-c: Low density lipoprotein cholesterol; M: Male; n: Number of patients.

Patients were always seen in the outpatient clinic in our department by the same physician (GAM-M). Visits were scheduled one month after baseline, every three months during the first year and every six months thereafter up to 7 years for the maximum follow-up. Treatment consisted of lifestyle reorganization (dietary and exercise related behavioral counseling) mainly focused on three key elements: avoidance of snacking and sweetened drink consumption, establishing a slow pace of food intake in meals and onset of scheduled daily physical activity. A daily recommendation for food group distribution was provided on a weekly basis in addition to the categorization of usual foods as recommended, non-recommended and allowed with limited frequencies/amounts. Self-monitoring of the fulfillment of the key elements of lifestyle reorganization was encouraged and specific documents for fulfillment registration provided.

Time of follow-up, drop-out rate and its causes, along with the patients' BMI Z-score, growth and pubertal evolution throughout follow-up were studied and their last available anthropometric and metabolic evaluation prior to the end of their follow-up were compared with those at baseline. To study the metabolic evolution, the last available metabolic analysis was used and only those patients that had an analysis at least 12 months after their baseline evaluation were included (available in 451 patients).

2.2. Excellent Responder Group

Two hundred and fifty-two patients (19.4% of the entire cohort) achieved a reduction in their BMI over 1.5 SDS and/or in their weight over 10% from baseline. Anthropometric and biochemical features for each patient after weight loss were compared with those at baseline, studying the eventual role of the time to attain weight loss on the observed changes. Additionally, the evolution of BMI in the 5 years after weight loss was analyzed.

2.3. Metabolically Healthy Group

According to their baseline features, patients were classified as: (1) "Metabolically healthy" (**MH**; n = 505; 38.8%) if they showed normal blood pressure, lipid profile (low density and high density (LDL-c, HDL-c) lipoproteins and triglycerides), and serum glucose and uric acid levels at diagnosis or (2) "Not metabolically healthy" (**No-MH,** n = 795, 61.2%) if one or more of these parameters were impaired. Additionally, patients were classified according to their fasting insulin levels as insulin resistant (**IR**, fasting insulin $\geq$ 15 µU/mL; n = 481; 37%) or **No-IR** (fasting insulin < 15 µU/mL n = 819, 63%).

Standardized BMI, blood pressure, fasting lipid profile, glucose, insulin, uric acid levels and HOMA index at baseline were compared between **MH** and **No-MH** patients, also accounting for the presence or absence of **IR**. In addition, the evolution of these features was studied by longitudinally comparing status at baseline and the end of follow-up, considering the eventual role of the background of **IR** at diagnosis.

2.4. Statistical Analysis

Data are shown as mean ± SD. For normally distributed parametric variables, comparison between two independent groups was performed using Student's *t* test, whereas *t*-test for related measurements was used for comparing patient features between different time-points. For those parametric variables with non-normal distributions, the Mann–Whitney U test and the Wilcoxon test were used. To compare non-parametric variables, Chi square tests (independent groups) and McNemar tests (paired samples) were used. The relationships between quantitative normal variables were studied by linear correlation analysis (Pearson's r), whereas Spearman's rho was used for non-normally distributed variables. A value of $p < 0.05$ was chosen as the level of significance. The software used was Statistical Package for Social Sciences (SPSS v. 15.0. MapInfo Corporation, Troy, NY, USA).

3. Results

3.1. Follow-Up Characterization

3.1.1. Time of Follow-Up and Drop-Out

Mean duration of follow-up in this cohort was 1.59 ± 1.60 years, with 59.9% patients stopping it unilaterally and 33.5% requesting the end of follow-up in their last visit (mainly due to the achievement of BMI or metabolic improvement). A progressive decrease in the study population was observed throughout follow-up with only 21 patients (7% of initial cohort) completing 7 years of follow-up (Figure 1). The drop-out rate before 6 months of follow-up was higher in Latinos (52% vs. 24% in Caucasians; $p < 0.001$), males (36% vs. 23% in females; $p < 0.05$) and prepubertal (32% vs. 26% in pubertal; $p < 0.05$). After 1 year, the interethnic difference in attrition rate persisted (47% in Latinos vs. 18% in Caucasians; $p < 0.001$). Among the patients dropping out, 84.1% had repeatedly not fulfilled the therapeutic recommendations in the visits prior to withdrawal and 5.4% argued familial/social difficulties. A total of 8% of the patients re-consulted after follow-up had stop (most after regaining lost weight).

It is of note that, among the patients abandoning follow-up, 11.2% did it after the initial clinical examination (not performing the complementary tests indicated) and 32.5% after their second visit once they received the results from the complementary examinations (total 43.7% patients abandoned prior to their third visit).

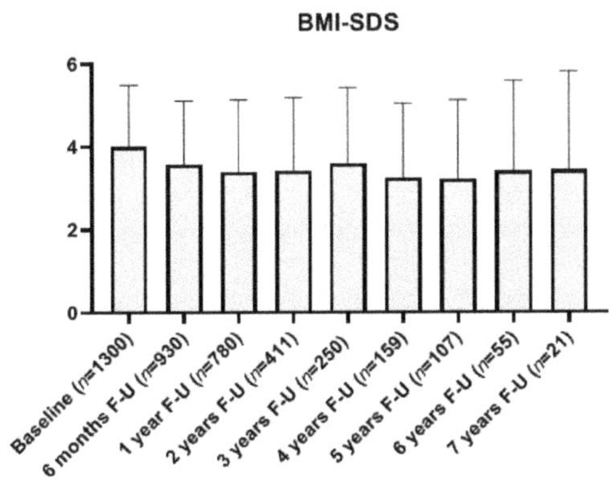

Figure 1. Evolution of patient retainment and their standardized BMI (expressed as SDS) throughout follow-up to a maximum of 7 years from their first evaluation. *Abbreviations:* BMI-SDS: Standardized body mass index (Z-score); F-U: Follow-up; n: number of patients retaining follow-up.

3.1.2. BMI Evolution and Lifestyle Changes

In the analysis of BMI evolution at 6 months, 66.8% of patients of follow-up had reduced their BMI (−0.89 ± 0.73 SDS), whereas 32.5% had increased it (+0.56 ± 0.53 SDS, both $p < 0.001$), reducing the mean cohort BMI in 0.41 ± 0.95 SDS compared to **baseline**

($p < 0.001$). At 12 months, mean cohort BMI was -0.63 ± 1.16 SDS below the initial BMI ($p < 0.001$), with 72.5% of the patients at follow-up showing BMI reduction from **baseline** (-1.11 ± 0.89 SDS, $p < 0.001$). After a significant decrease in mean cohort BMI in the first year of follow-up, a partial regain was observed at the second year, with later stabilization (Figures 1 and 2).

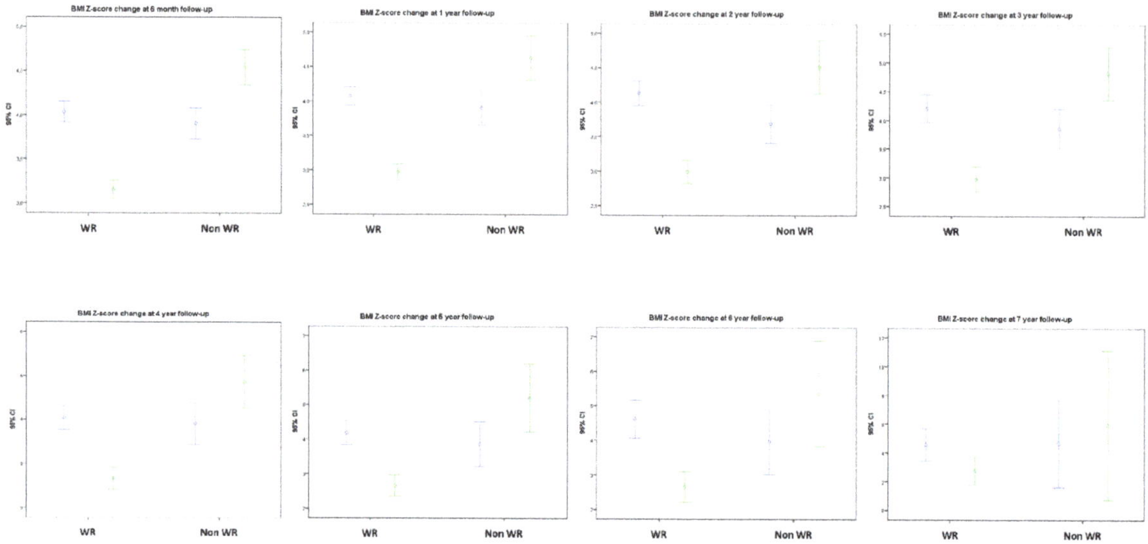

Figure 2. Evolution of BMI SDS at each time-point shown as a paired comparison with patients' BMI Z-score at baseline (taking into account exclusively those continuing follow-up at each timepoint) differentiating between those with weight reduction (WR) or increasing (Non WR) their BMI. *Abbreviations:* 95% CI: Confidence Interval 95%; Non WR: Not showing weight (or BMI) reduction; WR: Showing weight (and BMI) reduction. The percentages of patients showing WR among those retaining follow-up were, respectively: 66.8% at 6 months, 72.5% at 1 year, 71.6% at 2 years, 68.0% at 3 years, 73.1% at 4 years, 78.1% at 5 years, 72.2% at 6 years and 80.0% at 7 years (See Figure 1 for the number of patients in each time point).

The mean BMI at the end of follow-up ($n = 980$, $+3.59 \pm 1.87$ SDS) was lower than BMI at baseline (-0.37 ± 1.25 SDS; $p < 0.001$) with 62.65% patients having achieved some degree of BMI reduction (-1.04 ± 0.88 SDS; $p < 0.001$) but with 36.43% of patients increasing their BMI despite assistance ($+0.79 \pm 0.93$ SDS; $p < 0.001$). At the end of follow-up, 83.1% of patients still maintained their BMI above +2 SDS (obesity), with 10.3% shifting to the overweight category (BMI centile 90 to 97) and 6.6% normalizing their BMI (below centile 90).

The percentage of patients acknowledging snacking (eating in-between meals) at their baseline visit was 81.9% and this was reduced significantly ($p < 0.001$) at their second (55.9%) and last visit (57.2%). A similar pattern was observed for compulsive eating behavior (50.6% at the second visit and 47.3% at the last visit vs. 74.0% at baseline, $p < 0.001$). Additionally, the number of patients who did not perform any scheduled physical activity prior to their enrollment was 74.7%, with this improving significantly ($p < 0.001$) at their second (53.1%) and last visits (49.8%) (Table 2).

Table 2. Key behavioral items at baseline and after intervention.

	Baseline	Second Visit (p vs. Baseline)	Last Visit (p vs. Baseline)
Snacking	81.9%	55.9% ($p < 0.001$)	57.2% ($p < 0.001$)
Eating compulsivity	74.0%	50.6% ($p < 0.001$)	47.3% ($p < 0.001$)
Lack of scheduled physical activity	74.7%	53.1% ($p < 0.001$)	49.8% ($p < 0.001$)

3.1.3. Metabolic Evolution

Metabolic data at the end of follow-up were available for 451 patients and showed a significant decrease in HOMA index (−0.35 ± 2.07; $p < 0.001$) with a positive correlation between the parallel decrease in HOMA and BMI-SDS (r = +0.15; $p < 0.01$). This was also observed for triglyceride (−4.99 ± 53.54 mg/dL; $p < 0.01$/r = +0.12; $p < 0.01$) and LDL cholesterol levels (−4.89 ± 17.50 mg/dL; $p < 0.001$/r = +0.19; $p < 0.001$) whereas HDL cholesterol levels increased at the end of follow-up (+2.81 ± 8.72 mg/dL; $p < 0.001$/r = −0.20 with a change in BMI; $p < 0.001$). Despite no significant differences in mean uric acid levels between baseline and the end of follow-up, a direct correlation also existed between the change in uric acid levels and BMI SDS (r = +0.12; $p < 0.05$) as well as a decrease in the percentage of patients showing hyperuricemia (12.6% at the end of follow-up vs. 17.8% at baseline; $p < 0.05$).

3.1.4. Growth and Puberty throughout Follow-Up

In 81 patients (45 females and 36 males), follow-up encompassed their entire pubertal development (from its onset, or Tanner stage II, to its completion and attainment of adult height). Mean duration of puberty in this group was 3.23 ± 1.16 years, with no differences according to sex or race. In girls, the time from puberty onset (Tanner stage II) to menarche was 1.65 ± 0.91 years, again with no ethnicity-based differences. A negative correlation between the duration of puberty and baseline BMI-SDS was observed (r = −0.25; $p < 0.05$).

The pubertal growth spurt in this group was 16.29 ± 5.80 cm, with no differences between sexes and with a negative correlation between the degree of the growth spurt and the severity of obesity at baseline estimated by BMI-SDS (r = −0.38; $p < 0.01$).

In addition to these 81 patients, 227 additional patients achieved their final height during their follow-up (total 308 patients with available adult height). Their mean adult height was above their predicted target height (mean parental height +/− 6.5 for boys and girls, respectively) by +0.29 ± 0.94 SDS (+ 1.6 ± 5.4 cm; $p < 0.001$). In this group, adult height prediction using the Bailey Pinneau method using their bone age at their first visit was shown to overestimate the attained final height by +0.22 ± 0.78 SDS (+ 1.5 ± 4.56 cm, $p < 0.001$). This overestimation was greater in males and prepubertal patients.

3.2. The Excellent Responder Cohort

The characteristics of the 252 patients who achieved a reduction in their BMI of over 1.5 SDS and/or of their weight of over 10% from baseline are shown in Table 3. There was a higher proportion of prepubertal children among good responders (χ^2: 10.57; $p < 0.01$), whereas the relative percentages of the two main ethnicities was similar to those in the cohort at baseline.

Table 3. Clinical features of the excellent responder group at baseline.

Age (Years)	10.41 ± 3.19
BMI-SDS	4.24 ± 1.46
Ethnicity:	
- Caucasian	78.6
- Latino	18.1
- Others	4.3
Sex (%)	
Female	38.5
Male	61.5
Pubertal status (%)	
Prepubertal	57.10 (70.1% males/29.9% females)
Pubertal	42.90 (50.0% males/50.0% females)

Abbreviations: BMI-SDS: Standardized body mass index (Z-score).

The mean weight loss was 3.85 ± 5.92 kg, resulting in a mean BMI decrease of 1.59 ± 0.77 SDS. However, the mean body weight decrease needed to achieve the threshold set was higher in pubertal compared to prepubertal patients (−6.01 vs. −2.01 kg, respectively; $p < 0.001$). After weight loss patients experienced a significant increase in their HDL levels and a significant decrease in glucose, insulin, triglyceride, and LDL cholesterol, as well as in HOMA index (all $p < 0.01$, Table 4).

Table 4. Changes in BMI and metabolic parameters after weight loss compared to baseline.

	Baseline (*n* = 252)	**After Weight Reduction (*n* = 252)**	
BMI (SDS)	3.99 ± 1.43	2.69 ± 1.21	$p < 0.001$
Glucose (mg/dL)	94.39 ± 7.10	92.20 ± 6.78	$p < 0.01$
Insulin (mcU/mL)	15.25 ± 8.35	10.73 ± 5.28	$p < 0.001$
HOMA index	3.58 ± 2.07	2.47 ± 1.27	$p < 0.001$
Total cholesterol (mg/dL)	151.93 ± 29.99	146.35 ± 30.20	$p < 0.01$
LDL-c (mg/dL)	93.52 ± 27.92	87.76 ± 24.81	$p < 0.001$
HDL-c (mg/dL)	43.66 ± 10.06	46.13 ± 11.70	$p < 0.001$
Triglyceride (mg/dL)	74.03 ± 48.19	63.10 ± 37.58	$p < 0.001$
Uric acid (mg/dL)	5.05 ± 1.20	4.98 ± 1.14	N.S. ($p = 0.07$)
Ferritin (ng/mL)	39.00 ± 20.98	40.63 ± 20.76	N.S.
Total proteins (g/dL)	7.25 ± 0.42	7.24 ± 0.46	N.S.
Albumin (g/dL)	4.09 ± 0.27	4.17 ± 0.28	$p < 0.01$
25 [Vitamin D] (ng/mL)	22.54 ± 5.82	24.45 ± 6.90	N.S.

Abbreviations: BMI-SDS: Standardized body mass index (Z-score); F: Female; HDL-c: High density lipoprotein cholesterol; HOMA: Homeostatic model assessment; LDL-c: Low density lipoprotein cholesterol; n: number of patients; N.S.: Not significant.

The mean time from baseline to weight loss achievement was 0.94 ± 0.86 years, with 35.3% of patients attaining this goal at 6 months and 74.2% before 12 months of follow-up. No differences in time to weight loss were observed according to sex or pubertal status.

The longer the time needed to attain BMI reduction, the lower the amount of raw weight loss achieved ($r = -0.65$; $p < 0.001$). However, no correlation between the magnitude of changes in metabolic parameters and the time spent to achieve weight loss was observed.

Prospective follow-up showed that the BMI reduction was preserved and even enhanced after 6 months upon weight loss attainment but increased from the first to the third year after weight loss and later remained stable in those patients achieving 5 years of follow-up (Figures 3 and 4).

3.3. *"Metabolically Healthy" Cohort*

No differences in age, sex or pubertal distribution between the MH and No-MH groups were observed. However, the MH group showed a slightly lower mean standardized BMI (+3.78 ± 1.30) than No-MH (+4.15 ± 1.59 SDS; $p < 0.001$).

The degree of metabolic impairment categories observed in the entire cohort based on a fasting serum sample determinations and using the criteria previously described (12) are shown in Figure 5.

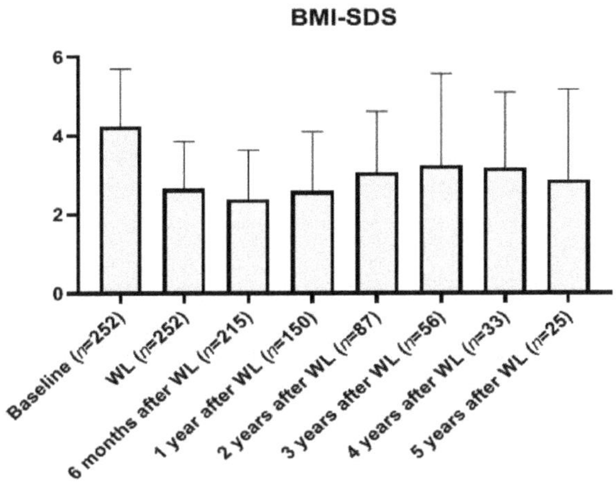

Figure 3. Evolution of patient retainment and their standardized BMI (expressed as SDS) in the five years following weight loss in the excellent responder group. *Abbreviations:* BMI-SDS: Standardized body mass index (Z-score); WL: Weight loss.

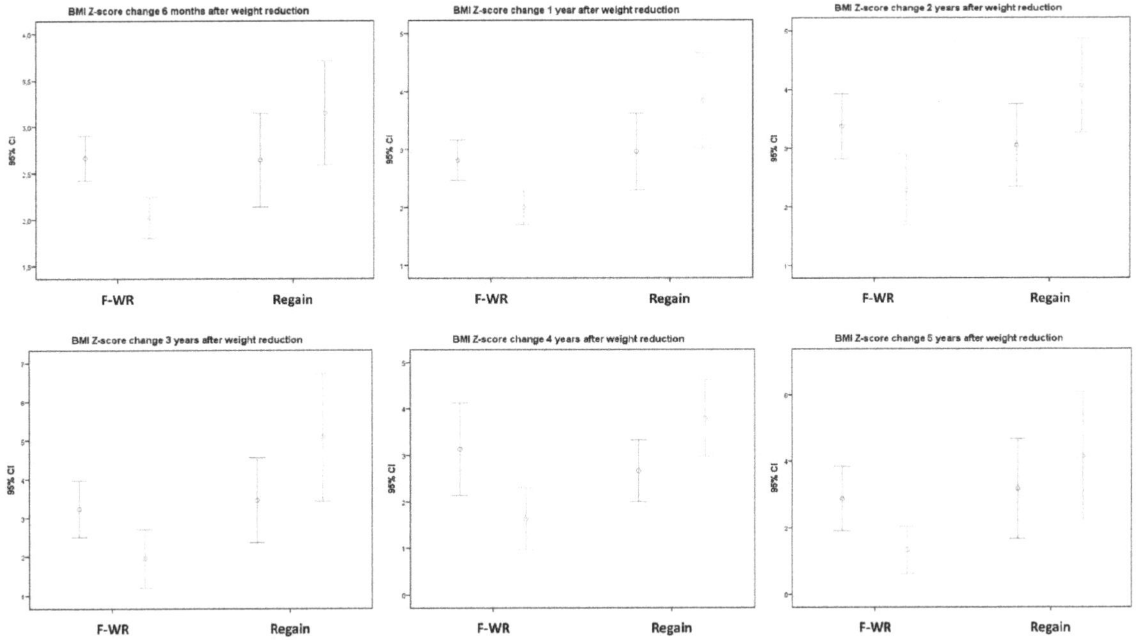

Figure 4. Evolution of BMI Z-score at every time-point throughout the 5 years following intense weight loss in the "excellent responder" group. Shown as the mean of a paired comparison with each patient's BMI Z-score at each timepoint compared to baseline (taking into account exclusively those retained at each follow-up) differentiating between those further reducing their BMI (F-WR) or regaining it (Regain) after the initial intense weight loss. *Abbreviations:* 95% CI: 95% Confidence interval; F WR: Further weight (and BMI) reduction; Regain: Showing weight (and BMI) increase after initial intense loss. The percentages of patients showing F-WR after initial weight loss among those retaining follow-up were 71.1% at 6 months, 63.9% at 1 year, 53.7% at 2 years, 61.3% at 3 years, 38.9% at 4 years, and 69.2% at 5 years.

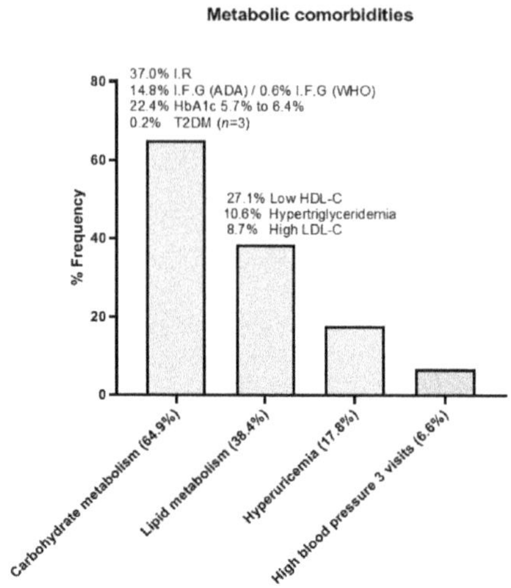

Figure 5. Prevalence of metabolic comorbidities in the entire study cohort at baseline based on fasting determinations. *Abbreviations:* ADA: American Diabetes Association (criteria for IFG: ≥100 mg/dL); HDL-c: High density lipoprotein cholesterol; IFG: Impaired fasting glucose; IR: Insulin resistance (fasting insulin ≥ 15 μU/mL); LDL-c: Low density lipoprotein cholesterol; T2DM: Type 2 diabetes mellitus (ADA criteria: ≥126 mg/dL, confirmed); WHO: World Health Organization (criteria for IFG: ≥110 mg/dL).

The prevalence of MH patients was lower in Latinos (30.4%) than in Caucasians (41.0%; χ^2 9.358; $p < 0.01$) and was also lower in IR (28.1%) compared to No-IR patients (48.0%; χ^2 46.003; $p < 0.01$). Consequently, the prevalence of IR (37.0% in the whole cohort) was higher in the No-MH group (44.8%) than in the MH patients (25.5%). Among MH patients, those with IR (n = 129) were older, more severely obese, and had higher systolic and diastolic blood pressure and glucose, uric acid and triglyceride levels and lower HDL-c levels than the MH patients without IR (Table 5).

Table 5. Clinical features of metabolically healthy (MH) patients and comparison according to the presence or absence of fasting hyperinsulinemia (Insulin ≥ 15 μU/mL vs. Insulin < 15 μU/mL).

All MH (n = 505)	Insulin < 15 μU/mL (n = 376)	Insulin ≥ 15 μU/mL (n = 129)	
Age (years)	10.14 ± 3.20	11.62 ± 2.58	$p < 0.001$
BMI-SDS	3.66 ± 1.25	4.12 ± 378	$p < 0.001$
SBP (mmHg)	113.46 ± 11.68	118.26 ± 12.57	$p < 0.001$
DBP (mmHg)	58.83 ± 6.89	61.68 ± 6.71	$p < 0.001$
Fasting glucose (mg/dL)	90.35 ± 5.32	91.68 ± 4.73	$p < 0.05$
Uric acid (mg/dL)	4.41 ± 0.79	4.63 ± 0.85	$p < 0.01$
HDL-cholesterol (mg/dL)	51.01 ± 9.15	48.41 ± 7.32	$p < 0.01$
Triglycerides (mg/dL)	55.54 ± 22.10	68.47 ± 24.27	$p < 0.001$

Abbreviations: BMI: body mass index; DBP: diastolic blood pressure; SBP: diastolic blood pressure; SDS: Standard deviation score. Data are shown as mean ± SD.

Metabolic data at the end of follow-up were available for 152 of the 505 MH patients at the onset of the study (30%). Among these, 73.7% remained MH whereas 26.3% had developed at least one metabolic comorbidity (independently of the presence or absence of IR at diagnosis). Among the No-MH patients (metabolic data at the end of follow-up were available in 29.8% [237/795]) 8.4% became MH by the end of follow-up, whereas 91.6% still showed at least one metabolic comorbidity.

A significant decrease in BMI from baseline to the end of the study was observed both in those patients who remained MH (+3.50 ± 1.02 to +2.76 ± 1.36 SDS, $p < 0.001$) as well as in those who resolved their initial comorbidities (+3.58 ± 1.57 to +2.69 ± 2.28 SDS, $p < 0.05$), but not in those developing comorbidities throughout follow-up or remaining No-MH.

4. Discussion

In this study we observed that a high attrition rate was the most relevant and limiting factor in our outpatient specialized assistance pediatric obesity clinic, with a very high drop-out rate in the early stages of intervention as well as a low mean duration of follow-up. We have seen how the fulfillment of behavioral counselling and the attainment of BMI reduction occurs most frequently in the first year of intervention, with a significant percentage of patients being very successful, and with metabolic improvement being attained independently from the time required to achieve weight loss and that can be sustained if follow-up is retained. We have also seen that controlled intervention does not affect growth or pubertal development, nor does it impair the attainment of the adult target height, although the timing and pace of growth are influenced by obesity and its severity. Finally, we saw that insulin resistance is related to metabolic status in patients with obesity, even before the onset of other metabolic alterations, and should be considered when defining whether a person is metabolically healthy, especially when considering that in childhood obesity the metabolic statis is a dynamic condition related to the evolution of the patient's BMI over time.

This study, similar to most preceding reports, highlights the evidence and relevance of the high attrition rate in intervention programs for childhood and adolescent obesity [8–11,28], with the number of patients in follow-up declining over time. Here, we found that 43.7% dropped out before their third visit and only 7% extended their visits up to 7 years. Around 60% of patients unilaterally decided to stop the follow-up. As might be expected, 84.1% of them had not fulfilled the therapeutic recommendations in their visits prior to withdrawal, whereas only 5.4% stated that they had difficulties to attend the programmed visits.

Several factors have been analyzed to predict and avoid a patient's dropout, including misperception of disease status, ethnicity, socio-economic or cultural determinants or unavailability to attend the visits [7,9–11,29]. Among these possibilities, misperception of the parents and children of their weight status or the conception that obesity is not a real disease is particularly important in our [30] and most western environments [31,32]. This underestimation of the pathogenicity of childhood obesity could, at least in part, explain why 11.2% of the patients in our cohort did not even perform the complementary test requested and withdrew after their first interview and clinical evaluation, even though they had been referred for specialized care by their primary care physician. This limited parental and child concern could also be involved in the high rate of patients not fulfilling the recommendations while in follow-up prior to attrition. Additionally, a large percentage of the population assumes that it is the onset of metabolic comorbidities, particularly type 2 diabetes or dyslipidemia, but not weight excess itself that confers the pathogenic potential to obesity [9]. This could influence the additional 32.5% of patients who dropped out at their second visit after getting the results from their metabolic evaluation.

This degree of acceptance of obesity is further enhanced if a positive background of familial obesity exists [31], with more severe obesity and higher prevalence of comorbidities observed in the offspring of parents with obesity at the time of consultation [33], with this being closely related to ethnic, socio-economic and cultural factors [31]. Although the parental academic level background distribution in our cohort was similar to that of the general population in our country [34], no family economic data were registered. These factors could potentially underly the significantly higher attrition rate observed in Latino patients compared to Caucasians at early stages of intervention.

Interestingly, up to one third (33.5%) of the parents asked to discontinue the visits, most after the children had improved their BMI or metabolic comorbidities. This early withdrawal from obesity intervention programs is thought to be a result of the misperception that the obesity was cured [35], which can result in weight regain and later re-consultation as observed in 8% of our patients, most of them after having regained previously lost weight.

Even assuming the high drop-out rate and the positive selection bias derived from a higher attrition rate in those patients not fulfilling therapeutical recommendations, mean follow-up duration in our cohort was similar to that reported in other long-term follow-up series [36], with a retention rate of 54.5% after 1 year; with 72% of the patients showing some BMI reduction (mean over −1 SDS) and with almost 20% being excellent responders (75% of these also in the first year). Subsequently, 31.6% and 15.4% of the cohort extended their follow-up over 2 and 3 years, respectively, resulting in a reduction in mean BMI at the end of follow- up of over 1 SDS in 62% of patients. The degree of fulfillment of the main behavioral recommendations, snacking avoidance, control of compulsive eating and scheduled physical activity, followed a parallel pace to patients' BMI evolution, significantly improving as early as the second visit and remaining stable to the end of follow-up. This reinforces the relevance of the changes attained in the early stages of the intervention to its final outcomes.

Our data show a higher retention rate and success in weight loss in this cohort compared to previous series [8,36], even though the proximity to the patient's home and the possibility of a greater frequency of contact, reported to positively influence behavioral outcome [29,37], is limited at the tertiary care level. These results could be influenced by the relevance that the parents place on being sent to specialized care by the primary care physician, the reduced mean age (10.46 years), the severity of the patient's obesity (mean BMI above +4 SDS) and the high prevalence of metabolic comorbidities in our cohort, all of which could enhance the parental perception of disease in their offspring. Consequently, this could underly the higher rate of excellent responders among prepubertal patients that can be more influenced by their parents' concerns compared to pubertal patients. Additionally, the development of the intervention in a socialized national healthcare system, with no economic factor biasing visit schedule, and the designation of the same physician for the successive visits of every patient could, among other factors, increase their loyalty and the retention rate once follow-up is settled [38].

The combined analysis of these data suggests that the first year of intervention is crucial to the final outcome and efforts should be focused on the attainment of the maximum BMI change in the first year of follow-up, as this increases the chances of sustaining the achieved weight loss, at least in the following 5 years, as seen in the excellent responder group. However, early weight loss can result in a "double edged sword"; that is, it can be the first step for sustained BMI improvement, but also can determine a misconception of definite success resulting in follow-up withdrawal and weight regain due to the return to unhealthy behaviors, which should be prevented [35]. Thus, rapid weight loss may not be the best option for every patient and an individualized strategy regarding the amount and pace of weight loss should be agreed upon in each singular case. This is supported by two observations: (1) among the excellent responders no correlation was observed between time to attain weight reduction and the magnitude of metabolic changes; (2) the excellent responders that required a longer time to achieve weight loss, thus reducing the influence of weight loss on growth, or those patients achieving a more modest weight reduction, independently of the time spent to attain it, also showed significant metabolic improvement.

Consequently, efforts must be made for the continuation of follow-up to consolidate the decrease in BMI, as its duration is an independent predictor of success [39]. Indeed, a duration of at least three years of follow-up has been proposed [17] and it is consistent with the maximum follow-up time observed for the majority of patients in our cohort. However, at the end of the intervention, only 6.6% of the patients normalized their BMI and 10.3% shifted to overweight, with 82.1% of them remaining above the threshold of obesity

(+2 BMI-SDS), which emphasizes the difficulties with reverting to this chronic condition and suggests that the coordinated assistance between specialized care (possessing resources and specialized units) and primary care (having proximity and accessibility) could enhance and prolong the benefits of obesity-oriented interventions [40].

4.1. Influence of Intervention and BMI Changes on Metabolic Comorbidities

The effect of BMI reduction on the improvement of metabolic status observed in the excellent responders might be expected. However, the mean decrease in HOMA index and lipid metabolism parameters observed in the 451 patients out of the total 1300 patient cohort reevaluated metabolically prior to the end of follow up, with a mean cohort decrease in BMI of −0.37 DSD, independently of the duration of follow-up, had a linear relationship with the magnitude of BMI decrease, which reinforces the idea that the change in BMI is the primary factor in metabolic health in children and adolescents with obesity. Furthermore, BMI reduction was observed in patients that became metabolically healthy during follow-up or that were already metabolically healthy at the onset of the study and/or at the last clinical visit; however, BMI was not reduced in patients that had persistent metabolic alterations or developed these alterations during the study.

Regardless of the criteria used for defining metabolically healthy in children with obesity [19–22], the results of this study reinforce the role of insulin resistance as the initial step for metabolic derangement in childhood obesity, even before any analytical abnormality in glucose, uric acid or lipid metabolism is detected [12,19], with metabolically healthy patients with IR showing significant differences in these metabolic parameters compared to those that are metabolically healthy without IR, even though this is not considered in the proposed consensus definition for this entity during childhood [20]. However, the consideration of insulin resistance, next to other elements such as inflammatory markers, adipokine levels or measurements of ectopic fat deposition, has been proposed in more recent revisions of this term [21,22] indicating that more precise analyses of body fat content and distribution (using DXA scan or abdominal MRI) should be considered to better describe the "metabolically healthy" phenotype in obesity. More importantly, our data indicate that during childhood, being classified as metabolically healthily obese is dynamic and mainly dependent on the evolution of the patient's BMI throughout childhood and adolescence. Additionally, the lower prevalence of metabolically healthy individuals in the Latino patients in our cohort, previously already shown to present higher insulin resistance, triglyceride levels and prevalence of liver steatosis when using our populational standards [12,41], should lead us to consider whether homogeneous standards are valid for every patient, or whether ethnic specific standards for these parameters should be advised.

4.2. Influence of BMI on Puberty and Growth

We have confirmed previous observations pointing to accelerated skeletal maturation in children with obesity, resulting in a standardized height over their target height and directly correlated with the severity of obesity [12,13]. Interestingly, the follow up of a significant number of our patients over an extended period of time, some of them encompassing their entire pubertal development and growth spurt, confirms the lack of impairment of obesity-oriented intervention on growth and the attainment of adult height, which was equal to or slightly above that expected according to parental heights [13,14]. Additionally, we observed that the mean pubertal growth spurt in obesity is lower and inversely correlated with the severity of obesity. At the same time the presence of obesity seems to abolish the differences between sexes in the degree of the growth spurt observed in physiological conditions. This could be related to the acceleration in skeletal maturation and the relative childhood overgrowth observed in these patients [12,13]. In contrast, the mean pubertal duration (3.23 years) and time from Tanner stage II to menarche in girls (1.65 years) were similar to that of the general population, despite the inverse correlation observed between obesity severity and duration of puberty. It is clear that several factors such as sex, severity of obesity or the degree of advancement in skeletal maturation determine the features of growth during childhood, and particularly during puberty. This should be taken into account when evaluating height, bone age and growth pace in children and adolescents with obesity as previously reported [12,23].

4.3. Study Limitations

The major limitation of this study derives from the fact that patient follow-up was performed during the regular outpatient clinic activity and not in an ideally controlled research design that would result in increased homogeneity in study time-points and data collection for all patients, particularly regarding the final follow-up time-point. Consequently, the high attrition rate observed and the modifications and delays in patient appointments, frequent in daily clinical practice, has resulted in a degree of heterogeneity in data collection. Additionally, the analysis of several obesity-related topics based on the regular activity in the clinical setting with a large number of patients throughout a long timeframe does not allow for the performance of specific examinations (i.e., body composition study) in all patients that would allow for a more thorough analysis of each aspect of auxological or metabolic affectation. However, at the same time this is one of the valuable singularities of this study, which represents the "real world" characteristics and difficulties of daily clinical practice and follow-up in childhood obesity in our environment. The simultaneity of the analysis of BMI evolution, attrition rate, metabolic changes, growth or puberty, though not exhaustive for each topic, will surely be useful for professionals involved in the care of these patients.

5. Conclusions

We can conclude that: (1) Behavioral management in an outpatient specialized clinic for childhood and adolescent obesity can be effective in a significant number of patients and it does not impair lineal growth (privative of this age range and absent in adult patients) that contributes to the effective achievement of BMI reduction. (2) The outcome of the intervention is conditioned by a high attrition rate whose predictive factors should be considered when individually designing the intervention schedule for each patient. (3) BMI reduction is the main determinant of metabolic improvement in children and adolescents with obesity, with the latter being achieved even after a sustained modest BMI reduction and not related to the time spent to achieve weight loss. (4) The best results in BMI reduction are attained during the first year of intervention, particularly in a subset of patients, and can be maintained if follow-up is retained. However, weight can be regained if intervention is stopped prematurely. Consequently, a sufficient follow-up duration must be ensured for these patients.

In summary, our observations support the concept that in a chronic disease such as obesity, long-term, if not life-long, treatment is often required and that the intervention to improve weight and metabolic status must be started at early ages in an attempt to achieve a healthy adulthood.

Author Contributions: Conceptualization, G.Á.M.-M. and J.A.; methodology, G.Á.M.-M. and J.A.; software, G.Á.M.-M., J.M.-V.F., A.F.-H. and Á.M.-R.; validation G.Á.M.-M. and J.A.; formal analysis, G.Á.M.-M., J.M.-V.F. and J.A.; investigation, G.Á.M.-M., J.M.-V.F., A.F.-H., Á.M.-R. and J.A.; resources, J.A.; writing—original draft preparation, G.Á.M.-M., J.M.-V.F. and A.F.-H.; writing—review and editing, G.Á.M.-M., J.M.-V.F., A.F.-H., Á.M.-R. and J.A.; visualization, G.Á.M.-M., J.M.-V.F., A.F.-H., Á.M.-R. and J.A.; supervision, G.Á.M.-M. and J.A.; project administration J.A.; funding acquisition, J.A. All authors have read and agreed to the published version of the manuscript.

Funding: This work was supported by CIBER Fisiopatología de la Obesidad y Nutrición (CIBERobn) and the Instituto de Salud Carlos III, FIS (FIS PI09/91060; FIS PI10/00747; FIS 13/01295 and FIS PI16/00485).

Institutional Review Board Statement: The study was conducted according to the guidelines of the Declaration of Helsinki, and approved by Ethics Committee of the Hospital Infantil Universitario Niño Jesús (protocol code R0014/10 and date of approval 29 June 2010).

Informed Consent Statement: Informed consent was obtained from parents or guardians of all subjects involved in the study.

Data Availability Statement: Data supporting reported results are preserved in investigators' records and available.

Conflicts of Interest: The authors declare no conflict of interest.

References

1. Srivastava, G.; Browne, N.; Kyle, T.K.; O'Hara, V.; Browne, A.; Nelson, T.; Puhl, R. Caring for US Children: Barriers to Effective Treatment in Children with the Disease of Obesity. *Obesity (Silver Spring)* **2021**, *29*, 46–55. [CrossRef] [PubMed]
2. Styne, D.M.; Arslanian, S.A.; Connor, E.L.; Farooqi, I.S.; Murad, M.H.; Silverstein, J.H.; Yanovski, J.A. Pediatric obesity-assessment, treatment, and prevention: An Endocrine Society clinical practice guideline. *J. Clin. Endocrinol. Metab.* **2017**, *102*, 709–757. [CrossRef]
3. Grupo de trabajo de la Guía de Práctica Clínica sobre la Prevención y el Tratamiento de la Obesidad Infantojuvenil; Centro Cochrane Iberoamericano, Coordinador. *Guía de Práctica Clínica sobre la Prevención y el Tratamiento de la Obesidad Infantojuvenil. Plan de Calidad para el Sistema Nacional de Salud del Ministerio de Sanidad y Política Social*; Guías de Práctica Clínica en el SNS: AATRM N° 2007/25; Agència d'Avaluació de Tecnologia i Recerca Mèdiques: Barcelona, Spain, 2009.
4. Smith, W.A.; Gray, E.; Jones, T.L.; Han, J.C.; Burton, E.T. Waitlist management in a pediatric weight management clinic: Implementing an orientation session. *BMC Pediatr.* **2021**, *21*, 416. [CrossRef] [PubMed]
5. Trujillo-Garrido, N.; Bernal-Jiménez, M.A.; Anti-Cano, M.J. Evaluation of Obesity Management Recorded in Electronic Clinical History: A Cohort Study. *J. Clin. Med.* **2020**, *9*, 2345. [CrossRef]
6. Johnson, V.R.; Bowen-Jallow, K.A.; Stanford, F.C. A call to action: Multi-disciplinary care and treatment of obesity in pediatrics. *Pediatr. Investig.* **2021**, *5*, 1–2. [CrossRef] [PubMed]
7. Dhaliwal, J.; Nosworthy, N.M.; Holt, N.L.; Zwaigenbaum, L.; Avis, J.L.; Rasquinha, A.; Ball, G.D. Attrition and the Management of Pediatric Obesity: An Integrative Review. *Child. Obes.* **2016**, *10*, 461–473. [CrossRef]
8. Reinehr, T.; Widhalm, K.; l'Allemand, D.; Wiegand, S.; Wabitsch, M.; Holl, R.W.; APV-Wiss Study Group and German Competence Net Obesity. Two-year follow-up in 21,784 overweight children and adolescents with lifestyle intervention. *Obesity (Silver Spring)* **2009**, *17*, 1196–1199. [CrossRef]
9. Oksel, E.; Gündüzoȷlu, N.Ç.; Topçu, S. The perception of obese persons: Cross cultural considerations. *Holist. Nurs. Pract.* **2015**, *29*, 225–231. [CrossRef]
10. Goode, R.W.; Ye, L.; Sereika, S.M.; Zheng, Y.; Mattos, M.; Acharya, S.D.; Ewing, L.J.; Danford, C.; Hu, L.; Imes, C.C.; et al. Socio-demographic, anthropometric, and psychosocial predictors of attrition across behavioral weight-loss trials. *Eat. Behav.* **2016**, *20*, 27–33. [CrossRef]
11. Yackobovitch-Gavan, M.; Steinberg, D.M.; Endevelt, R.; Benyamini, Y. Factors associated with dropout in a group weight-loss programme: A longitudinal investigation. *J. Hum. Nutr. Diet.* **2015**, *28* (Suppl. 2), 33–40. [CrossRef]
12. Martos-Moreno, G.A.; Martinez-Villanueva, J.; Gonzalez-Leal, R.; Chowen, J.A.; Argente, J. Sex, puberty, and ethnicity have a strong influence on growth and metabolic comorbidities in children and adolescents with obesity: Report on 1300 patients (the Madrid Cohort). *Pediatr. Obes.* **2019**, *14*, e12565. [CrossRef]
13. Holmgren, A.; Martos-Moreno, G.Á.; Niklasson, A.; Martínez-Villanueva, J.; Argente, J.; Albertsson-Wikland, K. The pubertal growth spurt is diminished in children with severe obesity. *Pediatr. Res.* **2021**, *90*, 184–190. [CrossRef] [PubMed]
14. He, Q.; Karlberg, J. BMI in childhood and its association with height gain, timing of puberty, and final height. *Pediatr. Res.* **2001**, *49*, 244–251. [CrossRef] [PubMed]
15. Moreno, L.A. Effects of diet on growth of children with obesity. *J. Pediatr. Gastroenterol. Nutr.* **2010**, *51*, S147–S148. [CrossRef] [PubMed]
16. Ford, A.L.; Hunt, L.P.; Cooper, A.; Shield, J.P.H. What reduction in BMI SDS is required in obese adolescents to improve body composition and cardiometabolic health? *Arch. Dis. Child.* **2010**, *95*, 256–261. [CrossRef]
17. Danielsson, P.; Svensson, V.; Kowalski, J.; Nyberg, G.; Ekblom, Ö.; Marcus, C. Importance of age for 3-year continuous behavioral obesity treatment success and dropout rate. *Obes. Facts* **2012**, *5*, 34–44. [CrossRef]
18. Smith, K.E.; Mason, T.B.; Wang, W.L.; Schumacher, L.M.; Pellegrini, C.A.; Goldschmidt, A.B.; Unick, J.L. Dynamic associations between anxiety, stress, physical activity, and eating regulation over the course of a behavioral weight loss intervention. *Appetite* **2021**, *168*, 105706. [CrossRef]
19. Primeau, V.; Coderre, L.; Karelis, A.D.; Brochu, M.; Lavoie, M.E.; Messier, V.; Sladek, R.; Rabasa-Lhoret, R. Characterizing the profile of obese patients who are metabolically healthy. *Int. J. Obes.* **2011**, *35*, 971–981. [CrossRef]
20. Damanhoury, S.; Newton, A.S.; Rashid, M.; Hartling, L.; Byrne, J.L.S.; Ball, G.D.C. Defining metabolically healthy obesity in children: A scoping review. *Obes. Rev.* **2018**, *19*, 1476–1491. [CrossRef]
21. Prince, R.L.; Kuk, J.L.; Ambler, K.A.; Dhaliwal, J.; Ball, G.D. Predictors of metabolically healthy obesity in children. *Diabetes Care* **2014**, *37*, 1462–1468. [CrossRef]
22. Vukovic, R.; Dos Santos, T.J.; Ybarra, M.; Atar, M. Children with metabolically healthy obesity: A review. *Front. Endocrinol.* **2019**, *10*, 865. [CrossRef]

23. Thomazini, F.; de Carvalho, B.S.; de Araujo, P.X.; Franco, M.D.C. High uric acid levels in overweight and obese children and their relationship with cardiometabolic risk factors: What is missing in this puzzle? *J. Pediatr. Endocrinol. Metab.* **2021**. [CrossRef] [PubMed]
24. Hernández, M.; Castellet, J.; Narvaiza, J.L.; Rincón, J.M.; Ruiz, I.; Sánchez, E.; Sobradillo, B.; Zurimendi, A. *Curvas y Tablas de Crecimiento*, 2nd ed.; Instituto de Investigación Sobre Crecimiento y Desarrollo, Fundación Faustino Orbegozo, Editorial Garsi: Madrid, Spain, 1988.
25. Cole, T.J.; Bellizzi, M.C.; Flegal, K.M.; Dietz, W.H. Establishing a standard definition for child overweight and obesity world-wide: International survey. *BMJ Evid. Based Med.* **2000**, *320*, 1240–1245.
26. National High Blood Pressure Education Program Working Group on High Blood Pressure in Children and Adolescents. The Fourth Report on the diagnosis, evaluation, and treatment of high blood pressure in children and adolescents. *Pediatrics* **2004**, *114*, 555–576. [CrossRef]
27. Greulich, W.W.; Pyle, S.I. *Radiographic Atlas of Skeletal Development of the Hand and Wrist*, 2nd ed.; Standford University Press: Standford, CA, USA, 1959.
28. Zeller, M.; Kirk, S.; Claytor, R.; Khoury, P.; Grieme, J.; Santangelo, M.; Daniels, S. Predictors of attrition from a pediatric weight management program. *J. Pediatr.* **2004**, *144*, 466–470. [CrossRef] [PubMed]
29. Walker, R.; Ramasamy, V.; Sturgiss, E.; Dunbar, J.; Boyle, J. Shared medical appointments for weight loss: A systematic review. *Fam. Pract.* **2021**, *18*, cmab105. [CrossRef]
30. Inclán-López, P.; Bartolomé-Gutiérrez, R.; Martínez-Castillo, D.; Rabanales-Sotos, J.; Guisado-Requena, I.M.; Martínez-Andrés, M. Parental Perception of Weight and Feeding Practices in SchoolChildren: A Cross-Sectional Study. *Int. J. Environ. Res. Public Health* **2021**, *18*, 4014. [CrossRef]
31. Blanchet, R.; Kengneson, C.C.; Bodnaruc, A.M.; Gunter, A.; Giroux, I. Factors Influencing Parents' and Children's Misperception of Children's Weight Status: A Systematic Review of Current Research. *Curr. Obes. Rep.* **2019**, *8*, 373–412. [CrossRef] [PubMed]
32. Bordeleau, M.; Leduc, G.; Blanchet, C.; Drapeau, V.; Alméras, N. Body Size Misperception and Dissatisfaction in Elementary School Children. *Child. Obes.* **2021**, *17*, 467–475.
33. Martínez-Villanueva, J.; González-Leal, R.; Argente, J.; Martos-Moreno, G.Á. Parental obesity is associated with the severity of childhood obesity and its comorbidities. *An. Pediatr. (Engl. Ed.)* **2019**, *90*, n224–n231. [CrossRef]
34. Martos-Moreno, G.Á.; Martínez-Villanueva, J.; González-Leal, R.; Argente, J. The importance of socioeconomic factors in obesity studies. Authors reply. *An. Pediatr. (Engl. Ed.)* **2019**, *91*, 424. [CrossRef] [PubMed]
35. Batterham, M.; Tapsell, L.C.; Charlton, K.E. Predicting dropout in dietary weight loss trials using demographic and early weight change characteristics: Implications for trial design. *Obes. Res. Clin. Pract.* **2016**, *10*, 189–196. [CrossRef] [PubMed]
36. Mameli, C.; Krakauer, J.C.; Krakauer, N.Y.; Bosetti, A.; Ferrari, C.M.; Schneider, L.; Borsani, B.; Arrigoni, S.; Pendezza, E.; Zuccotti, G.V. Effects of a multidisciplinary weight loss intervention in overweight and obese children and adolescents: 11 years of experience. *PLoS ONE* **2017**, *12*, e0181095. [CrossRef]
37. Vine, M.; Hargreaves, M.B.; Briefel, R.R.; Orfield, C. Expanding the Role of Primary Care in the Prevention and Treatment of Childhood Obesity: A Review of Clinic- and Community-Based Recommendations and Interventions. *J. Obes.* **2013**, *2013*, 172035. [CrossRef] [PubMed]
38. Zhou, W.J.; Wan, Q.Q.; Liu, C.Y.; Feng, X.L.; Shang, S.M. Determinants of patient loyalty to healthcare providers: An integrative review. *Int. J. Qual. Health Care* **2017**, *29*, 442–449. [CrossRef] [PubMed]
39. Jiandani, D.; Wharton, S.; Rotondi, M.A.; Ardern, C.I.; Kuk, J.L. Predictors of early attrition and successful weight loss in patients attending an obesity management program. *BMC Obes.* **2016**, *3*, 14. [CrossRef]
40. Caixàs, A.; Villaró, M.; Arraiza, C.; Montalvá, J.C.; Lecube, A.; Fernández-García, J.M.; Corio, R.; Bellido, D.; Llisterri, J.L.; Tinahones, F.J. SEEDO-SEMERGEN consensus document on continuous care of obesity between Primary Care and Specialist Hospital Units 2019. *Med. Clin.* **2020**, *155*, 267.e1–267.e11. [CrossRef]
41. Martos-Moreno, G.Á.; Martínez-Villanueva, J.; González-Leal, R.; Barrios, V.; Sirvent, S.; Hawkins, F.; Chowen, J.A.; Argente, J. Ethnicity Strongly Influences Body Fat Distribution Determining Serum Adipokine Profile and Metabolic Derangement in Childhood Obesity. *Front. Pediatr.* **2020**, *8*, 551103. [CrossRef]

nutrients

MDPI

Article

Lifetime Weight Course as a Phenotypic Marker of Severity and Therapeutic Response in Patients with Eating Disorders

Zaida Agüera [1,2,3,4,*], Cristina Vintró-Alcaraz [1,2,3], Isabel Baenas [1,2,3], Roser Granero [1,5], Isabel Sánchez [1,2], Jéssica Sánchez-González [2], José M. Menchón [2,3,6,7], Susana Jiménez-Murcia [1,2,3,6], Janet Treasure [8] and Fernando Fernández-Aranda [1,2,3,6,*]

1. Centro de Investigación Biomédica en Red Fisiopatología Obesidad y Nutrición (CIBERobn), Instituto de Salud Carlos III, 08907 L'Hospitalet de Llobregat, Spain; cvintro@bellvitgehospital.cat (C.V.-A.); ibaenas@bellvitgehospital.cat (I.B.); Roser.Granero@uab.cat (R.G.); isasanchez@bellvitgehospital.cat (I.S.); sjimenez@bellvitgehospital.cat (S.J.-M.)
2. Department of Psychiatry, University Hospital of Bellvitge, 08907 L'Hospitalet de Llobregat, Spain; jsanchezg@bellvitgehospital.cat (J.S.-G.); jmenchon@bellvitgehospital.cat (J.M.M.)
3. Psychiatry and Mental Health Group, Neuroscience Program, Institut d'Investigació Biomèdica de Bellvitge—IDIBELL, 08907 L'Hospitalet de Llobregat, Spain
4. Department of Public Health, Mental Health and Maternal-Child Nursing, School of Nursing, University of Barcelona, 08907 L'Hospitalet de Llobregat, Spain
5. Departament de Psicobiologia i Metodologia de les Ciències de la Salut, Universitat Autònoma de Barcelona, 08193 Barcelona, Spain
6. Department of Clinical Sciences, School of Medicine and Health Sciences, University of Barcelona, 08907 L'Hospitalet de Llobregat, Spain
7. Centro de Investigación Biomédica en Red de Salud Mental (CIBERSAM), Instituto de Salud Carlos III, 08907 L'Hospitalet de Llobregat, Spain
8. Department of Psychological Medicine, Institute of Psychiatry, Psychology and Neuroscience, King's College London, London WC2R 2LS, UK; janet.treasure@kcl.ac.uk

* Correspondence: zaguera@bellvitgehospital.cat (Z.A.); ffernandez@bellvitgehospital.cat (F.F.-A.); Tel.: +34-260-7227 (Z.A. & F.F.-A.)

Citation: Agüera, Z.; Vintró-Alcaraz, C.; Baenas, I.; Granero, R.; Sánchez, I.; Sánchez-González, J.; Menchón, J.M.; Jiménez-Murcia, S.; Treasure, J.; Fernández-Aranda, F. Lifetime Weight Course as a Phenotypic Marker of Severity and Therapeutic Response in Patients with Eating Disorders. *Nutrients* **2021**, *13*, 2034. https://doi.org/10.3390/nu13062034

Academic Editor: Lidia Santarpia

Received: 29 April 2021
Accepted: 10 June 2021
Published: 13 June 2021

Publisher's Note: MDPI stays neutral with regard to jurisdictional claims in published maps and institutional affiliations.

Abstract: The association between lifetime weight fluctuations and clinical characteristics has been widely studied in populations with eating disorders (ED). However, there is a lack of literature examining the potential role of weight course as a transdiagnostic factor in ED so far. Therefore, the aim of this study is to compare ED severity and treatment outcomes among four specific BMI profiles based on BMI-trajectories across the lifespan: (a) persistent obesity (OB-OB; (n = 74)), (b) obesity in the past but currently in a normal weight range (OB-NW; n = 156), (c) normal weight throughout the lifespan (NW-NW; n = 756), and (d) current obesity but previously at normal weight (NW-OB; n = 314). Lifetime obesity is associated with greater general psychopathology and personality traits such as low persistence and self-directedness, and high reward dependence. Additionally, greater extreme weight changes (NW-OB and OB-NW) were associated with higher psychopathology but not with greater ED severity. Higher dropout rates were found in the OB-OB group. These results shed new light on the BMI trajectory as a transdiagnostic feature playing a pivotal role in the severity and treatment outcome in patients with ED.

Keywords: body mass index (BMI) profiles; eating disorders; obesity; treatment outcome

1. Introduction

Eating disorders (ED) and obesity have frequently been considered as part of the same continuum of so-called extreme weight conditions [1–3]. This continuum is reinforced because both pathologies share risk and maintenance factors that have been widely described in the literature [4–6]. Furthermore, genetic factors underlying body mass index (BMI) have been associated with disordered eating behaviors and related cognitions, and these associations have also been mediated by BMI [7]. Among the different ED listed in the DSM-5 [8], binge eating disorder (BED) is the one with the highest prevalence of comorbid obesity [9,10] followed by bulimia nervosa (BN) [11]. Villarejo et al. [11] found that almost 30% of female patients with ED had lifetime obesity, and those patients were characterized by later age of onset, longer duration of the disorder, higher minimum and maximum-ever BMI, and higher eating-related and general psychopathological severity. Similarly, a continuum of severity has been described in which patients with obesity and BN show the highest symptomatology and psychopathology, followed by BED with obesity, with obesity without ED being the least severe [12].

The personality profiles of individuals with overweight or obesity have been widely reported in the literature, both in patients with [13,14] and without ED [15]. Patients with ED and lifetime obesity often present personality profiles characterized by a higher harm avoidance and lower scores in persistence, self-directedness, and cooperativeness than ED patients without obesity [11,12]. In addition, a systematic review on personality traits in obesity identified that high scores on reward sensitivity, impulsivity, and neuroticism may act as risk factors, whereas high self-directedness, persistence, and self-control would act as protective factors [15].

Weight trajectories [16] and fluctuations [17,18] have also been associated with disordered eating behaviors and may be of relevance as risk and maintaining factors [17,18]. Frequent weight fluctuations suggest some degree of dysregulation of weight homeostasis [19]. The difference between the premorbid weight before the onset of ED and current weight has been described as a risk factor for bulimic psychopathology [18,20]. It also appears as a predictor of weight gain during therapy [20,21] and poorer treatment outcomes [22]. Striegel-Moore et al. [23] found a rapid increase in weight trajectory two years prior to the onset of BED. Ivezaj et al. [24] also found that patients with BED and obesity reported a significant weight gain during the year before seeking treatment and this was associated with higher relapse rates, greater ED and affective psychopathology [24–26]. Furthermore, a large body of research has revealed that some ED-related characteristics such as emotional eating, binge eating behaviors, poor body image, and high body dissatisfaction are associated with weight fluctuations in patients with ED [27,28]. Indeed, some authors have described above-average weights and more fluctuation in adolescents prior to the onset of the ED (i.e.,) [29]. Likewise, severe weight cycling was more prevalent among adult women with obesity and was associated with higher reward sensitivity, and depressive-related symptomatology, and a higher prevalence of BED [30].

The relationship between weight suppression (WS) (defined as the difference between the highest adult weight and the current weight) and ED has also been the subject of interest in the literature. However, it is difficult to draw firm conclusions as the evidence is mixed. Some studies found no associations between WS and clinical variables [31,32], whereas others found that WS was related to more severe ED symptomatology, greater depression, poorer prognosis, and greater weight gain at post treatment [17,33–35].

To our knowledge, no study has examined groups of patients with ED based on lifetime weight trajectories. Therefore, the main goal of the present study was to examine whether obesity across the lifespan might be a transdiagnostic marker of ED severity and treatment outcome. A clinical sample of people with ED was post hoc distributed into four BMI profiles according to the period of obesity over adulthood: (a) with lifespan obesity (OB-OB), (b) with past obesity but currently normal weight (OB-NW), (c) with normal weight throughout their lifespan (NW-NW), and (d) with previous normal weight but current obesity (NW-OB). Therefore, two substudies were conducted. The first cross-sectional substudy aimed (1) to examine whether the different diagnostic categories of EDs are differentially distributed across the BMI profiles and (2) to compare the BMI profiles in terms of motivational stage, ED severity, general psychopathology, personality traits, and impulsive behaviors. The aim of the second prospective substudy was to examine whether the BMI profile predicted treatment outcome.

We hypothesized that the prevalence of patients with BED would be greater in BMI profiles with obesity. A second hypothesis was that patients with increased lifetime weight changes (i.e., OB-NW and NW-OB) would exhibit greater ED symptomatological and psychopathological severity, as a worse treatment outcome.

2. Materials and Methods

2.1. Participants

The clinical sample consisted of 1300 adult patients with ED. All the patients were consecutive referrals for assessment and treatment to the EDs Unit, Department of Psychiatry at the Bellvitge University Hospital (Barcelona, Spain). The sample was composed of 82 males and 1218 females meeting the criteria for BN (n = 719), BED (n = 211), and OSFED (n = 370). Patients admitted before 2013 were originally diagnosed according to DSM-IV-TR criteria [36]. All diagnoses were recoded post hoc using DSM-5 criteria [8].

The longitudinal substudy was conducted with 500 of the patients from the first substudy (91.6% females; 8.4% males) with available post-treatment data. Although differences were observed between the participants included and those not included in the longitudinal substudy in terms of diagnosis, sex, educational level, and employment status, it should be noted that they did not show significant differences in terms of the main clinical variables such as group distribution, age, age of onset of the ED, and symptomatological ED severity (see Supplementary Table S1).

The following exclusion criteria were applied to both substudies: (a) age below 18 years old; (b) having a diagnosis of AN or presenting with a BMI below 18.5 kg/m^2; (c) currently overweight (BMI: 25–29.9 kg/m^2). The last two exclusion criteria were made according to a clinical consensus to suit the standardized definitions of normal weight and obesity and to cluster the empirical groups accordingly. Figure S1 (Supplementary Materials) includes the flowchart with the sampling procedure. Additional analyses confirmed that there was no methodological bias since there were no significant differences between included and nonincluded participants in the distribution of the main variables such as sociodemographic variables (sex: $p = 0.065$, education level: $p = 0.127$, marital status: $p = 0.288$, and age: $p = 0.074$), age of onset of the disorder ($p = 0.986$), and psychopathological severity (SCL-90R PST: $p = 0.074$, SCL-90R GSI: $p = 0.075$, and SCL-90R PSDI: $p = 0.074$).

2.2. Assessment

Sociodemographic and clinical data were obtained by means of a face-to-face semistructured interview based on the SCID-5 [37] administered by clinical psychologists and psychiatrists specialized in ED. During this clinical interview, data on the presence of certain impulsive behaviors, such as nonsuicidal self-injury (NSSI) behaviors, suicidal ideation and/or attempts, alcohol abuse, and drug abuse were also retrieved from specific questions that have been previously used in previous research [38,39]. The evolution of weight was recorded by asking about the minimum and maximum weight attained throughout adulthood and at what age they reached this weight, as well as the current weight at the time of assessment. Additionally, the following commonly applied questionnaires in the field of ED were administered:

The Eating Disorder Inventory-2 (EDI-2) [40] is a 91-item self-reported questionnaire that assesses 11 ED-related cognitive and behavioral domains. A total score is also provided to report overall ED severity. This instrument has been validated in a Spanish population [41]. In the current sample, the internal consistency was excellent ($\alpha = 0.948$).

The Symptom Checklist-90-Revised (SCL-90-R) [42] contains 90 items that measure 9 primary psychopathological dimensions: somatization, obsession–compulsion, interpersonal sensitivity, depression, anxiety, hostility, phobic anxiety, paranoid ideation, and psychoticism; and includes three global indices: global severity index (overall psychological distress), positive symptom distress index (the intensity of symptoms), and a positive symptom total (self-reported symptoms). This scale has been validated in a Spanish population [43]. In the present study, internal consistency was excellent ($\alpha = 0.976$).

The Temperament and Character Inventory-Revised (TCI-R) [44] is a 240-item self-reported questionnaire that measures seven dimensions of personality: four temperament dimensions (harm avoidance, novelty seeking, reward dependence, and persistence) and three character dimensions (self-directedness, cooperativeness, and self-transcendence). The Spanish validation was carried out by Gutierrez-Zotes et al. [45]. Our internal consistency ranged from $\alpha = 0.797$ to $\alpha = 0.893$.

The motivation stage of change was evaluated by means of a visual analog scale, ranging from 0 to 8, which assessed the following five aspects: (1) subjective desire to receive treatment, (2) need for treatment, (3) perceived impairment, (4) self-concern, and (5) parental concern. Higher scores indicated greater worry and motivation to change. This scale has been previously described and applied in other studies [46].

2.3. Treatment

Treatment consisted of 16 weekly group outpatient sessions of cognitive behavioral therapy (CBT). There was a total of 8–10 patients per group. Although patients with BN, BED, and OSFED were placed in separate groups of therapy, all the treatment groups were based on the same CBT program. This program and its complementary material have already been manualized and published in Spanish [47] with demonstrated effectiveness [48–51].

Patients were reevaluated at discharge and categorized into the following DSM-5 categories [8]: full remission (total absence of symptoms meeting diagnostic criteria for at least 4 consecutive weeks), partial remission (substantial symptomatic improvement but with residual symptoms), and nonremission (poor outcome or exacerbation of symptoms). These categories were used to assess treatment outcomes in previously published studies [48,50,52–54]. Voluntary treatment discontinuation was categorized as dropout (i.e., not attending treatment for at least three consecutive sessions).

In accordance with the Declaration of Helsinki, the present study was approved by the Ethics Committee of our institution (The Clinical Research Ethics Committee (CEIC) of the Bellvitge University Hospital). All participants provided signed informed consent.

2.4. Statistical Analyses

Statistical analysis was carried out with Stata16 (StataCorp, College Station, TX, USA) LLC for windows [55]. The comparison between the four groups of the study (OB-OB, OB-NW, NW-NW, and NW-OB) was based on chi-square tests (χ^2) for categorical variables and analysis of variance (ANOVA) for quantitative variables.

The effect size for the difference between means was estimated through the standardized Cohen's d coefficient, considering null effect size for $|d| < 0.20$, low-poor for $|d| > 0.20$, moderate-medium for $|d| > 0.50$, and large-high effect for $|d| > 0.80$) [56]. The effect size for the difference between proportions was estimated through the standardized Cohen's h coefficient, which is interpreted similarly to Cohen's d measure and calculated through the arcsine transformation of the rates registered in each group (null effect size is considered for $|h| < 0.20$, low-poor for $|h| > 0.20$, moderate-medium for $|h| > 0.50$, and large-high for $|h| > 0.80$) [57].

An increase in Type-I error due to multiple significance tests was controlled with the Finner method [58], a family-wise error rate (FWER) stepwise procedure, which has proved more powerful than the classical Bonferroni correction. When controlling the k-FWER, a fixed number of k-1 of erroneous rejections is tolerated, and under the assumption that all the null hypotheses are equal, controlling the FWER at level α is equivalent to the problem of combining the original-unadjusted p-values to obtain single testing for the null hypothesis (H_0), which is at level α. For example, from a procedure R that controls the FWER at level α is equivalent to derive a single testing procedure of level α by rejecting the H_0 whenever R(p) is not empty (that is, whenever R(p) rejects at least one hypothesis). In practice, the Finner method is employed by adjusting the rejection criteria for each of the individual hypotheses fixing the FWER no higher than a certain prespecified significance level. The procedure starts sorting the p(unadjusted)-values (p1, ..., pk), achieved in k-independent null-hypothesis tests, into the order of lowest to highest. Then, the next algorithm is used: p(adjusted) = (1 − (1-p(unadjusted))^(total tests/position within the ordered tests).

3. Results

3.1. Comparison between the Groups for Sociodemographics, BMI, and Motivational Measures

Figure 1 displays the diagnostic profile within each grouping. The first block of Table 1 includes cluster, sociodemographic and diagnostic information type. The OB-OB BMI profile included mainly patients with BED, whereas patients with BN and OSFED diagnoses were within the OB-NW and NW-NW groups. The fourth BMI profile (i.e., NW-OB) consisted mainly of the BN and BED diagnostic types.

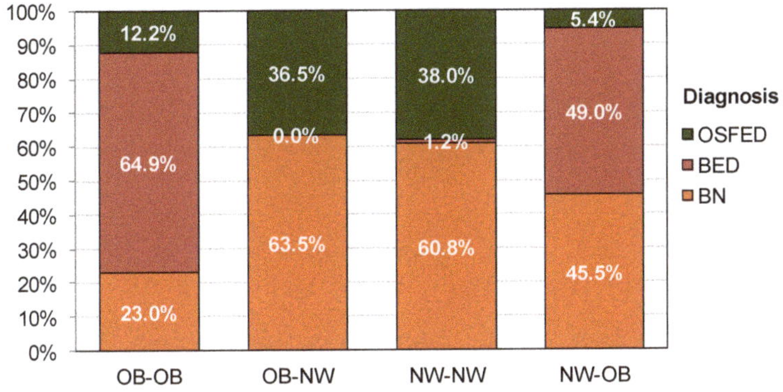

Figure 1. Distribution of the diagnostic subtype within the lifetime BMI profiles. Note: OB: obesity; NW: normal weight; BN: bulimia nervosa; BED: binge eating disorder; OSFED: other specified feeding or eating disorder.

The group with the highest prevalence of men was OB-NW, followed by OB-OB and NW-OB, only a small percentage of NW-NW patients were men.

Higher levels of educational achievement were attained in the NW-NW and NW-OB groups. A higher proportion of the NW-OB patients were married. Those in the OB-OB group were more often employed, and those in the NW-NW more often studying.

The NW-OB and OB-OB groups considered themselves to be most symptomatic and in need of treatment. Family members of NW-NW and OB-NW groups expressed most concern.

3.2. Comparison between the Groups for Clinical Measures

Table 2 contains the comparison between the groups for the clinical profiles. People in the NW-NW group were younger, with an earlier age of onset and shorter duration of the disorder. Those in the NW-OB group were older, with a later age of onset and longer duration.

The highest frequency of binges was noted within the NW-OB group, while the highest frequency of vomiting was noted in the OB-NW group. The OB-OB group had the lowest number of binges and vomiting episodes.

The highest eating psychopathology (EDI-2 total score) was in the OB-OB group, followed by NW-OB, OB-NW, and NW-NW groups. The most severe general psychopathological state (SCL-90R scores) was related to NW-OB, followed by OB-NW.

The OB-OB group had higher levels of harm avoidance, reward dependence, cooperativeness, and self-transcendence. The NW-NW group had higher levels of novelty seeking, persistence, and cooperativeness. The OB-NW group had lower levels of novelty seeking, reward dependence, and cooperativeness. The NW-OB group had higher levels of harm avoidance.

Table 1. Comparison between the BMI profiles on sociodemographics, clinical, and motivational measures.

	OB-OB $n = 74$		OB-NW $n = 156$		NW-NW $n = 756$		NW-OB $n = 314$		OB-OB vs OB-NW		OB-OB vs NW-NW		OB-OB vs NW-OB		OB-NW vs NW-NW		OB-NW vs NW-OB		NW-NW vs NW-OB	
	n	%	*n*	%	*n*	%	*n*	%	*p*	|*h*|	*p*	|*h*|	*p*	|*h*|	*p*	|*h*|	*p*	|*h*|	*p*	|*h*|
Diagnosis BN	17	23.0%	99	63.5%	460	60.8%	143	45.5%	**<0.001**	**0.90** †	**<0.001**	**0.83** †	**0.001**	**0.52** †	0.355	0.05	**<0.001**	0.37	**<0.001**	0.31
BED	48	64.9%	0	0.0%	9	1.2%	154	49.0%		**1.92** †		**1.84** †		0.32		0.16		**1.39** †		**1.32** †
OSFED	9	12.2%	57	36.5%	287	38.0%	17	5.4%		**0.59** †		**0.62** †		0.24		0.03		**0.83** †		**0.86** †
Gender Female	64	86.5%	124	79.5%	734	97.1%	296	94.3%	0.199	0.19	**<0.001**	0.39	**0.020**	0.27	**<0.001**	**0.57** †	**<0.001**	0.45	**0.027**	0.14
Male	10	13.5%	32	20.5%	22	2.9%	18	5.7%												
Education Primary	42	56.8%	89	57.1%	294	38.9%	156	49.7%	0.969	0.01	**0.009**	0.36	0.209	0.14	**<0.001**	0.37	**0.041**	0.15	**0.002**	0.22
Secondary	26	35.1%	53	34.0%	344	45.5%	108	34.4%		0.02		0.21		0.02		0.24		0.01		0.23
University	6	8.1%	14	9.0%	118	15.6%	50	15.9%		0.03		0.23		0.24		0.20		0.21		0.01
Civil status Single	42	56.8%	111	71.2%	654	86.5%	125	39.8%	**0.003** *	0.30	**<0.001**	**0.70** †	**0.026**	0.34	**<0.001**	0.38	**<0.001**	**0.66** †	**<0.001**	**1.11** †
Partner	27	36.5%	26	16.7%	68	9.0%	151	48.1%		**0.51** †		**0.69** †		0.24		0.23		**0.71** †		**0.96** †
separated	5	6.8%	19	12.2%	34	4.5%	38	12.1%		0.19		0.10		0.18		0.28		0.00		0.28
Unemployed	25	33.8%	63	40.4%	202	26.7%	160	51.0%	0.341	0.14	**<0.001**	0.15	**<0.001**	0.35	**<0.001**	0.29	**<0.001**	0.21	**<0.001**	**0.51** †
Student	18	24.3%	43	27.6%	385	50.9%	24	7.6%		0.07		**0.57** †		**0.51** †		**0.52** †		**0.54** †		**1.08** †
Employed	31	41.9%	50	32.1%	169	22.4%	130	41.4%		0.20		0.43		0.01		0.22		0.19		0.42
BMI measures	Mean	SD	Mean	SD	Mean	SD	Mean	SD	*p*	|*d*|	*p*	|*d*|	*p*	|*d*|	*p*	|*d*|	*p*	|*d*|	*p*	|*d*|
BMI current	44.95	9.46	22.16	1.74	20.81	1.66	36.54	5.25	**<0.001**	**3.35** †	**<0.001**	**3.55** †	**<0.001**	**1.10** †	**<0.001**	**0.80** †	**<0.001**	**3.67** †	**<0.001**	**4.04** †
BMI max.	48.45	9.50	34.72	4.94	22.76	1.43	38.48	5.79	**<0.001**	**1.81** †	**<0.001**	**3.78** †	**<0.001**	**1.27** †	**<0.001**	**3.29** †	**<0.001**	**0.70** †	**<0.001**	**3.73** †
BMI min.	33.41	3.17	19.92	2.55	17.99	1.88	21.89	2.17	**<0.001**	**4.69** †	**<0.001**	**5.92** †	**<0.001**	**4.24** †	**<0.001**	**0.86** †	**<0.001**	**0.83** †	**<0.001**	**1.92** †
Motivation: Intensity	6.14	1.62	5.64	2.17	5.12	1.97	6.24	1.75	0.069	0.26	**<0.001**	**0.56** †	0.667	0.06	**0.002**	0.25	**0.001**	0.31	**<0.001**	**0.60** †
Need treatment	6.74	1.48	5.87	2.28	5.71	2.18	6.74	1.66	**0.003**	**0.52** †	**<0.001**	**0.56** †	0.987	0.00	0.361	0.07	**<0.001**	0.44	**<0.001**	**0.53** †
Social impairment	5.18	2.56	4.90	2.55	4.69	2.36	5.32	2.36	0.410	0.11	0.099	0.20	0.630	0.06	0.335	0.08	0.069	0.17	**<0.001**	0.27
Self-concern	7.00	1.09	6.15	2.18	6.13	2.14	6.96	1.59	**0.003**	**0.51** †	**<0.001**	**0.51** †	0.881	0.03	0.871	0.01	**<0.001**	0.42	**<0.001**	0.44
Family concern	6.09	2.32	6.57	2.09	6.68	2.00	5.95	2.36	0.112	0.22	**0.023**	0.27	0.595	0.06	0.553	0.05	**0.003**	0.28	**<0.001**	0.33

Note: OB: obesity; NW: normal weight; BN: bulimia nervosa; BED: binge eating disorder; OSFED: other specified feeding and eating disorder; SD: standard deviation; * bold: significant comparison; † bold: effect size into the range mild/moderate (|*d*| > 0.50 or |*h*| > 0.50) to large/high (|*d*| > 0.80 or |*h*| > 0.80).

Table 2. Comparison between the groups for the clinical profile.

	OB-OB $n = 74$		OB-NW $n = 156$		NW-NW $n = 756$		NW-OB $n = 314$		OB-OB vs OB-NW		OB-OB vs NW-NW		OB-OB vs NW-OB		OB-NW vs NW-NW		OB-NW vs NW-OB		NW-NW vs NW-OB	
	Mean	SD	Mean	SD	Mean	SD	Mean	SD	p	$\lvert d \rvert$	p	$\lvert d \rvert$	p	$\lvert d \rvert$	p	$\lvert d \rvert$	p	$\lvert d \rvert$	p	$\lvert d \rvert$
Age (years-old)	32.70	10.56	29.12	9.01	24.91	7.60	37.61	10.77	**0.004 ***	0.36	**0.001 ***	**0.85 †**	**0.001 ***	**0.51 †**	**0.001 ***	**0.51 †**	**0.001 ***	**0.86 †**	**0.001 ***	**1.36 †**
Onset of ED	19.91	8.84	20.88	8.74	17.76	4.88	25.28	10.82	0.356	0.11	**0.018**	0.30	**0.001 ***	**0.54 †**	**0.001 ***	0.44	**0.001 ***	0.45	**0.001 ***	**0.90 †**
Duration of ED	12.80	8.62	8.27	7.21	7.19	6.95	12.41	10.01	**0.001 ***	**0.57 †**	**0.001 ***	**0.72 †**	0.708	0.04	0.122	0.15	**0.001 ***	**0.51 †**	**0.001 ***	**0.61 †**
Binges/week	3.98	4.94	3.97	6.13	4.11	5.77	6.16	5.59	0.988	0.00	0.850	0.02	**0.003 ***	0.41	0.775	0.02	**0.001 ***	0.37	**0.001 ***	0.36
Vomits/week	1.63	4.67	7.04	9.40	5.16	7.38	2.46	6.14	**0.001 ***	**0.73 †**	**0.001 ***	**0.57 †**	0.376	0.15	**0.003 ***	0.22	**0.001 ***	**0.58 †**	**0.001 ***	0.40
EDI-2: Total score	113.26	38.67	109.56	45.35	100.72	40.28	111.45	38.26	0.517	0.09	**0.011 ***	0.32	0.729	0.05	**0.013**	0.21	0.633	0.05	**0.001 ***	0.27
SCL-90R GSI	1.73	0.73	1.87	0.75	1.72	0.70	1.91	0.73	0.161	0.19	0.875	0.02	0.059	0.24	**0.014 ***	0.21	0.638	0.04	**0.001 ***	0.26
SCL-90R PST	62.12	16.26	65.42	18.65	64.78	17.00	66.32	15.82	0.167	0.19	0.196	0.16	0.054	0.26	0.669	0.04	0.583	0.05	0.174	0.09
SCL-90R PSDI	2.44	0.55	2.49	0.60	2.29	0.53	2.52	0.56	0.484	0.09	**0.032 ***	0.27	0.252	0.15	**0.001 ***	0.35	0.615	0.05	**0.001 ***	0.41
Novelty seeking	101.88	15.70	99.28	17.08	104.22	15.38	101.97	15.76	0.242	0.16	0.222	0.15	0.965	0.01	**0.001 ***	0.30	0.081	0.16	**0.033 ***	0.14
Harm avoidance	121.05	18.82	116.81	20.07	114.81	19.27	122.98	18.02	0.115	0.22	**0.007 ***	0.33	0.434	0.10	0.232	0.10	**0.001 ***	0.32	**0.001 ***	0.44
Reward dependence	104.08	17.36	99.02	14.53	102.35	14.85	102.31	15.68	**0.018 ***	0.32	0.348	0.11	0.366	0.11	**0.013 ***	0.23	**0.027 ***	0.22	0.969	0.00
Persistence	103.64	17.22	106.80	21.26	110.63	19.65	104.18	20.87	0.263	0.16	**0.004 ***	0.38	0.833	0.03	**0.030 ***	0.19	0.182	0.12	**0.001 ***	0.32
Self-directedness	114.07	19.96	113.45	19.45	115.94	19.61	111.05	20.23	0.824	0.03	0.436	0.09	0.238	0.15	0.151	0.13	0.216	0.12	**0.001 ***	0.25
Cooperativeness	132.88	18.23	130.37	16.32	133.36	15.23	132.57	16.65	0.264	0.14	0.803	0.03	0.881	0.02	**0.033 ***	0.19	0.158	0.13	0.458	0.05
Self-transcendence	68.95	15.31	64.28	14.21	64.98	14.20	66.58	15.82	**0.024 ***	0.32	**0.027 ***	0.27	0.213	0.15	0.585	0.05	0.109	0.15	0.104	0.11

Note: OB: obesity; NW: normal weight; SD: standard deviation; * bold: significant comparison; † bold: effect size into the range mild/moderate ($\lvert d \rvert > 0.50$) to large/high ($\lvert d \rvert > 0.80$).

3.3. Comparison between the Groups for Impulsive Behaviors

NSSI behavior, suicidal ideation and attempts, and substance use/abuse are shown in Table 3. The highest proportions of patients who reported NSSI behavior were in the OB-NW group, followed by NW-NW, NW-OB, and OB-OB groups. The highest prevalence of suicidal behavior (ideation and attempts) was registered among NW-OB and OB-NW groups. The lowest prevalence of alcohol and drug consumption was registered among the OB-OB group, while OB-NW and NW-NW groups reported the highest prevalence.

3.4. Association between Age of Onset of ED and Age of Maximum BMI

The age of the maximum BMI and age of onset of the ED are shown in Table 4, and a scatterplot of these data is shown in Figure 2. Most patients in the BMI profile of NW-OB and OB-OB registered the maximum BMI after the onset of the ED. Among OB-NW patients, 35.2% registered maximum-ever BMI prior to the onset of ED, 27.2% coinciding with the onset of ED, and 37.6% after the onset of ED. Among NW-NW patients, 24.6% registered maximum-ever BMI prior to the onset of the ED, 22.9% coinciding with the onset of ED, and 52.5% after the onset of ED.

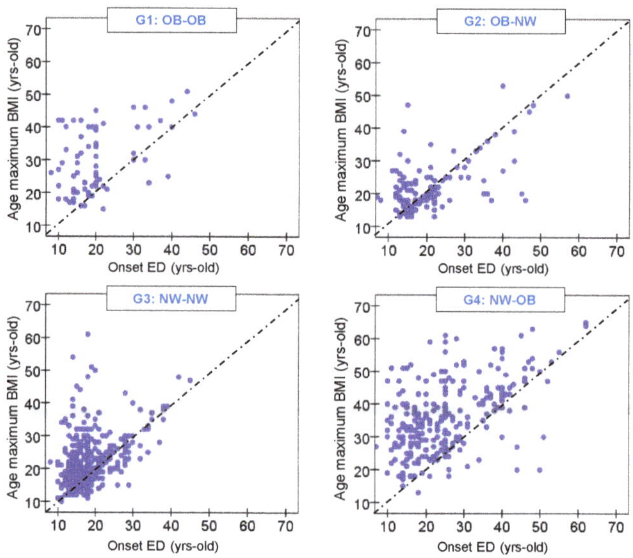

Figure 2. Scatterplot with the age of onset of the ED and the age of the maximum BMI.

3.5. Comparison of the CBT Outcomes between the BMI Profiles

Table 5 shows the distribution of the CBT outcomes between the groups (see also Figure 3). The OB-OB BMI profile registered the highest prevalence of dropouts and the lowest of non-remission. The NW-NW BMI profile presented the highest prevalence of non-remission. OB-NW and NW-OB groups achieved the highest prevalence of partial- or full-remission.

Table 3. Comparison between the groups for impulsivity measures.

	OB-OB G1; n = 74		OB-NW G2; n = 156		NW-NW G3; n = 756		NW-OB G4; n = 314		G1 vs G2		G1 vs G3		G1 vs G4		G2 vs G3		G2 vs G4		G3 vs G4	
	n	%	n	%	n	%	n	%	p	|h|	p	|h|	p	|h|	p	|h|	p	|h|	p	|h|
NSSI	18	24.3%	60	38.5%	257	34.0%	90	28.7%	**0.034** *	0.31	0.092	0.21	0.454	0.10	0.286	0.09	**0.032** *	0.21	0.090	0.12
Suicidal ideation	37	50.0%	85	54.5%	367	48.5%	181	57.6%	0.524	0.09	0.811	0.03	0.233	0.15	0.177	0.12	0.516	0.06	**0.007** *	0.18
Suicidal attempts	16	21.6%	39	25.0%	147	19.4%	80	25.5%	0.575	0.08	0.653	0.05	0.489	0.09	0.117	0.13	0.911	0.01	**0.028** *	0.14
Alcohol abuse	1	1.4%	16	10.3%	77	10.2%	24	7.6%	**0.016** *	0.39	**0.013** *	0.39	**0.047** *	0.31	0.979	0.00	0.339	0.09	0.195	0.09
Drugs abuse	8	10.8%	28	17.9%	157	20.8%	41	13.1%	0.164	0.20	**0.041** *	0.28	0.601	0.07	0.425	0.07	0.158	0.14	**0.003** *	0.21

Note: OB: obesity; NW: normal weight; NSSI: nonsuicidal self-injury; vs: versus; * bold: significant comparison.

Table 4. Age of onset of ED and age of maximum BMI.

	OB-OB G1; n = 69		OB-NW G2; n = 125		NW-NW G3; n = 558		NW-OB G4; n = 260		G1 vs G2		G1 vs G3		G1 vs G4		G2 vs G3		G2 vs G4		G3 vs G4	
Maximum BMI	n	%	n	%	n	%	n	%	p	|h|	p	|h|	p	|h|	p	|h|	p	|h|	p	|h|
Previous onset ED	7	10.1%	44	35.2%	137	24.6%	21	8.1%	**0.001** *	**0.63** †	**0.001** *	0.39	0.564	0.07	**0.008** *	0.23	**0.001** *	**0.70** †	**0.001** *	**0.51** †
Coincides onset ED	5	7.2%	34	27.2%	128	22.9%	12	4.6%		**0.55** †		**0.51** †		0.11		0.10		**0.65** †		**0.55** †
Posterior onset ED	57	82.6%	47	37.6%	293	52.5%	227	87.3%		**1.03** †		**0.68** †		0.13		0.30		**1.20** †		**0.82** †

Note: OB: obesity; NW: normal weight; vs: versus; * bold: significant comparison; † bold: effect size into the range mild/moderate (|h| > 0.50) to large/high (|h| > 0.80).

Table 5. Comparison for the CBT outcomes.

	OB-OB G1; n = 29		OB-NW G2; n = 60		NW-NW G3; n = 282		NW-OB G4; n = 129		G1 vs G2		G1 vs G3		G1 vs G4		G2 vs G3		G2 vsG4		G3 vs G4	
	n	%	n	%	n	%	n	%	p	|h|	p	|h|	p	|h|	p	|h|	p	|h|	p	|h|
Drop out	15	51.7%	21	35.0%	101	35.8%	36	27.9%	0.408	0.34	**0.038** *	0.32	**0.040** *	**0.51** †	0.105	0.02	0.290	0.15	0.081	0.17
Non-remission	1	3.4%	4	6.7%	49	17.4%	21	16.3%		0.15		**0.50** †		0.44		0.33		0.31		0.03
Partial-remission	4	13.8%	15	25.0%	69	24.5%	28	21.7%		0.29		0.27		0.21		0.01		0.08		0.07
Full-remission	9	31.0%	20	33.3%	63	22.3%	44	34.1%		0.05		0.20		0.07		0.25		0.02		0.26

Note: OB: obesity; NW: normal weight; vs: versus; * bold: significant comparison; † bold: effect size into the range mild/moderate (|h| > 0.50) to large/high (|h| > 0.80).

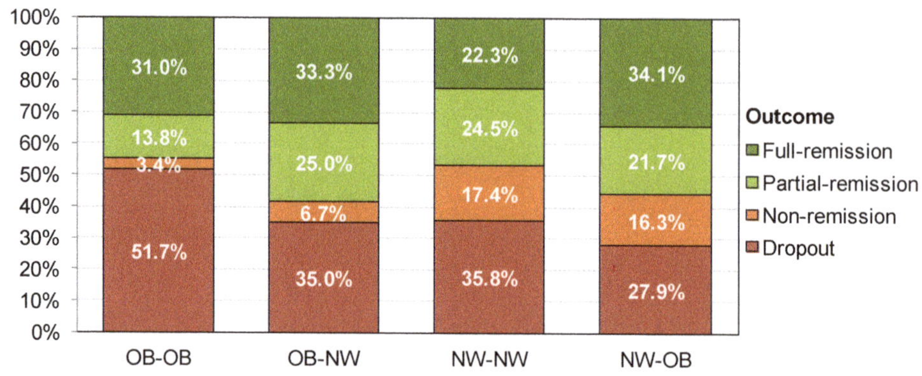

Figure 3. Distribution of the CBT outcome within the lifetime BMI profiles. Note: OB: obesity; NW: normal weight.

4. Discussion

The present study sought to address an important gap in the literature by examining whether the weight history of patients with ED could be a transdiagnostic marker of severity and treatment outcome. We analyzed the psychopathology and dysfunctional personality profiles of the different groups. We also examined whether these BMI profiles had a different response to therapy.

As expected, the main finding was that most patients with BED were in the BMI profile with current obesity. These results are in line with previous studies suggesting that BED is strongly associated with excessive body weight gain [11,59], due to the high-calorie overconsumption in absence of compensatory behaviors and the sedentary lifestyle frequently reported by these patients [10,60]. While most patients with OSFED were mainly represented in the BMI profiles with current normal weight (OB-NW and NW-NW), the patients with BN were more heterogeneous, and they were cited in all the BMI profiles but were mainly normal weight.

Patients with current obesity (i.e., those in OB-OB and NW-OB) reported the highest levels of motivation for change, specifically greater concern, and subjective intensity of their ED, and a higher desire for treatment. It may suggest that they consider their obesity related to the ED and, therefore, they are more motivated to seek treatment. This hypothesis would be reinforced by our results showing that most patients in the OB-OB and NW-OB BMI profiles recorded the maximum-ever BMI after the onset of the ED. On the other hand, it should be noted that these patients also had a longer duration or chronicity of the disorder, which has previously been related to increased motivation and perceived need for treatment [61].

The second main objective was to examine the clinical differences between the groups based on BMI changes over the lifetime. Our findings are partially in agreement with previous research on weight fluctuations. Consistent with previous studies, we found an association between lifetime weight changes (i.e., NW-OB and OB-NW) and a more severe general psychopathological state [24]. However, in contrast to other studies [24,25], we found no association between weight fluctuations and greater ED-related symptomatology. Nevertheless, according to previous research [11], our results corroborate that, overall, patients with lifetime obesity report greater ED and general psychopathology, compared to those without a history of obesity (namely NW-NW). This might suggest that lifetime obesity, rather than weight fluctuations, is associated with greater psychopathology, regardless of whether the obesity was before or after the development of the ED. Our findings show that patients who have never had obesity had higher novelty seeking, and were also higher in persistence and self-directedness than those with lifetime obesity. These findings are similar to those reported by Villarejo et al. [11] in which a more dysfunctional personality profile (characterized by high harm avoidance, and low scores on persistence, self-directedness, and cooperativeness) was described in patients with ED and lifetime obesity. Similarly, high persistence, self-directedness, and self-control have been identified as protective factors for weight gain or obesity development [15]. In addition, this research went a step further and identified the lowest scores on reward dependence and novelty seeking in the group of patients with previous obesity but current normal weight (i.e., OB-NW). Low scores on reward dependence are related to being independent, not influenced by others, nonconformist, socially detached, and insensitive to social pressures. Therefore, although this finding may seem striking, it is in line with a previous study suggesting that people who do not require social support and are more self-confident are more likely to achieve self-directed weight loss [62]. This finding supports the use of therapeutic tools targeted at improving self-reliance, especially in patients with lifetime obesity. On the other hand, our results reveal that patients who achieved a normal weight coming from obesity were those with the lowest scores on novelty seeking. This is consistent with a prior study suggesting that low novelty seeking was associated with weight loss in patients seeking treatment for obesity [63]. Therefore, this finding suggests that using techniques to reduce impulsivity would be useful in the treatment of patients with ED and obesity [64].

Our results also reveal that patients with more extreme weight changes across the lifespan (i.e., OB-NW and NW-OB) endorsed a higher frequency of suicidal ideation and attempts. These results are in line with previous studies reporting more depressive-related symptomatology and severe psychopathology in patients with lifetime weight fluctuations [22,24,30]. The OB-NW profile also engaged in more NSSI behaviors. Additionally, this group had the highest frequency of vomiting episodes, which is in line with previous findings suggesting that NSSI is strongly related to purging behaviors and both may serve similar functions in terms of emotion regulation [65]. The lowest prevalence of substance consumption (alcohol and drugs) was registered among OB-OB. As this BMI profile had the lowest frequency of vomiting, our results are also in agreement with previous studies that found a relationship between a higher frequency of purging behaviors and higher substance use [66,67].

Finally, the longitudinal data indicate that patients in both OB-NW and NW-OB groups had the best treatment outcomes, which is inconsistent with the previous literature that had found a relationship between greater weight fluctuations and lower therapeutic adherence and worse treatment outcome [17]. Patients in the OB-OB BMI profile had the highest dropout rates. This novel and noteworthy result calls into question the findings of previous studies reporting that patients with BED had rapid symptoms remission but also high dropout rates, compared to BN [48]. This previous study suggested that patients with BED, most of them with obesity, dropped out more frequently because their desire to lose weight was not addressed by standard CBT. In addition, the current research expands these findings and indicates differences within this type of patient. Although patients with BED were represented in both NW-OB and OB-OB BMI profiles, only those in the latter group presented a higher prevalence of dropout. One possible rationale could be that patients who have developed obesity after the ED onset may consider their weight gain as a consequence of the disorder and dependent on their recovery. Therefore, they may exhibit greater therapeutic adherence.

Limitations and Strengths

The present study should be considered within the context of several limitations. First, retrospective and self-report data collection (mainly regarding maximum and minimum weight) may limit the validity and reliability of our results. Participants who may have been underweight (BMI < 18.5 kg/m^2) in the past were not excluded in this study because of the difficulty of interpreting retrospective reports of age-associated BMI changes and the unavailability of height data. Further studies should exclude participants with a lifetime BMI less than 18.5 by controlling for weight and height at each time point. In addition, although we asked for the age of onset of ED and age of maximum and minimum BMI, our results do not allow us to state that weight changes are a cause or a consequence of the disorder. Second, the low representation of males did not allow for meaningful sex-related comparisons. However, this was representative of the proportion we routinely observe in clinical practice. Third, the motivational scale has not been validated, although it has been used in previous studies [46,49,61]. In this line, further studies should include validated instruments to measure the motivation stage of change. Finally, findings from the longitudinal substudy were based on symptomatological remission after the therapy but not recovery (which requires a long period of abstinence from ED symptomatology). Hence, additional longitudinal studies collecting follow-up data are needed to determine the long-term effect of the associations found.

Notwithstanding these limitations, the study also has several strengths that should be noted. To the best of our knowledge, this is the first study examining the potential role of BMI changes across the lifespan in the phenotypic characteristics and severity of patients with ED, as well as their association with therapeutic response.

5. Conclusions

In short, our findings provide support for considering the course of BMI as a transdiagnostic feature that serves as a possible marker of severity and treatment outcome. Our findings corroborate that lifetime obesity is associated with greater general psychopathology and with some personality traits such as low persistence and self-directedness, and high reward dependence (i.e., low self-confidence). Thus, more functional scores on these personality traits may act as protective factors against weight gain. Finally, a relevant finding from our research reveals that only a subgroup of patients with BED (namely, those in the OB-OB BMI profile) have significantly less treatment adherence and higher dropout rates, which might be because they do not link their obesity to the ED. Thus, the findings derived from this study might improve our ability to identify clinical features related to the symptomatic expression and prognosis of these patients (namely weight changes) and, thereby, aid in tailoring the best treatment targets.

Supplementary Materials: The following are available online at https://www.mdpi.com/article/10.3390/nu13062034/s1, Table S1: Comparison between the groups included and not in the substudy 2 of the treatment outcomes.

Author Contributions: Conceptualization, Z.A., C.V.-A., I.B., and F.F.-A.; methodology, Z.A. and R.G.; formal analysis, R.G.; investigation, Z.A., C.V.-A., and I.B.; data curation, Z.A. and R.G.; resources, F.F.-A.; writing—original draft preparation, Z.A., C.V.-A., I.B., and R.G.; writing—review and editing, Z.A., S.J.-M., I.S., J.S.-G., J.M.M., J.T., and F.F.-A.; supervision, Z.A. and F.F.-A.; funding acquisition, S.J.-M. and F.F.-A. All authors have read and agreed to the published version of the manuscript.

Funding: We thank CERCA Programme/Generalitat de Catalunya for institutional support. This research was partially supported by Instituto de Salud Carlos III (ISCIII; Grant Number: PI17/01167 and PI20/00132), by PERIS (Generalitat de Catalunya, SLT006/17/00246), and co-funded by FEDER funds/European Regional Development Fund (ERDF), a way to build Europe. C.V.-A. is supported by a predoctoral Grant of the Ministerio de Educación, Cultura y Deporte (FPU16/01453). I.B. was partially supported by a post-residency grant from the Research Committee of the University Hospital of Bellvitge (HUB; Barcelona, Spain) 2019–2020. CIBERobn and CIBERSAM are initiatives of ISCIII.

Institutional Review Board Statement: The study was conducted according to the guidelines of the Declaration of Helsinki and approved by the Ethics Committee of Bellvitge University Hospital (Protocol Code PR149/11, date of approval: 9 June 2011).

Informed Consent Statement: Written informed consent was obtained from all subjects involved in the study.

Data Availability Statement: Data are not available in any repository. Contact with corresponding authors.

Conflicts of Interest: Fernando Fernández-Aranda reports consultation fees from Novo Nordisk and the editor-in-Chief honorarium from Wiley. The funders had no role in the design of the study; in the collection, analyses, or interpretation of data; in the writing of the manuscript, or in the decision to publish the results. No other conflicts of interest are declared by the authors.

References

1. Ortega, F.J.; Agüera, Z.; Sabater, M.; Moreno-Navarrete, J.M.; Alonso-Ledesma, I.; Xifra, G.; Botas, P.; Delgado, E.; Jimenez-Murcia, S.; Fernández-García, J.C.; et al. Genetic variations of the bitter taste receptor TAS2R38 are associated with obesity and impact on single immune traits. *Mol. Nutr. Food Res.* **2016**, *60*, 1673–1683. [CrossRef]
2. Fagundo, A.; de la Torre, R.; Jimenez-Murcia, S.; Agüera, Z.; Granero, R.; Tárrega, S.; Botella, C.; Baños, R.; Fernández-Real, J.; Rodríguez, R.; et al. Executive functions profile in extreme eating/weight conditions: From anorexia nervosa to obesity. *PLoS ONE* **2012**, *7*, e43382. [CrossRef] [PubMed]
3. Marcus, M.D.; Wildes, J.E. Obesity: Is it a mental disorder? *Int. J. Eat. Disord.* **2009**, *42*, 739–753. [CrossRef] [PubMed]
4. Haines, J.; Neumark-Sztainer, D. Prevention of obesity and eating disorders: A consideration of shared risk factors. *Health Educ. Res.* **2006**, *21*, 770–782. [CrossRef] [PubMed]
5. Neumark-Sztainer, D. The interface between the eating disorders and obesity fields: Moving toward a model of shared knowledge and collaboration. *Eat. Weight Disord.* **2009**, *14*, 51–58. [CrossRef] [PubMed]
6. Rancourt, D.; McCullough, M.B. Overlap in Eating Disorders and Obesity in Adolescence. *Curr. Diabetes Rep.* **2015**, *15*, 1–9. [CrossRef]
7. Abdulkadir, M.; Herle, M.; De Stavola, B.L.; Hübel, C.; Santos Ferreira, D.L.; Loos, R.J.F.; Bryant-Waugh, R.; Bulik, C.M.; Micali, N. Polygenic Score for Body Mass Index Is Associated with Disordered Eating in a General Population Cohort. *J. Clin. Med.* **2020**, *9*, 1187. [CrossRef]
8. American Psychiatric Association. *Diagnostic and Statistical Manual of Mental Disorders: DSM-5*, 5th ed.; American Psychiatric Association: Washington, DC, USA, 2013.
9. De Zwaan, M. Binge eating disorder and obesity. *Int. J. Obes. Relat. Metab. Disord.* **2001**, *25* (Suppl. 1), S51–S55. [CrossRef] [PubMed]
10. Agüera, Z.; Lozano-Madrid, M.; Mallorquí-Bagué, N.; Jimenez-Murcia, S.; Menchón, J.; Fernández-Aranda, F. A review of binge eating disorder and obesity. *Neuropsychiatrie* **2020**, 1–11. [CrossRef]
11. Villarejo, C.; Fernández-Aranda, F.; Jimenez-Murcia, S.; Peñas-Lledó, E.; Granero, R.; Penelo, E.; Tinahones, F.; Sancho, C.; Vilarrasa, N.; Montserrat-Gil De Bernabe, M.; et al. Lifetime obesity in patients with eating disorders: Increasing prevalence, clinical and personality correlates. *Eur. Eat. Disord. Rev.* **2012**, *20*, 250–254. [CrossRef] [PubMed]
12. Villarejo, C.; Jimenez-Murcia, S.; Álvarez-Moya, E.M.; Granero, R.; Penelo, E.; Treasure, J.; Vilarrasa, N.; Gil-Montserrat de Bernabé, M.M.; Casanueva, F.F.; Tinahones, F.J.; et al. Loss of control over eating: A description of the eating disorder/obesity spectrum in women. *Eur. Eat. Disord. Rev.* **2014**, *22*, 25–31. [CrossRef]
13. Davis, C.; Levitan, R.D.; Carter, J.; Kaplan, A.S.; Reid, C.; Curtis, C.; Patte, K.; Kennedy, J.L. Personality and eating behaviors: A case-control study of binge eating disorder. *Int. J. Eat. Disord.* **2008**, *41*, 243–250. [CrossRef]
14. Peterson, C.B.; Thuras, P.; Ackard, D.M.; Mitchell, J.E.; Berg, K.; Sandager, N.; Wonderlich, S.A.; Pederson, M.W.; Crow, S.J. Personality dimensions in bulimia nervosa, binge eating disorder, and obesity. *Compr. Psychiatry* **2010**, *51*, 31–36. [CrossRef]
15. Gerlach, G.; Herpertz, S.; Loeber, S. Personality traits and obesity: A systematic review. *Obes. Rev.* **2015**, *16*, 32–63. [CrossRef]
16. Stemann Larsen, P.; Nybo Andersen, A.M.; Olsen, E.M.; Kragh Andersen, P.; Micali, N.; Strandberg-Larsen, K. Weight trajectories and disordered eating behaviours in 11- to 12-year-olds: A longitudinal study within the Danish National Birth Cohort. *Eur. Eat. Disord. Rev.* **2019**, *27*, 436–444. [CrossRef] [PubMed]
17. Gorrell, S.; Reilly, E.E.; Schaumberg, K.; Anderson, L.M.; Donahue, J.M. Weight suppression and its relation to eating disorder and weight outcomes: A narrative review. *Eat. Disord.* **2019**, *27*, 52–81. [CrossRef] [PubMed]
18. Thomas, J.G.; Butryn, M.L.; Stice, E.; Lowe, M.R. A prospective test of the relation between weight change and risk for bulimia nervosa. *Int. J. Eat. Disord.* **2011**, *44*, 295–303. [CrossRef] [PubMed]
19. Lowe, M.R.; Feig, E.H.; Winter, S.R.; Stice, E. Short-term variability in body weight predicts long-term weight gain. *Am. J. Clin. Nutr.* **2015**, *102*, 995–999. [CrossRef]
20. Lowe, M.R.; Davis, W.; Lucks, D.; Annunziato, R.; Butryn, M. Weight suppression predicts weight gain during inpatient treatment of bulimia nervosa. *Physiol. Behav.* **2006**, *87*, 487–492. [CrossRef] [PubMed]
21. Herzog, D.B.; Thomas, J.G.; Kass, A.E.; Eddy, K.T.; Franko, D.L.; Lowe, M.R. Weight suppression predicts weight change over 5years in bulimia nervosa. *Psychiatry Res.* **2010**, *177*, 330–334. [CrossRef]
22. Lowe, M.R.; Berner, L.A.; Swanson, S.A.; Clark, V.L.; Eddy, K.T.; Franko, D.L.; Shaw, J.A.; Ross, S.; Herzog, D.B. Weight suppression predicts time to remission from bulimia nervosa. *J. Consult. Clin. Psychol.* **2011**, *79*, 772–776. [CrossRef] [PubMed]
23. Striegel-Moore, R.H.; Franko, D.L.; Thompson, D.; Barton, B.; Schreiber, G.B.; Daniels, S.R. Changes in weight and body image over time in women with eating disorders. *Int. J. Eat. Disord.* **2004**, *36*, 315–327. [CrossRef]
24. Ivezaj, V.; Kalebjian, R.; Grilo, C.M.; Barnes, R.D. Comparing weight gain in the year prior to treatment for overweight and obese patients with and without binge eating disorder in primary care. *J. Psychosom. Res.* **2014**, *77*, 151–154. [CrossRef] [PubMed]

25. Barnes, R.D.; Blomquist, K.K.; Grilo, C.M. Exploring pretreatment weight trajectories in obese patients with binge eating disorder. *Compr. Psychiatry* **2011**, *52*, 312–318. [CrossRef] [PubMed]
26. Masheb, R.M.; White, M.A.; Grilo, C.M. Substantial weight gains are common prior to treatment-seeking in obese patients with binge eating disorder. *Compr. Psychiatry* **2013**, *54*, 880–884. [CrossRef] [PubMed]
27. Keller, C.; Siegrist, M. Ambivalence toward palatable food and emotional eating predict weight fluctuations. Results of a longitudinal study with four waves. *Appetite* **2015**, *85*, 138–145. [CrossRef]
28. Kjærbye-Thygesen, A.; Munk, C.; Ottesen, B.; Kjær, S.K. Why Do Slim Women Consider Themselves Too Heavy? A Characterization of Adult Women Considering Their Body Weight as Too Heavy. *Int. J. Eat. Disord.* **2004**, *35*, 275–285. [CrossRef]
29. Swenne, I. Changes in body weight and body mass index (BMI) in teenage girls prior to the onset and diagnosis of an eating disorder. *Acta Paediatr. Int. J. Paediatr.* **2001**, *90*, 677–681. [CrossRef]
30. De Zwaan, M.; Engeli, S.; Müller, A. Temperamental factors in severe weight cycling. A cross-sectional study. *Appetite* **2015**, *91*, 336–342. [CrossRef] [PubMed]
31. Van Son, G.E.; van der Meer, P.A.M.; Van Furth, E.F. Correlates and associations between weight suppression and binge eating symptomatology in a population-based sample. *Eat. Behav.* **2013**, *14*, 102–106. [CrossRef]
32. Zunker, C.; Crosby, R.D.; Mitchell, J.E.; Wonderlich, S.A.; Peterson, C.B.; Crow, S.J. Weight suppression as a predictor variable in treatment trials of bulimia nervosa and binge eating disorder. *Int. J. Eat. Disord.* **2011**, *44*, 727–730. [CrossRef] [PubMed]
33. Berner, L.A.; Shaw, J.A.; Witt, A.A.; Lowe, M.R. The Relation of Weight Suppression and Body Mass Index to Symptomatology and Treatment Response in Anorexia Nervosa. *J. Abnorm. Psychol.* **2013**, *122*, 694. [CrossRef] [PubMed]
34. Jenkins, P.E.; Lebow, J.; Rienecke, R.D. Weight suppression as a predictor variable in the treatment of eating disorders: A systematic review. *J. Psychiatr. Ment. Health Nurs.* **2018**, *25*, 297–306. [CrossRef] [PubMed]
35. Lavender, J.M.; Shaw, J.A.; Crosby, R.D.; Feig, E.H.; Mitchell, J.E.; Crow, S.J.; Hill, L.; Le Grange, D.; Powers, P.; Lowe, M.R. Associations between weight suppression and dimensions of eating disorder psychopathology in a multisite sample. *J. Psychiatr. Res.* **2015**, *69*, 87–93. [CrossRef] [PubMed]
36. American Psychiatric Association. *Diagnostic and Statistical Manual of Mental Disorders: DSM-IV-TR*; American Psychiatric Association: Arlington, VA, USA, 2000; Volume 4, ISBN 0890420254.
37. First, M.; Williams, J.; Karg, R.; Spitzer, R. *Structured Clinical Interview for DSM-5—Research Version (SCID-5 for DSM-5, Research Version SCID-5-RV)*; American Psychiatric Association: Arlington, VA, USA, 2015.
38. Gómez-Expósito, A.; Wolz, I.; Fagundo, A.B.; Granero, R.; Steward, T.; Jimenez-Murcia, S.; Agüera, Z.; Fernández-Aranda, F. Correlates of non-suicidal self-injury and suicide attempts in bulimic spectrum disorders. *Front. Psychol.* **2016**, *7*. [CrossRef] [PubMed]
39. Lozano-Madrid, M.; Bryan, D.C.; Sánchez, I.; Riesco, N.; Mallorquí-Bagué, N.; Jimenez-Murcia, S.; Treasure, J.; Fernández-Aranda, F. Impulsivity, Emotional Dysregulation and Executive Function Deficits Could Be Associated with Alcohol and Drug Abuse in Eating Disorders. *J. Clin. Med.* **2020**, *9*, 1936. [CrossRef]
40. Garner, D. *Eating Disorder Inventory-2*; Psychological Assessment Resources: Odessa, Ukraine, 1991.
41. Garner, D. *Inventario de Trastornos de la Conducta Alimentaria (EDI-2)*; TEA Ediciones: Madrid, Spain, 1998.
42. Derogatis, L.R. *SCL-90-R. Administration, Scoring and Procedures Manual*; Clinical Psychometric Research: Baltimore, MD, USA, 1990.
43. Derogatis, L.R. *SCL-90-R. Cuestionario de 90 Síntomas-Manual*; TEA Editorial: Madrid, Spain, 2002.
44. Cloninger, C.R. *The Temperament and Character Inventory–Revised*; Center for Psychobiology of Personality, Washington University: St. Louis, MO, USA, 1999.
45. Gutiérrez-Zotes, J.A.; Bayón, C.; Montserrat, C.; Valero, J.; Labad, A.; Cloninger, C.R.; Fernández-Aranda, F. Temperament and Character Inventory—Revised (TCI-R). Standardization and normative data in a general population sample. *ACTAS Esp. Psiquiatr.* **2004**, *32*, 8–15. [PubMed]
46. Casanovas, C.; Fernández-Aranda, F.; Granero, R.; Krug, I.; Jimenez-Murcia, S.; Bulik, C.M.; Vallejo-Ruiloba, J. Motivation to change in eating disorders: Clinical and therapeutic implications. *Eur. Eat. Disord. Rev.* **2007**, *15*, 449–456. [CrossRef]
47. Fernández-Aranda, F.; Turón, V. *Trastornos Alimentarios. Guia Basica de Tratamiento en Anorexia y Bulimia*; Masson: Barcelona, Spain, 1998.
48. Agüera, Z.; Riesco, N.; Jimenez-Murcia, S.; Islam, M.A.; Granero, R.; Vicente, E.; Peñas-Lledó, E.; Arcelus, J.; Sánchez, I.; Menchon, J.M.; et al. Cognitive behaviour therapy response and dropout rate across purging and nonpurging bulimia nervosa and binge eating disorder: DSM-5 implications. *BMC Psychiatry* **2013**, *13*, 285. [CrossRef]
49. Riesco, N.; Agüera, Z.; Granero, R.; Jimenez-Murcia, S.; Menchón, J.M.; Fernández-Aranda, F. Other Specified Feeding or Eating Disorders (OSFED): Clinical heterogeneity and cognitive-behavioral therapy outcome. *Eur. Psychiatry* **2018**, *54*, 109–116. [CrossRef]
50. Agüera, Z.; Sánchez, I.; Granero, R.; Riesco, N.; Steward, T.; Martín-Romera, V.; Jimenez-Murcia, S.; Romero, X.; Caroleo, M.; Segura-García, C.; et al. Short-Term Treatment Outcomes and Dropout Risk in Men and Women with Eating Disorders. *Eur. Eat. Disord. Rev.* **2017**, *25*. [CrossRef]
51. Fernández-Aranda, F.; Treasure, J.; Paslakis, G.; Agüera, Z.; Giménez, M.; Granero, R.; Sánchez, I.; Serrano-Troncoso, E.; Gorwood, P.; Herpertz-Dahlmann, B.; et al. The impact of duration of illness on treatment nonresponse and drop-out: Exploring the relevance of enduring eating disorder concept. *Eur. Eat. Disord. Rev.* **2021**, *29*. [CrossRef]

52. Agüera, Z.; Romero, X.; Arcelus, J.; Sánchez, I.; Riesco, N.; Jimenez-Murcia, S. Changes in Body Composition in Anorexia Nervosa: Predictors of Recovery and Treatment Outcome. *PLoS ONE* **2015**, *10*, 143012. [CrossRef]
53. Custal, N.; Arcelus, J.; Agüera, Z.; Bove, F.I.; Wales, J.; Granero, R.; Jimenez-Murcia, S.; Sánchez, I.; Riesco, N.; Alonso, P.; et al. Treatment outcome of patients with comorbid type 1 diabetes and eating disorders. *BMC Psychiatry* **2014**, *14*. [CrossRef]
54. Romero, X.; Agüera, Z.; Granero, R.; Sánchez, I.; Riesco, N.; Jimenez-Murcia, S.; Gisbert-Rodriguez, M.; Sánchez-González, J.; Casalé, G.; Baenas, I.; et al. Is food addiction a predictor of treatment outcome among patients with eating disorder? *Eur. Eat. Disord. Rev.* **2019**, *27*, 700–711. [CrossRef]
55. StataCorp. *Stata Statistical Software: Release 16*; StataCorp LLC: College Station, TX, USA, 2019; Available online: https://www.stata.com/company/ (accessed on 2 April 2021).
56. Kelley, K.; Preacher, K. On effect size. *Psychol. Methods* **2012**, *17*, 137–152. [CrossRef] [PubMed]
57. Cohen, J. *Statistical Power Analysis for the Behavioral Sciences*, 2nd ed.; Lawrence Earlbaum Associates: Hillsdale, NJ, USA, 1988.
58. Finner, H.; Roters, M. On the False Discovery Rate and Expected Type I Errors. *Biom. J.* **2001**, *43*, 985. [CrossRef]
59. Razzoli, M.; Pearson, C.; Crow, S.; Bartolomucci, A. Stress, overeating, and obesity: Insights from human studies and preclinical models Graphical abstract HHS Public Access. *Neurosci. Biobehav. Rev.* **2017**, *76*, 154–162. [CrossRef] [PubMed]
60. Vancampfort, D.; De Herdt, A.; Vanderlinden, J.; Lannoo, M.; Adriaens, A.; De Hert, M.; Stubbs, B.; Soundy, A.; Probst, M. The functional exercise capacity and its correlates in obese treatment-seeking people with binge eating disorder: An exploratory study. *Disabil. Rehabil.* **2015**, *37*, 777–782. [CrossRef] [PubMed]
61. Agüera, Z.; Riesco, N.; Valenciano-Mendoza, E.; Granero, R.; Sánchez, I.; Andreu, A.; Jimenez-Murcia, S.; Fernández-Aranda, F. Illness perception in patients with eating disorders: Clinical, personality, and food addiction correlates. *Eat. Weight Disord.* **2021**. [CrossRef] [PubMed]
62. Rafiei, N.; Gill, T. Identification of factors contributing to successful self-directed weight loss: A qualitative study. *J. Hum. Nutr. Diet.* **2018**, *31*, 329–336. [CrossRef] [PubMed]
63. Dalle Grave, R.; Calugi, S.; Compare, A.; El Ghoch, M.; Petroni, M.L.; Colombari, S.; Minniti, A.; Marchesini, G. Personality, attrition and weight loss in treatment seeking women with obesity. *Clin. Obes.* **2015**, *5*, 266–272. [CrossRef] [PubMed]
64. Schag, K.; Leehr, E.J.; Martus, P.; Bethge, W.; Becker, S.; Zipfel, S.; Giel, K.E. Impulsivity-focused group intervention to reduce binge eating episodes in patients with binge eating disorder: Study protocol of the randomised controlled IMPULS trial. *MJOpen* **2015**, e009445. [CrossRef]
65. Gonçalves, S.; Machado, B.; Silva, C.; Crosby, R.D.; Lavender, J.M.; Cao, L.; Machado, P.P.P. The Moderating Role of Purging Behaviour in the Relationship Between Sexual/Physical Abuse and Nonsuicidal Self-Injury in Eating Disorder Patients. *Eur. Eat. Disord. Rev.* **2016**, *24*, 164–168. [CrossRef]
66. Fouladi, F.; Mitchell, J.E.; Crosby, R.D.; Engel, S.G.; Crow, S.; Hill, L.; Le Grange, D.; Powers, P.; Steffen, K.J. Prevalence of alcohol and other substance use in patients with eating disorders. *Eur. Eat. Disord. Rev.* **2015**, *23*, 531–536. [CrossRef]
67. Bahji, A.; Mazhar, M.N.; Hudson, C.C.; Nadkarni, P.; MacNeil, B.A.; Hawken, E. Prevalence of substance use disorder comorbidity among individuals with eating disorders: A systematic review and meta-analysis. *Psychiatry Res.* **2019**, *273*, 58–66. [CrossRef] [PubMed]

nutrients

MDPI

Article

Neuropsychological Learning Deficits as Predictors of Treatment Outcome in Patients with Eating Disorders

Ignacio Lucas [1], Romina Miranda-Olivos [1,2,3], Giulia Testa [1,2,3], Roser Granero [1,3,4], Isabel Sánchez [1,2,3], Jessica Sánchez-González [1,3], Susana Jiménez-Murcia [1,2,3,5] and Fernando Fernández-Aranda [1,2,3,5,*]

1 Department of Psychiatry, Bellvitge University Hospital-IDIBELL, 08907 L'Hospitalet de Llobregat, Spain; ilucas@idibell.cat (I.L.); rmiranda@idibell.cat (R.M.-O.); gtesta@idibell.cat (G.T.); roser.granero@uab.cat (R.G.); isasanchez@bellvitgehospital.cat (I.S.); jsanchezg@bellvitgehospital.cat (J.S.-G.); sjimenez@bellvitgehospital.cat (S.J.-M.)
2 Psychiatry and Mental Health Group, Neuroscience Program, Institut d'Investigació Biomèdica de Bellvitge-IDIBELL, 08907 L'Hospitalet de Llobregat, Spain
3 Ciber Fisiopatología Obesidad y Nutrición (CIBERObn), Instituto de Salud Carlos III, 08907 L'Hospitalet de Llobregat, Spain
4 Department of Psychobiology and Methodology of Health Sciences, Autonomous University of Barcelona, 08193 Barcelona, Spain
5 Department of Clinical Sciences, School of Medicine, University of Barcelona, 08907 L'Hospitalet de Llobregat, Spain
* Correspondence: ffernandez@bellvitgehospital.cat; Tel.: +34-93-260-7227

Citation: Lucas, I.; Miranda-Olivos, R.; Testa, G.; Granero, R.; Sánchez, I.; Sánchez-González, J.; Jiménez-Murcia, S.; Fernández-Aranda, F. Neuropsychological Learning Deficits as Predictors of Treatment Outcome in Patients with Eating Disorders. *Nutrients* **2021**, *13*, 2145. https://doi.org/10.3390/nu13072145

Academic Editor: Stefano Erzegovesi

Received: 21 April 2021
Accepted: 17 June 2021
Published: 23 June 2021

Abstract: Eating disorders (EDs) are severe psychiatric illnesses that require individualized treatments. Decision-making deficits have been associated with EDs. Decision-making learning deficits denote a lack of strategies to elaborate better decisions that can have an impact on recovery and response to treatment. This study used the Iowa Gambling Task (IGT) to investigate learning differences related to treatment outcome in EDs, comparing between patients with a good and bad treatment outcome and healthy controls. Likewise, the predictive role of impaired learning performance on therapy outcome was explored. Four hundred twenty-four participants (233 ED patients and 191 healthy controls) participated in this study. Decision making was assessed using the Iowa Gambling Task before any psychological treatment. All patients received psychological therapy, and treatment outcome was evaluated at discharge. Patients with bad outcome did not show progression in the decision-making task as opposed to those with good outcome and the healthy control sample. Additionally, learning performance in the decision-making task was predictive of their future outcome. The severity of learning deficits in decision making may serve as a predictor of the treatment. These results may provide a starting point of how decision-making learning deficits are operating as dispositional and motivational factors on responsiveness to treatment in EDs.

Keywords: eating disorders; decision making; learning; treatment outcome

1. Introduction

Eating disorders (EDs) are important psychiatric illnesses that involve abnormal eating behavior. Patients affected with EDs may present excessive concern over food, body weight, and shape dissatisfaction. These conditions could also lead to serious physical problems and impaired psychosocial functioning [1]. Moreover, there is an increased risk of suicide in people with EDs compared to the non-ED population [2–5]. A recent systematic review regarding the diagnosis prevalence of EDs established that worldwide, around 8.4% of women and 2.2% of men will be diagnosed with this condition at some point in their lifetime [6]. The main treatments for EDs, which are based on cognitive–behavioral therapy (CBT), have been demonstrated to be useful in reducing symptoms [7,8]; however, these current treatments have not always reported successful outcomes [9–12].

A systematic review [13] reported ED remission rates between 18% and 62%. Several individual circumstances might underlie the response to treatment in EDs, increasing the risk of having bad treatment outcomes, resulting in low remission rates or poor adherence to treatment [14–19]; therefore, assessing which functions act as predictors for the treatment outcome of the ED is crucial in order to design optimized individual treatments [20–22].

Some of the most studied cognitive features in patients with EDs are their executive function impairments in comparison to the healthy population [16,23–28]. Executive functions optimize cognitive processes to solve demanding situations where instinct or intuition is insufficient [29]. Complex cognitive processes, such as decision making, are strongly related to executive functions [30]. Decision making involves high-level processes, including option generation, evaluation of risks and consequences, and choosing between different possibilities in order to achieve a certain personal objective [31]. Therefore, decision-making processes require complex high-level processing to make advantageous decisions taking different variables into account. These processes are commonly related to prefrontal cortex activity [32,33]. Psychiatric illnesses, such as EDs, are usually associated with significant impairments in prefrontal, fronto-limbic, and fronto-striatal neural systems [34].

Even though each ED subtype has been related to its own specific neurocognitive impairments [35], decision-making deficits have been found among all ED conditions [25,27,36–40]. Patients with EDs reported poor learning during decision-making paradigms [41,42], showing a tendency to persist in decisions/choices, despite negative consequences. Learning deficits in the decision-making tasks of patients diagnosed with EDs may be related to an excessive sensitivity to reward or punishment, which could be associated with the persistence of their dysfunctional behavior [42]. Some studies have hypothesized that in EDs, as reported in obsessive-compulsive disorders, observed impairments in decision making may be related to biological markers [26,43]; however, decision-making deficits in EDs do not have to be considered a completely permanent feature. Neurocognitive training on executive functions has been tested in patients with EDs, showing improvement in cognitive flexibility, inhibitory control, and working memory [16]. Furthermore, in another study, patients with anorexia nervosa showed great improvement in decision making after CBT treatment in patients in full remission of their ED symptoms but not in patients with no remission [40]. Just as patients with EDs who improve their symptoms showed an improvement in their performance post-treatment, it could be expected that better decision making at baseline would also predict a better treatment outcome; however, the literature examining neurocognitive predictors of treatment outcome in EDs is scarce [44] and there is a lack of studies focusing on neuropsychological profiles as predictors of therapy outcome [45]. Cavedini et al. [14] observed how the function of decision making might be linked to treatment outcomes in women with anorexia nervosa. Still, they pointed toward the necessity of understanding which neurocognitive feature linked to decision making can be used as a criterion for selecting the proper treatment.

Based on the facts described above, this research was designed with two aims: first, to assess baseline learning differences related to decision-making between patients with EDs who recovered from their symptoms and those who did not; second, to explore the predictive capacity of impaired learning performance on therapy outcome.

According to the above-mentioned aims, we propose two hypotheses. First, if learning decision-making skills influence treatment efficacy, EDs with bad treatment outcomes will show impaired learning performance, even before the treatment. Second, if there is an impaired neurocognitive functioning in ED patients with bad treatment results, the decision-making learning skill will help discriminate between having good or bad treatment outcomes.

2. Materials and Methods

2.1. Participants

A total of 424 participants were included in the present study: 341 women and 83 men, with a ratio similar to recent studies [6]. The ED group contained 190 women and 43 men, with a mean age of 30.52 (SD = 10.9), whereas the healthy control (HC) group (151 women and 40 men) had a mean age of 25.65 (SD = 8.5). In terms of the highest level of education, for the HC group, 5.8% attained a primary education, 56% attained a secondary education, and 38.2% attained a tertiary degree. For the ED group, 35.2% attained a primary education, 40.8% attained a secondary education, and 24% attained a tertiary degree. Table S1 (Supplementary Material) contains the sociodemographic characteristics of the groups at baseline. To avoid potential biases in the results, all the comparisons were adjusted for the covariates of age and education level at baseline. Patients with EDs were recruited from the Eating Disorders Unit at Bellvitge University Hospital in Barcelona, Spain. All patients within the ED group met the Diagnostic and Statistical Manual of Mental Disorders (DSM-5; American Psychiatric Association, Philadelphia, PA, USA) [46] criteria for EDs, following standardized structured interviews. The ED group was composed of 85 patients with anorexia nervosa (AN) restrictive subtype, 41 patients with AN bulimic/purging subtype, 44 with bulimia nervosa (BN), 45 patients with binge eating disorder (BED), and 18 patients with other specified feeding or eating disorder (OSFED). Once diagnosed, they were asked to voluntarily participate in this study. Neuropsychological and clinical assessments were conducted in the first week of their treatment. The exclusion criteria for the HC group were a body mass index below 18.5 or above 25 and a lifetime history of EDs, according to a semi-structured interview and following DSM-5 diagnostic criteria.

Data were collected between May 2008 and November 2020. All participants were adults, received information about the procedure, and signed an informed consent form. All procedures were approved by the Ethical Committee of the Bellvitge University Hospital in accordance with the Helsinki Declaration of 1975 as revised in 1983.

2.2. Procedure

Participants completed a computerized version of the Iowa Gambling Task (IGT) [47]. Additionally, the patients' psychopathology symptoms were evaluated via the Spanish version of the Symptom Checklist-Revised (SCL-90-R) [48], and their ED symptoms were assessed with the Spanish version of the Eating Disorders Inventory-2 (EDI-2) [49]. All these evaluations were conducted prior to the psychological treatment.

2.2.1. Decision-Making Assessment

The computerized version of the IGT was used to assess decision-making processes [50]. This task consists of 100 trials in which the participants must draw a card from one of the four presented decks (A, B, C, and D). Each card represents a monetary gain but can also result in monetary loss. There are two advantageous decks and two disadvantageous ones. The first ones produce less monetary incomes but with an overall gain, whereas the second presents larger gain amounts and an overall monetary loss. The participant has to gain as much as possible by the end of the task. It is subdivided into five blocks of twenty trials performed consecutively. The first blocks allow measuring decision making under ambiguity, whereas in the last blocks, the task switches to decision making under risk because the rules may have been figured out [51].

The test score for each block (IGT-1, 2, 3, 4, and 5) is calculated by subtracting the number of choices from disadvantageous decks to the number of choices from advantageous decks draws. The total task score (IGT-Total) is calculated by adding the scores of the five blocks. The task also allows us to calculate a learning score (IGT-Learning) and a risk score (IGT-Risk) [42]. IGT-Learning is calculated with the difference between the scores of the two first blocks and the two last ones. This approach/procedure allows us to assess the differences between the first and final blocks. The first blocks are assessed because the participant has not learned which decks are advantageous and disadvantageous; the last blocks are assessed because the experience gained through the trial can produce changes in choice patterns. Furthermore, IGT-Risk considers only the scores from the two last blocks, where a participant could have already detected which decks involve a risky choice.

2.2.2. Treatment

As described elsewhere [9,52], patients diagnosed with AN attended a day hospital treatment program, including CBT group therapy sessions, lasting 90 min each, for 15 weeks. Treatment for the other ED diagnosis (BN, BED, and OSFED) consisted of 16 weekly outpatients CBT group therapy sessions, lasting 90 min each. Patients were re-evaluated at discharge and categorized as either in full remission (i.e., total absence of symptoms meeting criteria for at least 4 weeks), partial remission (i.e., a substantial symptomatic improvement but with residual symptoms), and non-remission. These categories were previously used as the threshold to assess treatment outcomes in patients with EDs [9,19,52]. The treatment outcomes categories were based on the judgments of senior clinical staff considering normalization of nutritional dietary patterns, frequency of binge episodes and compensatory behaviors, weight restoration, and improvement in attitudes regarding weight and shape. Voluntary treatment discontinuation was categorized as dropout (i.e., not attending treatment for at least three consecutive sessions). Patients were subdivided into two groups depending on their treatment outcome. Those who showed full or partial remission of their symptoms were included in the good outcome group ($n = 166$; 71.2%), and those who did not show remission or abandoned the treatment were included in the bad outcome group ($n = 67$; 28.8%). The treatment results obtained were similar to those reported previously [53].

2.3. *Data Analysis*

Statistical analysis was done with Stata16 for windows (College Station, TX, USA). The association between the baseline measures with the CBT efficiency (bad versus good outcome) was based on the chi-square test (χ^2) for categorical measures and analysis of variance (ANOVA) for quantitative measures. An increase in the Type-I error due to the multiple significance tests was based on the Finner method [54], which is a family-wise procedure that has proved more powerful than the standard Bonferroni correction.

The comparison of the learning curves in the IGT was based on 3×5 mixed ANOVA (adjusted by the participants' age and education level), which is defined as the between-subjects factor of the group (bad CBT outcome, good CBT outcome, and control condition) and as the within-subjects factor for the score in each block. Polynomial contrasts for the within-subject factor assessed linear, quadratic, cubic, and quartic trends in the learning curves. Comparing the IGT-Learning score between the three groups was also based on analysis of variance, which was adjusted by age and education (ANCOVA).

The discriminative capacity of the IGT-Learning score to discriminate between good versus bad outcomes in the CBT was based on Receiver Operating Characteristics (ROC) analysis. This methodology is used in clinical areas to obtain the optimal cut-off in measurement tools using an external reference criterion. In this work, ROC analysis was applied within the ED subsample to obtain the best cut-off in the IGT index to discriminate between patients with bad versus good CBT outcomes. Since selecting the optimal cut-off depends on the prevalence of the criteria and the costs/risks of false classifications [55], the analysis was performed considering a distribution for the CBT outcome equal to the sample and a cost for a false negative double compared to the cost for a false positive.

Logistic regression valued the capacity of the optimal cut-off point in the IGT-Learning global measure to differentiate between bad and good outcomes. Goodness-of-fit was assessed with the Hosmer and Lemeshow test.

In this study, the effect size was based on the eta-squared coefficient (η^2) for quantitative measures (values of 0.06, 0.10, and 0.25 were interpreted as low–poor, moderate–medium, and large–high effect size) [56], and in Cramer's-V coefficient for categorical (values of 0.10, 0.30, and 0.50 were interpreted as low–poor, moderate–medium, and large–high effect size) [57].

3. Results

3.1. Comparison of the IGT Measures between the Groups

Table 1 contains the results obtained in the mixed ANOVA (adjusted by age and education) comparing the proficiency in the IGT between the groups (see also the first panel in Figure 1). The interaction of the within- and between-subjects factors was statistically significant ($F = 4.09$, $p < 0.001$, $\eta^2 = 0.019$), indicating that the learning curves had a specific shape depending on the group. No statistically significant differences between the blocks were found among patients in the bad outcome group ($F = 1.63$, $p = 0.166$, $\eta^2 = 0.015$), suggesting the absence of a learning curve. Within patients with a good outcome, significant linear ($F = 23.3$, $p < 0.001$, $\eta^2 = 0.124$) and quadratic ($F = 6.49$, $p = 0.012$, $\eta^2 = 0.038$) trends appeared: increasing means with blocks were registered (from −2.4 in block 1 to 1.2 in block 5), the difference being lower comparing blocks 4 versus 5 (1.23 versus 1.21). The same pattern was obtained in the control group: significant linear ($F = 79.71$, $p < 0.001$, $\eta^2 = 0.296$) and quadratic ($F = 27.99$, $p < 0.001$, $\eta^2 = 0.128$) trends.

Table 1. Performance learning curves in the Iowa Gambling Task (2 × 5 ANOVA adjusted by age and education).

	IGT Raw Scores											
	Block 1		**Block 2**		**Block 3**		**Block 4**		**Block 5**			
Group (outcome)	Mean	SD	Mean	SD	Mean	SD	Mean	SD	Mean	SD		
Bad (n = 67)	−2.45	3.85	−0.05	4.28	−0.87	5.82	−0.32	7.78	−0.41	7.64		
Good (n = 166)	−2.38	4.66	−0.61	5.53	0.24	5.87	1.23	7.42	1.21	8.45		
Control (n = 191)	−1.72	5.92	2.22	7.06	4.68	8.35	5.32	9.03	4.93	9.90		
Multivariate tests	F	df	p	η^2								
Int. BxG	4.09	8; 419	**0.001** *	0.019								
Block	0.80	4; 419	0.401	0.002								
Group	22.34	2; 419	**0.001** *	0.096								
Factor Block Within Group	F	p	η^2									
Bad	1.63	0.166	0.015									
Good	6.51	**0.001** *	0.059									
Control	30.89	**0.001** *	0.229									
Polynomial	Linear (order 1)			Quadratic (order 2)			Cubic (order 3)			Quartic (order 4)		
contrast for Block	F	p	η^2	F	p	η^2	F	p	η^2	F	p	η^2
Group: bad	1.14	0.289	0.017	3.94	0.051	0.056	1.20	0.277	0.018	1.73	0.193	0.026
Group: good	23.32	**0.001** *	0.124	6.49	**0.012** *	0.038	0.15	0.701	0.001	1.02	0.314	0.006
Group: control	79.71	**0.001** *	0.296	27.99	**0.001** *	0.128	0.55	0.457	0.003	0.53	0.468	0.003

Note. SD: standard deviation; * Bold: significant comparison (0.05 level); η^2: partial eta-squared.

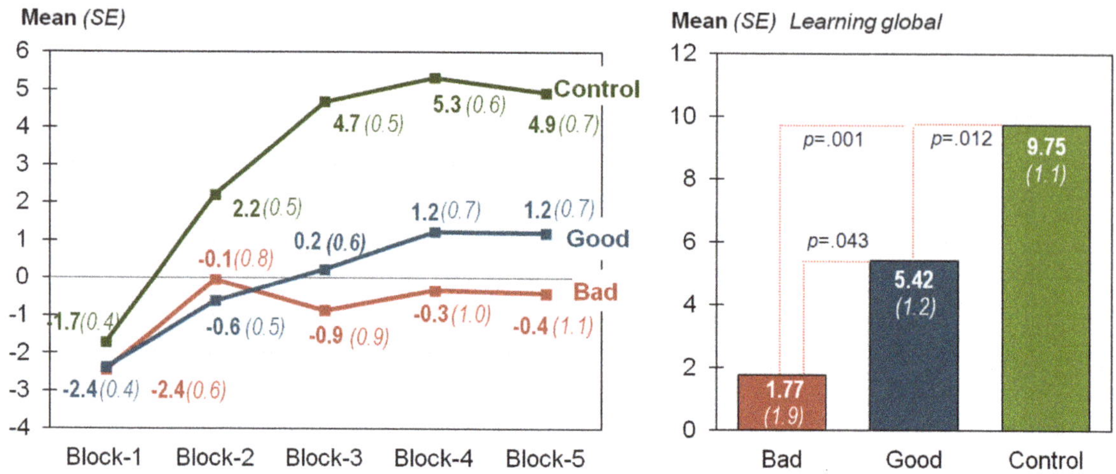

Figure 1. Iowa Gambling Task (IGT) performance–learning curves (**left**) and IGT global scores by group (**right**). Note. Sample size $n = 424$. SE: standard error.

Table 2 contains the results of the ANCOVA (adjusted by age and education) comparing the IGT-Learning score between the groups (see the second panel in Figure 1). Statistical differences between the groups appeared ($F = 7.14$, $p < 0.001$, $\eta^2 = 0.124$). Pairwise comparisons (contrasts between the groups) also achieved differences between all the groups.

Table 2. Comparison of the IGT learning global score: ANCOVA adjusted by age and education.

	Bad Outcome		**Good Outcome**		**Control**	
Descriptives	Mean 1.77	SD 14.04	Mean 5.42	SD 13.15	Mean 9.75	SD 16.67
Factor group	*F* 7.14	*df* 2; 423	*p* **0.001** *	η^2 0.033		
Pairwise comparisons	*F*	*p*	η^2			
Bad vs. good	4.84	**0.043** *	0.014			
Bad vs. control	12.93	**0.001** *	0.030			
Good vs. control	6.44	**0.012** *	0.015			

Note. SD: standard deviation; * Bold: significant comparison (0.05 level); η^2: partial eta-squared.

3.2. *Discriminative Capacity of the IGT-Learning Score*

Figure 2 contains the results of the ROC analysis obtained in the ED subsample. The optimal cut-off point in the IGT-Learning index to discriminate between good and bad CBT outcomes was 2, which achieved a sensitivity (Se), or true positive rate, of 64.2% and a specificity (SP), or true negative rate, equal to 54.8%.

Figure 3 shows the percentage of patients with a poor performance in the IGT in each group (based on the classification obtained for the cut-off = 2 in the global learning measure). The logistic regression (adjusted by age and education) valuing this cut-off's capacity for differentiating between the two groups achieved a significant parameter for differentiating between bad versus good groups (B = 0.754, SE = 0.301, OR = 2.12, $p = 0.012$). Goodness-of-fit was achieved (Hosmer and Lemeshow test: $\chi^2 = 5.95$, df = 8, $p = 0.653$).

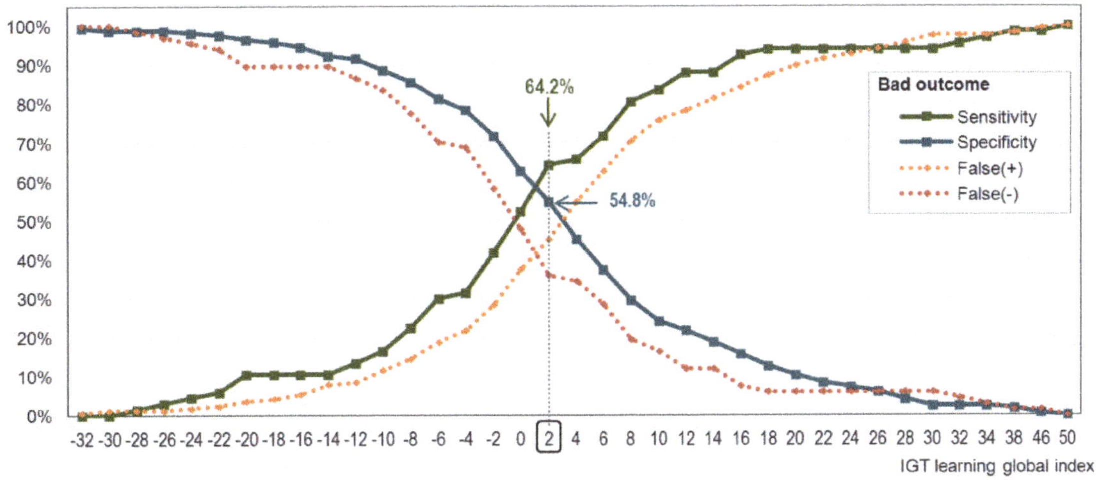

Figure 2. Valuation of the IGT-Learning raw score to predict the treatment outcome. Note. Results obtained for the ED subsample (n = 233).

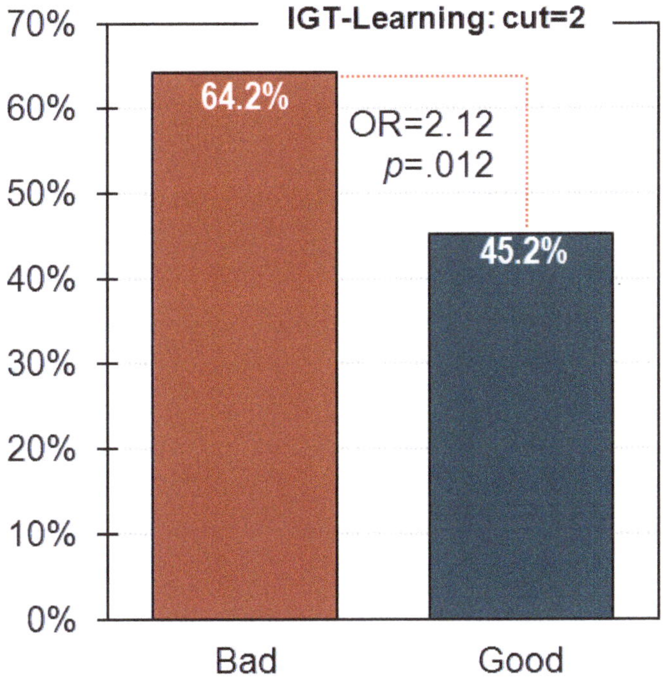

Figure 3. Capacity of the IGT-Learning score to predict the treatment outcome. Each bar represents the percentage of participants with poor IGT-Learning in each group with a cut-off point equal to 2. Note. Results obtained for the ED subsample (n = 233).

3.3. Variables Associated with the CBT Outcome

Table 3 contains the comparison between patients classified according to the CBT outcome (bad versus good) at baseline. No differences were found between groups in any of the variables.

Table 3. Association between baseline measures with the cognitive–behavioral therapy outcome.

		Bad Outcome (n = 67)		**Good Outcome** (n = 166)			
		n	%	n	%	p	V
Sex	Women	59	88.1%	131	78.9%	0.103	0.202
	Men	8	11.9%	35	21.1%		
		Mean	SD	Mean	SD	p	η^2
Chronological age (years-old)		28.99	9.50	31.13	11.39	0.174	0.008
Duration of disorder (years)		9.57	8.36	7.79	8.65	0.152	0.009
EDI-2: Drive for thinness		11.78	7.14	11.71	6.45	0.946	0.001
EDI-2: Body dissatisfaction		15.22	8.17	14.74	8.84	0.700	0.001
EDI-2: Interoceptive awareness		10.39	6.59	9.73	6.89	0.504	0.002
EDI-2: Bulimia		6.28	5.85	5.41	5.34	0.273	0.005
EDI-2: Interpersonal distrust		5.39	4.61	5.74	5.23	0.630	0.001
EDI-2: Ineffectiveness		10.84	7.08	9.40	7.24	0.169	0.008
EDI-2: Maturity fears		8.37	6.09	7.48	5.19	0.257	0.006
EDI-2: Perfectionism		6.07	4.89	5.05	4.08	0.103	0.011
EDI-2: Impulse regulation		5.43	5.30	5.36	5.81	0.925	0.001
EDI-2: Ascetic		6.70	4.24	6.05	4.25	0.289	0.005
EDI-2: Social insecurity		7.00	4.66	6.90	5.57	0.901	0.001
EDI-2: Total score		93.48	46.79	87.56	45.95	0.377	0.003
SCL-90R: Somatization		1.78	1.02	1.60	0.90	0.198	0.007
SCL-90R: Obsessive/compulsive		1.78	0.97	1.73	0.92	0.734	0.001
SCL-90R: Interpersonal sensitivity		1.90	0.99	1.88	1.00	0.848	0.001
SCL-90R: Depressive		2.25	0.98	2.06	0.99	0.196	0.007
SCL-90R: Anxiety		1.63	0.91	1.46	0.91	0.194	0.007
SCL-90R: Hostility		1.17	0.88	1.19	0.90	0.898	0.001
SCL-90R: Phobic anxiety		0.84	0.86	0.88	0.91	0.736	0.001
SCL-90R: Paranoid Ideation		1.43	0.89	1.28	0.84	0.253	0.006
SCL-90R: Psychotic		1.36	0.82	1.17	0.72	0.081	0.013
SCL-90R: GSI score		1.69	0.78	1.58	0.78	0.300	0.005
SCL-90R: PST score		61.43	19.63	60.36	18.86	0.697	0.001
SCL-90R: PSDI score		2.35	0.59	2.22	0.61	0.127	0.010

Note. EDI-2: V: Cramer's-V. η^2: partial eta-squared. Eating Disorders Inventory-2 [49]. SCL-90R: Symptom Checklist—Revised [48]. GSI: Global Severity Index. PST: Positive Symptom Total. PSDI: Positive Symptom Distress Index.

4. Discussion

We examined baseline differences in decision making in patients with EDs, differentiating between those who improved vs. those who did not after CBT, and analyzed its therapy outcome predicting value. As the first objective, our study addressed whether ED patients with different outcomes present learning differences related to decision making before the treatment. This study's main results showed how both the patients with good outcomes and the healthy control group showed a learning curve through the IGT task; however, the bad outcome group was the only group that did not show progression across the blocks. Based on these results, the first hypothesis is verified, as different outcomes present differences in learning, even before the intervention. The second main finding was that the IGT-Learning score predicted treatment outcome. These findings support our second hypothesis, as the capacity of learning through a decision-making task seems to discriminate between having a successful or a bad treatment outcome. There would be a chance that these learning deficits were related to higher depressive symptoms; nevertheless, there were no observed differences in depression between ED groups.

These results fit not only with previous studies that point toward decision-making deficits in patients with EDs [25,27,36,38–40] but also with the ones that report how individual differences correlate with distinct treatment outcomes [9,15–19]. Regarding a previous study that presented decision making as a predictor of treatment outcome in EDs [14], our study reported its predictive value using a bigger sample, with patients of both sexes and with different EDs subtypes. In addition, among the neuropsychological variables that discriminate between the treatment results, the learning skills showed differences depending on therapy outcomes and are good predictors of the treatment result. It is noteworthy to mention that patients with EDs who had a poor treatment outcome did not show changes in their answers across the IGT blocks; this could mean that perhaps they neither changed their behavior due to immediate rewards (as in disadvantageous decks) nor to delayed recompenses (as in advantageous decks) [36]. According to Hiroto and Seligman [58], this lack of change is probably related to learned helplessness, and therefore, they may not feel capable of changing the result of the task through their decisions. This behavior could explain why they do not believe in the possibility of improving their symptoms with psychological intervention, leading to poor treatment efficacy and less treatment adherence. Steward et al. [40] reported how patients with EDs who recover from their symptoms also improve their performance in decision-making tasks; therefore, they enhance their learning skills. If that is true, a potential treatment effect would be a patient believing in their ability to change negative situations via their actions and decisions. There were no observed differences in ED symptoms nor in general psychopathology, so, in this sample, the different treatment outcomes do not seem to be directly related to these parameters.

Previous research showed how patients with EDs tend to report high levels of sensitivity to punishment [42,59,60]; however, in our study, some of them still did not seem to learn from the negative feedback; this may be due to the fact that despite stimuli producing a great emotional impact, those patients do not change their behavior because they do not believe they can change situations via their decisions. The main characteristic of learned helplessness is that it highly correlates with depressive states [61,62]. Nevertheless, regarding our results, these learning impairments would be related to a worse treatment outcome independently from the depressive symptoms. The patients with EDs who show impaired learning behaviors and tend to have negative treatment outcomes would need to change their belief in the possibility of improving their symptoms; therefore, individualized treatments for those patients will require focusing on improving their locus of control.

Our study has certain limitations, and the results and conclusions of our study must take these into account. First, using a neuropsychological task such as the IGT may not be practical for the clinical assessment; it would be necessary to design more accessible tools to assess these impairments. Second, our sample size was limited to test the predictive role of IGT performance across ED subtypes. Therefore, inferences emerging from these results must be interpreted with caution considering no discrimination by ED diagnosis. Future studies with larger samples could elucidate the predictive role of decision-making learning in each ED subtype. Third, as seen in other psychological disorders, impaired motivation may influence the performance in cognitive tasks [63]. Future research should include some motivational measure to assess this effect. Fourth, it will still be necessary to evaluate whether there are differences between those patients who do not recover from their symptoms and those that show poor treatment adherence. This study presents an understanding of how neurocognitive deficits may underlie possible treatment outcomes in ED. Future studies should consider our results to develop individualized treatments so that patients with different features and symptoms can benefit from the treatment.

5. Conclusions

In sum, our results show how ED treatment outcomes could be related to cognitive functioning even before the treatment, as patients with different outcomes seem to present different learning skills related to decision making. This learning skill also demonstrated a predictive value for the treatment outcome, possibly indicating that patients who do not change their behavior despite its consequences tend to present greater difficulties with the treatment. It may indicate that these patients show a lack of belief in changing their situation through their behavior. These results point toward the importance of taking into account neuropsychological variables to develop and apply individualized treatments that successfully deal with EDs.

Supplementary Materials: The following are available online at https://www.mdpi.com/article/10.3390/nu13072145/s1, Table S1: Descriptives of the sample.

Author Contributions: Conceptualization, I.L., R.M.-O., G.T., S.J.-M. and F.F.-A.; methodology, I.L., R.M.-O., G.T., R.G., S.J.-M. and F.F.-A.; formal analysis, R.G.; data curation, R.M.-O., G.T., I.S. and J.S.-G.; writing—original draft preparation, I.L., R.M.-O., G.T. and R.G.; writing—review and editing, I.L., R.M.-O., G.T., R.G., S.J.-M. and F.F.-A.; supervision, S.J.-M. and F.F.-A.; funding acquisition, S.J.-M. and F.F.-A. All authors have read and agreed to the published version of the manuscript.

Funding: We thank CERCA Programme/Generalitat de Catalunya for institutional support. This manuscript and research was supported by grants from the Instituto de Salud Carlos III (ISCIII) (FIS PI14/00290, PI17/01167 and PI20/132), by the SLT006/17/00246 grant, funded by the Department of Health of the Generalitat de Catalunya by the call "Acció instrumental de programes de recerca orientats en l'àmbit de la recerca i la innovació en salut" (PERIS) and co-funded by FEDER funds/European Regional Development Fund (ERDF), a way to build Europe. CIBERObn is an initiative of ISCIII. The funders had no role in the study design, data collection and analysis, decision to publish, or preparation of the manuscript.

Institutional Review Board Statement: All procedures were approved by the Clinical Research Ethics Committee (CEIC) of Bellvitge University Hospital (ethic approval code: PR146/14) in accordance with the Helsinki Declaration of 1975 as revised in 1983.

Informed Consent Statement: Informed consent was obtained from all subjects involved in the study.

Data Availability Statement: Data are not available in any repository. Contact with the corresponding author.

Conflicts of Interest: The authors declare no conflict of interest. The funders had no role in the design of the study; in the collection, analyses, or interpretation of data; in the writing of the manuscript, or in the decision to publish the results.

References

1. Kerr-Gaffney, J.; Harrison, A.; Tchanturia, K. Social anxiety in the eating disorders: A systematic review and meta-analysis. *Psychol. Med.* **2018**, *48*, 2477–2491. [CrossRef]
2. Chesney, E.; Goodwin, G.M.; Fazel, S. Risks of all-cause and suicide mortality in mental disorders: A meta-review. *World Psychiatry* **2014**, *13*, 153–160. [CrossRef]
3. Foulon, C.; Guelfi, J.D.; Kipman, A.; Adès, J.; Romo, L.; Houdeyer, K.; Marquez, S.; Mouren, M.C.; Rouillon, F.; Gorwood, P. Switching to the bingeing/purging subtype of anorexia nervosa is frequently associated with suicidal attempts. *Eur. Psychiatry* **2007**, *22*, 513–519. [CrossRef]
4. Preti, A.; Rocchi, M.B.L.; Sisti, D.; Camboni, M.V.; Miotto, P. A comprehensive meta-analysis of the risk of suicide in eating disorders. *Acta Psychiatr. Scand.* **2011**, *124*, 6–17. [CrossRef]
5. Mandelli, L.; Arminio, A.; Atti, A.-R.; De Ronchi, D. Suicide attempts in eating disorder subtypes: A meta-analysis of the literature employing DSM-IV, DSM-5, or ICD-10 diagnostic criteria. *Psychol. Med.* **2019**, *49*, 1237–1249. [CrossRef]
6. Galmiche, M.; Déchelotte, P.; Lambert, G.; Tavolacci, M.P. Prevalence of eating disorders over the 2000-2018 period: A systematic literature review. *Am. J. Clin. Nutr.* **2019**, *109*, 1402–1413. [CrossRef] [PubMed]
7. Linardon, J.; Wade, T.D.; de la Piedad Garcia, X.; Brennan, L. The efficacy of cognitive-behavioral therapy for eating disorders: A systematic review and meta-analysis. *J. Consult. Clin. Psychol.* **2017**, *85*, 1080–1094. [CrossRef]
8. Vaidya, V. Cognitive behavior therapy in patients with binge eating disorder. *Eur. Psychiatry* **2011**, *26*, 739. [CrossRef]
9. Agüera, Z.; Sánchez, I.; Granero, R.; Riesco, N.; Steward, T.; Martín-Romera, V.; Jiménez-Murcia, S.; Romero, X.; Caroleo, M.; Segura-García, C.; et al. Short-Term Treatment Outcomes and Dropout Risk in Men and Women with Eating Disorders. *Eur. Eat. Disord. Rev.* **2017**, *25*, 293–301. [CrossRef] [PubMed]
10. Keel, P.K.; Brown, T.A. Update on course and outcome in eating disorders. *Int. J. Eat. Disord.* **2010**, *43*, 195–204. [CrossRef] [PubMed]
11. Radunz, M.; Keegan, E.; Osenk, I.; Wade, T.D. Relationship between eating disorder duration and treatment outcome: Systematic review and meta-analysis. *Int. J. Eat. Disord.* **2020**, *53*, 1761–1773. [CrossRef] [PubMed]
12. Jenkins, P.E. Treatment of anorexia nervosa: Is it lacking power? *Psychol. Med.* **2019**, *49*, 1055–1056. [CrossRef] [PubMed]
13. Nazar, B.P.; Gregor, L.K.; Albano, G.; Marchica, A.; Coco, G.L.; Cardi, V.; Treasure, J. Early Response to treatment in Eating Disorders: A Systematic Review and a Diagnostic Test Accuracy Meta-Analysis. *Eur. Eat. Disord. Rev.* **2017**, *25*, 67–79. [CrossRef] [PubMed]
14. Cavedini, P.; Zorzi, C.; Bassi, T.; Gorini, A.; Baraldi, C.; Ubbiali, A.; Bellodi, L. Decision-making functioning as a predictor of treatment outcome in anorexia nervosa. *Psychiatry Res.* **2006**, *145*, 179–187. [CrossRef]

15. Graves, T.A.; Tabri, N.; Thompson-Brenner, H.; Franko, D.L.; Eddy, K.T.; Bourion-Bedes, S.; Brown, A.; Constantino, M.J.; Flückiger, C.; Forsberg, S.; et al. A meta-analysis of the relation between therapeutic alliance and treatment outcome in eating disorders. *Int. J. Eat. Disord.* **2017**, *50*, 323–340. [CrossRef]
16. Juarascio, A.S.; Manasse, S.M.; Espel, H.M.; Kerrigan, S.G.; Forman, E.M. Could training executive function improve treatment outcomes for eating disorders? *Appetite* **2015**, *90*, 187–193. [CrossRef] [PubMed]
17. Preyde, M.; Watson, J.; Remers, S.; Stuart, R. Emotional dysregulation, interoceptive deficits, and treatment outcomes in patients with eating disorders. *Soc. Work Ment. Health* **2016**, *14*, 227–244. [CrossRef]
18. Stewart, C.S.; McEwen, F.S.; Konstantellou, A.; Eisler, I.; Simic, M. Impact of ASD Traits on Treatment Outcomes of Eating Disorders in Girls. *Eur. Eat. Disord. Rev.* **2017**, *25*, 123–128. [CrossRef]
19. Testa, G.; Baenas, I.; Vintró-Alcaraz, C.; Granero, R.; Agüera, Z.; Sánchez, I.; Riesco, N.; Jiménez-Murcia, S.; Fernández-Aranda, F. Does ADHD Symptomatology Influence Treatment Outcome and Dropout Risk in Eating Disorders? A longitudinal Study. *J. Clin. Med.* **2020**, *9*, 2305. [CrossRef]
20. Fernández-Aranda, F.; Casas, M.; Claes, L.; Bryan, D.C.; Favaro, A.; Granero, R.; Gudiol, C.; Jiménez-Murcia, S.; Karwautz, A.; Le Grange, D.; et al. COVID-19 and implications for eating disorders. *Eur. Eat. Disord. Rev.* **2020**, *28*, 239–245. [CrossRef]
21. Kan, C.; Cardi, V.; Stahl, D.; Treasure, J. Precision psychiatry—What it means for eating disorders? *Eur. Eat. Disord. Rev.* **2019**, *27*, 3–7. [CrossRef] [PubMed]
22. Murray, S.B.; Quintana, D.S.; Loeb, K.L.; Griffiths, S.; Le Grange, D. Treatment outcomes for anorexia nervosa: A systematic review and meta-analysis of randomized controlled trials. *Psychol. Med.* **2019**, *49*, 535–544. [CrossRef]
23. Boeka, A.G.; Lokken, K.L. The Iowa gambling task as a measure of decision making in women with bulimia nervosa. *J. Int. Neuropsychol. Soc.* **2006**, *12*, 741–745. [CrossRef] [PubMed]
24. Fagundo, A.B.; de la Torre, R.; Jiménez-Murcia, S.; Agüera, Z.; Granero, R.; Tárrega, S.; Botella, C.; Baños, R.; Fernández-Real, J.M.; Rodríguez, R.; et al. Executive functions profile in extreme eating/weight conditions: From Anorexia Nervosa to Obesity. *PLoS ONE* **2012**, *7*, e43382. [CrossRef]
25. Guillaume, S.; Sang, C.N.T.; Jaussent, I.; Raingeard, I.; Bringer, J.; Jollant, F.; Courtet, P. Is Decision Making Really Impaired in Eating Disorders? *Neuropsychology* **2010**, *24*, 808–812. [CrossRef]
26. Liao, P.C.; Uher, R.; Lawrence, N.; Treasure, J.; Schmidt, U.; Campbell, I.C.; Collier, D.A.; Tchanturia, K. An examination of decision making in bulimia nervosa. *J. Clin. Exp. Neuropsychol.* **2009**, *31*, 455–461. [CrossRef] [PubMed]
27. Perpiñá, C.; Segura, M.; Sánchez-Reales, S. Cognitive flexibility and decision-making in eating disorders and obesity. *Eat. Weight Disord.* **2017**, *22*, 435–444. [CrossRef]
28. Tchanturia, K.; Lounes, N.; Holttum, S. Cognitive remediation in anorexia nervosa and related conditions: A systematic review. *Eur. Eat. Disord. Rev.* **2014**, *22*, 454–462. [CrossRef]
29. Diamond, A. Executive functions. *Annu. Rev. Psychol.* **2013**, *64*, 135–168. [CrossRef]
30. Gleichgerrcht, E.; Ibáñez, A.; Roca, M.; Torralva, T.; Manes, F. Decision-making cognition in neurodegenerative diseases. *Nat. Rev. Neurol.* **2010**, *6*, 611–623. [CrossRef]
31. Del Missier, F.; Mäntylä, T.; de Bruin, W.B. Executive functions in decision making: An individual differences approach. *Think. Reason.* **2010**, *16*, 69–97. [CrossRef]
32. Yuan, P.; Raz, N. Prefrontal cortex and executive functions in healthy adults: A meta-analysis of structural neuroimaging studies. *Neurosci. Biobehav. Rev.* **2014**, *42*, 180–192. [CrossRef] [PubMed]
33. Arnstren, A.; Li, B. Neurobiology of executive functions: Catecholamine influences on prefrontal cortical functions. *Biol. Psychiatry* **2005**, *57*, 1377–1384. [CrossRef] [PubMed]
34. Vinogradov, S.; Fisher, M.; De Villers-Sidani, E. Cognitive training for impaired neural systems in neuropsychiatric illness. *Neuropsychopharmacology* **2012**, *37*, 43–76. [CrossRef] [PubMed]
35. Friederich, H.C.; Wu, M.; Simon, J.J.; Herzog, W. Neurocircuit function in eating disorders. *Int. J. Eat. Disord.* **2013**, *46*, 425–432. [CrossRef]
36. Brogan, A.; Hevey, D.; Pignatti, R. Anorexia, bulimia, and obesity: Shared decision making deficits on the Iowa Gambling Task (IGT). *J. Int. Neuropsychol. Soc.* **2010**, *16*, 711–715. [CrossRef]
37. Francesconi, M.; Flouri, E.; Harrison, A. Change in decision-making skills and risk for eating disorders in adolescence: A population-based study. *Eur. Psychiatry* **2020**, *63*, e93. [CrossRef] [PubMed]
38. Garrido, I.; Subirá, S. Decision-making and impulsivity in eating disorder patients. *Psychiatry Res.* **2013**, *207*, 107–112. [CrossRef]
39. Steward, T.; Mestre-Bach, G.; Vintró-Alcaraz, C.; Lozano-Madrid, M.; Agüera, Z.; Fernández-Formoso, J.A.; Granero, R.; Jiménez-Murcia, S.; Vilarrasa, N.; García-Ruiz-de-Gordejuela, A.; et al. Food addiction and impaired executive functions in women with obesity. *Eur. Eat. Disord. Rev.* **2018**, *26*, 574–584. [CrossRef]
40. Steward, T.; Mestre-Bach, G.; Agüera, Z.; Granero, R.; Martín-Romera, V.; Sánchez, I.; Riesco, N.; Tolosa-Sola, I.; Fernández-Formoso, J.A.; Fernández-García, J.C.; et al. Enduring Changes in Decision Making in Patients with Full Remission from Anorexia Nervosa. *Eur. Eat. Disord. Rev.* **2016**, *24*, 523–527. [CrossRef]
41. Danner, U.N.; Ouwehand, C.; Van Haastert, N.L.; Hornsveld, H.; De Ridder, D.T.D. Decision-making impairments in women with binge eating disorder in comparison with obese and normal weight women. *Eur. Eat. Disord. Rev.* **2012**, *20*, e56–e62. [CrossRef] [PubMed]

42. Giannunzio, V.; Degortes, D.; Tenconi, E.; Collantoni, E.; Solmi, M.; Santonastaso, P.; Favaro, A. Decision-making impairment in anorexia nervosa: New insights into the role of age and decision-making style. *Eur. Eat. Disord. Rev.* **2018**, *26*, 302–314. [CrossRef] [PubMed]
43. Galimberti, E.; Fadda, E.; Cavallini, M.C.; Martoni, R.M.; Erzegovesi, S.; Bellodi, L. Executive functioning in anorexia nervosa patients and their unaffected relatives. *Psychiatry Res.* **2013**, *208*, 238–244. [CrossRef] [PubMed]
44. Oldershaw, A.; Lavender, T.; Schmidt, U. Are socio-emotional and neurocognitive functioning predictors of therapeutic outcomes for adults with anorexia nervosa? *Eur. Eat. Disord. Rev.* **2018**, *26*, 346–359. [CrossRef]
45. Hemmingsen, S.D.; Wesselhoeft, R.; Lichtenstein, M.B.; Sjögren, J.M.; Støving, R.K. Cognitive improvement following weight gain in patients with anorexia nervosa: A systematic review. *Eur. Eat. Disord. Rev.* **2020**, *29*, 402–426. [CrossRef]
46. American Psychiatric Association. *Diagnostic and Statistical Manual of Mental Disorders*, 5th ed.; American Psychiatric Association: Philadelphia, PA, USA, 2013; ISBN 0-89042-555-8.
47. Bechara, A.; Damasio, A.R.; Damasio, H.; Anderson, S.W. Insensitivity to future consequences following damage to human prefrontal cortex. *Cognition* **1994**, *50*, 7–15. [CrossRef]
48. Derogatis, L.R.; Savitz, K.L. The SCL-90-R, Brief Symptom Inventory, and Matching Clinical Rating Scales. In *The Use of Psychological Testing for Treatment Planning and Outcomes Assessment*, 2nd ed.; Lawrence Erlbaum Associates Publishers: Mahwah, NJ, USA, 1999; pp. 679–724. ISBN 0-8058-2761-7. (Hardcover).
49. Garner, D. *Manual del EDI-2 Inventario de Trastorno de la Conducta Alimentaria*; TEA: Madrid, Spain, 1998.
50. Eisinger, A.; Magi, A.; Gyurkovics, M.; Szabo, E.; Demetrovics, Z.; Kokonyei, G. Iowa Gambling Task: Illustration of a behavioral measurement. *Neuropsychopharmacol. Hung.* **2016**, *18*, 45–55.
51. Brand, M.; Labudda, K.; Markowitsch, H.J. Neuropsychological correlates of decision-making in ambiguous and risky situations. *Neural Netw.* **2006**, *19*, 1266–1276. [CrossRef]
52. Riesco, N.; Agüera, Z.; Granero, R.; Jiménez-Murcia, S.; Menchón, J.M.; Fernández-Aranda, F. Other Specified Feeding or Eating Disorders (OSFED): Clinical heterogeneity and cognitive-behavioral therapy outcome. *Eur. Psychiatry* **2018**, *54*, 109–116. [CrossRef]
53. Fernandez-Aranda, F.; Treasure, J.; Paslakis, G.; Agüera, Z.; Giménez, M.; Granero, R.; Sánchez, I.; Serrano-Troncoso, E.; Gorwood, P.; Herpertz-Dahlmann, B.; et al. The Impact of Duration of Illness on Treatment Non-response and Drop-out: Exploring the Relevance of Enduring Eating Disorder (E-ED) Concept. *Eur. Eat. Disord. Rev.* **2021**, *29*, 499–513. [CrossRef]
54. Finner, H.; Roters, M. On the false discovery rate and expected type I errors. *Biom. J.* **2001**, *43*, 985–1005. [CrossRef]
55. Zhou, X.-H.; Obuchowski, N.A.; McClish, D.K. *Statistical Methods in Diagnostic Medicine*; Wiley Series in Probability and Statistics; John Wiley & Sons, Inc.: Hoboken, NJ, USA, 2011; ISBN 9780470906514.
56. Levine, T.R.; Hullett, C.R. Eta Squared, Partial Eta Squared, and Misreporting of Effect Size in Communication Research. *Hum. Commun. Res.* **2002**, *28*, 612–625. [CrossRef]
57. Cohen, J. *Statistical Power Analysis for the Behavioral Sciences*; Routledge: New York, NY, USA, 1988; ISBN 9780203771587.
58. Hiroto, D.S.; Seligman, M.E. Generality of learned helplessness in man. *J. Pers. Soc. Psychol.* **1975**, *31*, 311–327. [CrossRef]
59. Harrison, A.; Treasure, J.; Smillie, L.D. Approach and avoidance motivation in eating disorders. *Psychiatry Res.* **2011**, *188*, 396–401. [CrossRef] [PubMed]
60. Harrison, A.; O'Brien, N.; Lopez, C.; Treasure, J. Sensitivity to reward and punishment in eating disorders. *Psychiatry Res.* **2010**, *177*, 1–11. [CrossRef]
61. Miller, W.R.; Seligman, M.E. Depression and learned helplessness in man. *J. Abnorm. Psychol.* **1975**, *84*, 228–238. [CrossRef] [PubMed]
62. Dingemans, A.E.; van Son, G.E.; Vanhaelen, C.B.; van Furth, E.F. Depressive symptoms rather than executive functioning predict group cognitive behavioural therapy outcome in binge eating disorder. *Eur. Eat. Disorders Rev.* **2020**, *28*, 620–632. [CrossRef] [PubMed]
63. Fortgang, R.G.; Srihari, V.; Cannon, T.D. Cognitive effort and amotivation in first-episode psychosis. *J. Abnorm. Psychol.* **2020**, *129*, 422–431. [CrossRef]

nutrients

MDPI

Article

Nutrient Intake and Dietary Inflammatory Potential in Current and Recovered Anorexia Nervosa

Olivia Patsalos [1,*], Bethan Dalton [1], Christia Kyprianou [1], Joseph Firth [2,3,4], Nitin Shivappa [5,6,7], James R. Hébert [5,6,7], Ulrike Schmidt [1,8] and Hubertus Himmerich [1,8]

1 Department of Psychological Medicine, Institute of Psychiatry, Psychology & Neuroscience, King's College London, London SE5 8AF, UK; bethan.dalton@kcl.ac.uk (B.D.); christia.kyprianou1@nhs.net (C.K.); ulrike.schmidt@kcl.ac.uk (U.S.); hubertus.himmerich@kcl.ac.uk (H.H.)
2 Division of Psychology and Mental Health, Manchester Academic Health Science Centre, University of Manchester, Manchester M13 9PL, UK; joefirth@gmail.com
3 NICM Health Research Institute, Western Sydney University, Westmead, NSW 2145, Australia
4 Greater Manchester Mental Health NHS Foundation Trust, Manchester Academic Health Science Centre, Manchester M25 3BL, UK
5 Cancer Prevention and Control Program, Arnold School of Public Health, University of South Carolina, Columbia, SC 29208, USA; shivappa@email.sc.edu (N.S.); jhebert@mailbox.sc.edu (J.R.H.)
6 Department of Epidemiology and Biostatistics, Arnold School of Public Health, University of South Carolina, Columbia, SC 29208, USA
7 Department of Nutrition, Connecting Health Innovations LLC, Columbia, SC 29201, USA
8 South London and Maudsley NHS Foundation Trust, London SE5 8AZ, UK
* Correspondence: oliviapatsalos@gmail.com

Citation: Patsalos, O.; Dalton, B.; Kyprianou, C.; Firth, J.; Shivappa, N.; Hébert, J.R.; Schmidt, U.; Himmerich, H. Nutrient Intake and Dietary Inflammatory Potential in Current and Recovered Anorexia Nervosa. *Nutrients* **2021**, *13*, 4400. https://doi.org/10.3390/nu13124400

Academic Editors: Fernando Fernandez-Aranda, Janet Treasure and Empar Lurbe

Received: 31 October 2021
Accepted: 7 December 2021
Published: 9 December 2021

Abstract: Anorexia nervosa (AN) is characterised by disrupted and restrictive eating patterns. Recent investigations and meta-analyses have found altered concentrations of inflammatory markers in people with current AN. We aimed to assess nutrient intake in participants with current or recovered AN, as compared to healthy individuals, and explore group differences in dietary inflammatory potential as a possible explanation for the observed alterations in inflammatory markers. We recruited participants with current AN (n = 51), those recovered from AN (n = 23), and healthy controls (n = 49). We used the Food Frequency Questionnaire (FFQ), to calculate a Dietary Inflammatory Index (DII®) score and collected blood samples to measure serum concentrations of inflammatory markers. In current AN participants, we found lower intake of cholesterol, compared to HCs, and lower consumption of zinc and protein, compared to HC and recovered AN participants. A one-way ANOVA revealed no significant group differences in DII score. Multivariable regression analyses showed that DII scores were significantly associated with tumour necrosis factor (TNF)-α concentrations in our current AN sample. Our findings on nutrient intake are partially consistent with previous research. The lack of group differences in DII score, perhaps suggests that diet is not a key contributor to altered inflammatory marker concentrations in current and recovered AN. Future research would benefit from including larger samples and using multiple 24-h dietary recalls to assess dietary intake.

Keywords: anorexia nervosa; dietary inflammatory index; food frequency questionnaire; inflammation; nutrient intake

1. Introduction

Anorexia Nervosa (AN) is a severe psychiatric disorder characterised by low body weight, restrictive eating patterns, and body image disturbances. It has one of the highest standardised mortality [1,2] and relapse rates [3] of all psychiatric disorders and is frequently chronic in nature [4]. The underlying pathophysiology of AN is still poorly understood and research regarding its aetiology is ongoing. Meta-analyses have reported alterations in the immunological profile of AN patients, specifically increased concentrations of pro-inflammatory cytokines, which have been suggested as a potential contributing factor to the development and maintenance of the disorder [5,6].

Patients with AN lose weight through limiting their caloric intake and, for some, excessive physical exercise. Importantly, aside from the significantly reduced calorie intake, the macronutrient composition of their diets differs significantly from that of lean and healthy, or normal-weight people [7]. Research has shown that people with AN consume less fat, protein, and carbohydrates, but more fibre than their healthy peers [8,9]. Furthermore, it has been reported that even after treatment and weight restoration, recovered AN patients continue to exhibit suboptimal dietary intake of micronutrients and vitamins [10], as well as limited food variety [11].

Diet plays an important role in the regulation of inflammation [12] and associations between dietary patterns and inflammatory status have been reported [13]. For example, intake of dietary fibre has been associated with lower C-reactive protein (CRP), whereas consumption of saturated fatty acids has been associated with higher CRP concentrations [14,15]. It is widely accepted that the Mediterranean diet, which is generally plant-based and high in fibre and low in saturated fats, has anti-inflammatory effects and confers overall lower health risks as compared to a Western-style diet [16,17]. It also is recognised that poor nutrition significantly impacts immune function with many micronutrient deficiencies conveying profound alterations in the regulation of the immune system [18,19].

Given their highly disordered eating patterns and nutrition intake, AN patients often present with nutrient deficiencies [20]. For example, zinc deficiency has been consistently observed in AN patients and this deficiency has been associated with severe immune dysfunction, mainly affecting T-helper cells and delaying wound healing [21–23]. Another important nutrient is cholesterol: hypercholesterolaemia, which has been extensively studied in the context of cardiovascular disease, is frequently exhibited in people with AN and has wide ranging effects, including promoting inflammatory processes and the production of monocytes and neutrophils [24]. Crucially, sterols bind directly to several immune receptors, regulating cytokine expression [25]. It is possible, therefore, that the immunological alterations seen in AN patients could result in part from their disordered eating and patterns of nutrient intake.

In the last decade, there has been significant interest in the role of the immune system, particularly the role of cytokines in psychiatric disorders, including depression [26–31], anxiety [32–34], and post-traumatic disorder [35–37], all of which frequently co-occur with AN. Cytokines are small messenger molecules of the immune system involved in autocrine, paracrine, and endocrine signalling as well as brain functioning [38]. They are produced by a variety of cells including macrophages, as well as astrocytes and microglia [26] and have been shown to access the brain via humoral, neural, and cellular pathways [38]. In addition, they have been shown to play a role in appetite and feeding regulation via their influence on metabolic pathways and neurotransmitter signal transduction, as well as through modulating the hypothalamus-pituitary-adrenal (HPA) axis (see Himmerich et al. [29] for a review). Recent research has reported altered cytokine concentrations in AN patients compared to healthy comparison groups [39,40]. Additionally, when comparing people with current AN to those recovered from AN, significant differences in concentrations of several inflammatory markers have been reported, suggesting that some inflammatory markers could be state markers of the disorder and others trait markers of AN [41,42].

Given the evidence of cytokine alterations in AN, the reported effects of diet on inflammatory status and vice versa, and the disordered eating patterns of people with AN, we hypothesized that the documented altered inflammatory profile could result, at least partly, from their diet. Hence, primarily, we sought to compare the nutrient intakes of AN participants to people recovered from AN (recAN) and healthy controls (HC), and determine whether these groups differed in the inflammatory potential of their diet, using the Dietary Inflammatory Index (DII®) [43]. In addition, we explored the associations between DII scores and cytokine concentrations in participants with AN, recAN, and HC.

2. Materials and Methods

2.1. Participants

All participants were females over the age of 18 years. AN participants were required to have a current primary diagnosis of AN, according to the Diagnostic and Statistical Manual of Mental Disorders (DSM)-5 [44], and a body mass index (BMI) < 18.5 kg/m^2. For the recAN group, participants had to (i) have previously met AN diagnostic criteria based on the DSM-IV, (ii) have maintained a BMI > 18.5 kg/m^2 for at least 6 months prior to the study, (iii) menstruate, and (iv) have not binged, purged, or engaged in significant restrictive eating patterns for the last 3 months. Having previous alternative eating disorders diagnoses was not an exclusion criterion. AN and recAN participants were recruited via Specialist Eating Disorder Services in South London and Maudsley NHS Foundation Trust, online and poster advertisements at King's College London (KCL), the Beat eating disorder charity's research recruitment webpages, and through participation in other research projects. HCs were required to be of a healthy BMI (18.5–24.5 kg/m^2) without a history of or current mental health condition, including eating disorders (EDs), and were recruited via an e-mail circular to students and staff at KCL and through online and poster advertisements. Exclusion criteria for all participants were current pregnancy and the presence of acute or chronic inflammatory conditions e.g., asthma, psoriasis, Crohn's Disease, inflammatory bowel disease, arthritis.

Group classification (current AN, recAN or HC) was established using self-report and further assessed via a telephone screening. Screening questionnaires included the Eating Disorder Diagnostic Scale (EDDS) [45] to assess the presence of ED symptoms, and a brief inclusion/exclusion screen specific to this study, which included an assessment of physical health conditions. HC participants additionally completed the research version of the Structured Clinical Interview for DSM-IV Axis I Disorders [46] to assess the presence of current or past psychiatric disorders.

2.2. Measures

2.2.1. Food Frequency Questionnaire

We used the European Prospective Investigation of Cancer Study (EPIC)-Norfolk Food Frequency Questionnaire (EPIC-Norfolk FFQ) [47] to collect information on the average intake (e.g., frequency, portion size) of foods and beverages during the previous year. The EPIC-Norfolk FFQ [47,48] is a semi-quantitative self-report questionnaire and requests information on 290 foods. The food list in the EPIC-Norfolk FFQ is based on items from an FFQ widely used in the US [47,49], but it was modified to reflect differences in American versus UK food items and brand names. The questionnaire consists of two parts. Part 1 is a food list of 130 lines and the lines are either individual foods, combinations of individual foods or food types. Each line also has a portion size attached to it, which is a medium serving, standard unit or household measure. Respondents select an appropriate frequency of consumption for their average intake over the last year for each line. They can select from nine frequency categories ranging from "Never or less than once a month" to "6+ per day". Part 2 consists of several questions that ask for more detailed information about certain food lines in Part 1 (e.g., breakfast cereals). The EPIC-Norfolk FFQ has been widely used to assess dietary intake in large populations [48] and extensively validated [48,50].

We used the FFQ EPIC Tool for Analysis (FETA), an open source, cross-platform software tool, to convert EPIC-Norfolk FFQ data into nutrient and food group values [51]. Data were entered into a purposively designed comma-separated data input file following coding instructions (http://www.srl.cam.ac.uk/epic/epicffq/websitedocumentation.shtml) (accessed on 10 February 2020), which we then uploaded to FETA. The output from FETA provides an average daily nutrient and food group intake for an individual from all FFQ foods consumed; specifically, intake data for 46 nutrients and 14 basic food groups. This software produces similar nutrient and food group values to a previously validated, but less accessible tool (Compositional Analyses from Frequency Estimates (CAFÉ)) designed for converting EPIC-Norfolk FFQ data [52].

2.2.2. Dietary Inflammatory Index

We used the data from the EPIC-Norfolk FFQ, as calculated by FETA, to calculate the Dietary Inflammatory Index (DII) [43]. The DII is literature-derived, using a large-scale meta-analytic strategy to compute averaged inflammatory/anti-inflammatory effects for individual nutrient parameters that have sufficient evidence to capture their effect on inflammatory markers. The DII has been validated against several peripheral markers of inflammation, including interleukin (IL)-6 [53,54] and tumour necrosis factor (TNF)-α [55].

In the current study, the following 25 food and nutrient parameters were used: alcohol, β-carotene, total carbohydrate, cholesterol, fibre, iron, folate, energy, magnesium, niacin (vitamin B_3), total protein, retinol (vitamin A), riboflavin (vitamin B_2), selenium, thiamine (vitamin B_1), vitamin B_{12}, vitamin B_6, vitamin C, vitamin D, vitamin E, total fat, MUFA, PUFA, and SFA. For full details, on the steps to calculate the DII® [43], see Shivappa et al. [43]. Briefly, values of the nutrients listed above are standardised into a z score by subtracting the mean from the global database and dividing this by the standard deviation from the global database (global daily mean intakes and standard deviations listed in Shivappa et al. [43] for each nutrient). To minimise the effect of 'right skewing' this value is converted into a percentile score. To achieve a symmetrical distribution with values centred on 0 (null) and bounded between −1 (maximally anti-inflammatory) and +1 (maximally pro-inflammatory), each percentile score is then doubled and '1' is subtracted. The centred percentile value for each food parameter is then multiplied by its respective 'overall food parameter-specific inflammatory effect score', listed in Shivappa et al. [43], to obtain the 'food parameter-specific DII score'. Finally, all of the 'food parameter-specific DII scores' for the available nutrients are summed to create the 'overall DII score' for an individual. A higher DII score indicates greater inflammatory potential of an individual's diet. The DII score could range from +7.98 (maximally pro-inflammatory) to −8.87 (maximally anti-inflammatory) when calculated from all 45 food parameters for which the creators of the DII calculated an inflammatory score [56].

2.2.3. Blood Sampling and Inflammatory Marker Quantification

To quantify inflammatory marker concentrations, blood samples were collected by trained phlebotomists. Serum was separated by centrifugation and stored at −80 °C prior to use. All samples were anonymised and stored under secure conditions. Serum was thawed at room temperature for use. The concentrations of 36 cytokines were quantified simultaneously using multiplex ELISA-based technology provided by the Meso Scale Discovery V-PLEX Plus Human Biomarker 36-Plex Kit, following the manufacturer's instructions (Meso Scale Discovery, Rockville, MD, USA). Seven-point standard curves were run in duplicate on each plate to calculate absolute pg/mL values of cytokines for the samples assayed. Cases and controls were randomised across the plate. Plates were scanned on the Meso Scale Discovery MESO Quickplex SQ 120 reader at the Social, Genetic & Developmental Psychiatry Centre, Institute of Psychiatry, Psychology & Neuroscience, King's College London. For the purpose of the current study, only data on IL-6, IL-10, and TNF-α were used as the DII has been previously validated against these inflammatory markers and they were available on the assay. For the results on group differences for the 36 inflammatory markers measured, see Keeler et al. [42].

2.3. Procedure

Eligible participants attended a single research session at the Institute of Psychiatry, Psychology & Neuroscience at King's College London, lasting no longer than 1 and a half hours. After having their blood collected, participants had their height and body weight measured, from which BMI (kg/m^2) was calculated, and body composition was assessed using a portable and non-invasive Inbody S10 machine, Biospace Co., Ltd. Participants then completed a questionnaire pack, including questions on demographic characteristics, clinical characteristics for AN and recAN participants, and the EPIC-Norfolk FFQ. Participants also completed questionnaires on mental health, data for which have been presented elsewhere [42] and will not be included in the present study.

2.4. Statistical Analysis

All statistical analyses were performed in SPSS [57]. For normally distributed data, means and standard deviations are presented, and for non-normally distributed data, median and interquartile ranges (25th and 75th percentile) are provided. One-way ANOVAs were used to assess group differences in demographic characteristics and nutrient values. For significant results, post-hoc analyses were performed to determine specific group differences. Post-hoc analyses were adjusted for multiple comparisons using the Bonferroni correction. Multivariable regression analyses were performed to assess the association between DII scores and inflammatory marker concentrations.

3. Results

3.1. Participants

A total of 133 participants were recruited. Data from 10 participants were excluded from the analyses for the following reasons: four HCs and one recAN participant were not within the required BMI range, two HCs reported regular recreational drug use, two HCs did not provide FFQ data, and one HC had tonsillitis in the previous week. Therefore, data on nutrient intake were available for a total of 123 participants. Table 1 summarises participant demographic and clinical characteristics.

Table 1. Participant demographic and clinical characteristics with group comparisons.

	HC $n = 49$	**AN** $n = 51$	**RecAN** $n = 23$	**Group Comparisons**
Demographic characteristics				
Age [years] [median (IQR [a])]	22.5 (20.3, 25.8)	24 (21.0, 30.0)	24 (21.0, 30.0)	$H(2) = 4.003$ $p = 0.135$
Ethnicity [Caucasian/BAME] [n]	25/24	45/6	22/1	$F(2) = 5.96$ $p = 0.003$
Current smoker [n]	7	8	3	$F(2) = 0.068$ $p = 0.93$
BMI [kg/m^2] [median (IQR [a])]	21.0 (19.6, 22.5)	16.1 (15.1, 17.0)	20.7 (19.6, 21.3)	$H(2) = 84.121$ $p < 0.001$
Body fat [%] [mean ± SD]	23.9 ± 5.2	12.0 ± 5.2	22.3 ± 6.3	$F(2) = 69.33$ $p < 0.001$
Clinical characteristics				
AN subtype [AN-R/AN-BP] [n]		45/6		
Current treatment [none/outpatient/inpatient] [n]		20/30/1		
Disease Duration [years]		5.57		
Current antidepressant use [n]	0	21	6	$F(2) = 13.88$ $p < 0.001$
Current antipsychotic use [n]	0	6	2	$F(2) = 3.21$ $p = 0.04$

Statistically significant group comparisons at $p < 0.05$ are highlighted in bold. [a] 25th and 75th percentile reported. Abbreviations: HC = healthy controls; AN = anorexia nervosa; recAN = recovered anorexia nervosa; IQR = interquartile range; BAME = Black, Asian, and minority ethnic; n = number of observations; BMI = body mass index; AN-R = anorexia nervosa restricting type; AN-BP = anorexia nervosa binge-eating/purging type.

3.2. Nutrient Intake

Table 2 presents nutrient intake of 25 micronutrients and macronutrients (as reported in the FFQ) with group comparisons. One-way ANOVAs and post-hoc pairwise comparisons revealed group differences for cholesterol, monounsaturated fats (MUFA), polyunsaturated fats (PUFA), total protein, and zinc (Table 2). Both current AN and recAN participants had significantly lower intake of cholesterol than HCs (p = 0.001 and p = 0.028 respectively); AN participants reported lower protein (p = 0.033) and zinc (p = 0.015) intake than HCs, and lower MUFA and PUFA intake than recAN (p = 0.030 and p = 0.050, respectively).

Table 2. Between groups comparisons of individual nutrient and food component intake.

Nutrient	AN [SD] (n = 51)	RecAN [SD] (n = 23)	HC [SD] (n = 49)	Group Comparison	Post-Hoc Pairwise Comparison
Alcohol [g]	2.22 [4.35]	4.85 [7.05]	3.13 [3.37]	F (2) = 2.561 p = 0.081	HC—AN: p = 0.978 HC—RecAN: p = 0.436 AN—RecAN: p = 0.077
β-carotene [µg]	5239.39 [4561.55]	5701.02 [4846.22]	4387.41 [3068.63]	F (2) = 0.973 p = 0.381	HC—AN: p = 0.900 HC—RecAN: p = 0.619 AN—RecAN: p = 1.000
Total carbohydrate [g]	204.37 [108.67]	232.42 [99.08]	218.22 [118.02]	F (2) = 0.539 p = 0.585	HC—AN: p = 1.000 HC—RecAN: p = 1.000 AN—RecAN: p = 0.947
Cholesterol [mg]	168.56 [132.23]	181.90 [139.96]	294.07 [208.61]	F (2) = 7.72 p = 0.001	HC—AN: p = 0.001 HC—RecAN: 0.028 AN—RecAN: p = 1.000
Energy [kcal]	1553.64 [739.79]	1928.31 [875.55]	1823.68 [950.70]	F (2) = 2.0 p = 0.140	HC—AN: p = 0.350 HC—RecAN: p = 1.000 AN—RecAN: p = 0.250
Total fat [g]	57.43 [35.27]	81.07 [44.25]	72.16 [41.05]	F (2) = 3.375 p = 0.038	HC—AN: p = 0.192 HC—RecAN: p = 1.000 AN—RecAN: p = 0.055
Folate [µg]	323.52 [183.11]	375.31 [209.03]	310.05 [151.86]	F (2) = 1.094 p = 0.338	HC—AN: p = 1.000 HC—RecAN: p = 0.440 AN—RecAN: p = 0.736
Englyst fibre [g]	20.40 [11.41]	23.28 [13.94]	18.80 [10.47]	F (2) = 1.176 p = 0.312	HC—AN: p = 1.000 HC—RecAN: p = 0.385 AN—RecAN: p = 0.973
Iron [mg]	10.86 [5.21]	13.22 [6.54]	11.93 [5.90]	F (2) = 1.380 p = 0.256	HC—AN: p = 1.000 HC—RecAN: p = 1.000 AN—RecAN: p = 0.316
Magnesium [mg]	319.62 [129.58]	388.72 [202.81]	337.13 [170.24]	F (2) = 1.457 p = 0.237	HC—AN: p = 1.000 HC—RecAN: p = 0.627 AN—RecAN: p = 0.274
Monounsaturated fat [g]	21.03 [12.46]	30.93 [18.35]	27.75 [15.87]	F (2) = 4.279 p = 0.016	HC—AN: p = 0.083 HC—RecAN: p = 1.000 AN—RecAN: p = 0.030
Niacin (vitamin B_3) [mg]	20.51 [10.60]	22.32 [11.79]	21.97 [11.63]	F (2) = 0.299 p = 0.742	HC—AN: p = 1.000 HC—RecAN: p = 1.000 AN—RecAN: p = 1.000
Total protein [g]	63.91 [31.43]	73.61 [34.67]	83.85 [46.41]	F (2) = 3.325 p = 0.039	HC—AN: p = 0.033 HC—RecAN: p = 0.890 AN—RecAN: p = 0.959
Polyunsaturated fat [g]	11.91 [7.34]	17.01 [10.88]	13.22 [8.01]	F (2) = 2.965 p = 0.055	HC—AN: p = 1.000 HC—RecAN: p = 0.227 AN—RecAN: p = 0.050
Riboflavin (vitamin B_2) [mg]	1.87 [1.12]	1.97 [1.06]	1.82 [0.91]	F (2) = 0.174 p = 0.841	HC—AN: p = 1.000 HC—RecAN: p = 1.000 AN—RecAN: p = 1.000
Saturated fatty acids [g]	19.54 [14.91]	26.64 [16.07]	24.87 [15.50]	F (2) = 2.302 p = 0.104	HC—AN: p = 0.256 HC—RecAN: p = 1.000 AN—RecAN: p = 0.205
Selenium [µg]	50.83 [30.96]	54.35 [27.31]	63.16 [34.12]	F (2) = 1.954 p = 0.146	HC—AN: p = 0.162 HC—RecAN: p = 0.819 AN—RecAN: p = 1.000
Thiamin (Vitamin B_1) [mg]	1.51 [0.81]	1.94 [1.11]	1.59 [0.82]	F (2) = 1.957 p = 0.146	HC—AN: p = 1.000 HC—RecAN: p = 0.336 AN—RecAN: p = 0.163
Retinol (Vitamin A) [µg]	251.89 [368.00]	313.50 [358.19]	421.35 [398.41]	F (2) = 2.532 p = 0.084	HC—AN: p = 0.081 HC—RecAN: p = 0.786 AN—RecAN: p =1.000

Table 2. *Cont.*

Vitamin B_6 [mg]	1.83 [0.89]	2.12 [1.01]	2.23 [1.07]	F (2) = 2.168 p = 0.119	HC—AN: p = 1.000 HC—RecAN: p = 0.130 AN—RecAN: p = 0.735
Vitamin B_{12} [µg]	4.27 [3.69]	3.51 [2.87]	5.66 3.61]	F (2) = 3.527 p = 0.032	HC—AN: p = 0.151 HC—RecAN: p = 0.051 AN—RecAN: p = 1.000
Vitamin C [mg]	146.15 [90.44]	142.01 [91.63]	123.88 [69.78]	F (2) = 0.961 p = 0.385	HC—AN: p = 0.548 HC—RecAN: p = 1.000 AN—RecAN: p = 1.000
Vitamin D [µg]	2.04 [2.32]	2.11 [1.82]	2.73 1.98]	F (2) = 1.508 p = 0.225	HC—AN: p = 0.309 HC—RecAN: p = 0.720 AN—RecAN: p = 1.000
Vitamin E [mg]	12.58 [5.53]	15.44 [7.89]	12.45 [7.06]	F (2) = 1.813 p = 0.168	HC—AN: p = 1.000 HC—RecAN: p = 0.233 AN—RecAN: p = 0.268
Zinc	7.27 [3.23]	8.67 [4.35]	9.76 [5.26]	F (2) = 4.115 p = 0.019	HC—AN: p = 0.015 HC—RecAN: p = 0.971 AN—RecAN: p = 0.606

Abbreviations: AN = anorexia nervosa, HC = healthy controls, RecAN = recovered anorexia nervosa, n = number of observations.

3.3. Dietary Inflammatory Index

While the DII score was lower in the recAN compared to the current AN and HC groups (AN = 0.56 [SD = 1.86], recAN = 0.07 [SD = 1.73], HC = 0.60 [SD = 2.08]), a one-way ANOVA and an ANCOVA controlling for calorie intake revealed no significant group differences in DII score (F (2, 121) = 0.553, p = 0.577 and F (2, 121) = 1.797, p = 0.170, respectively). The DII score for the 25 nutrients investigated in the whole sample ranged from −3.26 to +3.63.

3.4. Association between DII Score and Inflammatory Markers

Multivariable regressions controlling for age and calorie intake showed that DII score was significantly associated with concentrations of TNF-α in our AN sample (β = 0.404, t = 2.396, p = 0.021). However, DII score was not significantly related to any other cytokines in the AN group nor any cytokines in the recAN and HC groups.

4. Discussion

Individuals with AN report altered nutrient intake [7–9] and recent immunological studies in AN have found altered levels of cytokines compared to healthy individuals [39,58]. In this study, we aimed to examine group differences in nutrient intake and explore whether the inflammatory potential of an individual's diet may be associated with inflammation.

4.1. Nutrient Intake

In our AN participants, we observed lower intake of cholesterol, protein, and zinc, compared to HCs, and MUFAs, compared to recAN participants. These findings could be explained by the food preferences of people with AN: research suggests that people with AN tend to prefer lower calorie options (e.g., avoid meat, dairy products, fried foods, and baked goods [59–62]) to prevent weight gain. It is important to note that we did not replicate well established findings, such as a reduced (total and saturated) fat intake in people with AN [8,61,63]. The lack of group differences may be accounted for by the large proportion of the AN sample who were receiving specialist ED treatment, as this aims to increase caloric consumption in a nutritionally balanced manner [61]. Methodological considerations associated with the FFQ may have also contributed to the findings, as will be discussed in Section 4.3.

We reported that both AN and recAN participants consumed significantly less cholesterol than HCs. This is unsurprising as people with AN tend to avoid foods that are high in cholesterol such as dairy products and meats [7,64]. Research on the lipid profile of AN patients has shown that they often exhibit hypercholesterolaemia [65,66]. This has been attributed to a diminished cholesterol and bile acid metabolism resulting from the reduced caloric intake [67,68] and suggests that, regardless of their dietary cholesterol intake, AN patients could be at risk of cardiovascular disease. With regards to recAN patients, research has found that they often make food choices based on their perceived health benefits [69]. Given the widely known health risks associated with high cholesterol, it is consistent with our recAN sample exhibiting lower cholesterol intake.

AN participants consumed significantly less protein than HCs in our study. Findings on consumption of protein in people with AN, compared to HCs, are mixed: some authors have reported increased protein intake [70,71], whereas others have reported lower intake [59,72,73]. Inadequate protein consumption can lead to decreased synthesis of visceral proteins, oedema, and muscle atrophy [74]. Indeed, oedema and muscle atrophy have been described in AN [75]. The lack of protein intake might have clinical implications for people with AN and a comorbid depressive or anxiety disorder. In AN, for example, recent studies found comorbidity rates of more than 50% for social anxiety disorder, about 40% for depression and 20–30% for generalized anxiety disorder [76,77]. Second-generation antidepressants such as selective serotonin reuptake inhibitors (SSRI) are the first-line pharmacological treatment for patients with depression and anxiety disorders [78,79]. However, SSRIs have not been found to have much benefit for depressive or anxious symptoms in the acute phase of AN [80]. The lack of proteins and amino acids has been suggested as a potential explanation because amino acids such as tryptophan are needed to produce neurotransmitters such as serotonin; and antidepressants, for example SSRIs, that act as reuptake inhibitors of neurotransmitters require the presence of neurotransmitters such as serotonin to be effective [81]. A comorbid depressive disorder may be a barrier to recovery from AN. Therefore, medications such as ketamine and esketamine which do not rely on the availability of amino acids have been suggested as treatment options for the treatment of a comorbid depressive disorder in malnourished patients with AN [82].

Zinc is perhaps the most studied micronutrient in AN, with previous research reporting deficient levels of zinc (<46 mcg/dL) in AN [59,72,83]. Our findings of lower zinc consumption in AN participants compared to HCs are consistent with some previous research [9]. However, some studies have reported no difference in zinc consumption, likely due to increased supplement use in AN [8]. Research has shown that people with AN are significantly more likely to be and/or have a history of being vegetarian, as compared to HCs [60,61]. As meat and fish are high in zinc, this may explain the present findings. The lack of zinc has also been suggested to play a role in the pathophysiology of depression and to contribute to therapy resistance during treatment with antidepressants; thus, zinc supplementation has been proposed as an adjunct to improve the efficacy of antidepressant treatment [84].

Compared to recAN participants, AN participants also consumed less MUFAs and PUFAs in this study. Indeed, people with current AN tend to restrict all types of dietary fats, whereas weight gain in AN has been associated with obtaining a higher percentage of total calories from fats, including unsaturated fats [85]. Overall, our results are in line with other studies showing essential fatty acid disturbances in current AN patients [86,87], as well as in chronically malnourished individuals [88,89]. However, it is perhaps surprising that group differences in total fat or saturated fat were not also identified, as it is well established that individuals with AN tend to prefer foods low in fat [8,64].

4.2. Dietary Inflammatory Index

Our analyses did not reveal any significant differences in DII score between the current AN, recAN and HC groups, despite the recAN participants having a lower DII score than the other groups. Given the few differences we identified in nutritional intake between groups, and the narrow range of inflammatory scores in the whole sample, this is perhaps to be expected.

We also explored whether DII score may be associated with cytokine concentrations in each of our groups. Inflammatory marker analysis revealed that DII score was associated with concentrations of TNF-α but only in the AN group (when controlling for age and calorie intake), such that a higher DII score was associated with increased concentrations of TNF-α. However, no other associations between DII score and inflammatory marker concentrations were found. Therefore, it may suggest that factors other than dietary intake regulate cytokines in current and recovered AN and be responsible for the alterations reported previously [5,6]. Indeed, there is likely a combination of factors that contribute to the observed altered concentrations of inflammatory markers in currently unwell AN patients. Alternative factors could include stress, genetics, and comorbid psychiatric disorders, as well as specifically AN-related factors like current recovery and refeeding status, recent weight gain, and current ED behaviours (e.g., self-starvation and compensatory mechanisms). Alongside this, other behavioural factors could also contribute to heightened concentrations of inflammatory markers observed in AN patients. Often correlated, health behaviours such as physical activity, tobacco smoking, and sleeping patterns [90,91] can impact on inflammatory status [92], and have previously been shown to be altered in people with eating disorders [93–95].

4.3. Strengths and Limitations

This is the first study to assess inflammatory potential of dietary intake in people with AN. However, the sample was relatively small, particularly in the recAN group, within which we performed multiple comparisons. Our sample size did not allow us to subdivide our AN participants according to their AN subtype (binge-eating/purging type or restricting type), which would have been of interest given likely differences in dietary patterns between the AN subtypes. Additionally, our sample was heterogeneous in demographic and clinical characteristics, including disease duration which ranged from 3 months to 35 years. Further issues and uncertainties to consider are that eating more food tends to be associated with lower DII scores, that findings seem to vary between studies depending on patterns of food intake within individual populations, and that there is often limited eating pattern variability within control groups [56]. Therefore, our results need to be interpreted with caution.

There are further methodological considerations that may have contributed to our findings, namely, the inherent strengths and limitations associated with the use of FFQs. The FFQ represents a good option for capturing dietary information as it is simple to self-administer, relatively low-cost, and may be a better representation of usual dietary patterns than 24-h recall or a few days of observation. However, there are also several limitations to this method of collecting data on nutritional intake. The EPIC-Norfolk FFQ requires participants to recall the frequency and portion size consumption over the last year. This is cognitively demanding and is often biased by their present dietary intake and patterns. Additionally, for AN participants who have been in treatment, it may have been difficult to record an average intake when their diet may have altered during this time frame, as nutrition restoration is a key component of treatment for AN. Further, food portion estimation is frequently imprecisely estimated and quantified: research has shown that people with AN tend to overestimate energy intake perhaps due to over-reporting of caloric intake; in contrast, HCs tend to consistently under-report caloric intake [72,96,97]. Hence, dependence on participant recall makes FFQs amenable to misrepresenting true dietary intake [98]. Finally, the FFQ is limited to a specific list of food items, which could be considered outdated given that it was designed approximately 20 years ago. Dietary habits have changed considerably over the last two decades [99,100]. For example, the list does not include non-dairy milk alternatives, consumption of which was reported by a large proportion of our contemporary participants.

5. Conclusions

In participants with current AN, we identified significantly lower intake of cholesterol, protein, and zinc, compared to HCs and MUFAs and PUFAs compared to participants recovered from AN. The DII score did not significantly differ between groups. Therefore, the findings from this study suggest that it is unlikely that a pro-inflammatory diet accounts for the alterations in cytokines and other inflammatory markers that have been observed in people with current AN. As this is the first study to assess dietary inflammation in AN, future research should further explore the use of the DII in samples with current and recovered AN, using multiple 24-h dietary recalls (to avoid problems associated with averaging intake over a long period of time).

Author Contributions: Conceptualisation, H.H., O.P. and B.D.; methodology, H.H., O.P. and B.D.; formal analysis, O.P.; investigation, O.P. and B.D.; data curation, O.P., C.K. and B.D.; writing—original draft preparation, O.P.; writing—review and editing, B.D., H.H., U.S., C.K., N.S., J.F. and J.R.H.; visualisation, O.P.; supervision, H.H. and B.D.; project administration, O.P. and B.D.; funding acquisition, H.H. All authors have read and agreed to the published version of the manuscript.

Funding: This research received no external funding.

Institutional Review Board Statement: The study was conducted according to the guidelines of the Declaration of Helsinki, and approved by the Ethics Committee of London City and East (Reference: 17/LO/2017).

Informed Consent Statement: Informed consent was obtained from all subjects involved in the study.

Data Availability Statement: The data presented in this study are available on request from the corresponding author. The data are not publicly available as they are still being used for analysis and manuscript writing.

Acknowledgments: O.P., U.S. and H.H. receive salary support from the National Institute of Health Research (NIHR) Mental Health Biomedical Research Centre (BRC) at South London and Maudsley NHS Foundation Trust (SLaM) and King's College London (KCL). B.D. was supported by a studentship awarded by the Department of Psychological Medicine, King's College London (KCL) and the Institute of Psychiatry, Psychology and Neuroscience (IoPPN), KCL. U.S. is also supported by an NIHR Senior Investigator Award. The views expressed in this publication are those of the authors and not necessarily those of the National Health Service, the NIHR, or the UK Department of Health. J.F. is supported by a University of Manchester Presidential Fellowship (P123958) and a UK Research and Innovation Future Leaders Fellowship (MR/T021780/1) and has received honoraria/consultancy fees from Atheneum, Parachute and Nirakara, independent of this work.

Conflicts of Interest: James R. Hébert owns controlling interest in Connecting Health Innovations LLC (CHI), a company that has licensed the right to his invention of the dietary inflammatory index (DII®) from the University of South Carolina in order to develop computer and smart phone applications for patient counselling and dietary intervention in clinical settings. Nitin Shivappa is an employee of CHI. The subject matter of this paper will not have any direct bearing on that work, nor has that activity exerted any influence on this project. The funders had no role in the design of the study; in the collection, analyses, or interpretation of data; in the writing of the manuscript, or in the decision to publish the results.

References

1. Arcelus, J.; Mitchell, A.J.; Wales, J.; Nielsen, S. Mortality Rates in Patients with Anorexia Nervosa and Other Eating Disorders. *Arch. Gen. Psychiatry* **2011**, *68*, 724. [CrossRef]
2. Papadopoulos, F.C.; Ekbom, A.; Brandt, L.; Ekselius, L. Excess mortality, causes of death and prognostic factors in anorexia nervosa. *Br. J. Psychiatry* **2009**, *194*, 10–17. [CrossRef]
3. Berends, T.; Boonstra, N.; van Elburg, A. Relapse in anorexia nervosa. *Curr. Opin. Psychiatry* **2018**, *31*, 445–455. [CrossRef]
4. Steinhausen, H.-C. The Outcome of Anorexia Nervosa in the 20th Century. *Am. J. Psychiatry* **2002**, *159*, 1284–1293. [CrossRef]
5. Solmi, M.; Veronese, N.; Favaro, A.; Santonastaso, P.; Manzato, E.; Sergi, G.; Correll, C.U. Inflammatory cytokines and anorexia nervosa: A meta-analysis of cross-sectional and longitudinal studies. *Psychoneuroendocrinology* **2015**, *51*, 237–252. [CrossRef] [PubMed]
6. Dalton, B.; Bartholdy, S.; Robinson, L.; Solmi, M.; Ibrahim, M.A.A.; Breen, G.; Schmidt, U.; Himmerich, H. A meta-analysis of cytokine concentrations in eating disorders. *J. Psychiatr. Res.* **2018**, *103*, 252–264. [CrossRef]
7. Van Binsbergen, C.; Hulshof, K.; Wedel, M.; Odink, J.; Coelingh Bennink, H. Food preferences and aversions and dietary pattern in anorexia nervosa patients. *Eur. J. Clin. Nutr.* **1988**, *42*, 671–678. [PubMed]
8. Misra, M.; Tsai, P.; Anderson, E.J.; Hubbard, J.L.; Gallagher, K.; Soyka, L.A.; Miller, K.K.; Herzog, D.B.; Klibanski, A. Nutrient intake in community-dwelling adolescent girls with anorexia nervosa and in healthy adolescents. *Am. J. Clin. Nutr.* **2006**, *84*, 698–706. [CrossRef] [PubMed]

9. Chiurazzi, C.; Cioffi, I.; De Caprio, C.; De Filippo, E.; Marra, M.; Sammarco, R.; Di Guglielmo, M.L.; Contaldo, F.; Pasanisi, F. Adequacy of nutrient intake in women with restrictive anorexia nervosa. *Nutrition* **2017**, *38*, 80–84. [CrossRef]
10. Pettersson, C.; Svedlund, A.; Wallengren, O.; Swolin-Eide, D.; Paulson Karlsson, G.; Ellegård, L. Dietary intake and nutritional status in adolescents and young adults with anorexia nervosa: A 3-year follow-up study. *Clin. Nutr.* **2021**, *40*, 5391–5398. [CrossRef]
11. Schebendach, J.E.; Mayer, L.E.; Devlin, M.J.; Attia, E.; Contento, I.R.; Wolf, R.L.; Walsh, B.T. Food Choice and Diet Variety in Weight-Restored Patients with Anorexia Nervosa. *J. Am. Diet Assoc.* **2011**, *111*, 732–736. [CrossRef] [PubMed]
12. Smidowicz, A.; Regula, J. Effect of nutritional status and dietary patterns on human serum C-reactive protein and interleukin-6 concentrations. *Adv. Nutr.* **2015**, *6*, 738–747. [CrossRef] [PubMed]
13. Wood, A.D.; Strachan, A.A.; Thies, F.; Aucott, L.S.; Reid, D.M.; Hardcastle, A.C.; Mavroeidi, A.; Simpson, W.G.; Duthie, G.G.; Macdonald, H.M. Patterns of dietary intake and serum carotenoid and tocopherol status are associated with biomarkers of chronic low-grade systemic inflammation and cardiovascular risk. *Br. J. Nutr.* **2014**, *112*, 1341–1352. [CrossRef]
14. King, D.; Egan, B.; Geesey, M. Relation of dietary fat and fiber to elevation of C-reactive protein. *Am. J. Cardiol.* **2003**, *92*, 1335–1339. [CrossRef]
15. Ma, Y.; Griffith, J.A.; Chasan-Taber, L.; Olendzki, B.C.; Jackson, E.; Stanek, E.J.; Li, W.; Pagoto, S.; Hafner, A.R.; Ockene, I.S. Association between dietary fiber and serum C-reactive protein. *Am. J. Clin. Nutr.* **2006**, *83*, 760–766. [CrossRef]
16. Esposito, K.; Marfella, R.; Ciotola, M.; Di Palo, C.; Giugliano, F.; Giugliano, G.; D'Armiento, M.; D'Andrea, F.; Giugliano, D. Effect of a Mediterranean-style diet on endothelial dysfunction and markers of vascular inflammation in the metabolic syndrome: A randomized trial. *J. Am. Med. Assoc.* **2004**, *292*, 1440–1446. [CrossRef] [PubMed]
17. Chrysohoou, C.; Panagiotakos, D.B.; Pitsavos, C.; Das, U.N.; Stefanadis, C. Adherence to the Mediterranean diet attenuates inflammation and coagulation process in healthy adults: The ATTICA study. *J. Am. Coll. Cardiol.* **2004**, *44*, 152–158. [CrossRef]
18. Maggini, S.; Wintergerst, E.S.; Beveridge, S.; Hornig, D.H. Selected vitamins and trace elements support immune function by strengthening epithelial barriers and cellular and humoral immune responses. *Br. J. Nutr.* **2007**, *98*, S29–S35. [CrossRef]
19. Childs, C.E.; Calder, P.C.; Miles, E.A. Diet and Immune Function. *Nutrients* **2019**, *11*, 1933. [CrossRef] [PubMed]
20. Palla, B.; Litt, I.F. Medical Complications of Eating Disorders in Adolescents. *Pediatrics* **1988**, *81*, 613–623. [PubMed]
21. Prasad, A.S. Zinc in human health: Effect of zinc on immune cells. *Mol. Med.* **2008**, *14*, 353–357. [CrossRef] [PubMed]
22. Dardenne, M. Zinc and immune function. *Eur. J. Clin. Nutr.* **2002**, *56*, S20–S23. [CrossRef] [PubMed]
23. Shankar, A.H.; Prasad, A.S. Zinc and immune function: The biological basis of altered resistance to infection. *Am. J. Clin. Nutr.* **1998**, *68*, 447S–463S. [CrossRef]
24. Tall, A.R.; Yvan-Charvet, L. Cholesterol, inflammation and innate immunity. *Nat. Rev. Immunol.* **2015**, *15*, 104–116. [CrossRef] [PubMed]
25. Fessler, M.B. The Intracellular Cholesterol Landscape: Dynamic Integrator of the Immune Response. *Trends Immunol.* **2016**, *37*, 819–830. [CrossRef] [PubMed]
26. Dantzer, R. Cytokine, Sickness Behavior, and Depression. *Immunol. Allergy Clin. N. Am.* **2009**, *29*, 247–264. [CrossRef]
27. Mills, N.T.; Scott, J.G.; Wray, N.R.; Cohen-Woods, S.; Baune, B.T. Research review: The role of cytokines in depression in adolescents: A systematic review. *J. Child. Psychol. Psychiatry* **2013**, *54*, 816–835. [CrossRef] [PubMed]
28. Herder, C.; Schmitt, A.; Budden, F.; Reimer, A.; Kulzer, B.; Roden, M.; Haak, T.; Hermanns, N. Association between pro- and anti-inflammatory cytokines and depressive symptoms in patients with diabetes-potential differences by diabetes type and depression scores. *Transl. Psychiatry* **2017**, *7*, 1. [CrossRef]
29. Himmerich, H.; Fulda, S.; Linseisen, J.; Seiler, H.; Wolfram, G.; Himmerich, S.; Gedrich, K.; Kloiber, S.; Lucae, S.; Ising, M.; et al. Depression, comorbidities and the TNF-alpha system. *Eur. Psychiatry* **2008**, *23*, 421–429. [CrossRef]
30. Maes, M.; Anderson, G.; Kubera, M.; Berk, M. Targeting classical IL-6 signalling or IL-6 trans-signalling in depression? *Expert Opin. Ther. Targets* **2014**, *18*, 495–512. [CrossRef] [PubMed]
31. Dowlati, Y.; Herrmann, N.; Swardfager, W.; Liu, H.; Sham, L.; Reim, E.K.; Lanctôt, K.L. A Meta-Analysis of Cytokines in Major Depression. *Biol. Psychiatry* **2010**, *67*, 446–457. [CrossRef] [PubMed]
32. Holden, R.J.; Pakula, I.S. Tumor necrosis factor-alpha: Is there a continuum of liability between stress, anxiety states and anorexia nervosa? *Med. Hypotheses* **1999**, *52*, 155–162. [CrossRef]
33. Tang, Z.; Ye, G.; Chen, X.; Pan, M.; Fu, J.; Fu, T.; Liu, Q.; Gao, Z.; Baldwin, D.S.; Hou, R. Peripheral proinflammatory cytokines in Chinese patients with generalised anxiety disorder. *J. Affect. Disord.* **2018**, *225*, 593–598. [CrossRef] [PubMed]
34. Costello, H.; Gould, R.L.; Abrol, E.; Howard, R. Systematic review and meta-analysis of the association between peripheral inflammatory cytokines and generalised anxiety disorder. *BMJ Open* **2019**, *9*, e027925. [CrossRef]
35. Waheed, A.; Dalton, B.; Wesemann, U.; Ibrahim, M.A.A.; Himmerich, H. A Systematic Review of Interleukin-1β in Post-Traumatic Stress Disorder: Evidence from Human and Animal Studies. *J. Interferon Cytokine Res.* **2018**, *38*, 1–11. [CrossRef] [PubMed]
36. Wang, Z.; Young, M.R.I. PTSD, a Disorder with an Immunological Component. *Front. Immunol.* **2016**, *7*, 219. [CrossRef]
37. Speer, K.; Upton, D.; Semple, S.; McKune, A. Systemic low-grade inflammation in post-traumatic stress disorder: A systematic review. *J. Inflamm. Res.* **2018**, *11*, 111–121. [CrossRef]
38. Capuron, L.; Miller, A.H. Immune system to brain signaling: Neuropsychopharmacological implications. *Pharmacol. Ther.* **2011**, *130*, 226–238. [CrossRef]

39. Dalton, B.; Leppanen, J.; Campbell, I.C.; Chung, R.; Breen, G.; Schmidt, U.; Himmerich, H. A longitudinal analysis of cytokines in anorexia nervosa. *Brain Behav. Immun.* **2019**, *85*, 88–95. [CrossRef]
40. Dalton, B.; Campbell, I.C.; Chung, R.; Breen, G.; Schmidt, U.; Himmerich, H. Inflammatory markers in anorexia nervosa: An exploratory study. *Nutrients* **2018**, *10*, 1573. [CrossRef]
41. Nilsson, I.A.K.; Millischer, V.; Göteson, A.; Hübel, C.; Thornton, L.M.; Bulik, C.M.; Schalling, M.; Landén, M. Aberrant inflammatory profile in acute but not recovered anorexia nervosa. *Brain Behav. Immun.* **2020**, *88*, 718–724. [CrossRef] [PubMed]
42. Keeler, J.L.; Patsalos, O.; Chung, R.; Schmidt, U.; Breen, G.; Treasure, J.; Himmerich, H.; Dalton, B. Reduced MIP-1β as a Trait Marker and Reduced IL-7 and IL-12 as State Markers of Anorexia Nervosa. *J. Pers. Med.* **2021**, *11*, 814. [CrossRef] [PubMed]
43. Shivappa, N.; Steck, S.E.; Hurley, T.G.; Hussey, J.R.; Hébert, J.R. Designing and developing a literature-derived, population-based dietary inflammatory index. *Public Health Nutr.* **2014**, *17*, 1689–1696. [CrossRef]
44. American Psychiatric Association. *Diagnostic and Statistical Manual of Mental Disorders*, 5th ed.; American Psychiatric Publishing: Arlington, VA, USA, 2013.
45. Stice, E.; Fisher, M.; Martinez, E. Eating disorder diagnostic scale: Additional evidence of reliability and validity. *Psychol. Assess.* **2000**, *12*, 123–131. [CrossRef]
46. First, M.B.; Spitzer, R.L.; Gibbon, M.; Williams, J. *Structured Clinical Interview for DSM-IV-TR Axis I Disorders, Research Version, Patient Edition*; (SCID-I/P); New York State Psychiatric Institute: New York, NY, USA, 2002.
47. Bingham, S.A.; Gill, C.; Welch, A.; Day, K.; Cassidy, A.; Khaw, K.T.; Sneyd, M.J.; Key, T.J.A.; Roe, L.; Day, N.E. Comparison of dietary assessment methods in nutritional epidemiology: Weighed records v. 24h recalls, food frequency questionnaires and estimated diet records. *Br. J. Nutr.* **1994**, *72*, 619–642. [CrossRef]
48. Bingham, S.A.; Welch, A.A.; McTaggart, A.; Mulligan, A.A.; Runswick, S.A.; Luben, R.; Oakes, S.; Khaw, K.T.; Wareham, N.; Day, N.E. Nutritional methods in the European Prospective Investigation of Cancer in Norfolk. *Public Health Nutr.* **2001**, *4*, 847–858. [CrossRef]
49. Rimm, E.B.; Giovannucci, E.L.; Stampfer, M.J.; Colditz, G.A.; Litin, L.B.; Willett, W.C. Reproducibility and validity of an expanded self-administered semiquantitative food frequency questionnaire among male health professionals. *Am. J. Epidemiol.* **1992**, *135*, 1114–1126. [CrossRef] [PubMed]
50. McKeown, N.M.; Day, N.E.; Welch, A.A.; Runswick, S.A.; Luben, R.N.; Mulligan, A.A.; McTaggart, A.; A Bingham, S. Use of biological markers to validate self-reported dietary intake in a random sample of the European Prospective Investigation into Cancer United Kingdom Norfolk cohort. *Am. J. Clin. Nutr.* **2001**, *74*, 188–196. [CrossRef]
51. Mulligan, A.A.; Luben, R.N.; Bhaniani, A.; Parry-Smith, D.J.; O'Connor, L.; Khawaja, A.P.; Forouhi, N.G.; Khaw, K.-T. A new tool for converting food frequency questionnaire data into nutrient and food group values: FETA research methods and availability. *BMJ Open* **2014**, *4*, e004503. [CrossRef]
52. Welch, A.A.; Luben, R.; Khaw, K.T.; Bingham, S.A. The CAFE computer program for nutritional analysis of the EPIC-Norfolk food frequency questionnaire and identification of extreme nutrient values. *J. Hum. Nutr. Diet.* **2005**, *18*, 99–116. [CrossRef]
53. Corley, J.; Shivappa, N.; Hébert, J.; Starr, J.; Deary, I. Associations between Dietary Inflammatory Index Scores and Inflammatory Biomarkers among Older Adults in the Lothian Birth Cohort 1936 Study. *J. Nutr. Health Aging* **2019**, *23*, 628–636. [CrossRef]
54. Shivappa, N.; Hébert, J.; Rietzschel, E.; De Buyzere, M.; Langlois, M.; Debruyne, E.; Marcos, A.; Huybrechts, I. Associations between dietary inflammatory index and inflammatory markers in the Asklepios Study. *Br. J. Nutr.* **2015**, *113*, 665–671. [CrossRef] [PubMed]
55. Shivappa, N.; Hebert, J.; Marcos, A.; Diaz, L.; Gomez, S.; Nova, E.; Michels, N.; Arouca, A.; Gil, E.M.G.; Frederic, G.; et al. Association between dietary inflammatory index and inflammatory markers in the HELENA study. *Mol. Nutr. Food Res.* **2017**, *61*, 1600707. [CrossRef]
56. Hébert, J.R.; Shivappa, N.; Wirth, M.D.; Hussey, J.R.; Hurley, T.G. Perspective: The Dietary Inflammatory Index (DII)–Lessons Learned, Improvements Made, and Future Directions. *Adv. Nutr.* **2019**, *10*, 185–195. [CrossRef] [PubMed]
57. IBM Corp. *IMB SPSS Statistics for Macintosh*; IBM Corp: Armonk, NY, USA, 2019.
58. Dalton, B.; Whitmore, V.; Patsalos, O.; Ibrahim, M.A.A.; Schmidt, U.; Himmerich, H. A systematic review of in vitro cytokine production in eating disorders. *Mol. Cell. Endocrinol.* **2018**, *497*, 110308. [CrossRef]
59. Lobera, I.J.; Ríos, P.B. Choice of diet in patients with anorexia nervosa. *Nutr. Hosp.* **2009**, *24*, 682–687.
60. Bardone-Cone, A.M.; Fitzsimmons-Craft, E.E.; Harney, M.B.; Maldonado, C.R.; Lawson, M.A.; Smith, R.; Robinson, D.P. The Inter-Relationships between Vegetarianism and Eating Disorders among Females. *J. Acad. Nutr. Diet.* **2012**, *112*, 1247–1252. [CrossRef]
61. Marzola, E.; Nasser, J.A.; Hashim, S.A.; Shih, P.A.B.; Kaye, W.H. Nutritional rehabilitation in anorexia nervosa: Review of the literature and implications for treatment. BMC Psychiatry. *BioMed Cent.* **2013**, *13*, 290. [CrossRef]
62. Moreiras-Varela, O.; Nunez, C.; Carbajal, A.; Morande, G. Nutritional status and food habits assessed by dietary intake and anthropometrical parameters in anorexia nervosa. *Int. J. Vitam. Nutr. Res.* **1990**, *60*, 267–274.
63. Mayer, L.E.S.; Schebendach, J.; Bodell, L.P.; Shingleton, R.M.; Walsh, B.T. Eating Behavior in Anorexia Nervosa: Before and After Treatment. *Int. J. Eat. Disord.* **2012**, *45*, 290. [CrossRef]
64. Vaz, F.J.; Alcaina, T.; Guisado, J.A. Food aversions in eating disorders. *J. Food Sci. Nutr.* **1998**, *49*, 181–186. [CrossRef]
65. Matzkin, V.B.; Geissler, C.; Coniglio, R.; Selles, J.; Bello, M. Cholesterol concentrations in patients with Anorexia Nervosa and in healthy controls. *Int. J. Psychiatr. Nurs. Res.* **2006**, *11*, 1283–1293.

66. Rigaud, D.; Tallonneau, I.; Vergès, B. Hypercholesterolaemia in anorexia nervosa: Frequency and changes during refeeding. *Diabetes Metab.* **2009**, *35*, 57–63. [CrossRef] [PubMed]
67. Nestel, P.J. Cholesterol Metabolism in Anorexia Nervosa and Hypercholesterolemia. *J. Clin. Endocrinol. Metab.* **1974**, *38*, 325–328. [CrossRef] [PubMed]
68. Weinbrenner, T.; Züger, M.; Jacoby, G.E.; Herpertz, S.; Liedtke, R.; Sudhop, T.; Gouni-Berthold, I.; Axelson, M.; Berthold, H. Lipoprotein metabolism in patients with anorexia nervosa: A case–control study investigating the mechanisms leading to hypercholesterolaemia. *Br. J. Nutr.* **2004**, *91*, 959–969. [CrossRef] [PubMed]
69. Dellava, J.E.; Hamer, R.M.; Kanodia, A.; Reyes-Rodríguez, M.L.; Bulik, C.M. Diet and physical activity in women recovered from anorexia nervosa: A pilot study. *Int. J. Eat. Disord.* **2011**, *44*, 376–382. [CrossRef]
70. Beumont, P.J.V.; Chambers, T.L.; Rouse, L.; Abraham, S.F. The diet composition and nutritional knowledge of patients with anorexia nervosa. *Int. J. Food Sci. Nutr.* **1981**, *35*, 265–273. [CrossRef]
71. Russell, G.F. The nutritional disorder in anorexia nervosa. *J. Psychosom. Res.* **1967**, *11*, 141–149. [CrossRef]
72. Hadigan, C.M.; Anderson, E.J.; Miller, K.K.; Hubbard, J.L.; Herzog, D.B.; Klibanski, A.; Grinspoon, S.K. Assessment of macronutrient and micronutrient intake in women with anorexia nervosa. *Int. J. Eat. Disord.* **2000**, *28*, 284–292. [CrossRef]
73. Gwirtsman, H.E.; Kaye, W.H.; Curtis, S.R.; Lyter, L.M. Energy intake and dietary macronutrient content in women with anorexia nervosa and volunteers. *J. Am. Diet. Assoc.* **1989**, *89*, 54–57. [CrossRef]
74. Bouquegneau, A.; Dubois, B.E.; Krzesinski, J.M.; Delanaye, P. Anorexia nervosa and the kidney. *Am. J. Kidney Dis.* **2012**, *60*, 299–307. [CrossRef]
75. Harrington, B.C.; Jimerson, M.; Haxton, C.; Jimerson, D.C. Initial Evaluation, Diagnosis, and Treatment of Anorexia Nervosa and Bulimia Nervosa. *Am. Fam. Physician* **2015**, *91*, 46–52.
76. Catone, G.; Pisano, S.; Muzzo, G.; Corrado, G.; Russo, K.; Maiorano, A.; Salerno, F.; Gritti, A. A glance into psychiatric comorbidity in adolescents with anorexia nervosa. *Minerva Pediatr.* **2020**, *72*, 501–507. [CrossRef] [PubMed]
77. Ulfvebrand, S.; Birgegård, A.; Norring, C.; Högdahl, L.; von Hausswolff-Juhlin, Y. Psychiatric comorbidity in women and men with eating disorders results from a large clinical database. *Psychiatry Res.* **2015**, *230*, 294–299. [CrossRef] [PubMed]
78. Bauer, M.; Severus, E.; Möller, H.-J.; Young, A.H.; WFSBP Task Force on Unipolar Depressive Disorders. Pharmacological treatment of unipolar depressive disorders: Summary of WFSBP guidelines. *Int. J. Psychiatry Clin. Pract.* **2017**, *21*, 166–176. [CrossRef]
79. Bandelow, B.; Zohar, J.; Hollander, E.; Kasper, S.; Möller, H.-J. World Federation of Societies of Biological Psychiatry (WFSBP) guidelines for the pharmacological treatment of anxiety, obsessive-compulsive and posttraumatic stress disorders. *World J. Biol. Psychiatry* **2002**, *3*, 171–199. [CrossRef] [PubMed]
80. Marvanova, M.; Gramith, K. Role of antidepressants in the treatment of adults with anorexia nervosa. *Ment. Health Clin.* **2018**, *8*, 127–137. [CrossRef] [PubMed]
81. Himmerich, H.; Kan, C.; Au, K.; Treasure, J. Pharmacological treatment of eating disorders, comorbid mental health problems, malnutrition and physical health consequences. *Pharmacol Ther.* **2021**, *217*, 107667. [CrossRef] [PubMed]
82. Keeler, J.L.; Treasure, J.; Juruena, M.F.; Kan, C.; Himmerich, H. Ketamine as a Treatment for Anorexia Nervosa: A Narrative Review. *Nutrients* **2021**, *13*, 4158. [CrossRef]
83. Casper, R.C.; Kirschner, B.; Sandstead, H.H.; Jacob, R.A.; Davis, J.M. An evaluation of trace metals, vitamins, and taste function in anorexia nervosa. *Am. J. Clin. Nutr.* **1980**, *33*, 1801–1808. [CrossRef] [PubMed]
84. Donig, A.; Hautzinger, M. Zinc as an adjunct to antidepressant medication: A meta-analysis with subgroup analysis for different levels of treatment response to antidepressants. *Nutr. Neurosci.* **2021**. ahead of print. [CrossRef]
85. Baskaran, C.; Carson, T.L.; Reyes, K.J.C.; Becker, K.R.; Slattery, M.J.; Tulsiani, S.; Eddy, K.T.; Anderson, E.J.; Hubbard, J.L.; Misra, M.; et al. Macronutrient intake associated with weight gain in adolescent girls with anorexia nervosa. *Int. J. Eat. Disord.* **2017**, *50*, 1050–1057. [CrossRef] [PubMed]
86. Holman, R.T.; E Adams, C.; A Nelson, R.; Grater, S.J.; A Jaskiewicz, J.; Johnson, S.B.; Erdman, J.W. Patients with anorexia nervosa demonstrate deficiencies of selected essential fatty acids, compensatory changes in nonessential fatty acids and decreased fluidity of plasma lipids. *J. Nutr.* **1995**, *125*, 901–907.
87. Shih, P.; Yang, J.; Morisseau, C.; German, J.; Scott-Van Zeeland, A.A.; Armando, A.M.; Quehenberger, O.; Bergen, A.; Magistretti, P.J.; Berrettini, W.; et al. Dysregulation of soluble epoxide hydrolase and lipidomic profiles in anorexia nervosa. *Mol. Psychiatry* **2016**, *21*, 537–546. [CrossRef] [PubMed]
88. Shimizu, M.; Kawai, K.; Yamashita, M.; Shoji, M.; Takakura, S.; Hata, T.; Nakashima, M.; Tatsushima, K.; Tanaka, K.; Sudo, N. Very long chain fatty acids are an important marker of nutritional status in patients with anorexia nervosa: A case control study. *BioPsychoSocial Med.* **2020**, *14*, 14. [CrossRef]
89. Humphries, L.; Vivian, B.; Stuart, M.; McClain, C.J. Zinc deficiency and eating disorders. *J. Clin. Psychiatry* **1989**, *50*, 456–459. [PubMed]
90. Sossa, C.; Delisle, H.; Agueh, V.; Sodjinou, R.; Ntandou, G.; Makoutodé, M. Lifestyle and Dietary Factors Associated with the Evolution of Cardiometabolic Risk over Four Years in West-African Adults: The Benin Study. *J. Obes.* **2013**, *2013*, 298024. [CrossRef]
91. Sabzwari, S.R.A.; Garg, L.; Lakkireddy, D.; Day, J. Ten Lifestyle Modification Approaches to Treat Atrial Fibrillation. *Cureus* **2018**, *10*, e2682. [CrossRef] [PubMed]

92. Firth, J.; Solmi, M.; Wootton, R.; Vancampfort, D.; Schuch, F.; Hoare, E.; Gilbody, S.; Torous, J.; Teasdale, S.B.; Jackson, S.E.; et al. A meta-review of "lifestyle psychiatry": The role of exercise, smoking, diet and sleep in the prevention and treatment of mental disorders. *World Psychiatry* **2020**, *19*, 360–380. [CrossRef]
93. Fairweather-Schmidt, K.; Wade, T. The relationship between disordered eating and cigarette smoking among adult female twins. *Int. J. Eat. Disord.* **2015**, *48*, 708–714. [CrossRef]
94. Bat-Pitault, F.; Da Silva, C.; Charvin, I.; Da Fonseca, D. Sleep disturbances in anorexia nervosa subtypes in adolescence. *Eat. Weight Disord.* **2021**, *26*, 1845–1852. [CrossRef] [PubMed]
95. Trott, M.; Jackson, S.; Firth, J.; Jacob, L.; Grabovac, I.; Mistry, A.; Stubbs, B.; Smith, L. A comparative meta-analysis of the prevalence of exercise addiction in adults with and without indicated eating disorders. *Eat. Weight Disord. Stud. Anorex. Boulimia Obeistyulimia Obes.* **2021**, *26*, 37–46. [CrossRef] [PubMed]
96. Schebendach, J.E.; Porter, K.J.; Wolper, C.; Walsh, B.T.; Mayer, L.E.S. Accuracy of self-reported energy intake in weight-restored patients with anorexia nervosa compared with obese and normal weight individuals. *Int. J. Eat. Disord.* **2012**, *45*, 570–574. [CrossRef]
97. Forbush, K.T.; Hunt, T.K. Characterization of eating patterns among individuals with eating disorders: What is the state of the plate? *Physiol. Behav.* **2014**, *134*, 92–109. [CrossRef] [PubMed]
98. Pérez Rodrigo, C.; Aranceta, J.; Salvador, G.; Varela-Moreiras, G. Food Frequency Questionnaires. *Nutr. Hosp.* **2015**, *31*, 49–56. [PubMed]
99. Huseinovic, E.; Hörnell, A.; Johansson, I.; Esberg, A.; Lindahl, B.; Winkvist, A. Changes in food intake patterns during 2000–2007 and 2008–2016 in the population-based Northern Sweden Diet Database. *Nutr. J.* **2019**, *18*, 36. [CrossRef] [PubMed]
100. Kearney, J. Food consumption trends and drivers. *Philos. Trans. R. Soc. B Biol. Sci.* **2010**, *365*, 2793–2807. [CrossRef] [PubMed]

nutrients

Article

Food Addiction in Eating Disorders: A Cluster Analysis Approach and Treatment Outcome

Lucero Munguía [1,2,†], Anahí Gaspar-Pérez [1,2,†], Susana Jiménez-Murcia [1,2,3,4], Roser Granero [2,4,5], Isabel Sánchez [1,2,4], Cristina Vintró-Alcaraz [1,2,4], Carlos Diéguez [4,6], Ashley N. Gearhardt [7] and Fernando Fernández-Aranda [1,2,3,4,*]

1 Department of Psychiatry, Universitary Hospital of Bellvitge, 08907 Barcelona, Spain; lmunguia@idibell.cat (L.M.); agaspape10@alumnes.ub.edu (A.G.-P.); sjimenez@bellvitgehospital.cat (S.J.-M.); isasanchez@bellvitgehospital.cat (I.S.); cvintro@bellvitgehospital.cat (C.V.-A.)
2 Psychoneurobiology of Eating Disorders and Addictive Behaviors Group, Neurosciences Programme, Bellvitge Biomedical Research Institute (IDIBELL), 08908 Barcelona, Spain; roser.granero@uab.cat
3 Clinical Sciences Department, School of Medicine, Barcelona University, 08907 Barcelona, Spain
4 CIBER Physiopatology, Obesity and Nutrition (CIBERobn), Health Institute Carlos III, 28029 Madrid, Spain; carlos.dieguez@usc.es
5 Department of Psychobiology and Methodology, Autonomous University of Barcelona, 08907 Barcelona, Spain
6 Department of Physiology, CIMUS, Instituto de Investigación Sanitaria, University of Santiago de Compostela, 15782 Santiago de Compostela, Spain
7 Department of Psychology, University of Michigan, Ann Arbor, MI 48109, USA; agearhar@umich.edu
* Correspondence: ffernandez@bellvitgehospital.cat; Tel.: +34-93-2607227; Fax: +34-93-2607193
† These authors contributed equally to this work.

Abstract: Background: A first approach of a phenotypic characterization of food addiction (FA) found three clusters (dysfunctional, moderate and functional). Based on this previous classification, the aim of the present study is to explore treatment responses in the sample diagnosed with Eating Disorder(ED) of different FA profiles. Methods: The sample was composed of 157 ED patients with FA positive, 90 with bulimia nervosa (BN), 36 with binge eating disorder (BED), and 31 with other specified feeding or eating disorders (OSFED). Different clinical variables and outcome indicators were evaluated. Results: The clinical profile of the clusters present similar characteristics with the prior study, having the dysfunctional cluster the highest ED symptom levels, the worse psychopathology global state, and dysfunctional personality traits, while the functional one the lowest ED severity level, best psychological state, and more functional personality traits. The dysfunctional cluster was the one with lowest rates of full remission, the moderate one the higher rates of dropouts, and the functional one the highest of full remission. Conclusions: The results concerning treatment outcome were concordant with the severity of the FA clusters, being that the dysfunctional and moderate ones had worst treatment responses than the functional one.

Keywords: food addiction; eating disorders; treatment outcome; cluster analysis approach

Citation: Munguía, L.; Gaspar-Pérez, A.; Jiménez-Murcia, S.; Granero, R.; Sánchez, I.; Vintró-Alcaraz, C.; Diéguez, C.; Gearhardt, A.N.; Fernández-Aranda, F. Food Addiction in Eating Disorders: A Cluster Analysis Approach and Treatment Outcome. *Nutrients* **2022**, *14*, 1084. https://doi.org/10.3390/nu14051084

Academic Editor: Zoltan Pataky

Received: 24 January 2022
Accepted: 2 March 2022
Published: 4 March 2022

1. Introduction

Even though food addiction (FA) has not being included as a formal mental disorder in the Diagnostic and Statistical Manual (DSM-5) [1], it is a concept of ongoing scientific interest and debate. According to the FA model, some foods, especially palatable ones, may be involved in producing both overeating and addictive-like behaviours, thus, phenomenological similarities with addictive disorders could been found [2].

FA has been mentioned as a potential subtype of obesity [3–5], and has been associated with Eating Disorders (ED), mainly in binge spectrum disorders as bulimia nervosa (BN) [6,7] and binge eating disorder (BED) [8,9]. It has been associated with higher body mass index (BMI), binge-eating episodes, higher eating psychopathology, more impulsive personality traits, and craving for highly palatable food [10–12], as well as poorer response to therapy [13,14].

Additionally, other predictors of developing severe symptomatology of food addiction are presenting dysfunctional personality traits, high emotional dysregulation, and high general psychopathology [15,16], and be women [17].

In a previous study, our group has assessed the heterogeneity within a group of subjects with positive FA (FA+) and have identified differential phenotypes and subgroups among the participants [18] considering general psychopathology, ED severity and personality traits. In the prior study, a sample of ED and obesity patients was included, and three clusters were obtained: (a) dysfunctional cluster (mainly represented by OSFED and BN), (b) moderate cluster (mainly represented by BN and BED patients) and (c) functional cluster (mainly represented by obesity and BED patients).

The obtained results of this study shed some light on the different clinical profiles within patients with ED and obesity who had FA+. However, there is a lack in the literature on how the treatment could be influenced by these severity and cluster groups. To have a deeper understanding of the FA construct, evidence related with treatment outcome could help to fill that gap, by knowing the relationship between treatment outcome, FA, psychopathological dimensions, and other variables.

Thus, based onto the prior study, the aim of the present research is to explore treatment response to Cognitive Behavioural Therapy in the ED sample of the different FA clusters found in the previous study [18]. We hypothesize that the functional cluster, will present better treatment outcomes and lower dropout rates than the moderate and dysfunctional ones. As well, due to belonging to a specific cluster provides information on the patients' profile in a broad collection of clinical measures, and that the present study only consider ED patients from the original sample, the analysis form the previous research, regarding psychopathological status, the personality traits, ED severity and the diagnostic subtype, will be done as well in this study.

2. Materials and Methods

2.1. Participants and Procedure

The initial sample was comprised of 234 participants of the original study [18]. The identification of the empirical clusters in this prior research was done through two-step-cluster procedure, using the log-likelihood distance measure (adequate for both quantitative and categorical indicators), and combining a multinomial probability mass function (non-metric data) and a normal density function (metric data). The clustering process was also based on an automatic selection of the number of cluster-classes, based on a large set of indicator variables including the ED severity level, global psychopathological state, personality profile and the diagnostic subtype.

The identification of the empirical clusters in this prior research was done through two-step-cluster procedure, using the log-likelihood distance measure (adequate for both quantitative and categorical indicators), and combining a multinomial probability mass function (non-metric data) and a normal density function (metric data). The clustering process was also based on an automatic selection of the number of cluster-classes, based on a large set of indicator variables including the ED severity level, global psychopathological state, personality profile and the diagnostic subtype, only the ED patients were selected. Therefore, the present study comprises a total of 157 adult women diagnosed with an ED (90 with bulimia nervosa (BN), 36 with binge eating disorder (BED), and 31 with other specified feeding or eating disorder (OSFED)) BN subtype, who presented for treatment to the Eating Disorder Unit within the Department of Psychiatry at Bellvitge University Hospital (HUB) (Barcelona, Spain) from May of 2016 and November 2018. Those patients with Anorexia Nervosa diagnosis were excluded, due to the low prevalence's of FA in this disorder. All participants included in the study were diagnosed according to the to the DSM-IV-TR criteria [19] through a semi-structured interview with experience clinical psychologist, and diagnoses were reanalysed and recodified post hoc using the DSM-5 criteria [1].

According to the Declaration of Helsinki, the present study was approved by the Clinical Research Ethics Committee (CEIC) of Bellvitge University Hospital, and written informed consent was obtained from all participants. All the assessments were conducted by experienced psychologist and psychiatrists.

2.2. Assessment

Alongside the assessment of several clinically relevant variables as age of onset, duration of the disorder, BMI (taking weight and height measures in the first visit to our center by trained staff, using the same device to all patients: Tanita MC 780-S MA portable scale: With segmental multifrequency. Bio Lógica Tecnología Médica SL, Barcelona, Spain), and sociodemographical characteristics such as age, income and marital status, the following Spanish validated instruments were used.

Eating Disorders Inventory 2 (EDI-2) [20], is a self-report questionnaire that assesses different cognitive and behavioural characteristics typical for ED in 11 subscales: Drive for Thinness, Bulimia, Body Dissatisfaction, Ineffectiveness, Perfectionism, Interpersonal Distrust, Interoceptive Awareness and Maturity Fears, Asceticism, Impulse Regulation and Social Insecurity. The measures consists of 91 items, answered on a 6-point Likert scale. The internal consistency of the total scale for our sample was 0.92 (coefficient alpha).

Symptom Checklist-90-Revised (SCL-90-R) [21] validated in Spanish population [22], is a questionnaire used to evaluate a broad range of psychological problems and symptoms of psychopathology considering nine primary symptom dimensions: Somatization, Obsession-Compulsion, Interpersonal Sensitivity, Depression, Anxiety, Hostility, Phobic Anxiety, Paranoid Ideation and Psychoticism; and includes three global indices: global severity index (overall psychological distress), positive symptom distress index (the intensity of symptoms) and a positive symptom total (self-reported symptoms). The global severity index can be used as a summary of the test. The measure consists of 90 items answered on a 5-point Likert scale. The internal consistency of the subscales for our sample range from 0.701 to 0.865, and the global indexes was 0.96 (coefficient alpha).

Temperament and Character Inventory-Revised (TCI-R) [23], validated in Spanish population [24], is a questionnaire that measures four temperament dimensions (Harm Avoidance, Novelty Seeking, Reward Dependence and Persistence) and three character dimensions (Self-Directedness, Cooperativeness and Self-Transcendence) of personality. The measure consists of 240-items and answered on a 5-point Likert scale. The internal consistency of the subscales for our sample range from 0.80 to 0.89 (coefficient alpha).

Yale Food Addiction Scale 2.0 (YFAS2.0) [25], validated in Spanish population [9], is a self-report questionnaire for measuring FA during the previous 12 months. Is based on DSM-5 Criteria and evaluates 11 symptoms and allows the establishment of symptom severity cutoffs: mild (2–3 symptoms), moderate (4–5 symptoms), and severe (6–11 symptoms). The score produce two measurements: (a) a continuous symptom count score that reflects the number of fulfilled diagnostic criteria (ranging from 0 to 11), and (b) a food addiction threshold based on the number of symptoms (at least 2) and self-reported clinically significant impairment or distress. This final measurement allows for the binary classification of food addiction (present versus absent). The measures consist of 35-items answered on a 8-point Likert scale. The internal consistency of the total scale for our sample was 0.93 (coefficient alpha).

2.3. Treatment

Patients received cognitive–behavioural therapy (CBT) treatment carried out by experienced psychologists at Bellvitge University Hospital (HUB), which consisted of 16 weekly outpatient group sessions of 90 min each and a follow-up period of 6, 12 and 24 months. A detailed description of the treatment applied could be found in [26], with the following main treatment objectives: cognitive restructuring, problem-solving, emotion management techniques, and normalisation of eating behaviour.

Treatment Outcome Assessment

The criterion for dropping out of treatment was not attending three consecutive sessions. Of those patients who completed treatment, the following categorisation, according to their symptomatology, was used: full remission (total absence of ED symptoms for at least 4 consecutive weeks), partial-remission (substantial symptomatic improvement, but with residual symptoms considering DSM-5 criteria. It could be an extinction of behavioural symptoms, as purging, or restriction, but residual cognitive distortions, or intense fear to gain weight, or, vice versa), and non-remission (still meeting full criteria for an ED) [1]. These categories to assess treatment outcome have also been used in prior published studies [27,28]. The assessment of treatment out for this study were performed at the end of the 16 treatment sessions.

2.4. Statistical Analysis

Statistical analysis was carried out with Stata17 for Windows (Stata-Corp, College Station, TX, USA) [29]. Firstly, the empirical clusters compared in this study were compared for the measures assessed at baseline, and for the ED diagnostic subtype, to provide information about the specific profile associated to each cluster. Next, the discriminative capacity of the empirical clusters on the treatment response was assessed.

Comparison between the clusters was based on chi-square tests (χ^2) for categorical variables and with analysis of variance (ANOVA) for quantitative variables. Effect size was calculated with the standardized Cohen-*h* for proportion differences and Cohen-*d* for mean differences (poor effect size was considered for absolute estimates lower than 0.50, mild-moderate effect size for absolute estimates higher than 0.50 and high-large for absolute estimates higher than 0.80) [30]. Control in Type-I error due to the multiple null-hypothesis statistical tests was done with Finner's method [31].

3. Results

Most participants in the study were single (n = 97, 61.8%) and had achieved secondary education levels (n = 74, 47.1%). Mean age was 33.2 years (SD = 11.9), mean age of onset of the eating problems was 21.1 years (SD = 9.4) and mean duration of the eating problems was 12.3 years (SD = 9.1). Table 1 includes the comparison between the groups for the descriptive variables. Considering the groups defined by the ED-subtype, BED included patients with the highest age and the oldest age of onset. Comparison between the clusters identified differences for age and onset for the dysfunctional cluster (C1), which had lower means compared to the moderate (C2) and the functional (C3) clusters.

Figure 1 displays the 100% stacked bar chart with the percentage of patients with a specific ED subtype within each cluster. Differences between the groups were found: The dysfunctional cluster (C1) included a high and similar distribution for BN and OSFED patients; the moderate (C2) cluster included mostly BN patients, following by a high percentage as well of BED; the functional (C3) cluster included a high proportion of BN patients, and similar percentage of BED and OSFED.

Table 1. Descriptive of the sample.

	BED (n = 36)		BN (n = 90)		OSFED (n = 31)			Cluster-1 (n = 37)		Cluster-2 (n = 69)		Cluster-3 (n = 51)		
	n	%	n	%	n	%	p	n	%	n	%	n	%	p
Civil status														
Single	14	38.9%	57	63.3%	26	83.9%	**0.005** *	29	78.4%	41	59.4%	27	52.9%	0.144
Married	16	44.4%	22	24.4%	3	9.7%		6	16.2%	20	29.0%	15	29.4%	
Divorced	6	16.7%	11	12.2%	2	6.5%		2	5.4%	8	11.6%	9	17.6%	
Education														
Primary	13	36.1%	31	34.4%	11	35.5%	0.688	13	35.1%	25	36.2%	17	33.3%	0.629
Secondary	14	38.9%	44	48.9%	16	51.6%		20	54.1%	32	46.4%	22	43.1%	
University	9	25.0%	15	16.7%	4	12.9%		4	10.8%	12	17.4%	12	23.5%	
	Mean	SD	Mean	SD	Mean	SD	p	Mean	SD	Mean	SD	Mean	SD	p
Age (years-old)	42.28	12.30	30.92	10.39	29.13	10.41	**0.001** *	28.14	8.86	34.74	12.89	34.71	11.62	**0.012** *
Onset (years-old)	27.72	11.45	18.98	7.89	19.29	7.44	**0.001** *	17.84	6.41	22.57	11.38	21.32	7.81	**0.046** *
Duration (years)	14.46	9.16	12.13	9.00	10.03	8.84	0.134	10.32	7.49	12.80	9.84	12.91	8.99	0.334

Note. BED: binge eating disorder. BN: bulimia nervosa. OSFED: other specified feeding and eating disorder. SD: standard deviation. Custer 1: dysfunctional cluster; Cluster 2: Moderate cluster; Cluster 3: Functional cluster. * Bold: significant comparison (0.05).

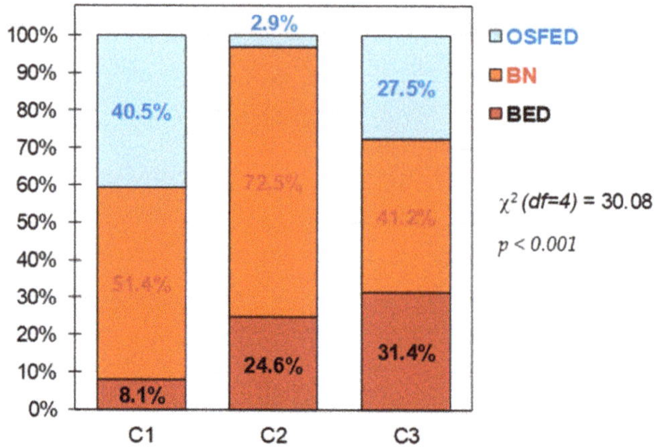

Figure 1. Composition of the clusters. Note. C1: cluster 1, dysfunctional cluster. C2: cluster 2, moderate cluster. C3: cluster 3, functional cluster. BED: binge eating disorder. BN: bulimia nervosa. OSFED: other specified feeding eating disorder. df = degrees of freedom. Sample size: $n = 157$.

The upper part of Table 2 shows the comparison between the clusters at baseline, and the lower part of the table shows the comparison for the CBT treatment outcomes. FA levels was higher in the moderate cluster (C2), followed by the dysfunctional one (C1), while the C3 (functional) presented the lower levels of FA. According to clinical characteristics, the dysfunctional cluster (C1) was characterized by the lowest mean for the BMI, the highest ED symptom levels (except for the EDI-2 bulimia scale), the worst psychopathology global state, and the highest levels in the personality domains of harm avoidance and self-transcendence. This cluster was also the one with the lowest percentage of participant with full remission (see also Figure 2). The functional cluster (C3) was the cluster with the lowest ED severity level, best psychological state, the lowest score in harm avoidance, and the highest scores in the personality traits of reward-dependence, persistence, self-directedness and cooperativeness. As well, this cluster also had the highest percentage of patients with full remission (Figure 2). C2, the moderate one, present intermediate levels of these clinical characteristics; however, it had the highest levels of dropouts.

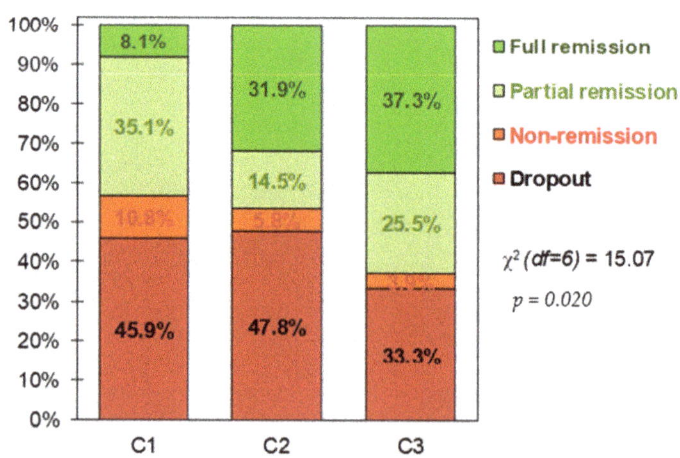

Figure 2. Distribution of the CBT outcomes within the clusters. Note. C1: cluster 1, dysfunctional cluster. C2: cluster 2, moderate cluster. C3: cluster 3, functional cluster. df = degrees of freedom. Sample size: $n = 157$.

Table 2. Comparison of clusters at baseline and CBT outcomes.

		Cluster-1 (*n* = 37)		Cluster-2 (*n* = 69)		Cluster-3 (*n* = 51)		Cluster-1 vs. Cluster-2		Cluster-1 vs. Cluster-3		Cluster-2 vs. Cluster-3	
	α	Mean	SD	Mean	SD	Mean	SD	*p*	|*d*|	*p*	|*d*|	*p*	|*d*|
BMI-FA													
BMI (kg/m^2)		25.96	7.44	29.42	8.54	30.77	10.15	0.057	0.43	**0.013** *	**0.54** †	0.411	0.14
YFAS total score	0.939	8.46	2.38	9.48	1.99	7.53	2.72	**0.034** *	0.46	0.068	0.36	**0.001** *	**0.82** †
EDI -2 Drive-thinness	0.767	18.03	2.71	15.94	4.77	14.14	4.94	**0.022** *	**0.54** †	**0.001** *	**0.98** †	**0.029** *	0.37
EDI-2 Body-dissatisfac.	0.850	21.30	5.73	20.59	6.52	16.96	7.17	0.600	0.11	**0.003** *	**0.67** †	**0.003** *	**0.53** †
EDI-2 Int-awareness	0.798	18.22	5.67	15.46	5.36	8.00	5.71	**0.016** *	**0.50** †	**0.001** *	**1.80** †	**0.001** *	**1.35** †
EDI-2 Bulimia	0.726	8.54	5.78	11.52	3.91	7.33	4.89	**0.002** *	**0.60** †	0.239	0.23	**0.001** *	**0.95** †
EDI-2 Interper-distrust	0.813	9.08	5.24	6.97	4.65	3.49	3.60	**0.022** *	0.43	**0.001** *	**1.24** †	**0.001** *	**0.84** †
EDI-2 Ineffectiveness.	0.848	17.38	6.55	14.88	5.70	6.88	4.68	**0.031** *	0.41	**0.001** *	**1.84** †	**0.001** *	**1.53** †
EDI-2 Maturity-fears	0.752	12.27	5.03	9.17	5.32	6.51	5.17	**0.004** *	**0.60** †	**0.001** *	**1.13** †	**0.006** *	**0.51** †
EDI-2 Perfectionism	0.740	6.95	5.12	6.14	4.24	4.65	3.97	0.371	0.17	**0.016** *	**0.50** †	0.066	**0.36**
EDI-2 Impulse-regulat.	0.730	13.22	5.28	7.57	4.37	3.18	3.18	**0.001** *	**1.17** †	**0.001** *	**2.30** †	**0.001** *	**1.15** †
EDI-2 Ascetic	0.702	10.35	2.99	8.77	2.92	5.61	3.11	**0.010** *	**0.54** †	**0.001** *	**1.56** †	**0.001** *	**1.05** †
EDI-2 Social Insecurity	0.752	12.76	4.78	9.41	4.17	4.49	2.82	**0.001** *	**0.75** †	**0.001** *	**2.11** †	**0.001** *	**1.38** †
EDI-2 Total score	0.923	148.1	27.28	126.4	20.73	81.24	22.63	**0.001** *	**0.89** †	**0.001** *	**2.67** †	**0.001** *	**2.08** †
SCL-90R GSI	0.966	2.67	0.33	2.07	0.35	1.28	0.36	**0.001** *	**1.80** †	**0.001** *	**4.03** †	**0.001** *	**2.22** †
SCL-90R PST	0.966	81.81	6.10	72.46	7.78	55.98	11.90	**0.001** *	**1.34** †	**0.001** *	**2.73** †	**0.001** *	**1.64** †
SCL-90R PSDI	0.966	2.94	0.33	2.58	0.36	2.04	0.34	**0.001** *	**1.05** †	**0.001** *	**2.70** †	**0.001** *	**1.54** †
TCI-R Novelty-seeking	0.806	103.5	16.07	98.4	17.27	102.7	15.88	0.133	0.31	0.811	0.05	0.168	0.26
TCI-R Harm-avoidance	0.887	133.7	14.52	126.4	17.00	109.0	16.24	**0.028** *	0.46	**0.001** *	**1.60** †	**0.001** *	**1.05** †
TCI-R Reward.depend.	0.831	97.5	17.30	98.3	14.06	104.8	15.59	0.797	0.05	**0.029** *	0.44	**0.023** *	0.44
TCI-R Persistence	0.896	102.8	22.46	100.8	20.27	108.4	19.78	0.633	0.09	0.213	0.26	**0.048** *	0.38
TCI-R Self-directed.	0.840	96.9	14.94	102.9	13.17	125.3	16.89	0.053	0.42	**0.001** *	**1.78** †	**0.001** *	**1.48** †
TCI-R Cooperativeness	0.861	127.8	20.24	133.7	17.15	139.3	11.88	0.082	0.31	**0.002** *	**0.69** †	0.067	0.38
TCI-R Self-transcend.	0.862	77.1	12.09	62.1	14.38	63.2	16.37	**0.001** *	**1.13** †	**0.001** *	**0.97** †	0.672	0.07
CBT outcomes		*n*	%	*n*	%	*n*	%	*p*	|*h*|	*p*	|*h*|	*p*	|*h*|
Dropout		17	45.9%	33	47.8%	17	33.3%	**0.010** *	0.04	**0.016** *	0.26	0.286	0.30
Non-remission		4	10.8%	4	5.8%	2	3.9%		0.18		0.27		0.09
Partial remission		13	35.1%	10	14.5%	13	25.5%		**0.51** †		0.21		0.28
Full remission		3	8.1%	22	31.9%	19	37.3%		**0.62** †		**0.74** †		0.11

Note. Cronbach's-alpha in the study. Custer 1: dysfunctional cluster; Cluster 2: Moderate cluster; Cluster 3: Functional cluster. SD: standard deviation; BMI: Body Mass Index; FA: food addiction; EDI: Eating Disorders Inventory; SCL: Symptom Checklist; GSI: Global Gravity Index; TCI: Temperament and Character Inventory; CBT: cognitive–behavioural therapy. * Bold: significant comparison (0.05). † Bold: effect size into the ranges mild-moderate to the high-large.

4. Discussion

The aim of the present study was to explore treatment responses in the different FA profiles identified by [18], considering only the ED sample. Clinical characteristics of these ED-focused clusters are similar to those previously found and were relevant for treatment outcome as well. As we hypothesized, the functional cluster (C3), do present better treatment response and lower dropout rates than the moderate (C2) and dysfunctional (C1) clusters. Several aspects of these results must be highlighted.

First, as in the prior study [18], FA levels were higher in the moderate cluster, followed by the dysfunctional one, and lower in the functional. The composition of each cluster regarding the diagnosis of the patients was maintained for the dysfunctional and moderate clusters, however, the composition of the functional one changed. In the prior study, this subgroup was highly represented by patients with obesity but no ED, while in this study non-ED participants were excluded. However, the clinical characteristics of the present and previous clusters were similar. This is, dysfunctional cluster (C1) had higher presence of BN and OSFED patients, higher severity of the disorder and worst psychopathological state, as well as low self-directedness and high harm avoidance. The functional cluster (C3) had more equilibrated proportion of diagnosis subtypes, with BN being more prevalent, and higher self-directedness and persistence, with lower levels of harm-avoidance. Finally, the moderate cluster (C2) had a heightened presence of BN (72.5%) followed by BED (24.6%), therefore, this cluster was particularly represented by binge ED subtypes; as well, this cluster had the highest levels of FA as in the first study.

Thus, what differentiates the dysfunctional cluster (C1) from the other clusters is the severity of it clinical characteristics (except FA), while the moderate (C2) group differs from the functional (C3) and dysfunctional cluster (C1) by a higher severity of FA, and the functional cluster (C3) differ from the dysfunctional (C1) and moderate (C2) one by the low severity of its clinical profile.

Treatment outcome was explored as well, not only to relate it with the presence of FA, being that other studies have already approach the subject [14,32], but to add to a better characterization of FA construct in well-defined phenotypes that consider FA presence and other clinical variables.

Low levels of full remission and higher rates of dropouts in the dysfunctional cluster (C1) were found. This subgroup was highly represented for OSFED patients, which have been reported to present low harm avoidance and self-directedness, as well as higher severity of ED symptomatology, aspects identified as predictors of high drop-outs and low full remission rates [28]. Additionally, similar personality traits that imply difficulties in following goals and higher levels of anxiety levels have been found in BN patients (also present in this cluster) [33]. This has also been associated with low levels of full remission after cognitive behavioural treatment (CBT) [26]. Therefore, patients within this cluster may benefit from treatments that target the reduction of the ED symptomatology and general distress, as well as favour the improvement in the establishment and following of objectives. It is also important to mention that younger patients with an earlier onset of the disorder were particularly present in this cluster; therefore, these aspects could be added as indicators of a more dysfunctional profile. Of note, early onset of the disorder has already been mentioned as a predictor of a longer maintenance of the ED [34].

In the moderate cluster (C2), the highest dropout rates were found, as well medium rates of full remission in comparison with the dysfunctional (C1) and functional clusters (C3). This cluster was characterized by the presence of binge spectrum ED patients and by the higher levels of FA, both aspects that could be involved in the response to treatment of the participants in this cluster. It is possible that the higher presence of FA symptomology in binge spectrum ED (relative to non-binge ED) may reflect the more frequent binge eating episodes and food craving associated with FA [35,36]. In the same line, it could be hypostatized that the high levels of FA could be related to the higher drop out percentage found here. This is consistent with prior studies that have found that FA predicts worse intervention response in BN patients [32], and that FA can act as a mediator between severity of ED in BN and BED patients and treatment outcome [14]. However, being that this cluster did not present levels of psychopathology and severity of the ED as high as the dysfunctional cluster (C1), this moderate cluster (C2) was more likely to reach full remission than the patients in C1. Therefore, it may be important to screen for severe FA (particularly for patients with diagnoses more represented in this cluster), to implement approaches that could reduce FA symptomatology. In this regard, several authors have suggested additional therapy aims of craving managements and increasing inhibitory control [37], and psychoeducation about the dietary patterns implicated in addictive eating [35,38]. As well, BED patients and FA patients present high levels of impulsivity, therapies aimed to reduce food related impulsivity could be implemented as well [39].

Finally, the functional cluster (C3) presents the higher levels of full remission and the lowest of drop out, as well as had the lowest levels of severity of FA. Further, this cluster is clinically speaking the most functional, presenting low ED severity and general psychopathology. It also had the highest levels of self-directedness and persistence, which may be associated with good compliance with the treatment. Patients within this subgroup may respond best to traditional CBT treatment and not need additive therapies to help them succeed. This groups overall FA severity level is low and other studies have found that FA symptoms can remit after traditional CBT [32]. Thus, specific targets for addictive mechanisms may not be needed for this cluster.

5. Strength and Limits

The present study has several strengths. Not only the relation of FA with ED treatment outcome was explored, a characterization of different phenotypes in ED patients that presents FA was confirmed. In this sense, it is important to consider that the clustering process was performed in the original study for a large set of indicators measured in the baseline (previously to the intervention), which included the ED severity level along with other variables (the comorbid psychopathological status, the personality traits and the diagnostic subtype). In this sense, belonging to a specific cluster provides wide information on the patients' profile in a broad collection of clinical measures. Since this work provides results for the comparison between these empirical profiles, this study can be conceptualized within a person-centred approach, characterized by the analysis of individuals who share multiple particular attributes (contrarily to the classical variable-centred approach, focused on assessing the specific contribution of isolated variables). Additionally, these clusters have specific clinical characteristics, which may inform precision therapies.

Even so, some limitations may be taken into account. The study was only performed in women patients, and the size of the sample was considerably reduced due to the exclusion of patients with obesity only (as the aim of this paper was on ED treatment response). These aspects affect the generalization of the results, and future studies should consider them.

6. Conclusions

The phenotypic characterization of FA proposed by the original study [18] (considering ED and obesity patients), and the present one (only considering ED patients), present similar clinical characteristics that again defined three clusters from a dysfunctional to functional one. The dysfunctional cluster had the lower rates in full remission, while the functional cluster had the higher proportions of full remission and the lowest of dropouts. Even though the moderate cluster presented the highest rate of dropouts, a higher percentage of participants in this cluster could reach full remission of their symptoms. Even though all participants presented FA symptoms, the differential characteristics of each cluster may be important to defining proper treatment approaches for ED patients with FA. For example, the dysfunctional cluster may benefit from treatments that target aspects of high severity ED symptoms and psychological distress; the moderate cluster may be specifically benefited by a focused treatment for the reduction of FA symptoms; finally, the functional cluster could continue with traditional approaches.

Author Contributions: Conceptualization: L.M., A.G.-P., S.J.-M., F.F.-A.; methodology: R.G.; formal analysis: R.G.; investigation: L.M., A.G.-P., I.S., C.V.-A.; resources: S.J.-M., F.F.-A.; data curation: R.G.; writing—original draft preparation: L.M., A.G.-P., S.J.-M., R.G., F.F.-A.; writing—review and editing: L.M., S.J.-M., A.N.G., F.F.-A.; supervision: L.M., S.J.-M., C.D., A.N.G., F.F.-A.; funding acquisition: S.J.-M., F.F.-A. All authors have read and agreed to the published version of the manuscript.

Funding: We thank CERCA Programme/Generalitat de Catalunya for institutional support. This manuscript and research was supported by grants from the Ministerio de Economía y Competitividad (PSI2015-68701-R), by the Delegación del Gobierno para el Plan Nacional sobre Drogas (2017I067 and 2019I47), by the Instituto de Salud Carlos III (ISCIII) (FIS PI17/01167 and PI20/132), by the SLT006/17/00246 grant, funded by the Department of Health of the Generalitat de Catalunya by the call "Acción instrumental de programes de recerca orientats en l'ambit de la recerca i la innovaci_o en salut", and cofounded by FEDER funds/European Regional Development Fund (ERDF), a way to build Europe. CIBERObn is an initiative of ISCIII.

Institutional Review Board Statement: The study was conducted according to the guidelines of the Declaration of Helsinki, and approved by the Ethics Committee of University Hospital of Bellvitge (PR205/17).

Informed Consent Statement: Informed consent was obtained from all subjects involved in the study.

Conflicts of Interest: F.F.-A. received consultancy honoraria from Novo Nordisk and editorial honoraria as EIC from Wiley. The rest of the authors declare no conflict of interest. The funders had no role in the design of the study; in the collection, analyses, or interpretation of data; in the writing of the manuscript, or in the decision to publish the results.

References

1. American Psychiatric Association. *Diagnostic and Statistical Manual of Mental Disorders*, 5th ed.; American Psychiatric Association: Washington, DC, USA, 2013.
2. Schulte, E.M.; Avena, N.M.; Gearhardt, A.N. Which foods may be addictive? The roles of processing, fat content, and glycemic load. *PLoS ONE* **2015**, *10*, e0117959. [CrossRef] [PubMed]
3. Cope, E.C.; Gould, E. New Evidence Linking Obesity and Food Addiction. *Biol. Psychiatry* **2017**, *81*, 734–736. [CrossRef] [PubMed]
4. Ferrario, C.R. Food Addiction and Obesity. *Neuropsychopharmacology* **2017**, *42*, 361–362. [CrossRef]
5. Gearhardt, A.N.; Boswell, R.G.; White, M.A. The association of "food addiction" with disordered eating and body mass index. *Eat. Behav.* **2014**, *15*, 427–433. [CrossRef]
6. De Vries, S.-K.; Meule, A. Food Addiction and Bulimia Nervosa: New Data Based on the Yale Food Addiction Scale 2.0. *Eur. Eat. Disord. Rev.* **2016**, *24*, 518–522. [CrossRef]
7. Meule, A.; Von Rezori, V.; Blechert, J. Food addiction and bulimia nervosa. *Eur. Eat. Disord. Rev.* **2014**, *22*, 331–337. [CrossRef] [PubMed]
8. Gearhardt, A.N.; White, M.A.; Masheb, R.M.; Morgan, P.T.; Crosby, R.D.; Grilo, C.M. An examination of the food addiction construct in obese patients with binge eating disorder. *Int. J. Eat. Disord.* **2012**, *45*, 657–663. [CrossRef] [PubMed]
9. Granero, R.; Jiménez-Murcia, S.; Gearhardt, A.N.; Agüera, Z.; Aymamí, N.; Gómez-Peña, M.; Lozano-Madrid, M.; Mallorquí-Bagué, N.; Mestre-Bach, G.; Neto-Antao, M.I.; et al. Validation of the Spanish version of the Yale Food Addiction Scale 2.0 (YFAS 2.0) and clinical correlates in a sample of eating disorder, gambling disorder, and healthy control participants. *Front. Psychiatry* **2018**, *9*, 321. [CrossRef]
10. Hauck, C.; Cook, B.; Ellrott, T. Food addiction, eating addiction and eating disorders. *Proc. Nutr. Soc.* **2020**, *79*, 103–112. [CrossRef]
11. Meule, A.; Gearhardt, A.N. Food addiction in the light of DSM-5. *Nutrients* **2014**, *6*, 3653–3671. [CrossRef]
12. Wolz, I.; Granero, R.; Fernández-Aranda, F. A comprehensive model of food addiction in patients with binge-eating symptomatology: The essential role of negative urgency. *Compr. Psychiatry* **2017**, *74*, 118–124. [CrossRef]
13. Fielding-Singh, P.; Patel, M.L.; King, A.C.; Gardner, C.D. Baseline Psychosocial and Demographic Factors Associated with Study Attrition and 12-Month Weight Gain in the DIETFITS Trial. *Obesity* **2019**, *27*, 1997–2004. [CrossRef]
14. Romero, X.; Agüera, Z.; Granero, R.; Sánchez, I.; Riesco, N.; Jiménez-Murcia, S.; Gisbert-Rodriguez, M.; Sánchez-González, J.; Casalé, G.; Baenas, I.; et al. Is food addiction a predictor of treatment outcome among patients with eating disorder? *Eur. Eat. Disord. Rev.* **2019**, *27*, 700–711. [CrossRef] [PubMed]
15. Brunault, P.; Ducluzeau, P.-H.; Courtois, R.; Bourbao-Tournois, C.; Delbachian, I.; Réveillère, C.; Ballon, N. Food Addiction is Associated with Higher Neuroticism, Lower Conscientiousness, Higher Impulsivity, but Lower Extraversion in Obese Patient Candidates for Bariatric Surgery. *Subst. Use Misuse* **2018**, *53*, 1919–1923. [CrossRef] [PubMed]
16. Burrows, T.; Kay-Lambkin, F.; Pursey, K.; Skinner, J.; Dayas, C. Food addiction and associations with mental health symptoms: A systematic review with meta-analysis. *J. Hum. Nutr. Diet.* **2018**, *31*, 544–572. [CrossRef] [PubMed]
17. Burrows, T.; Skinner, J.; McKenna, R.; Rollo, M. Food addiction, binge eating disorder, and obesity: Is there a relationship? *Behav. Sci.* **2017**, *7*, 54. [CrossRef] [PubMed]

18. Jiménez-Murcia, S.; Agüera, Z.; Paslakis, G.; Munguia, L.; Granero, R.; Sánchez-González, J.; Sánchez, I.; Riesco, N.; Gearhardt, A.N.; Dieguez, C.; et al. Food addiction in eating disorders and obesity: Analysis of clusters and implications for treatment. *Nutrients* **2019**, *11*, 2633. [CrossRef] [PubMed]
19. American Psychiatric Association. *Diagnostic and Statistical Manual of Mental Disorders*, 4th ed.; Text Revision (DSM-IV-TR®) No Title; American Psychiatric Association Publishing: Washington, DC, USA, 2010.
20. Garner, D.M. *Inventario de Trastornos de la Conducta Alimentaria (EDI-2)—Manual;* TEA: Madrid, Spain, 1998.
21. Derogatis, L.R. *SCL-90-R: Symptom Checklist-90-R. Administration, Scoring and Procedures Manuall—II for the Revised Version;* Clinical Psychometric Research: Towson, MD, USA, 1994.
22. Derogatis, L.R. *SCL-90-R. Cuestionario de 90 Síntomas-Manual;* TEA: Madrid, Spain, 2002.
23. Cloninger, C.R. *The Temperament and Character Inventory—Revised;* Center for Psychobiology of Personality, Washington University: St Louis, MO, USA, 1999.
24. Gutiérrez-Zotes, J.A.; Bayón, C.; Montserrat, C.; Valero, J.; Labad, A.; Cloninger, C.R.; Fernández-Aranda, F. Temperament and Character Inventory Revised (TCI-R). Standardization and normative data in a general population sample. *Actas Esp. De Psiquiatr.* **2004**, *32*, 8–15.
25. Gearhardt, A.; Corbin, W.; Brownell, K. Development of the Yale Food Addiction Scale Version 2.0. *Psychol. Addict. Behav.* **2016**, *30*, 113–121. [CrossRef]
26. Fernández-Aranda, F.; Treasure, J.; Paslakis, G.; Agüera, Z.; Giménez, M.; Granero, R.; Sánchez, I.; Serrano-Troncoso, E.; Gorwood, P.; Herpertz-Dahlmann, B.; et al. The impact of duration of illness on treatment nonresponse and drop-out: Exploring the relevance of enduring eating disorder concept. *Eur. Eat. Disord. Rev.* **2021**, *29*, 499–513. [CrossRef]
27. Agüera, Z.; Sánchez, I.; Granero, R.; Riesco, N.; Steward, T.; Martín-Romera, V.; Jiménez-Murcia, S.; Romero, X.; Caroleo, M.; Segura-García, C.; et al. Short-Term Treatment Outcomes and Dropout Risk in Men and Women with Eating Disorders. *Eur. Eat. Disord. Rev.* **2017**, *25*, 293–301. [CrossRef]
28. Riesco, N.; Agüera, Z.; Granero, R.; Jiménez-Murcia, S.; Menchón, J.M.; Fernández-Aranda, F. Other Specified Feeding or Eating Disorders (OSFED): Clinical heterogeneity and cognitive-behavioral therapy outcome. *Eur. Psychiatry* **2018**, *54*, 109–116. [CrossRef] [PubMed]
29. Stata-Corp. *Stata Statistical Software: Release 17;* Stata Press Publication (StataCorp LLC): College Station, TX, USA, 2021.
30. Kelley, K.; Preacher, K.J. On effect size. *Psychol. Methods* **2012**, *17*, 137–152. [CrossRef] [PubMed]
31. Finner, H.; Roters, M. On the False Discovery Rate and Expected Type I Errors. *J. Am. Stat. Assoc.* **2001**, *88*, 920–923. [CrossRef]
32. Hilker, I.; Sánchez, I.; Steward, T.; Jiménez-Murcia, S.; Granero, R.; Gearhardt, A.N.; Rodríguez-Muñoz, R.C.; Dieguez, C.; Crujeiras, A.B.; Tolosa-Sola, I.; et al. Food Addiction in Bulimia Nervosa: Clinical Correlates and Association with Response to a Brief Psychoeducational Intervention. *Eur. Eat. Disord. Rev.* **2016**, *24*, 482–488. [CrossRef] [PubMed]
33. Del Pino-Gutiérrez, A.; Jiménez-Murcia, S.; Fernández-Aranda, F.; Agüera, Z.; Granero, R.; Hakansson, A.; Fagundo, A.B.; Bolao, F.; Valdepérez, A.; Mestre-Bach, G.; et al. The relevance of personality traits in impulsivity-related disorders: From substance use disorders and gambling disorder to bulimia nervosa. *J. Behav. Addict.* **2017**, *6*, 396–405. [CrossRef] [PubMed]
34. Allen, K.L.; Byrne, S.M.; Oddy, W.H.; Crosby, R.D. Early onset binge eating and purging eating disorders: Course and outcome in a population-based study of adolescents. *J. Abnorm. Child Psychol.* **2013**, *41*, 1083–1096. [CrossRef] [PubMed]
35. Gearhardt, A.; White, M.; Potenza, M. Binge eating disorder and food addiction. *Curr. Drug Abus. Rev.* **2011**, *4*, 201–207. [CrossRef]
36. Van den Eynde, F.; Koskina, A.; Syrad, H.; Guillaume, S.; Broadbent, H.; Campbell, I.C.; Schmidt, U. State and trait food craving in people with bulimic eating disorders. *Eat. Behav.* **2012**, *13*, 414–417. [CrossRef] [PubMed]
37. Beitscher-Campbell, H.; Blum, K.; Febo, M.; Madigan, M.A.; Giordano, J.; Badgaiyan, R.D.; Braverman, E.R.; Dushaj, K.; Li, M.; Gold, M.S. Pilot clinical observations between food and drug seeking derived from fifty cases attending an eating disorder clinic. *J. Behav. Addict.* **2016**, *5*, 533–541. [CrossRef]
38. Murray, S.M.; Tweardy, S.; Geliebter, A.; Avena, N.M. A Longitudinal Preliminary Study of Addiction-Like Responses to Food and Alcohol Consumption Among Individuals Undergoing Weight Loss Surgery. *Obes. Surg.* **2019**, *29*, 2700–2703. [CrossRef]
39. Schag, K.; Leehr, E.J.; Meneguzzo, P.; Martus, P.; Zipfel, S.; Giel, K.E. Food-related impulsivity assessed by longitudinal laboratory tasks is reduced in patients with binge eating disorder in a randomized controlled trial. *Sci. Rep.* **2021**, *11*, 8225. [CrossRef] [PubMed]

nutrients

MDPI

Review

Ketamine as a Treatment for Anorexia Nervosa: A Narrative Review

Johanna Louise Keeler [1,*], Janet Treasure [1,2], Mario F. Juruena [2,3], Carol Kan [4] and Hubertus Himmerich [1,2]

1 Section of Eating Disorders, Department of Psychological Medicine, Institute of Psychiatry, Psychology & Neuroscience, King's College London, London SE5 8AF, UK; janet.treasure@kcl.ac.uk (J.T.); hubertus.himmerich@kcl.ac.uk (H.H.)
2 South London and Maudsley NHS Foundation Trust, Bethlem Royal Hospital, Monks Orchard Road, Beckenham BR3 3BX, UK; mario.juruena@kcl.ac.uk
3 Centre for Affective Disorders, Department of Psychological Medicine, Institute of Psychiatry, Psychology & Neuroscience, King's College London, London SE5 8AF, UK
4 Eating Disorder Service, Central and North West London NHS Foundation Trust, 1 Nightingale Place, Kensington & Chelsea, London SW10 9NG, UK; carol.kan@nhs.net
* Correspondence: johanna.keeler@kcl.ac.uk; Tel.: +44-(0)-20-7848-0187

Abstract: Anorexia nervosa (AN) is a highly complex disorder to treat, especially in severe and enduring cases. Whilst the precise aetiology of the disorder is uncertain, malnutrition and weight loss can contribute to reductions in grey and white matter of the brain, impairments in neuroplasticity and neurogenesis and difficulties with cognitive flexibility, memory and learning. Depression is highly comorbid in AN and may be a barrier to recovery. However, traditional antidepressants are often ineffective in alleviating depressive symptoms in underweight patients with AN. There is an urgent need for new treatment approaches for AN. This review gives a conceptual overview for the treatment of AN with ketamine. Ketamine has rapid antidepressant effects, which are hypothesised to occur via increases in glutamate, with sequelae including increased neuroplasticity, neurogenesis and synaptogenesis. This article provides an overview of the use of ketamine for common psychiatric comorbidities of AN and discusses particular safety concerns and side effects. Potential avenues for future research and specific methodological considerations are explored. Overall, there appears to be ample theoretical background, via several potential mechanisms, that warrant the exploration of ketamine as a treatment for adults with AN.

Keywords: anorexia nervosa; atypical psychedelics; eating disorders; esketamine; ketamine; narrative review; severe-enduring; treatment

Citation: Keeler, J.L.; Treasure, J.; Juruena, M.F.; Kan, C.; Himmerich, H. Ketamine as a Treatment for Anorexia Nervosa: A Narrative Review. *Nutrients* **2021**, *13*, 4158. https://doi.org/10.3390/nu13114158

Academic Editor: Stefano Erzegovesi

Received: 10 October 2021
Accepted: 18 November 2021
Published: 20 November 2021

1. Introduction: An Overview of Ketamine

Ketamine is an n-methyl-D-aspartate (NMDA) receptor antagonist that has traditionally been used for anaesthesia in larger doses [1]. It remains one of the two injectable anaesthetics under the World Health Organisation Model List of Essential Medicines, the other of which is propofol [2]. It is available in two enantiomers: the S(-) and racemic (R-) forms, referred to as esketamine and arketamine. However, when referred to as ketamine, this describes (R,S)-ketamine, which is a 1:1 racemic mixture of S- and R-ketamine enantiomers (see Figure 1 for the molecular structure). S-(Es)ketamine has an approximately four-fold higher affinity for the NMDA receptor site than R-ketamine and is three to four times as potent [3,4]. Moreover, esketamine generally produces fewer psychomimetic effects than R-ketamine. Ketamine can be administered via several routes that have varying bioavailability: intravenous (100%), intramuscular (90–95%), subcutaneous (90–95%), intranasal (30–50%), sublingual (20–30%), transdermal (10–50%) and oral (10–20%) [5]. Estimates of bioavailabilities increase when accounting for the contribution of norketamine; for example, in one study, the bioavailabilities of sublingual and oral ketamine increased from 32% to 54% and 23% to 59%, respectively [6]. Moreover, the area under the curve, peak plasma concentration and time to peak plasma concentration differ depending on the administration route and dosage (see Table 1).

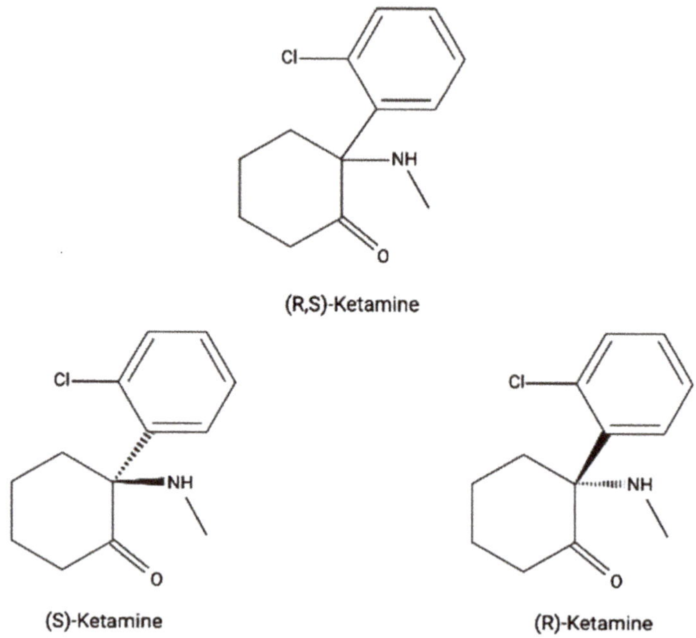

Figure 1. The molecular structure of ketamine, S-ketamine and R-ketamine.

Table 1. Single administration of ketamine: selected pharmacokinetic parameters.

Parameter	Administration Route		
	Intravenous	Sublingual	Oral
Dosage (mg)	10	25	25
C_{max} (μg/L) M ± SD	156 ± 161	28.6 ± 6.6	22.8 ± 12.8
T_{max} (h) M ± SD	0.24 ± 0.29	0.76 ± 0.51	0.96 ± 0.8
AUC/dose (μg.h/L.mg) M ± SD	13.4 ± 2.4	4.0 ± 1.9	3.1 ± 0.7

Notes: AUC = area under the curve, Cmax = peak plasma concentration, M = mean, SD = standard deviation and tmax = time to peak plasma concentration (adapted from [6]).

Ketamine is rapidly metabolised (the half-life is 2–4 h for racemic ketamine and 5 h for esketamine [5]), mainly by the liver, and is excreted renally through urine and faeces. Its by-products include hydroxyketamine, norketamine, dehydronorketamine and six hydroxynorketamine metabolites [7]. The main metabolic pathway is N-demethylation to an active metabolite norketamine by CYP3A4. There is increasing interest in the metabolites of ketamine. For example, research has demonstrated the importance of the (2S,6S;2R,6R)-hydroxynorketamine metabolite for the antidepressant effects of (R,S)-ketamine [7], which is independent of NMDA receptor activity.

The first human dosage of ketamine was in 1964 at the University of Michigan, where it was titrated from a subanaesthetic dose to full anaesthesia [8]. Patient reports of the experiences included feeling "strange" and having "no feeling in their arms or legs" [8]. These experiences contributed to its classification as a "dissociative anaesthetic" by Domino and Corssen [4]. In 1970, ketamine was approved by the Food and Drug Administration (FDA) for use as an anaesthetic in children, adults and the elderly. Four years later, in 1974, ketamine was used for the first time within a psychiatric setting as an adjunct to psychotherapy for depression in Argentina [9]. Since then, advances in the field of ketamine have led to randomised controlled trials investigating its use for the treatment of various psychiatric disorders, including depression [10], anxiety disorders [11], alcohol and substance use disorder [12–14] and post-traumatic stress disorder [15]. Unfortunately, this research was somewhat obscured by ketamine's classification as a class III substance in the US Controlled Substances Act due to it being popular as a recreational drug. However, in 2019, esketamine in intranasal form was licensed to treat treatment-resistant depression in the US and Europe by the FDA and European Medicines Agency (EMA), due to its rapid antidepressant effects.

Factors that contribute to the phenomenology of ketamine treatment include set (person factors) and setting (situational factors), terms introduced by Harvard psychologist Timothy Leary [16]. Set refers to the individual's internal state, such as the psychological preparation and intentions for the experience, as well as intrinsic factors such as mood, psychopathology, personality, fears and wishes [17]. Setting refers to any environmental factors, including the physical, social and cultural environments [18]. Importantly, the nature of the set and setting determine the ketamine experience; optimising both factors is important to minimise the chances of an adverse psychological experience (i.e., a "bad trip"). Set can be optimised by providing patients with "sitters", who help the patient prepare for the ketamine experience, set intentions, support them through the session and aid them in integrating its meaning afterwards. On the other hand, researchers and clinicians often optimise the setting by providing a calm and relaxing environment with minimal stimuli and bright light; an overly clinical or antiseptic environment may increase anxiety (for comprehensive guidelines, see [19]). Additionally, patients may be provided with eye shields and a carefully prepared music playlist and are guided to direct their attention inwards [20].

As aforementioned, the bioavailability of ketamine differs depending on the administration route, although it is unclear how or whether bioavailability is related to therapeutic effects [21]. Regardless, one study found dose-related antidepressant effects across all administration routes tested, including intravenous (IV), intramuscular (IM) and subcutaneous (SC) [22]. In this study, SC administration resulted in the fewest adverse events [22]. By comparison, IM and IV can be painful to administer, and intranasal ketamine can be uncomfortable if administered in the same nostril over 40 min [21]. Oral ketamine produces a bitter taste. However, oral, SC, IM and intranasal ketamine are more convenient than IV ketamine and can be used in everyday clinical care, as the latter requires an anaesthetist to be present for administration [21]. Overall, it is unclear which administration route is optimal within psychiatry, although within the context of treatment-resistant depression, intranasal esketamine alongside an antidepressant seems the most feasible and effective [5].

2. Materials and Methods

The purpose of this narrative review is to synthesise a theoretical rationale for the use of ketamine in the treatment of anorexia nervosa, integrating research across multiple disciplines (e.g., investigational research of ketamine for other psychiatric disorders). A literature search in the electronic databases MEDLINE and PubMed was performed until 15 September 2021, focusing on neurobiological models of anorexia nervosa and ketamine use within a psychiatric setting. An analysis of eligible publications using MeSH keywords such as "ketamine", "neuroplasticity", "anorexia nervosa" and "neurobiol" was conducted. Articles published in English were considered, and there were no restrictions on the type of article for inclusion; population-based studies, reviews, systematic reviews, meta-analyses, clinical trials and theoretical papers were included in this narrative review. Reference lists of publications were searched in order to identify additional eligible articles.

3. The Neurobiological and Psychological Effects of Ketamine

When administered at subanaesthetic doses, dissociative and mild psychological effects emerge within 15 min [23]. Psychological effects can include dissociation, alterations in perception, depersonalisation and derealisation, amongst others. These effects are transient and usually resolve within 90 min [24]. The antidepressant effects are rapid after the psychological effects dissipate, with effects on depressive symptoms persisting for a week in some patients [24]. This temporal sequence may indicate neuroadaptation to the effects of ketamine in the brain [25]. This aligns with studies revealing the positive influence of ketamine on neuroplasticity and, specifically, synaptogenesis.

Whilst ketamine is an NMDA receptor antagonist, its molecular action is more complex than a simple blockade of NMDA receptors. In fact, at low doses, ketamine paradoxically stimulates glutamate transmission [26]. This is achieved by both increased glutamate release and also increases in AMPA receptors at synapses, which are ionotropic transmembrane glutamate receptors [26]. This, in turn, causes increases in brain-derived neurotrophic factor (BDNF) release, which stimulates the mammalian target of rapamycin (mTOR) via Atk (protein kinase B) and ERK signalling. mTOR is a protein kinase that is important for the control of protein translation and contributes to long-lasting synaptic plasticity by increasing the number and density of synapses. Thus, the positive effect of ketamine on synaptogenesis is thought to reverse the reduced synaptic density that results from chronic stress and depression [27,28] and is implicated in its antidepressant effects.

As well as increasing synaptogenesis, rodent studies have indicated that ketamine increases neurogenesis and downregulates stress-induced inflammation. Adult neurogenesis refers to the birth of new neurons from stem cells, which occurs at a high rate in the hippocampus and is mediated by growth factors such as BDNF and vascular endothelial growth factor (VEGF). Studies in rodents have demonstrated increases in neurogenesis after ketamine administration both in vitro [29] and in vivo [30,31], which is thought to contribute to its sustained antidepressant effects [31]. Similarly, increases in BDNF and VEGF in the medial prefrontal cortex (mPFC) and hippocampus following ketamine administration are thought to contribute to this increase in neurogenesis [32].

Ketamine has also been shown to attenuate stress-induced inflammatory responses in rats. In one study, rodents exposed to chronic unpredictable mild stress exhibited greater hippocampal levels of proinflammatory cytokines (interleukin (IL)-1β, IL-6 and tumour necrosis factor (TNF)-α), which were reduced following a low dose of ketamine [33]. Notably, another study found decreases in proinflammatory cytokines in rodents exposed to stressors following ketamine administration but did not observe a reduction in corticosterone [34]. Thus, these effects may be independent of stress hormones. Whilst studies in humans are scarce, these findings have been replicated in patients with depression, with several studies finding decreases in various proinflammatory cytokines after ketamine treatment [35–37]. Whether the anti-inflammatory and antidepressant properties of subanaesthetic ketamine administration are related is debated, with some studies finding an association [36,37] and others finding no association [35,38]. Whilst more research is needed, it is possible that reductions in inflammation partially contribute to the therapeutic effects of ketamine.

4. Anorexia Nervosa

Anorexia nervosa (AN) has the highest mortality of any psychiatric disorder, with a standardised mortality rate of between 3.2 and 10.5 [39,40]. It is characterised by dietary restriction and weight loss behaviours (e.g., exercise), leading to significantly low weight. Prognosis is often poor, with estimates of relapse including 59% at nine years of illness [41] and 30% at 15 years of illness [42]. There are several biopsychosocial models that seek to explain the aetiology of AN, such as the Cognitive Interpersonal Maintenance Model [43]. Nevertheless, the neurobiological underpinnings of the disorder remain ambiguous. There are no approved psychopharmacological medications for AN, and the treatment options are otherwise limited [44]. Moreover, a large proportion of patients are treatment-resistant and therefore fail to gain weight. Treatment options are limited for this patient group [45], which has been described as a "crisis" in the field [46].

Psychiatric comorbidity is common in AN, even after the eating disorder has been resolved [47]. A study of 11,588 adults in eating disorder clinics in Sweden was conducted, with comorbidities including mood disorders (33–50%), generalised anxiety disorder (28–35%), social phobia (14–17%), obsessive-compulsive disorder (7–8%), post-traumatic stress disorder (PTSD; 3–7%) and substance use disorder (4–11%) [48]. Other data from separate geographical locations support similar prevalence rates [49–52], although other estimates of anxiety disorder comorbidity have been higher at ~55–85% of patients [53]. Features of autism spectrum disorder (ASD) are also highly prevalent in AN, with one study finding a 16.3% prevalence in a sample of 92 participants [54].

Patients with AN often report anhedonia, a lack of self-compassion, feelings of failure and suicidal ideation [49,55,56], and AN is associated with a higher risk of suicide [57]. Comorbid depression is linked to poor outcomes in patients, particularly those with severe-enduring AN (SE-AN), whereby patients with comorbid depression are six times more likely to remain unrecovered at a 22-year follow-up [58]. Individuals with AN often report that engaging in disordered eating behaviours allows them to cope with or avoid difficult emotions; affect regulation may be a maintaining factor for the disorder [59]. Additionally, anxiety is a feature within the syndrome of AN, with high levels of fear and anxiety around food, weight and body shape and stereotyped eating behaviours. In the majority of cases, symptoms of anxiety disorders (e.g., generalised anxiety disorder, social phobia and obsessive-compulsive disorder) precede the onset of AN [60,61]. Moreover, symptoms of anxiety as measured by the State-Trait Anxiety Inventory [62] often remain high even after recovery [63,64]. Another risk factor for the development of AN is childhood trauma, most of which are related to negative sexual experiences [65].

Genetic studies suggest overlapping aetiology between AN and some psychiatric comorbidities (e.g., depression and obsessive-compulsive disorder) [66–68]. However, psychopharmacological drugs often show little efficacy in terms of weight gain in AN; a meta-analysis found no benefit in the weight outcomes from both antipsychotics and antidepressants in comparison to the placebo [69]. New approaches to the management of comorbidities, such as depression, in AN are warranted, which may, in turn, alleviate eating disorder (ED) symptoms. The evidence for the use of ketamine in the treatment of each respective comorbidity will be addressed in the following sections.

5. The Use of Ketamine in Commonly Comorbid Psychiatric Disorders

5.1. Depression

Patients with treatment-resistant depression defined as those who have failed to achieve remission (or at least a 50% improvement in mood) after two antidepressants, are candidates for esketamine nasal spray therapy in conjunction with an antidepressant. Notably, the National Institute of Care Excellence (NICE) in the United Kingdom do not recommend nasal spray esketamine for depression on the grounds of poor cost-effectiveness [70]. This is currently being reviewed. In research, the most common administration route in clinical trials is intravenous (IV) ketamine [71]. Studies show that IV ketamine elicits a rapid antidepressant response in major depressive disorder and treatment-resistant depression, acting within 24 h and providing a response after a single IV administration of subanaesthetic doses (0.5 mg/kg) for 4–7 days [72]. There has been extensive research investigating ketamine as a treatment option for this population. For example, it has been found that a third of patients with treatment-resistant depression achieve remission [10], with higher rates of remission associated with repeated administrations. All symptoms of depression have been found to be reduced, including suicidality [25]. Additionally, improvements in aspects of memory and learning have been found in patients with depression after ketamine treatment, such as working memory and visual learning memory [73]. Studies of ketamine for depression have, for the most part, used adult samples, although a systematic review found reductions in depressive symptoms, suicidality and mood lability in adolescents given ketamine for treatment-resistant psychiatric conditions [74]. Thus, there is emerging evidence for its use in adolescents, although, notably, esketamine is only licensed for use in adult patients.

Whilst esketamine has fewer psychotomimetic effects than R-ketamine, it has been suggested that these psychotomimetic effects may increase the antidepressant efficacy [75,76]. Whilst considered a side effect, the psychotomimetic effects can have transformative psychological effects akin to those elicited from other psychedelic experiences (e.g., psilocybin [77,78]). Additionally, there have been concerns raised regarding the cognitive effects of ketamine, since it tends to produce impairments in cognitive function, although the majority of this evidence is in chronic users [79]. However, in acute doses, it appears that neurocognitive function is sustained or even improved [80]. More research should be conducted to ascertain the impact of therapeutic ketamine on cognition in patients with depression.

5.2. *Obsessive-Compulsive Disorder*

A systematic review of 11 studies of patients with OCD found that intravenous ketamine improves obsessive-compulsive symptomatology, with rapid effects that last from days to weeks [81]. Moreover, the effects of ketamine on OCD are prolonged if augmented with cognitive behavioural therapy (CBT). In an interesting case study of a patient with treatment-resistant depression, psychosis and OCD, oral esketamine was combined with deep brain stimulation targeting the ventral anterior limb of the internal capsule, demonstrating long-term benefits over 18 months [82]. Overall, there is a requirement for more research into the use of ketamine for OCD, although there is preliminary evidence for reductions in obsessive-compulsive symptomatology.

5.3. *Autism Spectrum Disorder (ASD)*

The evidence for using ketamine to treat the core symptoms of ASD (i.e., broadly, impairments in social interaction and restrictive/repetitive behaviours) is preliminary. One randomised controlled pilot study used two doses of intranasal ketamine and saline placebo in a crossover design on a population of young people with ASD [83]. There were no specific effects of ketamine on the clinician- and self-reported measures of autism; the rates went down both after the placebo and ketamine. Notably, ketamine was well-tolerated. However, a single case study found a dramatic reduction in the core symptoms of ASD for 36 h following a preoperative ketamine treatment [84]. Moreover, another single case study found improvements in depressive symptoms and the duration of eye fixation (an index of social skills) across 12 doses of intranasal ketamine in an individual with ASD and other psychiatric disorders [85]. Overall, the initial results were mixed, and further research is needed to ascertain whether ketamine is efficacious in addressing some of the core symptoms of ASD.

5.4. *Anxiety Disorders*

5.4.1. Generalised Anxiety Disorder and Social Anxiety Disorder

Several studies over the last ~5 years have demonstrated the efficacy of ketamine for the treatment of anxiety disorders such as generalised anxiety disorder (GAD) and social anxiety disorder (SAD). For example, a double-blind RCT in patients with SAD found greater reductions in the symptoms of SAD in patients given IV ketamine than patients given a saline placebo [11]. A later double-blinded RCT in patients with SAD and GAD compared subcutaneous ketamine to a midazolam placebo, finding a dose-responsive (0.25, 0.5 and 1 mg/kg) reduction in anxiety in those given ketamine within an hour of dosing, which persisted for a week [86]. Following this, Glue and colleagues investigated the safety, tolerability and efficacy of extended-release oral ketamine tablets in seven responders from their RCT [87]. Over 96 h, participants showed reductions in self-reported measures of fear, anxiety and depression. However, it is important to note that the small sample size meant that no inferential statistical analyses could be conducted, and the results should be considered preliminary but promising. To our knowledge, no studies have examined intranasal esketamine for anxiety disorders, nor have they paired ketamine with adjunctive therapy, which is a potential area for future research.

5.4.2. Post-Traumatic Stress Disorder

The fear response associated with a trauma-related stimulus may be targeted by ketamine. In addition, rodent models have demonstrated ketamine's ability to promote fear extinction, which is suggested to occur via mTORC1 signalling [88]. Thus, it may be appropriate as an adjunct to extinction therapies, whereby a fear-associated cue is exposed to patients with the aim to form a new memory associated with it via inhibitory learning [89]. In this way, ketamine treatment may be especially efficacious for PTSD when "harnessing a window of ketamine-induced neuroplasticity" [90].

Early studies of ketamine for PTSD in humans administered the drug immediately after exposure to trauma, which produced mixed findings [91]. Later studies have investigated its use to treat chronic PTSD, and whilst, to date, there are few randomised-controlled trials (RCTs), the results are promising. For example, in one double-blinded RCT of 41 chronic PTSD patients, the PTSD symptoms and depression improved in response to ketamine as opposed to midazolam [15]. Another study found increases in the length of the clinical response to a mindfulness-based extinction and reconsolidation cognitive therapy in patients given IV ketamine relative to a saline placebo [92]. Overall, these preliminary findings were promising, and ketamine is likely a viable treatment option for patients who have experienced trauma.

5.5. Substance and Alcohol Use Disorders

There have been several reviews, including one systematic review, detailing the anti-addiction properties of ketamine [12–14]. Collectively, the studies have suggested that ketamine improves cravings, motivations to quit, physiological reactions to withdrawal and, importantly, reduces or completely abolishes the self-administration of drugs/alcohol [13]. For addiction, ketamine is often administered alongside psychotherapy, termed "ketamine psychedelic therapy" (KPT), which generally consists of a preparation phase, dosing phase and integration phase. This allows patients to fully take advantage of a hyperplastic brain state. Interestingly, this idea has been harnessed by a study investigating the potential for ketamine to rewrite the maladaptive reward memories associated with alcohol and drugs [93]. Participants were presented with a glass of beer and then retrieved maladaptive reward memories through exposure to a beer-related cue. Participants administered ketamine directly after this reported lower alcohol consumption over 10 days over and above participants who were either given the retrieval task or ketamine alone. The authors suggested that the ketamine facilitated the rewriting of drinking memories, which occurred within a critical reconsolidation window [93]. This brings into light the potential role of ketamine in enhancing the efficacy of therapies or abolishing learned associations via neuroplastic mechanisms.

6. Ketamine and the Neurobiology of Anorexia Nervosa

6.1. Neurotransmitters

6.1.1. Serotonin

Serotonin, or 5-hydroxytryptamine (5-HT), is a monoamine neurotransmitter produced mainly in the gastrointestinal tract and also by the raphe nuclei, located in the brainstem. Thus, 5-HT has multifaceted functions and modulates food intake, body weight control, mood, cognition, learning and memory. There are many 5-HT receptors, ranging from 5-HT_1 to 5-HT_7, with a high density of receptors in the prefrontal cortex and hippocampus [94]. However, the 5-HT_1 and 5-HT_2 receptor families are of the most interest in the context of AN.

There is evidence for dysfunctions in the serotonin system in AN. For example, patients with AN show reduced levels of serotonin and markers of serotonin (e.g., tryptophan) in the acute stages, which normalise after recovery [95], together with depletions in 5-HT$_{1A}$ and 5-HT$_{2A}$ receptor densities [96]. However, some abnormalities persist after recovery. For example, 5-HT$_{2A}$ receptor activity has been found to be abnormal in individuals recovered from AN [97]. Additionally, there have been several studies indicating genetic differences related to serotoninergic activity in AN (e.g., the S allele of the 5-HTTLPR gene [98,99]), one of which is a polymorphism of the 5-HT$_{2A}$ receptor gene [100,101].

It is possible that the dietary restriction associated with AN leads to a depletion of the dietary supplies of tryptophan, which is an amino acid that is a chemical precursor to 5-HT. Alterations in serotonin signalling in limbic pathways (e.g., mesocorticolimbic pathway) and structures (e.g., the hippocampus, hypothalamus, amygdala and thalamus) may contribute to various features of AN, such as obsessiveness, body image distortions, low mood, anxiety, fear, dietary behaviour and their response to SSRIs [102].

Several studies have suggested that the antidepressant effects of ketamine are partially due to its effects on 5-HT, showing some similarities to traditional SSRIs. In vivo microdialysis studies in rodents given an acute subanaesthetic dosage of ketamine showed increases in 5-HT$_{ext}$ in the mPFC [103]. Additionally, a study in nonhuman primates demonstrated a downregulation of selective 5-HT transporters (SERT) after an acute IV ketamine injection [104]. Overall, there is evidence for the importance of 5-HT$_{1A}$ and 5-HT$_{1B}$ receptor agonism for the antidepressant effects of ketamine (see [105] for a review). It is thought that this may occur as a downstream effect of hippocampal NMDA receptor inhibition and AMPA receptor activation. This may normalise the aforementioned alterations shown in AN and improve mood and/or comorbid depression.

6.1.2. Dopamine

Dopamine is a neurotransmitter important in reward processing, produced mainly in the areas of the brain implicated in reward, such as the substantia nigra and ventral tegmental area. Reward constitutes three main processes: "liking" (a hedonic impact), "wanting" (incentive salience) and learning (habit formation and forming associations) [106]. Whilst dopamine is implicated in all reward processes, studies suggest that it is most important for "wanting" processes [107,108] and, thus, is a large feature in theories of addiction.

In AN, alterations in the dopaminergic reward system have been noted, although the findings are complex and often contradictory [109]. Overall, the findings suggest that alterations in dopamine in AN may drive difficulties in discriminating between punishment and reward, which is related to increased levels of anxiety and harm avoidance [110]. It has been suggested that AN-related cues and behaviours become rewarding over time, as increases in stress hormones attributable to food restriction can stimulate the dopamine reward system via the hypothalamic–pituitary–adrenal axis [111]. Repeated dopamine signalling may then aid in the transfer of these behaviours into habits [111,112]. Thus, it has been suggested that treatments focus on developing associations with recovery goals and egosyntonic aspects of the disorder rather than simply on food cues [110]. However, this is likely to be especially difficult in patients who remain underweight or have the treatment-resistant form of AN, as poor engagement in therapies and cognitive difficulties may interfere.

Ketamine has been found to modulate the brain circuits related to reward and motivation [113,114]. For example, resting-state functional magnetic resonance imaging (MRI) scans of patients with treatment-resistant depression two days post-ketamine infusion demonstrated increases in the frontostriatal connectivity in one study [115]. An additional study provided evidence for increases in synaptic plasticity in the hippocampus–accumbens pathway, which occurred partially due to the activation of D1 receptors [116]. Thus, it is possible that using the suggested psychological approaches above within a window of ketamine-induced neuroplasticity may instigate changes in reward functioning and reward-related associations with disordered cues.

6.2. Neuroplasticity and Neuromorphology

Neuroplasticity is regulated by the noradrenergic, serotoninergic, anticholinergic and glutamate systems [117,118]. Neuropsychological studies of AN indicate reductions in neuroplasticity, with decreased cognitive flexibility, memory and learning, which will be discussed in the following section. Malnutrition, chronic stress and the presence of psychiatric comorbidities can lead to reductions in BDNF and hippocampal volume, together with increases in proinflammatory cytokines. The presence of neuroinflammation has been noted in AN, with studies finding increases in proinflammatory cytokines (e.g., TNF-α, IL-6 and IL-1β [119,120]), some of which normalise after weight restoration (e.g., IL-6 [120,121]). Additionally, chronic psychosocial stress can alter the proinflammatory cytokine pathways [122,123]. Stressors include, but are not limited to, childhood adversities and life events, caregiver stress and loneliness, all factors that can be linked to the development of AN [124].

Stress-induced depression-like behaviours in rodents are associated with increases in proinflammatory cytokines but also with decreases in BDNF and neurogenesis [125–127]. Inflammation and aberrant concentrations of BDNF have been noted in several other psychiatric disorders that are often comorbid with AN, such as PTSD and depression [128–132]. Thus, comorbidities may contribute to neuroinflammation in AN. Similar to in depression, patients with AN show low levels of BDNF, which generally resolves following weight restoration [133].

In the acute stages of AN, global decreases in grey matter volume of 4% to 5% are observed [134,135], which are more apparent in certain structures such as the hippocampus [136]. This region is particularly vulnerable to long-term malnutrition due to its high levels of neurogenesis [137–140]. Additionally, a loss of white matter is observed [141], which is more pronounced in adolescents with AN, perhaps resultant from the high vulnerability of the brain during development [135]. Generally, the grey and white matter volumes increase following weight restoration, although they are not always fully normalised [141]. Notably, one study found that white matter volume loss at admission in adolescents was predictive of recovery at 1 year; the interruption of white matter tract development as a result of malnutrition may contribute to chronicity [142].

We have speculated in previous publications that the effects of chronic malnutrition and traumatic events and/or chronic social stress associated with living with AN may contribute to neuroinflammation and both impaired neuroplasticity and neurogenesis [136]. However, these speculations are yet to be confirmed with robust empirical research, and many questions remain. Whilst there is little research investigating neurogenesis in human patients with AN, a study using an activity-based anorexia (ABA) rodent model found decreases in cell proliferation in the dentate gyrus following three days of ABA [143].

In people with AN, many of these parameters often normalise following weight restoration and recovery. However, a proportion of patients fail to weight restore (i.e., are "treatment-resistant") and thus experience persistent impairments in neuroplasticity, which is a likely barrier to successful treatment. Targeting neuroplasticity in treatment is likely to increase its success in both acute and chronic cases of AN.

As aforementioned, the antidepressant effects of ketamine appear to be mediated by an increased glutamate release [144], which has been linked to downward increases in BDNF, neurogenesis and synaptic plasticity. Relatedly, a structural MRI study demonstrated increases in the hippocampal volume following a single dose of ketamine, which was associated with the treatment response [145]. Additionally, ketamine may mitigate the effects of chronic stress on the brain [146], as well as associated increases in inflammatory markers [33]. Ketamine treatment has been shown to have positive effects on the neuropsychological parameters of memory and learning, which will be discussed in the following section.

6.3. Neuropsychology

Patients with AN often have difficulties in several aspects of cognition that may be linked to reduced neuroplasticity and hippocampal function, such as memory, learning and cognitive flexibility. Apparent deficits in memory in AN include overgeneralising autobiographical memories [147,148], poor immediate and delayed recall of story details [149], recall of locations [150] and pattern recognition memory [151]. Patients with AN have a negative bias when constructing future-directed thoughts compared to healthy controls [152], which may be related to a negative bias in memory retrieval [153]; it has been hypothesised that generating future-directed thoughts is reliant on the flexible recombination of events from the past [154]. Relatedly, adults with AN show selective impairments in aspects of cognitive flexibility such as task switching, which are also apparent in adults recovered from AN [155]. Whilst such depletions in cognition may not be at a threshold to be deemed an "impairment" [155], they may be precipitating or maintaining factors and are likely to contribute to the significant difficulty in engaging with psychological therapies.

Amongst and related to ketamine's neurobiological actions, there are several qualities of ketamine that are likely to address the difficulties in several aspects of neuropsychology in AN. Ketamine has multifaceted effects on the memory [156], which is contingent on the dosage and length of use. For example, chronic ketamine abuse is associated with decrements in the episodic memory, working memory and semantic memory, the former two of which abate following drug cessation [156]. At subanaesthetic doses, ketamine has similar, albeit transient, effects. These effects have been harnessed in research examining whether ketamine as an adjunct to exposure therapy can be used to block the reconsolidation of trauma-related memories [157]. Reconsolidation refers to the process whereby the strength and course of existing memory traces are modified. Additionally, ketamine can facilitate extinction learning, which describes the process of a new memory being formed rather than an existing memory being modified; inhibitory learning is thought to antagonise the old memory [157]. Our team found preliminary evidence for generalised impairments in extinction learning in AN [158]. It is possible that ketamine may facilitate extinction learning against feared foods and food-related situations in patients with AN.

As aforementioned, individuals with AN often experience social anxiety [48]. Previous research has demonstrated that individuals with eating disorders have a higher vigilance for social signs of rejection and avoid social rewards [159]. Importantly, this sensitivity to interpersonal conflict and anxiety around social situations can interfere with the therapeutic bond and, thus, the outcomes of therapy. Ketamine has been reported to increase the social functioning of patients with depression, reducing rejection sensitivity, social avoidance, pessimistic thinking and a bias towards negative information, which facilitates a therapeutic bond [160].

Ketamine can induce alterations in bodily perceptions, including feelings of lightness and floating [161,162]. Patients with AN tend to report high levels of cognitive control and cognitive rigidity [163,164]. Patients also report that their eating disorders often feel intertwined with their identities [165] and report anguish at physically "taking up space" [166,167]. Additionally, disconnection from the self, others and the world is core to AN [168–170]. It is possible that ketamine may have an additional therapeutic impact for patients with AN by promoting flexibility, ego dissolution, detachment from one's internal dialogue and openness to experiences [162]. Moreover, the mystical and spiritual experiences that often manifest during ketamine treatment [162] may enable patients to connect with their spirituality and alter their perceptions of both themselves in the context of the wider world and of the universe itself.

7. Ketamine as a Treatment for Anorexia Nervosa

7.1. Current Research

To date, there have been few studies investigating the therapeutic use of ketamine for AN, most of which have been case series or reports. Table 2 provides an overview of the study characteristics and main findings; all studies found reductions in the main outcome measures, including depression scores, suicidality and eating disorder psychopathology [171–174]. To date, all investigations of ketamine as a treatment for AN have been in adult patients. We would recommend that initial RCTs use SE-AN samples, who are typically adults due to the long duration of the illness as a criterion for inclusion and often have comorbid depression. However, given that ketamine has been found to alleviate depression in adolescents [74], future studies may endeavour to use it in a younger sample of patients with AN.

Table 2. Characteristics and main findings of studies of ketamine as a treatment for patients with eating disorders.

Study [Ref]	Study Design	N	Diagnosis	Administration Route	Dosage	Main Findings
Dechant et al. [171]	Case study	1	SE-AN and MDD	IV R-Ketamine	9 × 0.5 mg/kg over 40 min	Reduction in depression and suicidality.
Mills et al. [172]	Case series	15	SE-AN	IV Ketamine	2–15 × 20 mg/h for 10 h	9/15 responded to treatment, with reductions in depression. and compulsive starving/eating.
Schwartz et al. [173]	Case series	4	SE-ED and TRD	IM/IV Ketamine	5–9 × 0.4–0.5 mg/kg	Improvements in depression, anxiety and eating disorder psychopathology over approx. days.
Scolnick et al. [174]	Case study	1	SE-AN and MDD	IV R-Ketamine	4 × 0.75 mg/kg over 40 min	Reduction in "anorexic voice" and depression and full and sustained remission.

Notes: IM = intramuscular, IV = intravenous, MDD = major depressive disorder, N = number, SE-AN = severe-enduring anorexia nervosa, SE-ED = severe-enduring eating disorders and TRD = treatment-resistant depression.

In all studies, no severe side effects were reported beyond those expected (e.g., transient headaches, mild nausea and sedation). However, as off-label, small and uncontrolled trials, these studies provided only preliminary evidence for its efficacy. To date, there have been no well-controlled feasibility studies using a large sample, although there is a pilot double-blinded crossover trial of oral ketamine versus midazolam registered on the Australian New Zealand Clinical Trials Registry (REG: ACTRN12618001393246p).

7.2. Side Effects and Safety Concerns

There are specific safety concerns when investigating pharmacological interventions for AN. Liver enzyme abnormalities, such as elevations in liver transaminases, are associated with a lower body mass index (BMI) and hypoglycaemia [175]. Repeated high doses of ketamine and prolonged ketamine abuse have been associated with hepatotoxicity and liver injury [176]. Whilst this causal pathway is not fully understood, it may be related to lipid peroxidation (oxidative damage) [177]. Liver function tests are therefore a necessary precursor to ketamine treatment in AN.

Moreover, upper and lower urinary tract dysfunctions are present in approximately 20–40% of recreational ketamine users [178–180], which tend to be discontinued following the cessation of ketamine use. There is a dose–response relationship between ketamine use and the probability of lower urinary tract symptoms, meaning that long-term usage may be a concern. This is a particular concern, as renal complications have been observed in patients with AN [181]. Thus, patients should be asked about polydipsia, haematuria, incontinence and pelvic pain; indicators of renal function in the blood (e.g., albumin to a creatinine ratio and glomerular filtration rate) should be monitored, and abnormalities would warrant the cessation of ketamine.

Cardiac complications/abnormalities are a notable feature of AN. For example, hypokaemia can be a consequence in patients who use self-induced vomiting as a compensatory behaviour to manage weight gain. This, in turn, can lead to prolonged QT intervals, markers of arrhythmias. Other cardiac complications include bradycardia/tachycardia, congestive heart failure and hypotension. Ketamine administration is associated with transient increases in the blood pressure and heart rate. The use of psychostimulants (e.g., amphetamines, methylphenidate, modafinil and armodafinil) should not be permitted, as they increase blood pressure. Moreover, patients on concomitant monoamine oxidase inhibitors (MAOIs) should have their blood pressure monitored closely, since MAOI usage has been reported to increase blood pressure [182]. Completing an ECG and measuring electrolytes prior to treatment may be recommended. Recent cardiovascular events or clinically significant cardiovascular conditions are also a specific contraindication of ketamine.

Other identified key side effects of ketamine include transient dissociative states, sedation, nausea and vomiting, dysgeusia (alterations in taste) and hypoesthesia (changes in touching sensation). Dissociation is more common in people with comorbid PTSD, which is likely due to it already being a feature of the disorder. Patients with comorbid PTSD should therefore be closely monitored, and studies should administer the Clinician Administered Dissociative States Scale (CADSS [183]) to investigate the incidence of dissociation in AN following ketamine treatment. The "setting" of the room should promote feelings of calm and relaxation, minimising bright lights and too many stimuli, and encouraging patients to focus on music and pleasant thoughts.

Psychosis may be a contraindication for ketamine; ketamine can induce psychotic episodes in people that have schizophrenia [184]. Sedation is more of a risk if patients are on opioids or benzodiazepines; thus, this should be considered when patients are screened for treatment. Nausea, vomiting and dysgeusia may be specific concerns in the context of AN, since they have the potential to be triggers. This will need to be examined closely in future research, although the aforementioned studies conducted so far have not indicated any of the above to be particular concerns.

8. Future Perspectives

AN is a particularly hard-to-treat population, and pharmacological trials in AN often suffer from a high dropout rate. People with AN have reported specific concerns around pharmacological interventions, such as fears around drug-instigating weight gain [185]. However, patients also report wanting medication to alleviate anxiety, eating disorder thoughts, poor concentration and sleep problems [185]. A recent survey conducted on 200 participants with eating disorders (n = 105 with AN) investigated views on psychedelic drugs as a treatment for eating disorders [186]. Approximately half of the participants expressed interest in participating in psychedelic interventional research in the context of various concerns. The concerns were mitigated when the participants were informed that esketamine was licensed for the treatment of treatment-resistant depression. Importantly, this survey highlighted important methodological considerations, including the need for collaboration with service users and those with lived experience in the design of trials. The participants emphasised the need for a safe, professional and controlled environment during the dosing, a good rapport with the research team, trust in the trial and trial team and the provision of psychoeducation about psychedelic drugs. They also emphasised the need for psychological preparation before the session and an assessment of the "set". Importantly, a third of the overall group reported that they would never take part in such research. Thus, establishing an ongoing dialogue with service users will be an essential consideration in the design of clinical trials.

Overall, it is apparent that future studies should first aim to establish a safety profile of ketamine for AN through well-controlled feasibility and pilot studies. The outcome measures should be agreed upon with service users. Investigational studies of neuromodulation (e.g., transcranial magnetic stimulation and deep brain stimulation) in severe-enduring AN have found proximal improvements in depression, with improvements in eating disorder psychopathology and weight taking 12–18 months to emerge [187–189]. Therefore, whilst the BMI is often the metric of success in interventional trials in AN, for patients with severe-enduring AN where weight gain is slow, other metrics of improvement such as depression scores, social connectedness and quality of life should be considered, and long follow-up periods should be implemented. Given the hypothesised role of ketamine in providing a window of neuroplasticity, it will be essential that ketamine is combined with psychotherapy in future trials. Whilst the antidepressant effects of ketamine are transient, there is emerging evidence that psychotherapies (such as CBT) can extend the duration of antidepressant effects [190]. Additionally, the experiential components of ketamine may facilitate the therapeutic bond between patient and clinician [160], which is known to be a predictor of response to treatments [191].

Ketamine-assisted therapy generally follows a three-stage process: (1) preparation, where the patient and client discuss the mindset going into the experience, treatment goals and expectations and set intentions; (2) dosing, where patients are given the ketamine administration; and (3) integration, where the ketamine experience is reflected upon, and insights/lessons gained during the experience are integrated into the self. In the treatment of AN, it may be useful to combine specific therapeutic strategies with ketamine, such as compassion-based meditation exercises, yoga, cognitive bias modifications and exposure therapies. Similarly, specific therapeutic approaches may work well with ketamine, such as compassion-focused therapy, the Maudsley Model of Anorexia Treatment for Adults (MANTRA), family-based interventions and other psychotherapies. However, it is important to note that a "one size fits all" approach is unlikely to be successful, and treatments should be tailored to the individual.

9. Conclusions

The current treatment options for AN show limited efficacy, and addressing severe-enduring cases presents a particular challenge to clinicians and researchers. This review gave an overview of a conceptual rationale for the use of ketamine in the treatment of AN. Ketamine has proven to be an effective treatment for a range of psychiatric disorders, including depression, anxiety disorders, addiction and PTSD. Relatedly, it was recently licensed for treatment-resistant depression as a nasal spray esketamine device. In AN, there are several compelling reasons for its application, which were discussed. Ketamine may promote neuroplasticity, neurogenesis and hippocampal volume, and mitigate neuroinflammation. As a rapid antidepressant, ketamine may also reduce depression in patients with AN, which may be a barrier to treatment. In combination with therapies, it may also promote cognitive flexibility, openness, open-mindedness and detachment from the self whilst also promoting a therapeutic bond. However, there are specific safety concerns that require consideration in the treatment of AN with ketamine, and future studies designed in collaboration with service users are warranted in order to establish its efficacy, acceptability and safety.

Author Contributions: Conceptualisation, J.L.K. and H.H.; validation, J.L.K., H.H., J.T., M.F.J. and C.K.; writing—original draft preparation, J.L.K.; writing—review and editing, J.L.K., H.H., J.T., M.F.J. and C.K.; visualisation, J.L.K. and supervision, H.H. and J.T. All authors have read and agreed to the published version of the manuscript.

Funding: J.K. acknowledges financial support from a Medical Research Council (MRC) funded Doctoral Training Partnership stipend (ref: MR/N013700/1). H.H. and J.T. acknowledge salary support from the National Institute for Health Research (NIHR) Maudsley Biomedical Research Centre (BRC) for Mental Health. M.J. is an Honorary Consultant at South London and Maudsley NHS Foundation Trust (SLaM) supported by the NIHR, BRC and SLaM.

Acknowledgments: The figure in this manuscript were created using Biorender.com, accessed on 15 September 2021.

Conflicts of Interest: M.J. has, within the last year, received honoraria for speaking from Janssen, Lundbeck, EMS, Neurocentrx and Daiichi Sankyo. M.J. also received the Wellcome Innovator award to study the first in-human, randomised, double-blinded, placebo-controlled study to investigate the safety and tolerability, PK and PD of oral ketamine in HV. C.K. has previously received salary support from the Lundbeck Foundation, NIHR, Novo Nordisk UK Research Foundation and Marie Curie Fellowship. H.H. has received a consulting honorarium from COMPASS pathways.

References

1. Kurdi, M.S.; Theerth, K.A.; Deva, R.S. Ketamine: Current applications in anesthesia, pain, and critical care. *Anesth. Essays Res.* **2014**, *8*, 283. [CrossRef]
2. World Health Organization. *World Health Organization Model List of Essential Medicines: 21st List*; World Health Organization: Geneva, Switzerland, 2019.
3. Mion, G.; Villevieille, T. Ketamine pharmacology: An update (pharmacodynamics and molecular aspects, recent findings). *CNS Neurosci. Ther.* **2013**, *19*, 370–380. [CrossRef]
4. Domino, E.F. Taming the ketamine tiger. *Anesthesiology* **2010**, *113*, 678–684. [CrossRef]
5. McIntyre, R.S.; Rosenblat, J.D.; Nemeroff, C.B.; Sanacora, G.; Murrough, J.W.; Berk, M.; Brietzke, E.; Dodd, S.; Gorwood, P.; Ho, R. Synthesizing the evidence for ketamine and esketamine in treatment-resistant depression: An international expert opinion on the available evidence and implementation. *Am. J. Psychiatry* **2021**, *178*, 383–399. [CrossRef]
6. Chong, C.; Schug, S.; Page-Sharp, M.; Ilett, K. Bioavailability of ketamine after oral or sublingual administration. *Pain Med.* **2006**, *7*, 469. [CrossRef]
7. Zanos, P.; Moaddel, R.; Morris, P.J.; Georgiou, P.; Fischell, J.; Elmer, G.I.; Alkondon, M.; Yuan, P.; Pribut, H.J.; Singh, N.S. NMDAR inhibition-independent antidepressant actions of ketamine metabolites. *Nature* **2016**, *533*, 481–486. [CrossRef] [PubMed]
8. Domino, E.F. Neurobiology of phencyclidine (Sernyl), a drug with an unusual spectrum of pharmacological activity. *Int. Rev. Neurobio.* **1964**, *6*, 303–347.
9. Fontana, A. Terapia atidpresiva con ketamine [Antidepressive therapy with ketamine]. *Acta Psiquiat. Psicol. Amer. Lat. Psychiatr. Psychol. Proc. Lat. Am.* **1974**, *20*, 32.
10. Wilkinson, S.T.; Toprak, M.; Turner, M.S.; Levine, S.P.; Katz, R.B.; Sanacora, G. A survey of the clinical, off-label use of ketamine as a treatment for psychiatric disorders. *Am. J. Psychiatry* **2017**, *174*, 695–696. [CrossRef] [PubMed]
11. Taylor, J.H.; Landeros-Weisenberger, A.; Coughlin, C.; Mulqueen, J.; Johnson, J.A.; Gabriel, D.; Reed, M.O.; Jakubovski, E.; Bloch, M.H. Ketamine for social anxiety disorder: A randomized, placebo-controlled crossover trial. *Neuropsychopharmacology* **2018**, *43*, 325–333. [CrossRef]
12. Ezquerra-Romano, I.I.; Lawn, W.; Krupitsky, E.; Morgan, C.J.A. Ketamine for the treatment of addiction: Evidence and potential mechanisms. *Neuropharmacology* **2018**, *142*, 72–82. [CrossRef] [PubMed]
13. Jones, J.L.; Mateus, C.F.; Malcolm, R.J.; Brady, K.T.; Back, S.E. Efficacy of ketamine in the treatment of substance use disorders: A systematic review. *Front. Psychiatry* **2018**, *9*, 277. [CrossRef]
14. Worrell, S.D.; Gould, T.J. Therapeutic Potential of Ketamine for Alcohol Use Disorder. *Neurosci. Biobehav. Rev.* **2021**, *126*, 573–589. [CrossRef] [PubMed]
15. Feder, A.; Parides, M.K.; Murrough, J.W.; Perez, A.M.; Morgan, J.E.; Saxena, S.; Kirkwood, K.; Aan Het Rot, M.; Lapidus, K.A.; Wan, L.B.; et al. Efficacy of intravenous ketamine for treatment of chronic posttraumatic stress disorder: A randomized clinical trial. *JAMA Psychiatry* **2014**, *71*, 681–688. [CrossRef] [PubMed]
16. Leary, T.; Litwin, G.H.; Metzner, R. Reactions to psilocybin administered in a supportive environment. *J. Nerv. Ment. Dis.* **1963**, *137*, 561–573.
17. Metzner, R.; Leary, T. On programming psychedelic experiences. *Psychedelic. Rev.* **1967**, *9*, 5–19.
18. Hartogsohn, I. Constructing drug effects: A history of set and setting. *Drug Sci. Policy Law* **2017**, 3, 2050324516683325. [CrossRef]
19. Johnson, M.W.; Richards, W.A.; Griffiths, R.R. Human hallucinogen research: Guidelines for safety. *J. Psychopharmacol.* **2008**, *22*, 603–620.
20. Carhart-Harris, R.L.; Roseman, L.; Haijen, E.; Erritzoe, D.; Watts, R.; Branchi, I.; Kaelen, M. Psychedelics and the essential importance of context. *J. Psychopharmacol.* **2018**, *32*, 725–731. [CrossRef]
21. Andrade, C. Ketamine for depression, 4: In what dose, at what rate, by what route, for how long, and at what frequency? *J. Clin. Psychiatry* **2017**, *78*, e852–e857. [CrossRef]
22. Loo, C.; Gálvez, V.; O'keefe, E.; Mitchell, P.; Hadzi-Pavlovic, D.; Leyden, J.; Harper, S.; Somogyi, A.; Lai, R.; Weickert, C. Placebo-controlled pilot trial testing dose titration and intravenous, intramuscular and subcutaneous routes for ketamine in depression. *Acta Psychiatr. Scand.* **2016**, *134*, 48–56. [CrossRef] [PubMed]
23. Dakwar, E.; Anerella, C.; Hart, C.; Levin, F.; Mathew, S.; Nunes, E. Therapeutic infusions of ketamine: Do the psychoactive effects matter? *Drug Alcohol. Depend.* **2014**, *136*, 153–157. [CrossRef]
24. Zarate, C.A.; Singh, J.B.; Carlson, P.J.; Brutsche, N.E.; Ameli, R.; Luckenbaugh, D.A.; Charney, D.S.; Manji, H.K. A randomized trial of an N-methyl-D-aspartate antagonist in treatment-resistant major depression. *Arch. Gen. Psychiatry* **2006**, *63*, 856–864. [CrossRef]
25. Krystal, J.H.; Sanacora, G.; Duman, R.S. Rapid-acting glutamatergic antidepressants: The path to ketamine and beyond. *Biol. Psychiatry* **2013**, *73*, 1133–1141. [CrossRef]
26. Duman, R.S.; Li, N.; Liu, R.J.; Duric, V.; Aghajanian, G. Signaling pathways underlying the rapid antidepressant actions of ketamine. *Neuropharmacology* **2012**, *62*, 35–41. [CrossRef] [PubMed]

27. Yang, B.; Zhang, J.-C.; Han, M.; Yao, W.; Yang, C.; Ren, Q.; Ma, M.; Chen, Q.-X.; Hashimoto, K. Comparison of R-ketamine and rapastinel antidepressant effects in the social defeat stress model of depression. *Psychopharmacology* **2016**, *233*, 3647–3657. [CrossRef] [PubMed]
28. Zhang, J.-C.; Yao, W.; Dong, C.; Yang, C.; Ren, Q.; Ma, M.; Han, M.; Hashimoto, K. Comparison of ketamine, 7, 8-dihydroxyflavone, and ANA-12 antidepressant effects in the social defeat stress model of depression. *Psychopharmacology* **2015**, *232*, 4325–4335. [CrossRef] [PubMed]
29. Dong, C.; Rovnaghi, C.R.; Anand, K.J. Ketamine affects the neurogenesis of rat fetal neural stem progenitor cells via the PI3K/Akt-p27 signaling pathway. *Birth. Defects Res. B Dev. Reprod. Toxicol.* **2014**, *101*, 355–363. [CrossRef] [PubMed]
30. Yamada, J.; Jinno, S. Potential link between antidepressant-like effects of ketamine and promotion of adult neurogenesis in the ventral hippocampus of mice. *Neuropharmacology* **2019**, *158*, 107710. [CrossRef]
31. Ma, Z.; Zang, T.; Birnbaum, S.G.; Wang, Z.; Johnson, J.E.; Zhang, C.L.; Parada, L.F. TrkB dependent adult hippocampal progenitor differentiation mediates sustained ketamine antidepressant response. *Nat. Commun.* **2017**, *8*, 1668.
32. Deyama, S.; Duman, R.S. Neurotrophic mechanisms underlying the rapid and sustained antidepressant actions of ketamine. *Pharmacol. Biochem. Behav.* **2020**, *188*, 172837.
33. Wang, N.; Yu, H.Y.; Shen, X.F.; Gao, Z.Q.; Yang, C.; Yang, J.J.; Zhang, G.F. The rapid antidepressant effect of ketamine in rats is associated with down-regulation of pro-inflammatory cytokines in the hippocampus. *Ups. J. Med. Sci.* **2015**, *120*, 241–248. [CrossRef]
34. Clarke, M.; Razmjou, S.; Prowse, N.; Dwyer, Z.; Litteljohn, D.; Pentz, R.; Anisman, H.; Hayley, S. Ketamine modulates hippocampal neurogenesis and pro-inflammatory cytokines but not stressor induced neurochemical changes. *Neuropharmacology* **2017**, *112*, 210–220. [CrossRef]
35. Kiraly, D.D.; Horn, S.R.; Van Dam, N.T.; Costi, S.; Schwartz, J.; Kim-Schulze, S.; Patel, M.; Hodes, G.E.; Russo, S.J.; Merad, M.; et al. Altered peripheral immune profiles in treatment-resistant depression: Response to ketamine and prediction of treatment outcome. *Transl. Psychiatry* **2017**, *7*, e1065. [CrossRef]
36. Zhan, Y.; Zhou, Y.; Zheng, W.; Liu, W.; Wang, C.; Lan, X.; Deng, X.; Xu, Y.; Zhang, B.; Ning, Y. Alterations of multiple peripheral inflammatory cytokine levels after repeated ketamine infusions in major depressive disorder. *Transl Psychiatry* **2020**, *10*, 246. [CrossRef] [PubMed]
37. Chen, M.H.; Li, C.T.; Lin, W.C.; Hong, C.J.; Tu, P.C.; Bai, Y.M.; Cheng, C.M.; Su, T.P. Rapid inflammation modulation and antidepressant efficacy of a low-dose ketamine infusion in treatment-resistant depression: A randomized, double-blind control study. *Psychiatry Res.* **2018**, *269*, 207–211. [CrossRef]
38. Park, M.; Newman, L.E.; Gold, P.W.; Luckenbaugh, D.A.; Yuan, P.; Machado-Vieira, R.; Zarate, C.A., Jr. Change in cytokine levels is not associated with rapid antidepressant response to ketamine in treatment-resistant depression. *J. Psychiatr. Res.* **2017**, *84*, 113–118. [CrossRef] [PubMed]
39. Birmingham, C.L.; Su, J.; Hlynsky, J.A.; Goldner, E.M.; Gao, M. The mortality rate from anorexia nervosa. *Int. J. Eat. Disord.* **2005**, *38*, 143–146. [CrossRef] [PubMed]
40. Franko, D.L.; Keshaviah, A.; Eddy, K.T.; Krishna, M.; Davis, M.C.; Keel, P.K.; Herzog, D.B. A longitudinal investigation of mortality in anorexia nervosa and bulimia nervosa. *Am. J. Psychiatry* **2013**, *170*, 917–925. [CrossRef]
41. Eddy, K.T.; Tabri, N.; Thomas, J.J.; Murray, H.B.; Keshaviah, A.; Hastings, E.; Edkins, K.; Krishna, M.; Herzog, D.B.; Keel, P.K.; et al. Recovery from anorexia nervosa and bulimia nervosa at 22-year follow-up. *J. Clin. Psychiatry* **2017**, *78*, 184–189. [CrossRef]
42. Støving, R.K.; Andries, A.; Brixen, K.; Bilenberg, N.; Hørder, K. Gender differences in outcome of eating disorders: A retrospective cohort study. *Psychiatry Res.* **2011**, *186*, 362–366. [CrossRef]
43. Treasure, J.; Willmott, D.; Ambwani, S.; Cardi, V.; Clark Bryan, D.; Rowlands, K.; Schmidt, U. Cognitive interpersonal model for anorexia nervosa revisited: The perpetuating factors that contribute to the development of the severe and enduring illness. *J. Clin. Med.* **2020**, *9*, 630. [CrossRef]
44. Treasure, J.; Oyeleye, O.; Bonin, E.M.; Zipfel, S.; Fernandez-Aranda, F. Optimising care pathways for adult anorexia nervosa. What is the evidence to guide the provision of high-quality, cost-effective services? *Eur. Eat. Disord. Rev.* **2021**, *29*, 306–315. [CrossRef]
45. Hay, P.J.; Touyz, S.; Sud, R. Treatment for severe and enduring anorexia nervosa: A review. *Aust. N. Z. J. Psychiatry* **2012**, *46*, 1136–1144. [CrossRef] [PubMed]
46. Wonderlich, S.A.; Bulik, C.M.; Schmidt, U.; Steiger, H.; Hoek, H.W. Severe and enduring anorexia nervosa: Update and observations about the current clinical reality. *Int. J. Eat. Disord.* **2020**, *53*, 1303–1312. [CrossRef]
47. Jagielska, G.; Kacperska, I. Outcome, comorbidity and prognosis in anorexia nervosa. *Psychiatr. Pol.* **2017**, *51*, 205–218. [CrossRef] [PubMed]
48. Ulfvebrand, S.; Birgegård, A.; Norring, C.; Högdahl, L.; von Hausswolff-Juhlin, Y. Psychiatric comorbidity in women and men with eating disorders results from a large clinical database. *Psych. Res.* **2015**, *230*, 294–299. [CrossRef] [PubMed]
49. Kennedy, S.H.; Kaplan, A.S.; Garfinkel, P.E.; Rockert, W.; Toner, B.; Abbey, S.E. Depression in anorexia nervosa and bulimia nervosa: Discriminating depressive symptoms and episodes. *J. Psychosom. Res.* **1994**, *38*, 773–782. [CrossRef]
50. Jordan, J.; Joyce, P.R.; Carter, F.A.; Horn, J.; McIntosh, V.V.; Luty, S.E.; McKenzie, J.M.; Frampton, C.M.; Mulder, R.T.; Bulik, C.M. Specific and nonspecific comorbidity in anorexia nervosa. *Int. J. Eat. Disord.* **2008**, *41*, 47–56. [CrossRef] [PubMed]

51. Hepp, U.; Spindler, A.; Schnyder, U.; Kraemer, B.; Milos, G. Post-traumatic stress disorder in women with eating disorders. *Eat. Weight Disord.* **2007**, *12*, e24–e27. [CrossRef] [PubMed]
52. Reyes-Rodríguez, M.L.; Ann Von Holle, T.; Thornton, L.M.; Klump, K.L.; Brandt, H.; Crawford, S.; Fichter, M.M.; Halmi, K.A.; Huber, T.; Johnson, C.; et al. Post traumatic stress disorder in anorexia nervosa. *Psychosom. Med.* **2011**, *73*, 491. [CrossRef] [PubMed]
53. Kaye, W.H.; Bulik, C.M.; Thornton, L.; Barbarich, N.; Masters, K.; Group, P.F.C. Comorbidity of anxiety disorders with anorexia and bulimia nervosa. *Am. J. Psychiatry* **2004**, *161*, 2215–2221. [CrossRef] [PubMed]
54. Inoue, T.; Otani, R.; Iguchi, T.; Ishii, R.; Uchida, S.; Okada, A.; Kitayama, S.; Koyanagi, K.; Suzuki, Y.; Suzuki, Y.; et al. Prevalence of autism spectrum disorder and autistic traits in children with anorexia nervosa and avoidant/restrictive food intake disorder. *Biopsychosoc. Med.* **2021**, *15*, 9. [CrossRef]
55. Bulik, C.M.; Sullivan, P.F.; Joyce, P.R. Temperament, character and suicide attempts in anorexia nervosa, bulimia nervosa and major depression. *Acta Psychiatr. Scand* **1999**, *100*, 27–32. [CrossRef] [PubMed]
56. Boehm, I.; Flohr, L.; Steding, J.; Holzapfel, L.; Seitz, J.; Roessner, V.; Ehrlich, S. The Trajectory of Anhedonic and Depressive Symptoms in Anorexia Nervosa: A Longitudinal and Cross-Sectional Approach. *Eur. Eat. Disord. Rev.* **2018**, *26*, 69–74. [CrossRef]
57. Pompili, M.; Mancinelli, I.; Girardi, P.; Ruberto, A.; Tatarelli, R. Suicide in anorexia nervosa: A meta-analysis. *Int. J. Eat. Disord.* **2004**, *36*, 99–103. [CrossRef]
58. Franko, D.L.; Tabri, N.; Keshaviah, A.; Murray, H.B.; Herzog, D.B.; Thomas, J.J.; Coniglio, K.; Keel, P.K.; Eddy, K.T. Predictors of long-term recovery in anorexia nervosa and bulimia nervosa: Data from a 22-year longitudinal study. *J. Psychiatr. Res.* **2018**, *96*, 183–188. [CrossRef]
59. Engel, S.G.; Wonderlich, S.A.; Crosby, R.D.; Mitchell, J.E.; Crow, S.; Peterson, C.B.; Le Grange, D.; Simonich, H.K.; Cao, L.; Lavender, J.M.; et al. The role of affect in the maintenance of anorexia nervosa: Evidence from a naturalistic assessment of momentary behaviors and emotion. *J. Abnorm. Psychol.* **2013**, *122*, 709–719. [CrossRef]
60. Raney, T.J.; Thornton, L.M.; Berrettini, W.; Brandt, H.; Crawford, S.; Fichter, M.M.; Halmi, K.A.; Johnson, C.; Kaplan, A.S.; LaVia, M.; et al. Influence of overanxious disorder of childhood on the expression of anorexia nervosa. *Int. J. Eat. Disord.* **2008**, *41*, 326–332. [CrossRef]
61. Bulik, C.M.; Sullivan, P.F.; Fear, J.I.; Joyce, P.R. Eating disorders and antecedent anxiety disorders: A controlled study. *Acta Psychiatr. Scand.* **1997**, *96*, 101–107. [CrossRef]
62. Spielberger, C.D.; Gorsuch, R.L.; Lushene, R.E. *Manual for the State-Trait Inventory*; Consulting Psychologists Press: Palo Alto, CA, USA, 1970.
63. Wagner, A.; Aizenstein, H.; Venkatraman, V.K.; Fudge, J.; May, J.C.; Mazurkewicz, L.; Frank, G.K.; Bailer, U.F.; Fischer, L.; Nguyen, V. Altered reward processing in women recovered from anorexia nervosa. *Am. J. Psychiatry* **2007**, *164*, 1842–1849. [CrossRef]
64. Kaye, W.; Bailer, U.; Frank, G.; Henry, S.; Price, J.; Meltzer, C.; Becker, C.; Ziolko, S.; Mathis, C.; Wagner, A. Serotonin transporter binding after recovery from eating disorders. *Psychopharmacology* **2008**, *197*, 521–522. [CrossRef]
65. Kong, S.; Bernstein, K. Childhood trauma as a predictor of eating psychopathology and its mediating variables in patients with eating disorders. *J. Clin. Nurs.* **2009**, *18*, 1897–1907. [CrossRef]
66. Wade, T.D.; Bulik, C.M.; Neale, M.; Kendler, K.S. Anorexia nervosa and major depression: Shared genetic and environmental risk factors. *Am. J. Psychiatry* **2000**, *157*, 469–471. [CrossRef] [PubMed]
67. Watson, H.J.; Yilmaz, Z.; Thornton, L.M.; Hübel, C.; Coleman, J.R.; Gaspar, H.A.; Bryois, J.; Hinney, A.; Leppä, V.M.; Mattheisen, M. Genome-wide association study identifies eight risk loci and implicates metabo-psychiatric origins for anorexia nervosa. *Nat. Genet.* **2019**, *51*, 1207–1214. [CrossRef]
68. Cederlöf, M.; Thornton, L.M.; Baker, J.; Lichtenstein, P.; Larsson, H.; Rück, C.; Bulik, C.M.; Mataix-Cols, D. Etiological overlap between obsessive-compulsive disorder and anorexia nervosa: A longitudinal cohort, multigenerational family and twin study. *World Psychiatry* **2015**, *14*, 333–338. [CrossRef]
69. de Vos, J.; Houtzager, L.; Katsaragaki, G.; van de Berg, E.; Cuijpers, P.; Dekker, J. Meta analysis on the efficacy of pharmacotherapy versus placebo on anorexia nervosa. *J. Eat. Disord.* **2014**, *2*, 27. [CrossRef] [PubMed]
70. Mahase, E. Esketamine for treatment resistant depression is not recommended by NICE. *BMJ* **2020**, *368*, m329. [CrossRef]
71. Short, B.; Fong, J.; Galvez, V.; Shelker, W.; Loo, C.K. Side-effects associated with ketamine use in depression: A systematic review. *Lancet Psychiatry* **2018**, *5*, 65–78. [CrossRef]
72. Fanta, S.; Kinnunen, M.; Backman, J.T.; Kalso, E. Population pharmacokinetics of S-ketamine and norketamine in healthy volunteers after intravenous and oral dosing. *Eur. J. Clin. Pharmacol.* **2015**, *71*, 441–447. [CrossRef]
73. Gill, H.; Gill, B.; Rodrigues, N.B.; Lipsitz, O.; Rosenblat, J.D.; El-Halabi, S.; Nasri, F.; Mansur, R.B.; Lee, Y.; McIntyre, R.S. The effects of ketamine on cognition in treatment-resistant depression: A systematic review and priority avenues for future research. *Neurosci. Biobehav. Rev.* **2020**, *120*, 78–85. [CrossRef]
74. Kim, S.; Rush, B.S.; Rice, T.R. A systematic review of therapeutic ketamine use in children and adolescents with treatment-resistant mood disorders. *Eur. Child Adolesc. Psychiatry* **2020**, *30*, 1485–1501. [CrossRef] [PubMed]
75. Sos, P.; Klirova, M.; Novak, T.; Kohutova, B.; Horacek, J.; Palenicek, T. Relationship of ketamine's antidepressant and psychotomimetic effects in unipolar depression. *Neuroendocrinol. Lett.* **2013**, *34*, 101–107.
76. Luckenbaugh, D.A.; Niciu, M.J.; Ionescu, D.F.; Nolan, N.M.; Richards, E.M.; Brutsche, N.E.; Guevara, S.; Zarate, C.A. Do the dissociative side effects of ketamine mediate its antidepressant effects? *J. Affect. Disord.* **2014**, *159*, 56–61. [CrossRef] [PubMed]

77. Belser, A.B.; Agin-Liebes, G.; Swift, T.C.; Terrana, S.; Devenot, N.; Friedman, H.L.; Guss, J.; Bossis, A.; Ross, S. Patient experiences of psilocybin-assisted psychotherapy: An interpretative phenomenological analysis. *J. Humanist. Psychol.* **2017**, *57*, 354–388. [CrossRef]
78. Griffiths, R.R.; Johnson, M.W.; Richards, W.A.; Richards, B.D.; McCann, U.; Jesse, R. Psilocybin occasioned mystical-type experiences: Immediate and persisting dose-related effects. *Psychopharmacology* **2011**, *218*, 649–665. [CrossRef]
79. Morgan, C.J.; Curran, H.V.; Independent Scientific Committee on Drugs (ISCD). Ketamine use: A review. *Addiction* **2012**, *107*, 27–38. [CrossRef]
80. Shiroma, P.R.; Thuras, P.; Wels, J.; Albott, C.S.; Erbes, C.; Tye, S.; Lim, K.O. Neurocognitive performance of repeated versus single intravenous subanesthetic ketamine in treatment resistant depression. *J. Affect. Disord.* **2020**, *277*, 470–477. [CrossRef]
81. Martinotti, G.; Chiappini, S.; Pettorruso, M.; Mosca, A.; Miuli, A.; Di Carlo, F.; D'Andrea, G.; Collevecchio, R.; Di Muzio, I.; Sensi, S.L. Therapeutic Potentials of Ketamine and Esketamine in Obsessive–Compulsive Disorder (OCD), Substance Use Disorders (SUD) and Eating Disorders (ED): A Review of the Current Literature. *Brain Sci.* **2021**, *11*, 856. [CrossRef]
82. Veraart, J.K.; Kamphuis, J.; Schlegel, M.; Schoevers, R.A. Oral S-ketamine effective after deep brain stimulation in severe treatment-resistant depression and extensive comorbidities. *BMJ Case Rep.* **2021**, *14*, e238135. [CrossRef]
83. Wink, L.K.; Reisinger, D.L.; Horn, P.; Shaffer, R.C.; O'Brien, K.; Schmitt, L.; Dominick, K.R.; Pedapati, E.V.; Erickson, C.A. Brief Report: Intranasal Ketamine in Adolescents and Young Adults with Autism Spectrum Disorder—Initial Results of a Randomized, Controlled, Crossover, Pilot Study. *J. Autism Dev. Disord.* **2021**, *51*, 1392–1399. [CrossRef] [PubMed]
84. Kastner, T.; Walsh, K.; Shulman, L.; Alam, F.; Flood, S. Ketamine and the core symptoms of autism. *Int. J. Disabil. Hum. Dev.* **2016**, *15*, 121–123. [CrossRef]
85. Wink, L.K.; Anne, M.; Shaffer, R.C.; Pedapati, E.; Friedmann, K.; Schaefer, T.; Erickson, C.A. Intranasal ketamine treatment in an adult with autism spectrum disorder. *J. Clin. Psychiatry* **2014**, *75*, 835–836. [CrossRef]
86. Glue, P.; Neehoff, S.; Sabadel, A.; Broughton, L.; Le Nedelec, M.; Shadli, S.; McNaughton, N.; Medlicott, N.J. Effects of ketamine in patients with treatment-refractory generalized anxiety and social anxiety disorders: Exploratory double-blind psychoactive-controlled replication study. *J. Psychopharmacol.* **2020**, *34*, 267–272. [CrossRef] [PubMed]
87. Glue, P.; Medlicott, N.J.; Neehoff, S.; Surman, P.; Lam, F.; Hung, N.; Hung, C.T. Safety and efficacy of extended release ketamine tablets in patients with treatment-resistant depression and anxiety: Open label pilot study. *Ther. Adv. Psychopharmacol.* **2020**, *10*, 2045125320922474. [CrossRef]
88. Girgenti, M.J.; Ghosal, S.; LoPresto, D.; Taylor, J.R.; Duman, R.S. Ketamine accelerates fear extinction via mTORC1 signaling. *Neurobiol. Dis.* **2017**, *100*, 1–8. [CrossRef]
89. Duek, O.; Kelmendi, B.; Pietrzak, R.H.; Harpaz-Rotem, I. Augmenting the treatment of PTSD with ketamine—A review. *Curr. Treat Options Psychiatry* **2019**, *6*, 143–153. [CrossRef]
90. Feder, A.; Rutter, S.B.; Schiller, D.; Charney, D.S. The emergence of ketamine as a novel treatment for posttraumatic stress disorder. *Adv. Pharmacol.* **2020**, *89*, 261–286.
91. Asim, M.; Bing, W.; Bo, H.; Xiaoguang, W. Ketamine For Post-Traumatic Stress Disorders And It's Possible Therapeutic Mechanism. *Neurochem. Int.* **2021**, *146*, 105044. [CrossRef]
92. Pradhan, B.; Mitrev, L.; Moaddell, R.; Wainer, I.W. d-Serine is a potential biomarker for clinical response in treatment of post-traumatic stress disorder using (R,S)-ketamine infusion and TIMBER psychotherapy: A pilot study. *Biochim. Biophys. Acta Proteins Proteom.* **2018**, *1866*, 831–839. [CrossRef]
93. Das, R.K.; Gale, G.; Walsh, K.; Hennessy, V.E.; Iskandar, G.; Mordecai, L.A.; Brandner, B.; Kindt, M.; Curran, H.V.; Kamboj, S.K. Ketamine can reduce harmful drinking by pharmacologically rewriting drinking memories. *Nat. Commun.* **2019**, *10*, 5187. [CrossRef] [PubMed]
94. Artigas, F. Serotonin receptors involved in antidepressant effects. *Pharmacol. Ther.* **2013**, *137*, 119–131. [CrossRef] [PubMed]
95. Gauthier, C.; Hassler, C.; Mattar, L.; Launay, J.M.; Callebert, J.; Steiger, H.; Melchior, J.C.; Falissard, B.; Berthoz, S.; Mourier-Soleillant, V.; et al. Symptoms of depression and anxiety in anorexia nervosa: Links with plasma tryptophan and serotonin metabolism. *Psychoneuroendocrinology* **2014**, *39*, 170–178. [CrossRef] [PubMed]
96. Bailer, U.F.; Kaye, W.H. Serotonin: Imaging findings in eating disorders. *Curr. Top. Behav. Neurosci.* **2011**, *6*, 59–79.
97. Bailer, U.F.; Price, J.C.; Meltzer, C.C.; Mathis, C.A.; Frank, G.K.; Weissfeld, L.; McConaha, C.W.; Henry, S.E.; Brooks-Achenbach, S.; Barbarich, N.C.; et al. Altered 5-HT 2A receptor binding after recovery from bulimia-type anorexia nervosa: Re-lationships to harm avoidance and drive for thinness. *Neuropsychopharmacology* **2004**, *29*, 1143–1155. [CrossRef]
98. Chen, J.; Kang, Q.; Jiang, W.; Fan, J.; Zhang, M.; Yu, S.; Zhang, C. The 5-HTTLPR confers susceptibility to anorexia nervosa in Han Chinese: Evidence from a case-control and family-based study. *PLoS ONE* **2015**, *10*, e0119378. [CrossRef] [PubMed]
99. Calati, R.; De Ronchi, D.; Bellini, M.; Serretti, A. The 5-HTTLPR polymorphism and eating disorders: A meta-analysis. *Int. J. Eat. Disord.* **2011**, *44*, 191–199. [CrossRef]
100. Nacmias, B.; Ricca, V.; Tedde, A.; Mezzani, B.; Rotella, C.M.; Sorbi, S. 5-HT2A receptor gene polymorphisms in anorexia nervosa and bulimia nervosa. *Neurosci. Lett.* **1999**, *277*, 134–136. [CrossRef]
101. Gorwood, P.; Ades, J.; Bellodi, L.F.; Cellini, E.; Collier, D.A.; Di Bella, D.; Di Bernardo, M.; Estivill, X.; Fernandez-Aranda, F.; Gratacos, M.; et al. The 5-HT 2A−1438G/A polymorphism in anorexia nervosa: A combined analysis of 316 trios from six European centres. *Mol. Psychiatry* **2002**, *7*, 90–94. [CrossRef]

102. Kaye, W.H.; Frank, G.K.; Bailer, U.F.; Henry, S.E.; Meltzer, C.C.; Price, J.C.; Mathis, C.A.; Wagner, A. Serotonin alterations in anorexia and bulimia nervosa: New insights from imaging studies. *Physiol. Behav.* **2005**, *85*, 73–81. [CrossRef]
103. Pham, T.; Mendez-David, I.; Defaix, C.; Guiard, B.; Tritschler, L.; David, D.; Gardier, A. Ketamine treatment involves medial prefrontal cortex serotonin to induce a rapid antidepressant-like activity in BALB/cJ mice. *Neuropharmacology* **2017**, *112*, 198–209. [CrossRef]
104. Yamanaka, H.; Yokoyama, C.; Mizuma, H.; Kurai, S.; Finnema, S.J.; Halldin, C.; Doi, H.; Onoe, H. A possible mechanism of the nucleus accumbens and ventral pallidum 5-HT1B receptors underlying the antidepressant action of ketamine: A PET study with macaques. *Transl. Psychiatry* **2014**, *4*, e342. [CrossRef] [PubMed]
105. Du Jardin, K.G.; Müller, H.K.; Elfving, B.; Dale, E.; Wegener, G.; Sanchez, C. Potential involvement of serotonergic signaling in ketamine's antidepressant actions: A critical review. *Prog. Neuropsychopharmacol. Biol. Psychiatry* **2016**, *71*, 27–38. [CrossRef]
106. Berridge, K.C.; Robinson, T.E. Liking, wanting, and the incentive-sensitization theory of addiction. *Am. Psychol.* **2016**, *71*, 670. [CrossRef] [PubMed]
107. Robinson, S.; Sandstrom, S.M.; Denenberg, V.H.; Palmiter, R.D. Distinguishing whether dopamine regulates liking, wanting, and/or learning about rewards. *Behav. Neurosci.* **2005**, *119*, 5. [CrossRef]
108. Berridge, K.C.; Robinson, T.E. What is the role of dopamine in reward: Hedonic impact, reward learning, or incentive salience? *Brain. Res. Rev.* **1998**, *28*, 309–369. [CrossRef]
109. Kontis, D.; Theochari, E. Dopamine in anorexia nervosa: A systematic review. *Behav. Pharmacol.* **2012**, *23*, 496–515. [CrossRef]
110. O'Hara, C.B.; Campbell, I.C.; Schmidt, U. A reward-centred model of anorexia nervosa: A focussed narrative review of the neurological and psychophysiological literature. *Neurosci. Biobehav. Rev.* **2015**, *52*, 131–152. [CrossRef] [PubMed]
111. Bergh, C.; Södersten, P. Anorexia nervosa, self-starvation and the reward of stress. *Nat. Med.* **1996**, *2*, 21–22. [CrossRef]
112. Zink, C.F.; Weinberger, D.R. Cracking the moody brain: The rewards of self starvation. *Nat. Med.* **2010**, *16*, 1382–1383. [CrossRef]
113. Sterpenich, V.; Vidal, S.; Hofmeister, J.; Michalopoulos, G.; Bancila, V.; Warrot, D.; Dayer, A.; Desseilles, M.; Aubry, J.M.; Kosel, M.; et al. Increased reactivity of the mesolimbic reward system after ketamine injection in patients with treatment-resistant major depressive disorder. *Anesthesiology* **2019**, *130*, 923–935. [CrossRef] [PubMed]
114. Kotoula, V.; Stringaris, A.; Mackes, N.; Mazibuko, N.; Hawkins, P.C.; Furey, M.; Curran, H.V.; Mehta, M.A. Ketamine Modulates the Neural Correlates of Reward Processing in Unmedicated Patients in Remission from Depression. *Biol. Psychiatry Cogn. Neurosci. Neuroimaging* **2021**, in press. [CrossRef]
115. Mkrtchian, A.; Evans, J.W.; Kraus, C.; Yuan, P.; Kadriu, B.; Nugent, A.C.; Roiser, J.P.; Zarate, C.A. Ketamine modulates fronto-striatal circuitry in depressed and healthy individuals. *Mol. Psychiatry* **2021**, *26*, 3292–3301. [CrossRef]
116. Belujon, P.; Grace, A.A. Restoring mood balance in depression: Ketamine reverses deficit in dopamine-dependent synaptic plasticity. *Biol. Psychiatry* **2014**, *76*, 927–936. [CrossRef]
117. Gu, Q. Neuromodulatory transmitter systems in the cortex and their role in cortical plasticity. *Neuroscience* **2002**, *111*, 815–835. [CrossRef]
118. Marzo, A.; Bai, J.; Otani, S. Neuroplasticity regulation by noradrenaline in mammalian brain. *Curr. Neuropharmacol.* **2009**, *7*, 286–295. [CrossRef] [PubMed]
119. Dalton, B.; Bartholdy, S.; Robinson, L.; Solmi, M.; Ibrahim, M.A.; Breen, G.; Schmidt, U.; Himmerich, H. A meta-analysis of cytokine concentrations in eating disorders. *J. Psychiatr. Res.* **2018**, *103*, 252–264. [CrossRef]
120. Solmi, M.; Veronese, N.; Favaro, A.; Santonastaso, P.; Manzato, E.; Sergi, G.; Correll, C.U. Inflammatory cytokines and anorexia nervosa: A meta-analysis of cross-sectional and longitudinal studies. *Psychoneuroendocrinology* **2015**, *51*, 237–252. [CrossRef]
121. Dalton, B.; Leppanen, J.; Campbell, I.C.; Chung, R.; Breen, G.; Schmidt, U.; Himmerich, H. A longitudinal analysis of cytokines in anorexia nervosa. *Brain Behav. Immun.* **2020**, *85*, 88–95. [CrossRef]
122. Elenkov, I.J.; Chrousos, G.P. Stress hormones, proinflammatory and antiinflammatory cytokines, and autoimmunity. *Ann. N. Y. Acad Sci.* **2002**, *966*, 290–303. [CrossRef] [PubMed]
123. Miller, G.E.; Cohen, S.; Ritchey, A.K. Chronic psychological stress and the regulation of pro-inflammatory cytokines: A glucocorticoid-resistance model. *Health Psychol.* **2002**, *21*, 531. [CrossRef]
124. Hänsel, A.; Hong, S.; Cámara, R.J.; Von Kaenel, R. Inflammation as a psychophysiological biomarker in chronic psychosocial stress. *Neurosci. Biobehav. Rev.* **2010**, *35*, 115–121. [CrossRef]
125. Kubera, M.; Obuchowicz, E.; Goehler, L.; Brzeszcz, J.; Maes, M. In animal models, psychosocial stress-induced (neuro) inflammation, apoptosis and reduced neurogenesis are associated to the onset of depression. *Prog. Neuropsychopharmacol. Biol. Psychiatry* **2011**, *35*, 744–759. [CrossRef]
126. Himmerich, H.; Fischer, J.; Bauer, K.; Kirkby, K.C.; Sack, U.; Krügel, U. Stress-induced cytokine changes in rats. *Eur. Cytokine Netw.* **2013**, *24*, 97–103. [CrossRef]
127. Krügel, U.; Fischer, J.; Bauer, K.; Sack, U.; Himmerich, H. The impact of social isolation on immunological parameters in rats. *Arch. Toxicol.* **2014**, *88*, 853–855. [CrossRef]
128. Miller, M.W.; Lin, A.P.; Wolf, E.J.; Miller, D.R. Oxidative stress, inflammation, and neuroprogression in chronic PTSD. *Harv. Rev. Psychiatry* **2018**, *26*, 57. [CrossRef] [PubMed]
129. Zhang, L.; Benedek, D.; Fullerton, C.; Forsten, R.; Naifeh, J.; Li, X.; Hu, X.; Li, H.; Jia, M.; Xing, G. PTSD risk is associated with BDNF Val66Met and BDNF overexpression. *Mol. Psychiatry* **2014**, *19*, 8–10. [CrossRef] [PubMed]

130. Suliman, S.; Hemmings, S.M.; Seedat, S. Brain-Derived Neurotrophic Factor (BDNF) protein levels in anxiety disorders: Systematic review and meta-regression analysis. *Front. Integr. Neurosci.* **2013**, *7*, 55. [CrossRef]
131. Michopoulos, V.; Powers, A.; Gillespie, C.F.; Ressler, K.J.; Jovanovic, T. Inflammation in fear-and anxiety-based disorders: PTSD, GAD, and beyond. *Neuropsychopharmacology* **2017**, *42*, 254–270. [CrossRef]
132. Raison, C.L.; Capuron, L.; Miller, A.H. Cytokines sing the blues: Inflammation and the pathogenesis of depression. *Trends Immunol.* **2006**, *27*, 24–31. [CrossRef] [PubMed]
133. Keeler, J.L.; Robinson, L.; Keeler-Schäffeler, R.; Dalton, B.; Treasure, J.; Himmerich, H. Growth factors in Anorexia Nervosa: A systematic review and meta-analysis of cross-sectional and longitudinal data. *World J. Biol. Psychiatry.* in press.
134. Seitz, J.; Bühren, K.; von Polier, G.G.; Heussen, N.; Herpertz-Dahlmann, B.; Konrad, K. Morphological changes in the brain of acutely ill and weight-recovered patients with anorexia nervosa. *Z. Kinder Jugendpsychiatr. Psychother.* **2014**, *42*, 7–18. [CrossRef]
135. Seitz, J.; Konrad, K.; Herpertz-Dahlmann, B. Extend, pathomechanism and clinical consequences of brain volume changes in anorexia nervosa. *Curr. Neuropharmacol.* **2018**, *16*, 1164–1173. [CrossRef] [PubMed]
136. Keeler, J.; Patsalos, O.; Thuret, S.; Ehrlich, S.; Tchanturia, K.; Himmerich, H.; Treasure, J. Hippocampal volume, function, and related molecular activity in anorexia nervosa: A scoping review. *Expert Rev. Clin. Pharmacol.* **2020**, *13*, 1367–1387. [CrossRef] [PubMed]
137. Pérez-García, G.; Guzmán-Quevedo, O.; Aragão, R.D.S.; Bolaños-Jiménez, F. Early malnutrition results in long-lasting impairments in pattern-separation for overlapping novel object and novel location memories and reduced hippocampal neurogenesis. *Sci. Rep.* **2016**, *6*, 21275.
138. Andrade, J.; Madeira, M.; Paula-Barbosa, M. Effects of long-term malnutrition and rehabilitation on the hippocampal formation of the adult rat. A morphometric study. *J. Anat.* **1995**, *187*, 379. [PubMed]
139. Neves, G.; Cooke, S.F.; Bliss, T.V. Synaptic plasticity, memory and the hippocampus: A neural network approach to causality. *Nat. Rev. Neurosci.* **2008**, *9*, 65–75. [CrossRef]
140. Eriksson, P.S.; Perfilieva, E.; Björk-Eriksson, T.; Alborn, A.-M.; Nordborg, C.; Peterson, D.A.; Gage, F.H. Neurogenesis in the adult human hippocampus. *Nat. Med.* **1998**, *4*, 1313–1317. [CrossRef]
141. Roberto, C.A.; Mayer, L.E.; Brickman, A.M.; Barnes, A.; Muraskin, J.; Yeung, L.K.; Steffener, J.; Sy, M.; Hirsch, J.; Stern, Y. Brain tissue volume changes following weight gain in adults with anorexia nervosa. *Int. J. Eat. Disord.* **2011**, *44*, 406–411. [CrossRef] [PubMed]
142. Seitz, J.; Walter, M.; Mainz, V.; Herpertz-Dahlmann, B.; Konrad, K.; von Polier, G. Brain volume reduction predicts weight development in adolescent patients with anorexia nervosa. *J. Psychiatr Res.* **2015**, *68*, 228–237. [CrossRef]
143. Barbarich-Marsteller, N.C.; Fornal, C.A.; Takase, L.F.; Bocarsly, M.E.; Arner, C.; Walsh, B.T.; Hoebel, B.G.; Jacobs, B.L. Activity-based anorexia is associated with reduced hippocampal cell proliferation in adolescent female rats. *Behav. Brain Res.* **2013**, *236*, 251–257. [CrossRef]
144. Yang, C.; Yang, J.; Luo, A.; Hashimoto, K. Molecular and cellular mechanisms underlying the antidepressant effects of ketamine enantiomers and its metabolites. *Transl. Psychiatry* **2019**, *9*, 280. [CrossRef] [PubMed]
145. Abdallah, C.G.; Jackowski, A.; Salas, R.; Gupta, S.; Sato, J.R.; Mao, X.; Coplan, J.D.; Shungu, D.C.; Mathew, S.J. The nucleus accumbens and ketamine treatment in major depressive disorder. *Neuropsychopharmacology* **2017**, *42*, 1739–1746. [CrossRef]
146. Aleksandrova, L.R.; Phillips, A.G.; Wang, Y.T. Antidepressant effects of ketamine and the roles of AMPA glutamate receptors and other mechanisms beyond NMDA receptor antagonism. *J. Psychiatry Neurosci.* **2017**, *42*, 222. [CrossRef] [PubMed]
147. Bomba, M.; Marfone, M.; Brivio, E.; Oggiano, S.; Broggi, F.; Neri, F.; Nacinovich, R. Autobiographical memory in adolescent girls with anorexia nervosa. *Eur. Eat. Disord. Rev.* **2014**, *22*, 479–486. [CrossRef]
148. Huber, J.; Salatsch, C.; Ingenerf, K.; Schmid, C.; Maatouk, I.; Weisbrod, M.; Herzog, W.; Friederich, H.C.; Nikendei, C. Characteristics of disorder-related autobiographical memory in acute anorexia nervosa patients. *Eur. Eat. Disord. Rev.* **2015**, *23*, 379–389. [CrossRef] [PubMed]
149. Nikendei, C.; Funiok, C.; Pfüller, U.; Zastrow, A.; Aschenbrenner, S.; Weisbrod, M.; Herzog, W.; Friederich, H.-C. Memory performance in acute and weight-restored anorexia nervosa patients. *Psychol. Med.* **2011**, *41*, 829–838. [CrossRef]
150. Kemps, E.; Tiggemann, M.; Wade, T.; Ben-Tovim, D.; Breyer, R. Selective working memory deficits in anorexia nervosa. *Eur. Eat. Disord. Rev.* **2006**, *14*, 97–103. [CrossRef]
151. Keeler, J.; Lambert, E.; Olivola, M.; Owen, J.; Xia, J.; Thuret, S.; Himmerich, H.; Cardi, V.; Treasure, J. Lower pattern recognition memory scores in anorexia nervosa. *J. Eat. Disord.* **2021**, *9*, 49. [CrossRef]
152. Godley, J.; Tchanturia, K.; MacLeod, A.; Schmidt, U. Future-directed thinking in eating disorders. *Br. J. Clin. Psychol.* **2001**, *40*, 281–295. [CrossRef]
153. Manuel, A.; Wade, T.D. Emotion regulation in broadly defined anorexia nervosa: Association with negative affective memory bias. *Behav. Res. Ther.* **2013**, *51*, 417–424. [CrossRef]
154. Schacter, D.L.; Addis, D.R. The cognitive neuroscience of constructive memory: Remembering the past and imagining the future. *Philos. Trans. R. Soc. B Biol. Sci.* **2007**, *362*, 773–786. [CrossRef]
155. Miles, S.; Gnatt, I.; Phillipou, A.; Nedeljkovic, M. Cognitive flexibility in acute anorexia nervosa and after recovery: A systematic review. *Clin. Psychol. Rev.* **2020**, *81*, 101905. [CrossRef]
156. Morgan, C.J.; Curran, H.V. Acute and chronic effects of ketamine upon human memory: A review. *Psychopharmacology* **2006**, *188*, 408–424. [CrossRef]

157. Veen, C.; Jacobs, G.; Philippens, I.; Vermetten, E. Subanesthetic dose ketamine in posttraumatic stress disorder: A role for reconsolidation during trauma-focused psychotherapy? In *Behavioral Neurobiology of PTSD*; Springer: Cham, Switzerland, 2018; pp. 137–162.
158. Lambert, E.; Treasure, J.; Purves, K.L.; McGregor, T.; Bergou, N.; Kan, C.; Breen, G.; Eley, T.C.; Cardi, V. Fear conditioning in women with anorexia nervosa and healthy controls: A preliminary study. *J. Abnorm. Psychol.* **2021**, *130*, 490. [CrossRef] [PubMed]
159. Cardi, V.; Matteo, R.D.; Corfield, F.; Treasure, J. Social reward and rejection sensitivity in eating disorders: An investigation of attentional bias and early experiences. *World J. Biol. Psychiatry* **2013**, *14*, 622–633. [CrossRef]
160. Hasler, G. Toward specific ways to combine ketamine and psychotherapy in treating depression. *CNS Spectr.* **2020**, *25*, 445–447. [CrossRef] [PubMed]
161. Stocker, K.; Hasler, G.; Hartmann, M. The altered-state-of-consciousness (ASC) aspect of a feeling of lightness is reported to be associated with antidepressant benefits by depressed individuals receiving ketamine infusions: A systematic analysis of internet video testimonials. *Psychother. Psychosom.* **2019**, *88*, 182–183. [CrossRef] [PubMed]
162. Mollaahmetoglu, M.; Keeler, J.; Ashbullby, K.J.; Argyri, E.K.; Grabski, M.; Morgan, C.J. "This is something that changed my life": A qualitative study of patients' experiences in a clinical trial of ketamine treatment for alcohol use disorders. *Front. Psychiatry* **2021**, *12*, 1356. [CrossRef]
163. Ehrlich, S.; Geisler, D.; Ritschel, F.; King, J.A.; Seidel, M.; Boehm, I.; Breier, M.; Clas, S.; Weiss, J.; Marxen, M.; et al. Elevated cognitive control over reward processing in recovered female patients with anorexia nervosa. *J. Psychiatry Neurosci.* **2015**, *40*, 307. [CrossRef] [PubMed]
164. Friederich, H.C.; Herzog, W. Cognitive-behavioral flexibility in anorexia nervosa. *Behav. Neurobio. Eat. Disord.* **2010**, *6*, 111–123.
165. Rich, E. Anorexic dis (connection): Managing anorexia as an illness and an identity. *Sociol. Health Illn.* **2006**, *28*, 284–305. [CrossRef]
166. Bowden, H. A phenomenological study of anorexia nervosa. *Philos. Psychiatry Psychol.* **2012**, *19*, 227–241.
167. Skårderud, F. Eating one's words, part I:'concretised metaphors' and reflective function in anorexia nervosa—An interview study. *Eur. Eat. Disord. Rev. Prof. J. Eat. Disord. Assoc.* **2007**, *15*, 163–174. [CrossRef]
168. Olatunji, B.O.; Levinson, C.; Calebs, B. A network analysis of eating disorder symptoms and characteristics in an inpatient sample. *Psychiatry Res.* **2018**, *262*, 270–281. [CrossRef] [PubMed]
169. Tantillo, M.; Sanftner, J.; Hauenstein, E. Restoring connection in the face of disconnection: An integrative approach to understanding and treating anorexia nervosa. *Adv. Eat. Disord.* **2013**, *1*, 21–38. [CrossRef]
170. Arkell, J.; Robinson, P. A pilot case series using qualitative and quantitative methods: Biological, psychological and social outcome in severe and enduring eating disorder (anorexia nervosa). *Int. J. Eat. Disord.* **2008**, *41*, 650–656. [CrossRef] [PubMed]
171. Dechant, E.; Boyle, B.; Ross, R.A. Ketamine in a Patient with Comorbid Anorexia and MDD. *J. Womens Health Dev.* **2020**, *3*, 373–375. [CrossRef]
172. Mills, I.H.; Park, G.R.; Manara, A.R.; Merriman, R.J. Treatment of compulsive behaviour in eating disorders with intermittent ketamine infusions. *QJM* **1998**, *91*, 493–503. [CrossRef]
173. Schwartz, T.; Trunko, M.E.; Feifel, D.; Lopez, E.; Peterson, D.; Frank, G.K.; Kaye, W. A longitudinal case series of IM ketamine for patients with severe and enduring eating disorders and comorbid treatment-resistant depression. *Clin. Case Rep.* **2021**, *9*, e03869. [CrossRef] [PubMed]
174. Scolnick, B.; Zupec-Kania, B.; Calabrese, L.; Aoki, C.; Hildebrandt, T. Remission from Chronic Anorexia Nervosa With Ketogenic Diet and Ketamine: Case Report. *Front. Psychiatry* **2020**, *11*, 763. [CrossRef]
175. Miller, K.K.; Grinspoon, S.K.; Ciampa, J.; Hier, J.; Herzog, D.; Klibanski, A. Medical findings in outpatients with anorexia nervosa. *Arch. Intern. Med.* **2005**, *165*, 561–566. [CrossRef]
176. Noppers, I.M.; Niesters, M.; Aarts, L.P.; Bauer, M.C.; Drewes, A.M.; Dahan, A.; Sarton, E.Y. Drug-induced liver injury following a repeated course of ketamine treatment for chronic pain in CRPS type 1 patients: A report of 3 cases. *Pain* **2011**, *152*, 2173–2178. [CrossRef]
177. Sear, J.W. Ketamine hepato-toxicity in chronic pain management: Another example of unexpected toxicity or a predicted result from previous clinical and pre-clinical data? *Pain* **2011**, *152*, 1946–1947. [CrossRef]
178. Li, C.-C.; Wu, S.-T.; Cha, T.-L.; Sun, G.-H.; Yu, D.-S.; Meng, E. A survey for ketamine abuse and its relation to the lower urinary tract symptoms in Taiwan. *Sci. Rep.* **2019**, *9*, 7240. [CrossRef] [PubMed]
179. Winstock, A.R.; Mitcheson, L.; Gillatt, D.A.; Cottrell, A.M. The prevalence and natural history of urinary symptoms among recreational ketamine users. *BJU Int.* **2012**, *110*, 1762–1766. [CrossRef] [PubMed]
180. Shahani, R.; Streutker, C.; Dickson, B.; Stewart, R.J. Ketamine-associated ulcerative cystitis: A new clinical entity. *Urology* **2007**, *69*, 810–812. [CrossRef]
181. Stheneur, C.; Bergeron, S.; Lapeyraque, A.-L. Renal complications in anorexia nervosa. *Eat. Weight. Disord. -Stud. Anorex. Bulim. Obes.* **2014**, *19*, 455–460. [CrossRef]
182. Cockhill, L.A.; Remick, R.A. Blood pressure effects of monoamine oxidase inhibitors—The highs and lows. *Can. J. Psychiatry* **1987**, *32*, 803–808. [CrossRef] [PubMed]
183. Bremner, J.D.; Krystal, J.H.; Putnam, F.W.; Southwick, S.M.; Marmar, C.; Charney, D.S.; Mazure, C.M. Measurement of dissociative states with the clinician-administered dissociative states scale (CADSS). *J. Trauma. Stress* **1998**, *11*, 125–136. [CrossRef]

184. Lahti, A.C.; Koffel, B.; LaPorte, D.; Tamminga, C.A. Subanesthetic doses of ketamine stimulate psychosis in schizophrenia. *Neuropsychopharmacology* **1995**, *13*, 9–19. [CrossRef]
185. Dessain, A.; Bentley, J.; Treasure, J.; Schmidt, U.; Himmerich, H. Patients' and Carers' perspectives of psychopharmacological interventions targeting anorexia nervosa symptoms. In *Anorexia and Bulimia Nervosa*; IntechOpen: London, UK, 2019; p. 103.
186. Harding, F.; Seynaeve, M.; Keeler, J.; Himmerich, H.; Treasure, J.; Kan, C. Perspectives on psychedelic treatment and research in eating disorders: A web-based questionnaire study of people with eating disorders. *J. Int. Neurosci.* **2021**, *20*, 551–560.
187. Dalton, B.; Lewis, Y.D.; Bartholdy, S.; Kekic, M.; McClelland, J.; Campbell, I.C.; Schmidt, U. Repetitive transcranial magnetic stimulation treatment in severe, enduring anorexia nervosa: An open longer-term follow-up. *Eur. Eat. Disord. Rev.* **2020**, *28*, 773–781. [CrossRef] [PubMed]
188. Arroteia, I.F.; Husch, A.; Baniasadi, M.; Hertel, F. Impressive weight gain after deep brain stimulation of nucleus accumbens in treatment-resistant bulimic anorexia nervosa. *BMJ Case Rep.* **2020**, *13*, e239316. [CrossRef] [PubMed]
189. Lipsman, N.; Lam, E.; Volpini, M.; Sutandar, K.; Twose, R.; Giacobbe, P.; Sodums, D.J.; Smith, G.S.; Woodside, D.B.; Lozano, A.M. Deep brain stimulation of the subcallosal cingulate for treatment-refractory anorexia nervosa: 1 year follow-up of an open-label trial. *Lancet Psychiatry* **2017**, *4*, 285–294. [CrossRef]
190. Krystal, J.H.; Abdallah, C.G.; Sanacora, G.; Charney, D.S.; Duman, R.S. Ketamine: A paradigm shift for depression research and treatment. *Neuron* **2019**, *101*, 774–778. [CrossRef] [PubMed]
191. Kazdin, A.E. Mediators and mechanisms of change in psychotherapy research. *Annu. Rev. Clin. Psychol.* **2007**, *3*, 1–27. [CrossRef]

nutrients

MDPI

Comment

Comment on Keeler et al. Ketamine as a Treatment for Anorexia Nervosa: A Narrative Review. *Nutrients* 2021, *13*, 4158

Maria Skokou

Department of Psychiatry, University Hospital of Patras, 26504 Patras, Greece; mskokou@upatras.gr;
Tel.: +30-6977-906161 or +30-2613-603241

Citation: Skokou, M. Comment on Keeler et al. Ketamine as a Treatment for Anorexia Nervosa: A Narrative Review. *Nutrients* 2021, *13*, 4158. *Nutrients* **2022**, *14*, 2118. https://doi.org/10.3390/nu14102118

Academic Editor: Stefano Erzegovesi

Received: 15 February 2022
Accepted: 27 April 2022
Published: 19 May 2022

Anorexia Nervosa (AN) represents a difficult therapeutic challenge, with up to 4% prevalence among females and increasing incidence among youth [1]. Approved pharmaceutical treatments are virtually absent, and emerging treatments [2] have not been translated in therapeutic options, setting the scene for clinicians' frustration [3]. Testing novel treatments, approved for frequent comorbidities of AN—for example depression—would seem reasonable, expecting that they might be effective on symptoms of AN.

Keeler et al. consider the case of using ketamine, currently approved for treatment-resistant depression, as a therapeutic option for severe, enduring AN, and describe the glutamergic and neuroplastic effects of the drug [4]. Taking this line of thought further, one could also consider the possible trial of other glutamatergic agents as effective for eating disorders, which could be lamotrigine, or vortioxetine.

Lamotrigine is a phenyltriazine thought to reduce excess glutamate release, as a result of blocking voltage-sensitive sodium channels, and subsequent influx of sodium ions [5]. Further, it has antiaspartate, antikindling, neuroprotective and procognitive effects, and exerts weak 5-HT3 antagonism [6]. Being a first-line agent for acute bipolar depression and depressive relapse prophylaxis, it is also used for treatment resistant schizophrenia, treatment resistant OCD, unipolar depression, PTSD, depersonalization disorder, affective dysregulation and behavioral dyscontrol, all of which are frequently encountered in the context of AN [6]. Efficacy is coupled with a favorable side effect profile, except for serious rash; a careful, slow titration can mitigate this risk.

Vortioxetine is a novel antidepressant drug, exhibiting serotonin transporter inhibition, 5-HT-1A agonism, 5-HT-1B partial agonism, and 5-HT-1D, 5-HT-3, 5-HT7 antagonism. The blockade of 5-HT-3 receptors on GABA interneurons is responsible for the increase of glutamate in the prefrontal cortex and hippocampus, thus enhancing neuroplasticity and ultimately showing procognitive and antidepressant actions [7]. Its unique pharmacodynamic profile is shown by its superior efficacy regarding cognitive symptoms—attention, memory, processing speed and executive deficits—as well as generally benign adverse effects [8]. Particularly, apart from treating comorbid depression, promoting cognitive flexibility with vortioxetine could be of substantial relevance for the fixed distorted self-image, calorie intake and weight preoccupations of anorexic patients.

To my knowledge, there are no studies testing the efficacy of lamotrigine or vortioxetine for eating disorders except for scarce reports of lamotrigine [9,10]. The advantages of both drugs are their neuroplastic and procognitive actions, along with excellent tolerance, at a lower cost than intranasal ketamine, which would have to be used in a hospital or specialized setting. Still, the hypothetical efficacy of all remains to be tested, either each alone or in combination. In the end, for a potentially lethal, disabling, chronic disorder with practically no available pharmaceutical treatments, such as severe and enduring AN, we seem to need all the help we can get.

Funding: This research received no external funding.

Conflicts of Interest: The author declares no conflict of interest.

References

1. Van Eeden, A.E.; Van Hoeken, D.; Hoek, H.W. Incidence, prevalence and mortality of anorexia nervosa and bulimia nervosa. *Curr. Opin. Psychiatry* **2021**, *34*, 515–524. [CrossRef] [PubMed]
2. Steffen, K.J.; Roerig, J.L.; Mitchell, J.E.; Uppala, S. Emerging drugs for eating disorder treatment. *Expert Opin. Emerg. Drugs* **2006**, *11*, 315–336. [CrossRef] [PubMed]
3. Abbate-Daga, G.; Amianto, F.; Delsedime, N.; De-Bacco, C.; Fassino, S. Resistance to treatment in eating disorders: A critical challenge. *BMC Psychiatry* **2013**, *13*, 282. [CrossRef]
4. Keeler, J.L.; Treasure, J.; Juruena, M.F.; Kan, C.; Himmerich, H. Ketamine as a Treatment for Anorexia Nervosa: A Narrative Review. *Nutrients* **2021**, *13*, 4158. [CrossRef] [PubMed]
5. Brodie, M.J. Lamotrigine. *Lancet* **1992**, *339*, 1397–1400. [CrossRef]
6. Naguy, A.; Al-Enezi, N. Lamotrigine Uses in Psychiatric Practice. *Am. J. Ther.* **2019**, *26*, e96–e102. [CrossRef] [PubMed]
7. Salagre, E.; Grande, I.; Solé, B.; Sanchez-Moreno, J.; Vieta, E. Vortioxetine: A new alternative for the treatment of major depressive disorder. *Rev. Psiquiatr. Salud Ment. (Engl. Ed.)* **2018**, *11*, 48–59. [CrossRef] [PubMed]
8. Gonda, X.; Sharma, S.R.; Tarazi, F.I. Vortioxetine: A novel antidepressant for the treatment of major depressive disorder. *Expert Opin. Drug Discov.* **2018**, *14*, 81–89. [CrossRef] [PubMed]
9. Trunko, M.E.; Schwartz, T.A.; Berner, L.A.; Cusack, A.; Nakamura, T.; Bailer, U.F.; Chen, J.Y.; Kaye, W.H. A pilot open series of lamotrigine in DBT-treated eating disorders characterized by significant affective dysregulation and poor impulse control. *Bord. Bord. Personal. Disord. Emot. Dysregulation* **2017**, *4*, 21. [CrossRef] [PubMed]
10. Trunko, M.E.; Schwartz, T.A.; Marzola, E.; Klein, A.S.; Kaye, W.H. Lamotrigine use in patients with binge eating and purging, significant affect dysregulation, and poor impulse control. *Int. J. Eat. Disord.* **2014**, *47*, 329–334. [CrossRef] [PubMed]

nutrients

MDPI

Reply

Reply to Skokou, M. Comment on "Keeler et al. Ketamine as a Treatment for Anorexia Nervosa: A Narrative Review. *Nutrients* 2021, *13*, 4158"

Johanna Louise Keeler [1,*], Janet Treasure [1,2], Mario F. Juruena [2,3], Carol Kan [4] and Hubertus Himmerich [1,2]

1 Section of Eating Disorders, Department of Psychological Medicine, Institute of Psychiatry, Psychology & Neuroscience, King's College London, London SE5 8AF, UK; janet.treasure@kcl.ac.uk (J.T.); hubertus.himmerich@kcl.ac.uk (H.H.)
2 South London and Maudsley NHS Foundation Trust, Bethlem Royal Hospital, Monks Orchard Road, Beckenham BR3 3BX, UK; mario.juruena@kcl.ac.uk
3 Centre for Affective Disorders, Department of Psychological Medicine, Institute of Psychiatry, Psychology & Neuroscience, King's College London, London SE5 8AF, UK
4 Eating Disorder Service, Central and North West London NHS Foundation Trust, 1 Nightingale Place, Kensington & Chelsea, London SW10 9NG, UK; carol.kan@nhs.net
* Correspondence: johanna.keeler@kcl.ac.uk; Tel.: +44-(0)-20-7848-0187

Citation: Keeler, J.L.; Treasure, J.; Juruena, M.F.; Kan, C.; Himmerich, H. Reply to Skokou, M. Comment on "Keeler et al. Ketamine as a Treatment for Anorexia Nervosa: A Narrative Review. *Nutrients* 2021, *13*, 4158". *Nutrients* **2022**, *14*, 2119. https://doi.org/10.3390/nu14102119

Academic Editor: Stefano Erzegovesi

Received: 9 April 2022
Accepted: 27 April 2022
Published: 19 May 2022

In response to our narrative review, which suggested the use of the glutamatergic n-methyl-D-aspartate (NMDA) receptor antagonist ketamine as a potential treatment for anorexia nervosa (AN) [1], Maria Skokou posed the question whether other glutamatergic medications (e.g., lamotrigine) might be effective in the treatment of eating disorders in general [2]. Therefore, we would like to develop the idea further that the glutamate system might be of relevance for the pathophysiology and the treatment of eating disorders.

Glutamate is the most common neurotransmitter in the central nervous system, as it is present in more than 80% of synapses in the brain. Glutamate unfolds its excitatory effects at synaptic and non-synaptic receptors on the membranes of neuronal and glial cells. Its receptors are important for synaptic transmission, plasticity, and development, learning and memory [3]. They can be categorised into voltage-sensitive ionotropic receptors such as NMDA, kainate, and alpha-amino-3-hydroxyl-5-methyl-4-isoxazole-propionate (AMPA) receptors and ligand-sensitive metabotropic glutamate receptors (mGluRs) [4]. Changes in glutamatergic signalling have been implicated in the pathophysiology of major psychiatric disorders such as depression, schizophrenia and autism spectrum disorder [5]. Glutamate receptors have specifically been suggested to be involved in the development of eating disorder symptoms. NMDA receptors have been implicated in the control of appetite and food preference [6]; and alterations in mGluRs, NMDA and AMPA receptors have been related to addictive behaviours towards food [7,8].

Various drugs and medications influence glutamate signalling including the following: the stimulant modafinil; the anaesthetic ketamine; the anxiolytic and antibiotic drug d-cycloserine; the novel antipsychotic lumateperone, antiepileptic drugs such as lamotrigine and topiramate; the antidementive drug memantine; the anti-craving medication acamprosate (e.g., [9]).

Some of these drugs have been tested in people with eating disorders, e.g., d-cycloserine, which is a partial agonist at the glycine recognition site of the glutamatergic NMDA receptor, as well as topiramate and lamotrigine, which both decrease glutamate release and signalling [10].

For d-cycloserine, we have conflicting results from small studies. Steinglass and colleagues [11] tested the administration of d-cycloserine before meal-exposure in AN. However, caloric intake did not increase. A similar trial by Levinson and colleagues [12] with a one-month follow-up resulted in an increase in body mass index under d-cycloserine compared to the placebo group.

Skokou [2] already mentioned the small case series which tested lamotrigine in people with bulimia nervosa (BN) [13,14], where lamotrigine treatment was associated with reductions in eating disorder symptoms. People with BN often experience problems with their mood, affect and impulsiveness. A recent study showed that the combination of lamotrigine and dialectical behaviour therapy (DBT) helps patients with bulimic-spectrum eating disorders regarding affective lability and impulsive behaviour [15]; in addition, it has been suggested that lamotrigine is helpful in co-morbid bipolar depression in people with BN and binge eating disorder (BED) [16].

However, the currently most promising glutamatergic agent in eating disorders seems to be topiramate. Two independent RCTs [17–19] showed superiority of topiramate to placebo in reducing the frequency of binge eating episodes and compensatory measures (e.g., vomiting and use of laxatives) in patients with BN. In BED, a large multi-centre, RCT with 407 patients [20] showed that topiramate significantly reduces binge eating frequency, leads to weight loss and improves BED symptoms compared to placebo. Two smaller RCTs [21,22] yielded similar findings. AN is a contraindication for topiramate though, because it leads to weight loss.

Taken together, we agree with Skokou [2] that the glutamate system might be highly relevant for the treatment of eating disorders. As explained in our previous paper [1], we particularly believe that ketamine might lead to a breakthrough in the pharmacological treatment of AN. Additionally, glutamatergic agents may help with psychiatric co-morbidities of people with eating disorders.

Funding: This research received no external funding.

Conflicts of Interest: The authors declare no conflict of interest.

References

1. Keeler, J.L.; Treasure, J.; Juruena, M.F.; Kan, C.; Himmerich, H. Ketamine as a Treatment for Anorexia Nervosa: A Narrative Review. *Nutrients* **2021**, *13*, 4158. [CrossRef] [PubMed]
2. Skokou, M. Comment on Keeler et al. Ketamine as a Treatment for Anorexia Nervosa: A Narrative Review. *Nutrients* 2021, 13, 4158. *Nutrients* **2022**, *14*, 2118. [CrossRef]
3. Riedel, G.; Platt, B.; Micheau, J. Glutamate receptor function in learning and memory. *Behav. Brain Res.* **2003**, *140*, 1–47. [CrossRef]
4. Stevens, L.; Rodin, I. Introduction to Drug Treatments. In *Psychiatry*, 2nd ed.; Stevens, L., Rodin, I., Eds.; Churchill Livingstone: Edinburgh, UK, 2011; pp. 20–21.
5. Olloquequi, J.; Cornejo-Córdova, E.; Verdaguer, E.; Soriano, F.X.; Binvignat, O.; Auladell, C.; Camins, A. Excitotoxicity in the pathogenesis of neurological and psychiatric disorders: Therapeutic implications. *J. Psychopharmacol.* **2018**, *32*, 265–275. [CrossRef] [PubMed]
6. Sasaki, T.; Matsui, S.; Kitamura, T. Control of appetite and food preference by NMDA receptor and its co-agonist d-serine. *Int. J. Mol. Sci.* **2016**, *17*, 1081. [CrossRef]
7. Hadad, N.A.; Knackstedt, L.A. Addicted to palatable foods: Comparing the neurobiology of Bulimia Nervosa to that of drug addiction. *Psychopharmacology* **2014**, *231*, 1897–1912. [CrossRef]
8. Yohn, S.E.; Galbraith, J.; Calipari, E.S.; Conn, P.J. Shared Behavioral and Neurocircuitry Disruptions in Drug Addiction, Obesity, and Binge Eating Disorder: Focus on Group I mGluRs in the Mesolimbic Dopamine Pathway. *ACS Chem. Neurosci.* **2019**, *10*, 2125–2143. [CrossRef]
9. Olive, M.F.; Cleva, R.M.; Kalivas, P.W.; Malcolm, R.J. Glutamatergic medications for the treatment of drug and behavioral addictions. *Pharmacol. Biochem. Behav.* **2012**, *100*, 801–810. [CrossRef]
10. Czapinski, P.; Blaszczyk, B.; Czuczwar, S.J. Mechanisms of action of antiepileptic drugs. *Curr. Top. Med. Chem.* **2005**, *5*, 3–14. [CrossRef]
11. Steinglass, J.; Sysko, R.; Schebendach, J.; Broft, A.; Strober, M.; Walsh, B.T. The application of exposure therapy and D-cycloserine to the treatment of anorexia nervosa: A preliminary trial. *J. Psychiatr. Pract.* **2007**, *13*, 238. [CrossRef]
12. Levinson, C.A.; Rodebaugh, T.L.; Fewell, L.; Kass, A.E.; Riley, E.N.; Stark, L.; McCallum, K.; Lenze, E.J. D-Cycloserine facilitation of exposure therapy improves weight regain in patients with anorexia nervosa: A pilot randomized controlled trial. *J. Clin. Psychiatry* **2015**, *76*, 4033. [CrossRef] [PubMed]
13. Trunko, M.E.; Schwartz, T.A.; Berner, L.A.; Cusack, A.; Nakamura, T.; Bailer, U.F.; Chen, J.Y.; Kaye, W.H. A pilot open series of lamotrigine in DBT-treated eating disorders characterized by significant affective dysregulation and poor impulse control. *Bord. Personal. Disord. Emot. Dysregulation* **2017**, *4*, 21. [CrossRef] [PubMed]
14. Trunko, M.E.; Schwartz, T.A.; Marzola, E.; Klein, A.S.; Kaye, W.H. Lamotrigine use in patients with binge eating and purging, significant affect dysregulation, and poor impulse control. *Int. J. Eat. Disord.* **2014**, *47*, 329–334. [CrossRef] [PubMed]

15. Reilly, E.E.; Berner, L.A.; Trunko, M.E.; Schwartz, T.; Anderson, L.K.; Krueger, A.; Yu, X.; Chen, J.Y.; Cusack, A.; Nakamura, T. Evaluating the use of lamotrigine to reduce mood lability and impulsive behaviors in adults with chronic and severe eating disorders. *Eat. Weight. Disord. Stud. Anorex. Bulim. Obes.* **2022**, 1–11. [CrossRef] [PubMed]
16. Himmerich, H.; Kan, C.; Au, K.; Treasure, J. Pharmacological treatment of eating disorders, comorbid mental health problems, malnutrition and physical health consequences. *Pharmacol. Ther.* **2021**, *217*, 107667. [CrossRef] [PubMed]
17. Hedges, D.W.; Reimherr, F.W.; Hoopes, S.P.; Rosenthal, N.R.; Kamin, M.; Capece, J.A. Treatment of bulimia nervosa with topiramate in a randomized, double-blind, placebo-controlled trial, part 2: Improvement in psychiatric measures. *J. Clin. Psychiatry* **2003**, *64*, 21395. [CrossRef] [PubMed]
18. Hoopes, S.P.; Reimherr, F.W.; Hedges, D.W.; Rosenthal, N.R.; Kamin, M.; Karim, R.; Capece, J.A.; Karvois, D. Treatment of bulimia nervosa with topiramate in a randomized, double-blind, placebo-controlled trial, part 1: Improvement in binge and purge measures. *J. Clin. Psychiatry* **2003**, *64*, 1335–1341. [CrossRef]
19. Nickel, C.; Tritt, K.; Muehlbacher, M.; Pedrosa Gil, F.; Mitterlehner, F.O.; Kaplan, P.; Lahmann, C.; Leiberich, P.K.; Krawczyk, J.; Kettler, C. Topiramate treatment in bulimia nervosa patients: A randomized, double-blind, placebo-controlled trial. *Int. J. Eat. Disord.* **2005**, *38*, 295–300. [CrossRef]
20. McElroy, S.L.; Hudson, J.I.; Capece, J.A.; Beyers, K.; Fisher, A.C.; Rosenthal, N.R.; Group, T.B.E.D.R. Topiramate for the treatment of binge eating disorder associated with obesity: A placebo-controlled study. *Biol. Psychiatry* **2007**, *61*, 1039–1048. [CrossRef]
21. Claudino, A.M.; de Oliveira, I.R.; Appolinario, J.C.; Cordás, T.A.; Duchesne, M.; Sichieri, R.; Bacaltchuk, J. Double-blind, randomized, placebo-controlled trial of topiramate plus cognitive-behavior therapy in binge-eating disorder. *J. Clin. Psychiatry* **2007**, *68*, 4857. [CrossRef]
22. McElroy, S.L.; Arnold, L.M.; Shapira, N.A.; Keck, P.E., Jr.; Rosenthal, N.R.; Karim, M.R.; Kamin, M.; Hudson, J.I. Topiramate in the treatment of binge eating disorder associated with obesity: A randomized, placebo-controlled trial. *Am. J. Psychiatry* **2003**, *160*, 255–261. [CrossRef] [PubMed]

MDPI
St. Alban-Anlage 66
4052 Basel
Switzerland
Tel. +41 61 683 77 34
Fax +41 61 302 89 18
www.mdpi.com

Nutrients Editorial Office
E-mail: nutrients@mdpi.com
www.mdpi.com/journal/nutrients

www.ingramcontent.com/pod-product-compliance
Lightning Source LLC
Chambersburg PA
CBHW061831210926
51850CB00006B/858